AMERICAN CONSPIRATORS.
PONTIAC.
BURR.
CALHOUN.
ARNOLD.
JOHN BROWN.

HISTORY OF AMERICAN CONSPIRACIES

BY

ORVILLE J. VICTOR.

HISTORY

OF

AMERICAN CONSPIRACIES:

A RECORD OF

TREASON, INSURRECTION, REBELLION, &c.

IN THE

UNITED STATES OF AMERICA,

FROM 1760 TO 1860.

BY ORVILLE J. VICTOR,

AUTHOR OF "HISTORY, (CIVIL, POLITICAL AND MILITARY,) OF THE SOUTHERN REBELLION."

New York:

JAMES D. TORREY, PUBLISHER,

13 SPRUCE STREET.

PREFACE.

The United States of America, in attaining their exalted position among nations, have not escaped local and national disorder. The history of Colonial times is rife with religious and political excitement, frequently associated with violence and revolution; the Aborigines have conspired, in numerous instances, for the extermination of their white foes; the Continental Confederation, accompanied with alarming distempers, was saved from a conflict of commonwealths only by the adoption of the Federal Constitution; and the Federation which made us one people has not accomplished its ends without occasional insurrections against its consolidated authority.

In this volume I have embraced the story of such conspiracies, insurrections and popular commotions as directly or indirectly affected the order of society, the destiny of States, or the political institutions of the Republic. The table of contents will show what I conceive to have been such events. Those minor or purely local disturbances, which, though exciting episodes in State or Colonial history, yet contributed nothing of change to the order of historic events, I have passed with but a brief allusion in the Preliminary Chapter.

Having for several years contemplated this work I entered upon its preparation with a good store of authorities, among which were several volumes of documents, letters, memoirs, &c., not accessible to the ordinary inquirer. These, with the generally available works on American History, have enabled me to produce what I hope will prove a satisfactory narrative of the interesting and important events considered.

In the composition of the chapters on Pontiac's Indian Conspiracy and the Paxton Riots I freely drew upon the thoroughly exhaustive work of Francis Parkman, Jr. His "History of the Conspiracy of Pontiac," is a very able and painstaking production. It has afforded to a class of scribblers for popular magazines matter for many an article, though the reader was not permitted to know who was plundered for their edification. The work of Mr. P. is one of the most valuable of all late contributions to American History.

The chapter on Wilkinson's Conspiracy doubtless will excite astonishment in the reader's mind—it being so much at variance with the popular estimates of the man and his services. I have studied the matter well, and conceive that the record here presented will stand the test of critical examination. If it does, then General James Wilkinson becomes one of the dishonored among our public characters.

Genet's Conspiracy and the Alien and Sedition Troubles I have treated as exhaustively as the subjects seemed to demand. If the version presented reflects discredit upon the Anti-Federal faction, it is because the proofs against Genet and his coadjutors, of a *design* to paralyse the administrations of Washington and Adams, if not to overthrow the Federal Constitution, are, to our apprehension, incontestible. It is not an agreeable task to discrown men whom the public long has worshipped; it is, indeed, presumptuous, even to attempt; but, no writer is warranted in suppressing truth, from personal considerations. If what is here set forth is not sustained in its assumptions and conclusions let it be put aside for what is better testimony, if such can be produced.

Of Aaron Burr's Conspiracy I have sought to present the most complete narrative yet published. Having access to a great mass of evidence bearing upon the subject, I have not hesitated to use whatever came well authenticated, no matter whom it affected. The reader will see that "pure and disinterested patriot," General James Wilkinson, in a new *rolé*—that of defender of the integrity of his country. The paper will be found to embrace much incidental matter of interest not hitherto presented in connection with the operations of Burr.

The Hartford Convention Conspiracy and the New England Discontents are subjected to a somewhat extended exposition. Their intimate and intricate relations to the general history of the country compels a constant recurrence to national affairs if the causes and effects of the discontent are to be clearly set forth. No local or partisan treatment of the subject can do it justice. I have endeavored to present it in its true historic light.

The Negro Insurrections of Denmark Vesey and Nat Turner are painful chapters to peruse, yet they possess a profound interest for all who care to understand the workings of the American slave system. In spite of a studious suppression of testimony by the authorities and the press, enough has transpired to show that the institution of involuntary servitude has rested upon the bosom of a volcano.

The Nullification Rebellion has had so much new light thrown upon it by recent events as to reduce its hitherto argumentative, and therefore undefined, position to the condition of absolute demonstration. In the Secession Revolution we have the *results* of the asserted "rights" upon which the Nullification theory was founded, and therefore have the exact relations of Calhoun's theory and acts to society and to government perfectly established. I have given the theme a full consideration, viewing it from a National rather than a local or State stand-point. Several hitherto unpublished documents are cited in this paper.

The story of the sectional struggle in Kansas is given at much length. It is the first exposition of the kind yet offered—being a complete political and social record of the matter. Like the first South Carolina rebellion, the struggle in Kansas finds a fresh and conclusive comment in the Secession Revolution. We see in its incipient stages the plans, not of patriotic men but of partisans bent upon perpetuating Southern predominance in the upper house of Congress; in the progress of the struggle we witness the humiliation of a National Executive and the triumph, for a season, of violence and bad faith; in its close we behold the futile efforts of Southern factionists in Congress to override their own asseverated principles of the rights of settlers in a Territory to form their own institutions. In the failure to make Kansas a Slave State the veil was flung aside. Southern arrogance became Southern treason. The struggle in Kansas was the culminating point in the Congressional history of slavery: it initiated the conflict between the two principles of freedom and servitude which deluged the land in blood.

The paper on John Brown's Conspiracy is as complete as it is possible at this time to make it. There is so mueh bad feeling existing toward those against whom he conspired and who succeeded in hanging him, that it is scarcely possible to do both parties justice. We have endeavored to present the subject in its true light—confining our record to those authenticated facts and incidents from which a correct judgment is to be formed.

In the Appendix will be found documents quite important to the student who would sift to the bottom each case presented.

That this volume is free from errors of fact or mistakes of judgment is not to be assumed. What works on American history can claim such positive qualities? What has been my aim is to present such a record as will bear the closest scrutiny, and to lay before the intelligent reader facts upon which he may form his own conclusions, and sustain or repudiate the opinions expressed by the author. No historian can hope successfully to suppress testimony, nor to pervert its interpretation; and he who writes for the present or for the future must be studious for the truth if he would retain the respect of friends and command the attention of foes.

O. J. V.

NEW YORK, Nov. 1st, 1863.

CONTENTS.

STEEL PLATE ILLUSTRATIONS.

WOOD CUTS.

HISTORY OF AMERICAN CONSPIRACIES.

PRELIMINARY CHAPTER.

In the production of this work,. as stated in the preface, we have considered only those conspiracies, rebellions, &c., which were more than local in their effects. Under this head we might, perhaps, have classed the several early Indian conspiracies of Opechancanough, in Virginia, (1622,) King Phillip, in New England, (1675,) and of the Tuscaroras, in the Carolinas, (1712,) but deemed the story of Pontiac's greater combination of savage tribes against the whites sufficient to illustrate that feature of our history.

Of local uprisings we have omitted to write of Clayborne's Maryland insurrection, 1745–46; of Nathaniel Bacon's seizure of the Government of Virginia (1676); of Jacob Leisler's usurpation and reign in New York (1689–91); of the revolution against the old proprietory in the Carolinas (1719). Though events of interest these belong purely to colonial history. So, also, the war of the New Hampshire Grants (1774–75), in which Ethan Allen figured conspicuously; the boundary troubles between Pennsylvania and Maryland, which resulted in the location of Mason and Dixon's line (1760–61); the "Old Court" and "New Court" emeute in Kentucky (1824–25); the "Toledo War" between Ohio and Michigan (1835)—all, are very interesting episodes in the developement of States, but possess no National interest.

Of Slave insurrections we have considered but those of Denmark Vesey and Nat Turner—these being the only conspiracies among the helots of the South of which sufficient data exists for a satisfactory record. That there have been frequent uprisings is not denied; but, the alarm felt by citizens, courts and press of the South has induced a studied secrecy. It was policy to suppress comment, which could have resulted only in convincing the slaves of their power to produce terror. Some evidence is in existence regarding Gabriel's insurrection in Virginia during the year 1800. But, the data is meagre and indefinite. "For the past week," said a letter writer from Southeastern Virginia, "we have been under momentary expectation of an uprising among the negroes, who have assembled to the number of nine hundred or a thousand and threatened to massacre all the whites. They are armed with desperate weapons and secrete themselves in the woods. God only knows our fate. We have strong guards every night under arms." This was the first general alarm sounded. Virginia, at that time, had in her bosom a powerful body of real anti-slavery men, among whom must be named Jefferson, whose "Notes on Virginia" was then having a wide circulation, as also had Judge Tucker's "Proposal for the Gradual Abolition of Slavery in Virginia." There was, *then*, a gradual drifting of the State toward a free constitution; but, even that slight agitation of the question was the very incentive needed to inspire the slave with ideas and hopes of freedom.

The insurrection above referred to was thoroughly organized and ready for explosion when discovered. Its first work was the capture of Richmond. September 1st was the "day of deliverance" chosen. The arrangements were for the blacks, under the general leadership of Gabriel, (a slave of Thomas Prosser, residing near Richmond,) to gather by night, to the number of eleven hundred, at a brook six miles from the capital. Then, having perfected their detail of disposition, the march upon Richmond was to be made by right and left wing and centre. The first division was to seize the penetentiary, at that time containing several thousand stand of arms; the second division was to capture the powder house. Then, united, the right and left were to press on to the Capitol building, and to retain it as their strong hold and central rallying point. Meanwhile the centre column, having all the arms first provided by the blacks, was to enter the city and commence the work of slaughter. Not a white, save the French inhabitants, was to be spared—all were to be massacred, young and old, male and female. The French were to have been saved—it was then assumed by the anti-Jacobins or anti-Jeffersonians—because they were known to the negroes as friends of freedom and equality; but, it is not certain that the slaves had so clear a conception of the French revolution and the French party in America. All things at first conspired to render the plot a success: Richmond was not even in a good defensive position; it was easy of siezure. Nothing, it would appear, stood between the negroes and a realization of their horrid dream but secresy. That was not wanting until the last hour, when the plot was divulged in full by two slaves, and active steps were taken to ferret out its leaders. The alarm which succeeded was painful in the extreme. Much of the State soon was under arms. Governor James Monroe, "impressed with the magnitude of the danger, appointed three aides-de-camp." Patrols were established in the towns; on plantations strict surveillance of negro quarters was practiced. Arrests, brief hearings and executions quickly followed—from five to fifteen slaves being hung at a time. Gabriel eluded arrest for a while. Three hundred dollars were offered for his apprehension. He was captured at length in Norfolk—having lain secreted in a schooner's hold for eleven days—and was hung October 7th. Gabriel was a resolute fellow, young but sagacious, and won admiration even from his foes, because of his firm bearing. He resisted all efforts of the Governor and the authorities to discover the extent of the plot, its originators, and those implicated. Certain it is that the slaves as far east as Norfolk, fully understood the programme. The negroes in all the south-eastern counties, it is supposed, were ready to rise—so well devised and extensive were the arrangements. Only a portion of those suspected were arraigned. Said a cotemporary journalist: "The trials of the negroes concerned in the late insurrection are suspended until the opinion of the Legislature can be had on the subject. This measure is said to be owing to the immense numbers who are interested in the plot, whose death, should they all be found guilty and executed, will nearly produce the annihilation of the blacks in this part of the country."

Gabriel's scheme quickly assumed a *political* aspect by the excessive partisanship of Democrats and Federalists. The latter charged that the negroes, from hearing the former continually ranting about "equality," "fraternity" and "human rights," learned their first lessons in revolution and only proposed to enforce French revolutionary ideas. This was a severe but plausible application of the teachings of Democratic and Jacobinical societies; still, it was unjust to assume that even the French partisans were in any degree responsible for that uprising. Its secret lay in the eternal injustice of the institution of slavery; and Gabriel, like Nat Turner and Denmark Vesey, but embodied the love of liberty which slumbers in every human breast. Human nature is rarely so abased as not to love liberty. To attain it, he who is not willing to sacrifice life itself is not worthy of the boon. It is the folly of wisdom which will not be wise that imputes a slave uprising to "bad teachings," to "incendiary pamphlets," &c. So long as there is a slave there will be rebellion, let the institution be ever so humanely ordered. But, brutally ordered as it has been, in the Southern States of the American Union, the wonder is that insurrections have not been more frequent and bloody.

The session of the Legislature which followed discussed the matter of the insurrection with closed doors. Nor, were the proceedings afterwards disclosed except in detached paragraphs, which it took thirty years to bring into consistency. From these we learn that steps were proposed for colonizing the blacks, thus reducing their numbers and opening a way for the emancipation and exportation of those deemed to be dangerous. Said John Randolph, in one of his impressive harangues, in Congress: "the night bell is never heard to toll in the city of Richmond but the anxious mother presses her infant more closely to her bosom." No doubt the people themselves were solicitous to banish from their midst such an element of terror. The Governor, by order and advice of the House of Delegates, entered into a secret correspondence with the President of the

United States upon the subject of securing a grant of land from the public domain upon which to colonize such negroes as gave trouble. Nothing came of this, at that time, though the matter still was agitated by the Virginians; and, finally, on January 22d, 1805, the following resolution passed the Legislature in secret session:

"Resolved—That the Senators of this State in the Congress of the United States be instructed, and the Representatives be requested to use their best efforts for obtaining from the General Government a competent portion of territory in the State of Louisiana, to be appropriated to the residence of such people of color as have been or shall be emancipated, or hereafter may become dangerous to the public safety."

It is somewhat remarkable that all this should have remained a profound secret even to the great mass of Virginians. It was both a confession of the weakness and of the wrong of slavery, coming from those most guilty; inspired by their fears, they desired to secure their own safety by thrusting upon the General Government the care of such blacks as should be given their liberty.

But, it was a secret movement out of which sprang nothing in results; and the resolution above quoted was not exhumed until 1816, when the matter was revived in the Virginia Legislature, and the resolution reaffirmed in substance. To assist this emancipation scheme the American Colonization Society was formed, under the Presidency of Henry Clay. Out of that movement, also, sprang nothing. The main reason why these several efforts were barren of good fruits was the constant appreciation in value of negro "stock." As Virginia lands grew less productive, and the "first families" found their old baronial splendors circumscribed by limited incomes, breeding slaves for market gradually assumed the condition of a business, and, by the time the Colonization Society was ready to relieve the State of its superabundant negroes, that superabundance was disposed of "to go South," at prices making slave breeding very profitable. Hence, the end was accomplished of ridding the State of its most dangerous blacks, while, at the same time, their sale compensated for the constantly depreciating resources of the soil. According to the Richmond *Inquirer*, the annual income of Virginia from the sale of negroes was equal to *four millions* of dollars. That journal very pertinently asked (when indicating the interest which Virginia had in the South, and to assist in deciding her course during the winter of 1860–61) what commerce of the North could compensate for the loss of that trade?

The Black Hawk (1831–32) war was, in no sense, a conspiracy. It originated in a purely local difficulty, and, though it required considerable exercise of military force, it was little else than a whiskey outbreak. Our Government having obtained by treaty with Keokuk, chief of the Sac and Fox Indians, title to their lands on the east side of the Mississippi river, opened it to settlers. Black Hawk, with a body of followers never exceeding six hundred—composed of the worst class of savages from several surrounding tribes—resolved not to leave Illinois territory, and kept his promise for over a year; but, at length, was thoroughly subdued and banished to the West.

The terrible riot in Philadelphia (1844) might, perhaps justly, have claimed a chapter in this volume; but, to have given it place would have been a precedent for recording the story of the outbreaks in Pittsburg, Cincinnati, Boston, &c. The Philadelphia tragedy was one of the most distressing and furious storms of passion which ever disgraced this country's annals—in some respects worse than the celebrated "draft" riots in New York city (1863). It sprung from the enmity of classes, and the animosity engendered by attempted political and social proscription. For several years prior to 1844 the foreign population of several of the Free States had become so powerful as to elect to office men of their kind. This ascendancy a large class of American-born citizens proposed to counteract, by the formation of a political party whose cardinal principle should be the exclusion of foreigners from office and the restriction of the elective franchise to those born in the country, or who had resided here for a term of twenty-one years. This party originated in Philadelphia, and there announced its first public meeting. That meeting, held Monday afternoon, May 6th, 1844, was assaulted by the Irish, and a riot followed, in which one American was killed and eleven wounded. The excitement quickly intensified; soon Philadelphia was lit up with incendiary fires. The reign of violence was supreme for two days, when, by a general arming of citizens and the introduction of the military, it was suppressed. A large number of buildings were burned or sacked, including several Roman Catholic churches, a Roman Catholic female seminary, &c., &c. Nothing came of this terrible episode except an increase of party animosities, and of the feeling against the Irish population. Time, which soothes all distempers, drew a vail over the days of May; but, it was years before those who had participated in the affair put aside their hates.

Excitement which succeeded the Mexican War convulsed the entire country. It was the old conflict for slave or anti-slave supremacy. The war with Mexico was but a scheme for territorial aggrandisement. It resulted favorably, and the South bid fair to acquire permanent ascendancy through the Slave States to be formed of Texas, California and New Mexico. But, the North would not yield to a slave representation the vast domain acquired. During the years 1848–49–50 the country was deeply agitated. The struggle in the halls of Congress assumed a very angry front. Northern free soil members sought to carry the 36-30 line across the continent—to engraft the Wilmot proviso upon territorial organization by which slavery was to be denied any recognition in a territory. Utah and New Mexico were held at arm's length during this protracted struggle, and remained in a kind of independent yet chaotic state. California, however, filled by the avalanch of gold seekers and adventurers, at once had leaped into a Free State's estate, and came clamoring for admission. But, Southern men resisted this turn of the tide, and refused to receive the new State with its free Constitution. The moment of peril had arrived. Section was arrayed against section, and neither would yield. It appeared as if the long predicted "final struggle" between slave and free ideas had come. At the moment of angriest discussion, Henry Clay, "the great compromiser," came forward with his plan of settlement (Jan. 29th, 1850), providing that the people of the territories should determine their own wishes in regard to slavery; stipulating for the more efficient enforcement of the Fugitive Slave law; defining the boundaries of Texas and New Mexico, and arranging for the organization of new territories. This, like his previous schemes of compromise, found men enough from both factions to carry it triumphantly through Congress. For a while the waters were stilled; but, the hateful spirit of Southern arrogance was bubbling beneath the surface, concocting its conspiracy to repeal the compromise of 1822. In 1854 the incendiary fires again were lit by the aggressors, when, suddenly, the country was convulsed as it never before had been. The movement assumed a social as well as political face, and therefore was productive of most intense feeling. It proposed to make slavery national and freedom sectional—a proposition at which Northern men, without much distinction of party, revolted. Only public distaste for slavery prevented the slave holder from "tarrying" with his slaves in Free States as long as he pleased—the Fugitive Slave law, under heavy penalties, making it the duty of every citizen to catch the slave should the poor wretch attempt to escape. But when, superadded to this deference to the "peculiar institution," came a demand to open all the vast region of the West to slave settlement, the prescription was too bitter for the lips of freemen. Yet, it was the effort of years to put away the unpalatable dose—so daring and persistent were the Conspirators against free institutions. *Their* efforts resulted in the formation of the Republican party, which, in 1860, elevated its candidate to the Presidential chair. Foiled in their desperate devices to retain their seventy years' supremacy—their "equilibrium" the partisans of slavery professed to call it—the Secession Revolution was inaugurated, to found a confederation of States whose corner stone should be the recognition of grades in society and the right of property in man.

THE CONSPIRACY OF PONTIAC.

Of conspiracies plotted by the Indians for the extirpation of the whites, that conceived by Pontiac, chief of the Ottawas, holds a prominent place. This savage seemed formed by nature for his bloody mission. Powerful in person, commanding in presence, resolute to an extraordinary degree, possessed of a rare gift of eloquence, sagacious and subtle as a beast of prey, he rightfully claimed the office of chief over many tribes and became the minister of vengeance for his race.

Pontiac first appears on the stage during the French and English war, in which he participated as the ally of the French. He was at the battle of the Heights of Abraham, though it does not appear that the English victors received as prisoners any Indians. But, to what extent he co-operated against the English, is not known. His sympathies all were with the French, whose policy toward the Indians almost uniformly had been one of fostering care and kindness. From them he had imbibed an implacable hatred of the Briton, which proved an inspiration of the conspiracy soon to see the light.

Following the fall of Quebec (September, 1759) one after another of the French possessions passed under the English sway. The trading posts and forts—Presque Isle (now Erie, Pa.), Miama (on the Maumee), Detroit, Michilmacinac, Green Bay, &c. — were occupied during 1760 by British troops. English traders, English laws, English insolence and English dishonesty quickly succeeded, to add fuel to the fires slumbering in the savage breast.

Major Rogers was dispatched in September, 1760, from Montreal, by Sir Jeffrey Amherst, to Detroit and Michilmacinac with two hundred men, who were to receive the capitulation of those posts and were to garrison the forts. Proceeding in row boats up Lake Erie he reached the mouth of Cuyahoga River, in Ohio, November 7th, where the Major determined to encamp for a few days to rest his wearied men. He had scarcely lit his camp fires ere a troop of Indians appeared, proclaiming themselves the messengers of Pontiac, and, in his name, ordering the English to proceed no farther. Rogers demanded an interview with the chief, who soon appeared, accompanied by an imposing retinue of warriors. It was here that the great conspirator first came forward into the full light of history. From Rogers' minute account of the interview, we have a clear conception of the Indian Attila. He approached with a haughty stride, gorgeously attired in his savage costume, demanding at once, in an imperious tone, to know by what authority the British officer presumed to enter the Indian country without permission or treaty. Rogers was not a man without nerve. He stood as unabashed before that son of the forest as he would have done before a great oak, surging and roaring in the wind. To the barbarian's demand Rogers answered that, the French having been conquered, he was commissioned to take possession of the upper forts—that his errand was one of peace, and his tarry at that point was for a brief season of rest. The chief answered: "I stand in your path until to-morrow morning," and then departed. A deputation of warriors soon returned to offer the whites provisions, which were accepted and paid for. On the succeeding day a long conference was held, in which Pontiac conceded the English permission to proceed, offering them, indeed, a guard—a highly important act, as the way was beset with constant peril from savages still on the war path.

Rogers re-embarked on the 12th of November, to find the savages in ambush at the mouth of Detroit river, ready to dispute his passage up stream. But, Pontiac's word scattered the braves, and the flotilla proceeded in safety to their first destination, to receive the capitulation of the French garrison, November 29th, 1760. The Wyandots and Pottawatomies, encamped below Detroit, on either side of the river, witnessed the change of masters in silence, and seemingly acquiesced in the transfer without anger; but they, like Pontiac's own immediate people—the Ottowas and Ojibwas—preferred to await the issue of events. Had the English then been wise enough to have scanned the future, and just enough to have inaugurated a conciliatory, fatherly policy in dealing with the Indians, much if not all the human suffering and sacrifice which followed might have been averted. But then, as since, Great Britain acted less from the dictates of a broad humanity than from the impulse of commercial gain.[1] In fixing the degree of responsibility for what followed we should, in order to be just, weigh well the causes which impelled the savages to the war path. If Great Britain could have appeased those tigers of the American forests, panting for blood, she should have done it; that she not only offered no conciliation but scorned and maltreated the untamed creatures, is to make her at least partially accountable for the conspiracy and its sad results.

The mutterings of the impending storm were heard early in the summer of 1761, when Captain Campbell, commanding at Detroit, was fully informed of a conspiracy among the tribes along the lakes and in the Ohio valley to rise simultaneously against all the forts, to massacre the garrisons, and then to combine and fall upon all settlements advanced over the eastern ridge of the Alleghanies. Expresses were at once dispatched to all the points menaced. This betrayal of their plot sufficed to postpone the attack for that season. Sir Jeffrey Amherst commanded extreme caution to be used at all posts, while the Indians were treated with a severity and suspicion which only served to strengthen their bitterness of feeling toward their foe.

---

[1] See Ms. letter cited by Parkman in his "History of the Conspiracy of Pontiac." See also Chap. VII. of Parkman's work for citations of facts bearing on this point. Concurrent annals are full of proofs to substantiate the conclusion here given.

This postponement gave time for further conferences among the tribes. Ambassadors from the Six Nations and Pontiac pierced to the Far West and to the South, everywhere receiving assurances of aid in any attempt to expel the English. Pontiac himself, it is probable, visited the tribes congregated in what are now the States of Illinois, Indiana, Ohio and Michigan, for the combination of those nations became complete during 1762, and the great leader's authority was quite generally acknowledged by them.

These proceedings were kept profoundly secret. Those conducting the plot dissimulated well. Crowds of men, women and children beset the forts and trading posts, eager for gunpowder, traffic and liquor; but, even in their drunken bouts, nothing escaped their lips to betray their murderous designs. A friendly savage would, at times, whisper a word of warning to some white who had won his confidence, and enough transpired to keep the English officers on their guard. The commandant at Fort Miami, on the Maumee river, was thus warned early in the year 1763. Messengers from the East had arrived in his neighborhood to inform the tribes of the hour of uprising, and the Miamis had consented to murder the garrison. The brave commander called the chiefs together, informed them of their bloody plot, and, by threats of dreadful retaliation, won from them a confession of its truth. This news was dispatched at once to Detroit, where Major Gladwyn held the chief command; but, the Major was so lulled into security by the apparently friendly nature of the Wyandots, Pottawatomies and Ottawas surrounding his post, that he discredited the report of a general uprising. He was only too soon made aware of his almost criminal disbelief.

The treaty between England and France was not signed until February 10th, 1763, while dispatches announcing its terms did not reach the Northern frontiers until the May following. Up to that time the French had plotted with the Indians, goading them on to the attack, and promising assistance in case of need. The savages were given to understand that King Louis favored their designs, and that assurance inspired a confidence which, otherwise, could not have been felt by

Pontiac and his coadjutors. By the terms of the treaty France relinquished all claims to her North American possessions east of the Mississippi and north of the Ohio. This forever extinguished any hope of French co-operation with the Indians, but its promulgation came too late—the dog feast and the war dance had been celebrated in an hundred villages, the war wampum had conveyed its final messages, and the Western woods swarmed with "braves" on the war path.

Three tribes gathered, during April, 1763, at their camping grounds on the little river Encores, which flows into the Detroit river from the west, opposite the head of Fighting Island. Wyandots, Pottawatomies and Ottawas were there, evidently *en route* from their winter hunt to reoccupy their old villages around and above Detroit. But, it was more than a chance gathering—it was a council convened for the decision of the great question of the combined attack upon every English post in the West. This council was held April 27th. It was attended by delegations of the tribes named, as also by Ojibwas, Miamis, Chippewas, Hurons and several Canadians. Pontiac was the ruling spirit. He was the conceded superior of all present; the chiefs of all the tribes represented were prepared to accept him as their oracle.[1]

The council fire being lit, and the warriors seated around it in circling rows, the pipe passed from mouth to mouth until all had smoked. This ceremony over Pontiac entered the charmed circle to divulge his secrets and expound his views. His speech is represented to have been very violent against the English, whom he characterised as robbers, tyrants and settled foes to the Indian race. Their rapacity was that of the wolf, their mercy that of grizzly bears, their truth that of the fox. They treated the warriors like dogs, the women like slaves, the children like wild animals. The land given to the Indian they conceived to be theirs; thus the aborigines were to be banished, their hunting grounds appropriated, their

---

1 See the Pontiac Ms. cited by Parkman, in the Appendix to his "History of the Conspiracy." Drake, in the composition of his work, "the History and Biography of the Indians of North America," does not appear to have known of the existence of this interesting document.

sources of supplies all cut off and starvation was to do for the tribes what the deadly rifle and "fire water" left undone.

This strain touched the wildest chord in the savage breast. The great assembly, stoic in its apparent apathy, broke out into grunts and muttered vows of vengeance as the great warrior progressed in his word-painting of wrongs heaped upon the suffering race. That it was a master-piece of forest eloquence tradition tells us. Long after the orator had passed away, tribes to the far West preserved the memory of that wonderful harangue.

But, this story of English rapacity and cruelty was only the peroration of the address. Having wrought upon the hearts of his fierce assembly until each seemed a cone of fire burning on the altar of vengeance, the wily chief informed his listeners of the French readiness to co-operate with the Indians for the expulsion of the intruders and robbers. A great belt of wampum was exhibited as coming to Pontiac from King Louis of France, in token of his mighty sympathy. The orator then represented that, even then, "big canoes" were on their way over the great waters to strike one more blow for the extirpation of the hated foe. Would the race of red men sit silently by their fires and see the French struggle alone? The spirits of their dead called them to the war path—their wrongs would be their food, their vengeance would be their strength.

Then, to confirm the impression of his stormy eloquence, and to leave on the mind of each hearer such an apprehension of the whole subject as would never fail to arouse the savage instinct for blood, the chief told this remarkable tale:[1]

"A Delaware Indian conceived an eager desire to learn wisdom from

[1] Parkman repeats this from the Pontiac Ms. How authentic that may be is only to be determined by its intrinsic evidence. Of the tale, Parkman observes: "Its precise origin is not easy to determine. It is possible that the Delaware prophet mentioned in a former chapter, may have had some part in it; or it might have been the offspring of Pontiac's heated imagination during his period of fasting and dreaming. That he deliberately invented it for the sake of the effect it would produce, is the least probable conclusion of all." If the legend were divested of the rhetoric and polish given it by the scribe who wrote it out from the meagre notes of the Pontiac Ms., it would be more apparently Indian, and therefore more likely Pontiac's own invention for the sake of effect. It was, we conceive, for *effect* solely that it was introduced.

the Master of Life: but, being ignorant where to find him, he had recourse to fasting, dreaming and magical incantations. By these means it was revealed to him, that, by moving forward in a straight, undeviating course, he would reach the abode of the Great Spirit. He told his purpose to no one, and having provided the equipments of a hunter —gun, powder-horn, ammunition and a kettle for preparing his food— he set forth on his errand. For some days he journeyed on in high hope and confidence. On the evening of the eighth day he stopped by the side of a brook at the edge of a small prairie, where he began to make ready his evening meal, when, looking up, he saw three large openings in the woods on the opposite side of the meadow, and three well-beaten paths which entered them. He was much surprised; but his wonder increased when, after it had grown dark, the three paths were more clearly visible than ever. Remembering the important object of his visit, he could neither sleep nor rest; and, leaving his fire, he crossed the meadow, and entered the largest of the three openings. He had advanced but a short distance into the forest, when a bright flame sprung out of the ground before him, and arrested his steps. In great amazement, he turned back, and entered the second path, where the same wonderful phenomenon again encountered him; and now, in terror and bewilderment, yet still resolved to persevere, he pursued the last of the three paths. On this he journeyed a whole day without interruption, when, at length, emerging from the forest, he saw before him a vast mountain of dazzling whiteness. So precipitous was the ascent that the Indian thought it hopeless to go further, and looked around him in despair: at that moment, he saw, seated at some distance above, the figure of a beautiful woman arrayed in white, who arose as he looked upon her, and thus accosted him: 'How can you hope, encumbered as you are, to succeed in your design? Go down to the foot of the mountain, throw away your gun, your ammunition, your provisions and your clothing; wash yourself in the stream which flows there, and you will then be prepared to stand before the Master of Life.' The Indian obeyed, and again began to ascend among the rocks, while the woman, seeing him still discouraged, laughed at his faintness of heart, and told him that if he wished for success, he must climb by the aid of one foot and one hand only. After great toil and suffering, he at length found himself at the summit. The woman had disappeared, and he was left alone. A rich and beautiful plain lay before him, and at a little distance, he saw three great villages, far superior to the squalid dwellings of the Delawares. As he approached the largest, and stood hesitating whether he should enter, a man gorgeously attired stepped forth, and taking him by the hand, welcomed him to the celestial abode. He then conducted him into the presence of the Great Spirit, where the Indian stood confounded at the unspeakable splendor which surrounded him. The Great Spirit bade him be seated, and thus addressed him:

"'I am the Maker of heaven and earth, the trees, lakes, rivers and all things else; I am the maker of mankind; and because I love you, you must do my will. The land on which you lived was made for you, and not for others. Why do you suffer the white men to dwell among you? My children, you have forgotten the customs and traditions of your forefathers. Why do you not clothe yourselves in skins, as they did, and use the bows and arrows, and the stone-pointed lances, which they used? You have bought guns, knives, kettles and blankets from the white men, until you can no longer do without them; and what is worse, you have drunk the poison fire-water, which turns you into fools. Fling all these things away; live as your wise forefathers lived before you. And as for these English—these dogs dressed in red, who have come to rob you of your hunting grounds, and drive away the game—you must lift the hatchet against them. Wipe them from the face of the earth, and then you will win my favor back again, and once more be prosperous and happy. The children of your great father, the King of France, are not like the English. Never forget that they are your brethren. They are very dear to me, for they love the red men, and understand the true mode of worshiping me.'

"The Great Spirit next instructed his hearer in various precepts of morality and religion, such as the prohibition to marry more than one wife, and a warning against the practice of magic, which is worshiping the devil. A prayer, embodying the substance of all that he had heard, was then presented to the Delaware. It was cut in hieroglyphics upon a wooden stick, after the custom of his people, and he was directed to send copies of it to all the Indian villages.

"The adventurer now departed, and returning to the earth, reported all the wonders he had seen in the celestial regions."

This relation is represented by those present to have created a profound impression. It struck at civilization by encouraging the savages to continue in barbarism—an idea not at all displeasing to them; while it fostered their hopes of carnage by ordering them to wipe out the English—the dogs dressed in red—from the face of the earth.

No record is preserved of other doings of the council, further than that the plan was adopted by which to effect the design of murdering the garrison and people of Detroit—the French only to be spared. The plan was for Pontiac, with a body of his best braves, to obtain admittance within the palisade under pretense of performing the calumet dance for the edification of the garrison and English commander, Major Gladwyn, whom they would honor, after their long absence during the winter. This was a preliminary for obtaining information regarding the fortification and garrison.

The council broke up at dusk. During the night the entire multitude of men, women and children struck their tents and disappeared, passing up the river to their old encampments near Detroit; and when morning came it was to find the red skin host suddenly installed in their lodges within sight of the fort. Their coming and going always were so mysteriously conducted that their reappearance at that time attracted no attention.

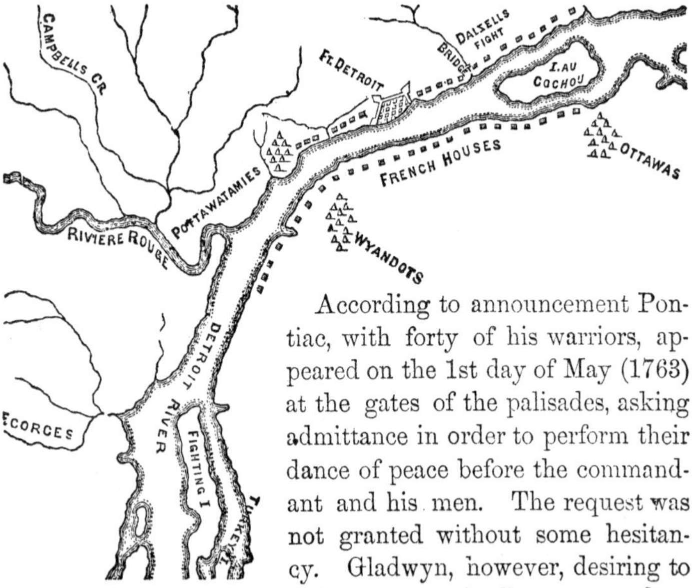

According to announcement Pontiac, with forty of his warriors, appeared on the 1st day of May (1763) at the gates of the palisades, asking admittance in order to perform their dance of peace before the commandant and his men. The request was not granted without some hesitancy. Gladwyn, however, desiring to preserve the good will of the savages, finally consented to their appearance, when the savages, decked and plumed in their gayest apparel, entered, in single file, Pontiac at their head. They at once proceeded to the house of Gladwyn, before which the dance was duly given, with all its aboriginal absurdity. All the Indians were not present, however, to assist in the ceremony. Ten of them dropped out of line, as they filed through the streets, and while the remaining thirty were engaged in the dance, the spies were at work with their eyes, penetrating to all accessible corners of the fortification, noting every thing regarding the strength and efficiency of the garrison. When they returned to the band the dance was discontinued and at once the entire forty filed out of the gates again. No suspicion had been excited. Gladwyn evidently regarded the visit as favorable to peace. The Indians found the garrison rather lax in discipline and comparatively weak in numbers. A surprise would accomplish all.

Detroit at that time was simply a fortified post standing in the midst of a village said, by Rogers, to contain twenty five hundred inhabitants—an estimate which must have included all the garrison and regular inhabitants and the lodges of traders, half breeds, &c., beyond the fort, within which were gathered about one hundred small houses, barracks, a church and a council house. The fortification consisted of palisades, twenty-five feet in heighth, planted in a great square, facing the river on the east, with bastions at each corner and block houses over the gateways. All were of wood, and not of a character designed to resist any formidable assault. The garrison consisted of but one hundred and twenty regulars and rangers, with about two score of traders and followers whose devotion was as little to be trusted as that of the Indian. Against this post and its feeble garrison the conspirator was to fling all the strength of his braves drawn from four tribes.[1]

The location of the several tribes around the post is indicated in the map. Pontiac, as Chief of the Ottawas, dwelt with them, though it is stated his own wigwam was on the Isle au Cochon, lying in the Detroit river near Lake St. Clair. The near contiguity of the tribes rendered frequent intercourse easy. After the visit to the fort, already referred to, a second general council was ordered by Pontiac. It convened in the Pottawatamie village May 3d, and was attended by all the

[1] It is known that many of the French Canadians were privy to the proceedings of the Indians, and that numbers of them openly co-operated with Pontiac, supplying him with arms, ammunition, food, &c., during the siege. So many of them, indeed, were compromised by the affair that Detroit village contained but five hundred and seventy-two inhabitants at the census of 1768—five years after the siege.

principal men of the three tribes, as well as by a number of delegates from other tribes, whose agents and runners were with Pontiac to receive his orders and to act in concert in the general warfare to be waged. Great circumspection was used, if we may credit the generally received accounts, to render the proceedings secret. Sentinels were stationed around the great council house, and no woman, nor warrior not entitled to a seat by the council-fire, was permitted to come within hearing distance. How the Ojibwa girl, hereafter mentioned, came to learn the secret of the session, we are not informed.

The great Chief unfolded his arrangements at length to the war chiefs before him. He addressed his fierce assembly in all the fervor of his burning passions—rekindling in their breasts the flame which feeds only on human blood. We can well imagine the picture presented: an hundred savages seated on the ground of a chamber but dimly lit by the fire in its centre—Pontiac in their midst, his terrible passions all aroused, thundering his poisoned words in their ears—the tiger-like ferocity of his hearers gleaming from each face as if already their tomahawks were reeking with the crimson flood: such was the scene which the chroniclers have drawn for our contemplation.

The plan divulged by Pontiac for the accomplishment of his scheme of murder was to demand an audience with Gladwyn, under pretext of discussing matters of great moment; sixty warriors were thus to gain admittance to his council house where all his officers would be assembled; each warrior was to be armed with knife, tomahawk and a rifle, whose barrel had been cut short so that all might be concealed beneath the blanket; outside were to be distributed as many carefully chosen braves as could well gain admittance within the gates, who, at the signal of a war shout from the council house, were to fall upon the garrison and English inhabitants, murdering men, women and children indiscriminately; the audience being granted, Pontiac was to address Gladwyn, holding forth a wampum belt—the signal for attack being the moment when the belt was reversed in his hand, when each warrior was to choose his victim and all whites present were to be butchered, at the same time giving the signal for their companions without.

This hideous design would have worked perfectly, had not the secret been betrayed. The story runs that Gladwyn had for a mistress an Ojibway girl, who, when not with him, dwelt with the Pottawatamies, probably as the wife of one of the braves of that tribe. This woman became possessed of the secret; and, as communication with the fort was unrestricted, she soon seized an opportunity to confer with Gladwyn. Historians have turned this incident to account by weaving around it the story of love and love's devotion. One authority has it:

"In the Pottawatamie village lived an Ojibwa girl who was the mistress of Major Gladwyn, and who loved him with the whole warmth of her generous soul. On the afternoon of the day, following the warning of M. Gouin, she came into the fort with a pair of elk-skin moccasins as a present to the commander. He noticed the saddened and pensive look she wore, but said nothing about it, and she withdrew. Still she lingered on the street, as if loth to depart until she had relieved her mind of some burden that was oppressing it. The sentinel, noticing her singular conduct, mentioned it to Gladwyn, who, recalling the girl, pressed her to reveal the cause of her trouble. She refused for a time to make any reply; but, after much urging and many promises not to betray her, she disclosed the whole murderous scheme. She said that on the morrow Pontiac, accompanied by sixty chiefs, would come to the fort. Each of these would have a short musket concealed under his blanket. Pontiac would make a speech as before mentioned, and at its close, offer a peace-belt of wampum, holding it in a reversed position. This would be the signal for the chiefs to shoot down the officers, and for the Indians upon the outside to commence their bloody work. The French were to be spared, but every Englishman was to be massacred."

This coincides with Parkman's version, though it is discredited by the statements of the French Priests' diary upon which the "Pontiac Ms." is founded. That authority expressly avers that a man of the Ottawa tribe made the disclosure. The truth seems to us to be this: The wife of a trader, M. St. Aubin, passed over to the Ottawa village on the afternoon of May 5th to find the Indians busily engaged in filing off their rifle barrels. This singular circumstance much excited her curiosity, and, from long association with the savages, she well knew it boded no good. Preserving a studied silence, as if she had not noticed the work, the woman returned to the village on the west side of the river, and at once reported the matter to M. Gouin, an old and influential trader. His suspicions were at once aroused. A dozen apparently trifling incidents were then recalled—all of which tended to confirm his alarm, and he hastened to the garrison to put it on guard against surprise. Gladwyn was, we are told, incredulous; the Indians were around the fort—men, women and children—daily, for gossip, barter and theft; no sign had been given of a spirit of war; hence he conceived an attack improbable.

The circumstance, however, served to inspire him with misgivings. The Ojibwa girl he probably questioned very closely, and doubtless obtained from her much to strengthen the impression made by M. Gouin's revelations. That she made some disclosures to him seems confirmed by the fact of Pontiac's having afterwards beaten her severely; but, this he may have done on the mere suspicion of her having revealed something to her "lover." Gladwyn unquestionably sought for information through his spies; that he obtained the detail from some warrior who was present at the Pottawatamie council is more probable than that he was saved by the devotion of his dusky mistress, who could, at best, have known very little about the great Chief's plans.

Be this as it may, the Major was on the alert for the promised visitation. His garrison was put in order for instant service—the men all being informed of the plot for their extirpation, to stimulate them to sleepless vigilance. During the night of the 5th, an attack was apprehended, but none was made; though the noise which came from the Indian camps gave evidence of unusual excitement among the savages.

On the morning of May 6th a large number of canoes were discovered crossing the river above the fort. In each was seen two or three savages, but the deeply ladened craft, rowed with great care, proved its load to have been that of eight or ten men in each. The common around the fort soon swarmed with Indian women and children, as if nothing unusual were on foot. Evidence was given that the cut-throats were about to play a game of ball. This was part of the programme of murder—to distract the attention of the whites. A few stalwart warriors, more respectable than the common herd, by being clad in blankets and tricked out in feathers, straggled up to the gates, and, one by one, were admitted. These were the fellows commissioned to do the outside butchery. They scattered to all parts of the village within the enclosure, as if having no concert or design in their movements. Even the malignant passions which had swayed their hearts for weeks were so far subdued as to leave their bronze faces as immobile as those of basilisks.

Pontiac passed over with his chosen sixty above the fort. They came down the river path, in solemn single file, making direct for the fort, which they reached about ten o'clock A. M. Gladwyn at once had the gates thrown open, and the delegation entered. To the dismay of the Chief he beheld the men all under arms; even the traders and *attaches* of the fort were in line, armed with cutlasses, pistols and muskets. Pontiac knew that his plans had been betrayed, and, for a moment, it is said, he was staggered with his consciousness of baffled hope and the storm of his indignation. Yet, with the stoicism of his race, he quickly assumed a haughty indifference, and passed through the lines of armed men to the council-house as if on a mission of honor. To the unflinching gaze of the soldiery the red skins returned the malignant fire of eyes scintillating like those of the rattlesnake when coiled for his stroke, while their ferocious faces, bedaubed with, vermillion, ochre, white lead and soot, served to add to the disgust which the English ever had entertained for the race.

Arrived at the council-house the Indians at once were given audience. They entered to find the officers there to receive them. In addition there stood a file of regulars, armed for duty. This reception looked as if the English were ready for the work of slaughter, while the brace of pistols in each officer's belt and the sword at his side, did not reassure the treacherous visitors of their own safety. But Pontiac preserved his courage and his temper. "Why," he asked of Gladwyn, "do I behold so many troops in the street?" The Major replied that his men were under arms for discipline and exercise. His air of confidence was perfect. Throughout the entire affair Gladwyn acted with great courage and tact.

At length the council was opened—a farce which must have galled the Indian's spirit like fire. To go through with it was, however, a necessity, if the Chief would not at once confess the truth of the English officer's suspicions. Pontiac therfore entered upon his formal speech, holding in his extended hand the wampum belt, which the conspirator had designed should play the important part in his proceedings. Before him sat and stood Gladwyn and his officers, with the bearing of men equal to and ready for the emergency—their eyes following the Chief's motions, and their hands ready to draw pistol at the first demonstration for reversing the belt. All this the orator perceived; he saw that even his private signal had been revealed; he was baffled. The clang of arms, the roll of the drum, the file of soldiers at command, taught him the propriety of prudence in demeanor as well as words. His speech was simply one of professed good will: he desired to seal the bond of amity and friendship which the Indians were solicitous ever should exist between them and the English; he asked that protection should be given them against traders and agents, and promised, in return, to make the tribes represented behave themselves well. During the utterance of these lying sentences the hand fell to his side which held the belt, nor did he extend it again. Once, it is stated, it was raised, when Gladwyn instinctively grasped his pistols and Pontiac at once closed his hollow harangue, discomfitted and overawed.

The commandant replied, in a tone and manner calculated to leave no doubt on the savage mind of his purposes. He assured them of confidence and protection as long as they merited it, but added that the first act of aggression—the first attempt at treachery—would be followed by vengeance. He advised the Chief and his followers to prudence, and said he should hold them to a strict accountability for every outrage which might be perpetrated by their tribes. With this he declared the council ended, and the baffled barbarians were forced to retire unsated with carnage. Their eyes gleamed like meteors in a leaden sky; their bedaubed visages could not conceal the commingled ferocity and disgust with which they were excited; yet they had to choke their passions down and passed out in silence. Pontiac alone, the last to leave, remarked to Gladwyn that he should soon visit him again, bringing along his squaws and children that they might all shake the hand of their English father. The Major made no reply to this, and the chief conspirator was permitted to depart to concoct further schemes of villainy. Why Gladwyn did not arrest him at once, along with his principle men, we are only left to conjecture. Doubtless he conceived it safest, considering his comparatively defenseless condition, to act leniently, nor do any act calculated to precipitate a war. His true course was to have held Pontiac as a hostage for the good behavior of his people, at least, until such time as Sir Jeffrey Amherst could place the garrison in a complete state of defense.

In extenuation of the Chief's infamous conduct in this affair, his biographer says: "Here and elsewhere the conduct of Pontiac is marked with the blackest treachery; and one cannot but lament that a nature so brave, so commanding, so magnanimous, should be stained with the odious vice of cowards and traitors. He could govern, with almost despotic sway, a race as unruly as the winds. In generous thought and deed he rivalled the heroes of ancient story, and craft and cunning might well seem alien to a mind like his. Yet Pontiac was a thorough savage, and in him stand forth, in strongest light and shadow, the native faults and virtues of the Indian race. All children, says Sir Walter Scott, are naturally liars, and truth and honor are developments of later education. Barbarism is to civilization what childhood is to maturity, and all savages, whatever may be their country, their color, their lineage, are prone to treachery and deceit." All of which, we suppose, means that Pontiac was no more responsible for his misdeeds than a child. The same philosophy would cover the tiger and the cobra de capello with the cloak of innocence. The truth is, he was simply a monster, and, though a barbarian, should have been held to a strict account for his acts. The English were not sinless in offering the provocation which aroused the fiend in the savage heart.

The warriors all withdrew beyond the palisades and quickly disappeared. Pontiac at once hastened to his island home, enraged, it is said, like a madman. But his mind was bent on the accomplishment of his scheme, and he determined to try the further use of treachery. With this object in view he repaired the next day to Gladwyn's quarters, accompanied by three warriors, bearing the pipe of peace, considered even by the savages an emblem sacred to honor and truth. His design was to convince the commandant that some bad bird had lied in his ears. "We stand before you," said the Chief, "as friends of the English, whom we love. We have therefore come, as chiefs, to smoke the pipe of peace." Whereupon all smoked, and Gladwyn did not say anything to excite suspicion among the Indians that he distrusted their truth. Before taking his leave Pontiac presented the calumet to Major Campbell—the second officer in command at the station—as a convincing assurance of his peaceful intentions. During the afternoon of that day a grand game of ball was played on the common before the palisades, by the several tribes, in further evidence of their good will. While it was in progress, however, Pontiac and the leading chiefs were in secret conclave, arranging for the furtherance of their plot. All was then arranged for an outbreak on the morrow and the installation of a siege, by which it was hoped to starve the garrison into a surrender. Runners were dispatched to the Southern and Western tribes, advising them of the attack, and urging them to the seizure of every post within their territory.

Monday morning, May 9th, the common to the west of the fort swarmed with savages, led by Pontiac in person. Advancing from their midst, with a large retinue of braves, he solicited leave to enter. The gates were barred against him. He demanded to know why he was refused admittance, when Gladwyn himself answered that the Chief alone might enter—not one of his followers, to which Pontiac replied that they wished to smoke with their English father. The commandant rejoined, in phrase more curt than courteous, that he wanted

7

none of them. This answer was the end of peace. Seeing that his hypocrisy and treachery were of no more avail, the Ottawa Chief strode haughtily away. His anger and chagrin were intense. He made at once for the river and embarked for his island, to prepare for the war path. His own disappointment was the signal for blood-letting, since the entire, half-concealed crowd leaped up, "shrieking like devils," and rushed away toward the first house on the common, where an old English woman and her two sons dwelt. In a few moments the scalp-yell warned the garrison that the work of death had, indeed, commenced. After this act the Indians hastened to their canoes, and the common was quickly deserted. Members of the Ottawa tribe hastened to the Isle au Cochou, where an Englishman named Fisher dwelt, in fancied security, under the protection of the great Chief. He was caught and scalped[1]—Pontiac being too much employed with his own wild thoughts to care for the defenceless man.

These atrocities were simply the premonitory symptoms of the storm to follow. All that night the village rang with the war whoop; the war dance was performed in several neighborhoods; paint and war adornments were brought into requisition to fit the braves for the war path. All night long the watchful garrison heard the appalling noise of preparation in the Indian villages. Sentinels strained eye and ear to detect the approach of the lurking cut-throats, whose general attack was expected momentarily. But no attack was made. The Ottawas were busy in transporting their lodges and property over the river, as ordered by Pontiac, that nothing but a path should stand between him and his enemies. Messengers came and went among the tribes. It is wonderful with

[1] Several Canadians passed over to the island, the next day, to give the body of Fisher burial. It was found and interred. Visiting the spot on the third day, the Canadians discovered the hands of the murdered man projecting from the ground, as if in an act of supplication. A second burial was, therefore made; but the spirit of the dead would not grant repose to his remains. Going to the grave on the fourth day the men were alarmed at beholding the hands again protruding from the earth. This inspired them with a fear of supernatural agency, and they hastened to their French priest, who went to the grave and with holy water and chaunt appeased the restless soul. A mass afterwards celebrated gave the body eternal quiet.

what rapidity news of the outbreak flew over the country. The savages of Lake Superior and those dwelling in the Wabash and Maumee vallies seemed to have received and acted upon the orders of Pontiac within a few days after the first demonstrations of the 9th. A little party, comprised of Sir Robert Davers and Captain Robertson, with their Canadian guides, was coming down the St. Clair river. It was waylaid and the two officers murdered—the Canadians in all instances being spared. One of these mongrel Frenchmen came in with the sad news during the evening of Monday, and also brought the further report that a large body of Ojibwas from Saginaw had joined Pontiac, eager for slaughter. If the Ottawas were the tigers of the forest the Ojibwas may be called the hyenas: a more detestable tribe of human beings never existed than those fierce people of the Saginaw woods.

Early dawn of Tuesday, May 10th, brought the expected assault. As the rosy light began to streak the east there came from the woods around Detroit such a shout as might be credited to the fiends of darkness. It was enough to appal the stoutest heart in the little garrison, for it proved that not a hundred but thousands of savages were on the war path thirsting for blood. A rain of rifle balls soon rattled against the wooden ramparts; soon every loop hole was rimmed with lead lodged in the logs by the unerring rifles of the assailants, who were distributed over the entire half circle of the fort's three points on the north, west and south. They lurked behind trees, stumps and logs, behind houses and barns, behind ridges in the ground and the crest of a hill to the west. From these coverts they fired in safety but without effect. Seeing this they took shelter behind a cluster of buildings within short range of the palisades, from which they threw a severe fire. A hat or jacket thrust before the openings, or above the pickets, was sure to be riddled with balls. Gladwyn's men soon entered with spirit into the contest, while the traders and employees answered the Indian yell with notes of defiance and scorn. Little firing was done by the garrison, though all were alert to pick off any savage who showed himself. An occasional shriek of agony told the death story for a "brave" who had been imprudent enough to betray enough of his person for a target.

The commandant, resolved to get rid of the buildings too close to the fort for comfort, opened on them with his cannon —of which he had two six-pounders, and one three-pounder, besides three bomb-mortars, but all of an inferior character. They served a good purpose, however, for the Indians stood in mortal fear of their terrible power. A few spikes were heated red hot and shot into the buildings referred to: in a few moments all were ablaze, and the red skins fled from them in the greatest terror. The sharp shooters were ready to pick off the rascals as they ran from cover, but, so odd was the sight, so ludicrous the fright and distortion of the savages, that the marksmen could only laugh.

Thus the morning wore away and Pontiac learned that such warfare could not accomplish any thing, further than to exhaust his supply of ammunition and to weary his patience. He therefore withdrew his force to concert more vigorous and united action. By noon of Tuesday all was still again save the occasional crack of the rifle of some brave still watching for his victim. This cessation led Gladwyn to think the affair some sudden outbreak only, which negotiation could reconcile; and, as he was in want of supplies for any siege which might be made, he resolved to open communication with Pontiac—hoping to obtain some corn if not any satisfactory explanation of the hostility shown. The Canadians, being neutrals, afforded a ready medium of intercourse with the Chief. During the afternoon La Butte, the French interpreter, accompanied by Chapeton and Godefroy, two old Canadians of good repute with the Indians, made his way up to the Ottawa village, then located only one mile and three-quarters away, over what is now called Bloody Run—a small stream emptying into the Detroit river just below the Isle au Cochou (now called Hog Island). These men were received by Pontiac without any show of anger, and their interview soon gave promise of such good results that La Butte made his way back to the fort to report the good tidings. Returning to the Ottawa village again he found the two Canadians hopeless: Pontiac was immovable as an oak, and refused every proposal for terms of peace, through professing to desire it. A conference of chiefs was finally held, when Pontiac declared their wish for a conference with their "English father"—mentioning Major Campbell, for whom the savages entertained a real respect. This proposal was laid before Gladwyn. Knowing so well the treacherous nature of Pontiac he opposed the mission; but Campbell, counting on his influence and good standing with the several tribes, begged permission to make the venture. He at length passed out of the fort, attended by Lieutenant McDougal, La Butte and several Canadians. Almost at the gates of the fort he was met by two messengers sent by M. Gouin to warn him of the treachery intended. This person had circulated through the Ottawa camp expressly to discover the designs on foot, and had learned enough to convince him of the perfidious nature of the proposal for a mission. But, Major Campbell was too strong in his convictions of safety in Pontiac's hands, and he refused to return. Passing on he soon came to the bridge over the creek leading into the Indian village. Once over it he had passed forever from retreat or friendly aid. He was quickly beset by a great crowd of women, children and half grown boys, who would have assaulted him at once had not the Chief come forward for his protection. Pontiac led the veteran officer and his aid to the central lodge where mats were laid for their comfort. The lodge was soon filed with warriors, who pressed in sullen silence in and around the place to hear what was said.

Campbell at once made a speech—stating his surprise at the breaking of the peace which had so long existed. He asked its cause, and said if any grievance existed the English fathers would consider it their duty to correct it. To this no reply was returned. Around the two men stood a wall of savages, silent as Sphinxes, and as heartless as the Aztec God of Sacrifice. For one long hour they sat there awaiting a response; yet none came. Campbell read his fate in that calm. He finally arose to his feet and declared his purpose to return to the fort, but, with a gesture of authority, the Chief bade him be seated again: "My father," he said significantly, "will sleep to-night in the lodges of his red children." Then the solemn silence was broken, and the Indians betrayed unmistakable signs of violence; but Campbell and McDougal were led away by the Chief and placed under guard in the house of a Canadian named Meloche. La Butte returned late in the evening to the fort to report his sad tidings: all present felt that their revered officer and friend were indeed lost to them forever. Two Ojibwas, then prisoners in the fort, were set apart as hostages for the Englishmen's safety.

This detention of an embassy which Pontiac himself had sought, is not the least perfidious of his many acts of dishonor. Had the officers been sent by Gladwyn, their detention as prisoners of war might not have been inadmissable in savage warfare; but, the detestable falsehood by which they were lured to the Indian camp, and their imprisonment to await the issue of events, reflect upon Pontiac's memory a stain which no special pleading for the "untutored mind" will wipe away. It was, like many others' of his proceedings, the work of a monster in perfidy.[1]

The imprisonment of Campbell was followed by active operations. Pontiac, having resolved to accept no terms save a total surrender of the garrison, post, property and the two armed vessels lying off the fort, prepared to press the siege so closely as to compel Gladwyn to surrender from the mere want of provisions—of which he knew a short supply only existed. A large body of Wyandots having become somewhat Christianized by the influence of a Jesuit priest had, thus far, refused to participate in the conspiracy. These non-combatants the great Chief threatened with dire vengeance if they longer refused to enter upon the war path. Stipulating that they should be permitted to attend the celebration of mass before dancing the war dance, these converts entered into the conflict

---

1 Major Campbell was not long afterwards murdered by the Chief of the Ojibwas. His body was horribly mutilated, and, it is stated, his heart—being that of a brave man—was eaten by his murderers to give them courage. It does not relieve Pontiac from the responsibility of the murder that he was so incensed at the Ojibwa Chief as to send him away to Saginaw.

with great zeal and became Pontiac's most tireless and efficient warriors.[1]

The disposition made by Pontiac of his forces was such as to invest the fort perfectly, except upon its river front. Off the fort, out in the stream, most fortunately for the garrison, lay two small vessels, both armed and ready for service as transports or for defense. These kept open the communication by water; all other approaches were closed by the savages, who, after May 12th, swarmed over the entire vicinity, occupying every position where a good shot might be likely to reward the vigilant brave.

Gladwyn, beholding these menacing preparations for his destruction, for the first time listened to the suggestions of his officers and men regarding an evacuation of the post, while it was yet possible, and an escape by the transports to Niagara. On the evening of the 12th, after sustaining a day's sharp fire from the assailing horde without, the commandant convened his officers to decide the question of evacuation. According

---

[1] Father Pothier's moral teachings seem to have struck no deeper into the savage heart than the teachings of evangelists since. The number of good Christians made out of the western and north-western tribes in one hundred years would only startle the reader by its absurd minuteness when contrasted with the efforts made. We may refer to a case which came under our own personal knowledge, as illustrative of the fact that despite all *apparent* civilization, the Indian never forgets his wild instincts:

A Wyandot, belonging to one of the leading families of his tribe, was educated in Northern Ohio, and proved to be a man of fine talents. After leaving school he studied law, was admitted to practice, married a most amiable and accomplished woman—the daughter of a leading elder in the Methodist church—and gave promise of a useful, perhaps a brilliant, career. He was, in time, put in nomination by the Whig party for the office of Prosecuting Attorney for which he was admirably fitted. At the election he was defeated, doubtless from the popular prejudice againss Indian blood. The defeat so stung his pride that the native spirit in a day overwhelmed his ambition and his civilization. He soon returned to his tribe (then living on the Wyandot Reservation near Upper Sandusky, Ohio), to become a common Indian in pursuits and tastes.

Similar cases are mentioned by historians. One, referred to we think by Stone, in his excellent "Life of Thayendanega" (Brandt) Chief of the Six Nations, where a young and talented Indian was educated for the ministry and entered with zeal upon his labors for some time; when suddenly he disappeared, leaving behind him all his "civilized" property in clothes, books, &c., to become one of his tribe again.

to a letter published in the old Pennsylvania *Gazette* (No. 1808) the Major alone is represented to have opposed the evacuation, and declared for holding out to the last extremity—hoping for reenforcements and supplies. This decision, it would appear, prevailed. Every arrangement was made for the defense. The scanty store of provisions—enough for about three weeks' sustenance upon close rations—was carefully gathered and put under lock and key, that not a morsel should be wasted. Water tanks were provided for use, in case of attempts by the savages to set the thatch roofs of the buildings on fire by means of arrows loaded with burning tow; while the most tireless vigilance was enjoined among officers and men. How that vigilance was enforced may be inferred from the letter of an officer of the garrison, written under date of July 6th, 1763 :

"We have been besieged here two Months, by Six Hundred Indians. We have been upon the Watch Night and Day, from the Commanding Officer to the lowest soldier, and have not had our Cloaths off, nor slept all Night since it began; we shall continue so til we have a Reinforcement up."

The indefatigable commandant had to use all his art to cope with his tireless foe. The vessels lying off shore were yet kept under the fort's guns, apprehending, as Gladwyn did, that Pontiac might try to effect their capture by boarding. Their guns swept the entire northern and southern face of the palisades—thus deterring the savages from any general assault. No occasion was lost for picking off every red skin who showed himself within range. Food was surreptitiously thrown into the place from over the river at night, by the aid of friendly Canadians. This beneficent act enabled the garrison to hold out, much to the astonishment of the Indians, who were, for a long time, kept in ignorance of the supplies sent over by boats. It was the Indians, indeed, who first wanted for food. Their improvidence had not been restricted by a state of war: they ate and wasted with the recklessness of fools. Thus their own stores of corn and cured meat was, ere long, exhausted, when they began to plunder the farm houses of the *habitans* to such a degree as compelled the Canadians to protest and demand protection of Pontiac. A deputation of fifteen old residents visited the Chief, laying their complaints before him, and threatening that when the French father came from Montreal "with his great army," he would punish the Indians as enemies.[1]

To this the Chief replied, extenuating the acts of the young men by reciting his own services in behalf of the Canadians, and particularly by referring to his co-operation, in the war with the Sac and Fox Indians, when he united with the French and assisted in defeating the Northern tribes—a war of which no historical record exists, though Parkman has succeeded in finding a confirmation of Pontiac's version of it in the Mss. of McDougal[2]—the officer who accompanied Major Campbell in his mission to Pontiac, May 10th. Pontiac repeated the story of a French army of invasion, and hoped that when it arrived all the Canadians who had assisted the English would be attended to. The Chief gave promise of protection but still reserved the right to provide himself and his warriors with food at the Canadians' expense. To this end, while his mandate was sufficient to protect the farmers from plunder, it was also potent enough to draw from their stores the supplies which the savages required. He established a depot at the house of Meloche, where, using several Frenchmen as assistants, the provisions were stored and issued in rations, to prevent improvidence. To the Canadians thus relieved of

---

[1] It would appear that, despite the news then generally disseminated throughout Canada and the Western posts, of the consummation of the treaty of February 10th, by which the French ceded to England all their possessions in the region named, there still prevailed a belief in the Canadas of a French invasion to regain their lost supremacy. This is referred to by Gladwyn—in a letter to Sir Jeffrey Amherst, dated July 8th, 1765—as the cause of the uprising among the Indians. Before the arrival of news regarding the treaty, Pontiac had dispatched agents to M. Neyou, French Commandant in the Illinois country, requesting his co-operation in the reduction of Detroit. Pontiac, however, knew before hostilities had progressed a month, that no co-operation could or would be extended by the French; but he preferred to keep the fires burning, by representing to the tribes of the vast section then seething in the throes of the conspiracy, that the French army would surely come to their aid. His falsehood and duplicity toward his own people were only exceeded in baseness by his treachery and cruelty toward his enemies.

[2] McDougal, it would appear, succeeded in effecting his escape from captivity among the Ottawas, and afterwards wrote out voluminous notes of the war. The documents are yet unpublished.

their property he gave notes or certificates of indebtedness, written on birch bark and signed by the Chief with his totem signet, the otter. The issue of these rough evidences of indebtedness is regarded by the Chief's biographers as indicative of remarkable intelligence in a savage. As the Chief was surrounded by men who well knew the value of, and the mode of preparing, notes of hand, it is to be presumed that, to reconcile the Canadians to the levies made upon them, he acceded to their demands for evidences, and simply gave what was required. No remarkable sagacity or intelligence were requisite for such an act.

We may, before pursuing the narrative of operations at and around Detroit, recur to the fall of those posts, in the then Indian country, against which the Conspiracy was directed.

Fort Sandusky was taken May 16th, by the treachery of the Wyandots. These Indians having been admitted freely to the fortification were regarded as friends. On the morning of the day named seven well known warriors applying for admission, were at once given an audience by Ensign Paully, commandant of the post. The visitors having seated themselves seemingly prepared for a smoke, when, a signal being given by one of the number stationed near the door, Paully was seized and disarmed. At the same moment a peculiar noise without informed him that the work of slaughter was going on among his men. He was soon led from the room to behold the parade strewn with the corpses of his troops. He was borne at once to the lake where canoes were in readiness, and his late friends paddled away for Detroit, offering the Ensign the sweet consolation of being burnt at the stake for Pontiac's edification. The light of his burning fort lit him on his way over the waters. He was conducted to the Ottawa camp, where for a season he served as a mark for the bludgeons and arrows of the women and children—a torture inflicted on all prisoners as preliminary to the severer tortures inflicted by the men. The poor prisoner was, however, saved from the fate in store, by being chosen as the husband of an old woman whose partner had died, and Paully became, to all intents and purposes, an Indian of the Ottawa tribe. He afterwards succeeded in escaping from the love embraces of his coffee-skinned spouse, and found refuge in Detroit.

The old post at St. Joseph fell on the 25th of May. Located on Lake Michigan, at the mouth of St. Joseph river, it was indeed far removed from civilization, yet but *fourteen* men garrisoned the place! A few runners of the Pottawatamies came during the evening previous, to "visit" that section of their tribe located near the fort. They bore Pontiac's order for the sacrifice of the garrison. On the morning of the 25th a great throng of savages (Pottawatamies) gathered around the place, and numbers found entrance within the garrison grounds, to play the usual game of perfidy and slaughter. The commandant, Ensign Schlosser, with three men, were spared and taken to Detroit to be exchanged for Indians then in Gladwyn's possession.

On the 27th of May, Fort Miami, on the Maumee river, in Ohio, (just above the present town of Maumee,) passed into the hands of the savages and Canadians. Its capture was accompanied by treachery of an unusual character. A Miami belle was the mistress of Ensign Holmes, then in charge of the post. His bronze beauty came to him on the morning of May 27th, representing a squaw to be dangerously ill, begging him to visit the wigwam, not far off. Holmes had suspected, from various signs, that the savages around him meditated treachery, and was on his guard; but, conceiving no perfidy to stain the heart of his companion, he at once followed her from the fort to the wigwams lying out of sight though not far from the fortification. Once within their precincts he was shot instantly. His sergeant, hearing the firing, and fearing the worst, passed out to reconnoitre, when he was seized. This left the post quite at the mercy of the savages. The garrison soon was summoned to surrender—the summons coming from white men, Canadians, who were engaged with the Indians. Having a promise of protection if no defense was made, the little garrison—isolated beyond hope of help or rescue, without a leader, and destitute, in some degree, of pluck—surrendered, and Fort Miami, holding the avenue of approach to the Wabash valley, was lost to the English.

Fort Ouatanon, on the Wabash river, in Indiana (below the present town of La Fayette,) was captured June 1st, by the Illinois, by stratagem, as its commandant reported in a letter to Gladwyn dated at that time. The Illinois, far removed from the influence of civilization, were comparatively a peaceful people. Acting under the influence of orders which they dare not disobey, they took the garrison prisoners and treated them kindly. This action proves how far-reaching was the power of the fierce Ottawa Chief.

Fort Michilmacinac fell June 4th, by the hands of the Ojibwas and Sacs. That most important post lay on the apex of the peninsula of Michigan, like a point of steel to serve as the entering wedge for civilization and commerce to the North. Its great importance and extreme isolation, however, did not see it properly garrisoned. It was held by about forty men under command of Captain Etherington. Nearly fifty other whites were at the post at the date of its fall, to partake of its disaster. The day preceding the fatal day, the Ojibwas informed the people of the garrison of their intention to play a game of ball—*baggatiway*—for a wager, inviting all to witness it. As the 4th was the King's birth day Captain Etherington permitted his men to enjoy the holiday, and very little caution was used in securing the fort. Discipline probably was forgotten. Captain Etherington and several of his officers passed out on the plain to witness the game, while the soldiers of the garrison flung open the gates and admitted a number of gaily clad squaws who were eager apparently for the society of the whites. They were conspirators in disguise; beneath each gaudy mantle was concealed the tomahawk soon to reek with the brains and blood of the unsuspicious victims. During the progress of the exciting game, in which four hundred savages participated, the ball was steadily pressed up toward the palisades, and, finally, with one tremendous stroke of the bat it was sent circling clear over the enclosure. With a wild shout and a furious rush the whole throng rushed to the gates, and, before officers or men were aware, the Indians were all within. Then came the work of slaughter. On the air arose the defiant war whoop. From beneath the squaws' blankets flew the iron hatchets and knives commissioned to the work of death, and, in a brief space of time, every English soldier on the parade was murdered and scalped. A trader who was present, escaped by the protection afforded by a French resident. We may quote a few paragraphs from his intensely interesting though appalling narrative:

"Going instantly to my window, I saw a crowd of Indians within the fort, furiously cutting down and scalping every Englishman they found. In particular, I witnessed the fate of Lieutenant Jemette.

"I had, in the room in which I was, a fowling-piece, loaded with swan-shot. This I immediately seized, and held it for a few minutes, waiting to hear the drum beat to arms. In this dreadful interval I saw several of my countrymen fall, and more than one struggling between the knees of an Indian, who, holding him in this manner, scalped him while yet alive.

"At length, disappointed in the hope of resistance made to the enemy, and sensible, of course, that no effort of my own unassisted arm could avail against four hundred Indians, I thought only of seeking shelter. Amid the slaughter which was raging, I observed many of the Canadian inhabitants of the fort looking calmly on, neither opposing the Indians nor suffering injury; and from this circumstance I conceived a hope of finding a place of security in their houses.

"Between the yard-door of my own house and that of M. Langlade, my next neighbor, there was only a low fence, over which I easily climbed. At my entrance, I found the whole family at the windows, gazing on the scene of blood before them. I addressed myself immediately to Langlade, begging that he would put me in some place of safety, till the heat of the affair should be over—an act of charity by which he might perhaps preserve me from the general massacre; but while I uttered my petition, M. Langlade, who had looked for a moment at me, turned again to the window, shrugging his shoulders, and intimating that he could do nothing for me: '*Que voudriez-vous que j'en ferais?*'

"This was a moment for despair; but the next, a Pani (Pawnee) woman, a slave of M. Langlade's beckoned me to follow her. She brought me to a door, which she opened, desiring me to enter, and telling me that it led to the garret, where I must go and conceal myself. I joyfully obeyed her directions; and she, having followed me up to the garret door, locked it after me, and, with great presence of mind, took away the key.

"This shelter obtained, if shelter I could hope to find it, I was naturally anxious to know what might still be passing without. Through an aperture, which afforded me a view of the area of the fort, I beheld, in shapes the foulest and most terrible, the ferocious triumphs of barbarian conquerors. The dead were scalped and mangled, and the dying were writhing and shrieking under the unsatiated knife and tomahawk, and from the bodies of some, ripped open, the savage butchers were drinking the blood, scooped up in the hollow of joined hands, and quaffed amid shouts of rage and victory. I was shaken not only with horror, but with fear. The sufferings which I witnessed, I seemed on the point of experiencing. No long time elapsed before—every one being destroyed who could be found —there was a general cry of 'All is finished!'"

All was indeed finished, so far as the destruction of the garrison was concerned. The officers were spared the general butchery by being run off into the woods. They were afterwards transferred to the keeping of the Ottawas from the Jesuit station of *L'Arbee Crocha*, twenty-six miles west of the fort. A good priest, Father Jonois, exerted all his influence in behalf of the captives, and, at Captain Etherington's request, made the arduous journey to Detroit to inform Gladwyn of the extent of the disaster. He arrived in Detroit June 19th, bearing a letter from the Captain in which, after detailing the events of the massacre, he begged for Gladwyn's immediate co-operation to regain the post—not knowing the extent of the latter commander's own great wants.

Although the post at Sault St. Marie was abandoned in the fall of 1762, its garrison did not escape the fate of Michilmacinac, for most of the men were victims in that massacre. A fire having partially destroyed their fortifications, they had been thrown into the fort on the south side of the Straits to await orders, or reenforcements before re-occupying the Sault station. Alas, they never returned!

The Green Bay station, though, by the prudence of its commanding officer, Lieutenant Gorell, it was spared the massacre of its garrison of seventeen men, was abandoned. After various trials the commander and his men succeeded in making their way by the Ottawa portage to Montreal—there to report to Sir Jeffrey Amherst as the only garrison of his western forts which had escaped destruction. Detroit alone held out, but how long could it escape the calamity impending?

The day succeeding Father Jonois' visit to Detroit, Gladwyn

received news of the loss, after an obstinate defense, of Presqu' Isle, on Lake Erie (now Erie, Pa.) This news was confirmed by the appearance, on the banks of the river opposite Detroit, of a band of prisoners—the remnant of the brave garrison. It was not until after the escape of Ensign Christie, several weeks later, from the Ottawas' village, that Gladwyn was informed of the full measure of the calamity. A band of Ottawas and Wyandots having been dispatched by Pontiac for the reduction of the post, appeared before the post on the 15th of June. The little band of defenders retired to the strong block house, where they made a defense quite memorable in the history of Indian wars. All day long, having the vantage ground of excellent breastworks, the savages pressed the assault so determinedly as to task the English to their utmost to save their fortress. A number of times it was in flames, which were only quenched by the use of the water preserved in barrels for the sustenance of the men. During the night the poor fellows had to work to sink a shaft for water, and, by morning, were rewarded for their exhausting endeavors. The precious fluid was needed, for early in the day of June 18th, the Indians having approached the garrison grounds by a mine, succeeded in firing the commandant's house, so near the block house as soon to set the little citadel again in flames. With the water, by great exertions, the place of refuge was once more preserved. During the 18th the fight was most obstinately waged, and night came to find Christie's men thoroughly prostrated from excessive labor. Still, they had to watch and fight on amid an atmosphere hot with fire and clogged with gunpowder smoke. At midnight a voice from without, in French, summoned the garrison to surrender, stating that preparations had been perfected for effectually firing the block house. After a brief parley an armistice was obtained for the night, when the men were permitted to sleep. In the morning, after ascertaining that the enemy had indeed prepared to roast the garrison alive, Christie surrendered, stipulating that himself and garrison should be permitted to make their way to the nearest post. When once within the hands of the Indians, however, the entire company was seized and borne to Detroit in captivity.

Pontiac kept them closely confined in defiance of the express terms of the surrender. As stated, Christie, ere long, by great daring escaped and reached Gladwyn in safety. The gallant fellow afterwards made a report, embodying the incidents of the defense.

The posts nearest Presqu' Isle were those of La Beuf, and Venango—both on the direct trail to Fort Pitt, now Pittsburg, Pa. The first was assailed on the evening of the 18th of June, by a detachment of the force then besieging Fort Presqu' Isle. It was soon in flames from fire arrows and flaming balls of pitch. The savages gathered around the gateway, waiting for the egress of their prey; but while the flames were roaring above and around him Ensign Price, the commandant, was cutting his way out through the rear walls. An opening having been effected he and his men all escaped, under cover of the darkness to the woods, proposing to find their way to Fort Pitt. They struck off into the wilderness leaving the savages dancing and yelling before the front gate, in the belief that the whites were roasting alive within. Price pressed on to Venango, where he arrived on the succeeding night to find nothing of that fort but embers, around which he was horror stricken to find the half consumed bodies of its little guard. It had been seized several days previously by the Senecas, who, having obtained admittance under pretence of friendship, butchered all the garrison except Lieutenant Gordon, the commandant. Him they reserved for the slow torture by fire. For several days, while the wretches feasted upon the garrison stores, and became infuriated over the whisky which always formed a leading article of supplies, they enjoyed their leisure moments in roasting the hapless commandant. He finally died under the torture, and, the stores having been consumed or wasted, the fiends set fire to the property and left that vicinity. Had Price and his little body guard arrived a day sooner it is horrible to think what must have been his fate. As it was, his command were great sufferers. Five of his thirteen men gave out on the way from Venango to Fort Pitt, and were left in the woods to perish of starvation. The Ensign and seven men reached Fort Pitt June 26th, in a distressed condition.

Beyond Fort Pitt, on the old Braddock trail to Cumberland were Forts Ligonier, Bedford and Cumberland, and Fort Augusta on the Susquehanna. All these posts were beset, but the savages were not in force enough to carry them. They seem only to have been after scalps and obtained many. Around most of these stations were settlements and farms. The Senecas and Delawares haunted the woods like hyenas, and carried terror along the whole frontier. These Indians united with the Shawnees, and for several weeks beset Fort Pitt, then commanded by Captain Ecuyer. Being in a position to hold his own against the assailants he answered their formal demands for a surrender, made July 26th (1763), by defiance and sarcasm. That night they invested the fortification, which stood facing the two rivers Alleghany and Monongahela, in whose forks it was built. Creeping up the banks of these two streams the savages dug burrows in the soft soil, and from their cover poured a severe fire into the fort above them. For several days this warfare continued, but was finally abandoned—the approach of Bouquet with his Highlanders, from the East, sending the savages in some haste to the wilderness.

We cannot here enter upon an account of the desolating war of the border which raged along the entire frontier, from the vales of Western Virginia to the Mohawk valley. Its story forms one of the most distressing chapters in our early history. Families which retired to rest in fancied security were awakened from their repose by the appalling war-whoop; fathers and brothers were slain in brave efforts to defend their loved ones; mothers shrieked for mercy in vain, or, after witnessing the braining of their little ones, were borne off into a captivity worse than death. Farms were desolated, buildings burned, stock slaughtered. The cry of wo and suffering went up from a thousand broken family circles. Men took to the war-path in defense, while their women and children were sent away to the east of the Susquehanna for safety. Then followed the subtle, relentless war of extermination. Settlers, mad with their losses, became as implacable as savages and neither asked nor gave quarter. The forests were haunted with pursuers and pursued, who flitted like evil spirits every where—seeking the darkest coverts for their enemies, and mingling in the hand to hand contest away off in labyrinths where the foot of the white man never before had trodden. The whoop of defiance, the shout of hate, the sharp crack of the rifle, the shriek of agony, were rapid episodes in the terrible drama. Then came the death struggle. If the dull sound of the tomahawk cleaving the skull was heard, and was followed by the dismal scalp-yell, it was a sign that the whites were overcome: if the rush of feet and the shouts of pursuit echoed through the woody fastnesses it was the good portent of victory to the settlers.

All through the summer and fall of 1763—through the months of 1764—this infernal warfare was waged; and not until after the successes of Bouquet and Bradstreet's expeditions against the Indian towns was quiet restored to the settlements on the eastern slope of the Alleghanies and in the Susquehanna vallies. It was not, indeed, until the year 1769 that the spirit of conspiracy was subdued and fears of a general massacre by the Indians allayed. Then followed a few years of repose, in which the settlements prospered, and the daring frontiersmen encroached rapidly upon the Indians' domain, only to be stayed by the storm of the War for Independence. That, for the while, arrested all progress, and placed the entire frontier again on the defense against the savages incited, by British gold and British promises, to the work of butchery.

Let us return from this inevitable digression again to Pontiac's own immediate operations against Detroit. Upon his success there seemed to hang the fate of his entire scheme. At least the pertinacity with which the siege was pressed would so seem to argue; and yet, when the Chief found that France would not embark in the war, what hope could he have had of any ultimate success? He evidently fought for the glory of leadership and from hate—not from the expectation of seeing his people restored to their hunting grounds and the whites driven over the Alleghanies. That he was ignorant of the power and resources of the English to crush him, is not at all admissable. He fought because he loved to fight.

Pontiac's force in the field, at first confined to the warriors of those sections of the three tribes—Ottawas, Wyandots and Pottawatamies—which were camping around Detroit, was rapidly augmented in June by warriors from other villages and tribes. His strength, however, was not formidable, at any time, had the garrisons not all been so weak. A force of one thousand trusty troops would have annihilated the horde of assassins which infested the neighborhood of Detroit, and that done, the same troops could have passed into Ohio, to punish the tribes there into obedience. The uprising was so well matured, the forts all were so rapidly assaulted, that no opportunity for reenforcements offered. The garrisons were destroyed ere help could have reached them. Then the conspiracy assumed such formidable dimensions as to render a general commonwealth organization of militia necessary, and several years passed away ere the punishment was inflicted which crushed out the fires lit by Pontiac's baleful influence.

About the middle of May (1763), the spring supply of provisions and ammunition was dispatched, in twenty small boats under command of Lieutenant Cuyler, from Fort Schlosser (just above Niagara Falls) to Detroit. No knowledge then was had of the hostility prevailing, and the boats' crews coasted up along the northern shore of Lake Erie in fancied security. Arriving at *Point au Pelee* island, May 28th, the boats all landed and the men proceeded to prepare fires. In a few moments an ambuscade of Wyandots—doubtless the identical band who had destroyed Sandusky twelve days before—opened on the troops, who at once formed as a cover to their boats; but, the savages becoming restless for their prey, and being in overwhelming force, broke from cover and dashed upon the lines. The English stood but a moment. The uplifted tomahawks, the hellish whoop, the bodies painted into hideousness sufficed to fill the hearts of the regulars with a sudden panic. Muskets were thrown away and a dash made for the boats, five of which were put afloat, filled to overflowing with the fear-stricken crowd. The savages seized two other boats and pursued, when three of the five little craft capitulated without defense. Two of the boats—one of which contained Lieutenant Cuyler—pulled for the adjacent islands (now called Put-in

Bay islands) and from thence to the fort at Sandusky, on Sandusky Bay. The fort, as already recorded, having been destroyed by the Wyandots, offered the fleeing men no refuge. Cuyler then started on his return to Niagara, following the southern shore of the Lake. He reached Presqu' Isle in safety and soon passed on to Niagara—to report the fall of Sandusky and his own losses.

It is sickening to contemplate the horrible end of the men seized in the three boats. After their capture the savages, with the entire flotilla of boats started for Detroit. On the morning of May 30th, a sentinel discovered the heavily ladened convoys rounding Montreal point. A great shout went up from the beleaguered garrison and a crowd of soldiers, *habitans* and traders at once rushed to the landing to welcome the relief. It was a moment of the wildest joy; but cheers and the booming of cannon were quickly succeeded by the most heart-rending depression. The answer to those notes of welcome was the appalling war-whoop, which came faintly over the water, while in every boat appeared a band of naked savages gesticulating and yelling like demons. The truth at once was evident to all, and the disheartened group on the landing returned, sickened, to the fort. Soon they were all excitement again. The boats gradually made their way up stream, pulled by the white men, over whom the savages held guard. When opposite the fort and the remaining vessel—one of the two vessels having then gone to Niagara to hasten up supplies—the crew in the first and leading small boat conceived the daring design of escape. The brave fellow acting as steersman grappled a stalwart Indian and flung him overboard, but the supple savage clung to the Englishman's garments and succeeded in pulling him into the deep river. They closed in the water, in a deadly struggle—the Wyandot using his knife with such fatal aim as soon sent his foe to the bottom. While this was transpiring the two remaining Indians leaped overboard, when the prisoners pulled for life toward the fort and vessel. The savages, with a loud cry of fury, struck out in pursuit; while the guard in all the boats, and the horde of Indians following along the eastern bank of the river, opened fire on the boat, wounding one of the three poor fellows in it. The chase became exciting in the extrem. Rifle balls cut the water all around into flecks of foam. Every moment the light canoes which had put out after the fugitives gained rapidly on the clumsy yawl. The fate of the soldiers seemed sealed, when, suddenly, the vessel opened on the pursuit with her six-pounders, and the three brave men were saved. The first ball cut the water close to the foremost canoe. Other shot which quickly followed caused the entire disappearance of the savages, who ever entertained a kind of supernatural dread of the "big bullets." The entire boats' crews were landed and the boats beached, while the wretched prisoners were marched around to the Ottawa camp above, to enter at once upon their tortures. Their corpses, blackened with fire and wounds, were cast into the river to float by the fortress and the vessels and thus warn the Englishmen of the fate reserved for all prisoners. A number of Canadians came, in terror to the fort, during the evening of that day (May 30th) to report such details of the sufferings of the prisoners as served to sicken and appal every listener. The Pontiac Ms. gives the following version of this awful affair:

"The Indians, fearing that the other barges might escape as the first had done, changed their plan of going to the camp. They landed their prisoners, tied them, and conducted them by land to the Ottawa village, and then crossed them to Pontiac's camp, where they were all butchered. As soon as the canoes reached the shore, the barbarians landed their prisoners, one after the other, on the beach. They made them strip themselves, and then sent arrows into different parts of their bodies. These unfortunate men wished sometimes to throw themselves on the ground to avoid the arrows; but they were beaten with sticks and forced to stand up until they were dead; after which those who had not fired fell upon their bodies, cut them to pieces, cooked and ate them. On others they exercised different modes of torment by cutting their flesh with flints, and piercing them with lances. They would then cut their feet and hands off, and leave them weltering in their blood till they were dead. Others were fastened to stakes, and children employed in burning them with a slow fire. No kind of torment was left untried by these Indians. Some of the bodies were left on shore; others were thrown into the river. Even the women assisted their husbands in torturing their victims. They slitted them with their knives, and mangled them in various ways. There were, however, a few whose lives were saved, being adopted to serve as slaves."

Such was the mercy meted out to helpless men by the "magnanimous savage"—as Pontiac's biographers have been pleased to term this monster of perfidy and cruelty.

It was but a few days after this that a procession of savages appeared on the eastern bank of the river bearing on poles the scalps of the Sandusky garrison. And from that time onward, until the fate of all the posts had been determined, Gladwyn was, at intervals, first made acquainted with new disasters by the sight of scalps or of prisoners exhibited on the Canada side of the stream. Thus the dreary monotony of the siege was stirred, though painfully, by episodes which served to redouble the vigilance of the beleagured men. What a fate was in reserve for them if Pontiac once became possessed of their defense!

All excitement was not, however, of a painful character. One of the two schooners anchored off the fort at the opening of the siege had been dispatched to Niagara for reenforcements and stores. The vessel missed Cuyler's convoy and passed down to Fort Schlosser, where she still remained at the date of Cuyler's return with his two boats' crews. She was then put in good trim and dispatched to Gladwyn's relief—Cuyler and his remaining men embarking in her. June 19th she had reached Detroit river and lay off Turkey island to await a favorable breeze with which to run the gauntlet that Cuyler knew was in store for them at the narrow channel along Fighting island. The vessel lay calm-bound below the island until June 23d, when a favorable breeze induced the commander to weigh anchor and to try the passage. The trip promised success, when, at the most critical moment, all wind died away leaving the little craft again becalmed. Anchor was cast in the narrowest part of the channel, as it would not do to drift down with the current for fear of grounding. All things were made ready for an attack. The banks swarmed with Indians, too eager for their prey to keep concealed. Over five hundred of the villains were on the bloody scent. Cuyler had learned caution, however, and so disposed his force as to be ready for any emergency. Night dropped down over all, not densely dark, for the stars gleamed out purely and the clear waters of the river reflected their light like a mirror. The sentinels were as sleepless as the stars, noting every shadow on the surface of the stream. Every log which floated lazily down the tide might shield the body of a savage whose eye-balls just peered above the water's surface to reconnoitre the point of attack. Every clump of grass, every nest of water reeds were felt to contain a living man ready to burst from cover at any moment when the rush should be ordered.

Just after midnight the forms of canoes were descried coming rapidly down stream. Their design evidently was to board the vessel so quickly as to give no opportunity for the use of the cannon. But, they were not successful. They came rushing down to find every man at his post. Swarms of savages sprang into the stream from each shore, making direct for the schooner. Cuyler waited calmly until the canoes and swimmers were within close musket range, when the signal was given and a fire opened with grape and musketry which crashed fearfully through the canoes and sent death over the waters. Fourteen savages were killed and large numbers wounded ere they could get beyond range. They fled howling to the shores and opened fire from a sand breastwork on the vessel. Cuyler dropped down stream a little distance, and was safe.

A second attempt to ascend, made two days later, was successful. She ran the gauntlet of a severe shore fire and gained the broad stream above Fighting island, to press on, with a good breeze to the fort. Passing the Wyandot village a murderous discharge of grape into the wigwams was the welcome which the vessel brought for the conspirators. To the garrison she brought gladness in many shapes. Not the least joyful intelligence was the conclusion, between England and France, of the Paris Treaty, by which the latter abandoned all claim to her old territory. This, it was thought, would compel the savages to give over all further hope of French aid and thus compel them to abandon their chimerical project of extirpating the English. But, there is every reason to think that Pontiac had not, after the first outbreak, counted upon French aid, although he studiously held out the idea of a great French army coming up the St. Lawrence in order to commit all the tribes under his influence to the war path.

Receiving help from no white source except from the half-breeds[1] and a few Canadians, Pontiac resolved at length to compel the French inhabitants along the river to take sides either for or against him—knowing that they would not do the latter for fear of consequences to their property and families. The Chief had but to give the command and involve all the *habitans* in one common massacre. A council was convened late in June, to which the leading French residents were summoned. It was largely attended by chiefs of the several tribes and by the Canadians. Pontiac's speech was somewhat violent. He said: "You claim to be friends and yet relieve and sustain the English by presents of provisions. You go through our camps and villages then report all to the English. You must be English or French. If you are French take up the war-belt and assist us: if you are English we shall declare war against you." To this an old Canadian replied by dissimulation. He confessed their willingness to aid the savages but held in his hand a copy of the treaty of Paris, by which they were bound not to war. He asked Pontiac, therefore, to say what they could do. The Chief was unable to answer; but his heart was gladdened by a number of "hard cases"—a set of whites whose long association with the Indians, as well as their brutal instincts, made them savages. How many of these rascals volunteered it is not stated. The council terminated satisfactorily: a great dog-feast followed, and the French ruffians were formally received into the tribes as members.

---

1 Half breeds became a quick growth in every tribe brought into contact with "civilization." As in the Slave States the great multitude of mulattos is proof positive not only of the waut of virtue among the negroes, but also of the gross sensuality of their white masters, so the presence in every tribe of Indians of great numbers of half breeds is evidence of the general absence of female virtue among the aborigines. The longer the contact with civilization the greater the demoralization which has followed. There are but few exceptions to this rule. Unpalatable as the statement may bc, our philanthropists and political economists will have to accept results even though they contravene theories and hopes of progress.

Night saw the renegades on the war-path. Proceeding to the fort, with a party composed of an equal number of Ojibwas, they threw up an entrenchment, under cover of the darkness, and early dawn found them in a position to worry the garrison. A squad of soldiers sallied from the fort at once and dislodged them—the white Indians running away at the first appearance of the troops. The Ojibways held their ground for a moment and then fled, leaving two of their number dead on the field. One of these, a soldier—who had been for seven years a captive among the Delawares, and who hated the race of red men with an intense hate—scalped, holding up the bleeding lock to the sight of the escaping savages. This act inspired the Ojibwas with unutterable rage. The red skin scalped was a nephew of Wasson, Chief of the Ojibwas. Wasson at once blackened his face in token of revenge, proceeded with a party of braves to the house of M. Meloche where the venerable Major Campbell still was confined, seized and murdered him on the spot, cut out his heart and ate it, then gave his body to the water, from which it was recovered by the Canadians and decently interred. This brutal murder so enraged Pontiac that Wasson and his party were compelled to flee to Saginaw for their lives. For the veteran Major the Ottawa Chief entertained a real respect, and the Conspirator doubtless held him in captivity to subserve his purposes in procuring terms of settlement, should the war prove disastrous to the Indian cause.

Affairs did not prosper under Pontiac's own immediate charge. The fort had not fallen and, after the arrival of the transport, more than ever defied his assaults. The two schooners so annoyed his villages by frequent bombardments early in July as to compel the savages, to their great discomfort, to move back into the woods. The smaller vessel having returned, a second time to Niagara, Pontiac determined to destroy the larger schooner. If her destruction could be effected the Chief had hopes of carrying the fort by assault. A fire-raft was constructed, composed of two floats loaded with combustibles. On the night of July 10th, it was fired and sent down stream. The vessel lay too close to shore for injury from the fire messenger; it passed down the stream harmlessly Not discouraged, the savage constructed a second and much larger raft, which was sent down on the night of July 12th. It was, evidently, directed by pilots, for it struck the shore current and followed closely down; only a steersman could have kept it from drifting out into the middle of the stream. The flame, too, was suppressed apparently until the moment when the pilots left the float; then the conflagration became quickly intense. The spectacle presented was one of sublimity. A vast tongue of flame leaped upward, circling around as if eager to catch the victim in its fiery folds. Against the background of the night it looked like an avenging demon out on its mission of devastation. Every farm house stood out in relief by its flame; every man on the fortress, every savage lurking on the shore, every canoe on the stream, were pictured in clear distinctness by that lurid glare, which penetrated far into the fastnesses of the woods around. Every heart in the fort throbbed wildly at the spectacle; each man stood in awe before that contrivance of devils to sweep away their chief defense and hope. But, the fear was only momentary. The artful pilots had over-done their work, for the raft passed in between the fort and the vessel, and floated grandly yet harmlessly away into the darkness below. As it slowly swept by a cannon boomed out on the night. A group of savages stood revealed on the river bank, watching the raft. The gunner trailed his piece on their dusky forms and a ball went hurtling into their midst. They vanished like spectres.

A third raft was then constructed, but Gladwyn took the precaution to anchor booms in the stream above the vessel thus completely outwitting the red rogues who, doubtless, acted in this matter under the advice, and with the assistance of their white coadjutors, before referred to.

The Indians now began to tire of their fruitless struggle. Although a large party of Shawnese and Delawares joined Pontiac's force in July, and about the same time, an Abenaki runner from Lower Canada came in with the news that the French were advancing up the St. Lawrence in a big fleet, the original confederates of the Ottawas grew disheartened and re

John H. Gowan Del. John Rogers sc.

PONTIAC'S FIRE RAFT.

J. D. Torrey Publisher 13 Spruce St. New York

solved to withdraw. The Wyandots first made proposals of peace and a truce was declared with them. They kept their word just three weeks. The Pottawatamies soon followed their example, and, after some trouble on account of the non-delivery of white prisoners held by their tribe, Gladwyn signified his amity with them. This apparently left the Ottowas and the fierce Ojibwas alone in the field. With the detachments of Shawnese and Delawares, and the French renegades, Pontiac still controlled a formidable force. The Wyandots and Pottawatamies were ready for the war-path at any moment which seemed propitious for scalps. Their treaties were the merest mockery.

Reenforcements at length reached the beleaguered garrison. Having received news of Cuyler's disaster, Sir Jeffrey Amherst —then at New York on his return to England—dispatched his aid-de-camp, Captain Dalzell, to Niagara, with orders to gather all the forces it would be safe to detach from the lower forts and with them to proceed to Gladwyn's relief. Dalzell, a brave but impetuous officer, who had shared with Israel Putnam in many of his adventures, accepted the service with pleasure. Early in July he was *en route* up the Lake, with two hundred and eighty men and twenty-two barges. A landing was made at the desolated posts of Presqu' Isle and Sandusky. From the latter he marched (July 26th) with a section of his force, upon the Wyandot town, a few miles to the south. This he destroyed, together with its cornfields and its orchards. The expedition then hurried on to the Detroit river. Under cover of a fog—rare, indeed, on that stream so late in the season—the flotilla passed up in safety during the night of July 28th and the morning of the 29th. The vicinity of the Wyandot and Pottawatamie villages was reached ere the convoy was discovered, when these savages at once forgot their late treaty, and a heavy attack was made. Fifteen of the troops were killed and wounded. Dalzell replied with musketry and boat howitzers, so hotly as to drive the red-skins from their coverts on the shore. The barges then pulled for the fort, where they were received with the wildest acclamations. The men were not made more welcome than the rich supply of stores and ammunition which they convoyed.

Dalzell, upon the day of his arrival, concerted an attack on the Ottawa village. Gladwyn discouraged the enterprise, conceiving it, doubtless, as rash and perilous to court disaster. Dalzell's importunity, however, bore down opposition and it became known throughout the garrison that an attack was to be made. This imprudent revelation was fatal to success. Two hours after it was known in the fort Pontiac was in possession of the plan, and, without delay, arranged to ambuscade the English.

The march to the Ottawa camp was along the river road to the creek, one mile and a half above the fort. Near the creek crossing was the house of Meloche. The Ottawa village had been located just beyond the bridge, on the ridges; but, scourged by the vessels' fire, it was removed up the creek, three miles away. Dalzell's plan was to march by night upon the village and surprise the savages: Pontiac's plan was to ambuscade the English at the bridge and surprise them with defeat. The English left the fort, at two o'clock on the morning of July 31st, two hundred and fifty strong. Two barges followed by the river, to co-operate with their swivels. The men pressed on to the creek. Over the little bridge the advance guard of twenty-five was passing when, from their front burst the war-whoop of two hundred savages, lurking in the darkness behind trees, fences, woodpiles, houses and stumps. The yells were followed by a discharge of rifles which brought down half the advance. It staggered before the unexpected blow and receded upon the centre. Dalzell rushed to the front, rallied the line and led the men in person over the bridge. Again the appalling whoop, followed by a volley which brought the troops to a stand. But they quickly recovered, and, led by Dalzell and Captain Gray, the centre of the detachment charged upon the ridges over the stream, on which the Indians had taken post. But the alert warriors glided away into the darkness; the troops charged in vain against woodpiles and fences; not a savage could be discovered until the sharp crack of a rifle, from some near cover, betrayed the momentary presence of an

Indian. This warfare with an invisible foe so disconcerted the men that Dalzell wisely resolved to withdraw to the south side of the creek, there to await day-light before pressing his advance. The retreat was made in good order, under a heavy and galling fire. Watchful as lynxes the Ottawa warriors kept close to their game, and, had the night been more favorable to true aim not a man of all that command would have been left alive by daybreak. The two barges, drawn up to the bridge, received the wounded and dead. Captain Grant in command of the rear detachment soon found that the assailants had crossed the creek, for they were upon his flank and rear almost as soon as the troops began to retire from the ridge. Having the cover of Meloche's house, orchard, fences and out-buildings, the assault was opened from them so sharply that Grant ordered his men to charge. As in every instance the bayonet found no enemy to pinion: the Indians glided away with the silence and rapidity of reptiles. In Meloche's house two Canadians were found who informed Grant of Pontiac's design of getting in between the English and the fort—thus to cut off all escape. The news was communicated to Dalzell, and quick steps taken to guard the road so as to keep up the line of retreat. The entire command soon began the retrograde movement—Grant on the lead and Dalzell covering the rear. The savages were now reenforced by bodies of Wyandots and Pottawatamies. These, with a body of Ottawas, Pontiac posted at a point where the attack would find the English compacted and less able to move in body, Arrived at this position the Indians attacked with great fury, throwing the regulars into a panic which well nigh proved fatal. Only Dalzell's great courage and power of command saved his men from butchery. The savages had grasped their tomahawks preparatory to a hand to hand struggle, when the column reformed again and was pushed forward in good order. Major Rogers, with his band of rangers, was ubiquitous. These men, skilled in Indian warfare, fought the red-men successfully. They lurked behind trees and fences, stole along through the grass, bounded around barns and houses sending their knives into many a savage breast.

This fierce struggle continued the entire distance to within range of the palisade guns. Captain Gray fell mortally wounded in a charge upon a fence; Dalzell was killed, and his reeking scalp torn from his head in sight of his men. Rogers finally flung his force into a house which commanded the road and thus effectually covered the retreat, after Dalzell's fall. Grant had also obtained a good position in an orchard, where he kept the savages at bay while the main body passed down the road. Here he was joined by Rogers and, together, these intrepid leaders so manœuvred from house to house as to hold the fortunes of the retreat safely. It was eight o'clock ere the last of that ill-fated expedition reentered the gates. [1]

The returns gave the losses as nineteen killed and forty-two wounded—a small number considering the nature of the contest. It would have been much greater had the darkness and the fog been less dense. Much was due, also, to the splendid manœuvering of Grant and Rogers, after day-light had come. The loss of the Indians could not have been great.

The result of this combat—called by historians the "battle of Bloody Run"—was to reinspire the Indians in their cause. They soon spread the news of their victory—magnified of course in its report of numbers—far and wide, receiving in return accessions from various tribes, until fully one thousand warriors invested Detroit. Yet, no assault was attempted. With the force then in the fort—fully three hundred strong—Gladwyn was in a position to defy his assailants; he had, apparently, only to await the passage of time to free him of his troublesome enemies.

---

[1] The account given by Drake in his work—"The Biography and History of the Indians of North America"—is singularly at variance with the version here adopted, though that author so far corrects the "popular version" as to publish Major Gladwyn's report of the "Battle of Detroit." That report varies in immaterial particulars from that given by Parkman, and which we have preferred to follow. The latter author recites many interesting incidents of the affair gathered from the descendants of persons then living in or around Detroit. General Lewis Cass having collected the material for a History of the Siege of Detroit, obtained much personal data, to which Mr. Parkman had access. The production of Parkman's work doubtless prevented General Cass from fulfilling his first design, though he had contributed several valuable papers to the Michigan Historical Society bearing on those interesting times and events. The celebrated Pontiac Ms. often referred to, is, we believe, deposited in the archives of the Society.

After the fight of Bloody Run nothing save occasional sharp-shooting occurred to break the monotony of the siege until September 5th, when the second arrival of the little schooner, dispatched to Niagara in July, gave the garrison fresh food for excitement, inasmuch as, during the previous night, she had been boarded by over three hundred savages, and yet had escaped. The story of that adventure was as follows:

The vessel, having a crew of eleven men—with six Mohawk Indians, sent by Amherst as spies and scouts—entered Detroit river on the 3d of September (1763). The succeeding morning the Mohawks were permitted to go ashore to scout. They never returned, but made their way direct to the villages above to give the alarm. The Captain felt keenly his danger, but contrary winds kept him from going up the stream. That night, about nine o'clock, a great number of canoes were seen rushing down upon him, and, almost before the bow gun could be discharged, the horde of savages was swarming over the bulwarks. Delivering one volley of musketry the crew threw down their guns and rushed upon the boarders with pike and cutlass. A furious hand-to-hand contest followed, in which it was soon apparent that the whites must be overpowered. The Captain being killed, the first mate—a very resolute fellow named Jacobs—held command. Seeing the savages about to accomplish their design, he ordered one of his men to fire the magazine and blow up the vessel. The order was understood by a "civilized" Wyandot, who repeated it in horror, and, with a loud yell, leaped overboard. In a twinkling the entire mass of red-skinned humanity was gone. Warriors decked in gay attire and bedaubed in artistic grease, soot and vermillion, dashed overboard like frogs, and, for a few moments were seen fluttering and ducking in the river in the most grotesque haste to avoid the expected explosion. They soon disappeared entirely; in less than ten minutes from the first gun, all was silent again. The crew's loss was two killed and four badly wounded. Eight savages were killed on the decks and about twenty wounded—of whom eight were reported soon to have died. The vessel passed on up the river the succeeding morning (Sept. 5th), reaching the fort in safety. For their bravery the crew was rewarded with silver medals struck by order of the commander-in-chief, commemorating the event.[1]

This second addition to the garrison's supplies quite disheartened the beleaguering host. Winter was approaching and their own necessities soon must drive them to the woods if they would save their families from starvation. Their ammunition also was fast running low, threatening to leave them powerless to secure their winter's food. Then came the news of a heavy reenforcement *en route* for Detroit, sufficient to carry the war into their villages. It was time for them to make peace, if only to gain time to recruit their energies for another year's work of slaughter. After conferences among the confedrates a chief of the Missisaugas—a branch of the great Ojibwa family—appeared at the fort October 12th. In a talk with Gladwyn he professed to represent the Ojibwas, Wyandots and Pottawatamies, who were sincerely sorry for their bad conduct and had sent him to beg forgiveness and peace. To this Gladwyn replied by granting a truce—a peace could only be secured through Sir William Johnson, His Majesty's Commissioner of Indian Affairs. The policy of this truce will be apparent when it is stated that Gladwyn's stores were even then at a starvation point—his men all being upon short allowance; and, should the promised reenforcement under Major Wilkins fail, by any mishap, to reach him, he would be compelled to evacuate the post. A truce opened communication, for a few days at least, with the *habitans* around; and Gladwyn used it so well that, ere a week had passed, the fort was supplied with meat, corn and potatoes enough for a winter's siege.

The Ottawas held aloof from this arrangement, although they did not, so far as we can learn, show hostility to their allies. Pontiac doubtless consented to it as the only means of

[1] The account given by Sir Jeffrey Amherst, of this gallant affair, represented the Indians to have been fairly repulsed by the crew, and no reference is made to the incident here recorded, of Jacobs' order to blow up the vessel. The incident is well authenticated, however, in the several Ms. accounts obtained by General Cass from the old Canadian inhabitants, as well as by several cotemporary writers. See Pennsylvania *Gazette* No. 1816. Drake's account of the event differs in almost every particular from the version here given. There evidently is a vast difference between his industry and care, and that exhibited by Parkman.

preserving any future authority over the tribes; he submitted to what he could not prevent. Still, the warriors of his tribe proudly kept up a show of hostility, more as a matter of pride than of effect. They sought to worry foraging parties, to cut off stragglers, and kept the fort under close surveillance, but accomplished little. How much longer Pontiac would have fretted against the bars shutting out even his hopes of success it is not hard to determine. On the last day of October (1763) he received answers to his demands for help, dispatched months before to the French stations in the Mississippi valley. M. Neyon, commander of Fort Chartres, the chief fort and depot in the Illinois country, wrote to the Ottawa Chief that the French being at peace with the English no assistance could be rendered, and he therefore advised Pontiac to cease a warfare which could do no good. This note was, it would appear, written by M. Neyon at the demand of Sir Jeffrey Amherst; and the fact that it was not written until so demanded shows the French to have connived at the war even if they could offer no aid. But, it is folly to presume that Pontiac had based his dreams upon the contingencies of their co-operation. We conceive it an improbable inference that, for the first time, after the receipt of M. Neyon's letter he beheld "his long cherished hopes of assistance from the French swept away at once," as Parkman has it. He knew, long before, of the treaty of Paris; he had received no voluntary assistance even from the Canadian *habitans*, save such as we have referred to as having been given by a few ruffians and half-breeds; and M. Neyon's letter added nothing to his "weight of disappointment." Parkman adds: "he saw himself and his people thrown back upon their own slender resources. In rage and mortification he left Detroit, and, with a number of his chiefs, repaired to the river Maumee, with the design of stirring up the Indians in that quarter and renewing hostilities in the spring." That letter, indeed, was propitious to the designs of the Chief, since it enabled him to deceive his followers once more by putting on the semblance of mortification and rage to cover his exit to the south.

The siege of Detroit by the savages thus was raised, to give place to the siege by winter's frosts, storms and snows—a siege dreaded even to this day, when the comforts of civilization are attainable even by the poor. The Indians of all the tribes scattered during October to the woods, in their depths to find the game required for their subsistence, and to court the shelter from storms which the grand old arches of the wilderness gave to all.

From this point the conspiracy proper is merged in the history of Sir William Johnson's diplomacy as Indian Commissioner General; of Bradstreet's campaign to Ohio and Detroit, from Niagara; of Bouquet's expedition into the Muskingum country from Fort Pitt, and of the mission of Captain Morris to the Wabash country—all of which transpired during the summer and fall of 1764. These several enterprises were concerted by the Lords of Trade, as preliminary to a new policy of kindness and conciliation to be pursued toward the Indians after they should be made to feel England's power. Sir William Johnson [1] and his deputy George Croghan were strenuous in their efforts to instate such a policy, but they conceded the impossibility of employing it until the savages were first

[1] Sir William Johnson was a man of remarkable traits. An Irishman by birth, he emigrated, when a young man, to the Mohawk valley, and there soon rose to wealth and importance, gaining a great influence over the Iroquois tribes, afterwards called the Six Nations. During the French war this influence was exercised so successfully for the English as to keep the Iroquois from the field except as allies of the English. He acted also as a Major-General in the war, and, with the Colonial troops and a small body of Iroquois, won an important victory over the French under Baron Deskau, at Lake George. This success gave him a baronetcy and a present of five thousand pounds sterling. He was then appointed Superintendent of Indian Affairs for the Northern tribes—an office for which he was admirably qualified, by courage, sagacity, knowledge of Indian character and influence over the savages. In 1759 by the death of Prideaux, the Commanding-General at Niagara, he was placed in the chief command, and, after a severe battle routed the French, planting the cross of St. George on the old stronghold. After the peace he so far maintained his power and ascendancy over the tribes in New York as to prevent them from joining in the Pontiac conspiracy—the Senecas only giving way to their thirst for blood, under the malign influence of the Delawares.

The late Colonel Wm. L. Stone, in the course of gathering materials for his most excellent Life of Brandt (Thayendanega) Chief of the Six Nations, became possessed of much valuable original data regarding Johnson. This he prepared with a view to its publication, but, unhapily for our historical literature, the author died before completing his task.

brought into subjection by force of arms. The programme laid out for 1764 was to put two armies in the field, one under Bouquet to reach the Delawares, Shawnese and Miamis; the other under Bradstreet to penetrate to Detroit, punishing every tribe which had shown hostility in Pontiac's war.

Prior to the departure of these two expeditionary armies, Johnson had sent out runners of the Iroquois, calling a grand council to assemble at Niagara. Those who would escape the impending blow he warned to make their peace by attending this council. Bradstreet arrived at Niagara late in July, 1764, to find a host of Indians encamped around—in answer to Johnson's summons. The baronet's messengers had penetrated to the North and West, finding all the tribes who had engaged in the war in a state of much destitution, owing to the sudden cessation of the fur trade and their losses by the war. They were therefore all the better disposed to a peace. Even the wild Ojibwas, who had then been summoned by Pontiac to again take the field before Detroit, preferred to accept Johnson's overtures and soon started their deputation to the council. Nor were the Ottawas unrepresented in that gathering of aboriginal notabilities—the section of the tribe at *L'Arbre Croche*, under the good priest Jonois, sending a deputation. But they were the "Christian Indians" whom Pontiac scorned: not a member of *his* people was at the council.

Johnson opened proceedings by first treating with the Indians separately—a tedious but politic process. In this manner he made peace with the Sacs, Foxes, Winnebagoes, Menomonies, Mississaugas, Caughnawagas, Ojibwas, the L'Arbre Croche Ottawas and a small deputation of the Detroit Wyandots. From these he extracted solemn promises of good faith, and they returned to their peripatetic homes filled with rum and loaded with presents. All were well pleased with the interview. The Shawnese and Delawares sent to the council the insulting message that they would treat for peace out of pity for the "old women" (the English).

These proceedings ended, Bradstreet started for the West, accompanied by a large body of the Iroquois and by many Canadians. His orders were to proceed first to Sandusky, carrying war into the villages and country of the Wyandots, Ottawas and Miamis. Arriving near Presqu' Isle, August 12th, the expedition was forced, by a storm of wind and rain, to land. There Bradstreet was met by a band of savages, who, proclaiming themselves to be Shawnese and Delawares deputies, sought terms of peace for those tribes. They were a band of warriors out on the war-path, who assumed the guise of agents for the purpose of testing the mettle of the English commander. He appears to have been a self-willed, unsagacious man. Against the advice of his officers, against the protest and warning of his Indian allies, that the pretended deputies were spies, he entered into a preliminary treaty to refrain from attacking their tribes—they stipulating to meet him with all their white prisoners at Sandusky, there to conclude a definitive treaty. As Bradstreet was not empowered to treat at all—as the Shawnese and Delawares were not in his province—as Bouquet was especially commissioned to act against these tribes, Bradstreet's conduct certainly merited the censure afterwards bestowed upon it by the Commander-in-Chief, General Gage. Bradstreet sent word to Bouquet, then preparing to advance from Fort Pitt (now Pittsburg), that he might forego his expedition as the Shawnese and Delawares were already reduced to terms! The vigorous and sagacious Bouquet treated the affair as it deserved—with contempt, and hastened to push into the territory of the treacherous and relentless Southern Ohio tribes. Even while these pretended emissaries had stipulated for peace their warriors were marching along the whole Pennsylvania and Virginia frontier; nor did they abate in atrocity until Bouquet's bayonets had forced the demons to a full submission and the rendition of every white captive in their keeping.

After this exploit Bradstreet rowed along shore with his great flotilla until Sandusky was reached. There the same wretched farce was gone through with of accepting the "submission" of the Wyandots; while Captain Morris, with a small body guard of Canadians and Indians, was dispatched to the Maumee country to treat with Pontiac, with orders also to proceed on up to the Wabash country there to treat with the Miamis. Garrisoning Fort Sandusky Bradstreet pushed on to Detroit, arriving there August 26th, 1764. He was received with a frenzy of joy by the long beleaguered garrison, who were at once relieved from duty. The siege of Detroit was raised. A grand council was at once called, and on the 7th of September he met, in the open air, a full delegation of the Wyandots, and a single deputy, the Chief Wasson, who represented the Ottawas, Pottawatamies, Ojibwas, Miamis and Sacs. These he addressed through a *French* interpreter—an act which so incensed his allies, the Iroquois, that they refused to shake hands, to confirm terms which they did not understand. That simple act, together with Bradstreet's generally pusillanimous conduct, so unpleasantly impressed them that when they sought their homes it was in disgust and anger; nor could Sir Wm. Johnson's potent influence reconcile them. They became sullen though not hostile—a state of affairs particularly to be regretted at that time when a general reconciliation and fraternization was hoped for. Bradstreet readily obtained from the obsequious savages the promises he demanded.

Pontiac had invested Detroit with many of his warriors during the spring and summer, keeping the garrison in a constant state of alarm. At Bradstreet's approach he withdrew to the Maumee country, there to keep the fires of vengeance burning by the power of his great influence and his resistless eloquence. There Captain Morris found him, and at his hands received such a welcome as proved the Chief to be little inclined to peace. Dispatched, in August, to the Maumee country, Morris proceeded from Sandusky by the Lake to Maumee, and thence by canoes up that stream until the vicinity of the Ottawa villages was reached. He encountered a horde of braves whose feeling toward the Englishman was made strikingly manifest by menacing gestures and rough usage. At the village he was confronted by Pontiac in person. The Chief scowled ominously at the missionary and refused to accept his extended hand. "The English are liars!" he ejaculated, at the same time producing a letter purporting to have been written by the King of the French to him, promising aid and co-operation. This epistle of course was a forgery, but it served to give the Chief a tangible excuse for his continued hostility. Morris could obtain no hearing; his party were stripped of their property, though he was permitted to pursue his journey to the country above. At old Fort Miami he barely escaped murder at the hands of the Miamis. The fort was in possession of some Canadian traders, who desired to offer him protection, and did so, although it was apparent that his life might be sacrificed at any moment. A deputation from the blood-thirsty Shawnese and Delawares had arrived with war-belts, but a short time before him; Morris, hence, found the Miamis ready to co-operate in the general war proposed. These treacherous tribes were treating with the too-easily duped Bradstreet for peace at the very moment they were stirring up the western Indians to an exterminating war. Their proceedings with Bradstreet and their efforts to stay the progress of Colonel Bouquet's force were solely to gain time for a general uprising—a scheme in which we can readily conceive Pontiac to have entered with a leader's zeal. Morris was finally taken from the fort by two Miami warriors, stripped and led bound to the great village, passing to what he deemed his martyrdom at the stake. He was surrounded by the rabble and received with an uproar of epithets. Two of his Canadian attendants followed, resolved to save him at the risk of their lives. A leading Miami chief, named Swan, also interposed, and, sustained by a young chief—a nephew of Pontiac—severed the bonds of the captive.[1] Morris then took courage and essayed to speak, when a chief named White Cat again seized him and bound him fast by his neck to the faggot post. At this a chief, named Peccane, interposed and, in great fury, bade them to go for English meat to Detroit. The Englishman came as an ambassador and should be protected. He was released, yet only escaped the fury of his persecutors by being closely protected. He was at length permitted to return

[1] This act, it is probable was a stroke of policy. Godefroy, one of Morris' Canadian attendants, told the Indian that Gladwyn had a number of Ottawa warriors in his hands as prisoners, and that any harm to Morris would be the signal for their death. This fact, expressed by the Canadian boldly, doubtless saved Morris from the stake.

to Maumee—several chiefs acting as a body-guard, in addition to his faithful Iroquois and Canadian attendants, who never, for a moment, had failed to sustain him.

Thus the "embassy" was ended. Morris returned exhausted and dispirited to Detroit—arriving there Sept. 17th, 1764, to find Bradstreet gone. Having dispatched garrisons to re-occupy the posts at Green Bay, Michilmacinac and Sault Ste Marie, and leaving with Gladwyn a force sufficient for effective defense, the Colonel returned to Sandusky, with the main body of his troops, to complete his arrangements with the deputies of the Shawnese and Delawares, with whom, it will be remembered, he had stipulated to treat. Arriving at Sandusky he awaited several days over the appointed time, but no deputies, with their promised train of white captives, appeared. A few warriors, lurking upon his track as spies, appeared in the British camp and begged a further delay, promising that, if Bradstreet would remain quiet for another week the prisoners should be forthcoming. The foolish commander acceded to their request; instead of seizing the rascals as hostages for the fulfilment of their promises, he allowed them to depart on their mission of arousing the savages to oppose any march into the country. Had Bradstreet essayed to penetrate to their villages he would have found the Ottowas, Miamas, Wyandots and Shawnese in his war-path in such numbers as would have rendered his track a bloody one, even if the army was not overcome. During that week's delay, however, Bradstreet was put in possession of General Gage's rebuke, already referred to, repudiating his proceedings and ordering him to proceed without delay to execute his orders on the Sandusky tribes, then to push for the Sciota country, there to effect a junction with Bouquet. Then soon came the journal kept by Captain Morris, dispatched from Detroit. Bradstreet's eyes were now fully opened to his folly, yet he had not the courage to obey orders and march to the Sciota country. Conceiving various excuses for inaction after several weeks longer tarry at Sandusky Bay he started to return to Niagara with his entire force—a company of regulars being left to garrison the fort. The flotilla had scarcely emerged from the beautiful bay into the open lake beyond Cedar Point ere a storm gathered and for three days the expedition was tempest-tossed. Many of the boats were beached, others were leaky. Re-gathering his forces, it was found that the barges were too few to convey the troops. Most of the Iroquois and a detachment of provincial militia were thereupon ordered to march along the shore, to Niagara—a distance of over two hundred and thirty miles, through jungles, over streams and swamps, with no equipments and provisions except such as they could carry on their backs. It was an inhuman order, and, had the Shawnese been in the vicinity, the entire band must have perished. As it was, they reached Niagara, after a seventeen days' march, the provincials in miserable plight, and the Iroquois so thoroughly infuriated and disgusted as to be rendered enemies of the English instead of friends. Thus this expedition, promising auspiciously at the outset, ended with half-accomplished purposes. It had reinvigorated Detroit, regarrisoned several of the forts taken by the savages, and distracted the Indian confederation so far as to drive Pontiac into Ohio for his allies; but, the formidable Chief was neither brought to a treaty nor forced to submission; those hyenas of the woods, the Shawnese, and the equally implacable Delawares, still were on the war-path, desolating the border and keeping alive the fires of the conspiracy. Bradstreet is justly censured for his short comings, which were serious indeed. Had Sir William Johnson's influence been less the entire Iroquois confederacy (Six Nations) might have drifted into the league of savages against the whites, so dissatisfied were they with the English military commander.

But, good came of Bouquet's conduct of the campaign into the Muskingum territory. Into the forest fastnesses beyond the Muskingum river the Shawnese and Delawares had removed their villages, preparatory to a vigorous prosecution of their war of extirpation. All the long summer those savages continued their butcheries penetrating to the *east* of the Alleghanies with torch and tomahawk. Villages supposed to be secure; quiet vallies, up and down whose slopes stretched farms and dwellings; old trading posts, given over to decay as too near the haunts of civilization—all were made to feel the terror of Shawnee and Delaware visitation. To stay this barbarous butchery the efforts of the settlers and local forces were powerless:[1] it was necessary to carry the war into the Indian country, to burn their villages, to ravage their corn-fields and to crush the warriors in battle, in order to compel the blood-thirsty wretches to terms. To this work Bouquet was assigned. A better man could not have been chosen. His experience during the previous year at the sanguinary battle of Bushy Run proved him to be of the right *mettle*, while his discretion and wisdom were known and trusted. The savages feared him as they soon learned to despise Bradstreet; and when it was found that the latter's order for the other to discontinue his expedition from Fort Pitt was to be disregarded—that Bouquet was to carry the war into their very villages, the barbarians first began to think of peace.

Bouquet, with his five hundred Highlanders, one thousand provincials and a strong body of skilled Virginia and Maryland border men, penetrated to the wilderness where several offending tribes had deemed their families safe. The middle of October found him over the Muskingum river, prepared to carry devastation into every village. His enemy, beholding the ruin and suffering in store for them, convinced that no perfidy and treachery could avail to save them from punishment, hastened to make terms of peace. A narrative of the ceremonies and negotiations which followed forms a very interesting chapter in the history of the war. By the prudence, the stern decision, the sagacity and the justice of Bouquet every object of his mission was accomplished without destroy-

[1] Among other measures adopted to encourage the settlers and others to hunt the Indians the Governor of Pennsylvania issued a proclamation offering a bounty on the scalps of Indian men and women. This act has by some been regarded as a barbarous measure; but, when it is known that the "braves" were sustained on the war-path by the labor and prowess of their squaws—that the squaws never failed to wreak a horrible vengeance upon every captive—that, when occasion offered, the Indian women assisted in massacre—it must be a very Quaker conscience which can censure the proclamation. The Indian women were as ferocious as the Indian men, and it could be scarcely expected that settlers whose hearth-stones were yet warm with the blood of their murdered wives and innocent little ones would submit to a *partial* punishment of their detested foe.

ing a single field of corn or the injury of a single family. Shawnese, Delawares, a seceded section of the Senecas, a village of the Tuscaroras, all were brought to humiliation and subjection. Captives to the number of two hundred, embracing men, women and children, were restored; some of the women having been taken by the savages as wives, their children by the unnatural alliance were not permitted to remain—all were restored to civilization and their homes. What a painfully joyous meeting must it have been when those long-lost ones were restored to their broken households! Alas, how many never returned! [1] Parkman, in his narrative of Bouquet's expedition, dwells at considerable length upon the scenes and incidents which transpired during these interesting and eventful moments of reunion.

Where was Pontiac? In the midst of all these calamities to his cause the proud Chief still held a defiant front. One by one his allies left his side—the Ojibwas, Pottawatamies and Wyandots first; then the Shawnese and Delawares, upon whose strength he rested in security. He witnessed the movements of Bradstreet and Bouquet, powerless to oppose them; but, his fertile mind was concocting new combinations to carry on his wild crusade against civilization. In the fall of 1764 we find him once more on the scene of operations. His restless spirit, undaunted by discouragement, now arose in mighty majesty; his Conspiracy took new form; his power once more became formidable to the English.

His plan now was to unite all the warriors of the Mississippi valley in a league of hostility against the English, to prevent them from taking possession of the forts in that section ceded by the treaty of Paris. With four hundred warriors, composed of chiefs and noted braves of several tribes who scorned to make peace—of Miamis, Ottawas, Shawnese, Delawares, Senecas and Wyandots—the Conspirator started in the autumn of 1764 on a grand embassy to the West. The route lay through

---

[1] Many cases are well authenticated where young girls were wooed and won by bronze lovers, and so attached did the "wives" become to their dusky partners that they refused to leave their wigwams. This class of persons, though females, always exercised considerable influence in every village.

the country of the Miamis, Kickapoos, Piankishaws and of the Illinois tribes. In every village his imperious spirit found utterance in words winged with the eloquence which ever stirs a savage breast, and the war-song went up along his path. Arrived in the country of the Illinois he found himself in the midst of French whose hatred of the English was little less than his own. By these men he was cajoled with promises of aid never destined to fulfilment. They represented matters in very false colors, and, it is said, really impressed Pontiac with the belief in aid from the King of the French. In expectation of this aid the Chief visited Fort Chartres, on the Mississippi river, where the French were still in command and possession. M. Neyon de Villiers, angered and humiliated at the cession of French possession, in the Illinois country to the detested English, had withdrawn from his post and gone down to New Orleans, where he fondly supposed the French were to remain masters. His command was turned over to M. St. Ange de Bellerive, an old officer who had spent a lifetime in this Indian service. This officer was greatly perplexed at the anomalous state of affairs which surrounded him. A French commander, with a French garrison, surrounded by French trading posts and Indians all devoted to the French interest, he was only awaiting a relief garrison to transfer all to English possession. He could therefore do nothing but wait. Beset by savages clamorous for their usual supply of powder and guns, by traders soliciting aid he could not give, by agents stirring up the Indians to hostility against those to assume the control of affairs, his position was one of perplexity from which there was no escape. It was not rendered any the less intolerable by the sudden advent of Pontiac and his band of four hundred resolute warriors. The haughty Chief was prepared to demand aid as his right, and did so in terms which St. Ange could not mistake. But the French commander really was powerless to comply with the request for arms and ammunition, and so answered, much to the Chief's anger and disgust. The stern warriors encamped around the Fort, evidently resolved to make it their resting place to await the appearance of the English, when the fires of warfare were again to be lit.

The delay at this point was, for another reason, somewhat imperative. When the embassy first started for the West Pontiac prepared an immense wampum belt, which was dispatched to the tribes of the South, by the hands of a delegation of well-known Shawnee, Delaware, Miami and Ottawa chiefs. This belt was borne down the Mississippi river to all the tribes along its boundaries. Everywhere it was received with great ceremonies, and, in every instance, so far as the record exists, did not fail to stir up the spirit of strife. Pontiac's name was well known to every warrior of note even among those living in the far South, and his embassy was accredited with all the respect due to a chief whom the savages all acknowledged as their superior. The wampum, after having visited all available tribes, was finally borne to New Orleans, there to lay it before the French Governor, and, in Pontiac's name, to demand of him aid in guns, ammunition and stores, with which to carry on the war against the English. The accredited warriors appeared in the Southern city at an unpropitious time. They were, indeed, most unwelcome. The French Governor, M. D'Abbadie, was then very ill from excitement and chagrin. But a few weeks previous to the Indian advent the news was promulgated that, by a secret convention, France had transferred to Spain all her possessions in the Louisiana territory. This filled the cup of bitterness for the proud and really able Frenchman at the head of affairs, and he awaited the arrival of the Spanish garrison and Governor to quit the country in disgust.

Pontiac's messengers were not to be deterred from pressing their claims upon D'Abbadie, and a council was granted, to which a number of English officers were admitted. A Shawnee chief, displaying the great war-belt, spake for the embassy. Parkman thus reports the speech:

"These red dogs" alluding to the English, "have crowded us more and more, and, when we ask them by what right they come, they tell us that you, our French fathers, have given them our lands. We know that they lie. These lands are neither yours nor theirs, and no man shall give or sell them without our consent. Fathers, we have always been your faithful children, and we now have come to ask you that you will give us guns, powder and lead, to aid us in this war."

The extreme feebleness of D'Abbadie prevented much of a reply. He strove to appease their evident excitement and dismissed them with orders to have them cared for as his guests. That night he died, and, at the council of the succeeding day, his successor, M. Aubry, failed to answer satisfactorily to the Indians' demand. A Miami chief made a fierce speech, full of bitterness toward the French for being conquered, and of hate toward the English. "As for you," he exclaimed, turning toward the English officers present, "our hearts burn with rage when we think of the ruin you have brought on us." M. Aubry declared it his wish that the Indians should be at peace —that the English meant no harm and would treat them well if they behaved well. A few presents were distributed among the thoroughly infuriated ambassadors, and, early on the morrow, they were paddling their canoes up the Mississippi, their hearts thoroughly surcharged with the fury of disappointed hope and disgust at the impotence of their old friends and fathers, the French. They bore in their keeping the words which must forever dash Pontiac's hopes of aid from any source; and, without arms, how powerless was he even with ten thousand braves at his call!

The embassy reached Fort Chartres on its return in February, 1765. Pontiac had awaited the coming of his agents with much anxiety. We can imagine the rage which filled his proud and defiant soul at the request sent by the French Governor of New Orleans for him to make peace with the English. Yet, what could he do? The all conquering English were pressing in from the East. Croghan, the deputy of Sir William Johnson, was, even then, after immeasurable peril, in the Illinois country, having entered successfully on his mission of pacification. One by one the Western tribes passed from the power of his savage control to accept the terms tendered by the English agent. There remained for the Chief but two courses to pursue: one, escape to the west of the Mississippi, where dwelt the wild and powerful Dacotah, the remorseless and intractable Sioux, the subtle and suspicious Osages—not one of whom would confess the other brother, or war together in any common cause. Pontiac could hope to do little with them, even with his powerful eloquence, and might, at any moment, excite jealousies which would cost him his life. To the North were tribes ready to obey his will, but what were they if alone pitted against the strong foe? He might, indeed, banish himself, with a proud remnant of his people, to the regions of Lake Superior, but, what an end to all his dreams of power!

The second alternative opened for his choice was that of peace—to accept the terms of amnesty and reconciliation extended by Croghan and to abide the issue of events—hoping that, in the unsettled order of affairs a disorder might arise propitious to his further attempts at aboriginal consolidation. This alternative he resolved to adopt. How must his turbulent spirit have revolted at such a step! Yet, we can well believe he found consolation in his perfidious heart. Duplicity, treachery, insincerity, were weapons kept in reserve when all others failed: upon their potency he relied, with a savage obliviousness to honor, to carry him through even the humiliations of a peace.

Croghan's mission was one full of wild adventure and danger. It required not only a stout heart to penetrate the Indian country, but great prudence in managing the savages over whom the wand of peace was to be waved. These qualities the deputy of Sir William Johnson appears to have possessed in a bountiful degree. Though attacked by the Kickapoos on the Ohio, just below the mouth of the Wabash, and two-thirds of his party killed or wounded, the leader was spared and borne a prisoner to Vincennes, where he found a kind reception from Canadian traders, and the chiefs friendly to the objects of his mission. From Vincennes, though a prisoner, he was permitted to proceed up the Wabash to Fort Ouatanon, arriving there June 23d, 1765, to find the old fort tenanted by a motly crowd of traders and savages of both sexes. By these he was made welcome; and the news, which soon spread by messengers, of his presence and the powers with which he was clothed, soon served to surround him with deputations from all the adjacent tribes and sub-tribes. These Indians all smoked and made peace, swearing eternal fealty to the English. One tribe of the Illinois dispatched a messenger—a Frenchman—to Ouatanon with the polite request for the Indians at the post to burn the deputy; but, peace was already made, and no Pontiac was there to perpetrate the atrocious act.

The news of Croghan's arrival and labors soon reached St. Ange at Fort Chartres, whose disagreeable position already has been adverted to. Surrounded by Pontiac's hungry and defiant warriors, all the winter and spring the French commander had lived in daily expectation of an outbreak. Day by day he had kept his weary watch over the stream which flowed away in its wonderful tide to the Gulf, hoping to see the cross of St. George bearing up to his relief; but, though two expeditions started from New Orleans they were abandoned as impractical, and, up to the date of Croghan's arrival, no English force had reached Fort Chartres. St. Ange, hence, welcomed the agent and dispatched a messenger to hasten his visit to the Illinois country. Arrangements were soon made for the journey. No longer a prisoner he was attended by a large body of warriors and chiefs as an honorary guard and the march to Fort Chartres commenced. When but a few miles on the way, Croghan was surprised by encountering the formidable Ottawa Chief, who, it appeared, was *en route* with a large body of his leading men for Ouatanon, to make peace with the agent. All returned to the Wabash, where a council at once was convened and the terms of a treaty soon arranged. Pontiac treated the Englishman with a dignity becoming a great brave. He acknowledged that he had been deceived by the French, but failed to concede to any white man rights to soil.

This practically ended the objects of the mission to the Illinois country. Accompanied by Pontiac and a large retinue of his warriors, Croghan bent his way to Detroit, by way of Fort Miami and the Maumee river, holding conferences at numerous villages on the route. He reached Detroit August 17th, to find great numbers of Ottawas, Pottawatamies and Ojibwas in the vicinity, all eager to enter into covenants for peace.

Their sufferings through a total cessation of the fur trade, by which their many wants of blankets, guns, ammunition, kettles, &c., had been supplied, their losses in battle, and the absence of their usual supply of rum, all conspired to make the red-men repentant and anxious for Croghan's coming. He quickly convened the chief men of all the tribes in the old Pottawatamie council chamber. There Pontiac had lit the fires of conspiracy, and there it was meet that they should be quenched. Even the blood-thirsty wretch who had led the massacre at Michilmacinac was present to ask terms of reconciliation. Pontiac was a comparatively quiet spectator, taking but small part in the ceremonies, though lending his influence to a consummation of the objects of the mission. He, to all appearances, acted in good faith, though it is not to be conceived that his thoroughly perfidious nature was capable of acting from any other impulse than of policy. On the 28th of August, in reply to Croghan's formal speech of congratulation and fraternity made on the previous day, Pontiac declared his peace to be permanently made, and closed with an eloquent exordium that the rum-barrel might be opened and his warriors be permitted to quench their thirst.

The conferences were not finally ended until late in September, when Croghan returned to Niagara to report the success which had attended his labors. His journal, written out with much care, still is preserved in the State Office at Albany. It was perused, at the date of his return, by Sir William Johnson and General Gage, Commander-in-Chief, with great satisfaction. It was the record of the close of the great Conspiracy.

Our narrative would properly close here, but we may be permitted briefly to recur to the succeeding career of Pontiac.

Early in the summer of 1766 the Ottawa Chief, agreeable to promise made to Broghan, started upon a visit to Sir William Johnson. Attended by sixty of his chosen warriors and several chiefs from the confederated tribes, he passed down Lake Erie from the Maumee river, on which stream he had located his people. The voyage was made in birch-bark canoes along the southern shore of the great Lake, over which the mighty fleets of the all conquering race were, ere another half century, to sweep. Could the proud savage have had the veil lifted—could he have beheld the coming of the mighty host scattering great cities in its train, how would his barbarian spirit have raved in its impotence! He really stood upon the threshhold, only a shadow of the past—a type of the darkness doomed to pass away before the white skinned civilization coming.

Arriving at Schlosser canoes and packs were taken on the shoulders of the bronze braves and borne down Niagara river past the falls to Lake Ontario at Fort Niagara. From thence, after a brief tarry, the little fleet pursued its way down to Oswego, where Sir William Johnson awaited the Ottowa's coming. How he was informed of that coming we are not advised, but he was present, with an imposing body of Iroquois, to receive the Western deputation.

The first meeting of welcome took place July 23d, 1766.[1] The formal grand council opened on the succeeding day and was continued until July 31st. It was attended with the usual Indian ceremonials and forms, but proved highly interesting in its matter and manner of discourse. All things were arranged satisfactorily, and the council ended by a distribution of numerous gifts to the embassy. Johnson, throughout the entire proceedings, acted with his usual keen judgment, and apparently, gained over the mind of Pontiac and his followers influence like that which he had won over the Iroquois. That it was only a passing influence was demonstrated ere a year had fled, when the West again resounded with threatenings which were soon to be followed by the second war of the border—a prelude to the sacrifices and massacres of the Revolution.

Pontiac does not appear upon the stage again except like a portentous shadow flitting hither and thither through the Western wilderness to excite the anxiety of garrisons and traders. Though it is not known that he actually incited the

[1] From the Minutes of Proceedings now preserved in the State Office at Albany, we learn that chiefs of the Ottawas, Hurons, Chippewas (Ojibwas) and Pottawatamies were present. Pontiac in his reply to Johnson's address, said among other things: "I speak in the name of all the nations to the Westward, of whom I am the master." And again: "When you address me, it is the same as if you addressed all the nations of the West."

savages to a perpetuation of their rancor toward the English, it is certain that his influence was not exerted to fulfil the terms of his treaty; every commander, agent and trader in the West, from Fort Pitt, Presqu' Isle, Detroit, to Michilmacinac and Fort Chartres, felt that his influence was bad; he was everywhere, and, apparently with good reason, regarded with distrust. Had he been spared to the period of the War of the Revolution, with what joy would his treacherous heart have welcomed the British Government's call of the savages to the field! Well, indeed, for the border settlements in 1777 and 1778 that the great Conspirator was dead.

He was murdered in 1769 by a member of one of the Illinois tribes. Accounts are, however, quite conflicting regarding the time and place of his death. Parkman gives confidence —properly so, we think—to the precise statements of the late Pierre Chouteau, of St. Louis, who, through all his after life, recalled the incidents distinctly. He stated that Pontiac, with a number of his chiefs, had visited the Illinois country—for what reason is not known. In April, 1769, he spent several days in St. Louis, then a Spanish post. There, he was so favorably received as to add to the anxiety of the English regarding his presence. He, at length, passed over the river to Cahokia, where the Illinois Indians always were congregated in considerable numbers. Cahokia was an old French settlement, whose Creole inhabitants had so far assimilated with the red race as to seem like their veritable "brothers." Pontiac found a warm welcome at their hands. A feast followed and, in common with all his warriors, the Ottawa Chief became drunk. The moment for the English to rid themselves of their detested and dreaded foe seemed to have arrived. A trader named Wilkinson, then in the village, resolved to see the deed of assassination consummated, and, with a barrel of whisky bribed a vagabond brave of the Kaskaskia tribe to kill the Chief. The favorable opportunity was not long wanting. Pontiac, loaded with liquor, reeled away into the woods, chaunting as he staggered along the medicine song of the race of magicians, to which the Chief was reputed to belong. This was the last ever seen of the great warrior alive. His dead body was, in a brief time discovered. Then followed a scene which beggars description. From hamlet to hamlet the intelligence flew. The air resounded with the wails of the Ottawa warriors. Soon these wails were changed to the wild war-whoop, and the warriors, swinging aloft their tomahawks, cried aloud for vengeance. The Kaskaskias drew their weapons for the onslaught, apparently eager to annihilate the whole Ottawa band. But, no bloodshed followed. Pontiac's followers bounded off into the woods, to bear to the tribes of the East and North news of his death, and to call them to the war-path. The murdered Chief was left weltering in his gore until the body was claimed by St. Ange—then commanding at St. Louis—who buried it with martial ceremony near the Spanish fort.

Parkman observes, of the war which followed: "Could his shade have revisited the scene of murder his savage spirit would have exulted in the vengeance which overwhelmed the abettors of the crime. Whole tribes were rooted out to expiate it. Chiefs and sachems, whose veins had thrilled with his eloquence—young warriors, whose aspiring hearts had caught the inspiration of his greatness, mustered to revenge his fate, and from the North and East their united bands descended on the villages of the Illinois. Tradition has but faintly preserved the memory of the event; and its only annalists, men who held the intestine feuds of the savage tribes in no more account than the quarrels of panthers or wild cats, have left but a meagre record. Yet enough remains to tell us that, over the grave of Pontiac, more blood was poured out in atonement than flowed from the hecatombs of slaughtered heroes on the corpse of Patroculus; and the remnant of the Illinois who survived the carnage remained forever after sunk in utter insignificance." If such was the vengeance of savages towards their own race, it is not to be wondered at that their vengeance toward the whites was characterised by a cruelty and ferocity which would have shocked the barbarian hordes who swept down from the North to destroy Roman civilization. It was well for the destiny of the American colonies that Pontiac's Conspiracy was powerless to roll back the tide of civilization setting in toward the boundless West. Had the great Conspirator succeeded in preserving his ascendancy the wilderness and prairies of what is now the grain garden of the world must have long remained a haunt for wild beasts and savages. Let us be rejoiced that he did not appear one century earlier.

THE PAXTON "RIOTS."

PENNSYLVANIA was the scene of intense excitement during the winter of 1763–64. In the settlements along the Eastern slopes of the Alleghanies and the upper vallies of the Susquehanna, Indian barbarities that are sickening to contemplate had scarcely ceased when a spirit of revenge sprang into life which, for a brief season, threatened the total subversion of all order in society if not all order in government. It originated primarily in hostility to the Indian race, and, secondarily, in the Quaker policy of the Pennsylvania Assembly. While it supported from public monies bodies of Christianized Indians, the Assembly, owing to its Quaker majority, refused to sustain the hardy border men in resisting incursions of the savages. The awful sufferings of the frontier settlements; the tardy, almost heartless, co-operation of the Assembly; the protection and support given to the Moravian and Conestoga Indians; the bitterness existing between the Quakers and the Presbyterians—all conspired to excite the frontier men to a course which, though reprehensible, had strong extenuating circumstances.

A remnant of an ancient section of the Iroquois still remained (in 1762) at the "Manor" of Conestoga, below Lancaster on the Susquehanna. A treaty made with William Penn, and ratified by succeeding Governors, had guaranteed to the Indians their possessions in the manor; there they had lived, undisturbed, for many years—decreasing in numbers as the red race usually does when brought into contact with civilization.[1] At the date under notice the entire community comprised only twenty persons—men, women and children, who obtained the means of sustenance through the manufacture by the women of baskets, brooms, bead-work, and by the rude cultivation of small corn patches. The men (six in number) were veritable vagabonds, who, at any moment, would sell their squaws' honor for a dram of rum. They were considered by their white neighbors simply as a social nuisance, perfectly harmless, and not considerate enough of their own welfare to do any thing requiring exertion of any kind.

The massacres along the Susquehanna above Lancaster, during 1763, had so thoroughly exasperated the people that no quarter was given to any savage caught on the war-path. The woods were infested with the tireless warriors, who crept like snakes upon their prey, indiscriminately butchering men, women and children—a few only of the females being spared to be borne off into captivity. All the year long a great cry of sorrow went up from the region, now so beautiful in its richness, comprised in the counties of Cumberland, Dauphin, York, Lancaster and Berks. The people ceased to cultivate lands; estates and tenements were deserted, the fugitives seeking safety in the eastern and southern settlements; everywhere along the frontier only the hardy border man tarried, to care for his little property or to hunt the savage. Even in villages not then remote from the thickly settled district tireless vigilance

---

[1] We say "civilization" for want of a true term by which to express a painful fact. Contact with the whites almost uniformly carries vice to the Indian household and community. It debauches the females and debases the males, both to a degree incomprehensible when we consider that the red race has a quick and penetrating intelligence, that it loves independence and, in its native state, possesses noble traits of honor and virtue. Palpable reasons for this vice are offered; as, for instance, the Indian love for liquor—the female love of adornment—the disinclination of the males to labor—the native love for a vagabond life. But, all these are incidental faults; they never were displayed until the white man came with his "civilization", and, by all the laws of logic they are therefore chargeable to that civilization. In his most primitive state, when his passions are those of the tiger—playful when at peace but remorseless when on the war-path—the savage is infinitely preferable, in the great scale of humanity, to the creature that he becomes after association with the white race.

was used to prevent surprise; every man carried his fire-arms to church, to the field, in his visits, and kept them by his bed-side at night.

Among the places sacked and its inhabitants butchered during the French War (1755) was Paxton—a little settlement on the Susquehanna, near the present site of Harrisburg. It was, in 1763, one of the most exposed of villages. Its people were relatives of those murdered in the first onslaught of the savages, and in their bosoms burned a hatred of the red race to be quenched only with the annihilation of their detested foe. In common with most of the border hamlets it was peopled by Presbyterians of North-of-Ireland descent—a race of men about equally addicted to scripture, to dislike of Quakers and to eagerness for a "set to" with any kind of an antagonist. They were not lacking in the material for a riot, nor did they lack for reasons which offered them, at the time, enough excuse for their violence to find many sympathisers among men in high station.

We have here the two ingredients of the outbreak which followed. The Paxton, men confident that the Conestoga vagabonds were leagued with the hostile Indians, acting as spies for them and giving them shelter, resolved upon the "wiping out" the entire twenty—men, women and children. During the second week of December a Paxton scout reported that an Indian guilty of crimes on the frontier had been traced to Conestoga, where he was entertained by the manor families. This fired the combustible materials of the "riot." Matthew Smith, a recognised leader among the Paxton people, called five of his trusty fellows to the saddle and they proceeded to the manor to reconnoitre. Reaching it early in the night Smith himself approached the cabins, and, peering into those in which fires were burning, discovered what he reported to be armed savages. Thus the worst suspicions of the settlement were confirmed, and it was resolved no longer to delay the oft-threatened extirpation. Gathering about fifty men, well armed and mounted, Smith led the way to the cabins, reaching them early on the morning of December 14th. The party picketing their horses in the woods, approached stealthily on foot through the snow, but not so noiselessly as to give no alarm. The susceptible ear of an Indian caught the muffled tread of feet. He issued from one of the cabins to reconnoitre. A rifle ball brought him to the ground, shot by one of the band who professed to recognise the savage as the one who had killed his (the border man's) mother. A wild shout rent the air and the borderers passed into the little tenements to kill every red-skin found. Only six were there—all the others having, as if in premonition of their fate, scattered throughout the neighborhood during the previous day. These six were horribly mutilated—the white men, for the moment, becoming veritable savages. The cabins were then rifled of whatever of value they contained and the torch applied. By the light of the flames the "avengers" made their way, through the deep snow, toward Paxton.

An alarm soon spread. The light of the burning log houses lit up the sad scene and brought many neighbors to the spot. These gathered the half consumed bodies of the dead and gave them decent burial. The sheriff of Lancaster, being on the ground at once, gathered the fourteen remaining Indians from the farm houses in the neighborhood and had them borne for protection to the Lancaster jail. Excitement over the tragedy ran high. The general voice then condemned the murder as atrocious and uncalled for, though a few, with the old hate of the race still rankling in their breasts, extenuated the deed of blood as an excusable revenge for wrongs suffered. The news quickly flew to Philadelphia. Governor Penn offered, by proclamation, a reward for the discovery of the murderers, and, for a few days, there was an earnest purpose on the part of the authorities to ferret out every man concerned in the crime.

But, all this scarcely affected the bold fellows who had resolved upon wiping out the Conestoga tribe—fourteen of whom still remained, though safely protected by the strong walls of the stone jail in Lancaster. A spy was dispatched to the jail, by the Paxton men, to ascertain if, among the Indians in the jail, there was one suspected of having killed a relative to a member of the men in arms. The spy reported favorably to the suspicion; when the band determined upon a visitation to the jail, under the guidance of one Lazarus Stewart. Smith, the former leader, accompanied the second expedition—which, it is stated by some authorities, was only for the seizure of the suspected savage, who was to be borne to Carlisle, and, if identified of the crime attributed to him, was there to be hung. If the leader entertained such a design his men certainly were not of his mind; they enlisted to consummate the horrible work commenced at the cabins of exterminating the wretched outcasts.

Having arranged all for a sudden descent on Lancaster the band left Paxton December 27th, 1763—all well mounted and armed. In starting from the village they were confronted by their pastor, Rev. John Elder, whose influence though great could not dissuade the men from their purpose. Pushing on to Lancaster, at three in the afternoon the Paxton rangers rode rapidly into the town, turned their horses loose in a yard and, without a moment's delay, rushed to the jail. The door of the strong building offered but a moment's resistance; soon the entire mob of desperate men was inside. The fourteen Indians were, at that moment, in the jail yard. They cowered before the sudden storm and read their fate at a glance. Two or three of the red-men seized billets of wood as if to defend themselves, but there was no defense against the rifles and tomahawks of fifty savage whites, intent on blood. Crowding into the yard they quickly completed the work of death. It was a revolting act: men, women and children were involved in the common massacre. Did any show signs of life a dozen rifles and tomahawks were made to do service on the helpless victim. Not one was spared; the spot which, a few moments before, was their friendly shelter, became the altar of their sacrifice.

So quickly was the deed consummated that the alarm could not be given in season to arrest the perpetrators: they were on their horses, flying out of town before the people were aware of what had transpired. The chief magistrate, Edward Shippen, and most of the leading citizens, were at church celebrating a Christmas service, which had been deferred from the previous day. In the midst of the service a man burst open the door and shouted "murder—jail—Paxton men

—Indians!" The audience rushed tumultuously forth and from the house of worship passed into the presence of death—death in its most horrible aspects. There lay the victims, scattered around through all parts of the yard, mangled shockingly, heads blown to pieces, bodies pierced, limbs lacerated—the work of men professing to be Christian. It was a sight from which all turned in horror. A decent burial was given the remains, outside the town limits, where the bones were permitted to remain until eighty years afterwards, when a railway excavation first disturbed their repose.

This shocking butchery sent a wild thrill of horror to the bosoms of the Quakers in the province. Their indignation found vent in a wholesale denunciation of the murderers and their alleged friends, the Presbyterians, who, it was asserted, defended the two murderous expeditions by citations from scripture.[1] This inculpation soon heightened the wrath long existing between the two sects, and from that hour for many years they became as irreconcileable as two positive poles of a voltaic battery. Governor Penn issued a second proclamation, offering what was then deemed to be heavy rewards for the detection and arrest of the murderers; but none were arrested, though no concealments of their share in the butchery were practiced by those who did the deed: they rather boasted of their act as one of proper retributive and religious justice. No arrest could have been made except by a heavy force of military; but no such force was available. Indeed, it is presumed that, feeling, as all soldiers then did, a deadly hatred of the entire Indian race, they would not have acted as a *posse comitatus* to hunt the hardy Paxtonians.

There was, however, but brief respite for enforcing legal processes. Successful in exterminating the Conestoga vagabonds, the Paxton men were emboldened to conceive themselves constituted ministers of vengeance, and, in the plenitude of their assurance, they resolved to finish the Moravian Indians—thus to save the peaceful missionaries all trouble of civilizing the barbarians. To this precious project of wholesale butch-

[1] Deuteronomy vii. 2, was particularly cited by the rioters themselves as a pious defense of their act.

cry it is true that a majority of border men lent a willing ear, moved by their irreconcileable hate of the Indian, their disgust of the non-combatant Quakers, and their indignation toward a General Assembly which appropriated public money to support missions, yet offered a beggarly assistance to those struggling against the horrors of savage visitation on the frontier.[1] In the Assembly were only ten representatives from the five counties of Lancaster, York, Cumberland, Berks and Northampton, while the counties of Philadelphia, Chester and Bucks had twenty-six members—the majority of whom were Quakers. As the counties first named were settled chiefly by Irish and Scotch Presbyterians, their minority in the Chamber placed them and their prosperity quite at the mercy of the drab coated, broad brimmed majority. In consequence, the wrath of the frontier men waxed strong in proportion to the wrong conceived to have been done by the Quakers.

The Moravian Indians, two months prior to the Conestoga affair, had been so threatened by the border men that their missionaries had been impelled to consolidate their three communities and to remove to a place of safety. Nazareth was first chosen; but, from thence, owing to the continual public excitement, the General Assembly ordered their removal to some spot near Philadelphia where, being entirely disarmed, it would be out of their power to do harm. Gathered for their exile they numbered about one hundred and forty, of all ages and conditions. Everywhere along the route to Philadelphia they were received with jeers and threats by all except the Quakers, who stood firm as friends to the forlorn band. Reaching the capital excitement ran so high that their destruction seemed inevitable. Quarters had been assigned them in the barracks,

---

[1] In the Memorial afterwards addressed to the Governor and General Assembly, by Matthew Smith and James Gibson, the grievances of the frontier men were set forth at some length. Nine specifications were offered of wrongs and inflictions under which they suffered. The points taken appear to have been well grounded in fact. The Memorial discloses the purpose of the "rioters" to have been of a somewhat revolutionary character. The Moravian Indians were to be disposed of, but that was only a redress of one of nine disabilities alleged to exist—all of which the "Paxton boys" were bound to "wipe out." Their movement, therefore, on the then capital of Pennsylvania was both insurrectionary and revolutionary.

by order of the Governor; but the soldiers of the station positively refused to receive their detested guests. All day long the Indians stood out on the square in front of the barracks; and no command of Governor or officer could open the doors of the buildings. Only the presence of a large number of Quakers, many of them persons of influence, prevented the mob from violence toward the thoroughly frightened exiles.

Late in the afternoon it was arranged to send the Indians down to Province island, where temporary protection could be offered them; and thither they proceeded, followed by the infuriated mob, but protected by a strong body of Quakers. Once quartered on the island they remained in comparative security, cared for by the benevolent. It was thought all danger and suffering were past. But, the awful tragedy at Lancaster jail stirred the fires anew. The alarm spread to Philadelphia and the terrible Paxton men were reported to be *en route* for Province Island, resolved upon the murder of every red-skin there. A number of boats were sent down to the island and every Indian was embarked, to be borne further down the river. That alarm was groundless, and the trembling creatures were restored to their quarters only to be soon turned out again. This time they were, agreeable to orders of the Assembly, dispatched to New York, there to be placed in charge of Sir William Johnson—an order which the Assembly had no right to make without the consent of the Governor of New York and of the Indian Agent. There was danger, however, in the red people remaining; any day might see the border madmen down upon the city—a visitation dreaded as Rome must have dreaded the coming of the Goths. The terror which prevailed in the city was painful to behold, yet it had, behind all, a background of humor and satire. If the city was menaced why did not the people arm and boldly confront the violators of law and order? Quaker non-combativeness seemed nothing but abject pusillanimity; and the act of sending off the unoffending Moravian converts to another province, capped the climax of their absurd timidity. The poor victims, starting at midnight, January 4th, 1764, were marched over New Jersey, everywhere to receive nothing but insults at the hands of the people—so general was the hate of the red race. Arriving at Amboy, after a weary tramp by way of Trenton, the agents of Pennsylvania were astonished to receive from Governor Colden, of New York, a message forbidding the Indians to step foot on his territory. Other orders from General Gage and the New York city authorities, arrested all further progress; once more the exiles were without a resting place. A messenger soon came from Governor Franklin, of New Jersey, ordering the Indians from his territory. Under an escort of one hundred and seventy troops, dispatched by General Gage to the assistance of Governor Penn against the rioters, the men, women and children returned to Philadelphia. Their ill usage and a sense of danger from the border men had worked a change in the soldiers' hearts toward the helpless band, and they were given quarters in the city barracks.

The moment was one of great excitement, for the Paxton men were, in truth, advancing upon the city. Seeing that there was no other way to avert the danger than boldly to confront it—to match rifle with rifle and sword with tomahawk, the Quakers made a virtue of necessity and became as combatant as the most devoted martinet could have desired. The Assembly voted arms and supplies; it proclaimed the English riot act and no longer had any qualms of conscience about the proper use of powder and ball. Benjamin Franklin moved his fellow-citizens, the animating genius of the crisis. He then betrayed that sagacity, prudence, indomitable will and true courage which afterwards made him one of the safest guides through the stormy period of the Revolution.

The Paxton men, under command of Matthew Smith, James Gibson and others, after gathering from their several rendezvous, started for Philadelphia about the first of February, increasing in numbers as they progressed, until nearly or quite one thousand men composed the motly mob. Their advance appeared at Germantown February 4th, and the alarm was at once given in the city. The bells rang and citizens flocked to the barracks, determined to defend the Indians to the last. The troops sent by Gage, and a small body of Highlanders, were under arms ready for duty. A spirit of resistance prevailed which must have drenched the streets in blood, had the "regulators" then attempted a descent upon the barracks. But no invasion of the city limits followed. All night long, in a drenching rain, the citizens stood under arms, alert for an attack expected at any moment. The following day (Sunday) a barricade was thrown across the square before the barracks, upon which were mounted a number of cannon, so disposed as to sweep all approaches. The city fairly swarmed with men in arms—conspicuous among whom were drab coats and broad brimmed hats. Spies from the border men circulated freely throughout the place, to report the belligerent state of affairs to their somewhat surprised brother cut-throats; they had not expected such a reception at the hands of the Quakers.

Nothing occurred during the Sabbath to cause further alarm. Still preferring the use of the tongue to the sword, the citizens dispatched a squad of clergymen to the Paxtonians, hoping to prove that it was not their duty to butcher the heathen, according to command in Deuteronomy. This mission the ministers do not appear to have executed with commendable zeal, since Matthew Smith, that night, seized Swedes Ford, over the Schuylkill, preparatory to a march upon the city. But no advance was made. Ready as the Paxton men were to cut the throats of one hundred and forty bronze men, women and children, they were not prepared to face the music of twelve cannon and two thousand muskets. So they remained quietly at Germantown, and, during Monday, were visited by a number of the more adventurous citizens. An unexpected change had come over the spirit of the border men's dreams. Though "clad in blanket coats and moccasins," and "armed with rifles and tomahawks and some with pistols stuck in their belts," they were as non-combative as disciples of George Fox. No violence was offered, and numbers of those who had volunteered to bring the Quakers to terms, returned home to consider matters. This peaceable attitude induced the authorities to a trial of negotiation, much against the desires of the regulars and of the citizens in arms, who seemed to prefer the bayonet for an arbiter in suppressing such an insurrection. The voice of the elders prevailed, and Franklin, with three other eminent citizens, sought the Paxton camp. His negotiations ended satisfactorily, assurances having been given of a redress of grievances, as well as safety being guaranteed to those of the Paxton men who might enter the city as deputies. Matthew Smith and John Gibson were chosen by their men to represent their cause. They at once drew up two papers, a Remonstrance and a Declaration of Grievances—the latter of which is referred to in foot note page 109—which the Governor was to lay before the Assembly. Upon this settlement of the affair the citizen-soldiers were dismissed and quiet was restored. On the succeeding day thirty of the frontier men entered the city much to the alarm of its people, who again swarmed into the streets with arms in their hands: but the thirty were on a peaceful mission of observation and to boast of their exploits in having participated in the Conestoga and Lancaster murders. The act was one of singular bravado considering the fact that rewards were then out for their arrest; but, none of all that city of brave men were presumptuous enough to lay hands on the desperate fellows. They visited the barracks to identify Indians whom they swore they had seen in arms against the settlers and who had fought against Colonel Bouquet; but none were recognised. The Paxton men soon withdrew; Germantown was relieved of their thieving and riotous presence; only Smith and Gibson remained in Philadelphia to care for the interests of their constituents before the Assembly.

Thus ended the "Paxton Riots"; but there followed a war of words which, for a season, so absorbed all classes as to render them oblivious to the original cause of the disturbance. Quaker was pitted against Presbyterian. Argument and appeal soon gave place to threat and invective. Pamphlets, satires, poems, letters, addresses, communications, flew around as thickly as snow flakes. Everybody seemed to be drawn into the vortex of passion. Friends became enemies—enemies, friends. The "subject" invaded the precincts of the pulpit, the bar, the school room, the family circle and the counting house. Shoemakers hammered their opponents instead of hammering sole-leather; tailors thrust rhetorical daggers into Presbyterian or Quaker, instead of stitching away eight honest hours at jean garments; painters stopped daubing houses to daub their enemies' character and prospects; lawyers forgot their briefs in lengthy tirade, against some equally wordy antagonist. Preachers "pitched into" one another like experts from a Donnybrook fair. It was a veritable reign of reason run mad; and stands on the page of history as an illustration of the folly and the weakness of human nature.

Nothing came of the labors of Smith and Gibson to secure more equality in representation, to obtain guarantees of protection for the borders, to compel a change of policy toward friendly Indians, and to secure immunity from trial for those engaged in the Conestoga massacre. The warlike attitude of affairs, by which even the interior was threatened with the tomahawk of blood-thirsty demons compelled the Assembly to vote troops and supplies; but no concessions were made to the Paxton men, and they remained under the ban of the law through their lives. No arrests, singularly enough, were made, save that of Lazarus Stewart, eight years after the Lancaster jail tragedy, when he was placed in confinement in the same building where the unhappy Indians had sought safety. To insure conviction the Quakers had arranged to transfer his trial to Philadelphia. This attempt to force him from Lancaster—where Stewart, it would appear, was quite willing to be tried—impelled him to break jail and escape. At Paxton he rallied a band of resolute fellows who set the officers of the law at defiance. He issued an address of justification to the people, setting forth his services and the justice of his acts. With his followers he retired to Wyoming, in whose tragic history his name and those of his brave rangers mingle in honorable connection. The Moravian Indians remained in Philadelphia during the Indian war, supported by appropriations from the public treasury and by contributions. In the year 1765 they were removed to the Susquehanna, not far from their old settlements, and there founded a very prosperous colony.

THE CONSPIRACY OF BENEDICT ARNOLD.

"FOREVER be his name accursed of men, and his crime be the associate of his memory!" was the malediction which followed the traitor after the exposure of his stupendous villany.

The story of Arnold's treason is, to American readers, familiar as a household word; yet, like the narrative of Guy Fawkes' attempt to blow up the English Parliament, it has a perennial interest, not only because of its momentous nature as a conspiracy against the cause of the Colonies, but also from the drama which followed involving the fate of André. We consider it, in this volume, simply in the light of a conspiracy, leaving to historians and to romance that detail of collateral and incidental events which serve more as embellishments to, than as adjuncts of, the attempted betrayal of West Point.

Arnold, throughout the Revolutionary War, up to 1780, had acted both an honorable and a dishonorable part. His character was turbulent; his temper quick; his pride imperious; his principles bad; his integrity doubted. He fought well but acted ill; he was courageous to an astonishing degree but unreliable, jealous, quarrelsome and captious. He fought for glory from no higher motive than the love of adulation and power; he was not sound at heart. To such a nature, thwarted in its hopes of advancement, or distempered by wrongs real and imaginary, treason was not a crime—it was simply an instrument of revenge. It needed but the pretext for him to commit and excuse the commission of a hideous act; and we much doubt if, in the whole course of his after life, the traitor ever felt any compunctions of conscience for the course he had pursued toward his country. Such men exist in all communities; they need only favoring circumstances to strip them of their disguise and to show them as they are—purely selfish and unprincipled. It is not strange that Arnold should have appeared on the stage at the proper time and place to give his name to eternal infamy; it is, rather, strange that he should stand quite alone—that, out of that great contest for human liberty, so few should have proved recreant to trust and corruptible. Many were disloyal among the people, and not a few engaged in the contest were lukewarm in the cause; but, to Arnold alone attaches the dishonor of an American officer of high command endeavoring to sell his birthright and to betray his country.[1] Washington said: "Arnold's conduct is so villainously perfidious that there are no terms that can describe the baseness of his heart." He also said: "He wants feeling. From some traits of his character which have lately come to my knowledge, he seems to have been so hackneyed in villainy, and so lost to all sense of honor and shame, that, while his faculties will enable him to continue his sordid pursuit, there will be no time for remorse." A severity of judgment which time has not failed to confirm. Sabine, in his American Loyalist says: "I am inclined to believe that Arnold was a finished scoundrel from early manhood to his grave. Nor do I believe he had any real, true-hearted attachment to the Whig cause. He fought as a mere adventurer, and took sides from a calculation of personal gain and chances of plunder and ad-

[1] The case of Major-General Charles Lee is, by many writers, assumed to be somewhat analagous to that of Arnold; but, we are not prepared to impute to him the crimes charged to his memory. His devotion to the American cause was, like that of many other officers and statesmen high in position, governed much by his ambition. He conceived the daring design of superceding Washington, for whom he entertained no regard, and whose military abilities he conceived to be overestimated. He caballed against him, and fought badly at Monmouth in order to procure defeat that Washington might be the sufferer. For this conduct he was court martialed and driven into exile in Virginia; but, it is not yet *proven* that he deliberately plotted to betray the army or to sell his *adopted* country—for he was an Englishman by birth, education and association, having arrived in America only two years previous to the events of 1775. His crime was that of all the faction who, under the leadership of Conway, endeavored to ruin Washington.

vancement." This was written with all the weight of testimony which sixty years had produced.

At the second memorable battle of Saratoga, October 7th, 1777, Arnold's leg was broken, and he was incapacitated for service for several months. He joined Washington at Valley Forge in May, 1778, and was present at the entrance of the Continental army into Philadelphia, June 17th, 1778. Washington placed Arnold in command as military Governor—a remarkable trust when we consider Washington's prudence and sagacity and Arnold's well known character for rashness, insubordination, cruelty and dissoluteness. Of all places Philadelphia then required a wise, discreet, humane government, and of all men Arnold was the worst agent who could have been chosen. It is true Arnold was to act under specific instructions, enforcing the executive resolves of Congress, respecting the civil rights of the State and the municipality, and executing the wishes of Washington; but, what were orders and wishes to him? Three days after he took command he entered into a secret copartnership for the purchase and sale of goods, by which he at once controlled trade, and, obtaining extraordinary prices, soon realized a large revenue out of the necessities of the people. He set the municipal and State authorities at defiance, espousing, in a local quarrel, the cause of those notoriously disloyal—an alliance designed to further his schemes of rapacity. He, ere long, wooed and won the daughter of a wealthy loyalist, Edward Shippen—she a beauty of eighteen, he a widower of forty. Margaret Shippen was gay, witty, accomplished, a fashionable flirt; her suitor was low-born, rude, vicious in his propensities: by what means or influences the engagement was effected we are only left to conjecture. The intrigue and duplicity which afterward came near to success in betraying his post certainly were equal to the task of catching a belle. His style of living was truly magnificent for those days: his establishment was almost royal in its appointments. It was necessary to marry wealth to sustain enormous expenditures which even his speculations could not support. But, long before he could call Margaret his bride and instal her as mistress of the elegant old Penn mansion, its doors were besieged by importunate creditors. The choice of General Joseph Reed to the Presidency of the Executive Council of Pennsylvania, brought matters to a crisis. He was not disposed to see the course and acts of the military Governor of Philadelphia covered up by Arnold's fame, and by the powerful faction which stood forth in the Governor's support.

We need not here narrate in detail the investigations which followed: results will suffice for our purposes. Arnold was finally, after great delays, convicted, before a military tribunal, on two comparatively minor specifications and sentenced to be reprimanded by the Commander-in-Chief—a sentence confirmed by Congress February 12th, 1780, and soon executed by Washington, with remarkable good taste and kindliness. The charges first preferred by Reed were of a character to overwhelm Arnold with disgrace, but they were rejected by Congress, in the report of a special committee, March, 1780. A very thorough examination had been given the matter, and an acquittal at the hands of the committee would seem to argue that, whatever may have been his sins, they were not such as to deprive him of the confidence of Congress or of Washington. Five days after this acquittal he was married to Miss Shippen —having first resigned the military Governorship. But the report was not called up for discussion, and the whole matter, without further consideration, was referred anew to a joint committee of the Assembly and Council of Pennsylvania and of Congress. The report of this committee was soon ready. It was considered at length, eliciting much warmth of discussion and was finally disposed of by resolving that Washington should convene a court martial for the military trial of such charges as were of a nature to be cognizable by such a court.[1]

[1] Hamilton, in his "History of the Republic," thus construes this matter: "In the exercise of an invidious duty thus confided to him, Arnold incurred great displeasure. The Government of the State interposed. Charges were made of an abuse of his powers, and civil prosecutions were threatened. A sharp controversy ensued and an appeal was preferred to Congress. The result was a vindication of Arnold from criminal conduct. Upon a statement that the full testimony had not been produced, Congress, in concert with the authorities of Pennsylvania, decided to submit to a court martial such charges as were cognizable by a military tribunal. This procedure Arnold charged to be the act of Reed, the President of the State, and was supposed to have produced his ultimate criminality."

This court the Commander-in-Chief appointed to meet May 1st, but, owing to various causes, it could not convene until the beginning of 1780, when it resulted as above stated, in a verdict of reprimand.

Having resigned his command in Philadelphia, Arnold was without employ, but his restless spirit had not been in repose. It was in the fall of 1779 that he conceived the design of passing over to the enemy. By means of a disloyal preacher in Philadelphia, named Odell, he found means of communicating with Sir Henry Clinton, then holding New York. Clinton turned the matter over to John André, his Adjutant General, who at once set himself about discovering who the volunteer correspondent was. He was not long in identifying his man. During the winter several letters passed, but none of a nature looking to definite results. Commercial terms were used as a disguise. Arnold was "Gustavus," and André "John Anderson." After the reprimand the leaven of treason worked more rapidly in Arnold's heart. His indignation at the usage meted out by Congress and by the Pennsylvania authorities, his exceedingly straitened circumstances, his inability to obtain from Congress an allowance of his claims for expenses incurred, all contributed to turn his thoughts more directly to the British for aid and honors. Having married Miss Shippen, through her he could communicate with André without suspicion, since she was an old friend and confidant of the gay adjutant. But, he still proceeded with excessive caution. The commercial parlance used offered a perfect cloak from detection. "Invoices," "adventures," "sums needed," "disbursement," "debt and credit," were convenient terms to cover the contemplated sale of a soul to the devil and of body to Sir Henry Clinton.

Goaded by his wants Arnold, in his extremity, appealed for aid to M. de Luzerne, French Minister to the Revolutionary Government. It was, evidently, his last bid for favor and help. With strong words he pictured to the Minister the hardships of his case, the wrongs he had suffered by persecutions and slights, the injustice of keeping back payment of his claims, the damage sustained by the sacrifices he had made for his country; he adverted to the necessity he would be under of abandoning the service, unless he could then obtain a loan sufficient to clear him from the burden of his debts. This loan he represented it must be for the interest of the French Government to extend, thus securing to the cause of France and the American Colonies his continued services. This bold bid for a purchase of his loyalty to his country the Frenchman rejected as incompatible with personal honor or public prosperity. He said:

"When the envoy of a foreign power gives, or, if you please, *lends* money, it is ordinarily to corrupt those who receive it, and to make them the *creatures* of the sovereign whom he serves. Or, rather, he corrupts without persuading; he buys yet does not secure. But, the league entered into between the King and the United States is the work of justice and of the wisest policy. It has for its basis a reciprocal interest and good will. In the mission with which I am charged, my true glory consists in fulfilling it without intrigue or cabal; without resorting to any secret practices and by the force alone of the conditions of the alliance."

It is assumed by some writers who have sought to relieve Arnold's name from some of its load of obloquy, that he, in good faith, sought this aid in order to save him from the necessity of accepting British gold; but, all the evidence afforded by his subsequent career goes to prove that, had he obtained it, the "arrangement" with André would have been consummated. For several months the correspondence regarding his "commercial venture" had been going on, and Arnold had fully committed himself to treason. His desire to obtain the money was to enable him to pay off his debts, and, by a good use of his gold and his influence, to secure such a command as would render his defection, at the proper moment, most calamitous to the American cause and most worthy of a rich reward from the British Government. But he failed, and was left for a season to the importunities of creditors and the cold consideration generally awarded to all claimants by Congressmen and public officials.

His plans matured rapidly. Washington having been invested with dictatorial powers, with an advisory council of three, and news of French aid soon to arrive having been received, active operations promised for the summer. This called the various commanders to duty. Arnold wrote to General Schuyler, one of the three advisers who was about to join Washington, that he desired to return to the service but would be precluded from active duty owing to his wounds which, he said, were yet painful. He intimated the wish to be assigned to West Point, clearly foreseeing that, in event of a combined French and American attack upon New York, West Point would prove the key to the campaign: its betrayal would quite destroy the Patriot programme for the summer if not entirely ruin the American cause. It was the prize to be sought for, and, with the cool calculation of an adept in villainy, Arnold laid his plans to gain possession of the post.

Schuyler replied (June 2d) to Arnold's note, after having conferred with Washington, saying in substance that the Commander-in-Chief regarded the application for service with much pleasure and would give it proper consideration in his arrangements for the campaign. This reply did not guarantee West Point; hence Arnold set influences to work to have that assignment made. His partizans in and out of Congress were numerous and powerful, but it would not do for the Conspirator to press his point too urgently—it might excite opposition in others quite anxious for the important command. Robert R. Livingston wrote for the post for Arnold, urging his wounds and his fitness for such a service as the strong points to be considered. Nothing was done, however. Washington never yielded to any suggestion except upon its merits; and the application remained unanswered until the campaign was fairly inaugurated in July.

Washington having moved his little army of four thousand men from Morristown, New Jersey, up to the Hudson, had concerted an attack on New York—the French fleet under the Chevalier de Ternay and the French army under Count de Rochambeau co-operating. The arrival of Admiral Graves in New York harbor, July 13th, with six superb ships of the line, gave Sir Henry Clinton such reenforcements as rendered the proposed combined operations impracticable, and the French and American commanders resolved to await reenforcements then on the way before moving on the city. Of all this Clinton was fully informed—by what means is not known. He therefore planned a counter-expedition against the French, then at Newport, Rhode Island. His plan was to march six thousand men to Throg's Neck, on the Sound, from whence, transports having been provided by Admiral Arbuth not, the descent was to be made on Newport, Arbuthnot's fleet co-operating. Of this move Washington soon obtained information, when he at once threw his now increased force over the Hudson at Peekskill, preparatory to moving down by way of King's Bridge. In the midst of these stirring preparations Arnold appeared. He addressed Washington to know what place had been assigned to him. The Commander-in-Chief replied that he had resolved to place him in command of the left wing.[1] Arnold was silent, and, by his acts, expressed chagrin. All who witnessed the scene were surprised at his evident dissatisfaction—it being supposed that such a field of duty would have best pleased his daring and restless spirit. Further conference at headquarters resulted in Arnold's choice to the command of West Point "and its dependencies." What influences were brought to bear by the Conspirator to obtain the post we are not informed. Robert Livingston, as we have remarked, had urged Arnold for the place; Hamilton, in his "History of the Republic," states that Schuyler "concurred"; while we can well understand that the leg wounded at Saratoga was a most powerful intercessor. The command assigned included West Point and the posts from Fishkill to King's Ferry, together with the forces—infantry and cavalry—then holding the east side of the Hudson river. Washington's advance upon New York was frustrated by Sir Henry Clinton's abandonment of his expedition against Newport after his march to Throg's Neck; and the bulk of the American army was withdrawn, by Dobbs' Ferry, to the west of the Hudson river, there to await any movements of the British, or the concert of operations with their allies which Washington strove, at once,

---

[1] Hamilton, in his "History of the Republic," gives the impression (vol. ii. page 52) that Arnold was assigned to the left wing command soon after his reprimand. He received no intimations from Washington until the occasion above stated. See Irving's Washington, vol. iv. page 81.

to effect. Arnold's force therefore consisted of the men manning the forts and redoubts surmounting the heights and a body of about six hundred infantry and two hundred cavalry posted on the eastern side of the river on outpost, scout and skirmish duty.

The fortifications of West Point comprised, at that time, a fort on the north-east face of the plateau, while west of it and surmounting the heights beyond was Fort Putnam—a very powerful and well conceived redoubt. Both of these works, however, were very illy equipped and ordered—so much so, that, in a report made by an engineer, ten days after Arnold took possession, it was said: "the whole appears, at present, under the care of ungovernable and undisciplined militia, like a wild Tartar's camp, instead of that shining fortification all America thinks not only an insurmountable barrier against the incursion of the enemy, but likewise an easy defense in case of an unforeseen disaster to its army." This picture must have been a sad one for Washington to contemplate, and doubtless offers one reason for his placing Arnold there: he hoped that that officer's well known character for sternness would at least reduce all to order and efficiency. In the campaign then pending it was all important that West Point should be ready for stern duty, for it would, in event of any reverse to the American arms, have been instantly assailed by the British Commander-in-Chief. It was the barrier against British communicatron with Canada, while it kept open the direct route of passage for the Americans from tha New England States to the South. If, therefore, it were lost, a terrible blow woeld be given to the Patriot cause—then at its lowest point of discouragement. That Arnold chose it and that particular moment for the consummation of his scheme, proves him to have sought the entire ruin of his country and its subjugation to the foreign yoke.

The Conspirator took possession of the command by orders dated August 3d, 1780. His instructions were to hasten the completion of the works, to place them in a state of efficiency, and to use every measure of precaution to prevent surprise or a knowledge of his disposition and force. Washington's headquarters were at Tappan, on the Jersey side of the river. All that Arnold did was done under the eye of his chief. He, therefore, had to proceed with extreme caution; the sagacious instincts of the Commander-in-Chief were never asleep. Arnold proceeded to the eastern bank of the river, taking up headquarters at Robinson's House—a fine mansion located on a rich plateau nearly opposite West Point. It was the confiscated property of Colonel Beverly Robinson, then in Clinton's service, and a coadjutor of André in forwarding the game of treason.

Washington, eager to fall upon New York, held much correspondence with the French, who still remained inactive at Newport. Nothing definite was determined upon during August—the French being disconcerted by the non-arrival of the second division of their army of co-operation, which the British, with admirable zeal, had blockaded in the port of Brest, France, thus preventing its departure. Rochambeau also was disappointed by the non-arrival of Count de Guichen, with his West India squadron—a reenforcement necessary as a counterpoise to Arbuthnot's fleet, then sustaining Clinton. The Patriot Commander-in-Chief, as his published papers show, was exceedingly anxious in regard to the loss of time, yet he could do literally nothing without French aid. His little host of about five thousand tried men, sustained by nearly as many new levies, was no match for the British army and navy. Still, he kept unwearied watch over the country around New York, alert to catch any opportunity for a stroke at his adversary. Lucifer was at his side, walking with him unseen to thwart his great purposes of serving and saving his country. The Devil assumed the disguise of Benedict Arnold. That creature of darkness, learning all things regarding Washington's designs, apprised Clinton of every matter of importance. His correspondence with André, during August and September, was unremitted. Once fully in possession of his post he began preparations for its betrayal by first regulating the *price* which was to be paid in hand for his stupendous crime. André and Clinton do not, to our apprehension, stand out in the guise of heroes in this transaction: both were principals in the crime, by all the laws of honor and the usage of courts: they did not aid and abet the act, but became co-equals and instigators. André, had he been a man of honor, would have left to baser men that bargaining for a human soul. His whole procedure, in spite of the sympathy so freely bestowed upon his memory, was that of a *particeps criminis*, and as such he deserves the execrations of those who scorn treason and despise treachery. As in the War for the Union, those in rebellion deemed it honorable to break oaths of allegiance and strictly proper to practice every species of dissimulation and treachery toward their enemy, so André and his employer assumed a new law of moral obligation to cover their wretched practices. But, neither men nor angels can stay the inexorable judgments of time: they ever have covered, and ever will cover, dishonor with dishonor, perfidy with perfidy. The poet says: "let the dead Past bury its dead"; History says: let the living Past christen its dead.

September 18th–20th, Washington repaired to Hartford, Conn., accompanied by Lafayette, General Knox, Hamilton, McHenry and several others. The army was left in command of General Greene. The Commander-in-Chief crossed the river at Verplanck's Point in Arnold's barge—Arnold being with him and riding as far as Peekskill in his company, doubtless to learn everything possible regarding the movements which it was Washington's special mission to Hartford to concert. It will be seen by Hamilton's account, which we quote, that, in crossing the river, Arnold sought to account for the presence of the British sloop-of-war *Vulture*, which then lay off Teller's Point, just below Haverstraw. That vessel was then co-operating in the game of treason. Seven days previously (Sept. 11th) an interview between André and Arnold had been arranged to be had at Dobbs' Ferry, which was then on "neutral ground", where, if André were surprised he could not be treated as a spy, not being within the American lines. Arnold had arranged to have the British agent introduced to the Robinson House as the bearer of intelligence, under the feigned name of John Anderson, but André, well aware of the desperate nature of his intrigue, refused to enter the lines. The interview therefore was arranged for at Dobbs' Ferry. André and Colonel Robinson were on hand, at the appointed time, but Arnold's barge in coming down the river, not being covered by a flag, was chased by the British guard-boats, and the Conspirator was compelled to pull back, in some haste, to the protection of a battery on the west side of the river. The *Vulture* therefore was sent up stream to cover the proposed interview. How it was effected the reader will see.

Washington having proceeded to Hartford, a conference was there held, Sept. 22d, with Count Rochambeau and Admiral Ternay, to make arrangements for operations against New York, in event of de Guichen's arrival with his West India squadron, which had been reported as on its way to New England. But, news coming that the squadron had actually sailed for France, the French commander refused to enter into arrangements for the fall campaign; and Washington returned at once to the Hudson, two days sooner than was expected by Arnold—two Providential days. The return, however, was not direct to Peekskill, but to the river above, at Fishkill, with the design of inspecting fortifications then constructing or completed along the river above West Point. The party was detained on the night of Sept. 23d at Fishkill, but started off before daylight on the morning of the 24th, designing to breakfast with Arnold at the Robinson House. A courier, with the baggage, had proceeded in advance to Arnold's headquarters to apprise him of the General's coming with his suite, for breakfast. Arnold, thunderstruck at this unexpected advent of his chief, knew not what an hour would bring forth. Two days more and he would have surrendered his garrisons to a detachment ef the British army!

Most unfortunately, Washington did not proceed direct to the breakfast table, but turned aside, when within one mile of the Robinson House, to go down to the river and inspect the works at that point. Lafayette jocosely reminded him that Mrs. Arnold probably was in waiting for them, the Chief replied: "Ah, Marquis, you young men are all in love with Mrs. Arnold. I see you are eager to be with her as soon as possible. Go you and breakfast with her, and tell her not to wait for me. I must ride down and examine the redoubts on this side of the river, but will be with her shortly." He therefore passed on down to the river, accompanied by Lafayette and Knox, while Alexander Hamilton and James McHenry, his aids, proceeded to the House, where breakfast was soon served. Mrs. Arnold was gay-hearted, totally unconscious, evidently, of the awful thunder-stroke impending. Arnold was so fearfully impressed with the sense of his peril as to be unable to hide his emotion: he was abstracted and sullenly depressed. The crisis was approaching more rapidly than he could have guessed.

In the midst of the repast the blow fell. A horseman rode up in great haste bearing a dispatch from Lieutenant-Colonel Jameson, commanding at North Castle, one of the lower stations, stating that a spy named John Anderson had been arrested, having in his possession important papers. André arrested, the papers discovered, no British army near, Washington on the ground! Surely, a heart less insensible to fear than that which Benedict Arnold bore in his breast, would have sunk under its load of guilt and its sense of danger. But, the bold bad man was not paralyzed to inaction. Summoning, with his finger, Mrs. Arnold from the breakfast table to her private room, he hastily told her that he was a ruined man and must flee for his life. She evidently apprehended the worst and fell into a swoon. He hastened from the room, dispatched the bearer of the message from Colonel Jameson to her assistance, (doubtless to prevent him from conversing with Hamilton and McHenry,) seized the messenger's horse and was soon plunging, at a headlong pace, to the river, where his barge lay moored, but ever ready for service. Into it he sprang and bidding the oarsmen pull away at their best speed, as he must hasten his return to meet Washington, he sped like an arrow down the river toward the British sloop-of-war which lay below Teller's Point, awaiting André's return to her decks. The first intimation Colonel Robinson had of André's fate was from Arnold, whose barge, bearing a flag of truce, having safely passed the battery at Verplanck's Point, came dashing up to the *Vulture's* sides just before noon of that eventful day.

The traitor sprang to her decks, turned over his faithful boat's crew as prisoners of war and hastened to the cabin to pen to Washington a letter begging for considerate attentions to Mrs. Arnold, whom he protested was "as good and innocent as an angel, and as incapable of doing wrong." This was one scene in the first act of that dreadful drama.

Let us bring up the narrative of André's adventures by quoting from the account given of the matter by Alexander Hamilton in a letter written, after André's execution, to his friend Laurens. It is at once personal, concise and clear, and, coming from Hamilton's hand, possesses a double interest.

* * * "The twentieth of last month, Robinson and André went up the river in the *Vulture* sloop-of-war. Robinson sent a flag to Arnold with two letters, one to General Putnam, enclosed in another to himself, proposing an interview with Putnam, or in his absence with Arnold, to adjust some private concerns. The one to General Putnam was evidently meant as a cover to the other, in case, by accident, the letters should have fallen under the inspection of a third person.

"General Washington crossed the river on his way to Hartford, the day these dispatches arrived. Arnold, conceiving he must have heard of the flag, thought it neeessary for the sake of appearances, to submit the letters to him, and ask his opinion of the propriety of complying with the request. The General, with his usual caution, though without the least surmise of the design, dissuaded him from it, and advised him to reply to Robinson, that whatever related to his private affairs must be of a civil nature, and could only properly be addressed to the civil authority. This reference fortunately deranged the plan, and was the first link in the chain of events that led to the detection. The interview could no longer take place in the form of a flag, but was obliged to be managed in a secret manner.

"Arnold employed one Smith to go on board the *Vulture* the night of the twenty-second, to bring André on shore with a pass for Mr. John Anderson. André came ashore accordingly, and was conducted within a picket of ours to the house of Smith, where Arnold and he remained together in close conference all that night and the day following. At daylight in the morning, the commanding officer at King's Ferry, without the privity of Arnold, moved a couple of pieces of cannon to a point opposite to where the *Vulture* lay, and obliged her to take a more remote station. This event, or some lurking distrust, made the boatmen refuse to convey the two passengers back, and disconcerted Arnold so much, that by one of those strokes of infatuation which often confound the schemes of men conscious of guilt, he insisted on André's exchanging his uniform for a disguise, and returning in a mode different from that in which he came. André, who had been undesignedly brought within our posts, in the first instance, remonstrated warmly against this new and dangerous expedient. But Arnold, persisting in declaring it impossible for him to return as he came, he at length reluctantly yielded to his direction, and consented to change his dress, and take the route he recommended. Smith furnished the disguise, and in the evening passed King's Ferry with him, and proceeded to Crompond, where they stopped the remainder of the night, (at the instance of a militia officer,) to avoid being suspecteb by him. The next morning they resumed their journey, Smith accompanying André a little beyond Pine's Bridge, where he left him. He had reached Tarrytown, when he was taken up by three militia men, who rushed out of the woods and seized his horse. At this critical moment, his presence of mind forsook him. Instead of producing his pass, which would have extricated him from our parties, and could have done him no harm with his own, he asked the militia men if they were of the upper or lower

---

Fac similie of the Pass given by Arnold to André.

Head Quarters Robinsons
House Sepr. 22d. 1780

Permit Mr. John Anderson to pass the
Guards to the White Plains, or below
if He Chuses. He being on Public
Business by my Direction

B. Arnold M Genl

party, distinctive appellations known among the refugee corps. The militia men replied that they were of the lower party; upon which he told them that he was a British officer, and pressed them not to detain him, as he was upon urgent business. This confession removed all doubt; and it was in vain he afterwards produced his pass. He was forced off to a place of greater security; where, after a careful search, there were found concealed in the feet of his stockings, several papers of importance delivered to him by Arnold. Among these there were a plan of the fortifications of West Point; a memorial from the engineer, on the attack and defense of the place; returns of the garrison, cannon and stores; and a copy of the minutes of a council of war held by General Washington a few weeks before, &c. The prisoner at first was inadvertently ordered to Arnold; but, on recollection, while still on the way, he was countermanded and sent to old Salem.

"The papers were enclosed in a letter to General Washington, which, having taken a route different from that by which he returned, made a circuit, that afforded leisure for another letter, through an ill-judged delicacy, written to Arnold, with information of Anderson's capture, to get to him an hour before General Washington arrived at his quarters, time enough to elude the fate that awaited him. He went down the river in his barge to the *Vulture*, with such precipitate confusion, that he did not take with him a single paper useful to the enemy. On the first notice of the affair he was pursued, but much too late to be overtaken.

"There was some color for imagining it was a part of the plan to betray the General into the hands of the enemy.[1] Arnold was very anxious to ascertain from him the precise day of his return, and the enemy's movements seem to have corresponded to this point. But, if so it was very injudicious. The success must have depended on surprise, and as the officers at the advanced posts were not in the secret, their measures might have given the alarm, and, General Washington taking command of the post, might have rendered the whole scheme abortive. Arnold, it is true, had so dispersed the garrison, as to have made a defense difficult, but not impracticable; and the acquisition of West Point was of such magnitude to the enemy, that it would have been unwise to connect it with any other object, however great, which might make the obtaining of it precarious.

"Arnold, a moment before setting out, went into Mrs. Arnold's apartment, and informed her that some transactions had just come to light,

[1] We infer that it was no part of Arnold's plan to betray Washington. There is no proof to sustain Hamilton's suspicions in this respect. Arnold's anxiety about Washington's return was upon his (Arnold's) own behalf. He would consummate the scheme before the Commander's return—as after it there would be little opportunity for any further conference of the conspirators.

which must forever banish him from his country. She fell into a swoon at this declaration, and he left her in it to consult his own safety, till the servants, alarmed by her cries, came to her relief. She remained frantic all day, accusing every one who approached her with an intention to murder her child, (an infant in her arms,) and exhibiting every other mark of the most genuine and agonizing distress. Exhausted by the fatigue and tumult of her spirits, her frenzy subsided towards evening, and she sunk into all the sadness of affliction. It was impossible not to have been touched with her situation: everything affecting in female tears, or in the misfortunes of beauty, everything pathetic in the wounded tenderness of a wife, or in the apprehensive fondness of a mother, and, till I have reason to change the opinion, I will add, everything amiable in suffering innocence, conspired to make her an object of sympathy to all who were present. She experienced the most delicate attentions, and every friendly office, till her departure for Philadelphia.[1]

"André was, without loss of time, conducted to the headquarters of

[1] See Parton's "Life of Aaron Burr," pages 126–27, for apparent proof of Mrs. Arnold's complicity in the whole plot. After quoting from Hamilton's account as given above, the author says: "It fell to Burr's lot to become acquainted with the repulsive truth. He was sitting one evening with Mrs. Prevost when the approach of a party of horse was heard, and, soon after, a lady, vailed and attired in a riding habit burst into the room, and hurrying toward Mrs. P. was on the point of addressing her. Seeing a gentleman present, whom, in the dim light of the apartment she did not recognize, she paused and asked in an anxious tone:

"'Am I safe? Is this gentleman a friend?'

"'Oh yes,' was Mrs. F.'s reply, 'he is my most particular friend, Colonel Burr.'

"'Thank God!' exclaimed Mrs. Arnold, for she it was: 'I've been playing the hypocrite and I'm tired of it.'

"She then gave an account of the way she had deceived General Washington, Colonel Hamilton and the other American officers, who, she said, believed her innocent of the treason and had given her an escort of horse from West Point. She made no scruple of confessing the part she had borne in the negotiations with the British General, and declared it was she who had induced her husband to do what he had done. She passed the night at Paramus, taking care to resume her acting of the outraged and frantic woman whenever strangers were present,"

This extraordinary statement would at once settle the question of Mrs. Arnold's guilt were it reliable, which it is not. Burr was not present at that reputed interview, but was told of it after his marriage with Mrs. Prevost. Even supposing he was present, as stated, would Mrs. Arnold, as a shrewd, designing woman, have cast off her disguise and avowed all to a Colonel then commanding in the American army? The entire story is unsustained by evidence sufficient to give it authority. Irving, in his "Life of Washington," evidently refers to the above story when he says: "In recent years it has been maintained that Mrs. Arnold was actually cognisant and participant of her husband's crimes; but, after carefully examining all the proofs adduced, we remain of opinion that she was innocent."

the army, where he was immediately brought before a board of General officers, to prevent all possibility of misrepresentation or cavil on the part of the enemy."

Washington's conduct throughout this affair was admirable in the extreme. He passed all the morning of the fatal day in inspecting West Point—having first breakfasted at Arnold's. No suspicion of the real state of affairs crossed his mind, though several things tended to excite his surprise. Colonel Jameson, when André was brought before him by Paulding, Van Wert and Williams—the captors of the spy—was quite disconcerted by the nature of the affair. In "Anderson's" pass he at once detected Arnold's complicity in the game of treason, and, supposing Washington to be still at Hartford, at once started André off, under a guard, to Hartford—also sending along the important papers discovered. Yet, as if to give Arnold the alarm, Jameson dispatched a courier to the Robinson House, where he arrived, as we have seen, on the morning of the 24th—a piece of folly only accounted for on the supposition that he did not clearly apprehend the true state of the case. Major Tallmadge, the next in command at North Castle, coming in soon after the dispatch of the prisoner and the couriers, perceived the great mistake made, and, at his earnest remonstrance, André was stopped at Salem, but Jameson failed to recal the courier then on his way to the Robinson House. The courier to Hartford having learned that Washington had returned to West Point, turned upon his track and, at Salem, was given a letter from André to Washington, confessing his name and rank, and offering a vindication for having assumed the character of a spy. That letter was Major Tallmadge's first intimation of the true character of his prisoner. It, and the dispatches by the courier, reached the Robinson House just before noon of the 24th. Hamilton, as Washington's aid and secretary, broke the seals. That was their first apprisal of the act committed. Hamilton hastened out of the house to seek Washington, over the river, but, meeting the General, on his return, the two proceeded together to the house, where the full extent of the crime was soon comprehended. The Chief, though astounded, was not disconcerted. He ere long reappeared, and made confidants of Lafayette and Knox. To others the discovery was not revealed. "Whom can we trust now?" was Washington's sad, solemn inquiry.

To secure Arnold was his first thought; then care for the defenses became his source of anxiety. How many in and out of the garrison were implicated—how fully the scheme had been perfected—how quickly the British might move up the river for the assault, none knew. The suddenness of the discovery, the surprise, the extent of the villainy premeditated, the distrust of those around—all conspired to make Washington's subordinates doubly eager to relieve the Chief's mind of its weight of apprehension. Hamilton hurried to Verplanck's Point, on horse, hoping to reach there in season to open guns on Arnold's barge; but, the Conspirator already had flown beyond reach: at that moment, so expeditious had been his movements, he was on the *Vulture*, and his bargemen were prisoners of war. Hamilton returned to headquarters, bearing to Washington two letters sent ashore by flag of truce, from the British vessel—one from Arnold, already referred to, and one from Colonel Robinson, André's coadjutor in the enterprise of infamy. The latter letter interceded for André's release, saying that he was on shore under the protection and sanction of a flag of truce, by order of Arnold, who was authorized to give the permit.

Washington dispatched a messenger to Greene, then in command of the American army at Tappan, New Jersey, ordering up troops for immediate service in the garrison. Greene at once dispatched that most trusted of men, Anthony Wayne,[1]

---

[1] Wayne's opinion of Arnold should be cited. He wrote to a friend in Congress: "There were a few gentlemen, who at a very early period of this war, became acquainted with his true character. When you asked my opinion of that officer last winter, I gave it freely, and, I believe, you thought it rather strongly shaded. I think I then informed you that I had the most despicable idea of him, both as a gentleman and a soldier, and that he had produced a conviction in me in 1776 that honor and true virtue were strangers to his soul; and, however contradictory it might appear, that he never possessed either genuine fortitude or personal bravery, and that he rarely went in the way of danger but when stimulated by liquor even to intoxication." Wayne then cites cases of Arnold's peculative operations, which would seem to confirm Governor Reed's charges of Arnold's dishonest small practices.

with his Pennsylvania brigade. That inflexible patriot, writing of the affair on the 27th, said:

"At twelve o'clock of the morning of the 25th, an express reached General Greene from his Excellency, (who had fortunately arrived at West Point on his return from Hartford,) to push on the nearest and best disciplined troops, with orders to gain the defile or pass over the Dunderburg before the enemy. The first Pennsylvania brigade moved immediately; and, on the arrival of the second express, I was speedily followed by our gallant friend General Irvine, with the second brigade. Our march of sixteen miles was performed in four hours, during a dark night, without a single halt or a man left behind. When our approach was announced to the General, he thought it fabulous; but when assured of the reality of his tenth legion being near him, he expressed great satisfaction and pleasure.

"The protection of this important place is committed to the division under my command until a proper garrison arrives. We will dispute the approaches to the works inch by inch, at the point of the bayonet, and, if necessary, decide the fate of the day in the gorge of the defiles at every expense of blood."

There was patriotism in that man's heart. Had the British attempted to carry the works, we can well believe that "Mad Anthony" and his resolute ranks would have perished to a man before yielding up the fortress. No attempt, however, was made. André alone held the order of arrangements in his keeping; and, though Clinton had troops awaiting André's orders, they were not used. Rodney's flotilla, which had been gathered with much care for the ascent of the river, was abandoned. No doubt exists that great confidence was felt by Clinton in the success of André's negotiations, and he had arranged to strike quickly and strong ere the American army at Tappan could move.

Efforts to rescue André from his fate were numerous and earnest. Clinton wrote from New York on the 26th, demanding the release of his officer on the ground that he was protected and covered by the pass of Arnold—that, having visited the American lines under a flag of truce at the request of Arnold, then having a right to make the request, he was entitled to be considered as covered by that flag. These were the grounds urged, as we have seen, by Colonel Robinson from the *Vulture's* cabin, but whose force Washington did not see.

Arnold also wrote out his views, in a note to Sir Henry, sustaining his position in the matter. He said:

"I commanded at that time, at West Point; had an undoubted right to send my flag of truce to Major André, who came to me under that protection, and, having held conversation with him, I delivered to him confidential papers in my own hand-writing to deliver to your Excellency. Thinking it much properer he should return by land, I directed him to make use of the feigned name of John Anderson. * * All of which I then had a right to do, being in the actual service of America, under the orders of General Washington, and Commanding-General of West Point and its dependencies."

As if his orders to take command at West Point covered the *right* to conspire for its betrayal! As if André, disguised and secretly plotting for the ruin of his enemy within that enemy's lines, could be *protected* even by a "pass" of Washington himself! The demand was a sublime assurance on Clinton's part, while Arnold's plea was that of a very great scoundrel. Still, Clinton was involved in the matter, for, under his full sanction the "negotiations" had been carried on; under his sanction the *Vulture* had gone up the river with André and Robinson; and, though André had gone ashore from the vessel on his own responsibility, against the wishes of Robinson—although he had gone within the American lines and had taken treasonable correspondence in his keeping without orders—although he had, on his own judgment, taken a disguise and sought to return to New York by a long ride through the American lines—all these are but *incidents* to the one great crime permitted if not authorised by Clinton. Therefore his hand was not guiltless of André's fate. He felt the weight of his responsibility, and though he must have known, from the first announcement of the Major's arrest, that he would be tried as a spy and hung as a spy, yet he resolved to leave neither plea or threat untried to avert his merited fate.

André was tried by a board of General officers—six Major-Generals and eight Brigadiers—General Greene presiding. The hearing was upon the citations of Washington, which Hamilton gives as follows:

"Major André, Adjutant-General to the British army, will be brought before you for your examination. He came within our lines in the night on an interview with Major-General Arnold, and in an assumed character; and was taken within our lines, in a disguised habit, with a pass under a feigned name, and with the enclosed papers concealed upon him. After a careful examination, you will be pleased, as speedily as possible, to report a precise state of his case, together with your opinion of the light in which he ought to be considered, and the punishment that ought to be inflicted. The Judge Advocate will attend to assist in the examination, who has sundry other papers relative to this matter, which he will lay before the board."

"When brought before the board" Hamilton wrote, "he met with every mark of indulgence and was required to answer no interrogatory which would even embarrass his feelings. On his part, while he carefully concealed everything that might implicate others, he frankly confessed all the facts relating to himself, and, upon his confession, without the trouble of examining a witness, the board made up their report." Briefly surveying the circumstances of the case, the board was of opinion that Major André, Adjutant-General of the British army, ought to be considered a spy from the enemy, and, agreeably to the law and usage of nations, ought to suffer death. This decision Washington approved and ordered the execution to take place October 1st. André comported himself with firmness and evinced gratitude for the considerate manner in which he had been treated. By his gentlemanly deportment, his unflinching resolution, his anxiety for others, he won the hearts of all. Not an American officer but would have rejoiced at some pretext for his exchange or acquittal. Even after the sentence it was intimated by Lafayette, to Captain Ogden—bearer of dispatches to the British, apprising Clinton of André's fate—that if Arnold were given up André would be exchanged for him. This intimation Ogden was authorised to make to the enemy and did so in his interview with the British officer commanding at Paulus' Hook. The matter was laid before Clinton who rejected the suggestion as inadmissable with honor or principle.

Receiving the report of the military board, and learning of the sentence of execution, Clinton again wrote to Washington (Sept. 30th) assuming that the board had not been rightly informed of all the circumstances upon which to form a correct judgment; and that, in order to have the matter properly represented he urged a suspension of proceedings until his commissioners could be heard. October 1st was fixed for André's execution, but the request of Clinton was granted and proceedings were stayed to await the issue of this professedly fuller information. On the morning of October 1st, three persons, viz: Lieutenant-Governor Elliott, Chief Justice Smith (brother of the Smith at whose house the treason was consummated) and Lieutenant-General Robertson, accompanied by Colonel Robinson, André's confidant, went up to Dobbs' Ferry by vessel. The commission asked a safe conduct to Washington, but General Greene who was in attendance, would only permit Lieutenant-General Robertson to come ashore—he being the only military officer in the embassy. A long conference followed. Robertson had nothing new to offer; he only

André's Pen Photograph of himself, made the day after his capture.

urged the points already made in André's defense—all of which Greene declared inadmissable. Robertson solicited permission to see Washington, but Greene—doubtless by orders of the Commander-in-Chief—refused permission and reported the matter to his superior. Robertson delivered to Greene a second letter from Arnold to Washington, which was properly delivered. It reasserted his (Arnold's) right as commanding officer of the department to cover André's admission to the American lines, that his power to issue a pass fully covering André's person was indisputable. He insisted that he had a commander's right to transact the business in which André was concerned, and then added this remarkable threat:

"If after this just and candid representation of Major André's case, the board of General officers shall adhere to their former opinion, I shall suppose it dictated by passion and resentment; and if that gentleman should suffer the severity of their sentence, I shall think myself bound, by every tie of duty and honor, to retaliate on such unhappy persons of your army as may fall within my power, that the respect due to flags and to the laws of nations may be better understood and observed.

"I have further to observe that forty of the principal inhabitants of South Carolina have justly forfeited their lives, which have hitherto been spared by the clemency of his Excellency, Sir Henry Clinton, who cannot in justice extend his mercy to them any longer, if Major André suffers; which, in all probability will open a scene of blood at which humanity shudders.

"Suffer me to entreat your Excellency, for your own sake and the honor of humanity, and the love you have of justice, that you suffer not an unjust sentence to touch the life of Major André. But if this warning should be disregarded, and he suffer, I call heaven and earth to witness that your Excellency will be justly answerable for the torrent of blood that may be spilt in consequence."

This note excited only indignation in Washington's breast: it was worthy of Arnold but unworthy of Clinton, to whom its contents must have been known. Greene soon dispatched a brief epistle to Robertson, stating that the Commander-in-

Chief's conclusions were not modified by his (Robertson's) representations. To this the commissioner replied, assuming that Greene could not have reported the matter fully. He therefore addressed Washington, stating his views and points at length. They were, however, fruitless, and André was executed on the succeeding day. His bearing to the last was that of a man conscious of having done only his duty. He made no recriminations, uttered no protests, but walked to death as a soldier should. If his conscience arraigned him for the base part he had played it was not made apparent. He died on the scaffold, and forthwith was canonized by the British nation as a martyr in its behalf.

The story of Arnold's career, after his safe arrival in the British camp, is one of dishonor. His first efforts were directed toward the release of André; these failing, he next issued an "address" to the people of America. In this document he sought to vindicate his memory, falsifying and dissimulating to the end. He said that in the beginning he had only taken up arms to secure a redress of grievances; a falsehood, because he had entered the field as all other patriots did—to drive the British from American soil, and, had asseverated his right to promotion because of the services rendered in the cause of independence. He regarded the Declaration of Independence as precipitate, while subsequent offers of the British Government had rendered it unnecessary—a statement as unpatriotic as it was dastardly in one who had never lisped such words until branded with infamy by his countrymen. He inveighed against the Continental Congress for its rejection of terms offered by the British Crown without submitting those offers to the people—a singular charge considering the brutal excesses committed by the British to *enforce* their "overtures." His last grievance—that which had most stirred his honorable pride and Christian principle, was the alliance with France, the enemy of Protestantism and of liberty. That alliance had filled the cup of his indignation and had determined his course! What to the mass of American patriots was succor in time of their greatest need—what to them was a new lease of life and hope—to Benedict Arnold was a humiliation. It were better even for *his* name that that excuse for his defection from the cause of liberty and honor had not been offered.

He forgot to state, in this address, the amount of British gold and the military commission paid for his desertion.

This document was accompanied by a proclamation addressed especially to the officers and soldiers of the Continental army, inviting them to rally under the Cross of St. George and to fight for the true interests of their country and for liberty. To such as would come to his embraces large bounties and generous subsistence supplies were volunteered, as well as compensation for all the accoutrements and implements of war which they might steal and bring in with them.

It is needless to say the address and proclamation only heightened the disgust felt for the miscreant and poltroon. Washington said: "I am at a loss which to admire most, the confidence of Arnold in publishing it, or the folly of the enemy in supposing that a production signed by so infamous a character will have any weight with the people of these States, or any influence upon our officers abroad." A few cut-throats and renegades then within the British lines answered his call —just enough to give him a body guard adapted in character for his special service.

His wife was made to feel the weight of his crimes. Though given a safe escort to Philadelphia she was quickly ordered, by the Executive Council, to leave the State, not to return during the war. Fourteen days only were allowed for preparation. This order was issued in the firm conviction that she was privy to the plot, and had acted a part in the affair with André. But, to add to the supposition of her guiltlessness it is stated that, before the order of banishment was issued, she had determined to procure a legal separation from her husband "to whom" Irving says "she could not endure the thought of returning after his dishonor." Irving also quotes from a letter written at that time by one of her relatives, who said: "We tried every means to prevail on the Council to permit her to stay among us, and not to compel her to go to that infernal villain, her husband. Mr. Shippen (her father) had promised the Council, and Mrs. Arnold had signed a writing to the same purpose, engaging not to write to General Arnold any letters whatever, and to receive no letters without showing them to the Council, if she were permitted to stay." But, to no purpose. Public and private opinion set in so strongly against her that she was forced to proceed to New York, where she rejoined her husband, and thereafter—without a murmur as far as any evidence exists—shared his fortunes. It must have been a dreadful decree if she indeed were guiltless of complicity in his crime.

Thus ends the chapter of Arnold's Conspiracy. We might, with interest to the reader, pursue the traitor's fortunes; might advert to his desolating and terrible visitation upon Virginia, and to his destruction of New London in his native State; might trace his after career in St. John's, N. B., in the West Indies and in England—the most despised and shunned of men; but all these matters belong rather to general history and to biography than to our province. We may, however, refer to the efforts made, with Washington's consent, to secure the person of the traitor.

The defection of Arnold resulted in a wide spread suspicion that others were engaged in the conspiracy, and names were whispered to Washington which gave him great uneasiness, as well as pain. General St. Clair's was mentioned so confidently as Arnold's confederate, that the Commander-in-Chief resolved to investigate the implicatory charges. To this end, by secret emissaries, he reached New York, penetrated to Sir Henry Clinton's confidence and wormed the truth from Arnold. Nothing was learned to implicate any others. St. Clair was thus relieved of an odious imputation, which, if it had not been wiped away at that time might hhve stained his name forever. Washington felt great relief at the result of the investigations.

Major Henry Lee, who conducted the investigation, it would appear, conceived a plan for Arnold's abduction. So earnest was the desire of all, both officers and men, to secure the traitor for punishment that any enterprise however hazardous, which had for its purpose Arnold's capture, would have found ready volunteers. But, secure within the British lines, no plan was feasible which necessitated the open use of force. Lee's ready mind turned to stratagem. His agents were instructed to learn all about the traitor's place of residence, his habits, and, if possible, his plans—an injunction faithfully performed, since, through his faithful spies, he became possessed of all information necessary to perfect the project for his capture. Having conceived his plan of operations, Lee consulted with the Commander-in-Chief, and, after much canvassing of the affair, obtained from him the necessary consent to put his scheme on foot.[1]

John Champe, Sergeant-major of cavalry in Lee's legion of light horse, was the chosen instrument of the enterprise. He was a resolute, cool and sagacious man, admirably fitted for such a service, which he undertook only after much persuasion. In its execution, it would be necessary for him to cover his name with the dishonor of a deserter and to link himself to Arnold's hated person—an ordeal that the patriotic dragoon shrank from encountering. His consent being won it was arranged that he should desert to the enemy, make his way to New York, there to seek Arnold's household and obtain service in it in such a capacity as would place him near the traitor's person. In this he had a confederate—a New Jersey boatman who had long acted as a spy and, from being accounted a friend of the British, had easy access by boat to the city, bearing news and fresh provisions to the officers. Between these two it was planned to seize Arnold at night, in one of his solitary walks in the garden, to bear him to the boat moored in the river at the foot of the garden, and to pull out in the darkness for the Hoboken shore, where Lee was to be in attendance with a guard and horses to spirit the prisoner away

[1] Irving says the plan was formed at Washington's suggestion. He is in error. Lee's emissaries, by reporting that Arnold resided in a place bordering on the Hudson, suggested the idea, to the bold Major of dragoons, of Arnold's capture. Laying the plan before the Commander-in-Chief it was approved by him. Lee, therefore, should have the credit of having conceived the enterprise. Washington expressly stipulated that Arnold should be brought in alive. He said: "No circumstance whatever shall obtain my consent to his being put to death. The idea which would accompany such an event would be that ruffians had been hired to assassinate him. My aim is to make a public example of him." To all of which both Lee and Champe assented.

to Washington's headquarters. The chief difficulty in the outset was for the Sergeant to effect his escape in safety. So vigilant were the troopers that, to elude their pickets was almost impossible, while, if discovered and pursued, capture was almost inevitable. If captured, the poor fellow would be under the necessity of appealing to the clemency of his drum-head court by confessing the whole affair, if he would escape being shot—a confession mortifying to make since it would implicate both Washington and Lee, while it was not then desirable to make the design for the traitor's capture known.

All worked well. Champe, after close pursuit succeeded in taking refuge in a British guard-boat on the Hudson—barely escaping capture at the hands of his indignant comrades. Lee's dilatoriness in ordering the pursuit saved his messenger from recapture. Once in the British lines the dragoon made his way to Arnold, and, by representing that he had deserted from the famous light horse corps, was at once attached to the service of his intended victim. The seizure was arranged for an early consummation. The Jerseyman apprised Lee of everything, and all things promised success. Arnold walked nightly in the garden: the nights were not light; Champe and his confederate could penetrate to the place, and thus the moment of abduction was definitely fixed. But, alas for the happy issue so confidently contemplated! The day before his projected seizure Arnold moved his quarters and that night witnessed the total miscarriage of the hazardous enterprise. Lee waited on the Hoboken shore all night long for the expected boat, with its prize, but waited in vain. He returned to headquarters at Tappan, to report a failure to Washington. The Commander-in-Chief was much concerned in regard to the matter, apprehending that Champe had been detected, and would, in consequence, suffer death for his devotion to orders. But, no harm came to the bold sergeant further than that he was made to embark, as one of Arnold's American legion, in the Virginia expedition, to participate in an outrage upon his native State, which history has not failed to condemn. He succeeded, eventually, in effecting his escape, and after nearly a year's absence returned to his comrades, to receive their congratulations and the thanks of the Commander-in-Chief. The army and the people that scorned the name of Arnold delighted to honor that of Champe, the humble Sergeant-major of cavalry.

REVOLT OF THE PENNSYLVANIA LINE.

THE winter of 1780–81 was one of depression to the Patriot cause. To want of success in the field came that of disappointment in the effect of French co-operation, upon which much reliance had been placed by Washington, by Congress, by the army and by the people. Public finances were at their lowest ebb of credit: a handfull of Continental bills being the value of a dinner. The army, illy clothed and worse paid, was discontented and turbulent. Many troops, whose term of enlistment had expired, excited dismay at their clamors for a proper requital for their services. "Commerce was almost exhausted; there was not sufficient natural wealth on which to found a revenue; paper currency had depreciated through want of funds for its redemption until it was nearly worthless. The mode of supplying the army by assessing a proportion of the productions of the earth had proved ineffectual, oppressive and productive of alarming opposition. Domestic loans yielded but trifling assistance. The patience of the army was nearly exhausted; the people were dissatisfied with the mode of supporting the war, and there was reason to apprehend that, under the pressure of impositions of a new and odious kind, they had only exchanged one kind of tyranny for another."[1] Washington, Hamilton, Greene, Wayne, Lafayette, apprehending the worst, plead Congress in terms which to us now seem even pitiful, for action to relieve the depression and dissatisfaction so generally prevalent. Under the stress of their petition John Laurens was dispatched (by commission dated Dec. 28th, 1780) to Versailles, there to seek the aid in means and men

---

[1] Irving's "Washington," vol. iv. page 210.

which alone seemed able to avert the impending disintegration of the army and the consequent failure of the Revolution.

Brigadier-General Anthony Wayne, then commanding the First Pennsylvania brigade, as early as September 17th, 1780, wrote to President Reed, of Pennsylvania, as follows:

"When I look to a period fast approaching, I discover the most gloomy prospects and distressing objects presenting themselves; and when I consider the mass of people who now compose this army will dissolve by the first of January (except a little corps enlisted for the war, badly paid and worse fed) I dread the consequence, as these melancholy facts may have a most unhappy influence on their minds when opposed to a well appointed, puissant and desolating army."

To other influential men of his State he wrote in a similar strain. To Robert Morris, the great financier (Nov. 9th), after referring to the disasters which must follow to American arms if the troops were not immediately cared for, he said:

"Let me, therefore, as a friend and fellow-citizen, call upon you, in the most solemn manner, to meet the other part of the Assembly and Council with temper. Let party prejudices subside. Meddle not now with the Constitution, as the time is drawing nigh when the *magnum concilium* of Pennsylvania will be necessarily convened to decide upon its case. Exert every power for the immediate completion of your quota of troops; establish magazines of provisions; adopt some efficacious measure to procure a quantity of specie; and, at all events, find means to clothe the soldiers belonging to the State by the first of January."

In another letter he said:

"Poorly clothed, badly fed and worse paid—some of them not having received a paper dollar for near twelve months; exposed to winter's piercing cold, to drifting snows and chilling blasts with no protection but old, worn-out coats, tattered linen overalls and but one blanket between three men. In this situation the enemy begin to work upon their passions, and have found means to circulate some proclamations among them."

These were indeed 'times which tried men's souls.' There must have been a tremendous weight of patriotism upon the breasts of the patriot soldiers generally to have kept down their griefs and to have soothed their absolute sufferings. The case of the Pennsylvania line troops, however, was peculiar, and the revolt here recorded in all probability would not have occurred had their only cause of complaint been scanty rations, poor clothing and no pay. These men had enlisted for "three years or during the war." Their three years expired in the fall of 1780, but they were refused their discharge, on the ground that their term of service was not for three years, but during the war—a construction at variance with the plain meaning of the stipulation and one rejected by all authorities: it meant three years if the war should last so long. Irving calls the construction made, *chicanery.*

The brigade of Wayne[1] went into winter quarters at Morristown, New Jersey, where the troops proceeded to erect huts for their protection—a labor in which the officers participated to cheer their shivering men. Wayne said: "the officers in general, as well as myself, find it necessary to stand for hours every day exposed to wind and weather among the poor naked fellows while they are working at their huts and redoubts, often assisting with our own hands in order to procure a conviction to their minds that we share, and more than share, every vicissitude in common with them, sometimes asking to participate in their bread and water. The good effect of this conduct is very conspicuous, and prevents their murmuring in public; but the delicate mind and eye of humanity are hurt, very much hurt, at their visible distress and private complainings." This temporary obedience to orders soon gave way before the growing discontent. A spirit of insubordination spread rapidly, encouraged as it was by a few riotous characters and by secret emissaries of Sir Henry Clinton—who was fully informed of the critical state of affairs, and sought by every means to profit by it. The men from being sullen, became insolent. They committed all manner of excesses among the surrounding farmers, and threatened retaliation upon any officer who questioned their right to "help themselves." In Wayne they found a sympathizing fellow-soldier, but a stern, unflinching commander—one who would be obeyed. He arrested and severely punished the marauders. Strong sentinels were stationed around the encampment, and every out-going or returning soldier was rigidly examined; if his pass was not authentic he was seized and sent to the guard-house for trial.

[1] Wayne's brigade was the First—Irvine's the Second of the Pennsylvania line (regular) troops. The revolt was confined to the First brigade.

Every hut was visited by the inspection-guard nightly, after tattoo-beating, to see that all the inmates, whose names were inscribed on the door, were there. Washington wrote Wayne from his headquarters at New Windsor, 28th of December, expressing great satisfaction at the arrangements of the camp, and the course being pursued. He advised that he had ordered 800 of 2000 shirts (donated by the Philadelphia ladies) to be forwarded to Wayne's brigade. The letter did not reach him in time to stay the storm, so long anticipated, of an open insurrection. Between the hours of nine and ten, on the evening of Jan. 1st (1781), the men rushed from their huts, seized upon arms, ammunition and provisions, secured six pieces of artillery, and horses from the stables.[1] This formidable step was followed by the declaration that they not only were going to abandon their quarters but were determined to march upon Philadelphia and redress their grievances by their guns.

The officers flew to arms. Wayne rushed among the men, followed by his aids. Cocking his pistols he threatened death to the leaders of the mutiny. Instantly a platoon of muskets were leveled at his breast. One of the leaders spoke out: "We love you, we respect you, but you are a dead man if you fire. Do not mistake us. We are not going to the enemy. On the contrary, were they now to come out, you would see us fight under your orders, with as much resolution and alacrity as ever." He did not fire, but attempted to use his authority to disperse the men. Three regiments, still true to their General, were paraded under arms. A conflict ensued, in which numbers were wounded on both sides and one Captain (Bitting) killed. The mutineers were so strong as, not only to overcome all opposition, but to compel the three regiments named to join their ranks; when, numbering 1300 strong, the march was taken up for Philadelphia *via* Princeton. Wayne immediately dispatched two of his leading officers to Philadelphia, to

---

1 Irving says the men were under the influence of liquor. We do not know his authority for this statement. If they had had an additional glass of grog, in honor of the New Year, it was not the cause of the outbreak which, evidently, had long been contemplated, and arranged for the day upon which they should have been according to their interpretation of their enlistment) discharged.

R. Thew, Sculp

REVOLT OF WAYNE'S BRIGADE.

apprise Congress of the movement. He wrote hurriedly to Washington detailing the particulars of the affair, and then followed on after the men, striving by all the means in his power to bring them back to duty—or, at least, to forego their desertion of their quarters, until deputies could be sent to Congress to arrange all difficulties. They would not be stayed. Wayne, gallantly assisted by Colonels Butler and Stewart, then ordered out the militia. "Alarm-fires were kindled upon the hills; alarm-guns boomed from post to post," says Irving; "the country was soon on the alert." Advancing to Princeton a halt was there made by the leaders of the insurrectionists—fearing to pass beyond that point, and feeling strong in it.

Philadelphia was thrown into consternation by the news. Congress immediately dispatched a committee to meet the insurgents. President Reed and other State officers also hastened forward to the scene of excitement, halting at Trenton, along with the committee, in order to confer with Wayne, who still was with the troops, in an equivocal position, being neither their commander, nor yet utterly without authority. The Governor wrote to Wayne, soliciting an interview four miles from Princeton—remarking that, after the indignities heaped by the men upon General St. Clair, the Marquis Lafayette and Colonel Laurens (whom they had ordered out of the camp at short notice) he could not place himself in a position to receive similar treatment. This letter Wayne read aloud to the men on parade. It touched their pride to the quick: to think that their own beloved President, who had come to redress their injuries, could not trust himself in their hands! The good leaven of reason and confidence began to work. At this moment two of Clinton's agents arrived on the spot, making the most enticing overtures to the troops for their services. This fired their indignation and their patriotism. They seized the emissaries of the British commander as spies, handing them over to Wayne, by whom they were afterwards hanged, at Trenton cross-roads.

President Reed, on the morning of the 7th, however, at Wayne's request, ventured into the encampment. All there was precision and order, and Reed was respectfully saluted as he passed. Through Wayne, the President proceeded to offer terms of accommodation. Through Wayne, the insurgents replied. They still trusted their old commander entirely. After considerable correspondence terms were arranged, which proved that kindness was more potent than the sword. The insurrection was at an end. Some were discharged from service; some on forty days' furlough; all were to be supplied with specified clothing; certificates were granted for such depreciation in the currency as the troops had been compelled to suffer from; arrears of pay were to be provided for as soon as possible. This arranged, the brigade dissolved and was soon entirely dispersed.

These terms were distasteful to Washington, for he apprehended that, as a precedent, the settlement under compulsion would be bad. So it proved. A portion of the Jersey line stationed at Pompton revolted, on the night of Jan. 20th, claiming the same terms granted the Pennsylvania line. As in the previous revolt Clinton's agents were ready with tempting offers to turn the troops from their allegiance to the patriot cause. This second revolt, however, the Commander-in-Chief determined to suppress by force of arms, at all hazards, and to shoot the leaders as a warning against future attempts. Major-General Howe, with a detachment from the trusty Massachusetts line, surprised the mutineers early one morning, in their huts. Only five minutes were granted to parade without arms and surrender the leaders. This surprise, and the determined bearing of the officer, compelled them to his terms. Two of the ringleaders were instantly shot. Thus an effectual end was put to further insurrections. Washington proved to the army that his mercy could never be tempered to mutineers: obedience to allegiance first—accommodation of differences afterwards, was his policy. As he wrote [see p. 173] regarding the insurrection in Massachusetts: "*influcnce* is not *government.*" His life was order and symmetry itself, and his course of action was such as to reduce disorder by a display of the hand of authority. Such men are made to *govern.*

THE "STATE OF FRANKLIN" EMEUTE.

"By such rash and irregular conduct, a precedent is formed for every district, and even for every county in the State, to claim the right of separation and independency for any supposed grievance of the inhabitants, as caprice, pride and ambition shall dictate, at pleasure, thereby exhibiting to the world a melancholy instance of a feeble or pusillanimous Government, that is either unable or dares not restrain the lawless designs of its citizens. I know, with reluctance, the State will be driven to arms; it will be the last alternative to imbrue her hands in the blood of her citizens; but if no other ways or means are found to save her honor and reclaim her headstrong, refractory citizens but this last sad expedient, her resources are not yet so exhausted or her spirits damped but she may take satisfaction for this great injustice received, and regain her government over the revolted territory, or render it not worth possessing."

These were the words of a proclamation issued by the Governor of North Carolina, April 25th, 1785, addressed to the people of the "Washington District." Lying on the western slope of the Alleghanies, in the vallies of the Holston and the Wautaga rivers, it was a 'world to itself,' shut in by the great Appalachian ridges on the north, east and west. Thus isolated its settlers had, prior to the Revolution, formed for themselves a government—primitive and crude, yet substantial—which they called the "Watauga Government." This was represented by four delegates in the Convention assembled at Halifax, North Carolina, 1772. In 1777 one of these delegates, John Sevier, was a member of the North Carolina "House of Commons," and procured for the Watauga people a full recognition of their claims as an integral section of the State. Their territory—afterwards comprised in the three counties of

Washington, Greene and Sullivan—was made a judicial district, and called the "Washington District." It now reposes in the quiet regions of East Tennessee, disturbed in its pristine valley-silence only by the whirr of wheels and the shrieks of the rushing messengers of trade and travel. During the War of Independence its inhabitants were not drawn much into the contest until during the fall of 1780, when they suddenly swooped down upon Cornwallis' advance under Ferguson, and, at the glorious battle of King's Mountain (Oct. 7th), performed signal service under the leadership of Sevier.[1] Surrounded as they were by hostile Indians, the inhabitants of the District were not permitted to enter into the Continental service as a distinct military body, though many of them found their way over the mountains to mingle in the struggle for liberty.

In 1785 they were in revolt against the State, whose authority over them ever had been the merest form, and whose benefits had been truly nominal. The District, by the voice of the people, through their delegates in Convention assembled, voted to *secede* from North Carolina, and to erect a commonwealth of their own, to be called the "State of Franklin." In this act the hydra of Secession was born:[2] how it was viewed

---

[1] Irving, in his "Life of Washington," vol. iv. pages 187–93, refers, in terms of high praise, to those "warriors of the wilderness."

[2] We have said in another work [" History of the Southern Rebellion" vol. i. pages 12, 13, 16] that Jefferson, by his Kentucky resolutions, became the author of Secession. He was such, in effect, though Sevier and his co-workers were first to act upon the higher-law principle of "popular sovereignty." Jefferson talked for States; Sevier used the right assumed by the Great Lawgiver as inhering to the State to apply also to *parts* of a State. Jefferson taught the superiority of the State over the National Government; Sevier fought for the superiority of three counties over the State. Jefferson concocted the phrases and forms of political and social disintegration; Sevier enforced the principle. The Virginian may have learned of Seveir; Sevier certainly did not learn of Jefferson. The "Governor" of the "State of Franklin," however, struck the keynote of inter-State revolution too soon—before the General Government and National Executive had existence; Jefferson struck it in 1798, and, therefore, may be regarded as wet nurse of the infant dragon; his voice taught it to lisp its numbers and to use its relentless teeth. Fortunately for Jefferson's succeeding course he was abroad in 1778—as our Minister to France. Had he been in Virginia he might have had to commit himself on the question of Secession, as some of his coadjutors had to do in suppressing the

by the Governor, Council and Legislature of North Carolina, may be inferred by the quotation above given from the proclamation of April 25th.

This movement for separation originated in the act of the North Carolina Legislature ceding to the Confederation all territory west of the Alleghanies. This cession was in response to a call of Congress for such an appropriation by all the States having untenanted lands, which were to be used as a resource for liquidating the then enormous public debt. The Confederation was but a rope of sand; its Congress virtually had no power whatever over the States; both lived simply by the sufferance of the people. Even the expenses of Congress, from 1782 to '87, were unprovided for—no authority existing to levy taxes for its sustenance! The States volunteered aid or withheld it, as they saw fit.[1] They enacted laws at variance with the interests of other States and of the Confederation.[2] Their Governors assumed prerogatives of supreme executors, and looked with disdain upon a Congress without power.[3] Dissolution and civil war seemed imminent. Yet Congress struggled desperately to maintain the Government, to sustain its credit, and to place its Departments in a condition of efficiency. It enacted laws of a salutary character, though many of its enactments necessarily were merely speculative, or were dead letters from want of power to enforce them. It called upon the States, again and again, to uphold the Confederate treasury and executive. It levied assessments, imposts, excise, to receive but the shadow of a return. It borrowed with no power to pay. It issued bonds which found few purchasers at any price.

---

fires kindled in the south western counties by Sevier's ideas. Patrick Henry, as Governor of Virginia, was, during 1785, called upon to threaten all unlawful combinations with the punishment due to all who disturbed the harmony and offended the majesty of the State. Had Jefferson occupied Henry's seat he might have committed himself against the revolutionary idea.

[1] See author's "History of Southern Rebellion," vol. i. page 207, for the proportion contributed by each of the States toward the general expenses.

[2] See Hamilton's "History of the Republic," vol. iii. chap. xlii. Also Irving's "Washington," vol. iv. chap. xxvi.

[3] See Hamilton, vol, iv. page 238.

North Carolina answered the call for aid as stated. But, this transfer of soil without consent aroused the hardy and somewhat turbulent population of the territory ceded to an indignant opposition. The cession was made in June, 1784; in August, the same year, a Convention of the people of the three counties (Washington, Greene and Sullivan) assembled to take action in the matter. Sevier was a ruling spirit. He advocated a rejection of the right of cession and claimed the right of secession. His views prevailed; the Convention declared, by a unanimous voice, the independence of their counties from all State relations and control. This declaration apparently gave popular satisfaction, since, aside from the Legislature's action in giving away their territory, the people of the District had several grievances of an exciting character to stir up bitterness against that Legislature. August 24th a declaration and "form of government" were issued setting forth, in true secession style, the glories to attend upon the new State. It was provided that contiguous counties in Virginia might participate in the movement and become joint heirs to prosperity. A "provisional government" was arranged; yet, more honest than the secession revolutionists of 1860–61, the delegates did not presume to instate it until the people actually had accepted it through a second Convention. Public officers were directed to retain all public monies then in their keeping until the succeeding Convention could assume the responsibility of their disposal in the "fair and equitable settlement" which it was proposed to make with the old State.

Thus matters rested in the District, until the meeting, two months later, of the second Convention. The sober second thought had begun to work; while the State, troubled at the schism, hastened to correct its ways by legislating backward. The act of cession to the Confederation was repealed; the western counties were made into an exclusive judicial district and granted an assistant judge and attorney-general for the State Superior Court; while Sevier, the gallant but turbulent patriot, was commissioned a Brigadier-General! These signs of returning sense on the part of the old State authorities and lawgivers, disarmed the seceders of their professed "wrongs," leaving them without an excuse for further insurrection. Sevier was reconciled.

But, not so with the people. They had been excited with the blandishments of secession and were bound to taste of the forbidden fruit. They set aside the conservatives, or submissionists, and inaugurated the "provisional" Government. It at once proclaimed an election for members of a General Assembly, and otherwise legislated for the "permanent" order of things. With true revolutionary precipitation an election for the Assembly was held at once; its members elect met at Jonesborough, early in 1785, opening the "Senate" and "House of Commons" with due form. The Assembly's first act was the appointment of Sevier as provisional Governor, the instation of provisional Courts and the inauguration of all necessary machinery of State. Their new commonwealth was then christened "The State of Franklin." This done, Sevier, by act of the Assembly, duly, and in official form, informed Martin, Governor of North Carolina, of the action of the western counties, whose people "no longer considered themselves under the sovereignty and jurisdiction of the parent State." Receiving this quit-notice Governor Martin immediately convened his Council (April 22d, 1785). After three days' solemn deliberation the Legislature was convoked to meet at Newbern, June 1st, in extraordinary session, and the proclamation (quoted at the opening of our paper) was issued—not published. It was circulated in manuscript form to give it the force of a special and personal consideration by the people of the three counties, by whom it was generally read and thoroughly canvassed. It began to work among the more reflecting, and again excited the "submissionists" to life. But Sevier—"in for a penny in for a pound"—resolved to throw down the gauntlet of defiance. This he did in a manifesto to the people, encouraging them to loyalty to the new State, and threatening all malcontents with his dire displeasure. To this manifesto the new Governor of North Carolina, Caswell, rejoined, repeating his purpose to enforce the just authority of the State.

But, notwithstanding all this show of war, the *people* of the old State apparently gave the matter little heed. Even the

Legislature summoned to meet at Newbern forgot to come together; and, generally, the affair was treated as a joke. Profiting by this reception, the secessionists proceeded to strengthen their movement and their Government, by meeting in Convention at Greenville, Nov. 14th, 1785, to adopt a permanent Constitution.[1] After a noisy and not particularly harmonious 'comparison of views' between the men of property and those owning only a horse, hunting-shirt and rifle, the Convention adopted the North Carolina Constitution, with slight modifications. This organic law was at once put in motion in seven counties so far as legislation went, though the want of money, of taxable products, of commercial communication with the North and East, all contributed to render the new State literally a state of suspense. The need for money, however, was obviated in a novel manner. By law the price of beaver, otter, mink, deer and other skins—of whisky, bacon, maple sugar and homespun linen—was fixed; and these commodities, thereafter, took the place of money—became the "circulating medium." It was provided that "all salaries and allowances hereby made shall be paid by any treasurer, sheriff or collector of public taxes to any person entitled to the same—to be paid in specific articles (referring to skins, &c.) as collected and at the rates allowed by the State for the same," &c. Lossing observes: [2]

> "It has been jocularly declared that the salaries of the Governor, Officers of State and Judges were paid in fox skins, and those of sheriffs, constables and inferior officers in mink skins. This currency was accepted as good, and no one thought of fluctuation or depreciation until confidence in it was shaken by daring counterfeiters. Opossom skins were almost worthless, while raccoon skins were valued at one shilling and six-pence. The counterfeiters sewed raccoons' tails upon oppossum skins, passed the mongrel as genuine "coons," and thus brought discredit upon the whole currency of Franklin."

All this procedure did not pass, however, unnoticed by the North Carolina authorities. The Legislature convened in reg-

---

[1] Greenville has since become classic ground in the cause of the Union. It was there that the great Convention of Unionists was held in June, 1861, to protest against secession and treason.

[2] See article "Early Secessionists" in Harper's Magazine for March, 1862.

ular session in the fall of 1785, pursued a very conciliatory course toward the disaffected counties. An act was passed granting amnesty and oblivion for all the past providing the people returned to their allegiance and disavowed the Sevier government. They were authorised to vote for representatives in the State Assembly, while judges were appointed for the courts. This act of clemency again gave strength to the old State party, and at once created a clear issue. Sevier was firm and his partisans were in the majority; but the opposition numbered some of the staunchest men in the District. Led by Colonel John Tipton the anti-Secessionists soon stood forth and boldly refused all recognition of the revolutionary Governor and Government. Party lines were drawn and personal feuds followed. Sevier denounced Tipton while Tipton denounced Sevier. Tipton stood for an election to the North Carolina Senate and others stood for the Lower House; judges were appointed under the amnesty act, and the counties soon witnessed the extraordinary spectacle of two systems inaugurated for their government. The State of Franklin Assembly legislated, its courts decreed, and its bailiffs collected taxes: the State of North Carolina did the same. This of course quickly created a conflict. During 1786 the entire District, and particularly Washington county, was the scene of much excitement, which, at times, culminated in violence. The old State courts established their sessions for Washington county at Buffalo, within ten miles of Jonesborough. Colonel Tipton, with a number of his partisans, made a descent on the county court there in session, seized papers and ejected judge and jurors. Sevier immediately did the same thing for the court at Buffalo. The two leaders finally met, and from words descended to blows. A regular hand to hand fight followed, in which large numbers participated: the submissionists were beaten and had to retire.

Such a state of affairs could not long endure. Sevier either had to abdicate or obtain the aid of arms to enforce his authority. This latter he sought to effect. He applied first to the sage, Benjamin Franklin, for advice, but received not a word. He sought an alliance with Georgia, with no success. He parleyed with the counties in South Western Virginia, whose secession schemes Patrick Henry had nipped in the bud by a rigid show of authority, but not a word of comfort could he extort in return. He finally appointed Commissioners to "treat" with the State authorities for a separation; but they were not recognised at Newburn. A delegate had, previously, been appointed to the Continental Congress, but Congress knew no "State of Franklin," and gave the delegate no admittance. Thus rebuffed Sevier did not despair. He summoned the militia to his aid. His Assembly fully empowered him to act. It passed laws imposing severe penalties upon any who should presume to act, within the State of Franklin, under the authority of the State of North Carolina. This was in conformity with Sevier's expressed resolve made to Governor Caswell, upon the return of the Commissioners sent to treat for separation. He then wrote:

> "I had the fullest hopes and confidence that that body would have either agreed to the separation on honorable principles and stipulations, or otherwise have endeavored to have reunited us upon such terms as might have been lasting and friendly; but I find myself and the country entirely deceived; and if your Assembly have thought their measures would answer such an end, they are greatly mistaken. * * We shall continue to act as independent, and would rather suffer death in all its various and frightful shapes than conform to anything that is disgraceful."

Caswell's reply was admirable. It was highly conciliatory and conveyed the assurance that, in proper season and under favorable auspices, a new State would be formed out of the territory west of the Alleghanies. He therefore begged the people to forbear, and await the issue of events as good and orderly citizens. This note was the severest blow that then could have been inflicted: it drove from Sevier's support many of his partisans, leaving him but a minority. The old State party grew, thence, rapidly. It elected members to the North Carolina Assembly and refused to countenance the election of members to the insurgent Legislature. In consequence, elections were not held in several districts, and, when the showing of strength was finally made, it was ascertained that Sevier really had but two out of the seven counties of the new State with him.

This compelled the Governor to seek for terms of accommodation consistent with a retreat without dishonor. He therefore solicited the Governor of Georgia to "mediate" for a settlement between the old State and the new—an office which the Georgian refused to accept. Sevier then dispatched a second commission to Newbern to treat with the Governor, but Caswell would give them no recognition as commissioners, though he treated them well as citizens. The Governor of North Carolina seemed willing to let events take their course, clearly foreseeing that the people themselves would rectify their errors. He acted wisely, for the last Sevier Legislature me tin September, 1787. Failing to elect a State Council, it hovered on the verge of dissolution for a few weeks, hoping to see the way clear for an honorable surrender of their delegated authority; but, finally expired of mere inanition. Governor Sevier alone remained. He did not surrender his authority, nor yet did he offer opposition to the rapid displacement of his officials by the old State party, and the authorities. He kept the field, however, evidently too proud and obstinate to give over to his enemies. Colonel Tipton, resolving to bring matters to a crisis and thus to get rid of the Governor, concocted the seizure of Sevier's negroes. They were taken on his farm on the Nolachuky river and borne by the Sheriff of Washington county to Tipton's farm on the Watauga river. Sevier and his friends were aroused to a state of frenzy. They gathered to the number of one hundred and fifty and proceeded to Tipton's house, which was surrounded and an order made for its surrender. But fifteen men were with Tipton, yet he replied defiantly to the summons. Sevier then sent in to him a written demand, as Governor of the State of Franklin, for his unconditional surrender. This document Tipton dispatched to Colonel Maxwell, in an adjoining county, begging the Colonel to come to his aid. Maxwell replied by immediately gathering a large body of partizans, with whom he fell upon Sevier's men and a severe fight ensued. Two men were mortally wounded, and Sevier's two sons were taken prisoners. Tipton resolved to hang them at once, and was only dissuaded by the earnest interposition of friends. Sevier's party suffered utter defeat, and the Governor became a kind of exile amid his own people. His restless spirit kept all in a ferment, until, finally (in July, 1789) the Governor of North Carolina issued an order for his arrest, charging him with being guilty of high treason. This order was issued at a moment when Sevier was on the frontier protecting the settlers against the Indians. He had gathered a strong body of armed men and proceeded toward the Creek country, but it was surmised that the chastisement of Indians was only a cover for his real design, to secure a powerful band of confederates and with them to co-operate with Miro, Spanish Governor of Louisiana, and his agent, General James Wilkinson, in transferring the country west of the Alleghanies to the Spanish rule. Evidence which afterwards transpired, proved that Sevier had really contemplated such a transfer as a last resort in resistance of the power of North Carolina.[1]

Sevier was secured, by the aid of Tipton, and borne in irons

---

[1] The Spaniards themselves had conceived a plan for dismembering the Union. In this project General James Wilkinson became involved—the same individual who acted the part of informer against and betrayer of Aaron Burr, in 1806-7. To his complicity in the scheme for transferring Kentucky to the Spanish domination we devote one paper of this volume. Sevier's complicity is also established. On the 12th of Sept., 1788, he wrote to Gardequi, Spanish Minister to the United States, informing him that the inhabitants of Franklin were unanimous in their vehement desire to form an alliance and treaty of commerce with Spain, and to *put themselves under her protection*. He therefore begged for ammunition, money, and any other assistance which Miro, Governor of Louisiana, would bestow, to aid in the contemplated separation from North Carolina, pledging the faith of the State of Franklin for the payment of whatever sums Spain might advance, and whatever expenses she might incur in an enterprise which would secure to her such durable and important results. He said in conclusion:

"Before concluding this communication it is necessary that I should mention that there cannot be a moment more opportune than the present, to carry our plan into execution. North Carolina has refused to accept the new Constitution proposed for the Confederacy, and therefore a considerable time will elapse before she becomes a member of the Union if that event ever happen."

This extract shows how deeply Sevier plotted. He falsified in saying that the people of Franklin were unanimous in their wish to form an alliance with Spain: the *people* really knew nothing of his ambitious, or rather of his desperate designs, to sustain his course. We shall advert to this phase of Sevier's treason in a succeeding paper: See "The Conspiracy of General James Wilkinson."

to the jail at Jonesborough. Fearing a rescue he was conveyed secretly over the mountains to Morgantown, in Burke county. This deportation aroused the mountain men and his old confederates in arms, and they were soon on his track in large numbers, resolved upon a rescue. The trial quickly followed. Sevier was arraigned for high treason and everything promised his conviction. But his partisans were there in the great crowd. One friend, Major Evans, had brought with him the fallen Governor's fleetest mare and stood with her before the Court House door. Another friend named Cozby entered the Court room and confronted the judges. Sevier evidently knew the programme. "Are you done with this man?" said the fearless Cozby, in a stentorian voice, addressing the judges. A scene of tumult followed, and ere a minute Sevier was astride of his fleet mare, flying like a whirlwind toward the mountains. He escaped, but only to be outlawed and hunted. But his treason was not such as to deprive him of sympathy. Out of his persecutions sprang a spirit which sustained him even in the face of persecution. His old friends rallied in force: his enemies were not vengeful, and he was elected to the North Carolina Legislature by an overwhelming vote! In November, 1789, he was in Fayetteville to attend the Assembly session. No feeling prevailed against him; on the contrary Governor and Assembly seemed eager to reenstate him to citizenship and honor! A special act restored him to a citizen's rights and soon after he was clothed with the old commission of Brigadier-General. The Legislature also passed an act to validate all marriages contracted and letters of administration issued under the State authority of the insurgent administration.

Such was the finale of the Franklin State emeute—at once an insurrection and a revolution, though amounting to little more than the fabled tempest in the teapot. Sevier was afterwards honored with offices of trust and served his constituency with satisfaction. He was elected in 1790 to Congress—having no competitor, and took his seat as the first representative from the west of the Alleghanies. Having again been ceded by North Carolina to the General Government (1790) the magnificent domain west of that State to the Mississippi river, was erected into a territory. A Convention called at Knoxville, in 1796, formed a State Constitution and General Sevier was elected its first Executive. The State of Tennessee was admitted into the Union June, 1796. For two terms Sevier was the chosen Governor of the State—revered and honored by all men. In 1811 he was returned to Congress from the Knoxville district, and, during the war of 1812–15, served on the House Committee on Military Affairs. In 1815 President Madison named him Commissioner to run the boundary lines of territory ceded by the Creek Indians to the General Government. In the performance of that duty he was seized with a fever and died in September. The people of Tennessee, mindful of his name and deeds, erected a monument to his memory in the cemetery at Nashville. The monument does not allude to his contemplated treason against his country in endeavoring to pass his "State" over to the Spanish King.

SHAYS' REBELLION.

COLONEL Humphreys writing to General Washington under date of November 1st, 1786, said:

"The trouble in Massachusetts still continue. Government is prostrated in the dust, and it is much to be feared that there is not energy enough in the State to re-establish the civil powers. The leaders of the mob, whose fortunes and measures are desperate, are strengthening themselves daily, and it is expected that they will soon take possession of the Continental magazine at Springfield, in which there are from ten to fifteen thousand stand of arms in excellent order.

"A general want of compliance with the requisitions of Congress for money seems to prognosticate that we are rapidly approaching a crisis. Congress, I am told, are seriously alarmed and hardly know which way to turn or what to expect. Indeed, my dear General, nothing but a good Providence can extricate us from the present condition."

General Knox, then Secretary of War, visiting Massachusetts to look after the threatened revolution, thus wrote of the malcontents:

"Their creed is that the property of the United States has been protected from the confiscation of Britain by the joint exertions of all and therefore ought to be the common property of all, and he that attempts opposition to this creed is an enemy to equity and justice, and ought to be swept off the face of the earth. * * * They are determined to annihilate all debts, public and private, and have agrarian laws, which are easily effected by the means of unfunded paper which shall be a tender in all cases whatever."

The achievement of independence did not bring with it social and political peace. The throes of a revolution were felt in tremors through all the States. Society was ill at ease. Public confidence in the stability of affairs was wanting. State animosities and jealousies became apparent, threatening future relations. Ambitious men intrigued for power and turbulent men defied authority. It was a season of great agitation, full of speculation and suspicion even among the most patriotic. It was evident to the observant that a great change was impending: the country either must drift into anarchy or a more solid and efficient government must be evolved. Still, the men whose judgment and devotion had brought the country safely through the War for Independence struggled to maintain their Government. The heart of those well known in the councils and the field was right; all wished for solidarity of government and labored to accomplish that close union which alone, by suppressing the vicious spirit of State supremacy, could give the whole country one government—render the whole people one nation, and the nation one power. None were more earnest to accomplish that consolidation than Washington. His calm judgment clearly foresaw disaster, disintegration and civil commotion in the near future. To James Warren he wrote:

"The Confederation appears to me to be little more than a shadow without the substance, and Congress a nugatory body; their ordinances being little attended to. To me, it is a solecism in politics, indeed it is one of the most extraordinary things in nature that we should confederate as a nation, and yet be afraid to give the rulers of that nation (who are creatures of our own making, appointed for a limited and short duration, and who are amenable for every action and may be recalled at any moment, and are subject to all the evils which they may be instrumental in producing) sufficient powers to order and direct the affairs of the same. By such policy as this the wheels of government are clogged, and our brightest prospects, and that high expectation which was entertained for us by the wondering world, are turned into astonishment; and from the high ground on which we stood, we are descending into the vale of confusion and darkness."

To another he said:

"I have ever been a friend to adequate powers in Congress, without which it is evident to me we never shall establish a national character, or be considered as on a respectable footing by the powers of Europe. We are either a united people under one head and for Federal purposes, or we are thirteen independent sovereignties, eternally counteracting each other. If the former, whatever such a majority of the States as the Constitution points out, conceives to be for the benefit of the whole, should, in my humble opinion, be submitted to by the minority. I can foresee no evil greater than disunion; than those *unreasonable* jealousies

(I say unreasonable because I would have a *proper* jealousy always awake, and the United States on the watch to prevent individual States from infracting the Constitution with impunity) which are continually poisoning our minds and filling them with imaginary evils for the prevention of real ones."

In reply to a very despondent letter from Judge Jay, then Secretary of Foreign Affairs, we quote:

"We have errors to correct. We have probably had too good an opinion of human nature in forming our Confederation. Experience has taught us that men will not adopt and carry into execution measures the best calculated for their own good, without the intervention of coercive power. I do not conceive we can exist long as a nation, without lodging, somewhere, a power which will pervade the whole Union in as energetic a manner, as the authority of the State Governments extends over the several States. To be fearful of investing Congress, constituted as that body is, with ample authorities for National purposes, appears to me the very climax of popular absurdity and madness. Could Congress exert them for the detriment of the people, without injuring themselves in an equal or greater proportion? Are not their interests inseparably connected with those of their constituents? By the rotation of appointments must they not mingle frequently with the mass of the citizens? Is it not rather to be apprehended, if they were not possessed of the powers before described, that the individual members would be induced to use them, on many occasions, very timidly and inefficaciously, for fear of losing their popularity and future election? We must take human nature as we find it; perfection falls not to the share of mortals.

"What then is to be done? things cannot go on in the same strain forever. It is much to be feared, as you observe, that the better kind of people, being disgusted with these circumstances, will have their minds prepared for any revolution whatever. We are apt to run from one extreme to another. * * * I am told that even respectable characters speak of a monarchical form of government without horror. From thinking proceeds speaking, thence acting is often but a single step. But how irrevocable and tremendous! What a triumph for our enemies to verify their predictions! What a triumph for the advocates of despotism to find that we are incapable of governing ourselves, and that systems, founded on the basis of equal liberty, are merely ideal and fallacious! Would to God that wise measures may be taken in time to avert the consequences we have but too much reason to apprehend."

These views so wise then are not without significance now, when that detested and truly anarchial principle of "State rights" is again made the rallying cry of demagogues and aspirants to office. The *people* should read Washington's views of government, should understand just what "State rights" mean, should see the future as it would be under a system where each State or district in a State, was a law unto itself, before committing themselves to the dangerous principles which are the germ of secession and revolution. Let them read, in the story of Shay's rebellion, just what must follow upon individual attempts to override or suppress laws enacted for the good of the whole.

The debt, at the close of the War for Independence, contracted by Congress in the prosecution of the war was seventy millions of dollars—a sum at that date equivalent to a debt of ten thousand millions in 1860. The debt of Massachusetts alone was five millions; that of other States, if not proportionately great, was very heavy. That old New England State had been first in the field; had furnished more men for the war than Virginia—then the first in population, wealth and political influence; had more ably and efficiently sustained Congress than Virginia or New York by contributions, loans and taxes, and when the war was over she stood nobly forth, even with her tremendous burthen of debt, to sustain the credit of the common country. Governor James Bowdoin, the sturdy patriot and unflinching man of integrity, urged the Legislature to meet the urgent *appeals* of Congress for aid by assuming Massachusetts' share of the sum required in 1786 to meet the public debt—one million and a half of dollars! This act of assumption was voluntary, for in Congress existed no power to enforce its behests. The Legislature, however, was not of the Governor's mind entirely. It represented, to no small degree, the turbulent element seething and bubbling under the surface of affairs, and threatening at any moment to break forth in an eruption of violence. The desire to be relieved of taxation; to stay the collection of debts; to make money plenty by State emissions of paper; to enact laws discriminating against the products or revenues of other States, found embodiment in representatives, who gave the insurrectionary portion of the people encouragement by catering to their lawlessness Still, this class was not in the ascendant, most fortunately for the whole country; and Governor Bowdoin, having succeeded in his wish to sustain the calls of Congress and in suppressing the vicious paper money scheme, adjourned the Legislature from July, 1786 to January, 1787.

Hamilton in his "History of the Republic," says: "The firmness of the Legislature put in motion every active and turbulent spirit. Combinations were formed entertaining desperate designs, and conventions of delegates from extensive districts of the State were held which adopted the most violent resolutions, censuring every measure that had been taken to fulfil the public engagements; declaring open hostility to the ministers of justice; calling for an abolition of all existing contracts; claiming an equal distribution of property; and, at the same time professing that their proceedings were Constitutional!" These turbulent assemblages, indeed, became so frequent and so violent during August and September that Governor Bowdoin called an extra session of the Legislature to consider the alleged grievances and to take steps for suppressing the insurrectionary spirit. The remonstrances, petitions, manifestoes, citations and resolutions sent in were numerous enough to assure the authorities that, whatever the justice of their cause, the malcontents were numerous enough to give trouble if not appeased. Their complaints were as manifold as the petitions were numerous. The heavy poll tax; the excise; costs of court proceedings; high valuation of farm lands; the assumption of National obligations; the riches of lawyers; the high salaries paid public office holders—all came in for an almost general denunciation; while many of the more significant resolutions of the "popular conventions" aimed a blow at the existence of the Senate, of Courts of Common Pleas, of several provisions of the State Constitution—all of which, it was claimed were useless and burthensome and should be abolished. It was of these revolutionary demands that Humphrey and Knox wrote. The scheme of agrarian commonalty of property, adverted to by Knox, was the growth of a later month, when the movement passed out of the hands of demagogues into the hands of the mobs they had called into existence.

A convention held late in July at Hatfield, in Hampshire county, comprised delegates from about fifty towns. This important assembly initiated the violence which soon after took form in the suppression of the Court-sittings at Northampton. It gave the insurrection the form of a popular movement for correcting grievances and disabilities unnecessarily imposed by law-givers. Acting under its declarations other conventions followed; while the mob, as stated, acted out the spirit of their resolves by suppressing the Northampton Court. These seditious movements and act induced Bowdoin to issue a proclamation forbidding such assemblages, and calling upon all good citizens to sustain the constituted authorities in suppressing such combinations. This really temperate manifesto from the Chief Magistrate only fired the lawless to further seditious acts. Their strength grew daily, particularly in the counties of Worcester, Berkshire, Middlesex and Bristol, and, imitating the example of the Hampshire ruffians, the Worcester insurrectionists, on the 1st of September, suppressed the sittings of their County Court. They then concerted a movement upon Springfield to suppress the sittings of the Supreme Court, then about to be held there. This high handed procedure was under the guidance of one Daniel Shays, late a Captain in the Continental army—a resolute, unscrupulous, and ambitious person, who, unquestionably sought to upturn the whole order of society.

Bowdoin ordered out the militia to protect the Supreme Court from interruption; and Major-General Shepard, gathering six hundred reliable men, surrounded the Court House for its protection. Shays appeared on the ground, with a force much heavier than that of the militia men, but did not dare to challenge the ordeal of blood ready for him. He essayed to communicate with the judges, but his messages were given no notice. Three days of the session were thus passed; but, on the morning of the fourth, apprehending a general collision, the Court adjourned, and Shays' horde of ruffians dispersed, much to the relief of the terrified people whom they had shamelessly robbed during their three days' stay.

A similar proceeding was arranged by the insurrectionary

leader to suppress the Bristol county Court, over which Major-General Cobb presided as Chief Justice. Bowdoin authorised Cobb to call out his forces, which he did. At the opening of the Court at Taunton, the insurgents appeared in great force, but Cobb's demeanor, and the determination of his troops, awed the disorganizers. The terror inspired among the towns-people at the attitude of affairs induced Cobb to adjourn the sitting. A few days after the Supreme Court met at the same place. Its sittings were to have been broken up, but Cobb with his militia kept the precincts of the bench sacred from intrusion. The Middlesex County Court was less fortunate. It was not protected by the militia and its sittings were, in consequence, broken up.

It was these acts that induced the reconvention of the Legislature, which assembled late in September to take action in the premises—to redress grievances, and to clothe the Governor with full power to meet the crisis. Bowdoin laid before the Legislators a full history of the incendiary proceedings and asked to be empowered to act as the case seemed to demand. The Legislature, while it did so empower him and pledge its entire power and resources to sustain the majesty of the law, acted upon the petitions of the insurrectionists by passing several acts of a specific nature, calculated to appease the clamors of the mob. This deference to clamor, however, was not accompanied by any expression of mercy or leniency toward those in arms. The privileges of the *habeas corpus* were suspended for a period of eight months, to secure the rigor of the law from interference and obstruction. An address was issued, in which the people were reminded of their National as well as State obligations, and duty to the country, while they were enjoined to discourage all acts not consistent with law and order.

But, the spirit of violence was not to be laid by the exorcism of legislative edicts. Shays and his coadjutors labored zealously to fan the incendiary fires; nor did they labor in vain. Even during that session of the Legislature the insurgents were moving and combining in a menacing manner. The sittings of the Supreme Court in Middlesex county had to be protected during November; a force was called out so strong as to keep the insurgents quiet.

The commotion produced throughout the country by this state of affairs in Massachusetts may be inferred from Washington's correspondence on the subject. Even before the adjournment of the Legislature in December, after its six weeks' session, the insurrectionists became so evidently bent on revolution that Governor Bowdoin was forced to place the militia of the State on a war footing. Whereupon Washington wrote:

"What, gracious God! is man, that there should be such inconsistency and perfidiousness in his conduct. It was but the other day, that we were shedding our blood to obtain the Constitutions under which we now live; Constitutions of our own choice and making; and now we are unsheathing the sword to overturn them. The thing is so unaccountable, that I hardly know how to realize it, or to persuade myself that I am not under the illusion of a dream."

To the fears of Knox he replied:

"I feel, my dear General Knox, infinitely more than I can express to you, for the disorders which have arisen in these States. Good God! who, beside a tory, could have foreseen, or a Briton predicted them? I do assure you that, even at this moment, when I reflect upon the present prospect of our affairs, it seems to me to be like the vision of a dream. * * * After what I have seen, or rather what I have heard, I shall be surprised at nothing; for, if three years since, any person had told me that there would have been such a formidable rebellion as exists this day against the laws and Constitution of our own making, I should have thought him a bedlamite, a fit subject for a mad-house."

And to James Madison he addressed this powerful plea for unity and strength in the Central Government—a plea which we may commend to the consideration of every 'democrat' who sees in his dogma of State sovereignty a cure for all the evils which government is heir to:

"How melancholy is the reflection that in so short a time we should have made such large strides toward fulfilling the predictions of our transatlantic foes! 'Leave them to themselves, and their Government will soon dissolve.' Will not the wise and good strive hard to avert this evil? Or will their supineness suffer ignorance and the arts of self-interested and designing, disaffected and desperate characters, to involve this great country in wretchedness and contempt? What stronger evidence can be given of the want of energy in our Government than these disorders? If there is not power in it to check them, what security has a man for life, liberty, or property? To you, I am sure I need not add aught on the subject. The consequences of a lax or inefficient Government are too obvious to be dwelt upon. Thirteen sovereignties pulling against each other, and all tugging at the federal head, will soon bring ruin on the whole; whereas, a liberal and energetic Constitution, well checked and well watched, to prevent encroachments, might restore us to that degree of respectability and consequence to which we had the fairest prospect of attaining."

How he would treat insurrectionists we learn from his letter to Colonel Lee, then a member of Congress:

"You talk, my good sir, of employing influence to appease the present tumults in Massachusetts. I know not where that influence is to be found, or, if attainable, that it would be a proper remedy for the disorders. *Influence* is not *government.* Let us have a government by which our lives, liberties and properties will be secured, or let us know the worst at once. There is a call for decision. Know precisely what the insurgents aim at. If they have *real* grievances, redress them, if possible; or acknowledge the justice of them, and your inability to do it at the moment. If they have not, employ the force of Government against them at once. If this is inadequate, *all* will be convinced that the superstructure is bad and wants support. To delay one or other of these expedients is to exasperate on the one hand or to give confidence on the other. * * * Let the reins of Government then be braced and held with a steady hand, and every violation of the Constitution be reprehended. If defective, let it be amended; but not suffered to be trampled upon while it has an existence."

The insurgents gathered, during December, in strong force, particularly in the western counties, where their meetings were violent in opposition to the Executive and Legislature. A general resolve was made to resist the enforcement of such laws as they, "the people," did not like. This wild and precipitate rejection of all law was simply the result of their first professions of opposition to payment of debts, public and private. Once assuming the right to nullify one law it was easy to repudiate all law. The Governor's call for the militia hastened the crisis. The insurgents were then to test their power to cope with the Government. They gathered, under the general leadership of Shays, to meet the trial with a desperate resolve not to succumb. The insurrection then took on the forms and accepted the immense responsibilities of a revolution.

Early in December a movement was concerted upon Cambridge, with the ultimate design of holding that place until terms were obtained of the Governor satisfactory to those in arms. The ostensible object of this movement was to obstruct the Court sitting, though it is surmised by many writers that the leaders really proposed to take Boston, to seize the public archives and to instal a provisional government. If such a *coup d'etat* was meditated it failed miserably. Even its conception savored so strongly of folly as to be pronounced absurd. What could Shays and his friends hope to accomplish even by a suppression of the Court sittings at Cambridge, under the very shadow of the Capitol? It must be confessed that they over-estimated their own strength or under estimated the spirit of loyalty which animated seven-eighths of the people of the State. It is presumed by some authorities that the conspirators, alarmed at the dead certainty of their destruction as soon as the militia were well in the field, conceived the idea of a march toward Boston to obtain terms of amnesty and concession by menacing the capital. This seems probable.

But they mistook both the temper of the Governor and the power he could bring to bear on them. They gathered at Concord during December, where it was proposed to gather a host so formidable in numbers as to carry terror to all opposition. The crowd did not assume the proportions designed. Many of those disaffected withdrew from the treasonable movement, and a want of concert in action paralyzed the conduct of the force gathered. Bowdoin dispatched the Sheriff of Middlesex county, with a strong *posse comitatus*, to the insurgent quarters and succeeded in arresting three of the mob leaders, who were soon immured in Boston jail. This unsuspected stroke somewhat disconcerted the insurgent programme, but only for a season. Shays led a large body of his men against Worcester, where the Court was in sitting. This he suppressed, while he billetted his vagabonds upon the terrified and unresisting people. They soon cleared the town of its provisions. Shays then revived his scheme for seizing Boston;

under pretence of releasing his three comrades, then in jail in the capital, he proposed at once to march into the city. His project was received with favor by all his adherents; for a few days it seemed as if Boston was seriously in danger. But, Bowdoin was stirring. The veteran General Lincoln, of Revolutionary fame, was placed in command of the militia summoned for the defense of the city. He soon made such dispositions of forces and guns as compelled Shays to retire from Worcester to Rutland, where he found quarters for his army of rag-a-muffins in the old Continental barracks. Here starvation stared them in the face, and Shays was forced to action to save his force from immediate disbandment. He therefore marched upon Springfield, where the County Court was to open its sessions December 26th. The insurgents arrived there on the 25th, and at once warned the Judges against opening the session, taking possession of the Court House for their quarters. This, of course, prevented the sitting for that term.

Bowdoin was resolved to use the full power of the State to end this insurrection. He therefore made a call for 4400 militia, to serve thirty days. Two artillery companies, of good material, were put in requisition. General Lincoln assumed the field. Two thousand men were ordered to muster at Boston; the rest in other parts of the State; and all were to move upon Shays at Springfield in concert, to prevent his escape. Bowdoin issued a proclamation characterised by kindness but firmly expressing his purpose to compel a submission to the laws and constituted authorities.

These formidable preparations did not intimidate the insurrectionary leader. He prepared for resistance, and, by exciting appeals, as well as by the use of threats, gathered a very strong force around him. He appealed in a published address to his "suffering fellow citizens" to rally in defense of their rights, setting forth the wrongs for which they had obtained no redress. He then prepared to arm his rapidly increasing forces by a seizure of the Government arsenal at Springfield, where were stored about twelve thousand stand of arms in good order. This danger to the arsenal Bowdoin and the Continental Government had foreseen, and had commissioned

General Shepard of the Hampshire district to gather the militia in its protection. There were soon over one thousand excellent troops in Springfield ready for his orders. The arsenal was then deemed safe, and the Court proposed to assume its session; but Shays, calling in his forces from the various rendezvous, prepared for an attack and capture of the arsenal before Lincoln could arrive. To this end he mustered full eighteen hundred fellows, most of them real desperadoes; and made his combinations for assault on or before the 25th of January, as Lincoln was then at Worcester, only fifty miles distant. Shays marched upon Shepard, at four o'clock on the afternoon of the 25th, approaching in open column. The General sent out his flag of truce, warning Shays not to approach, but it was not respected—the insurgents continuing to approach. A second warning was given by Shepard; it also was received derisively. The artillery was then brought to bear on the approaching mob, and a blank cartridge fired. It had no effect, except to extort a laugh and a shout of defiance. The guns were then shotted and fired. Three of Shays' men were killed and one wounded. This earnest of the reception that awaited them sent a thrill of dismay into the insurgent ranks; and soon, despite all efforts, they were on the run for Ludlow, ten miles away, through the deep snow. Shays, reenforced by a fresh detachment under Luke Day, rallied enough, however, to make a second attempt upon the arsenal. Before he could arrange matters, Lincoln, by a forced march, reached Springfield with four regiments, artillery and a troop of cavalry. This saved the place, to the great relief of the alarmed inhabitants.

Lincoln, determined to dissipate the entire insurgent army, marched a detachment over the Connecticut river—then firmly frozen—to West Springfield, whence the vagabonds of Day retreated in confusion to Northampton. Shepard moved, at the same time, direct up the river against Shays' own force, which retired to Amherst. In its vicinity and at Pelham the malcontents gathered in such force that it was not found practicable to march against them during the inclemency of the weather, which was very rigorous even for that region. Late in January the State forces took up quarters at Hadley, from whence the old General addressed a last warning to the insurrectionary leader, informing him that defiance to law was open rebellion which would surely be punished as high treason. To this Shays answered with apparent boldness, proposing a cessation of hostilities, an unconditional pardon for all engaged in the "controversy" and a hearing of the points at issue before the Legislature—terms which the General was not empowered to concede. The insurgents, assisted by a section of society which exists in every State—of those who, under the guise of "peace men," "compromisers," "conservatives," covertly use their influence to cover assaults upon the Government, or upon the order of communities—were encouraged to strengthen their opposition as the best means of securing a pardon and of compelling the Legislature to adopt laws favorable to the agrarian and loose desires of the mob. The armistice asked for by Shays was only to give him time for consolidating his force and to strengthen the movement by creating a formidable "peace party," upon whose influence he might count in securing pardon for all. This Lincoln comprehended, and he purposed to end the matter before it could gain much momentum or shield its abettors by raising up friends in their behalf. Not only the State but the Continental Congress looked to him for safety, and he resolved to strike finishing blows to the dangerous combination.

The insurgents having moved to Petersham, late in January, there awaited the Legislature's action on a petition signed by Shays and other leaders of the rebellion, in which they acknowledged their mistake in taking up arms against the State in redresss of grievances which they desired to correct, and promised to lay down their arms if a guarantee of pardon to all were given. Upon this no action was taken, though the peace men strove to call it up by every parliamentary stratagem. Bowdoin had adapted his means to ends and found the Legislature ready to sustain him in forcing the rebels to terms and in bringing the guilty leaders to trial. Steps were taken for strengthening the force in the field. But, before these reenforcements reached him, Lincoln had struck the fatal blow which really ended the "rebellion." He moved by night from Hadley, upon Petersham, and, after a forced march of thirty miles through a heavy snow, with the cold at zero, reached the insurgent quarters early the next day, surprising the rebels completely, when they incontinently fled without firing a gun. Shays and other leading spirits made their escape. One hundred and fifty of his followers were secured by the State troops as prisoners. The "army" of Shays was broken, but the spirit of resistance to law was not entirely allayed, for it kept parts of the State in a ferment for several months thereafter, to the intense disgust and anger of all the better portion of the people. In Berkshire county the lawlessness of the mob continued to such a degree that the better class of citizens formed a home guard to give safety to themselves and order to communities. They acted with such determination as to break up the several insurrectionary bands which still retained their organization in that section, inspired by the leaders and most guilty abettors of the rebellion, who had fled to New York, Vermont and New Hampshire, to escape arrest and trial for treason.

Congress was then holding its session in New York, whither many of the insurgent leaders took refuge. On the 18th of February, 1787, General Schuyler, in the Senate, moved for a proclamation to issue for their apprehension. The alarm felt by Congress was great. None knew how quickly the fires of insurrection might kindle in other sections. The then incipient Federal party—laboring for a stronger Government, a new Constitution and a more consolidated Union—seized the moment to press their ideas, and to encourage the call for a Convention to propose the necessary changes in the organic structure of the Union. It was a period of extreme excitement, particularly in all the New England and Middle States. The Government was on the verge of ruin: the "independence" of States and the power of faction threatened a condition of anarchy. Shays' rebellion was but the eruption of a disease in the body politic which could not be reached by the outward application of restoratives or palliatives: the root of the disease must be stricken—the remedy must be a radical renovation of the system. How the hearts of patriots must have suffered in those days of almost hopeless suspense! In the letters saved to us of the correspondence of Washington, Adams, Madison, Hamilton, Jay, Livingston, Ames, Pinckney, &c., we see how those worthies struggled to stem the tide of disorganization that was fast drifting the Union toward a condition of vassalage to the British crown which it had bled through a seven years' war to shake off. There were, thank God, of pure and far seeing minds enough to lead the wild elements into the only true way necessary to save the country.

In this period it is inspiring to turn to the conduct of Massachusetts. She stood forth as a model of courage, patriotism and clear sighted conception of the crisis. She not only suppressed the rebellion within her borders, but sustained the General Government in a gratifying manner. She lent her voice to the convention for the adoption of a new Constitution. She labored with her great heart and mind to perfect the Union and to strengthen a Nationality which only needed consolidation to make it one of the most powerful governments on the earth. Her record is indeed a noble one; and if a very few of her citizens, at a later day, advocated the pernicious doctrines of nullification and secession, it may be imputed less to her want of patriotism than to her detestation of a line of policy calculated to injure the *whole* country.

The "rebellion" was ended. Bowdoin made application to the Governors of adjoining States for the arrest of fugitive citizens harbored within their jurisdiction. The Legislature commanded special sessions of the Supreme Judicial Court to be held in the several disaffected counties for the trial of all who had participated in the insurrection. Sheriffs were busy in seizing and securing the rebels, aided, in several instances, by strong bodies of citizens. Three Commissioners were named to proceed to the several county seats for a revisal of the proceedings to be instituted against those under arrest. They used their authority to pardon over three hundred, who, it appeared, were simply the deceived tools of designing demagogues. Fourteen were turned over to the Courts, tried for high treason and sentenced to death. A considerable number (among them several justices of the peace) were tried for, and convicted of, seditious practices; these were punished by fine and imprisonment. One member of the Legislature was tried for open opposition to the civil authorities. He was fined heavily and was made to sit upon the public gallows for a day. Of those convicted of high treason eight were pardoned by the Governor upon assurances of their contrition; the other six were respited conditionally. Shays, escaping to New York State, was not discovered for several months. He never returned to Massachusetts, but settled at Sparta, Livingston county, New York, where he led a peaceful life and died in 1825, at the good age of eighty-five.

CONSPIRACY OF GENERAL JAMES WILKINSON.

GENERAL Arthur St. Clair, in a letter to his old companion in arms, Major Dunn, dated Dec. 5th, 1788, said:

"I am very much grieved that there are strong dispositions on the part of the people of Kentucky to break off their connection with the United States, and that our friend Wilkinson is at the head of this affair. Such a consummation would involve the United States in the greatest difficulties, and would completely ruin this country. Should there be any foundation for these rumors, for God's sake make use of your influence to detach Wilkinson from that party."

Wilkinson, the party here referred to, in a secret dispatch to Mirò, Spanish Governor of Louisiana, under date of February 14th, 1789, wrote:

"Herein inclosed you will find two Gazettes which contain all the proceedings of our last Convention. You will observe that the memorial to Congress was presented by me, and perhaps your first impression will be that of surprise at such a document having issued from the pen of a good Spaniard. But, on further reflection, you will discover that my policy is to justify in the eye of the world our meditated separation from the rest of the Union, and quiet the apprehensions of some friends in the Atlantic States, the better to divide them, because, knowing how impossible it is that the United States should obtain what we aspire to, not only did I gratify my sentiments and inclinations, but I also framed my memorial in such a style as was best calculated to excite the passions of our people; and convince them that Congress has neither the power nor the will to enforce their claims and pretensions. Thus having energetically and publicly represented our rights and lucidly established our pretensions, if Congress does not support them with efficacy (which you know it cannot do, even if it had the inclination), not only will all the people of Kentucky, but also the whole world, approve of our seeking protection from another quarter."

To comprehend more fully the character of Wilkinson's intrigue we may add to these two quotations another from Mirò's dispatch to Madrid, dated April 11th, 1789:

"In the paragraph B, you will find an account of the bold act which General Wilkinson has ventured upon, in presenting his first memorial in a public convention. In so doing, he has so completely bound himself, that, should he not be able to obtain the separation of Kentucky from the United States, it has become impossible for him to live in it, unless he has suppressed, which is possible, certain passages which might injure him. Nevertheless, on account of the opposition made by Marshall and Muter to Wilkinson's plan, the Convention determined that new memorials be presented to Virginia and to Congress, to obtain the independence or Kentucky, its admission into the Union, and the free navigation of the Mississippi."

Spain came into possession of the Louisiana territory, as stated in the "Conspiracy of Pontiac," (page 94) by a secret Convention in 1762. She did not, however, take possession until 1779. An attempt to assume the government in 1766 brought with it extreme excitement, which culminated, in 1768, in an open insurrection, by which the colonists and old French residents entirely drove out the Spaniards. The arrival of O'Reilley in the same year with a strong force soon restored the Spanish authority. His reign of blood quickly suppressed all ideas of any further revolt; and thenceforward, to 1803, the country remained under the dominion of Spain. The territory, understood to be comprised in their domain, reached from St. Genevieve and St. Louis, to the Gulf a vast, undefined region on the west of the Mississippi river, with some possible claims to territory on the east, low down, on the Gulf.

New Orleans, with a population in 1765 of 4960, Natchez 1550, Mobile 746, St. Louis 897, were their principal towns, though the territorial census of 1765 gave a total population of 31,433. During the War of the Revolution the Spanish Governor, Galvez, had made a glorious campaign against the British posts on the river and Gulf—an episode of that war too little known to the mass of readers. Baton Rouge, Natchez, Mobile, Pensacola, all were wrested from Great Britain by the gallant Spaniard. These conquests gave to his possessions territory east of Mississippi. It was a portion of these acquired possessions which Georgia claimed, extending from

Loftus' Heights, toward the north, for about three hundred miles. That State in 1785 sent Commissioners to New Orleans to reclaim possession—a demand which was referred to the authorities of the two Governments, Spain and the American Congress, for adjudication. Aside from this claim there was no right of soil urged by the American Government, or any of the States, against the Spanish possessions of Louisiana.

But the "manifest destiny" principle of aggrandisement began to show itself at that early day. Hardly had the American Revolution ended before the eyes of capitalists, adventurers and statesmen looked longingly down the Mississippi, while the tide of emigration began to pour, in one steady stream, into Kentucky, Western Pennsylvania, Western Virginia and Tennessee—all States watered by rivers whose outlet was the Mississippi. The commerce of all that vast region, drained by the Tennessee, Cumberland and the confluents of the Ohio, necessarily centered at New Orleans. No treaty stipulations having been entered into between Spain and the American Congress to regulate that trade great dissatisfaction soon prevailed. Every flat-boatman and trader who returned home to the North and East, after his long voyage, had his story to tell of impositions practiced upon him by the New Orleans officials. Schemes for the seizure of that post was freely canvassed during the years 1786–88.[1]

The Spaniards, alive to the threatened danger of subversion, soon conceived a counter plot, which not only would break the ascendancy of the Federal Union to the West, but would perpetuate Spanish power. This plan was to erect Louisiana into a viceroyalty, similar to that of Mexico, and, by offering immense inducements to emigration, to fill up the territory with a hardy and reliable population, who, as planters and traders, would give order and solidity to the new power. Gayarré, in his "History of the Spanish Domination in Louisiana," says:

"Well informed of the condition of things then existing, Governor Mirò, in Louisiana, and the Spanish Minister, Gardoqui, at Philadel-

---

[1] See Judge Martin's "History of Louisiana," vol. ii. page 101, for reference to five different schemes or propositions entertained by the Western men to obtain control of the Mississippi.

phia, were both pursuing the same object, which was—to draw to Louisiana as much of the Western population as could be induced to emigrate, and even to operate, if possible, a dismemberment of the Confederacy, by the secession of Kentucky and of the other discontented districts from the rest of the United States. Both these Spanish functionaries were partners in the same game, and yet they were unwilling to communicate to each other the cards they had in hand. Each one was bent upon his own plan, and taking care to conceal it from the other; each one had his own secret agents unknown to the colleague whom he ought to have called to his assistance. There was a want of concert, arising perhaps from jealousy, from the lack of confidence, from ambition, from the desire of engrossing all the praise and reward in case of success, or from some other cause. Be it what it may, the consequence was, that the schemes of these two men frequently counteracted each other, and resulted in a series of measures which were at variance and contradictory, and which seemed inexplicable to him who had not the key to what was going on behind the curtain."

General James Wilkinson here comes upon the historic stage to act his part of Conspirator, spy and dissimulator. He had done honorable service in the War for Independence, as may be inferred from the tone of General St. Clair's letter, quoted at the opening of this paper; but he had not obtained any distinctive position in that contest; and, had he not come forward in his western intrigues with Governor Mirò and with Aaron Burr, his fame would have passed into the common but honorable catalogue of the Revolutionary fathers. He appears to have been an ambitious and an unscrupulous man, gifted with rather unusual powers of dissimulation, but with less judgment than should belong to characters who would emulate Talleyrand. In the history of his intrigues with Mirò, to carry Kentucky over to the Spanish interest, he made, for several years, a liberal use of prophecies and promises; he labored assiduously in a field of diplomacy in which few men would have discovered much fruit; he conceived castles which proved to be less real than structures of air; yet he found it possible to deceive Mirò, to dupe the Spanish Minister, to conciliate the United States; and, if his projects all failed, it was not from the lack of talent for trickery but rather from want of judgment in correctly apprehending men and circumstances.

Wilkinson appeared in New Orleans, early in the year 1787,

as a trader—having ventured down the Mississippi from Kentucky with a flat-boat load of flour, tobacco, butter and bacon. The usual offensive tariff-customs levied upon all such ventures were remitted in his case, by Governor Mirò, after a long interview. The supposition is that, having conceived the project for a large trade, he let Mirò into his secret concerning the destiny of Kentucky, and together they then hatched the scheme which, in some of its aspects, recalls John Law's celebrated "Mississippi Bubble," which was first based upon the trade and resources of this very same Louisiana territory. Having sold his cargo with great advantage to himself the adventurer devoted three months to "interviews" with Mirò. Gayarré says: "Many wondered at the intimacy which had grown up, during this time, between Mirò and Wilkinson, and sly hints and insinuations were thrown out as to its nature and tendency." Butler, in his "History of Kentucky," gives us some inkling of the subjects canvassed by the two worthies. It transpired that Wilkinson had given his "views" in writing respecting the political interests of Spain and the inhabitants of the United States dwelling upon the Western waters. These views, written out at considerable length, were designed to show the good policy of opening trade with the North by liberal arrangements and an encouraging policy. He alluded to the surpassing richness of the regions watered by the rivers flowing to the South—assuming that the people had a natural right to the use of the river as a highway. One or two allusions were rather novel. Thus, as reported by Butler: "he describes the general abhorrence with which they (the western people) received the intelligence that Congress was about to sacrifice their dearest rights by ceding to Spain, for twenty years, the navigation of the Mississippi; and represents it as a fact that they are on the point of separating themselves entirely from the Union on that account." He thereupon proceeded to show how easily it would be for the Americans and British, united, to wrest the Louisiana territory from Spain. This document was addressed to Governor Mirò though really designed for the Spanish Minister, Valdez, having supervision of foreign and colonial affairs. "But it leaked out," says Gayarré, "and passed current among those who pretended to be well informed, that Wilkinson had delivered to the Spanish Governor a memorial containing other representations which were kept from the public eye." What this other document was soon appeared. Gardoqui, in pursuance of *his* plans, dispatched his agent, Pierre Wower d'Arges, to the Cumberland and Kentucky region to "invite" the people to emigrate to the Florida District of Lower Louisiana. The agent executed his mission; and, he being empowered to make most liberal grants of land, rights in slaves, free admission of farming implements, as well as to grant liberal commercial privileges, he succeeded in securing a number of American families, who proceeded to the South and became subjects of Spain. This movement on the part of the Spanish Minister to the American Confederation, at once awoke all the jealousy of Mirò, who saw in it danger to his own and Wilkinson's projects. What these projects were had to come forth to the light. January 8th, 1788, the Governor wrote to Valdez at some length to show that Gardoqui's operations must prove disastrous to the larger and more important enterprise of Wilkinson. "I fear that they may clase with Wilkinson's principal object," he said, and proceeded to demonstrate how important it would be to make the two act in concert. "I have been reflecting for many days whether it would not be proper to communicate to d'Arges Wilkinson's plans, and to Wilkinson the mission of d'Arges, in order to unite them and to dispose them to work in concert. But I dare not do so, because d'Arges may consider that the great project of Wilkinson may destroy the merit of his own, and he may communicate them to some one who might cause Wilkinson to be arrested as a criminal, and also because Wilkinson may take offence at another being admitted to participate in confidential proceedings, upon which depend his life and honor, as he expresses himself in his memorial."

"Confidential proceedings!" There was then a secret memorial. What was its purport? We can infer from the following words which occur in the Governor's protest to Valdez: "The *delivering up of Kentucky into his Majesty's hands, which is the main object to which Wilkinson has promised to devote him-*

self entirely, would forever constitute this province a rampart for the protection of New Spain."

This revealed something of Wilkinson's plot. More evidence was soon forthcoming. In April Mirò sent forward another dispatch announcing the arrival of letters from his coadjutor, from one of which he quoted as follows:

"I have collected much European and American news, and have made various interesting observations for our political designs. It would take a volums to contain all that I have to communicate to you. But I dispatch this letter with such haste, and its fate is so uncertain, that I hope you will excuse me for not saying more until the arrival of my boats; and, in the mean time, I pray you to content yourselves with this assurance: all my predictions are verifying themselves, and not a measure is taken on both sides of the mountains which does not conspire to favor ours. I encountered great difficulties in crossing the mountains."

This letter also contained a paragraph highly illustrative of the duplicity which was the ruling principle of Wilkinson's strategy. He wrote:

"Considering that Gardoqui has spies all over the United States, I thought that, in order to prevent his suspicions, and divert his investigations from the quarter to which they might be directed, it was prudent on my part to write him a complimentary letter, in which I broached some ideas which may give rise to a correspondence between us, and the result of which I shall communicate to you."

On the 5th of May another letter was dispatched by Wilkinson to his confederate in New Orleans, by the hand of Major Dunn—the officer to whom General St. Clair addressed the letter given at the beginning of this paper. We now learn fully of the *process* by which the plan was to be carried into execution. We shall see them thus:

"Major Isaac Dunn, the bearer of this dispatch, and an old military companion of mine, came to settle in these parts during my absence. The reliance which I put in his honor, his discretion and his talents, has induced me, after having sounded his dispositions with proper caution, to choose him as a fit auxiliary in the execution of our political designs, which he has embraced with cordiality. He will therefore present himself in order to confer with you on those points which require more examination, and to concert with you those measures which you may deem necessary to expedite our plan; and, through him, I shall be able to receive the new instructions which you may deem expedient to send me. I have also chosen him to bring me back the product of the present cargo of my boats. For these reasons, permit me to recommend him as one worthy of your entire confidence, and as a safe and sagacious man, who is profoundly acquainted with the political state of the American Union, and with the circumstances of this section of the country. I desire that he be detained in Louisiana as little as possible.

"On the first day of January of the next year, 1789, by mutual consent, this district will cease to be subjected to the jurisdiction of Virginia. It has been stipulated, it is true, as a necessary condition of our independence, that this territory be acknowledged an independent State by Congress, and be admitted as such into the Federal Union. But a Convention has already been called to form a Constitution of this section of the country, and I am persuaded that no action on the part of Congress will ever induce this people to abandon the plan which they have adopted, although I have recent intelligence that Congress will, beyond a doubt, recognize us as a Sovereign State.

"The Convention of which I have spoken will meet in July. I will, in the mean time, inquire into the prevailing opinions, and shall be able to ascertain the extent of the influence of the members elected. When this is done, after having previously come to an understanding with two or three individuals capable of assisting me, I shall disclose so much of our great scheme as may appear opportune, according to circumstances, and I have no doubt but that it will meet with a favorable reception; because, although I have been communicative with no more than two individuals, I have sounded many, and wherever it has seemed expedient to me to make known your answer to my memorial, it has caused the keenest satisfaction. Colonel Alexander Leatt Bullit and Harry Innis, our attorney-general, are the only individuals to whom I have intrusted our views, and, in case of any mishap befalling me before their accomplishment, you may, in perfect security, address yourselves to these gentlemen, whose political designs agree entirely with yours. Thus, as soon as the new government shall be organized and adopted by the people, they will proceed to elect a governor, the members of the legislative body and other officers, and I doubt not but that they will name a political agent with power to treat of the affair in which we are engaged, and I think that all this will be done by the month of March next. In the meantime, I hope to receive your orders, which I will do my utmost to execute.

"I do not anticipate any obstacle from Congress, because, under the present Federal compact, that body can neither dispose of men nor money, and the new government, should it establish itself, will have to encounter difficulties which will keep it weak for three or four years, before the expiration of which I have good grounds to hope that we shall have completed our negotiations, and shall have become too strong to be subjected by any force which may be sent against us. The only fears I have, proceed from the policy which may prevail in your Court. I am afraid of a change in the present ministry, and in the administration of Louisiana, of the possibility of which event you are better judges than I can be, and I beg you to be explicit with me on the subject. * * *

"I have applied to Mr. Clark, my agent in New Orleans, with regard to sending me merchandise by the way of the Mississippi. This is of the utmost importance for the accomplishment of our wishes, because the only tie which can preserve the connection of this country with the Atlantic States is the necessity under which we are, to rely on them altogether for the supply of such articles as are not manufactured among us; and when this people shall find out that they can procure them more conveniently through this river, the dependent state in which they are will cease, and with it all motives of connection with the other side of the Apalachian mountains. Our hopes will then be turned toward you, and all obstacles in the way of our negotiations will have been removed."

This important document was further illuminated by Mirò's comments accompanying its remission to Spain. He said: "This Major confirms all of Wilkinson's assertions, and gives it out as certain, that, next year, after the meeting of the first assemblies in which Kentucky will act as an independent State, she will separate entirely from the Federal Union; he further declares that he has come to that conclusion from having heard it expressed in various conversations among the most distinguished citizens of that State: that the direction of the current of the rivers which run in front of their dwellings points clearly to the power to which they ought to ally themselves, but he declares that he is ignorant of the terms on which this alliance will be proposed. The said Brigadier-General, in a private letter addressed to me, adds that he flatters himself with the prospect of his being the delegate of his State to present to me the propositions offered by his countrymen, and that he hopes to embrace me in April next."

Mirò begins to suspect his agent, at this stage of their proceedings, it would appear, for he states that Wilkinson had borrowed three thousand dollars, which the cargo sent down by Major Dunn was to repay. The rest of the cargo was to pay for the tobacco, which he had bought on credit, and to give him money to "support himself without embarrassment." The Governor thereupon adds: "Although his candor, and the information which I have sought from many who have known him well, seem to assure us that he is working in good earnest, yet I am aware that it may be possible that his intention is to enrich himself at our expense, by inflating us with hopes and promises which he knows to be vain."

It would require a volume to trace their Conspiracy through all its tortuous ways. That it was a deeply laid plan of the Spanish Government to break up the Union, important documents which have lately come to light tend fully to prove. Wilkinson was confidential operator, spy and agent of the Spaniards in Louisiana, while d'Argès received instructions direct from Madrid to do all in his power to procure the dismemberment of the American Union.[1] Gardoqui gave powers of colonization to Colonel George Morgan, late of the Continental army, who proposed to establish a large colony at some point below the mouth of the Ohio. This he succeeded in doing, founding the town of New Madrid, now in Missouri, as a Spanish settlement. On the 3d of November, 1788, Mirò wrote to Valdez to say that the "affair"—the dismemberment of the Union—"proceeds more rapidly than I had presumed, and some considerable impetus is given to it by the answer of Congress to the application of Kentucky to be admitted into the Union as an independent State." "Rest assured" he further wrote "that Brown (a delegate to Congress from Kentucky), on his arrival in Kentucky (he was then in attendance upon Congress) finding Wilkinson and his associates disposed to surrender themselves up to Spain, or at least to put themselves under her protection will easily join them; and it is probable, as Wilkinson has already foretold it, that, next spring, I shall have to receive here a deputation appointed in due form." This deputation, however, never arrived. Wilkinson wrote under date of February 12th, 1789, to Mirò, from Lexington, Kentucky, saying:

"Immediately after having sent you my dispatch by Major Dunn, I devoted all my faculties to our political designs, and I have never since turned aside from the pursuit of the important object we have in view. If subsequent events have not come up to our expectations, still I con-

[1] See Gayarré's "Spanish Domination," pages 216–17.

ceive that they are such as to inspire us with flattering hopes of success in due time, and, although in the conjectural opinions which I presented to you and Navarro, I may, in some particulars, have been deceived, you will yet see that, in the main, I expressed myself with a prophetic spirit, and that important events have occurred, to confirm the accuracy of my sentiments.

"When Major Dunn left Kentucky, I had opened myself only to the Attorney General Innis, and to Colonel Bullitt, who favor our designs, and indirectly I had sounded others, whom I also found well disposed to adopt my ideas. But, having made a more strict examination, I discovered that the proposed new Government of the United States had inspired some with apprehensions, and others with hopes—so much so that I saw that this circumstance would be a cause of some opposition and delay. I also perceived that all idea that Kentucky would subject itself to Spain must be abandoned for the present, and that the only feasible plan to the execution of which I had to direct my attention was that of a separation from the United States, and an alliance with Spain, on conditions which could not yet be defined with precision. I considered that, whatever be the time when the separation should be brought about, this district being then no longer under the protection of the United States, Spain might dictate her own terms; for which reason, I embraced without delay this last alternative.

"The question of separation from the United States, although discussed with vehemence among the most distinguished inhabitants of this section of the country, had never been mentioned, in a formal manner, to the people at large, but now was the time for making this important and interesting experiment, and it became my indispensable mission to do so. I had to work on a ground not yet prepared for the seed to be deposited in it, and I felt that, to produce a favorable impression, I had to proceed with reserve, and avoid with the utmost care any demonstration which might be calculated to cause surprise or alarm. For these motives, I gave an equivocal shape to the expression of my design, speaking of it in general terms, as being recommended by eminent politicians of the Atlantic coast, with whom I had conversed on this affair; and thus, by indirect suggestions and arguments, I inspired the people with my own views, without presenting them as such, because it would have been imprudent in me to divulge them under the existing circumstances, and I can give you the solemn assurance that I found all the men belonging to the first class of society in the district, with the exception of Colonel Marshall, our surveyor, and Colonel Muter, one of our Judges, decidedly in favor of separation from the United States and of an alliance with Spain."

He then proceeds to detail proceedings of much interest in regard to the political operations of the year consequent on

Kentucky's endeavor to form a State, and then adds in justification of the two-faced part which he played:

"To consolidate the interests and confirm the confidence of our friends, to try our strength, to familiarize the people with what we aim at, to dissipate the apprehension which important innovations generally produce, and to provoke the resentment of Congress with a view to stimulate that body into some invidious political act, which might excite the passions of the people; these are the motives which influenced me, and on which I rely for my justification."

Wilkinson, in this important communication, lifts the vail upon the secession scheme which he encouraged, while he secretly plotted to transfer the State to the keeping of Spain. After divulging the machinations which he had set on foot, and betrayed the results of an interview held with an emissary of Lord Dorchester, Governor-General of Canada (who proposed to assist the men of the West in driving Spain from her Louisiana possessions), Wilkinson came to the confessional thus:

"After having read these remarks, you will be surprised at being informed, that lately I have, jointly with several gentlemen of this country, applied to Don Diego Gardoqui for a concession of land, in order to form a settlement on the river Yazoo. The motive of this application is to procure a place of refuge for myself and my adherents, in case it should become necessary for us to retire from this country, in order to avoid the resentment of Congress. It is true that there is not, so far, the slightest appearance of it, but it is judicious to provide for all possible contingencies."

In his relation of the interview with Colonel Connelly, the British emissary to provoke a descent upon New Orleans for its seizure, we have the character of the Conspirator well delineated. After Connelly had divulged his whole information and secret proffers of assistance, Wilkinson resolved to get rid of him at once; and, for that purpose, hired a hunter to waylay the agent with the apparent intent to murder him in revenge for excesses committed by the English and Indians in the War of the Revolution. As Wilkinson held the office of "Civil Judge," the hunter was brought before him and committed. "I availed myself," says the upright judge, "of this circumstance to communicate to Connelly my fear of not being able to answer for the security of his person, and I expressed my doubts whether he could escape with life. It alarmed him so much that he begged me to give him an escort to conduct him out of our territory, which I readily assented to, and, on the 20th of November he recrossed the Ohio on his way back to Detroit." From Connelly he obtained full particulars of the British design to drive Spain from her possessions in the West. If the messenger of Lord Dorchester represented truly, then Great Britain must have been willing to enlist in a war against France and Spain, since any active co-operation in sustaining, with arms, munitions and stores, a campaign against New Orleans, must have resulted in a state of hostilities between the three great powers.

In a private communication written to M. Mirò, two days after the above lengthy dispatch the spy, the Conspirator makes still further divulgements, which prove that if he did not succeed in transfessing Kentucky to Spain it was not for lack of rascality in trying to consummate his scheme. He made known the following precious items of news:

"Don Diego Gardoqui, about the month of March last, received from his court ample powers to make with the people of this district the arrangements he might think proper, in order to estrange them from the United States and induce them to form an alliance with Spain. I received this information, in the first place, from Mr. Brown, the member of Congress for this district, who (since the taking into consideration of our application to be admitted into the Union has been suspended) entered into some free communications on this matter with Don Diego Gardoqui. He returned here in September last, and, finding that there had been some opposition to our project, he almost abandoned the cause in despair, and positively refused to advocate in public the propositions of Don Diego Gardoqui, as he deems them fatal to our cause. Brown is one of our deputies or agents; he is a young man of respectable talents, but timid, without political experience, and with very little knowledge of the world. Nevertheless, as he firmly perseveres in his adherence to our interests, we have sent him to the new Congress, apparently as our representative, *but in reality as a spy on the actions of that body.* I would myself have undertaken that charge, but I did not, for two reasons: first, my presence was necessary here, and next, I should have found myself under the obligation of swearing to support the new Government, which I am in duty bound to oppose."

The letter-writer then proceeds to show up Gardoqui. In his true character of informer and dissimulator, Wilkinson seeks by his items of news and his special version of Gardoqui's operations, to inflame Mirò against the minister. Yet, despite this, he (Wilkinson) was seeking for favors from the minister—thus acknowledging his authority for granting lands, passes and commercial favors in the Louisiana territory. He (W.) confessed that himself, Brown, Major Dunn and others, had petitioned to Gardoqui for the grant of land to establish a colony on the Yazoo, above Natchez, as already referred to, that the conspirators, in case of disasters, might have a place of retreat. "With a view to removing every cause of distrust or unfavorable impression from Gardoqui's mind I wrote him a letter of which I send you a copy," said Wilkinson; while, in trying to extenuate his application to the minister for the Yazoo grant, he said: "Our intention is to make an establishment on the ground mentioned in my communication of the 12th, *to estroy the plan of a certain Colonel Morgan.*"

What duplicity is here! Seeks to cajole the Spanish minister into giving a grant for a colony which the colonists propose to found in order to thwart Gardoqui's own agent, Morgan, in founding a colony above! As if, only two days previously, he (Wilkinson) had not assured Mirò that the special purpose in securing the grant was to obtain a place of refuge! Mirò was further informed that a spy was on Morgan's track who would keep him thoroughly informed of his rival's movements and operations. He seemed determined to crush out the New Madrid settlement of Morgan, saying: "probably it will destroy the noble fabric of which we have laid out the foundations and which we are endeavoring to keep." To a general defamation of Morgan's character and of his enterprise he added his warning, thus:

"I am informed that Morgan intends visiting you, as soon as he shall have finished the survey of the lands conceded to him. Permit me to supplicate you, my most esteemed of friends, not to give him any knowledge of my plans, sentiments or designs. It is long since he has become jealous of me, and you may rest assured that, in reality, he is not well affected towards our cause, but that he allows himself to be entirely ruled by motives of the vilest self interest, and therefore that he will not scruple, on his return to New York, to destroy me. One of the objects of Major Dunn, in seeing Gardoqui, is to sound him on this affair, and I doubt not but that he will do so successfully."

The letter to Gardoqui, referred to above as having been written by Wilkinson, has been found in the archives at Madrid. A copy was made for the State of Louisiana—in whose State library it and all other documents obtained by the special commission appointed for that purpose, were deposited. Our space forbids its reproduction. It was very friendly; full of assurances of consideration; apparently made a full avowal of his (Wilkinson's) designs, &c.; and yet, as we learn by the private letter to Mirò, it was all false—was designed simply to deceive the Ministers! How could the Governor of Louisiana trust such a great rogue? He himself was an intriguant and desired to use his "friend" as an instrument, trusting to his own shrewdness to outwit any Yankee game which Wilkinson might attempt to play. That the Conspirator was playing successfully for his own interests pecuniarily is evident, for Mirò, in his dispatches to Madrid, of April 11th, 1789, recommended the Minister to repay Wilkinson the sum of five thousand dollars which he (W.) declared he had spent in the cause of Spain; also that the Ministry intrust him (W.) with two thousand and five hundred dollars as asked for, with which *to corrupt* Marshall and Muter [see page 191]! Mirò also informs the Ministry that *he* had bought of W. on account of the royal treasury, 235,000 pounds of tobacco, which transaction he requested the government to approve "on the ground that it was important to keep the General contented." The General was certainly operating to his own advantage.

At this stage of the conspiracy a new agent appears on the scene—Dr. James White—a representative of Gardoqui to the inhabitants of Frankland (Sevier's "State of Franklin,") to arrange for their transfer of allegiance to Spain. This was in answer to Sevier's letter referred to in foot note page 162. After visiting Sevier and other plotters of treason in the Cumberland region White wrote to Mirò as follows, under date of April 18th, 1788:

"With regard to Frankland, Don Diego Gardoqui gave me letters for the chief men of that district, with instructions to assure them that, if they wished to put themselves under the protection of Spain and favor her interests, they should be protected in their civil and political government, in the form and manner most agreeable to them, on the following conditions:

"1st—It should be absolutely necessary, not only in order to hold any office, but also any land in Frankland, that an oath of allegiance be taken to his Majesty, the object and purport of which should be to defend his government and faithful vassals on all occasions, and against all his enemies, whoever they might be. 2d.—That the inhabitants of that district should renounce all submission or allegiance whatever to any other Sovereign or power. They have eagerly accepted these conditions, and the Spanish minister has referred me to your favor, patronage and assistance to facilitate my operations. With regard to Cumberland, what I have said of Frankland applies with equal force and truth."

Mirò advanced White four hundred dollars "to facilitate his dealing decently and commodiously with those he was to influence," and, in his official capacity, authorised special trade arrangements to be made with the people of those districts. But, he disavowed any purpose to assist or foment the scheme of secession then acting, "on account of the good harmony which exists between his Catholic Majesty and the United States"—a qualification which sounds ludicrous when we consider that White was supplied with money to help on the emeuté, that special trades' regulations were extended to the people, and that the grand scheme of the Governor and Wilkinson contemplated the robbery from the United States of the entire Kentucky region. The explanation is found in the fact that Mirò preferred to have Gardoqui's influence cast overboard and his own substituted—as we are informed by the Governor's private letters to Wilkinson, giving him a full account of the efforts of Dr. White and of others operating in the Territory of Mirò—as the Cumberland district was called by the intriguants. And Mirò, in his dispatches to Madrid of April 30th, 1789, alluded to the affair with Sevier's government, saying:

"The answer which I have given to White, and which he is to show to the principal men of Mirò and Frankland, is so framed, that, should it miscarry, it will afford no cause of complaint to the United States; but verbally, I have energetically recommended to him to use the most strenuous efforts to procure the desired separation."

Nothing came of this affair. The reverse in Governor Sevier's fortunes and the loyalty of the people to their State, precluded all hopes of Spanish domination in Franklin and Cumberland. A change appears to have come over the Conspirators' hopes of the Kentucky people. On the 20th of January, 1790, Wilkinson wrote to Mirò to say that "the general permission to export the products of this country through the Mississippi river, on paying a duty of 15 per cent., has worked the consequences which I feared, because, every motive of discontent having thus been removed, the political action has subsided, and to-day there is not one word said about separation." And again: "The pruriency of emigration has been soothed and allayed by the spirit of trade which engrosses general attention." But, trade alone was not the most powerful agent at work to cut asunder the Conspirators' webs and snares for betraying Kentucky. George Washington was then at the head of affairs. His influence began to permeate through all society; the strong arm of Government began to be felt and recognised; the head of faction and discontent disappeared; treason began to fear for its reward. Wilkinson wrote:

"On my arrival here, I discovered a great change in those who had been our warmest friends. Many, who loudly repudiated all connection with the Union, now remain silent. I attribute this, either to the hope of promotion, or to the fear of punishment. According to my prognostic, Washington has begun to operate on the chief heads of this district. Innis has been appointed a Federal judge with an annual salary of one thousand dollars; George Nicholas, district attorney; Samuel McDowell, son of the president of the Convention, and Marshall, have been appointed to offices somewhat resembling that of Alguazil Mayor; and Payton Short, the brother of our chargé d'affaires at Versailles, is made a custom-house officer. But he has resigned, and probably will visit you in the spring. I do not place much reliance on George Nicholas and Samuel McDowell. But I know that Harry Innis is friendly to Spain and hostile to Congress, and I am authorized to say that he would much prefer receiving a pension from New Orleans than from New York. Should the King approve our design on this point, it will have to be broached with much delicacy, caution and judgment, &c. * * * And I fear that we can rely on a few only of my countrymen, if we cannot make use of liberal donations," &c.

At a later date he expressed these characterist sentiments:

"I am justified in saying that Congress strongly suspects my connection with you, and that it spies my movements in this section of the

25

country. Consequently, an avowed intention on my part to induce these people here to separate from the Union, before the majority of them show a disposition to support me, would endanger my personal security, and would deprive me of the opportunity of serving you in these parts. My situation is mortally painful, because, while I abhor all duplicity, I am obliged to dissemble. This makes me extremely desirous of resorting to some contrivance that will put me in a position, in which I flatter myself to be able to profess myself publicly the vassal of his Catholic Majesty, and therefore to claim his protection, in whatever public or private measures I may devise to promote the interest of the Crown."

All of which proved to Mirò that Anglo-Saxon "manifest destiny" already had swept away forever his scheme of aggrandisement. Yet he seemed to struggle against the uncomfortable conclusion. He wrote under date of April 30th, 1790:

"I therefore confidently hope that, with your characteristic perseverance, making use of the information which I give you, and which will be confirmed by your countrymen on their return, you will be able to revive our political designs, by sowing broad-cast, and causing to germinate among your people, such ideas as will seem to you best calculated to establish the conviction, that the welfare of the inhabitants of Kentucky depends, either on their forming a close and strong connection with Spain, or on their seeking to better their fortune by becoming denizens of Louisiana."

And, in regard to that passage of Wilkinson's letter already given, where he avows himself an object of suspicion, Mirò thus caustically gave his views:

"I much regret that General Washington and Congress suspect your connection with me, but it does not appear to me opportune that you declare yourself a Spaniard, for the reasons which you state. I am of opinion that this idea of yours is not convenient, and that, on the contrary, it might have prejudicial results. Therefore, *continue to dissemble and to work as you promise, and as I have indicated.*"

There is little more here to be written to illustrate this record of the General's complicity with the Spaniards to dismember the country. We could add, perhaps profitably to the reader, several pages, concerning the rise, progress and success of the South Corolina Company, but we should not be warranted in absorbing more space with this theme. Wilkinson, it was soon discovered, not only had failed to accomplish the proposed work in Kentucky, but was intriguing to obtain an influence in this new Company, in which Spain found a formidable opponent to her plans of empire. Mirò, in his dispatches of May 22d, 1790, wrote to express his extreme disappointment at the rather disgraceful termination to his three years' machination and intrigue. He added:

"Nevertheless, I am of opinion that said Brigadier-General ought to be retained in the service of his Majesty, with an annual pension of two thousand dollars, which I have already proposed in my confidential dispatch No. 46, because the inhabitants of Kentucky, and of the other establishments on the Ohio, will not be able to undertake anything against this province, without his communicating it to us, and without his making at the same time all possible efforts to dissuade them from any bad designs against us, as he has already done repeatedly."

And then concluded with a recommendation of a pension for Sebastian, "because I think it proper to treat with this individual, who will be able to enlighten me on the conduct of Wilkinson, and on what we have to expect from the plans of the said Brigadier-General."

O most impotent conclusion! says the reader. It is so truly, simply because the conspiracy was a failure, and it stands as such in the history of our country. But, it was a gigantic scheme of plotting against the integrity of this government, as well as against the liberties of the people; and, despite its failure, forms a very exciting and important chapter in the story of American Conspiracies. Wilkinson, the chief aid and abettor of the Spaniards, again comes on the stage in his connection with Aaron Burr's designs upon the old Spanish dominion. The chapter here given will so inform the reader of his true character that the story of his connection with Burr's plans of empire will receive a new interest.

The reader is not to infer that, with Kentucky's admission to the Union (1792) all danger of conspiracy in her borders passed away. The French Minister to the United States, Genet—a name offensive to every American patriot's mind—had so deeply stirred the turbulent element of our democracy that, for years after his recall, the people of the Ohio and Mississippi valleys were in a state of almost constant ferment. In 1794 the democratic society of Lexington, Kentucky, opened a correspondence with the people of the East for the purpose of uniting them in a crusade against Spain and against the President and Congress for not seizing the Louisiana territory and opening the Mississippi river to free navigation A remonstrance drawn up and sent in to Congress was highly indecorous and threatening. They demanded, in peremptory words, the free navigation of the great river, alluding to their past moderation in not having already used the means in their power to assert their "rights"—that is, in declaring their independence and in forming a league of States west of the mountains. This was but an indication of the strong undercurrent prevailing against the General Government, and which came near to plunging this country into a war with Spain and Great Britain. To this conspiracy of the French faction and the democratic societies we devote a paper, to which we call the attention of those who would be fully informed of the dangers through which the Union has passed.

A second attempt was made by Carondelet, Mirò's successor, to seduce the Territory of Kentucky into Spanish embraces. Carondelet dispatched Powers and Sebastian to Philadelphia, from whence Powers returned, in the Summer of 1796, with an elaborate plan of operations for carrying the State over to Spanish possession. But, though making an apparently feasible and powerful appeal to the cupidity of the people, it failed. Wilkinson having been made Major-General in the place of Wayne, (who had died in December, 1796,) was approached with a bribe of ten thousand dollars; but, though appealed to as the "Washington of the West," he did not see success enough in store to warrant a transfer of his army and services to the cause of disunion. Carondelet's attempt to seduce the State from its allegiance was the last made by the Louisiana (Spanish) Governors.

THE WHISKEY INSURRECTION.

AFTER his tour through the Southern States, in the Spring and Summer of 1791, President Washington wrote (July 20th): "As this law (the excise) came in force only on the first of this month, little can be said of its effects, from experience; but, from the best information I could get on my journey, respecting its operation on the minds of the people—and I took some pains to obtain information on this point—there remains no doubt but it will be carried into effect, not only without opposition but with very general approbation in those very parts where it was foretold that it would never be submitted to by any one. It is possible, however, and perhaps not improbable that some demagogue may start up, produce and get signed some resolutions declaratory of their disapprobation of the measure."

Even while the revered Washington was thus traveling for information, and was conferring with leading men of the South, Thomas Jefferson, then Secretary of State, was traveling through the Northern States concerting those measures of opposition to the Federal Administration which resulted in the formation of the "Democratic" party and the election of himself and Aaron Burr to the offices of President and Vice President of the Federal Government. "Anti-Federal" ideas had existed to a considerable extent, during the first two years of Washington's term; but, the success of his administration—the astonishing vitalization infused into the new government by him—the great confidence rapidly following upon Hamilton's financial conduct of the Treasury Department—served to allay opposition, and the Spring of 1791 found the people quite reconciled to the Administration's measures. This unity Jefferson secretly essayed to break. Washington he dare not assail directly; but, his fertile mind soon conceived the ways and means of an opposition to the Federalism of Washington, Hamilton, Marshall, Adams and Franklin, through the medium of a party. With issues pandering to the tastes and prejudices of the masses; with representations of bugbears of aristocratic monsters cloaked beneath the forms of law; with expressions of sympathy for "the people" which he assumed the Federalists could not and did not feel, it was not an arduous task to excite an opposition to the policy of the men named. In May, 1761, accompanied by Madison, Jefferson visited New York to concert with Aaron Burr, Clinton and Chancellor Livingston—the three personal opponents of Hamilton and Schuyler. With these three confirmed intriguants, Jefferson and Madison matured their plans for an open and active opposition to the Federalist party. In those men[1] were found the "demagogue" whom Washington feared might arise to excite animosity against his measures. To their loose principles regarding National and State relations; regarding the right of the individual to sit in judgment on the acts of the Executive and of Congress; regarding the integrity of oaths of National fealty; regarding the right of government to *enforce* law and to suppress sedition—do we owe, and shall continue to owe, in a great measure, the existence of treason and rebellion in our midst.

Upon the assumption, by the Federal Government, of debts incurred by States in their War for independence, it became necessary to provide for the interest, and gradual liquidation of the principal, of that debt—making $826,000 to be added to the *annual* tax list in support of the Federal Government. This sum, Alexander Hamilton, then Secretary of the Treasury, proposed to raise by an "excise" tax on distilleries, and by additional duties on imported liquors. In confirmation of the Treasurer's recommendation, the Congress of 1791–92 enacted laws imposing upon all imported spirits a duty varying from

[1] Aaron Burr succeeded Schuyler in the U. S. Senate (1791) and was Vice President during Jefferson's first term: Clinton was Vice President during Jefferson's second term. Livingston was made Minister to France.

twenty to forty cents a gallon.[1] The excise to be collected on domestic spirits varied, with their strength, from nine to twenty-five cents per gallon on those distilled from grain, and from eleven to thirty cents when the material was molasses or any other imported product, thus allowing considerable discrimination in favor of the exclusively "home product." For the collection of these duties each State was made an inspection district, with its supervisor, and each district was subdivided into surveys of inspection, each with its inspector. All distillers were required to enter their distilleries at the nearest office of inspection, with a complete description of all their buildings—which buildings were to be subject to the constant examination of an inspector appointed for that purpose, who was to guage and brand the casks. All duties were to be paid before the removal of the spirits from the distillery. But, to save expense and trouble to both parties in this constant oversight, small stills not located in any town or village, were to pay an *annual* rate of sixty cents per gallon on the capacity of the still. All casks containing spirits not properly branded and certified were liable to forfeiture. These were the leading features of the law against which the Pennsylvanians proposed to protest by force of arms.

Pennsylvania at that time manufactured great quantities of whiskey. Indeed, it was manufactured liberally by all the States, and became so common as a beverage as to be reckoned one of the actual necessaries of life! Its tax, and consequent

---

[1] See Hildreth's "History of the United States," Second Series, vol. ii. pages 254–55. The law was very strenuously opposed in and out of Congress. The Pennsylvania Legislature passed strong resolutions against its passage. Findley, Smiley, Snyder and Gallatin, members of that body and opponents of the law, were afterwards deeply implicated in the insurrection. During the debate in Congress, pending the passage of the law, a North Carolina representative, Steele, stated that the consumption of liquor in his State was greater, by ten times, than that of Connecticut—making it appear that whiskey was a prime necesslty. The law finally passed the U. S. House of Representatives by a vote of 35 to 21. The feeling against it at once became very violent in North Carolina, Virginia, Maryland and Pennsylvania—States most affected by its operations. In the latter State, there were nearly or quite five thousand public and private stills in 1790. The large majority of farmers manufactured all their marketable corn and rye into whiskey. It was at once the staple and the curse of the country.

enhancement of cost to the consumer, created as much feeling as if flour and bacon were to become agents in replenishing an exhausted treasury. But, in Pennsylvania, west of the Alleghany mountains, the excitement soon assumed the tone of a menace. In that particular section the chief grain grown was rye, which, in the shape of whiskey, could be transported to the east and there be exchanged for every needed commodity. Whiskey thus became a kind of *currency*. To tax it was regarded as an arbitrary assumption which it was as just and necessary to repudiate as to resist the tea and stamp tax imposed by the British Parliament.

The opposition party which was then forming seized upon Western Pennsylvania as a fertile field. The secret "democratic societies" vied with the emissaries of France in exciting a spirit of opposition to the Federal Government. Although a member of Washington's cabinet, it is proven beyond all question that Jefferson's influence contributed to foster the spirit of license and dislike of restraint which was developed rapidly by the factionists, during the years 1791–94. In Western Pennsylvania the immediate pretext for opposition was the excise; but, the disease had another instigator beside whiskey. Washington gives us the key to that other agent of disturbance—the "Democratic" societies, of which Mr. Jefferson ultimately became the recognized head—in a letter to Judge Jay:

"'The self-created societies who have spread themselves over this country have been laboring incessantly to sow the seeds of distrust, jealousy, and, of course, discontent, hoping thereby to effect some revolution in the Government, is not unknown to you. That they have been the fomenters of the western disturbances admits of no doubt in the mind of any one who will examine their conduct. But, fortunately, they have precipitated a crisis for which they were not prepared, and thereby unfolded views which will, I trust, effect their annihilation sooner than it might have happened. An occasion has also been afforded for the people of this country to show their abhorrence of the result, and their attachment to the constitution and laws; for I believe that five times the number of militia that were required would have come forward in support of them had it been necessary.'

"In his speech to Congress, after praising the alacrity with which persons came forward in support of the laws and Government, Washington said:

"'To every description, indeed, of citizens, let praise be given; but let them persevere in their affectionate vigilance over that precious depository of American happiness, the Constitution of the United States. Let them cherish it, too, for the sake of those who, from every clime, are daily seeking a dwelling in our land, And when, in the calm moments of reflection, they have retraced the origin and progress of the insurrection, let them determine whether it has not been fomented by combinations of men, who, careless of consequences, and disregarding the unerring truth that those who rouse cannot always appease a civil convulsion, have disseminated from ignorance or perversion of facts suspicions, jealousies and accusations of the whole Government.'"

The United States Senate, in its reply to Washington's speech at the opening of Congress, Nov. 19th, 1794, said:

"Our anxiety, arising from the licentious and open resistance of the laws in the western counties of Pennsylvania, has been increased by the proceedings of certain self-created societies relative to the laws and administration of the Government. Proceedings, in our apprehension, founded in political error; calculated, if not intended, to disorganize our Government, and which, by inspiring delusive hopes of support, have been instrumental in misleading our fellow-citizens in the scene of insurrection."

We here have a hint as to the *true* source of the uprising against the General Government—the same source which inspired Shays' rebellion, viz:—a set of demagogues, who, to elevate themselves to power *created* popular disaffection, and, by compelling the Government to *defend* itself, gained the title of "people's champion" by being recognised as opposed to "tyranny." We have not been without this class of men since that time, and, in the State Rights administration of 1860, witnessed the final culmination of their pernicious influence.

Those chiefly instrumental in exciting the people to resistance were Bradford, prosecuting attorney for the District; Brackenridge, Judge of the Supreme Court of Pennsylvania; Findlay, member of Congress, and late a member of the State Legislature; Albert Gallatin, an emigrant from Switzerland, a large landholder and a man of great personal influence; Marshall, Registrar of the District. Others were implicated among those holding office under the State and General Governments: like certain other patriots of a later day, they did not hesitate

26

to take the money of, while they were conspiring against, their employer. These men so succeeded in inflaming the public mind that combinations were formed in the four western counties to resist by force the execution of the law. A convention of leading citizens assembled at Redstone Old Fort, (now Brownsville,) July 26th, 1791, to take the subject of opposition to the law into consideration. It resolved the act of Congress to be "unequal in its operation, immoral in its effects, dangerous to liberty, and especially oppressive to the inhabitants of the western country." Arrangements were perfected for the organization of county committees which were to assemble at Pittsburgh on the 7th of September, to concert uniform action. The committee for Washington county assembled on the 23d of August. Among its members were the County Registrar, the Deputy Attorney-General for the State, Judge of the Supreme Court, and other public functionaries. The spirit of this body of regulators may be inferred from their declaration "that any person who had accepted, or may accept an office under Congress, in order to carry the law into effect, would be considered as inimical to the interests of the country"; and the committee "recommended the citizens of Washington county to treat every person who had accepted such office, or might thereafter accept, with contempt; and absolutely refuse all kind of communication or intercourse with the officers, and to withhold from them all aid, support and comfort."

The general meeting of the County Committee was held at Pittsburg, Sept. 7th. The day previous, Johnson, collector of revenue for Alleghany county, was seized by a body of men in disguise, shaved, tarred and feathered and ordered out of the District. This only preluded the feeling of the convention, which, beside condemning the excise and its enforcement, branched out into a general censure of the General Government, complaining of the exorbitant salaries of officers, of the unreasonable interest of the public debt, of the non-discrimination between original holders and transferees of that debt, of the institution of a National Bank, &c. &c. The Committee betrayed an unmistakably seditious spirit, to which the mass of people seemed eager to respond. On the 8th, processes were obtained for the arrest of those guilty of the outrage upon Johnson, the collector. The marshal dispatched his writs to a deputy for service, when the messenger was caught, whipped, tarred and feathered, led naked to the woods, where he was tied, blindfolded, to a tree. His horse was stolen and he left to perish miserably. But he was accidentally discovered and released. Other outrages followed—several of which were characterised by great cruelty, and, so great became the fear of violence that officers could neither be found to arrest the guilty nor to enforce the collection of the excise. The law, therefore, was a dead letter in that section during 1791. No means existed whereby the National authorities could enforce the National laws; aside from court processes and the action of marshals no power rested with the Executive to compel obedience to the laws. Such had been the fears of the State-rights' politicians that the General Government had not yet been clothed with authority to sustain its own dignity. It was not until April, 1792, that Congress passed the National Militia law which (in 1863) was, with slight modification in each State, the law of the land. That act empowered the President to call forth the militia of any State or surrounding States in case of invasion by any foreign nation or Indian tribe, or imminent danger thereof; or in case of insurrection in any State, *application being made by its Legislature or Executive;* or, in case of combinations to resist the laws of the United States too strong to be suppressed by the ordinary course of justice—such fact being first certified by the Federal Judge for the District, or by one of the Judges of the Supreme Court of the United States. This act was passed by the Federalists, in view, not only of the danger of resistance to the excise, but of revolution which, at any moment, the French party and the "democratic societies" might precipitate.

A considerable modification of the excise and its enforcement was made by Congress at the suggestion of Hamilton, Secretary of the Treasury. The duties were diminished from one to seven cents per gallon, according to proof and kind—the highest duty being fixed at twenty-five cents per gallon and the lowest at seven cents. Small country distillers were allowed to pay a monthly instead of a yearly rate upon the capacity of their stills and to take out licenses for any period which pleased them. The offices for executing the law were so modified as to render them as little annoying as possible.

These changes, however, like most compromises with an insurrectionary spirit, produced only renewed hostility to the revenue measure. "Opposition subsided" it was said, "in several districts where it before prevailed; and the hope was indulged that the refractory parts of Pennsylvania would gradually acquiesce in the execution of the law." But, it was a fallacious hope. The insurrectionists had no idea of giving in to the Government. Their "democratic societies" preferred to make an issue with the administration, and used the excise as a convenient protest—just as the secessionists of 1861–62 used the legal election of an anti-Slavery man to the Presidency as a pretext for their diabolical scheme to found a pure Slave confederacy. Albert Gallatin was one of the leading spirits in fomenting this continued hostility to the Government. He and his friends resolved that no officer of inspection should be permitted to exercise his functions in each county. This openly expressed antagonism induced the preparation, by Hamilton, of an address to the people, explaining the law and endeavoring to reconcile the discontented to its operations. Though widely circulated and canvassed in the four counties, it failed to appease the turbulent passions aroused by whiskey and the democratic leaders. An Inspector of Revenue obtained a house, after much effort, in Washington county. Its owner, a captain in the regular army, was entrapped by a body of regulators, and, under threats of tar, feathers and the scalping knife, and the burning of his house, was made to promise to eject the inspector, and so did. This implacable hostility to the law so painfully convinced Hamilton of the necessity for action, that, early in August, he wrote to Washington (then at Mount Vernon) urging a vigorous exertion of the law against the malcontents. "If" Washington replied, "after these (new) regulations are in operation, opposition is still experienced, and peaceable procedure is no longer effectual, the public interest and my duty will make it necessary to enforce the law respecting this matter; and, however disagreeable this would be to me, it must nevertheless take place." Action of an imperative character, it was soon evident, would be required.

August 21st, 1792, a new Convention gathered at Pittsburg, at which Gallatin (soon after elected to the U. S. Senate) acted as secretary. It was violent in its resolutions; counselled a determined opposition, by all "legal"(?) forms, to the enforcement of the law; appointed a committee to correspond with committees of a similar character that might be selected in other parts of the United States.[1] Such other steps were taken as were calculated to defeat the operation of the law.

In view of this public and open combination, Hamilton at once drafted a proclamation with a design of sending it to the President for his signature.[2] George Clymer, Supervisor of the District, was ordered forthwith to repair to the survey, to "collect evidence in regard to the violence which had been committed, in order to a prosecution of the offenders," to ascertain the particulars of the meeting at Pittsburg, to encourage the officers of the revenue to continue their labors, &c. The Attorney General, Edmund Randolph, of Virginia,[3] was consulted by the Secretary of the Treasury for an opinion as to whether an indictable offence had been committed by the delegation to that (Pittsburg) Convention, with a view of having their case brought before the Supreme Court then about to open its sessions at Yorktown, if the President thought an arraignment expedient.[4] In asking for this opinion Hamilton

[1] See Marshall's "Washington," vol. ii. page 273. See also Hamilton's "History of the Republic," vol. v., chap. lxxxi.

[2] See Randall's "Jefferson," vol. ii., pages 94, 95.

[3] It will be observed that the predominance of Virginia was acknowledged, by Washington's conferring *two seats* in the Cabinet to citizens of that State, viz.: Jefferson, Secretary of State, and Randolph, Attorney General. As the President also was a Virginian, *one half of the Administration* was from that Commonwealth. It was many years before that extraordinary predominance was equalized—so potent was the "diplomatic" influence of Jefferson, Madison and Munroe—every one of whom became, in succession, Presidents of the United States. From 1789 to 1825 (thirty-six years) Virginians occupied the Presidential chair the *entire time*, except the four years of John Adams' single term!

[4] See Hamilton's Works (Congressional Edition), vol. iv., page 284. See same, pages 286–88, for the letters of Washington, Hamilton and Randolph, covering the

expressed his conviction to Washington that "it was indispensable, if competent evidence could be obtained, to exert the full force of the law against the offenders," and, if the "processes of the courts were resisted—as was rather to be expected—to employ those means which, in the last resort, were put in the power of the Executive." He also conceived, in his letter to Washington (Sept. 1st) submitting the form of the proclamation, that moderation enough had been shown—that it was time to assume a different tone. Randolph, while he did not oppose the proclamation, suggested amendments to its phraseology. He wished no harm to his friends—for such, it afterwards appeared, the leaders of the insurrection were. His collusion with them and with the French faction will be alluded to hereafter. [See note at close of this paper.] Jefferson, then visiting his Monticello estate, took no part in these preliminary proceedings. Washington remitted for his signature (it then being the custom for the Secretary of State to countersign all Executive documents) the proclamation. Jefferson gave it his countersign, and suggested the same amendments advised by Randolph, but, in no way committed himself to any endorsement of the course determined upon by Washington. At a later stage of the proceedings, after his withdrawal from the cabinet, he condemned the "invasion" of Western Pennsylvania and the "coercion" of its citizens by Federal arms.[1] The Secretary of State, before the affair was settled, was, like Randolph, discovered to be, if not in direct league with Gallatin

---

entire matter of the proclamation. The opinions therein enunciated stand as a valuable precedent for procedure in all similar cases of insurrection against the General Government. Had the "Democratic" Administration of James Buchanan in 1860, been as firm and wise as the Federalist Administration of Washington, how fortunate had it been for the country!

[1] In a letter to Madison Jefferson said: "Hamilton says there is no possibility of getting the law executed there and that probably the evil (of insurrection) will spread. A proclamation is to be issued—another instance of my being forced to appear to approve what I have condemned uniformly from its first conception." Washington wrote to Hamilton that the reason he sent the proclamation to Jefferson for his signature was his desire to conform to previous practice and, "for another reason which has some weight in my mind." What that "other reason" was is, doubtless, indicated by Jefferson in the last sentence of the extract above quoted in his letter to Madison.

and Findley, yet not inimical to them. His feeling was openly expressed, when he came into the Executive chair, by appointing Gallatin his Secretary of the Treasury.

The proclamation, as drawn by Hamilton and amended by Jefferson, was issued Sept. 15th, 1792. After stating that opposition to laws made pursuant to an express provision of the Constitution was subversive of good order and dangerous to the very being of Government—alluding to the moderation of the Government and the disposition manifested by the Legislature (Congress) to obviate the causes of objection—the proclamation admonished and exhorted all persons to refrain and desist from all unlawful combinations to obstruct the operation of these laws, and charged the magistrates to exert their powers to enforce them. Not a very bellicose mandate, truly; yet, both Jefferson and Randolph, as we have seen, did not favor even this exercise of the National Executive authority. Hamilton's purpose was to prosecute the offenders for violation of the law, and for resistance to its officers. With this view he consulted Randolph, as legal adviser of the Government. To the Treasurer's surprise he was informed that the Pittsburg Conventionists were not indictable; and the first prosecution attempted, under Clymer's efforts, was abandoned from evident want of *authority* to impress local courts with National ideas. This failure only confirmed the opposition in its contempt of a General Government which was powerless to enforce its laws and to protect its servitors. A *denouement* so mortifying illustrated the power of faction and the weakness of the National authority. Hamilton, however, resolved to see the law enforced, as was his duty. He conceived another plan to attain his object—ingenious and politic, but it also proved powerless, in view of the fact that no excise officers dared to exercise their functions in the disaffected region—so completely did the mob rule.

Thus matters stood, up to the opening of Congress, Nov. 5th, 1792, when Washington, in his speech, alluded to the failure of efforts to enforce the law. He assured Congress that "nothing within Constitutional and legal limits" would be "wanting to assert and maintain the just authority of the laws." "In fulfilling this trust I shall count entirely upon the full co-operation of the other departments of the Government and upon the zealous support of all good citizens," said the President.

Nothing came however of efforts to enforce the law, but violence and excitement. The President shrunk from the ordeal of calling in the military to assist in enforcing the law. He sought, by every means, to appease the malcontents. But even Washington's great influence did not suffice to obtain respect for the law or for the Government. Both were reviled with all the bitterness of vicious men conscious of power. The democratic societies were busy; ceaselessly their leaders labored to bring discredit upon the Government and to breed contempt for its laws. Armed men soon organized into patrols. As "regulators," these umpires visited every section of the four counties to punish every distiller who might seek to comply with the law, and to dispose summarily of any officer who should persist in exercising his functions. Tar and feathers were freely administered; several houses were burned; a local newspaper (the "Pittsburg Gazette") was pressed into the revolutionary service; no man dared to defend the law for fear of violence to his person: anarchy reigned supreme. One John Holcroft, a ruffian sustained by the democratic societies, assumed a leadership of the armed patrol, which, from its acts in "tinkering" the stills that would pay the law obedience, won the name of "Tom the Tinker." It became, during the Fall of the year 1793, a terror to all loyal citizens and a scourge to all officers of the Government. Holcroft was, in fact, a *sans culotte* of brutality and impudence, before whose power, all authority, both State and National, soon quailed. Even those leaders of the insurrection who had trifled with the law from the sordid motive of personal popularity, were affrighted at the monster which their own lawlessness had evoked.

During 1794, the Administration having previously appointed John Neville insp tor of the district, resolved to press prosecution against those who had failed to comply with the law —being empowered by a special act of the late Congress to call the delinquents to account. Neville, a very influential man of wealth and family position, resolved to see the laws of Con-

H. W. Herrick del. John Rogers, sc.

TARRING & FEATHERING AN EXCISE OFFICER.

J. D. Torrey, Publisher, 13 Spruce St. New York

gress obeyed and assumed office to perform his duties at all hazards. Through his exertions indictments were found against thirty distillers who had neglected to enter their stills. Warrants were issued against each offender and all except one were served by the marshal, in company with Neville. On the road to the last delinquent, the marshal and inspector were met by a party of "tinkers," who at once fired upon the officers and caused them to fly for their lives. Neville returned to his fine mansion, eight miles from Pittsburg, whither he was pursued by the regulators. On the morning of July 16th, 1794, his house was assailed, by forty of the ruffians. Neville was prepared for them. Having armed his negroes and others in the house, he repulsed the assailants, wounding six of them, one mortally. The ruffians withdrew and gave out that they would "finish the job" on the morrow. The inspector appealed to two magistrates, and to the county militia commanders, for protection, but obtained for answer that they were powerless to give it. He then summoned a guard from Fort Pitt. Eleven regulars, under Major Fitzpatrick, were detailed to protect the house in case of assault. The regulators appeared on the ground July 17th, with a force numbering nearly five hundred desperadoes, all fully armed. They were under the leadership of one McFarlane, formerly a lieutenant in the Continental army. Neville's surrender was demanded, but the inspector had escaped, foreseeing the too evident result if he remained. When informed of this, McFarlane demanded admittance to the house, with five others, to search for papers connected with Neville's office and operations. This demand was refused, when the insurgents ordered the women and children to withdraw from the house. The attack quickly followed. It was answered with spirit by the regulars. McFarlane was killed and several of his men wounded. Infuriated, the "tinkers" at once fired the outbildings. The mansion was soon in flames, when the regulars capitulated—three of them having been wounded. The fine dwelling and outbuildings were consumed, and the grounds around laid waste. The marshal and Neville's son, appearing on the ground, were seized and rather roughly used but not injured. The officer was dismissed only after having given his solemn promise to serve no more processes west of the mountains.

Neville and the marshal having taken refuge in Pittsburg, were followed by two delegates from the mob. A demand was made for the first to resign his office and for the marshal to deliver up all warrants and processes in his possession—a demand peremptorily refused. The ferment which followed was threatening. Neville would have retired to the fort, but such demonstrations were preparing for an outbreak as induced the inspector and marshal to slip down the river to Marietta. From thence they passed over the mountains to Philadelphia, to report an end to all peaceful measures for enforcing the law.

These proceedings were followed by the wildest excitement throughout the four counties. A public meeting was called at Mingo creek meeting house, July 23d. Bradford, Brackenridge and Marshall were present. The first proposed to take up arms and to defy the Government. The second declared against such violence as had been shown. He preferred not to involve those friendly to the best interests of their section by endorsing the late riot. The "tinker" faction was in the ascendant, but Brackenridge succeeded in effecting a call for a convention, to be composed of delegates from all townships west of the mountains and from the adjoining counties of Maryland and Virginia. This convention was to meet at Parkinson's Ferry, on the Monongahela river, in three weeks. During this period it was impossible for the insurrectionary spirit to remain quiet. Three days after the Mingo meeting, by Bradford's order, the mail bound east from Pittsburg was seized (July 26th). It contained, as was expected, letters to the United States authorities, implicating those most guilty in the late transactions. Bradford, Marshall and others at once issued a circular to all commandants of militia in the western counties, to muster as many men as possible and to rendezvous at Braddock's Field with arms and four days' rations. The reason urged for this summons was that, in the intercepted mail, a discovery had been made which rendered a resort to action necessary. August 1st found not less than *seven thou-*

sand armed men at the place of rendezvous. A meeting was organized. Says Hildreth: "Colonel Cook, one of the judges of Fayette county, a member of the first popular convention held in Pennsylvania at the commencement of the Revolution, distinguished for his opposition to the excise, having repeatedly presided at the public meetings called to protest against it, was chosen president of the armed assembly. Albert Gallatin, the late rejected Senator,[1] was appointed secretary, Bradford, to whom everybody cringed, assumed the character of Major-General and reviewed the troops." The gathering, however, was a discomfiture to the wild men who had called it. It seemed to have had no specific objects, further than to inflame the military ardor of the people.

The robbed mail had placed the insurrectionists in possession of information regarding the "spies" in their midst. Most of these already had been expelled; but, the meeting resolved upon exiling two more citizens of Pittsburg. The entire mob then marched into that city, were feasted by the people, and, after "a good drunk," disbanded—having done no serious harm. Only the more persistent of the mob remained in the field, resolved to punish Major Fitzpatrick, and, if possible, to seize the fort; but, after a few days, they dispersed, having succeeded only in burning the Major's barn. It was, unquestionably, Bradford's design to excite the mob, to march upon Pittsburg, to seize the fort and munitions, and then to proclaim the "independence" of Western Pennsylvania. Against this Gallatin, Brackenridge and others protested, while the most responsible among the militia commanders positively refused to be parties to such a treasonable step. This temporarily frustrated Bradford's ambitious scheme for the "secession" of the Western counties.[2]

---

[1] Gallatin was chosen, by the "democratic" majority of the Pennsylvania Legislature, to the United States Senate (1794) but was denied his seat in the Senate owing to his ineligibility under the Constitution—being a foreigner of only eleven years' residence in the country.

[2] The combined operations of the democratic societies and the French faction had, by this time, brought on a crisis in the affairs of the West. Kentucky stood ready to "secede," with a view of wresting from the Spaniards all their Louisiana possessions. The French previously had landed forces at St. Mary's, Florida, to

There followed, however, a few days in which every excess was committed by the regulators against all persons suspected of *disloyalty* to the insurrectionary cause. Upon all sides, even into Western Maryland and Virginia, the lawless spirit spread. No citizen dared to condemn the recent proceedings nor to sustain the cause of the National Administration. Every remaining excise officer was expelled from the country, some being badly maltreated, their houses burned and their horses and cattle stolen. All law for the moment was suspended save the law of a mob: "democratic societies" were tasting the fruit of the tree which they had planted.

Where was the Governor of Pennsylvania during these lawless proceedings? the reader asks. Miflin, like Jefferson and Randolph, was an anti-Federalist, and, like them, doubted the propriety of *enforcing* submission. After the outrages just enumerated he issued a circular letter to the State officers in the disaffected region in which, after having expressed his indignation at the lawless proceedings, he enjoined them to exert their utmost authority to suppress the tumults and to punish the offenders. Of what use was such a mandate when all avenues of law were closed?

But, in General Knox, Secretary of War; Alexander Hamilton, Secretary of the Treasury; and William Bradford, then Attorney General, Washington found advisers equal to the emergency. These members of his Cabinet, aroused by the dangers of the crisis, earnestly advised the President to exercise his fullest powers in suppressing the insurrection before it became a revolution. Washington resolved to use his autho-

---

seize that colony and to add it to the Louisiana domain. A gigantic game of commingled impudence, fraud and treason, hatched by the French Minister, Genet, and sustained by the democratic and Jacobin associations of the Atlantic States, was then (in the Summer of 1794) just ready to burst upon the country, bringing in its train a war with Great Britain and a division of the Confederacy. The Whiskey Insurrection was part of this gigantic game; and Bradford, by declaring the "independence" of Western Pennsylvania, only anticipated the events which he and his confederates conceived were sure to follow. Most fortunately for the country a President occupied the chair too incorruptible, too brave, too wise for the intrigues of foreign and domestic foes. He drew the sword and treason fled abashed. We devote a paper [see "The Conspiracy of Genet"] to the intrigues of the French Minister and his emissaries.

rity to the utmost, to exact obedience to the laws. Governor Miflin, and Randolph, Secretary of State, doubted his constitutional right to *coerce* the people, and prophesied the worst results from introducing the militia of other States into Pennsylvania. But, the President's resolution was taken. The majesty of the National Government had been insulted, assailed and scorned: if there was any power in that Government to support its dignity the moment had arrived to assert it. All constitutional quibbles and tender apprehensions of results were set aside; only the great end to be attained was regarded. To *enforce* a compliance with the laws and an acknowledgement of the supremacy of the General Government was a duty imperative as the salvation of the country. It was a critical moment in the destiny of the republic—a sublime moment in the career of George Washington.

Having become assured that Miflin could not, in his capacity of Governor, suppress the revolt, Washington, acting under authority of the Militia Law of the session of 1791–92, and also by virtue of a special act of the session of 1793–94, obtained a certificate from one of the Supreme Judges that a state of insurrection existed in the Western counties too powerful for the judicial authorities to suppress. The statutory proclamation announcing this state of affairs, and requiring those in revolt to desist and disperse, was put forth Aug. 7th, followed by a requisition upon the Governors of Pennsylvania, Maryland, Virginia and New Jersey, for the aggregate of thirteen thousand men (afterwards increased to fifteen thousand) —a force deemed sufficient to cope with the large body of insurgents which it was presumed Bradford and his co-conspirators could summon to the field. Brackenridge and Gallatin, alarmed at this climax to their disloyal machinations against the General Government, sought, by all means, to prevent the consummation of Washington's programme. They were aided, so far as it was good policy to offer aid, by Randolph, then Secretary of State[1] and Governor Miflin, though neither of

[1] Jefferson retired from the Cabinet of Washington at the close of the year 1793, and suggested Randolph, then Attorney General, as his successor. Randolph was thus nominated and William Bradford of Pennsylvania, became Attorney General.

these anti-Federalist leaders cared to assume any *open* justification of the insurrectionists. Both were patriotic enough to desire no harm to the Federal Government, but were too solicitous for popularity with the powerful democratic societies and with the French faction to give Washington's measures their unqualified endorsement.[1] Randolph laid before the Cabinet a letter from Brackenridge, to a "friend in Philadelphia," in which it was assumed that the Western counties were not only able to defend themselves but would, in all probability, be aided by the people east of the mountains, who would offer resistance to any march of Federal troops over their soil, to be used for coercing the people. The letter writer also alluded to the possibility of an *application to Great Britain for aid*, and hinted at the idea of a march upon Philadelphia! As Brackenridge was a leading actor in, and authority among, the democratic societies these confessions indicate quite clearly the disgusting disloyalty at the bottom of these organizations. The letter, doubtless, *was written for Randolph's use* in the Cabinet: how powerless it was even to modify Washington's purposes was soon evident. The militia were ordered to be ready to move by the first of September (1794).

To exhaust every means of amicable settlement prior to a resort to arms, Washington had delegated (August 7th) three commissioners, to proceed in advance of the army, with discretionary authority to effect a settlement of difficulties. U. S. Senator from Pennsylvania Ross; the Attorney-General Bradford; and Judge Yates, of the Pennsylvania Supreme Court, constituted the commission. The time allowed for a settlement was up to September 14th, when, if an effectual submission to the laws had not taken place, the military must assume the field. As coadjutors, Governor Miflin named Chief Justice McKean and General Irving, to act on the part of the State, with the Commissioners. The Governor also issued two proclamations—one convening the Legislature and one addressed to the insurgents, requiring them to submit to the laws and

[1] Jefferson afterwards complained, in a letter to Madison of Randolph's duplicity, averring that he gave to him (Jefferson) the shells and to Hamilton the oysters.

announcing his determination to obey the President's call for troops.[1]

To return to the insurgents. The meeting at Mingo creek meeting house, it will be remembered, appointed a general convention of the townships of the four counties, to assemble at Parkinson's ferry, August 14th. The townships responded, with two exceptions. Delegates, to the number of two hundred and fifteen, were present at the appointed time. It was a very important gathering—composed largely of the most violent faction, yet numbering many persons of influence who were resolved to bring matters to a peaceful settlement. Among this latter class were Gallatin and Brackenridge, both of whom were thoroughly alarmed at the portentous fortunes evidently in store for them. Judge Cook, president of the Mingo meeting, and Gallatin, secretary of that preliminary assemblage, were called to the same positions in this second convention, whose proceedings, if typified by the mottoes on the liberty pole, bid fair to be revolutionary enough. "No asylum for cowards and traitors!" "Liberty and no excise!" flaunted from the staff, over which floated the American flag. We may quote from Hildreth's lucid account[2] of the proceedings from this point:

"A series of resolutions was offered by Marshall, of which the first, against taking citizens out of the vicinity for trial, passed without objection. The second resolution proposed the appointment of a committee of public safety, empowered to 'call forth the resources of the Western country to repel any hostile attempts against the citizens.' After a speech, in which he denied any danger of hostilities, the only danger being that of legal coercion, Gallatin proposed to refer this resolution to a select committee. But, though there were many persons present whose chief object, like Gallatin's it was to extricate the people from the disastrous consequences of a violent opposition to the laws, which they themselves had done so much to stimulate, no one dared to second the motion. Marshall, however, already began to waver; and he presently

[1] The idea that he would not, being an anti-Federalist, obey the call was generally entertained by the opponents of the Administration. The Governor was too loyal for such a course, much as he disliked Hamilton and his financial budget and Washington's executive views.

[2] Hildreth's "History of the United States of America," vol. i., second series, chapter vii.

offered to withdraw the proposition, provided a committee of sixty was appointed, with power to call another meeting, This was readily agreed to, as was also the appointment of a sub-committee of fifteen, to confer with the Federal and State commissioners. For the purpose of being remodeled, the resolutions were referred to a committee, consisting of Bradford, Gallatin, Brackenridge and Herman Husbands, then a very old man, a leader formerly among the North Carolina 'Regulators.' The determination expressed in one of these resolutions, not to submit to the excise, was struck out on Gallatin's motion. But, neither he nor any body else went so far as to advocate obedience to it. A promise to submit to the State laws was, however, inserted. This business being disposed of, the exercise of some address secured a dissolution of the meeting, the assembly of the committee of sixty being fixed for the 2d of September.

"A few days after, as had been arranged, the committee of fifteen met the commissioners at Pittsburg (Aug. 21). Among the members of this committee were Bradford, Marshall, Cook, Gallatin and Brackenridge, the whole, except Bradford, being inclined to an accommodation. [A condidate for Congress for the Pittsburg district, in his anxiety to secure votes, Brackenridge had hitherto gone so far as to make the insurgents believe he was on their side. But, he was well aware of the folly and hopelessness of their cause, and at bottom was not less anxious than Gallatin to escape out of the present dilemma. In a book which he afterwards published, he excused the part he had taken as necessary to protect himself against the violence of the insurgents.] The demands of the commissioners were exceeding moderate. They required from the committee of sixty an explicit declaration of their determination to submit to the laws, and a recommendation to the citizens at large to submit also, and to abstain from all opposition, direct or indirect, and especially from violence or threats against the excise officers or the complying distillers. Primary meetings were required to be held to test the sense of the citizens in these particulars. Should satisfactory assurances be given on or before the fourteenth of September, the commissioners promised a suspension till the next July of all prosecutions for offences prior in date to this arrangement; and, in case the law, during that interval, should be generally complied with, in good faith, a final pardon and oblivion of all such offenses.

"The committee of fifteen pronounced these terms reasonable; and, to give more time to carry out the arrangement, they agreed to anticipate by four days the calling together of the committee of sixty. Meanwhile a report spread that the conferees had been bribed; indeed, that charge was made in express terms in a letter of 'Tom the Tinker' to the Pittsburg Gazette, which the printer, as was the case with other communications of that anonymous personage, did not dare to omit to publish. While the members of the committee of sixty were collecting at Brownsville, the place appointed for the meeting, an armed party of horse and foot entered the town with drums beating. The friends of submission were so intimidated that, but for Gallatin, they would have abandoned all thoughts of urging an accommodation. Bradford insisted on taking the question at once: but, by the exercise of some address, the matter was postponed till the next day; meanwhile the armed party were persuaded to return to their homes.

"Gallatin opened the business the next morning in a speech, in which the motives to submission were judiciously urged. He was followed by Brackenridge, who now came out strongly on the same side. Bradford, in an extravagant harangue, urged continued resistance, and the organization of an independent State. Not daring to expose themselves by an open vote, the friends of submission had prevailed that the decision should be by secret ballot. They were thus enabled to carry, by a very lean majority, a resolution that it would be for the interest of the people to accede to the terms offered by the commissioners. But, they did not dare to propose what the commissioners had demanded, a pledge from the members of the committee themselves to submit to the law, and arrangements for obtaining, in primary meetings, a like pledge from the individual citizens. After appointing a new committee of conference, the committee of sixty adjourned without day.

"The new conferees asked of the commissioners, Sept. 1, further delay till the 10th of October, to ascertain the sense of the people; but, this was declined as being beyond their authority. They now required that meetings should be held in the several townships on the eleventh of September, any two or more members of the late committee of sixty, or any justice of the peace to preside, at which the citizens should vote yea or nay on the question of submitting to and supporting the law, all those voting in the affirmative to sign a declaration to that effect, which was to secure them an amnesty as to past offenses. The third day after the vote, the presiding officers were to assemble in their respective county court houses, to ascertain the number of votes both ways, and to declare their opinion in writing whether the submission was so general that excise inspection offices could be re-established with safety; all the papers to be forwarded to the commissioners at Union Town by the sixteenth of the month.

"Meetings were held under this arrangement in many of the townships, but the result, on the whole, was quite unsatisfactory. Most of the more intelligent leaders were careful to provide for their own safety by signing the required submission; but many of those who had taken no active part in resisting the law refused to attend, or to pledge themselves to obedience. As they had committed no offense, such was their argument, they ought not to be required to submit—as if winking at the violation of law and neglecting to assist in its enforcement were not among the greatest of offenses! In some townships the meetings were violently broken up and the papers torn to pieces. Such was the case in the town in which Findley resided, who, it seems, was personally insulted on the occasion. From Allegany county no returns were received. The judges of the vote in Westmoreland expressed the opinion that excise inspection offices could not be safely established in that county. In the other two counties the expression of any direct opinion was avoided; but these counties had always been more violent than Westmoreland. The better disposed part of the population had begun to form associations for mutual defense, and the opinion among them was quite universal that the presence of the troops was absolutely necessary."

This result of their mission left the President no other course than to use the strong arm of military power. The troops required had been furnished with alacrity, by the several Governors. Those from Pennsylvania were last in the field. The Legislature had offered bounties for volunteers, while Miflin made the tour of the lower counties—then the most populous in the State—where, by his remarkable popular eloquence, he soon obtained recruits enough to fill his quota. None were more astonished than the "democratic societies" to see the Governor thus "up in arms against his own people and party." But, the shrewd Governor was as patriotic as politic, and chose the right course at the right moment. The old war-horse of the Revolution, General Daniel Morgan, led the Virginia forces; General William Smith, then a member of Congress from Baltimore, led those of Maryland. These two latter bodies composed the "left wing" of the army, and assembled at Cumberland, Maryland, from whence they were to move across the mountains by Braddock's road. The troops of Pennsylvania and New Jersey, composing the "right wing", and led by Governors Miflin and Howell, rendezvoused at Bedford. The Command-in-Chief was given to Governor Henry Lee of Virginia—"Light-Horse Harry" of the Revolution. Washington and Hamilton also determined to proceed with the army.

This formidable assertion of authority sent consternation into the ranks of the insurgents—few of whom cared to court the ordeal of blood to defend their right to free whiskey. But, prior to the actual appearance of the troops in the field, many evidences of the "tinkers" became visible, even to the east of the mountains. At Carlisle the two Pennsylvania commissioners had stopped, to require bonds of a party who had run up a barrel of whiskey on the liberty pole, as an insult and a menace to the commission. The Judge and the General had scarcely left town when a large body of armed men rode into Carlisle to capture the two commissioners. Finding them gone, the mob proceeded to burn them in effigy, and gave many other evidences of the existence of "democratic societies" in that section. Similar feeling betrayed itself in several counties of Maryland, but it was suppressed by a volunteer corps of dragoons, who seized and imprisoned in the Hagerstown jail more than a hundred of the malcontents.

But, these spasms of the disease were of brief duration. The desire for peace became so strong that a second convention was called, by the efforts of Gallatin, Brackenridge and Findley, at Parkinson's Ferry, Oct. 2d, at which the declaration was made that the failure to obtain written pledges, as stipulated by the commissioners, was owing chiefly to the want of time and of information. The mass of voters, it was stated, assuming their innocence of any hostile acts against the Government, argued that to sign the required pledge was an implication of the existence of their guilt which they could not consent to sustain. Hence, the failure of the commissioners' proposals. This declaration and other messages of contrition were confided by the assembly to Findley and a person named Redick, who were ordered to hasten over the mountains, to stay, if possible, the march of the army against the Western counties. The two delegates lost not a moment in their embassy. They met the right wing of the Federal forces at Carlisle, where Washington then was. The President received the embassadors but failed to accept their proffers of peace. He advised Findley to return and reassemble the convention, that, if a settlement really was desired, the insurrectionists might have it by sueing in proper terms and by giving full assurances of entire submission to the laws. The troops were ordered forward to the rendezvous at Bedford, where, the President stated, he would receive the expected answer of the convention.

Findley, inspired with the zeal of fear, succeeded in exciting a like apprehension among all of the most intelligent of those who had participated in the insurrection, or who had affiliated with the democratic societies. The convention reassembled October 24th. "Resolutions were passed," said Hildreth, "declaring the competency of the civil authorities to enforce the laws, recommending all delinquents who had not already secured an indemnity to surrender for trial, and expressing the conviction that offices of inspection might be opened with safety, and that the excise duties would be paid. Findley hastened back with these resolutions, but before he reached the army the President had already returned to Philadelphia. Hamilton, however, remained behind, and was believed to act as the President's deputy. The troops crossed the Alleganies in a heavy rain, up to their knees in mud, and not without severe suffering, which occasioned in the end a good many deaths. The two wings formed a junction at Union Town, and, as they advanced into the disaffected counties, the re-establishment of the authority of the law became complete. Having arrived at Parkinson's Ferry, Lee issued a proclamation, Nov. 8th, confirming the amnesty to those who had entitled themselves to it, and calling upon all the inhabitants to take the oath of allegiance to the United States.

"A few days after, arrangements having been previously made for it, there was a general seizure, by parties detached for that purpose, of persons supposed to be criminally concerned in the late transactions. But, as those against whom the strongest evidence existed had either fled the country or taken advantage of the amnesty, this seizure fell principally on persons who, without taking an active part, had been content with encouraging and stimulating others. Many were dismissed at once for want of evidence; and of those who were bound over for trial at Philadelphia, the greater part were afterwards acquitted. Among those thus bound over, Brackenridge was one; but, instead of being tried, he was used as a witness against the others. These people complained loudly of the inconvenience to which they had been put, and of the harsh treatment which, in some few cases, had been experienced at the hands of the military parties by whom the arrests had been made. But, such evils were only the natural consequences of lying quietly by and allowing resistance to the laws to aggravate itself into rebellion."

Morgan, with a portion of the Virginia troops remained in the disaffected region during the winter, as a military guard to secure implicit obedience to the laws. Of those seized, as in the case of those implicated in Shays' Rebellion, none were made to answer with their lives for their crime against the Government. The great majority were found guilty of treason, upon trial before the Circuit Court at Philadelphia; but, exercising his prerogative of pardon, Washington ultimately bade even those most guilty to "go, and sin no more."

This insurrection illustrated two things, namely—first, the revolutionary nature of all asserted rights of a State in contradistinction with, and as supreme to, the rights of the Union; and, second, the power of the National Executive to enforce the National laws. The country breathed more freely; the cause of the Constitntion became more fixed; the assumed supremacy of the State retreated to the background, only to be occasionally dragged forth by malcontents, nullificators and secessionists, for the same end as in 1794—for humiliating the National authority. Could the country always be blessed with a President as wise as George Washington it would have but little to apprehend from the element of insurrection which, confounding liberty with license, has become one of the fixed facts in our democratic society.

NOTE.—Reference has been made, in this paper to the connection of the "democratic societies'" affiliation with the Jacobinical faction existent in this country after the advent of Genet, Minister from the "Republic" of France to the United States, April, 1793; also to the intercepted dispatch of M. Fauchet, successor of Genet. Some little light will be thrown upon the history of 1794 by a further reference to this dispatch of Fauchet, to the Commissioner of Foreign Relations, dated October 31st, 1794. This minister, having succeeded Genet, inherited much of that intermeddler's contempt for the Federal Government. As an intriguant he was more subtle, less impudent but not less unscrupulous. He was at once a spy and an agent to create a division among our people, by which to advance the interests of France—then still in the throes of its ever memorable revolution. The dispatch alluded to was caught *in transitu* on the "Jean Bart," a French privateer, overhauled in the British Channel by a British frigate. According to instructions the dispatch box was cast into the sea, when its capture became imminent; but, an Englishman—a captain of a merchantman captured by the "Jean Bart"—suspecting the character of the contents, leaped overboard and sustained the box until it was secured by a boat from the frigate. The important and interesting nature of the dispatch caused the British Government to send it to their minister to the United States, by whom it was brought to the attention of the Administration. That the disclosure astonished and angered Washington is not strange. The President, though aware of the incendiary nature of French influence, was not prepared to learn that a member of his own Cabinet was in league with the anarchical faction, and plotting for his (Washington's) humiliation. We quote from the document such passages as throw light upon the secret influences at work, during the early stages of the Republic, to unsettle the public mind and to plunge the country into a foreign war. Fauchet wrote:

"CITIZEN—1. The measures which prudence prescribes to me to take with respect to my colleagues, have still presided in the digesting of the dispatches signed by them, which treat of the insurrection of the western countries, and of the repressive means adopted by the Government. I have allowed them to be confined to the giving of a faithful, but naked recital of events. The reflections therein contained scarcely exceed the conclusions easily deducible from the character assumed by the public prints. I have reserved myself to give you, as far as I am able, a key to the facts detailed in our reports. When it comes in question to explain, either by conjectures or by certain data, the secret views of a foreign government, it would be imprudent to run the risk of indiscretions, and to give one's self up to men, whose known partiality for that government, and similitude of passions and interests with its chiefs, might lead to confidences, the issue of which is incalculable. Besides, the precious confessions of Mr. Randolph alone throw a satisfactory light upon every thing that comes to pass. These I have not yet communicated to my colleagues. The motives already mentioned lead to this reserve, and still less permit me to open myself to them at the present moment. I shall then endeavor, Citizen, to give you a clew to all the measures, of which the common dispatches give you an account, and to discover the true causes of the explosion, which it is obstinately resolved to repress with great means, although the state of things has no longer any thing alarming.

"2. To confine the present crisis to the simple question of the excise, is to reduce it far below its true scale; it is indubitably connected with a general explosion for some time prepared in the public mind, but which this local and precipitate eruption will cause to miscarry, or at least check for a long time. In order to see the real cause, in order to calculate the effect and the consequences, we must ascend to the origin of the parties existing in the State, and retrace their progress."

He then proceeds to show that the "parties" existing are Federalists and anti-Federalists—the first aiming to *monarchise* the Government and the latter to democratise it. The explosion of the Whiskey Insurrection he declared had been *premature;* unfortunately for the latter class it had served only to strengthen the Administration. Monsieur then descants upon Hamilton's financial schemes, which he assumed were but gigantic stock-jobbing, creating an aristocracy of speculators especially antagonistic to the agricultural interests of the country. In these financial projects the emissary of Robespierre beheld the further fruition of aristocratic ideas. He proceeds in his luminous essay:

"8. In the mean time, the popular societies are formed;[1] political ideas concentrate themselves; the patriotic party unite, and more closely connect themselves; they gain a formidable majority in the Legislature; the abasement of commerce, the slavery of navigation, and the audacity of England strengthen it; a concert of declarations and censures against the government arises, at which the latter is even itself astonished."

After elaborating on the discontent prevailing, upon the enormity of the offenses of the party in power, the minister recurs to the excise revolt as a further evidence of the tyranny of the Government and of its unjust impositions. He adds:

"But why, in contempt of treaties, are they left to bear the yoke of the feeble Spaniard, as to the Mississippi for upwards of twelve years? Since when has an agricultural people submitted to the most unjust capricious law of a people explorers of the precious metals? Might we not suppose that Madrid and Philadelphia mutually assisted in prolonging the slavery of the river; that the proprietors of a barren coast are afraid lest the Mississippi, once opened, and its numerous branches brought into activity, their fields might become deserts; and, in a word, that commerce dreads having rivals in those interior parts as soon as their inhabitants shall cease to be subjects? This last supposition is but too well founded; an influential member of the Senate, Mr. Izard, one day in conversation undisguisedly announced it to me."

It is unnecessary to follow the loquacious intriguant through all his allusions and illusions. That portion which most interests our readers we subjoin:

"It appears, therefore, that these men, with others unknown to me, all having without doubt Randolph at their head, were balancing to decide on their party. Two or three days before the proclamation was published, and of course before the Cabinet had resolved on its measures, Mr. Randolph came to see me with an air of great eagerness, and made to me the overtures, of which I have given you an account in my No. 6. Thus, with some thousands of dollars, the republic could have decided on civil war or peace! Thus the consciences of the pretended patriots of America have already their price! It is very true that the certainty of these conclusions, painful to be drawn, will forever exist in our archives. What will be the old age of this Government, if it is thus early decrepid?"

Dispatch "No. 6" referred to did not help Mr. Randolph's case, nor serve to create additional sympathy for the democratic societies. It was written in August, and, according to Fauchet's owu confessions afterwards extorted in Randolph's defense, contained the following piece of news:

"Scarce was the commotion known (i. e. the uprising in the West during July and August, 1794) when the Secretary of State (Randolph) came to my house. All his countenance was grief. He requested of me a private conversation. 'It is all over,' he said to me: 'a civil war is about to ravage our unhappy country. Four men, by their talents, their influence, their energy, may save it. But, debtors of English merchants, they will be deprived of their liberty if they take the

---

[1] Formed by Genet, predecessor of Fauchet. Dallas, Secretary of the State of Pennsylvania, was at the head of them, and was the principal agent in their formation.

smallest step. Could you lend them instantaneous funds to shelter them from English persecution!' This inquiry, the dispatch continued, astonished me. It was impossible for me to render a satisfactory answer. You knowing my want of power, and my defect of pecuniary means, I shall withdraw myself from the affair by some common place remarks, and by throwing myself on the pure and disinterested principles of the republic."

"*Four* men by their talents may save it." Who were they? Miflin, Dallas, Randolph and Jefferson!

A precious mass of evidence, truly, to come to light at that crisis, when Washington, by the happy issue of his proceedings against the malcontents—by the increased confidence felt in public credit—was more than ever trusted. "Jefferson, on whom the patriots cast their eyes *to succeed the President* * * prudently retired, &c." And Mr. Randolph also "prudently retired," when Washington placed the dispatch in the hands of his until then trusted adviser for explanations. Randolph retired from the Cabinet, not like Jefferson "in order to avoid making a figure against his inclinations," but to write out his Vindication, to become the enemy of George Washington and the adviser of "the patriots" who were "casting their eyes" toward Jefferson as Washington's successor.

In Randall's "Life of Jefferson," vol. ii., chapters iii., iv., v., will be found the best presentment yet made of the anti-Federalist view of the "Whiskey War" and the affair of the Fauchet dispatch. Mr. Randall's defense of the democratic societies, and his chief points of exculpation of Mr. Jefferson for the part he played in fomenting the public disquietude, rest upon the absurd assumption of the monarchical tendency of the Federal party. The biographer evidently proceeds upon the theory that, because Jefferson hated Hamilton therefore it is necessary for Jefferson's biographer to believe every suspicion hatched in the Virginian's fierce partizan brain.

THE CONSPIRACY OF M. GENET.

FRENCH intrigue in the United States during the early administrations enters largely into the history of that period. In fact, it ramified through the entire structure of our Government and our society, being at once the cause of alarm among Federalists and the source of partisan strength to their opponents. To Washington it became a constant agent of unhappiness; to his successor, Adams, it contributed one unceasing flow of mortifying and aggravating circumstances; to Jefferson it offered less annoyance simply because he was of the French party, because the question of neutrality had been settled by Washington and Adams, and because another object of the intrigue—the dispossession of Spain in the Louisiana territory—was quieted by the cession of that territory to Napoleon and its purchase by the United States' Government; to Madison it only ruffled the surface of affairs, though the pressure of the French faction had much to do in drawing this country into the war against Great Britain in 1812–14.

France having contributed by arms and means to the independence of the American States, her ministers to this country assumed a creditor's right in the premises, acting arrogatingly to our Government and patronizingly to the people. Even before the adoption of the Constitution the seeds of French disquietude appeared in our midst. Jefferson, when Minister to France, contributed to the overthrow of Louis XVI.—the Monarch whose benefactions had sustained the Colonies in their struggle against British tyranny; he became a coadjutor of the revolutionists, opening his doors freely to the Jacobins and agents of Condorcet. His sympathy was repeated among a large class on this side of the sea, who entered into the foreign revolution with more than the ardor of friends—with the frenzy of partizans; and when "Citizen Genet" came to this country, in April, 1793, as the accredited representative of the French "Republic," then under the reign of the Girondins, he found such a welcome as scarcely could have been extended to Lafayette[1] had he reappeared on our shores. He landed at Charleston, S. C., April 9th, 1793, where his reception was enthusiastic on the part of the State authorities and the people; his journey to Philadelphia was one continued ovation. The country was then aglow with hopes of liberty for Europe which the French revolution had excited. In that revolution they beheld a regeneration of society and of governments; hence, notwithstanding its phases of horror, infidelity and brutal excesses, it was regarded as the messenger of a new order of things. Genet arrived on our shores to find France the guest of American homes, from the seaboard to the frontier. He was fêted, not as the man but as the Minister from the regenerated nation.

With his coming came trouble indeed to the administration of Washington. Scarcely had Genet arrived in Charleston and received the ovations of Governor Moultrie and his people, ere he began the issue of commissions, for privateers, to American citizens. France having declared war against Great Britain, Genet was instructed, it afterwards appeared, to draw this country into co-operation with its old ally against its old foe. The Convention had proceeded, with singular indifference to American rights, to clothe their representative with extraordinary powers. He not only commissioned American citizens, but at once authorised French consuls throughout the United States to constitute themselves a court of admiralty for adjudicating upon such prizes as French cruizers, or those operating under his commissions, might bring into American ports! This sublime assurance ere long was aggravated by

[1] Lafayette was then a fugitive from France. As the head of the army he had protested against the reign of terror and Jacobinical overthrow of the Constitution. He had to flee before the storm and soon found himself in an Austrian dungeon—a victim of the Jacobinical societies,

Genet's continued refractoriness, until, at length, he presumed to despise and defy Washington's authority and threatened to appeal from him to the people! He actually menaced the Executive with threats of a revolution, if his (Genet's) proceedings were countermanded. The emissary should have been sent in chains to France.

News arrived in New York of the declaration of war by France against Great Britain five days prior to the French minister's appearance in Charleston. This news gave Washington much uneasiness. He hastened from Mt. Vernon to Philadelphia, summoning a Cabinet council, determined to place this country in an attitude of strict *neutrality*. Such an attitude, in the face of the powerful sympathy existing in all the States for France and hate of Great Britain, was calculated to excite Gallic partizans fiercely. The decree of neutrality issued April 22d, 1793, to find anything but a favorable reception at the hands of those friendly to the revolutionists. The proclamation warned citizens to avoid all acts not in consonance with an *impartial neutrality* toward the belligerents; declaring the resolution of the Federal Government not only "not to interpose on behalf of those who might expose themselves to punishment or forfeiture under the law of nations by aiding or abetting either of the belligerents, but to cause all such acts done within the jurisdiction of the United States to be prosecuted in the proper courts." Genet's proceedure in issuing commissions, and in constituting prize courts, was, therefore, in contempt of the Administration; but, sustained by a powerful section of society, a thorough enthusiast in defying all "tyranny" (and every step taken to circumvent his machinations was regarded as a 'tyrannical assumption of authority') reckless of results, the apostle of revolution pursued his audacious game without ceasing. Scarcely a day passed in which some act was not committed calculated to annoy the National authorities.

But, we cannot here trace the course of this madcap, in all its diplomatic and undiplomatic windings. The record of his intrigues, his audacity, his impertinence, his folly would fill a volume. To one immediate result of his labors we may recur.

In the Philadelphia *National Gazette*, edited by Philip Freneau, clerk in the State Department, Genet and the "opposition" found a most available instrument of incendiarism and disaffection. Previous to the arrival of the French embassador it had been distinguished for its "war on the monocrats," as Jefferson approvingly termed it, and day by day grew in virulence toward the Administration in whose employ he remained. His aim was especially to shake confidence in Hamilton's financial measures and to alarm the people of the monarchical tendencies of the Government. Washington, as the head of Government, was not spared. His name and measures were traduced; his integrity questioned; his devotion to liberty derided. So virulent became its course after the arrival of Genet, that the President, in an interview with the Secretary of State, insinuated that Freneau ought to be discharged from Government employ, not alone because of his base defamation of the Administration, but for the additional reason that, in his position as translating clerk, Freneau obtained much secret and valuable information which he used to the detriment of the State The malignant journalist was not discharged nevertheless. "*That*, I would not do," said Jefferson in his "Ana" of confidential disclosures published after his decease. His excuse was that the *Gazette* had saved the Constitution, then in danger of subversion by the monarchists! [If Jefferson sincerely loved Washington, as we have every reason to believe he did, must it therefore be said that he showed his greater love for his country in keeping Washington's libeller in his employ and confidence because Freneau had "saved the Constitution"? If Jefferson's biographers will insist upon *this* construction they must accept the inevitable conclusion, i. e.: that Washington was one of the enemies of the Constitution. This bare inference, now that we have the full light of history upon those times—times which, even more than the seven years' war, 'tried men's souls'—proves how absurd were Jefferson's "apprehensions" regarding the monarchical sympathies of his adversaries.]

Washington's great sin was in throwing his august influence across the path of the disintegrators of society and government, then as now known as the champions of State Rights; and when he sought to repress the spirit of license and French infidelity which threatened all order and law with destruction, he committed, in the eyes of these "champions of the people," an outrage too great for forgiveness.[1]

The Frenchman's gold flowed freely in all channels where it could breed corruption. He sought and obtained advances from the United States Government on the debt due to France—all of which he disbursed with the power and irresponsibility of an Emperor. Jacobin clubs flourished; democratic societies spread like a leprosy on the body politic; "opposition journals," cherished and fostered by the French partizans, and countenanced by the faction inimical to Hamilton's financial measures, soon joined their influence to hurry the country into a war with Great Britain. Neutrality was assailed with unceasing rancor and "Federal usurpation" was a term of constant use.

In all of this storm of passion, prejudice and folly, Genet rode, the master spirit. His influence was supreme. He was the Eolus who tapped the mountain and loosed the winds, which, with omnipotent enthusiasm, he conceived were to sweep away all opposition. Disgusted, annoyed and alarmed at the marplot's power for mischief, Washington at length determined to rid the country of his presence. To this end he succeeded in obtaining from his Cabinet an assent to his wish

---

[1] Washington took these persecutions calmly though at times he expressed his annoyance at their insolence. So long as he continued in office they did not cease. Freneau and his echoes, thoroughly demoralized by their anarchical principles, left no stone unturned to give the great and good man pain. As late as 1796, writing to Jefferson of these 'democratic' persecutions, he said:

"Accused of being the enemy of America, and subject to the influence of a foreign country, and to prove which every act of my administration is tortured, and the grossest and most insidious misrepresentations of them made by giving one side only of a subject, and that too in such exaggerated and indecent terms as could be scarcely applied to a negro, to a notorious defaulter, or even to a common pickpocket."

It has been the fortune of many eminent men to be thus calumniated by those incapable of appreciating virtue and unselfish patriotism. That Washington did not escape is to encourage others less august to continue in well doing even against the aspersions of their generation: history will do them justice.

for Genet's recal. Jefferson, Minister of State, was called upon to prepare the papers in the case and did so with great good judgment, forwarding to the French Assembly documents setting forth the irregularity of the embassador's conduct in such terms as, eventually, effected the purpose required. Genet was recalled in January, 1794.

Pending an answer to this demand for his recal the indefatigable revolutionist set on foot two expeditions—one for the conquest of Florida, organized in South Carolina, and one for the conquest of New Orleans, organized in Kentucky. Government was soon apprised of these criminal enterprises, which seemed to excel in insolence all previous craft of the French Conspirator. It was ascertained that four agents of Genet had gone West and South, late in the year 1793, to carry out his projects of conquest. These men were empowered to give commissions, to enlist men, to make contracts for supplies, and, in event of success, even to make terms with the Spanish authorities. In the renowned George Rogers Clarke the Conspirator found, unfortunately for that patriot's memory, a man to lead the Kentucky army of invasion. Says his biographer:

"The insolent Frenchman, Genet—supported, it must be confessed, by some of our own statesmen high in station—attempted to establish a proconsulship in the United States, and to reduce our country to the rank of a mere satellite of the French Republic, George Rogers Clarke accepted at his hand a commission of Major General in the armies of France, and Commander-in-Chief of an expedition to be organized in violation of the laws of his country, and in defiance of the proclamation of Washington, for the purpose of attacking the Spanish provinces in the South. A proclamation, which, it is to be hoped, was not Clarke's composition, was issued in his name, offering the plunder of an inoffensive people as a bribe to the reckless adventurers of the West to enlist under the tri-colored flag. A counter-revolution in France, however, saved Clarke from the disgrace of carrying out this programme, and merging the character of a patriot soldier in that of a filibustering adventurer. The party that had been raised to power in Paris by the revolution of Thermidor disavowed all the acts of Genet and his agents, and annulled the commissions granted by him; and Clarke again sank back into the obscurity from which he had thus been for a short time elevated."

This is but an unsatisfactory reference to that interesting era in Kentucky history. The same writer says truly: "Kentucky was at that time, a hot bed of intrigues and intriguers. We do not believe a country can be named whose history reveals such an amount of secret and underhand dealing. Her whole early history, between the year 1783 and the breaking out of the late war with England, consists, when closely examined, of one perplexing mass of secret machinations and treasonable and dishonorable intrigues. One of the most deeply implicated in many of these was that political and military Proteus, General James Wilkinson, whose character and career is even yet a mystery."

When made aware of these filibustering devices Washington acted promptly for their suppression. In reference to that against New Orleans, Jefferson, as Secretary of State, at once was directed by Washington to communicate with the Governor of Kentucky (Isaac Shelby), desiring him to use all lawful means for obstructing and preventing the expedition; while General Knox, Secretary of War, also wrote to say that, if such preventive means should fail, it was the President's wish that effectual military force should be employed to stay the expedition. The Governor's reply to the communications illustrates the turbulent and independent spirit which animated the Western people. While, in convention assembled, they had not hesitated to *demand* of Congress, in language both indecorous and dictatorial, the immediate and unconditional opening of the Mississippi river (then controlled by Spanish possession of its mouth), they had not refrained to show their contempt of the General Government by threats of secession, by encouraging, in their midst, the spirit of sedition and by aiding, openly, the several conspiracies hatched for the dismemberment of the Union and the erection of a new power in the West. Governor Shelby, after confessing his knowledge of the expedition against New Orleans, said:

"I have great doubts, even if they do not attempt to carry their plan into execution, (provided they manage their business with prudence,) whether there is any legal authority to restrain or punish them, at least before they have actually accomplished it: for, it is lawful for any one citizen of this State to leave it—it is equally so for any number of them to do it. It is also lawful to carry with them any quantity of provisions, arms, ammunition, and if the act is lawful in itself, there is nothing but the particular intention with which it is done, that can make it unlawful. But I know of no law which inflicts a punishment on intention only; or any criterion by which to decide what would be sufficient evidence of that intention, if it was a proper subject for legal censure.

"I shall, upon all occasions, be averse to the exercise of any power which I do not consider myself as clearly and explicitly invested with; much less would I assume power to exercise it against men whom I consider as friends and brethren, in favor of a man whom I view as an enemy and a tyrant. I shall also feel but little inclination to take an active part in punishing or restraining any of my fellow citizens for a supposed intrusion only, to gratify or remove the fears of the Minister of a Prince who openly withholds from us an invaluable right, and who secretly instigates against us a most savage and cruel enemy."[1]

From the hour of Wilkinson's appearance among them the people of the Western territories had cherished ideas of independence and empire not in consonance with loyalty to the Union and the Constitution; and when the agents of Genet were made to play upon their passions and their lust for dominion they were less inclined than ever to submit to orders from the departments of the National Government. To show the extent and motive of the intrigues instigated by the Minister we may recur to the address of the Jacobin club of Philadelphia, in January, 1794, directed to the inhabitants of Louisiana. It was headed:

"LIBERTY, EQUALITY.

"The Freemen of France to their Brothers in Louisiana:

"2d year of the French Republic."

These "Freemen of France" comprised many American citizens, although members of that Jacobin club. The address, in impassioned language, strove to stir up revolution against Spanish domination. It encouraged the idea of complete independence and empire. We quote its close:

"You quiver, no doubt, with indignation; you feel in your hearts the desire of deserving the honorable appellation of Freemen, but the fear of not being assisted and of failing in your attempt deadens your zeal. Dismiss such apprehensions: know ye, that your brethren the French, who have attacked with success the Spanish Government in Europe,

[1] How nearly this corresponds in sentiment to the language of the Governor of Kentucky in April, 1861, in answer to the President's call for troops to suppress insurrection!

will in a short time present themselves on your coasts with naval forces; that the republicans of the Western portion of the United States are ready to come down the Ohio and Mississippi in company with a considerable number of French republicans, and to rush to your assistance under the banners of France and Liberty; and that you have every assurance of success. Therefore, inhabitants of Louisiana, show who you are; prove that you have not been stupified by despotism, and that you have retained in your breasts French valor and intrepidity; demonstrate that you are worthy of being free and independent, because we do not solicit you to unite yourselves with us, but to seek your own freedom, when you shall have the sole control of your actions, you will be able to adopt a republican constitution, and being assisted by France so long as your weakness will not permit you to protect or defend yourselves, it will be in your power to unite voluntarily with her and your neighbors—the United States—forming with these two republics an alliance which will be the liberal basis on which, henceforth, shall stand our mutual political and commercial interests. Your country will derive the greatest advantages from so auspicious a revolution; and the glory with which you will cover yourselves will equal the prosperity which you will secure for yourselves and descendants. Screw up your courage, Frenchmen of Louisiana. Away with pusillanimity—ça ira—ça ira—audaces fortuna juvat."

This inflamatory document was distributed by Genet's agents throughout all the territory; it was read by all and created, as might have been expected, much sensation. August de la Chaise, a native of Louisiana, was Genet's chief emissary in promoting the Kentucky invasion, though Clarke was to have been commander-in-chief of the expedition. De la Chaise was a person of winning manners, of inconquerable zeal and chivalric devotion to the cause of "liberty and equality," and he labored during the winter of 1793–4 with consummate address, to avert the consequences threatened by Washington's determined action.

After the reception of Governor Shelby's refusal to enforce the Admistration's orders Washington took steps to arrest the expedition Major-General Anthony Wayne, then "Commander-in-Chief" of the regular army,[1] was pressing his event-

[1] The "regular army," then denominated "the Legion of the United States," consisted of one Major-General, four Brigadiers and their several staffs, the necessary commissioned officers and five thousand one hundred and twenty non-commissioned officers and privates! With this army Wayne was expected to sustain, and did so, the fortunes of the Republic in the Great West.

ful campaign against the savages of the North-west Territory. He was at once instructed to use military force in order to prevent any passage down the river of the armed host. For that purpose he fully garrisoned Fort Massac, on the Ohio, (Kentucky side,) thirty-eight miles above its mouth. Wayne also was instructed to hold a body of troops ready for service at his headquarters at Hobson's Choice, near Cincinnati. All this argued Washington's determination to use every means in his power to sustain the supremacy of his authority.

The expedition fortunately failed; not, as Clarke's biographer assumes, because of the counter-revolution in France, but from the *want of funds* with which to sustain the heavy expense of his revolutionary adventure. Genet, having obtained one large instalment of the debt due from the United States to the French Government—to the *Crown* of France—sought, in order to obtain funds for his Spanish conquest, to cajole Hamilton into accepting drafts for the instalments due in 1794–95. But, the Treasurer had no idea of placing funds in the trick ster's hands to be employed against the peace and good faith of the Government. He replied that, in his view, the amount due in 1794 already had been paid; while any payment of the instalment of 1795 must depend upon the success of loans yet to be negotiated in Europe—an answer too conclusive for offensc even to the now thoroughly exasperated French partisans, whose dislike of Washington, and hate of Hamilton, did not abate with their success, the first in preserving the country in its attitude of neutrality and the second in consummating his plans of finance. The one saved the honor of the country by protecting its dignity and asserting its power; the other saved the credit of the country by a vitalization of its finances to a degree deemed incredible even by the most able minds of the age. That these true patriots should have been the subjects of calumnies unstinted may well excite our surprise.[1]

[1] We have given Washington's estimate of this "opposition," but may subjoin, as more fully illustrative of the feeling of the French faction toward him, an extract from Tom Paine's "Letter to George Washington," written and published in Paris in the Summer of 1793, after reception of the President's Proclamation of Neutrality:

"Elevated to the chair of the Presidency you assumed the merit of every thing

Upon the failure of the Kentucky expedition De la Chaise addressed the democratic society of Lexington a note[1] from which we learn the full measure of the conspiracy contemplated. He said:

"Citizens: Unforeseen events, the effects of causes which it is unnecessary here to develop, have stopped the march of two thousand brave Kentuckians, who, strong in their courage, in the justice of their rights, in the purity of their cause, and in the general assent of their fellow-citizens, and convinced of the brotherly dispositions of the Louisianians, waited only for their orders to go and take away, by the irresistible power of their arms, from those despotic usurpers the Spaniards, the possession of the Mississippi, secure for their country the navigation of it, break the chains of the Americans and of their French brethren in the province of Louisiana, hoist up the flag of liberty in the name of the French republic, and lay the foundations of the prosperity and happiness of two nations destined by nature to be but one, and so situated as to be the most happy in the universe.

"Citizens: The greater the attempts you have made toward the success of that expedition, the more sensible you must be of the impediments which delay its execution, and the more energetic should your efforts be toward procuring new means of success. There is one from which I expect the greatest advantages and which may be decisive—that is, an address to the National Convention, or to the Executive Council of France. In the name of my countrymen in Louisiana, in the name of your own interest, I dare once more ask you this new proof of patriotism.

---

to yourself, and the natural ingratitude of your constitution began to appear. You commenced your Presidential career by encouraging and swallowing the grossest adulation, you travelled America from one end to the other, to put yourself in the way of receiving it. You have as many addresses in your chest as James the IId. Monopolies of every kind marked your administration, almost in the moment of its commencement. The lands obtained in the Revolution were lavished upon partisans: the interest of the disbanded soldier was sold to the speculator: injustice was acted under the pretense of faith; and the Chief of the army became the patron of the fraud.

"And as to you, Sir, treacherous in private friendship, and a hypocrite in public life, the world will be puzzled to decide whether you are an apostate or impostor; whether you have abandoned good principles, or whether you ever had any."

Jefferson had strenuously pressed Tom Paine for Post Master General in Washington's Cabinet. The President's refusal to accept the reckless infidel's services doubtless had something to do with his hostility. Jefferson remained, to the last, a warm friend of Paine.

[1] See American State Papers, vol. i., page 931.

"Being deprived of my dearest hopes, and of the pleasure, after an absence of fourteen years and a proscription of three, of returning to the bosom of my family, my friends, and my countrymen, I have only one course to follow—that of going to France and expressing to the representatives of the French people the cry, the general wish of the Louisianians to become part of the French republic—informing them, at the same time, of the most ardent desire which the Kentuckians have had, and will continue to have for ever, to take the most active part in any undertaking tending to open to them the free navigation of the Mississippi.[1]

"The French republicans, in their sublime constitutional act, have proffered their protection to all those nations who may have the courage to shake off the yoke of tyranny. The Louisianians have the most sacred right to it. They are French, but have been sacrificed to despotism by arbitrary power. The honor, the glory, the duty of the National Convention is to grant them their powerful support.

"Every petition or plan relative to that important object would meet with the highest consideration. An address from the Democratic Society of Lexington would give it a greater weight.

"Accept, Citizens, the farewell, not the last, of a brother who is determined to sacrifice everything in his power for the liberty of his country, and the prosperity of the generous inhabitants of Kentucky. Salut en la patrie. AUGUSTE LA CHAISE."

The agent had no opportunity of serving again in the "cause of Kentucky." With Genet's recal, and Washington's firm repressive policy, nothing was left for the revolutionists in Kentucky but submission to the Executive will.

The Florida expedition also was abortive from the want of means. The Governors of Georgia and South Carolina co-operated with Washington to prevent American citizens from embarking in the invasion. A number of arrests were made of Genet's emissaries and the rendezvous in Georgia broken up. As late as April, 1794, a force of French troops landed on the Spanish side of the river St. Mary—the van of the army of conquest; but, none others followed. Genet's recal, and the absorption of funds in other more pressing directions, compelled the French National Convention soon to give over the idea

[1] Marshall states that intercepted letters showed several members of the French National Convention to have approved of the Minister's scheme of conquest. M. Genet was, as Major-General to be Commander-in-Chief of all forces raised on the American continent. The scheme was not given over by the French for several years—though nothing more was done to accomplish its ambitious ends.

of absorbing American territory Marshall in his "Life of Washington" says: "This intelligence (of the two expeditions) seemed to render a further forbearance incompatible with the dignity, perhaps with the safety of the United States. The question of superseding the diplomatic functions of M. Genet, and depriving him of the privileges attached to that character, was brought before the Cabinet (January, 1794) and a message to Congress was prepared, communicating these transactions, and avowing a determination to adopt that measure within — days, unless, in the meantime, one or the other House should signify the opinion that it was not advisable so to do. In this state, the business was arrested by receiving a letter from Mr. Morris (our Minister to France) announcing, officially, the recal of this rash minister (Genet)."

His successor, M. Fauchent, arrived in Philadelphia, February, 1794. Genet left for France, at once, but not until he had received congratulations, addresses of sympathy and other marks of respect from numerous public societies and individuals. The "opposition" ever regarded him as a martyr in the cause of Liberty! Many, however, of those who at first had favored his principles and his projects, became disgusted at his course. The indignity heaped, by the foreigner, upon Washington and his Administration brought its reward of indignation from thousands of those who, though French partizans and members of the democratic societies, were, nevertheless, too patriotic to sustain French assumption at the expense of American self-respect. Washington's conduct throughout the ministry of Genet and his successor, was admirable. To his great prudence, his firmness, his power to breast the popular storm, excited by the Minister, did the country owe its second preservation. Had it made cause with France, it must have been involved in the fearful struggle which shook Europe to its base.

The "Whiskey Insurrection" which Washington was called upon to suppress by force during the latter part of the year 1794, was one of the legitimate results of Genet's machinations. Many writers will have it that the turbulent uprising in Western Pennsylvania was due alone to the excise; but, it is a narrow view of the case. The *first* fruit of Genet's procedure was to bring odium upon the National Government—to render his partisans disobedient citizens. The 'democratic societies' were but the Jacobin clubs reproduced: though organized by the anti-Federalists professedly to oppose what Jefferson called the Monocrats, these societies were ultra "State Rights" champions and proved their disloyalty to the General Government in every conceivable way. They contemned Washington, hated Hamilton, scorned John Adams, abused Marshall and assailed Jay with extreme malignity. The Pennsylvania troubles received an impetus from the excise, but their exciting cause was the 'democratic societies,' their leaders were 'democratic' leaders, their ultimate aim was the independence of Western Pennsylvania and the formation of a Confederacy or a league of States upon the plan of the Kentucky secessionists—to unite with France in opening the Mississippi, and to form part of a French American republic, or to remain in alliance with such a republic yet retaining their State independency. The insurrection had been brewing for several years; it was simply one eruption of that conspiracy concocted by the disunionists and afterwards directed by the French ministers, to override the General Government and to denationalise the national existence. The party there born of the spirit of turbulence, has existed to this day, and doubtless will continue to exist so long as there are demagogues to fan the flames of incendiarism under the hollow pretense of "defending and perpetuating popular rights." In a people's government like ours, where there are knaves to lead there are fools to follow; and, for the coming century, we may expect to see "popular" outbreaks every decade. With a central Executive strong enough to maintain its ascendency and to enforce its authority we have nothing to fear; but, if it ever should come to pass that our National authorities are powerless to resist and to suppress disloyal combinations our liberties are gone and a mob must rule. Let American citizens, then, guard well their liberties, and preserve them by sustaining the Government and the Laws against all enemies.

THE ALIEN AND SEDITION TROUBLES.

It is not possible for the people of this generation to conceive of the excitement in social and political circles during the terms of Washington, Adams and Jefferson. Discontent arising from State enmity of the new National Government which had absorbed their supremacy in its own; opposition to laws of Congress not acceptable to people of certain sections; hostility to the schemes of finance pressed to a successful initiation by Alexander Hamilton; insane partisan sympathy for France and hate of Great Britain; the uprising of a party implacable in its opposition to the Federalists, whom it characterized as "Monocrats";—all conspired, during Washington's second term, to create divisions which it took years to heal. In previous papers [see "Whiskey Insurrection" and "Genet's Conspiracy"] we have alluded to the influences at work to unsettle the public mind. After a suppression of the Western discontents and the recal of Genet, the seeds sown by Jacobin clubs and democratic societies spread like thistles and bore fruit prolific of passions, hates and distempered minds. Sympathy for the French revolutionists continued to grow, in spite of Washington's neutrality injunctions. Jefferson, who had, with the beginning of the year 1794, withdrawn from Washington's Cabinet to "contemplate the tranquil growth of his lucerne and potatoes" at Monticello, soon became the recognised head of the opposition. James Madison, James Monroe and Aaron Burr were his partisans. All three cast the weight of their great influence in the scale of the French faction, and inaugurated that hostility to Great Britain which was the fruitful theme of popular discourse for twenty years. They did more: they perfected plans for overthrowing the ascendancy of the Federalists; and the fact that each of the first three were President in turn, and the last Vice President, proves how successfully they manipulated public opinion.

Washington, in his last speech to Congress, August 7th, 1796, said:

"While in our external relations some serious inconveniences and embarrassments have been overcome and others lessened, it is with much pain and deep regret I mention that circumstances of a very unwelcome nature have lately occurred. Our trade has suffered and is suffering extensive injuries in the West Indies from the cruisers and agents of the French Republic; and communications have been received from its minister here, which indicate the danger of a further disturbance of our commerce by its authority; and which are in other respects far from agreeable. It has been my constant, sincere and earnest wish, in conformity with that of our nation, to maintain cordial harmony and a perfectly friendly understanding with that Republic. This wish remains unabated; and I shall persevere in the endeavor to fulfil it to the utmost extent of what shall be consistent with a just and indispensable regard to the rights and honor of our country; nor will I easily cease to cherish the expectation, that a spirit of justice, candor and friendship, on the part of the Republic, will eventually ensure success."

The spirit of "justice, candor and friendship" did not visit the hearts and minds of men intoxicated with a new-found liberty; nor did the existence, in this country, of a powerful party which sustained French interests in opposition to the wishes of the National Administration, serve to lessen the hostility of the French Convention toward the party and policy then supreme. Yet Washington strove to effect a reconciliation by every means in his power short of a virtual surrender to the insane French faction. Early in January, 1797, he requested the Secretary of State, Mr. Pickering, to address a letter to the newly appointed Minister to France, C. C. Pinckney, reviewing the then freshly reiterated allegations of M. Adet, French Minister to the United States, made against the policy and acts of Washington's Administration,[1] "exam-

---

[1] These allegations were made by M. Adet in a letter addressed to Mr. Pickering —a copy of which letter was sent, at once, by the Frenchman, to the notorious *Aurora* newspaper (Philadelphia) for publication! Its preparation and publication were designed to influence the then pending Presidential election, hoping to

ining and reviewing the same, and accompanying the statement with a collection of papers and letters relating to transactions therein adverted to."

This letter was prepared with great care and dispatched by Mr. Pinckney. He arrived in France only to be ordered, with his letter, out of French territory! Mr. Monroe, the retiring Minister, was addressed, at the audience of leave with M. Barras, President of the Directory, in these extraordinary terms:

"The French Republic hopes that the successors of Columbus, of Raleigh, and of Penn, ever proud of their liberty, will never forget that they owe it to France. * * * * In their wisdom, they will weigh the magnanimous benevolence of the French people with the artful caresses of perfidious designers, who meditate to draw them back to their ancient slavery. Assure, Mr. Minister, the good American people that, like them, we adore liberty; that they will always have our esteem, and that they will find in the French people the republican generosity which knows how to accord peace, as it knows how to make its sovereignty respected.

"As to you, Mr. Minister Plenipotentiary, you have fought for the principles, you have known the true interests of your country. Depart with our regrets. We give up, in you, a representative of America, and we retain the remembrance of the citizen whose personal qualities honor that title."

This insulting address was followed by other steps which left no alternative but to swallow it in humiliation or to resent it. John Adams, as Washington's successor, convened Congress in extra session May 15th, 1797. His opening speech to the two Houses made this reference to the attitude of France:

"The speech of the President (M. Barras) discloses sentiments more alarming than the refusal of a minister, because more dangerous to our independence and union; and, at the same time, studiously marked with indignities toward the Government of the United States. It evinces a disposition to separate the people from their Government; to persuade them that they have different affections, principles and interests from those of their fellow citizens, whom they themselves have chosen to manage their common concerns, and thus to produce divisions fatal to our peace. Such attempts ought to be repelled with a decision that

---

strengthen the French party and thus elect Thomas Jefferson as Washington's successor. The publication was an outrage upon all diplomatic usage; and yet the act was in perfect keeping with the insolent course uniformly pursued toward the Administration by the French embassadors.

shall convince France and the world, that we are not a degraded people, humiliated under a colonial spirit of fear, and sense of inferiority, fitted to be the miserable instruments of foreign influence, and regardless of national honor, character and interest."

Adams, doubtless influenced by the tremendous outcry raised by the French partizans, and adopting also the wishes of the Vice President, Thomas Jefferson, determined upon dispatching a special mission to France, whose object he announced to be "to dissipate umbrages, remove prejudices, rectify errors, and adjust all differences, by a treaty between the two powers." Washington, from his retirement, beheld this state of affairs with alarm—apparently seeing in the conduct of the French Directory a design to force this country into the embraces of France, thus to render the American Republic its ally in the tremendous war which followed the downfall of the old règime. "Things cannot," he wrote to a friend, "and ought not to remain any longer in their present disagreeable state. Nor should the idea that the Government and the people have different views, be suffered any longer to prevail at home or abroad; for it is not only injurious to us, but dirgraceful also, that a Government constituted as ours is, should be administered contrary to their interest, if the fact be so."

He did not conceive that any good would come of the mission. "It is hardly to be expected" he further wrote, "that the Directory will acknowledge its errors and tread back its steps immediately. This would announce at once that there has been precipitancy and injustice in the measures they have pursued." He judged truly.

The three ministers extraordinary named—Pinckney, Marshall and Gerry—assembled in Paris October 4th, 1797, but were not recognised in their official capacity. Their report[1] revealed at once the baseness and the insincerity of the French authorities. Talleyrand, through his secret agents—many of whom he ever employed—demanded a heavy sum as a *douceur* preliminary to the opening of negotiations! Several attempts to obtain recognition and to open the conferences failed; at each interview the agent of the French Minister of State in-

[1] American State Papers, vols. iii., iv.

sisted upon his bribe. Irving thus chronicles the conduct of the mission:

"On the 20th of October, the same subject was resumed in the apartments of the plenipotentiary, and on this occasion, beside the secret agent, an intimate friend of Talleyrand was present. The expunging of the passages in the President's speech was again insisted on, and it was added that, after that, money was the principal object. 'We must have money—a great deal of money!' were his words.

"At a third conference, October 21st, the sum was fixed at 32,000,000 francs (6,400,000 dollars), as a loan secured on the Dutch contributions, and 250,000 dollars in the form of a *douceur* to the Directory.

"At a subsequent meeting, October 27th, the same secret agent said: 'Gentlemen, you mistake the point, you say nothing of the money you are to give—you make no offer of money—on that point you are not explicit.' 'We are explicit enough,' replied the American envoys. 'We will not give you one farthing; and before coming here, we should have thought such an offer as you now propose, would have been regarded as a mortal insult.'

"On this indignant reply, the wily agent intimated that if they would only pay, by way of fees, just as they would to a lawyer, who should plead their cause, the sum required for the private use of the Directory, they might remain at Paris until they should receive further orders from America as to the loan required for Government.

"Being inaccessible to any such disgraceful and degrading propositions, the envoys remained several months in Paris unaccredited, and finally returned at separate times, without an official discussion of the object of their mission."

Thus were the doors closed against a settlement; while the Directory, further to exasperate the people of this country, as well as to strengthen the French party in America, passed a decree confiscating *neutral* vessels and their cargoes if any portion of their loads should consist of British fabrics or productions! This struck a severe if not fatal blow at the commerce of the United States, then the "great neutral carriers of the world."

War now seemed inevitable, and preparations were made accordingly. The great mass of American intelligence stood by the Government, and were prepared to resent French arrogance to the last. Washington—who had sought Mt. Vernon, there to pass his remaining years in repose—was made Commander-in-Chief, an appointment seemingly called for by the alarming emergency. Not only were the French to be met on land and sea, but the French party in the States, strong in numbers, powerful in leaders, moved by a common sympathy for the interests of France and hate of the Federalists, were to be taught loyalty and forced to sustain the war measures. Washington alone was the nation's hope. Hamilton, writing to him to beg his acceptance of the position to which President Adams had called him, said: "I use the liberty which my attachment to you and the public authorizes, to offer you my opinion that you should not decline the appointment. It is evident that the public satisfaction at it is lively and universal. It is not to be doubted that the circumstances will give an additional spring to the public mind, will tend much to unite, and will facilitate the measures which the conjuncture requires."

Irving adds:

"It was with a heavy heart that Washington found his dream of repose once more interrupted; but his strong fidelity to duty would not permit him to hesitate. He accepted the commission, however, with the condition that he should not be called into the field until the army was in a situation to require his presence; or it should seem indispensable by the urgency of circumstances."

Hamilton was named by Washington second in command, and C. C. Pinckney third. General Knox was named fourth, but refused to serve under his juniors—a point of etiquette which the veteran companion-in-arms of Washington lived to regret. Every arrangement was made during the Summer of 1798 to place the troops, called into the field, in a state of high efficiency.

Yet, affairs "hung fire," greatly to Washington's astonishment. His commissions were issued so slowly, and the Government seemed so apathetic, that the Commander-in-Chief was much perplexed and chagrined. The solution of the mystery was afterwards given in the fact that secret overtures of settlement were being made. Talleyrand, with his usual sagacity and non-committalism, becoming alarmed at the belligerent attitude of the United States, after badgering Mr. Gerry, and courting the offices of several "democratic" but unofficial emissaries, wrote to the *secretary* of the French Minister at the Hague, intimating that, should the United States send a plenipotentiary to France, to adjust differences, he would unquestionably be received "with the respect due to the representative of a free, independent and powerful nation." This information the secretary at once communicated to the American Minister to Holland, William Vans Murray, who, in turn, hastened to remit it to the President. of the United States. Mr. Adams, rejoiced at this offering for an accommodation, laid the letter before the Senate along with his nomination of Mr. Murray as minister plenipotentiary to the French Republic (Feb. 18th, 1799). Two others by the pressure of the Senate were added, viz.: Oliver Ellsworth and Patrick Henry, but Mr. Henry declining, Mr. Wm. R. Davis was substituted. These three envoys, after various and somewhat inexplicable plots and counter plots, succeeded in effecting a treaty, which was signed Sept. 3d, 1800. Mr. Adams' conduct throughout the affair brought down upon him a storm of censure from all parties—censures which, even to this day, have weight with those who essay to pronounce upon this patriot's merits.

All this is but preliminary to an understanding of the theme of this paper, namely, the Alien and Sedition Laws' excitement, and their consequents, the Kentucky resolutions of 1798.

The French partisans were variously termed "anti-Federalists," "Republicans," "French Democrats," &c. All these most strenuously opposed the attitude of defiance at length shown to France. They clamored in public and private against the Federalists for "precipitating a collision;" they disapproved the called session of Congress, May, 1797; they organized their forces, during that session, for a determined resistance to all war measures; they opened the batteries of the press with a virulence unexampled in the history of free journalism; they schemed, intrigued, slandered, falsified; played the sycophant or the censor as the occasion required; and contributed, by all means in their power, to stir up the most violent elements of opposition to the Administration. On the part of Jefferson the hostility shown sprang quite as much from his detestation of the Federalists as for sympathy with France. Patriot as he was, he could but denounce Talleyrand's treatment of our Ministers; yet, in the preparation for resenting that treatment and the wrongs inflicted upon our commerce by French vessels of war and French privateers, the patriot was swallowed up in the Virginia politician. In the train of evils to flow from a war, he beheld an increased public debt, increased taxation, increased war establishment and increased list of army officials. The latter must contribute to the increased strength of the Federalists. These were good issues with which to go before the people, and they were used to the utmost. His partisans, in and out of Congress, marshaled by Burr, Madison, Gallatin, Nicholas, the New York Livingstons, Findley, Giles, Smith of Maryland, and others, labored assiduously to fix a stigma upon all proceedings looking to the creation of a war establishment under any pretext; while, in Jay's treaty with Great Britain, (which they had bitterly opposed and denounced in all its stages, before and after its confirmation,) they beheld at once the sole cause and a justification of French irritation.

From this opposition sprang a feeling of resentment in the breasts of the war party something akin to that felt in the Northern States against the "copperhead" faction of 1863. This hostility of the opposition soon resolved itself into a malignant persecution of men and measures, from the President to the humblest citizen. The *Aurora*, of Philadelphia, edited by Bache, a grandson of Benjamin Franklin, fairly blazed with the lightning of its wrath against the Federalists and their "accursed policy"; it stole State secrets, pryed into Cabinet mysteries, invented stories at will of the most outrageous character; and never, for a single issue, intermitted its abuse of all concerned in sustaining the dignity of our flag.[1] It was the recognised organ of the anti-Republicans; and, as the people,

[1] This sheet wrote thus on Washington's retiring from office: "The man who is the source of all the misfortunes of our country is this day reduced to a level with his fellow-citizens and is no longer possessed of power to multiply evils upon the United States. If ever there was a period for rejoicing this is the moment." And much more in the same spirit. His sin, in this journal's estimation, seemed to consist in the fact that Washington was the bulwark behind which the Federalists were intrenched. The *Aurora* then was Jefferson's accredited exponent, and so remained during the life of Bache (who died in August, 1798), and of his successor, James Duane, an Irishman, under whose auspices its malignancy and powers of vituperation measurably increased.

during 1798, began to centre more closely around the President, to resent the indignities heaped on their country by France, it unbottled new vials of wrath and gall. The *Aurora* was also the organ of Adet, the French Minister, and received from his hand important documents which that functionary had communicated to our Government, and which alone held the right of their publication. These State documents the newspaper would parade before the people even before our Government had considered them! They were thus published in the spirit of arrogance and desire for discord which had rendered M. Genet so offensive to Washington's Administration; and all partisans of the French faction, instead of resenting the insult designed to the National authorities, by the foreigner, applauded. This we instance as one of many acts which demonstrated the abasement of that public sentiment which was arraigned as the "opposition" to Adams' war measures. That there were many good men and true patriots among those who opposed all steps and acts favoring an appeal to arms is undeniable; but, the leading men of the factionists were demagogues who intrigued for power more from want of principle than from any well defined system of opinions. The *Aurora* found echoes in several other journals—the *Examiner*, of Richmond, the *Argus*, of New York, the *Chronicle*, of Boston, &c., all of which became arsenals of assault on the dominant party. What their "principles" were—if such it be slaimed they had—we learn from Jefferson's letter to Mazzei, the Italian patriot. Under date of January 25th, 1797, he wrote:

"Our political situation is wonderfully changed since you left us. Instead of that noble love of liberty and that republican government which triumphantly carried us through the war, an Anglo-monarchio-aristocratic party has arisen, whose avowed object is to draw over us the substance, as they have already done the forms, of the British Government. Nevertheless, the principal body of our citizens remain faithful to their republican principles. All our proprietors of lands are friendly to these principles, as also the great mass of talents. Against us are the Executive power, the Judiciary power (two out of three branches of our Government), all the officers of the Government, all who are seeking office, all timid men who prefer the calms of despotism to the tempestuous sea of liberty, British merchants and Americans trading on British capital, speculators and those interested in the public funds, banks invented for purposes of corruption and for assimilating us in all things, rotten as well as sound, to the British model. I should give you a fever were I to name the apostates who have embraced these heresies, men who were Samsons in the field and Solomons in the council,[1] but whose hair has been shorne off by the harlot of England. They would wrest from us that liberty which we have obtained with so much peril and labor, but we shall preserve it." &c., &c.

This remarkable indictment was drawn up by Jefferson while yet in Washington's confidence; but, its most unexpected publication by Mazzei, alienated Washington from a person who could so play at once the friend and the foe. The letter brought forth volumes of controversy, and served to intensify animosities rapidly growing against the French partisans, who were regarded by the Federalists as little else than anarchists and disintegrators of Government, alike dangerous to morals and to liberty.

The Paris *Moniteur*, in publishing the above letter, used it as an evidence of the hostily of the Government (Federal) but as a proof that the *people* in America were with France. It said: "there is no doubt it (the action of the French Government in ordering Mr. Pinckney out of their territory) will give rise in the United States to discussions which may afford a triumph to the party of good republicans, the Friends of France." This expression discloses the design of all French intrigue in this country, and the cause of the overbearing insolence toward our authorities practiced by Genet, Fauchent and Adet. Assuming that the people made the Government and that the people were with them, the French authorities therefore were

---

[1] Washington is here specifically referred to. In his (Jefferson's) letter to Madison, (March 27th, 1796.) he had said of the President: "I wish that his honesty and his political errors may not furnish a second occasion to exclaim 'Curse on his virtues, they have ruined his country.'"

justified in setting the Federal authorities at defiance! Never, for one moment, did the French ministers intermit their endeavors to precipitate a collision between the people and their Administration; and in this nefarious work History has it to record that they received the utmost sympathy and co-operation from Jefferson, Burr, &c., which it was *politic* to bestow. No whitewashing of their memories ever will cover this stain on their escutcheon.

Affairs became so dangerously exciting, and the French faction so irreconcilably malignant, that Congress, early in 1798, began to consider the necessity of a Sedition Law, to punish the incendiarism of the press, and to protect the authorities and leading men from the effect of its most shocking libels. It was a fact that the most venomous of these journalists were *foreigners*—"unwilling exiles" from their own countries, where they had so outraged society as to be compelled to take refuge in America. Their most active supporters also were foreigners—persons who, having been driven from Europe by the storm of revolution sweeping over that continent, had flown to America to add greatly to the opposition prevailing against the constituted authorities under the guise of a hate of Federalism. These refugees, chiefly from Ireland and France, almost to a man were hostile to the neutral attitude of the Government, and everywhere formed an element of society turbulent if not dangerous. Against these legislation was proposed—so incensed did the Federalists become at the course pursued by the emigrants. Jefferson, writing to his confidant, Madison, under date of April 28th, 1798, said of the projected legislative action:

"One of the war party, in a fit of unguarded passion, declared some time ago that they would pass a citizen bill, an alien bill and a sedition bill. Accordingly, some days ago, Coit laid a motion on the table for modifying the citizen law. Their threats pointed at Gallatin, and it is believed they will endeavor to mark him by this bill. Yesterday Hillhouse laid on the table of the Senate a motion for giving power to send away suspected aliens. This is understood to be meant for Volney and Collot. But it will not stop there when it gets into a course of execution. There is now only wanting to accomplish the whole declaration before mentioned, a sedition bill, which we shall certainly soon see proposed. The object of that is the suppression of the Whig presses. Bache has been particularly named. That paper, and also Carey's totter for want of subscriptions. We should really exert ourselves to procure them, for if these papers fall, Republicanism will be entirely browbeaten. The popular movement in the Eastern States is checked as we expected, and war addresses are showering in from New Jersey and the great trading towns. However, we still trust that a nearer view of war and a land tax will oblige the great mass of the people to attend. At present the war-hawks talk of Septembrizing, deportation and the examples for quelling sedition set by the French executive. All the firmness of the human mind is now in a state of requisition."

Here we are informed of the acts contemplated, and also have the evidence of Jefferson's anxiety to sustain the two most offensive newspapers. It darkens the halo around the head of the writer of the Declaration of Independence to learn that the author of that glorious instrument became the *patron* of journals too indecent and too revolutionary for admission to respectable circles. The action adverted to quickly followed. As the Constitution secured the right of naturalization and consequent citizenship to foreigners, there remained for Congress only the power to fix the time and terms of qualification to enjoy the constitutional right. This power it exercised by the passage of an act amending the Naturalization law, extending the previous necessary term of residence from five to fourteen years, requiring five years previous declaration of intention to become a citizen instead of three years, as originally stipulated. But, "alien enemies" were not to be admitted to citizenship at all. "A register was to be kept of all aliens resident in the country, who were to report themselves under certain penalties; and in case of application to be naturalized, the certificate of an entry in this register was to be the only proof of residence whenever that residence commenced after the date of this act."

This did not, however, reach the evil most decried, viz.: the residence here of numerous French and Irish emigrants, not citizens, said to entertain designs against the peace of the country, and suspected of, or known to be, in co-operation with external enemies. Hildreth says: "Alarm on this score was by no means groundless. Talleyrand was believed to have acted during the latter part of his residence in the United States as a spy for the French government, and others of the exiled French were objects of a similar suspicion. The late attempts to set on foot French expeditions in Georgia and the West were not forgotten. Davis, the representative from Kentucky, stated that the commissions issued on that occasion were yet in existence, and that a certain Frenchman, resident in Kentucky, through whose hands they had passed, was still very busy in alienating the affection of the people from the United States. Indeed, it was strongly suspected, and probably not without reason, that Volney had not been engaged in exploring the Western country solely with scientific views. Like Micheaux, the botanist, a few years before, he had, perhaps, been employed as a French government agent to obtain information; and possibly too in forming connections of which advantage might be taken in case of a rupture with the United States, to procure a dismemberment from the Union of the trans-Alleghany settlements, and their junction with Louisiana, which it was believed that France already had or soon would re-acquire." To meet the case of these parties a second act was passed, limited to two years in its operation, bestowing upon the President authority to order out of the country all such aliens as he might judge dangerous to the peace and safety of the United States, or suspect to be concerned in any treasonable or secret machinations. This second ordinance, known as the *Alien Act*, was most strenuously opposed in Congress, passing the House by a vote of forty-six to forty. Out of Congress it was received with anathemas loud and ceaseless. It was regarded as an unconstitutional interference with the right secured to the existing States to admit, prior to 1808, the importation or emigration of any such persons as they might think proper; and also as an unconstitutional interference with the right of trial by jury.

A third act also was added to provide for public safety in event of war declared by, or an invasion of, the United States, whereby all resident aliens, natives or citizens of the hostile nation, might, upon a proclamation to that effect (to be issued at the President's discretion) be apprehended, and secured or removed.

These three acts exasperated those inimical to the Administration; but their exasperation was measurably heightened, when, a few days later, Lloyd, Senator from Maryland, brought in his bill to define more precisely the crime of treason, and to define and punish the crime of sedition. The original bill was modified and finally passed, as amended, in the House by the close vote of forty-four to forty-one. As passed it provided: First, that it is a high misdemeanor, punishable by fine, not exceeding five thousand dollars, for any persons to conspire against the Government of the United States to impede the operation of the law, or to commit, advise or attempt to procure any insurrection, riot, unlawful assembly or combination. The second section subjected to a fine, not exceeding two thousand dollars, the publishing of any false, scandalous or malicious writings against the Government of the United States, or either house of Congress, or the President, with intent to defame them or bring them into disrepute, or to excite against them the hatred of the people of the United States, or to stir up sedition, or to excite any unlawful combination for opposing any law of the United States, or to encourage any hostile designs of any foreign nation against the United States. The act was to continue in force until 25th of June, 1800.

In its original shape Alexander Hamilton opposed the act on patriotic and individual grounds. He regarded it as highly exceptionable, and apprehended that it might induce just the evil, civil war, which it was especially intended to avert. "Let us not" said he, "establish tyranny; energy is a very different thing from violence. If we make no false step we shall be eventually united; but, if we push things to extremes, we shall then give to faction body and solidity." These views were quickly proven to be sound; since, in spite of the apparent provocation for this proscriptive legislation, they were so alarmingly effective in their nature, that every class of citizen affected by them united in their condemnation, while the "republican" leaders, the French sympathisers, the society of United Irishmen and the Roman Catholic element—all combined, in one body, to bring odium upon the laws and their makers. So powerfully, indeed, did the enemies of the Administration use the acts that they were made instrumental in exalting Jefferson to the Presidency and Aaron Burr to the Vice Presidency, March 4th, 1801; while the Congress elected to meet Dec. 7th, 1800, showed the Federalists to be heavily in the minority. The Senate stood eighteen "Republicans" to fourteen Federalists; the House sixty-nine "Republicans" to thirty-six Federalists.

Thus sagaciously did the opposition use their opportunities. Though the Alien law was not enforced, and the Sedition law expired, *by limitation*, in June, 1800, the "republican" leaders made the most of the proscriptive principles involved in the acts, fixing upon the Federalists a purpose to circumscribe citizenship and to repress the free utterance of opinion—charges well calculated to consolidate and harmonise the half-dozen turbulent opposition elements which, until that moment, had not decidedly united.

But six prosecutions were made under the Sedition act. As many more were attempted but abandoned. The death of Washington (1799), the peaceful adjustment (1800) of our affairs with France by the advent of the Bonapartists to power; the division in the Federalists' ranks owing to the mingled rashness, folly and implacability of John Adams, and to his war with Alexander Hamilton; the Alien and Sedition laws; the severity of taxation, &c.—all conspired to drive from power a party which gave character to the Government in its most perilous and trying moments, and stamped upon our institutions the features of central, self-sustaining power which alone have perpetuated the Union and made us great as one people.

The excitement engendered during the years 1797–98 was but one manifestation of the *sectional* animosity prevailing between the Northern and the Southern States. New England then was Federalist overwhelmingly; New York and Pennsylvania were nicely balanced, though soon overwhelmingly democratic; Virginia and the South were democratic, or anti-Federalist. It was this growing spirit of local enmity, as well as the general discord prevailing, which induced Washington to accept the Presidency for a second term. Urging him to take the office, Governor Randolph, of Virginia, said that those who had opposed the Federal Constitution from "a hatred of the Union," *never could be reconciled to it;* while others would "push the construction of Federal power to every tenable extreme;" and added that the Republican (anti-Federalist) party had then adopted "the fatal error that the *State Assemblies* were to be resorted to as the engines of correction to the Federal Administration." The "Democratic Societies", already referred to, [see "Whiskey Insurrection"], were positively disloyal to the General Government, but were not more so than the foreign factionists. The opposition, indeed, were so powerful, that Jefferson wrote to Madison (Dec. 1794): "Separation is now near and certain, and determined in the minds of all men." This disunion spirit Washington's great influence was barely able to suppress; and, in preparing his "Farewell Address," this truly great man sought to show the value of Union and the necessity for its preservation. The election which followed really was a contest between those desiring to solidify and to strengthen the Union, and those desiring to render it but the mere creature of convenience, without authority in, and possessing no rights supreme to, the States. This latter section Jefferson represented: he was its candidate for the Presidency (1796), and so nearly succeeded that Adams triumphed only by *three electoral votes* (71 to 68). Had the ballots thrown for Aaron Burr (also a "Republican") been cast for Jefferson, he would have been elected President by twenty-seven majority.[1]

The evidence of Jefferson's antagonism to the Federal idea of the National "compact" ere long came forth in many ways. He labored, however, with extreme caution. Much of his correspondence, now made public, was not designed to see the light; he worked incessantly, both in secret and openly, to accomplish his ambitious political aims—the overthrow of the

[1] The vote of the Electoral College was: John Adams, 71; Thomas Jefferson, 68; Thomas Pinckney, 59; Aaron Burr, 30; Samuel Adams, 15; Oliver Ellsworth, 11; George Clinton, 7; John Jay, 5; James Iredell, 3; George Washington, 2; John Henry, 2; S. Johnson, 2; C. C. Pinckney, 1. Sixteen States voted.

Federalists, the triumph of the "Republicans," and the exaltation of himself to the Presidency. That that *was* his aim, we now have the "cloud of witnesses" which carries conviction.

The history of the Kentucky Resolutions of '98 is as follows: Mr. Jefferson, then Vice President of the United States, was visited at Monticello, in October, 1798, by George Nicholas, of Kentucky, and his brother, Wilson C. Nicholas, soon afterwards chosen United States Senator from Virginia, chiefly through Jefferson's influence. These persons, just from Philadelphia—then the seat of National Government—represented that the leading Republicans in Congress, "finding themselves useless there," being "brow-beaten by a bold and overwhelming majority in that body," had concluded to retire from that field and take a stand in the State Legislatures. Their programme was to reassert the doctrines of State Supremacy, so earnestly struggled for in the Convention which formed the Constitution, and maintained up to that moment by a large body of the people. Their views of government were against centralization, and, for that reason, they had opposed, in their Legislatures, the adoption of the Constitution. Once adopted, however, they were powerless except to triumph over the friends of that Constitution at the ballot box, and then to seek, by legislation, what they had failed to accomplish in Convention—the denationalization of the General Government. But, they labored in vain during Washington's term of office, though, with their numerous popular rallying cries against taxation, against the excise, against Hamilton's banking schemes, against the Jay treaty with Great Britain, and, finally, against the Alien and Sedition laws, they obtained a vantage ground which soon gave them almost unbroken control of the Government for forty years. Jefferson, after canvassing the matter with the Nicholas brothers, finally consented to draw up a set of resolutions embodying the "Republican" idea of State and National relations; these resolutions were to be sanctioned by some State Legislature and sent by such Legislature to other States for action. Being Vice President, ought he to engage in the work proposed, which was especially designed to weaken the strength and to circumscribe the authority of the Government? He had, only in the previous month of June, written to a Virginian, John Taylor, to prove to him the impolicy of any scheme of disunion—of "estimating the separate mass of Virginia and North Carolina with a view to their separate existence." Yet, Jefferson was a politician as well as a patriot; and, seeing the way open for a broad, clear enunciation of doctrines which had in them the elements of popular success, he did not shrink from the responsibility, particularly as he was not to be known as the author of the work. Under a pledge of secrecy the celebrated State Rights Resolutions of '98 were wrought, and that pledge was faithfully kept until twenty years later, when, constrained by Nicholas' son to avow the authorship, he wrote: "I would have wished this rather to have remained, as hitherto, without inquiry." No doubt of it, since those resolutions make him the parent of that brood of dragons which has afflicted, and doubtless will continue to afflict, this Government with threats of political disintegration.

The resolutions as prepared by Jefferson were more *vicious* and radically revolutionary than even the Kentucky Legislature could bear, and were, therefore, changed—the original 8th and 9th being discarded and new 8th and 9th substituted by Nicholas. As amended they were presented in the Legislature, Lower House, by John Breckenridge, and were adopted Nov. 10th, 13th, by an almost unanimous vote.[1]

The first assumed that the Federal Constitution is a *compact* between the States *as* States [—an assumption not founded in fact, because the preamble to the Constitution declares positively to the contrary: "We the *people of the United States*" is its enacting clause—] by which is created a General Government for special purposes, each State reserving for itself the residuary mass of power and right, and "that, as in other cases of *compact* between parties *having no common* judge, EACH PARTY has an EQUAL RIGHT *to judge for itself*, as well of infractions as of *the mode and manner of redress.*" [Herein was laid the egg which hatched the dragons of nullification and secession. South Carolina in 1832 and 1860 only exercised the "rights" here set forth—nothing more.[2] And the Hartford Convention, which

[1] See Appendix for Resolutions at length, as adopted.

[2] See Appendix for Madison's defense and disclaimer.

Jeffersonian "democrats" never tire of stigmatising as a convention of traitors, only repeated, as its fundamental principle of action, the "right" patented if not invented by Thomas Jefferson. It is only when "Federalists" propose to exercise that right that it is treason?]

This premise taken for granted the succeeding six resolutions applied the right of State judgment to three acts of the last Congress, viz: to punish counterfeiters of the bills of the United States Bank, the Sedition law and the Alien law—all of which were pronounced "*not* law, but *altogether void and of no force.*" [This was the "tub" to those affected with the anti-National Bank mania, and to those foreign and domestic malcontents whose discrimination between liberty and license was not particularly apparent.]

The seventh of the series as drawn by Jefferson postponed "to a time of greater tranquility" the "revisal and correction" of sundry other acts of Congress, also assumed to be founded upon an unconstitutional interpretation of the "right to impose taxes and excises to provide for the common defense and welfare and to make all laws necessary and proper for carrying into execution the powers vested in the Government" of the United States. [This was the "tub" to those who proposed to drink whiskey free of an excise, and who preferred to live without the annoyance of being taxed on what little property they might possess, for the support of a "General" Government.]

The eighth of Mr. Jefferson's series, directed the appointment of a committee of conference and correspondence to communicate the resolutions to the several States, and to inform them that the commonwealth of Kentucky, with all her esteem for her "co-States" and for the Union, was *determined* "to submit to undelegated, and, consequently, unlimited powers *in no man or body of men on earth;* that, in cases of an abuse of the delegated powers, the members of the General Government being chosen by the people, a change by the people would be the constitutional remedy; but, where powers are assumed which have not been delegated, *a nullification of the act is the right remedy; and that every State has a natural right, in cases not within the compact, to nullify, of their own authority, all assumptions of power by others within their limtts.*" This extraordinary "higher law" assumption was justified, with much effort to prove that it was the only doctrine consistent with liberty—that, to appeal to Congress, in such a case, would be out of place, since Congress was not a party to the "compact" (the Constitution) but merely its creature; therefore, the committee of correspondence and conference was to call upon these "co-States" "to concur in declaring these acts void and of no force, and each to take measures of its own for providing that neither of these acts, nor any other of the General Government not plainly and intentionally authorized by the Constitution, shall be exercised within their respective territories." [Here was the "tub" to the big whale—to all that large class, who, disliking restraint upon their actions or their principles, preferred to sail where and how they pleased. If any pilot boat or Federal ship seeking supplies, should be caught in their waters, she was to be scuttled and sunk. This promised a plentiful harvest of popular excitement, and, if enforced, would rend the Union to atoms.]

The ninth resolution, as drawn by Jefferson, gave to the committee of correspondence power to correspond with like committees to be appointed by the "co-States"—the committee being required to report all such correspondence at the next session of the Legislature.

There never was a conspiracy concocted against the Union more fatal to its peace and to its life than that wrought in the library at Monticello; and, if George Nicholas afterwards extracted some of the fangs of the dragon before daring to present the monster for the caresses of the public, it does not make Thomas Jefferson any the less responsible for what he attempted to perform. *Fiat justitia et ruat cœlum!*

It will be perceived, by reference to the resolutions as introduced and adopted, that the original first seven resolutions were accepted by Nicholas, but for the eighth and ninth Nicholas substituted others which, as contrasted with Jefferson's production, resembled a dagger with its point broken off and its edges well dulled. The substitutes merely directed that the preceding resolutions be laid before Congress by the Kentucky senators and representatives, who were "to use their best endeavors to procure at the next session a repeal of the aforesaid unconstitutional and obnoxious acts;" the Governor meanwhile to transmit copies to the Legislatures of the several States, to whom an earnest argumentative appeal was addressed, borrowed partly from Jefferson's eighth resolution, for an expression of opinion as to the Alien and Sedition laws, and for their concurrence with Kentucky in declaring these laws void and of no force, and in requesting their repeal at the next session of Congress.

These resolutions were responded to quickly by a similar series—prepared by Madison at Jefferson's instigation—introduced to the Virginia Legislature by the John Taylor already referred to as a disunionist. We give the series as adopted, in the Appendix. It will be seen that, though briefer and apparently less de-National, they nevertheless inculcate the same baleful idea of overriding Congress and of making the General Government subordinate to the States. The resolutions, as passed, were deprived of much of their original anti-National animus. Indeed, in order to secure their passage at all, the most "representative" sections were eradicated; the whole were so *toned down* as to render them less inimical to the General Government and more considerate of Congress. The resolutions only passed, after a spirited and somewhat protracted debate—in the House of Delegates Dec. 21st, by a vote of one hundred to sixty-three, and in the Senate Dec. 24th, by fourteen to three. Then as ever since, up to 1861, the aristocratic element of Virginia's population—the old families with vast estates and many slaves—were extremely hostile to the idea of any authority supreme to that of Virginia. The "democratic" element was, therefore, largely in the ascendant; and, from that day forward, not only Virginia, but all the Southern States presented the anomaly of its most exclusive and tyrannical element being most devoted to the democratic idea! History furnishes few parallels for this incident in our national experience wherein the two extremes—the most liberty hating and liberty loving portion of society—act and vote in unison.

Northern democrats have, from Jefferson's time down, voted with Southern aristocrats.

These Virginia resolutions were sent forth to the States, accompanied by an address, prepared by Madison with all the ability of an adroit rhetorician, setting forth the causes of complaint against the Federal Government, and giving reasons at length for the adoption of the resolutions. This address called forth a counter address, signed by fifty-eight of the minority, in which it was declared that the awful crisis had arrived, lamenting the existence of the revolutionary resolutions, and justifying their own course in opposing them by declaring their apprehension of "the evils which *disunited* America must inevitably suffer." The minority address also put forth the sentiment that "America is *one nation*, and, therefore, the State Governments are restrained from interfering with the great acts of sovereignty of the General Government." This address was presented by the minority to the Legislature, to be printed and circulated with the Madison paper; but, it was, by a vote of the majority, denied the light, and was afterwards published in the newspapers, in which it had a wide circulation, with good effect on the public mind, as showing that Virginia was not all disloyal. Indeed, the resolutions and the address so alarmed many a patriot who had conscientiously opposed the adoption of the Constitution, that numbers of hitherto "republicans" came forth to sustain the Government by their influence against these evidently revolutionary proceedings. Patrick Henry, though in ill health and indisposed to any further public service, took the field in an active canvass for the Legislature for the purpose of fighting down the iniquitous scheme concocted by the "republican" leaders to bring discredit upon the National Government. He did not then know how deeply Madison and Jefferson were implicated in the matter; but, he did behold the appalling dangers awaiting the States and the Union if the doctrines embodied in the resolutions prevailed. Wirt, in his life of Henry, gives a report of one of his speeches made during the canvass for his election, in which he assumed that, in daring to pronounce upon the validity of Federal laws the State had quitted the sphere in which she had been placed by the

Constitution, had gone *out* of her jurisdiction in a manner not warranted by any authority, and, in the highest degree, alarming to every considerate man; and he declared that such opposition to the General Government as that proposed *must* beget the enforcement of the laws by military power. This shows how the most intelligent minds construed the character of those resolves; and, though both Madison and Jefferson, alarmed at the monster which they had evoked, gave, in after life,[1] ample evidence that they, too, repudiated the heresies of nullification and secession, their efforts in the two Legislatures were alarmingly revolutionary, in theory at least. The principles embodied in their resolves have constituted, ever since, the chief defense of all enemies of the Union.

The address and resolves only elicited from the States marks of disapproval. No responsive echo came from any Legislature save that of uneasy Kentucky. Maryland, Delaware, Pennsylvania, New Jersey, New York, Connecticut, Rhode Island, Massachusetts, New Hampshire and Vermont all expressed their dissent in resolves denying the right assumed of a State Legislature deciding upon the validity of acts of Congress. The reply of Massachusetts was characteristic of her old heart of loyalty. She maintained the constitutionality of the Alien and Sedition laws and declared them to be justified by the exigency of the moment and by the power of Congress to provide for the common defense. This earnest denial of the State Rights' assumption, by men who had well considered the entire question in their labors upon the Constitution and in their canvass for its adoption, would seem to be conclusive upon one point, viz.: if States which had just merged their su-

[1] Jefferson was no sooner in the Presidential chair than he virtually repudiated his Kentucky programme. He said in his inaugural address that "the preservation of the General Government in its whole constitutional vigor, was the sheet anchor of our peace at home and safety abroad:" that "absolute acquiescence in the decisions of the majority was the vital principle of republics, from which there is no appeal but to force, the vital principle and immediate parent of despotism." The published works of both Madison and Jefferson contain many things which it is very hard to reconcile with the two series of resolves to which they gave the paternity of their great names. See Appendix for a letter not given in Madison's published works, wherein he denounces secession and gives his own views of the resolutions of '98.

premacy in that of the Union, denounced the right to sit in judgment on acts of Congress and to call the General Government to an account at their will, that right must be regarded as a constitutional heresy. The burden of proof that it is not a heresy is, therefore, thrown upon those who oppose the Constitution as expounded by those who constructed that instrument or assisted in its inauguration. We have but to cite the testimony of "the Fathers" to prove that the State rights dogmatists really stand in an attitude of revolution.

But, after all, these bold resolves were not meant for a future generation. As we have said, they seem simply to have been an invention of a shrewd politician, in a moment interesting to the fortunes of his party, whereby to consolidate the several elements of opposition to the party in power, with a view to its overthrow and the consequent promotion of Thomas Jefferson to the Presidency. Chief Justice Marshall, writing of the debates in the Virginia Legislature on the resolves, said:

"The debates on these subjects were long and animated. In the course of them sentiments were declared and (in my judgment) views were developed of a very serious and alarming extent. To me it seems that there are men who will hold power by any means rather than not hold it, and who would prefer a dissolution of the Union to the continuance of an administration not of their own party. They will risk all the ills which may result from the most dangerous experiments rather than permit that happiness to be enjoyed which is dispensed by other hands than their own."

Though written by an administration man, this was the view of a clear head and a just mind. It was confirmed by subsequent events. Those who intrigued were all the recipients of offices and honors at the hands of the popular party. Jefferson became President; Burr, Vice President; Madison, Secretary of State; Albert Gallatin, Secretary of the Treasury; and John Breckenridge, Attorney General. Madison, next had his turn at the Presidency, to be followed by Monroe, also a Virginian and a partisan of the Jefferson school.

Referring to the Kentucky and Virginia resolves Edward Everett has correctly said: "They did their work—all they were intended or expected to do—by shaking the Administration. At the ensuing election, Mr. Jefferson, at whose instance the entire movement was made, was chosen President by a very small majority; Mr. Madison was placed at the head of his Administration as Secretary of State; the obnoxious laws expired by their own limitation; and Mr. Jefferson proceeded to administer the Government upon constitutional principles quite as lax, to say the least, as those of his predecessors."

Quite as "lax." A great many things deemed unconstitutional when out of power were found to be constitutional when in power. Indeed, when assuming the reins of government he said, (in his inaugural): "Every difference of opinion is not a difference of principle. We have called by different names brethren of the same principle. *We are all Republicans —all Federalists.*" Remarkable confession when coming from him who, of all others, had fixed the stigma of monarchy and usurpation upon those just driven from the executive and seats of legislation. And when he added: "If there be any among us who would wish to dissolve this Union, or to change its republican form, let them stand undisturbed as monuments of the safety with which errors of opinion may be tolerated when reason is left to control it," we are constrained to exclaim: "can this be the same man who, but a few months previously, sought to array the States against the General Government and Congress?"

In weighing all the circumstances which gave rise to the obnoxious enactment, of 1798, we are surprised less at their severity than at their moderation. It is the chronic failure of partisan writers, of the Jeffersonian faith, to belittle the dangers which then existed and to magnify the bad character of the offending statutes. The truth is undeniable that, if the laws were proscriptive and of unmeasured severity, the provocation was great. Irish patriots and French revolutionists, having only radical conceptions of liberty, used their freedom of speech and of the press to villify and debase. Their papers, which still are preserved, are positively foul with libels and abuse; liberty to them consisted in perfect unrestraint; old patriots and Federalists, for seeking to give the National Government power and executive force, were assailed as aristocrats, and, everywhery were the subjects of malignant abuse by foreigners many of whom had but just landed on our shores. The entire foreign element conspired with the worst elements of our native population to discredit law and to disseminate vicious principles of politics, public morals and religion. It was a carnival of license; and if the Federalists struck boldly at the evil it was because the evil existed in a shape to defy all ordinary restraints. Let us, in passing judgment on the measures adopted, consider the provocation offered for severity of legislation, ere we utter maledictions against the legislators.

THE CONSPIRACY OF AARON BURR.

PRECEDING papers have informed the reader in regard to disunion intrigues in the West. Wilkinson's treasonable alliance with the Spaniards, and his labors with tongue, pen and Spanish gold to divorce Kentucky from its allegiance to the Federal Government, deeply unsettled the minds of all concerned in the Ohio valley, inspiring them with dreams of empire which it required two generations to forget. His intrigues were succeeded by the disloyal "democratic societies," and these, in turn, were followed by the machinations of Genet, whose emissaries proposed to wrest Louisiana and Florida from the Spaniards. Their eloquence, their promises of vast commercial rewards, and their gold, measurably added to the disunion distemper. Almost every domicil, particularly of that large class which lived by their wits,[1] became the centre of excitement, which first the Spanish and then the French emissaries swayed to their ambitious projects. Gradually, however, love for the Union quieted the old spirit of secession, and the year 1800 saw Kentucky an outwardly contented State. By the cession of Louisiana to the United States (1803) the last source of discontent was removed. The mouths of the Mississippi were opened to commerce, and, thenceforward, the boundless West only had to unloose its energies to grow into greatness.

[1] See Hall's "Sketches of History, Life and Manners in the West," for an interesting exposition of Kentucky character at the date now under notice. A large number of Kentucky settlers having pursued the life of hunters and guides, or served in the field under Boone, Hardin, Clarke, Scott, &c., were thoroughly infused with the spirit *militaire*, and formed, with the professional boatmen, a strong *background* for the labors of those plotting military and commercial enterprises. A more courageous, hardy and restless set of men never lived.

But, the old fires were there; only some master spirit was required to set them all aflame. That Prince of Marplots, General James Wilkinson, was appointed by Mr. Jefferson Governor of Louisiana, and to Louisiana the ostracised democratic ex-Vice President of the United States turned his eyes. Though a fugitive from justice, and cast from the high estate of the Vice Presidency to that of the outcast, Aaron Burr neither lost his astonishing equanimity nor forgot his subtle skill for intrigue; and he turned to the West as naturally as if his movements had been determined in that direction for years.

Burr, as a politician, instinctively gravitated to the "opposition" party. His talent for dissimulation, his indifference to principle in politics, his innate love of intrigue, his disregard of all moral restraints, led him to associations with those whose ideas of liberty were synonymous with license. He became the confidante of Jefferson, and not only co-operated with him but directed for him those secret and open movements which were to end in their triumph. As a return he came within one vote of being made "republican" President of the United States. Jefferson only obtained the Presidency, after seven days of intense excitement, by the casting vote of a Federalist. Burr thereupon assumed the Vice Presidency. The history of that seven days' ballotting forms one of the most remarkable episodes in our political annals. It served to divide the republicans into two factions, but, so powerful were they that, even in division they were stronger than their opponents, the Federalists. Burr took the second position gracefully; served his office with ability and plotted for the Chief Magistracy quietly but confidently. For this reason he soon grew to be Jefferson's most powerful and most dreaded antagonist. It behooved the President to be rid of such a competitor for democratic favor; therefore all the tremendous machinery of his well organised party system was brought to bear. Burr was out-manœuvered and failed of a nomination at the hands of the democracy even for the Vice Presidency.[1] But, not to be thwart-

[1] Prior to the election of 1804 the Constitution had been so amended as to make the offices of President and Vice President each separately elective. Up to the election of 1800 the rule had been to make him President who had most electoral

ed, Burr threw himself into the canvass, a candidate for the Executive chair of New York (1804,) and must have been elected had not Alexander Hamilton cast his powerful local influence against the man whom he regarded as a dangerous friend and a treacherous foe. In that defeat was recorded the fate of Hamilton. There long had rankled in the bosom of Burr a hate of the great Federalist leader. Words, written and spoken in the heat of an unusually exciting canvass, offered, according to the duello's code, apparent cause for a hostile meeting. The defeated man challenged his political enemy to mortal combat. By avoiding even the possibility of a settlement, Burr forced the unwilling Hamilton to place his body as a target for the unerring weapon of his implacable adversary. They met July 11th, 1804. Burr, taking the most deliberate aim, shot his antagonist. Hamilton did not design to fire, though his pistol exploded from the convulsive motion of his finger on the trigger when Burr's ball struck his bosom. Burr fled, while the execrations of a nation followed him. He tarried a few days in secret, in Philadelphia, to pursue an intrigue with one of his many female victims; but, the outcry becoming appalling even to his unfeeling heart, he sought a brief residence, "until the storm should pass over," in the Southern States, where a successful duelist ever possessed a passport to public and private favor. From thence he journeyed back to Washington to preside, up to March, 1805, over the Senate. In Virginia he had a most enthusiastic public reception, at a moment when two warrants were out for his arrest as a murderer, one in New York and one in New Jersey. At Washington he was received, Parton says, with more deference than usual. The President, now beholding his antagonist crushed and powerless, could afford to offer him civilities.

votes and the second on the list Vice President. The difficulties of this rule were made so apparent by the seven days' contest in the House of Representatives that the Constitution was amended as stated. The vote in the Electoral College (1800) stood: Thomas Jefferson, 73; Aaron Burr, 73; John Adams, 65; C. C. Pinckney, 64; John Jay, 1--sixteen States voting. There being a tie the election was thrown into the House, where a tie also occurred, until, after seven days' ballotting, the vote of Bayard, Federalist, of Delaware, was cast for Jefferson. That vote made the President.

Madison, Secretary of State, rode out with him; Gallatin, Secretary of the Treasury, visited him freely; a leading democratic member of the House said: "Our little David of the Republicans has killed the Goliah of Federalism and for this I am willing to reward him." He was the idol of those whose hate of Hamilton and Federalism conquered their self-respect and their respect for law. At his instance Jefferson named Wilkinson to the office of Governor of Louisina. In soliciting that appointment the Vice President was taking the initial step for his Western schemes. For years these two men had corresponded *in cypher;* Burr was fully informed of the General's Spanish services, and, without doubt, had sounded him so far as to feel that, in the ex-stipendiary of Mirò, he had the coadjutor most to be desired.

When his term of office had expired Burr's Western plans were so far perfected, that, had he not been detained "by some trifling, important concerns of business" in financial matters, he would have been off at once, for the West, in pursuit of his Utopia.

Writing from Philadelphia to his son-in-law, Joseph Alston, under date of March 22d, 1805, he said: "Though in my former letters I did not, in express terms, inform you that I was under ostracism, yet it must have been inferred. Such is the fact. In New York I am to be disfranchised, and in New Jersey hanged. Having substantial objections to both I shall not, for the present, hazard either, but seek another country." A few days later, writing to Mrs. Alston (his daughter Theodosia), he said: "In ten or twelve days I shall be on my way westward. My address, until further orders, is at Cincinnati, Ohio, care Hon. Jno. Smith. As the objects of this journey, not mere curiosity, or *pour passer le tems*, may lead me to Orleans, and perhaps further."

These extracts indicate first, his reason for "seeking a new country," and, second, that he had a *special* object in view, which might lead him to New Orleans, or *further*. Throughout all his correspondence, indeed, construed by the light of subsequent events, we find many hints and allusions which tend to show that he had arranged before hand, so far as he could so do, all the leading ideas of his secret mission down the Mississippi. Parton says:

"A variety of projects lay half formed in his mind—projects of land speculations, of canal making, of settling in some rising city of the West in the practice of the law, of beginning anew his political life as the representative of a new State in Congress. If more ambitious schemes agitated him they were concealed; neither in his diary, nor in his voluminous correspondence, published or unpublished, is there the slightest reference to any but ordinary and legitimate objects during the year 1805."

All of which may be true: but, there is strong inferential evidence that his "ambitious schemes" were conceived in the Winter of 1804–5; that Wilkinson's appointment was one step toward their inauguration; that Burr's voyage down the Ohio and Mississippi rivers, his visits to and proven conferences with influential revolutionists of the West and South, his return by land from New Orleans to Nashville and Kentucky, for a second prolonged interview with men known to be ready for a crusade against the Spanish dominions, his journey to St. Louis for a further conference with Wilkinson, all are circumstantial proofs which it is hard to rule out in making up a judgment in his case. The efforts made by Wilkinson and Matthew Lyon, member of Congress from Kentucky, to secure Burr's return to Congress from the Nashville district, and Burr's *apparent* endorsement of their wishes, do not militate against any inference which assigns to Burr a clear comprehension of his work in hand. Indeed, his election from Tennessee or, as was contemplated by him—his return from New Orleans as a delegate to Congress—would have impeded, in no degree, the prosecution of his plans; it might, on the contrary, have furthered them. Nothing that has been offered in evidence disproves the idea that Burr had definite designs in his first visit to the western country.

On the 30th of April, 1805, Burr embarked from Pittsburg, on his first trip down the great river. The journey was made on a flatboat, well fitted for comfort and the entertainment of guests. The floating house dropped down stream with the current, striking shore at all points where its proprietor desired. The diary kept by him for his daughter Theodosia, and the letters reprinted by Davis, in his "Life of Burr," give us a pleasing picture of people and incidents on the way. He was, in almost all instances, enthusiastically received. At Marietta, Ohio, he landed, nominally to explore the ancient mounds in its vicinity, but really to come in contact with leading men of that old town. At Blennerhassett's island, a few miles below, he landed, apparently without design, and there first met with the owners of the place. By his winning discourse and polished manners he quite captivated the too-credulous couple whose fortunes were to be so intimately and disastrously affected by their relations with the *voyageure.* At Cincinnati he found several old friends and many ardent admirers. John Smith, U. S. Senator from Ohio, and Jonathan Dayton, late U. S. Senator from New Jersey, were there to receive him and to participate in his counsels.[1] After a day's tarry at Smith's house the excursionist drifted on his way down to Louisville. There he found Matthew Lyon. From Louisville he proceeded by land to Nashville, at which city his welcome was that of a public guest. He was domiciled with Andrew Jackson. Matthew Lyon said: "the newspapers described his arrival and reception there as one of the most magnificent parades that had ever been made at that place. They contained lists of toasts and great dinners given in honor of Colonel Burr, everybody at and near Nashville seeming to be contending for the honor of having best treated or served Colonel Burr." These demonstrations must have impressed the visitor favorably concerning the availability of the western people for use in his enterprises, when the hour should come to enlist them. Returning to the Ohio river in a boat supplied by Jackson, he found his own flatboat at the mouth of the Cumberland river. At Fort Massac, sixteen miles below, he not unexpectedly met Wilkinson. A four days' conference ensued (June 6th, 10th,) when Burr abandoned his slow moving ark, and, provided by Wilkinson "with an elegant barge, sails, colors, and ten oars,

[1] Judge Burnet, in his "Notes" disclaims for Smith any knowledge of Burr's designs. The Judge produces evidence which leaves a very unpleasant impression on the reader's mind in regard to the conduct of the prosecutions which followed Burr's arrest.

with a sergeant and ten able, faithful hands," the trip to New Orleans was accomplished by June 25th. There he tarried until July 10th, in secret conference with the rich merchant Daniel Clark, who, it afterwards was proven, was then successfully enlisted in Burr's "land speculations," and in his Mexican expedition. Burr bore a letter of introduction from Wilkinson to Clark, in which it was said: "If the persecutions of a great and honorable man can give title to generous attentions he has claims to all your civilities and all your services. * * To him I refer you for many things improper to letter, and which he will not say to any other." His reception exceeded in enthusiasm every demonstration yet made. Dinners, public and private; balls; fetes; receptions, made the guest forget the dead Hamilton and the persecutions he had left behind. But, in the midst of all those festive offerings, Burr was secretly busy; and here it is that vague speculation as to his purposes begins to take a consistent form. What were those purposes? We may give Parton's presentment as being the best yet made in Burr's behalf. He says:

"The question has been answered, first, by Wilkinson in his ponderous Memoirs; secondly, by Clark in his angry octavo, entitled, 'Proofs of the Corruption of General James Wilkinson, and of his Connection with Aaron Burr;' thirdly, by Matthew L. Davis, speaking for Burr himself. Wilkinson says the reference in his letter of introduction, was simply to the election scheme. Clark declares that Burr confided nothing to him whatever. He says he liked Burr exceedingly, invited him to dinner, showed him every possible civility, but had not a syllable of confidential conversation with him. In the most positive and circumstantial manner, he denies that he had then, or ever had, any participation in, or knowledge of, Burr's designs.[1] Davis, on the con-

[1] Clark's own comments on Wilkinson's letter are as follows: "The things which it was improper to letter to me are pretty plainly expressed in a communication made about the same time (by Wilkinson) to General Adair. The letter is dated, Rapids of Ohio, May 28th, 1805, 11 o'clock, and contains these expressions: 'I was to have introduced my friend Burr to you, but in this I failed by accident. He understands your merits, and reckons on you. Repair to me and I will tell you *all*. We must have a peep at the unknown world beyond me.' The letter to me I think fully proves that some secret plan of Burr's was known to Wilkinson in May, 1805. That to General Adair leaves no doubt on the subject. Immediately after this he went to St. Louis, where his very first act, before he had broken bread in the territory, was an endeavor to bring Major Bruff into his plans. He

trary, asserts that Clark and Wilkinson were both ardently engaged with Burr; and that Clark agreed to advance fifty thousand dollars in furtherance of the great project. Other friends of Burr say that Clark made two voyages to Vera Cruz, to spy out the enemy's country. Clark admits having made the voyages (one in September, 1805, the other in February, 1806); admits having collected information in Mexico respecting the strength of the fortresses, the number of the garrisons and the disposition of the people; but asserts that his voyages had none but commercial objects, and that his inquiries were only prompted by curiosity. A witness deposed to having heard Clark say, that he would willingly join in a private scheme for the conquest of Mexico, provided the adventurers could turn their backs for ever on the United States. 'You, for example, might be a duke,' was one expression which the witness swore he had heard Clark use in the course of the same conversation.

"My own impression, after reading all the procurable documents, is, that neither Clark nor Wilkinson were embarked in Burr's Mexican scheme; though both, up to a certain point, may have favored it. Nor do I think that, during this visit to New Orleans, Burr himself did more than collect information, and cast a very wistful eye across the river to the domain of the hated Spaniards, who still held the western bank of the Mississippi."

Having accomplished the first objects of his mission, and satisfied himself that New Orleans was ripe for any *coup d'etat* he might determine upon, Burr proceeded by land to Nashville by way of Natchez, reaching General Jackson's hospitable home August 6th, where he remained one week—the recipient of attentions, public and private, of the most flattering character. He then journeyed into Kentucky by way of Frankfort and Lexington, evidently "feeling" of men and public opinion. From Louisville he directed his steps to St. Louis, for another conference with Wilkinson. The General, in his account of that interview, afterwards said:

"Burr seemed to be revolving some great project, the nature of which he did not disclose. Speaking of the imbecility of the Government, Colonel Burr said: 'it would molder to pieces, die a natural death,' or words to that effect; adding 'that the people of the Western country were ready for revolt.' To this I recollect replying, that if he had not

tells him that he had a '*grand scheme*,' that 'would make the fortunes of all concerned;' and though Major Bruff's manner of receiving this overture put a stop to any further disclosures, yet we may judge of its nature, for it was introduced by a philippic against democracy, and the ingratitude of republican governments."

profited more by his journey, he had better have remained at Washington or Philadelphia. For surely, said I, my friend, no person was ever more mistaken! The Western people disaffected to the Government? They are bigoted to Jefferson and democracy! and the conversation dropped."

This would appear, upon its face, to exculpate Wilkinson from all *previous* knowledge of Burr's schemes, and go to demonstrate that he (W.) was a patriotic devotee of the Union. A knowledge of the man, however—as learned from his prior services in behalf of the Spaniards—and the fact that from that time (Sept. 1805) to the following May, six cypher letters were written by Burr to him, every one of which were in the highest degree confidential and important, prove to us that Wilkinson acted in his old character of dissimulator in his record of what passed at the interview held at St. Louis. Davis says:

"The great object of Burr was the conquest of Mexico. With this view he conferred with General Wilkinson, who was ardent in the cause. Wilkinson's regular force, about six hundred men, was intended as a nucleus, around which the followers of Burr were to form. They were the only disciplined corps that could be expected. As W. was the American Commander-in-Chief (General-in-Chief) and stationed upon the borders of Mexico, he possessed the power and was pledged to strike the blow whenever it should be deemed expedient. This commencement of the war would thus have been apparently under the sanction and authority of the American Government, and would have drawn to the standard of Burr numerous volunteers from the Western States. Such, undoubtedly, was the plan; Burr entertained no suspicion of Wilkinson's treachery toward him until his interview with Swartwout."

This is true. Burr wrote in reassured confidence to Wilkinson, acted in confidence, concerted in confidence, until first informed of his (W.'s) treachery by the issue of Jefferson's proclamation for his (Burr's) apprehension, Nov. 27th, 1806. Probably no word, no hint, no act of the General, ever gave the watchful Burr even a suspicion of treachery.

From St. Louis Burr proceeded eastward, by way of Vincennes, there calling upon General William Henry Harrison. He reached Washington early in November, and at once entered upon an elaborate system of intrigue, calculated to enlist in his projects some of the most trusty men in the army and

35

navy. The moment seemed propitious. A war with Spain threatened. The Dons beyond the Mississippi (west side) and on the Sabine, had committed many acts calculated to arouse the western people to a war of extermination. Everywhere throughout the West Burr found a spirit of intense rancor prevailing against the Spanish, who yet retained several important posts in the old Louisiana territory as well as in Florida. For several years prior to 1805 the people were only restrained from proceeding to extremities with their Roman Catholic neighbors by the constant vigilance of the authorities at the National Capital. Burr ever had been an advocate of a determined course toward the crown of Spain—for which reason he was greeted with favor; and his visit to the West, during 1805, was regarded by the people as having *something* to do with the foreigners on our borders. Jefferson, apprehending the resentment of France in event of a war with Spain, had pursued a policy characterized by timidity and deference to the power of Napoleon; but, so great became the causes of complaint, during 1805, that, in his messages of Dec. 3d–9th, 1805, the President was constrained to use strong terms of denunciation. When Burr arrived from the West it was to find the war spirit running high—so high, indeed, that, for months, a declaration of hostilities was daily expected. He seemed to read his future by the light of the fires then kindled. That he labored assiduously to gather resources for his majestic plans of conquest, we can well imagine. If before he had conceived a stroke for Mexico feasible, it now seemed near its realization under auspices of a state of actual war. His plans took a wider range, or, what had been merely dreams of power, became established principles of action, if we may credit his revelations to General Eaton, to which reference will hereafter be made. Having been "dined" by Jefferson, and treated with distinguished consideration by the authorities at Washington, he left the new Capital, with its sparse population and its dreary distances, to take up headquarters in the old Capital, Philadelphia, then the recognized social and political centre. He rented a small house in a retired part of the city that he might pursue his labors unobserved, and, being divorced from society, could devote his entire time to labor. The little dwelling ere long became a rendezvous for men of high and low degree, whom the Conspirator received, in almost all instances, *singly*. Captivating in manner, gifted with wonderfully seductive powers of speech, using fact, fancy and fabrication in a way to confound every opposing circumstance or element, he had no difficulty in gathering to his net great numbers of the adventurous spirits, willing to stake fortune, honor and happiness on his cast. He had a special word for all. Each visitor, regarding himself sole confidant of the wily ex-Vice President, withdrew from the little dwelling to labor in his behalf, or to preserve the secret of the enterprise proposed until the propitious moment. And yet, it is quite certain that Burr committed to none, if we except General Eaton, the daring purposes which apparently underlaid his adventure. He wrote much and talked little, scarcely appearing in public. Even his most trusted political partisans were ignorant of the grand designs revolving and perfecting in his busy brain. To them he still was the political intriguant, planning, devising, scheming for their own as well as for his own advancement. Missions, embassies, local offices were talked of for him, while he, in turn, used his influence to obtain those places for others. He thus appeared in a two-fold character, ready for political place and power, but never for one moment deserting the dazzling object of his ambition—the conquest of Spanish dominions.

Confidant, at length, of ultimate success in that direction, the conspirator dropped his mask for a moment and broke the seal of secrecy to General Eaton, then late U. S. Consul to Tripoli. This individual, having planned the romantic expedition against Derne, was upon the point of seeing his work consummated, when a treaty, unexpectedly concluded with Tripoli, dashed his hopes and ended his labors. He returned to the United States quite out of temper with Government for its inefficient conduct of the Tripolitan war and for its neglect of his claims for monies expended in the Derne enterprise. Burr approached him, doubtless conceiving the high spirited man ready for a second adventure promising rewards commensurate with his merits as a dashing leader and with the claims of his broken pecuniary fortunes. As we learn from Eaton's testimony, given at the trial of Burr, the ex-Vice President approached him first with propositions to embark in the expedition against Mexico, into which he (Eaton) enlisted, understanding that it was countenanced by the Administration, with whom Burr still sustained cordial relations. After having secured the General's consent to the invasion adventure, Burr, so Eaton testified, finally developed a project for revolutionizing the Western country, establishing a monarchy, organizing a force of ten or twelve thousand volunteers; when, having secured the co-operation of the marine corps at Washington and gaining over Truxton, Preble, Decatur and others, he intended to turn Congress out of doors, assassinate the President, seize on the Treasury and Navy, and declare himself the Protector of an energetic government! All of this extraordinary programme Eaton swore was clearly and unequivocally detailed to him. Wilkinson was declared by Burr to be a party to the scheme—was to bring over to it his army in the West and South, and was to act as General-in-Chief, while Eaton was to have the second command.

As Eaton, according to his own testimony, expressed abhorrence of this revolutionary plot, and utterly refused to participate in it, the question naturally occurs why did he not at once divulge the matter? He was under no bond to secrecy. He had position enough to sustain his word against that of Burr, should the latter deny the impeachment. The excuse offered was that he was fearful to put his own reputation for veracity against that of the Conspirator; yet, he confesses to have advised with Jefferson in regard to a foreign appointment for Burr! We may quote from the testimony:

"On the solitary ground upon which I stood, I was at a loss how to conduct myself, though at no loss as respected my duty. I durst not place my lonely testimony in the balance against the weight of Colonel Burr's character; for, by turning the tables upon me, which I thought any man, capable of such a project, was very capable of doing, I should sink under the weight. I resolved, therefore, with myself to obtain the removal of Mr. Burr from this country in a way honorable to him; and on this I did consult him, without his knowing my motive. Accordingly, I waited on the President of the United States, and after a desultory conversation, in which I aimed to draw his view to the westward, I took the liberty of suggesting to the President that I thought Colonel Burr ought to be removed from the country, because I considered him dangerous in it. The President asked where we should send him? Other places might have been mentioned, but I believe that Paris, London and Madrid, were the places which were particularly named. The President, without positive expression (in such a matter of delicacy), signified that the trust was too important, and expressed something like a doubt about the integrity of Mr. Burr. I frankly told the President that perhaps no person had stronger grounds to suspect that integrity than I had; but that I believed his pride of ambition had so predominated over his other passions, that when placed on an eminence, and put on his honor, a respect to himself would secure his fidelity. I perceived that the subject was disagreeable to the President, and to bring him to my point in the shortest mode, and at the same time point out the danger, I said to him that I expected that we should in eighteen months have an insurrection, if not a revolution, on the waters of the Mississippi. The President said he had too much confidence in the information, the integrity, and attachment to the Union of the citizens of that country, to admit any apprehensions of that kind. The circumstance of no interrogatories being made to me, I thought imposed silence upon me at that time and place."

Commodore Truxton confessed to having had propositions from Burr to embark in a scheme, "legitimate in war," as B. averred, against Mexico—that nothing more was proposed. Upon Eaton's testimony and that of the Morgan's, hereafter mentioned, stands the charge of treason and revolution.[1]

During the winter and spring several letters passed between Burr and Wilkinson in cypher—all containing allusions more

[1] In the cross examination this testimony of Eaton's was so skilfully ventilated by Burr as to cast suspicion upon its truthfulness. Just after the arrest of Burr and the strange proceedings in New Orleans of Wilkinson in suspending the writ of *habeas corpus*, incarcerating persons *suspected* of being able to testify, &c.—all of which was understood to have been done with Jefferson's approbation, if not by his direct orders—Eaton received ten thousand dollars from Government as indemnity for his Barbary losses. It was in the midst of excitements caused by Wilkinson's proceedings that he came forward with published affidavits to expose Burr. His statements tended, of course, to create a public sentiment against Burr, and to sustain the conduct of Wilkinson. That the money paid to him had any thing to do in eliciting his testimony is not probable. The money had long been due.

or less direct to their plans, yet too obscure or general in terms to afford any clue as to their exact significance. One thing they did prove—that Wilkinson was deeply concerned in whatever was proposed. No effort of his friends, no confidence of the Administration in his patriotism and fidelity, could whitewash from his Gubernatorial and military escutcheon the stains of these mysteriously confidential notes. We may quote from one written in the spring of 1806:

"The execution of our project is postponed till December. Want of water in Ohio rendered movement impracticable: other reasons rendered delay expedient. The association is enlarged, and comprises all that Wilkinson could wish. Confidence limited to a few. Though this delay is irksome, it will enable us to move with more certainty and dignity. Burr will be throughout the United States this summer. Administration is damned, which Randolph aids. Burr wrote you a long letter last December, replying to a short one deemed very silly. Nothing has been heard from the Brigadier (Wilkinson) since October. Is Cusion (Colonel Cushing) et Portes (Major Porter) right? Address, Burr, at Washington."

Parton observes: "That Wilkinson *knew* what Burr proposed, I cannot doubt; but that he had unequivocally engaged to join in the projected speculation, is a question upon which there may be two well sustained opinions."

It is hardly possible to conceive that he knew what Burr proposed and yet did not lend himself to the scheme fully. All collateral evidence goes to show that he did engage in the "speculation," and that Burr, when he stated to Eaton, Truxton and others that Wilkinson was enlisted in the enterprise as first in military command, spoke authoritatively. We are not disposed, knowing what we now do in regard to that General-in-Chief's duplicity, even to ascribe to Burr the chief merit of the Mexican enterprise: Burr's only *originality* in the matter appears to have been his *superadded* idea of annexing the Western States of the Union to his Spanish estate, with a remote possibility of turning the Government at Washington out of doors. Matthew Davis says:

"Daniel Clarke, of New Orleans, entered into the Mexican project. He engaged to advance fifty thousand dollars; but subsequently, from disappointments, he was unable to fill his contract. General Wilkinson detailed to Colonel Burr all the information he possessed respecting that country, and pointed out the facilities which would probably be afforded by the inhabitants in effecting a revolution. Without Wilkinson's troops, Burr declared most solemnly, a short time before his death, that he would not have made the attempt on Mexico; that he was perfectly aware the men he would collect, so far as it respected military operations, would be at first little better than a mob.

Colonel Burr had repeated conferences on the subject with Mr. Merry, the British Plenipotentiary resident in the United States. Mr. Merry communicated to his government the project of Mr. Burr. Colonel Charles Williamson, the brother of Lord Balgray, went to England on the business, and, from the encouragement which he received, it was hoped and believed that a British naval squadron would have been furnished in aid of the expedition. At this juncture Mr. Pitt died. Wilkinson must have heard of the death of the premier late in the spring or early in the summer of 1806. From this moment, in Mr. Burr's opinion, Wilkinson became alarmed, and resolved on an abandonment of the enterprise at the sacrifice of his associates.

"On the suggestion of Wilkinson, Mexico was twice visited by Daniel Clark. He held conferences and effected arrangements with many of the principal militia officers, who engaged to favor the revolution. The Catholic bishop, resident at New Orleans, was also consulted, and prepared to promote the enterprise. He designated three priests of the order of Jesuits, as suitable agents, and they were accordingly employed. The bishop was an intelligent and social man. He had been in Mexico, and spoke with great freedom of the dissatisfaction of the clergy in South America. The religious establishments of the country were not to be molested. Madame Xavier Tarjcon, superior of the convent of Ursuline nuns at New Orleans, was in the secret. Some of the sisterhood were also employed in Mexico. So far as any decision had been formed, the landing was to have been effected at Tampico."

A careful study of the testimony adduced at Burr's Richmond trial, and by subsequent developments, leads us to the belief that Wilkinson himself led Colonel Burr on to these plans of conquest, taking the initiative, so far as he dared to, in missions to Mexico, and in intrigues in the South. His (W's) own testimony to the contrary, as written out in his "Memoirs," has but little weight, in our mind, where not sustained by corroborative or collateral evidence of a conclusive nature—such is our want of faith in the man's integrity. When we reflect upon the proofs now existing of his duplicity and dishonesty, it seems incredible that he should have won and retained the confidence of Thomas Jefferson, President of the United States.

If Jefferson's enemies make use of his intimate relations with Tom Paine, Wilkinson and other men of blunted moral perceptions, to prove his own indifference to moral principles, they certainly are not without strong grounds, at least inferential, of justification. It is the application of Esop's *haec fabula docet* in the fable of the goose and the buzzards.

Burr's movements in the spring and summer of 1806 were governed by our relations with Spain. An actual state of war would *legitimise* his operations. He could then proceed openly in his plans so far as the invasion of Mexico was concerned. "As spring advanced," says Parton, "affairs in the South-west looked more and more threatening. The Spaniards added aggression to insolence. It had been agreed between the two governments, that until the boundary line should be settled by negotiation, each party should retain its posts, but establish no new ones, nor make any military movements whatever within the limits in dispute. But, after making several petty encroachments, the Spanish commander, early in June, advanced a force of twelve hundred men to within twenty miles of Nachitoches Instantly, General Wilkinson took measures for the defense of the frontier. He had only six hundred regulars under his command, most of whom were hurried forward to the scene of expected warfare. The forts of New Orleans were hastily repaired. Every militiaman in the West was furbishing his accoutrements, and awaiting the summons to the field. On the 4th of July, 1806, there were not a thousand persons in the United States who did not think war with Spain inevitable, impending, begun! The country desired it. A blow from Wilkinson, a word from Jefferson, would have let loose the dogs of war, given us Texas, and changed the history of the two continents."

But, the war did not follow, nevertheless. Pitt, the British Prime Minister, having died, (Jan. 6th, 1806,) Napoleon was, for the moment, doubly reassured as master of the situation: —a stroke upon our part against Spain was to incur his hostility—a contingency which Mr. Jefferson did not care to accept. Hence, no aggressive step followed; Wilkinson's menace on the Sabine was that and nothing more.

Pitt's death, as stated by Matthew Davis, was a severe blow to Burr's arrangements, dashing, as it did, all hopes of British naval operations against Vera Cruz and Tampico. These several disappointments, it would appear, directed Burr's mind more strongly to his second resource, viz.: the purchase of an immense body of land in the South-west, where to gather his forces, to intrigue and arrange for his Spanish invasion at his leisure. Davis says: "Previous to the cession of Louisiana to the United States, Baron P. N. Tut Bastrop contracted with the Spanish Government for a tract of land exceeding thirty miles square near Nachitoches. By the terms of the contract he was, within a given period of time, to settle upon these lands two hundred families. Subsequently Colonel Charles Lynch made an arrangement with Bastrop for an interest in this contract. Burr purchased from Lynch nearly four hundred thousand acres, lying between the Sabine and Nachitoches. On the trial at Richmond this purchase was established, and the actual payment to Lynch by Burr of five thousand dollars was also proved."

General Adair, however, intimates that it was not until after the discovery, by Burr, of Wilkinson's defection, in the fall of 1806, that he "turned his attention altogether towards strengthening himself on the Wachita,[1] and waiting a more favorable crisis." This doubtless is true as qualified: "turned his attention *altogether*," Adair says; prior to that time it was the "*second* string to his bow," artfully used to cover his real purposes. Of this purchase, made *in July*, 1806, Davis writes:

"The grant of the Spanish government to Bastrop amounted to 1,200,000 acres. Six-tenths of this grant was conveyed to Colonel

---

[1] There is great discrepancy in the location of this purchase. Davis expressly states the Bastrop cession to have been a tract of land thirty miles square near Nachitoches, and that Burr's purchase of Lynch was four hundred thousand acres lying *between the Sabine and Nachitoches*. General Adair refers to the estate as on the *Wachita* river, which lies considerably to the *east* of Nachitoches, and Parton refers to it in general terms as "far to the South-west, beyond the Mississippi, on the banks of the river Wachita, a branch of the Red river." The correct location is thus given by Hildreth: "Situate on the *upper* waters of the Wachita, not many miles distant from the left bank of the Mississippi, *just below the mouth of the Arkansas river*." This places the lands many leagues away from the Sabine country, to the *west* of Nachitoches, to which Davis consigned the Bastrop purchase.

Lynch, and cost him about one hundred thousand dollars. As the time within which two hundred families were to be settled on the land was rapidly drawing to a close, Lynch conveyed one half his right to Burr for fifty thousand dollars. In this purchase many private citizens of worth and respectability were interested. The two projects, however, became in some degree blended."

In regard to the "many private citizens of worth and respectability" here referred to, Parton says:

"In this purchase, several persons participated, most of whom were near relatives or connections of Burr. One of his relatives in Connecticut, a descendant of Jonathan Edwards, advanced a great part of his savings for this purchase. Mr. Alston, probably, furnished money; it is certain he endorsed paper for his father-in-law. Burr's connections in New York were not backward in aiding him. From one source and another, a sum was raised which, as I conjecture, did not exceed forty thousand dollars, though more was to be forthcoming when needed.

"Who were his confederates? Before all others, his daughter, who was devoted to the scheme heart and soul. To achieve a career, and a residence, which she, her husband, and her boy could share, were the darling objects with which Burr had gone forth to seek a new country. She caught eagerly at his proposal. She saw in it the means whereby her father could win a glorious compensation for the wrongs she felt he had endured, and obtain a conspicuous triumph over all his enemies. Her husband, whose mind Burr had aided to form, and who tenderly loved Theodosia, entered into the enterprise with energy. In New York, it found adherents among the young ambitious men who had surrounded him in the days of his glory. The Swartwouts were in it. Marinus Willet, who was afterward Mayor of New York, was one of its promoters. A score or two of other New Yorkers were involved in a greater or less degree. Doctor Erich Bollman, a German, who had distinguished himself by a gallant attempt to rescue Lafayette from prison, was one of Burr's most trusted confederates. Dayton was another. Colonel Dupiester was one of the leading spirits. General Jackson, a thorough-going hater of Spaniards, was enthusiastic in the cause. General Adair, of Kentucky, deep in Burr's confidence, approved his plans heartily, but was not personally engaged in them. Blennerhassett was completely captivated by an enterprise which was to enrich him and his children without his being subjected to disagreeable exertion. Upon his island the first rendezvous was to be made. Mrs. Blennerhassett, no less ardent, was preparing to entertain the chief and his daughter at her fantastic mansion; for it was settled that Theodosia should accompany her father, and that both she and Mrs. Blennerhassett should go with the expedition as far as Natchez or New Orleans; there to await the issue. Alston was to follow in a few weeks. Probably five hundred persons in all, knew something of Burr's plans, and had entered into some kind of engagement to follow his fortunes. There were, also, four or five thousand whose names were on Burr's lists, and who, he thought, would hasten to his standard, as soon as he should obtain a foothold on Spanish soil."

There can, then, be no question of the immense influence which Burr wielded: that he should have embarked so many persons of ability and good character in his projects is a con clusive tribute to his tact, his industry and his profound dissimulation.

Burr was not ready to move before the latter part of July. Previous to starting from Philadelphia he wrote in cypher to Wilkinson a communication detailing the *processes* of the plot, quite minutely, betraying to his coadjutor the full extent of his contemplated work, and the programme for its execution. This most interesting and important letter he dispatched by the hands of two couriers, Samuel Swartwout, and a son of Matthew Ogden, of New Jersey. The two young men proceeded West by way of Pittsburg to St. Louis, where Burr supposed Wilkinson still to be. But, the General-in-Chief was not there: he was down in Lower Louisiana, at Nachitoches—a fact which materially affected the consummation of the concerted movement—Burr having arranged to have him (W.) move *down* the Mississippi, as a distinct section of the expedition. We shall see how the presence of Wilkinson in Louisiana, in advance of Burr's coming, caused the explosion of the whole enterprise.

Six days after the couriers left, Burr started for Pittsburg, accompanied by Theodosia, Colonel Dupeister and two others. His departure from the East excited comparatively little attention, nor did the gossips "snuff the air" until two months later, when word came back from the West of the din of preparation on the Ohio river which followed his advent. A newspaper printed at Lexington, Kentucky, called the *Western World*, edited by Wood, historian of "John Adams' Administration," first sounded the alarm. Becoming confident that some grand scheme of revolution was afoot, Wood and his friends (among whom were Humphrey Marshall and Jo Daviess) zealously struck at those supposed to be in command, unveiling as much of the old Spanish intrigues of Wilkinson, Sebastian, Innis and others as could be dragged to the light. Hence, soon after Burr reached the Ohio country he found himself suspected by the then few persons who still preserved their Federalism, and connected their old distrust of the ends and aims of "democratic societies" with the new movements. A "democratic" paper at Pittsburg, the *Commonwealth*, immediately after Burr's appearance in the West opened its columns to a discussion of Western claims to independency, laboring zealously to enkindle the old Whiskey insurrection spirit. These articles soon were responded to by a series published in the *Ohio Gazette*, printed at Chilicothe, then the State capital, over the signature of "Querist," furnished by Blennerhasset but afterwards ascribed to the tireless pen of Burr. "Querist" labored to show the necessity for separation from the Union east of the mountains, and to establish a Confederation composed of States west of the Alleghanies, embracing also as much of the South as should give the new Confederacy entire control of the Mississippi and the Gulf ports. By September 1st the public mind in Kentucky and Ohio was thoroughly aroused, and Aaron Burr's name was linked with every report of disunion and the conquest of Spanish dominion.

Wilkinson, though afar off in Louisiana, heard these mutterings on the Ohio; his name was connected with the indefinable greatness coming. It is quite probable that, *then* weighing the chances of promotion and honor in the scale, he resolved to break with Burr, and, by defeating his projects, to win the reputation of a deliverer.

Burr, floating down the Ohio, stopped at points indicated in his lists as favorable for securing recruits. A visit was paid to old Colonel Morgan, the Revolutionary patriot and pioneer, living, with his two sons, near Cannonsburg, Ohio. It was the Conspirator's design to secure the Colonel and his boys to his interest; but, over confident from his hitherto almost uniform success, he found, in the old man's home, hearts which he could not move. Morgan was a friend of Burr, sympathising with him in the Hamilton duel affair. The sons were sent forward by the father to conduct their august guest to the farm house.

On the road Burr opened his mind to one of the young men in a manner at once startling and confounding. He stated that the Union was near its dissolution, and that it ought to fail—that the West having no interests in common with the East, should set up for itself. He also made minute inquiries concerning the militia of the county, their disposable force, arms, &c. This conversation was the preliminary of what followed after dinner. Morgan's testimony taken at the Richmond trial we may repeat, in part:

"Colonel Burr said, that with two hundred men he could drive Congress, with the President at its head, into the river Potomac; or that it might be done; and he said with five hundred men, he could take possession of New York. He appealed to Colonel Dupiester, if it could not be done: he nodded assent. There was a reply made to this by one by my sons, that he would be damned if they could take our little town of Cannonsburg with that force. Some short time after this, Colonel Burr went out from the dining-room to the passage, and beckoned to my son Thomas. What their conversation was, I cannot say. soon after, a walk was proposed to my son's mill, and the company went out. When they returned, one (or both of my sons) came to caution me, and said: 'You may depend upon it, Colonel Burr will this night open himself to you. He wants Tom to go with him.' After the usual conversation, Colonel Burr went up stairs, and, as I thought, to go to bed. Mrs. Morgan was reading to me (as is usual, when the family have retired), when about eleven o'clock, and after I had supposed he had been an hour in bed, she told me that Colonel Burr was coming down, and as she had heard my son's conversation, she added, 'You'll have it now.' Colonel Burr came down with a candle in his hand. Mrs. Morgan immediately retired. The Colonel took his seat by me. He drew from his pocket a book. I suppose it was a memorandum-book. After looking at it, he asked me if I knew a Mr. Vigo, of Fort Vincent, a Spaniard. I replied, yes; I knew him; I had reasons to know him. One was that I had reasons to believe that he was deeply involved in the British conspiracy of 1798, as I supposed; the object of which was to separate the States; and which General Neville and myself had suppressed. I called it a nefarious thing to aim at the division of the States. I was careful to put great emphasis on the word '*nefarious.*' Colonel Burr, finding what kind of a man he had to deal with, suddenly stopped, thrust into his pocket the book which I saw had blank leaves in it, and retired to bed. I believe I was pretty well understood. The next morning Colonel Burr and Colonel Dupiester went off before breakfast, without my expecting it."

The old patriot, anxious and dissatisfied, proceeded to town and returned with two judges from the Court then in session there. To these he detailed minutely all the circumstances of Burr's visit. A letter thereupon was drawn up, directed to the President of the United States, giving information in regard to the matter and suggesting that the adventurer be closely watched. That letter, Mr. Jefferson stated, was the first intimation which he had of Burr's designs. In his special message of Jan. 22d, 1807, he said that, in the latter part of September he had "received intimations that designs were in agitation in the Western country, unlawful and unfriendly to the peace of the Union." "It was not," he further said, "till the latter part of October that the objects of the conspiracy began to be perceived, but still so blended and involved in mystery that nothing distinct could be singled out for pursuit." Having then had the Cannonsburg letter at least one month he adopted the suggestion to watch Burr's movements, and dispatched a confidential agent thither, who, of course, did not reach Ohio until far in November. The President certainly was not ignorant of affairs in the West up to the dates mentioned. Who better than himself was informed of the working of the disunion elements in Kentucky? Who can doubt that copies of the *Western World* and of the Pittsburg *Commonwealth* were quickly placed in his hands? The vigilant Jo Daviess we know kept the President "posted"; and, knowing all about Aaron Burr's movements, it is rather singular, to say the least, that no steps were taken *then* to arrest the schemer's programme. It is highly probable that the President, approving of Governor Shelby's version of the Constitutional right for American citizens to filibuster [see pages 237–38], preferred to wait until Burr had openly rendered himself amenable to arrest before proceeding to extremity. After he did let loose the thunders of the law upon the little Conspirator, all "Executive usurpations" of Washington and Adams were put to shame by the rigors of Jefferson's patriotic frenzy.

Leaving Morgan's place Burr proceeded to Marietta, where he found the militia attending a "general training." Riding to the field he exercised the men in evolutions and made a fine impression. At a ball given that evening the beautiful Theodosia mingled with the motley throng in the dance and confirmed the good impression made by the father. It soon was noised around that the ex-Vice President was *en route* for a new realm, and that he would accept volunteers. The idea was given that, in his proceedings, Burr had the sanction of his Government, which left all persons at liberty to second his movements, and Marietta soon became the centre of military activity, in forwarding and directing of which Herman Blennerhasset soon became the responsible agent. This credulous Irishman and his ambitious lady had not seen Burr for a year, but, by correspondence, had arranged to embark in his adventure—never dreaming for a moment, it was afterwards testified, that treason lay lurking in the background. Parton says:

"Leaving his daughter upon Blennerhassett Island, Burr bent all his powers to preparing for the expedition. Contracts for fifteen large batteaux, to be capable of transporting five hundred men, were entered into at Marietta, and the work forthwith began. Quantities of flour, pork and meal were purchased. On the island kilns were constructed for drying the corn. Men were daily added to the rolls, They appear to have been engaged for an object which was to be explained to them afterwards, but were all to come equipped and armed, and to each was promised, as part of the compensation for his services, one hundred acres of land on the Wachita. Blennerhassett was busy enough. To prepare the Western mind for future contingencies, he wrote a series of articles in a neighboring newspaper, in which the advantages of a separation of the Western States from the Eastern were discussed and exhibited. His island resounded with the din of preparation. Mrs. Blennerhassett, happy in the society of Theodosia, full of confidence in her father's talents, was all aglow with pleasant expectation. Burr was everywhere; now at Marietta; now at Chillicothe; then at Cincinnati; through Kentucky and Tennessee; everywhere gaining adherents, and enlarging his acquaintance with men of influence; received always as the great man. Six boats were set building on the Cumberland, and four thousand dollars deposited with General Jackson to pay for them. In October, Mr. Alston arrived, and soon after, he, Theodosia and Blennerhassett, journeyed, by easy stages, to Lexington, in Kentucky, leaving the energetic wife of Blennerhassett upon the island, to superintend the great concerns there going forward. On their journey they found the country full of rumors respecting Burr, and some scheme he was said to have in hand; but they also observed that these rumors were generally believed to be groundless; and attributed to the malice of Burr's old enemies, the Federalists."

Taking advantage of this near approach of Burr, the United States Attorney for the District of Kentucky, Jo Daviess, resolved to face public opinion, and, without instructions from Washington, to call Burr into court to answer the charge of being engaged in an enterprise contrary to the laws of the United States and designed to injure a power with which the Federal Government was at peace. The motion was made Nov. 3d, in the District Court at Frankfort, before Judge Innis—one of Wilkinson's *confreres* in Spanish intrigue. This motion fell like a thunder clap upon the public ear. Any other man than Jo Daviess must have quailed before the fury it invoked from seven-eighths of the people. But, the heart of that remarkable wild-woods' lawyer was of too stern stuff to shrink from duty. He read Burr and despised him. Burr read Daviess and feared him, but, with his usual effrontery, prepared to meet the danger. The motion, after two days reserve for consideration, was denied; but, Burr was quickly on hand to challenge an examination. With surprising self-possession he asked the Judge to grant the motion, in order that it might not trouble him at another moment. It was a master stroke, which gave the little man the vantage ground of an overwhelming public sympathy; but Daviess gladly closed with the proposition and set his day for a hearing. Burr was present at the appointed time (the Wednesday succeeding Nov. 5th). Much to his chagrin, Daviess had to ask for an extension of time. John Floyd, an important witness, was absent, and Nov. 25th was fixed upon for the hearing. What a moment in which to try the nerves of the immobile Conspirator! Time so precious to him—so all-important for success, thus to be wasted in awaiting the attendance of witnesses! What might not happen before Nov. 25th? Word having flown from Ohio to Washington an order for his arrest might arrive ere that time, and thus dash his prospects forever. By that time the State authorities might become aware of his deception in assuming that he acted with the consent of the Federal authorities; and, by siezing his flotilla, strip him of every resource. Yet, he betrayed not a single sign of impatience or of uneasiness. He addressed the Court at some length. "He hoped the good people of Kentucky would dismiss their apprehensions of danger from him, if any such really existed. There was really no ground for them, however zealously the attorney might strive to awaken them. He was engaged in no project inimical to the peace or tranquillity of the country; as they would certainly learn whenever the attorney should be ready, which he greatly apprehended would never be. In the mean time, although private business urgently demanded his presence elsewhere, he felt compelled to give the attorney one more opportunity of proving his charge, and would patiently await another attack."

Henry Clay appeared as Burr's counsel, having first received from him the most solemn assurance that he entertained "no design to intermeddle with or disturb the tranquillity of the United States, nor its territories, nor any part of them. He had neither issued, nor signed, nor promised a commission to any person for any purpose. He did not own a single musket, nor bayonet, nor any single article of military stores, nor did any other person for him, by his authority or knowledge. His views had been explained to several distinguished members of the Administration, were well understood and approved by the Government. They were such as every man of honor, and every good citizen must approve."

[The same and even stronger assurances were given to Governor Harrison under date of Nov. 27th. General Jackson, alarmed at the attitude of affairs, had to be appeased, and Burr also reassured him in the most unequivocal manner.]

It is not strange that, after such avowals, the people should deem the adventurer a persecuted man. Daviess, for a few weeks, carried upon his shoulders a load of obloquy and defamation which no other man in the West could sustain. He was a Federalist—one of that class then special objects of 'democratic' dislike; and now, that he was *persecuting* the man regarded by the masses as one of the chief founders of the democratic party, the District Attorney could hope for nothing less lenient than a coat of tar and feathers. But, what man in Kentucky dared to lay violent hands on Jo Daviess!

Again a postponement of the hearing, to Dec. 2d. Floyd

still being absent. When this latter day came Floyd was present, but John Adair (General Adair, one of Burr's confidants) was absent, and Daviess was forced to ask for a further postponement—the Grand Jury to remain impanneled. This Clay resisted. Collins, in his "History of Kentucky" says: "Burr, upon the present occasion, remained silent, and entirely unmoved by anything that occurred. A most animated and impassioned debate sprung up, intermingled with sharp and flashing personalities, between Clay and Daviess. Never did two more illustrious orators encounter each other in debate. The enormous mass which crowded to suffocation the floor, the galleries, the windows, the platform of the judge, remained still and breathless for hours, while these renowned and immortal champions, stimulated by mutual rivalry, and each glowing in the ardent conviction of right, encountered each other in splendid intellectual combat. Clay had the sympathies of the audience on his side, and was the leader of the popular party in Kentucky. Daviess was a Federalist, and was regarded as persecuting an innocent and unfortunate man from motives of political hate. But he was buoyed up by the full conviction of Burr's guilt, and the delusion of the people on the subject; and the very infatuation which he beheld around him, and the smiling serenity of the traitor who sat before him, stirred his great spirit to one of his most brilliant efforts. All, however, was in vain. Judge Innis refused to retain the grand jury, unless some business was brought before them; and Daviess, in order to gain time, sent up to them an indictment against John Adair, which was pronounced by the jury 'not a true bill.' The hour being late, Daviess then moved for an attachment to compel the presence of Adair, which was resisted by Burr's counsel, and refused by the court, on the ground that Adair was not in contempt till the day had expired. On the motion of Daviess, the court then adjourned to the following day."

On the following day Daviess demanded permission to attend the grand jury in their room for the purpose of examining witnesses—a claim resisted by Clay as unprecedented, and denied by Judge Innis. The grand jury retired, examined such witnesses as were sent up to them, and, on the 5th of December, returned "not a true bill." This return was accompanied by a written declaration signed by every juryman in which, in view of all the evidence placed before them, they exonerated Burr from any design inimical to the peace or well being of the country.

This acquittal was received with extraordinary demonstrations of satisfaction. Collins says: "The acquittal of Burr was celebrated at Frankfort by a brilliant ball, numerously attended; which was followed by another ball given in honor of the baffled attorney, by those friends who believed the charge to be just, and that truth, for the time, had been baffled by boldness, eloquence and delusion. At one of these parties the editor of the *Western World*, who had boldly sounded the alarm, was violently attacked, with a view of driving him from the ball-room, and was rescued with difficulty."

Thus freed from legal restraint, the adventurer hastened to perfect his arrangements for a descent of the river. He proceëded, in company with General Adair, to Nashville, where he became the recipient of new honors. The section of the expedition to move from Nashville down the Cumberland he was to lead in person. At the mouth of the Cumberland he would be joined by Blennerhessett's, Floyd's and Tyler's sections, when the whole would proceed on the Southern voyage. This was the plan.

But, delays had wrought the evils apprehended. Jefferson's messenger reached Marietta about Nov. 15th, and, by practising a little art, soon learned from the enthusiastic Blennerhassett enough to make action necessary. He proceeded quickly to Chillicothe, the State capital, where the Legislature was in session. An act was passed, without delay, empowering the Governor to call out the militia, to seize the boats building on the Muskingum, and to take all necessary steps to break up the expedition. The boats accordingly were seized early in December. The President's proclamation soon followed, to add zest to the pursuit of the now outlawed crusaders. A section of the expedition, fitting out at Beaver, Pennsylvania, hastened its departure. Four boats, under command of Colonel Tyler, reached Blennerhassett's island Dec. 10th. Finding that, not only were his own boats seized, but that the militia were to move down to seize those of Colonel Tyler, Blennerhassett hastily embarked, on the night of Dec. 13th, in Tyler's batteaux, with such of the men as chose to adhere to the enterprise. On the 14th a posse of militia with three justices of the peace visited the island, only to find there a company of gay young fellows just arrived from New York city. These, the justices "tried," but soon released from want of any evidence of their participation in Burr's enterprise. Mrs. Blennerhassett, with her children, having failed to obtain from the Marietta authorities her own specially furnished boat, dropped down to the island during the day (14th) and was rather roughly treated by the "citizen soldiery," who, having access to the wine cellar, soon became uproarous in their conduct. The New Yorkers offering the still resolute woman passage in their boat, she accepted the substitute for her own barge of state and fled down stream to join her husband. That beautiful house was quickly reduced to a ruin. Its grounds, its costly furniture, its expensive works of art—all were a wreck, ere a week had passed.

Hastening from Chillicothe, Graham, the Government's agent, proceeded to Frankfort, Kentucky, to find the Legislature in session and a state of high excitement prevailing. Jo Daviess had succeeded in obtaining a committee of investigation upon charges of corruption and Spanish pensions preferred against Sebastian, Judge Innis, George Nicholas, [the same who assumed the paternity of Jefferson's resolutions of '98] then deceased, and others. The disclosures which followed were startling enough; yet, strange as it may appear, the greatest sinner of all the "pensioners," General Wilkinson, escaped exposure. Graham arrived at the moment of these disclosures, and readily succeeded in securing the passage of an order for the arrest of all inculpated in Burr's enterprise. A few seizures only were made. Such a marvellous change had a few days made that, out of the great multitudes of those who had applauded and sustained the ex-Vice President, not a beggarly dozen could be found who did not now denounce him! Jo Daviess' hour of triumph indeed had come.

Burr, at Nashville, heard of Graham's mission, and precipitately fled, with but two boats, down the Cumberland, on the night preceding the arrival of orders for his arrest. General Adair at the same time started overland to New Orleans. Reaching (Dec. 24th) the mouth of the Cumberland, the fugitive found Blennerhasset, Floyd and Tyler already there, awaiting his coming. Some delay was made in that then wild and distant spot, awaiting the arrival of other boats which it was supposed would escape from Cincinnati and other points. But, the zeal of Burr's late friend, United States Senator Smith, and the activity of the Ohio and Kentucky authorities, prevented the embarkation of recruits. No reenforcements, therefore, were forthcoming. Burr did not despair. He at once commenced an intrigue to secure the garrison of Fort Massac, (located on the Ohio, nearly opposite the Cumberland mouth). A sergeant only was obtained under the false plea that he was required for a special mission to St. Louis.

A count of heads showed the "expeditionary force" to consist of sixty men and ten boats. With this array the monarch of undefined realms floated away down stream, on the route to New Orleans and—Richmond. Not one of the men knew whither they were bound. They were a jolly set, who loved nothing so much as whiskey and a fiddle—two commodities with which they were well supplied. The silences of the great Father of waters were strangely disturbed by the merry-making of that band of brothers.

January 3d, 1807, the flotilla brought up at the Chicksaw Bluffs (Memphis) a military post, having a small garrison. Burr sought to enlist the services of its commanding officer and nearly succeeded; but, the officer, after consultation with friends, refused his co-operation and Burr proceeded on his way without a single recruit from that station. January 10th he reached the settlement of Bayou Pierre, thirty miles above Natchez, and there from a newspaper first learned, to his great amazement and indignation, that Wilkinson had proven false and was even then preparing New Orleans to resist the grand climax of horrors which his eager fancy had painted as coming in the train of Aaron Burr's advent. The country was all ablaze with excitement. The Governor of Mississippi already had out a proclamation denouncing the expedition and calling upon all to assist in its suppression. In the hurried glance over that newspaper the Conspirator read his doom: his Mexican castle was gone and a prison stared him in the face.

We may now recur to Wilkinson's operations. The two messengers dispatched by Burr, after nine weeks' incessant traveling, reached the mouth of the Red river to learn that Wilkinson was at Nachitoches. Ogden went on down to New Orleans, while Swartwout, with the important letter in cypher, pushed on for the United States' camp, arriving there October 8th. After some little delay the precious package was placed by the bearer in Wilkinson's hands. The letter, as interpreted by the General-in-chief, and as given in evidence, read:

"Yours, post-marked 13th of May, is received. I, Aaron Burr, have obtained funds, and have actually commenced the enterprise. Detachments from different points, and under different pretenses, will rendezvous on the Ohio, 1st November—everything internal and external, favors views; protection of England is secured. T—— is going to Jamaica to arrange with the admiral on that station; it will meet on the Mississippi. ——, England, ——, navy of the United States are ready to join, and final orders are given to my friends and followers: it will be a host of choice spirits. Wilkinson shall be second to Burr only, Wilkinson shall dictate the rank and promotion of his officers. Burr will proceed westward, 1st August, never more to return; with him goes his daughter; the husband will follow in October, with a corps of worthies.

"Send forth an intelligent and confidential friend with whom Burr may confer; he shall return immediately with further interesting details; this is essential to concert and harmony of movement. Send a list of all persons known to Wilkinson, west of the mountains, who may be useful, with a note delineating their characters. By your messenger send me four or five commissions of your officers, which you can borrow under any pretense you please; they shall be returned faithfully. Already are orders to the contractors given to forward six months' provisions to points Wilkinson may name: this shall not be used until the last moment, and then under proper injunctions. The project is brought to the point so long desired. Burr guarantees the result with his life and honor, with the honor and fortunes of hundreds of the best blood of our country.

"Burr's plan of operation is, to move down rapidly from the Falls on the 15th of September, with the first 500 or 1,000 men in light boats, now constructing for that purpose, to be at Natchez between the 5th and 15th of December; there to meet Wilkinson; there to determine whether it will be expedient in the first instance to seize on or pass by Baton Rouge. On receipt of this send an answer. Draw on Burr for all expenses, etc. The people of the country to which we are going, are prepared to receive us. Their agents, now with Burr, say, that if we will protect their religion, and will not subject them to a foreign power, that in three weeks all will be settled. The gods invite to glory and fortune; it remains to be seen whether we deserve the boon. The bearer of this goes express to you; he will hand a formal letter of introduction to you from Burr. He is a man of inviolable honor and perfect discretion; formed to execute rather than to project; capable of relating facts with fidelity, and incapable of relating them otherwise. He is thoroughly informed of the plans and intentions of Burr, and will disclose to you as far as you inquire and no further. He has imbibed a reverence for your character, and may be embarrassed in your presence. Put him at ease, and he will satisfy you."

Accompanying this was a brief but very significant note from ex-Senator Dayton. It ran:

"Dear Sir: It is now well ascertained that you are to be displaced in next session. Jefferson will affect to yield reluctantly to the public sentiment, but yield he will. Prepare yourself, therefore, for it. You know the rest. You are not a man to despair, or even despond, especially when such prospects offer in another quarter. Are you ready? Are your numerous associates ready? Wealth and glory, Louisiana and Mexico! I shall have time to receive a letter from you before I set out for Ohio. OHIO. Address one to me here, and another in Cincinnati. Receive and treat my nephew affectionately as you would receive your friend DAYTON."

Here, then, were the results of his connection with Burr. What should be done? It was stated on evidence that the letter was decyphered during the night, and that, early the next morning, the General announced to Colonel Cushing its important contents, at the same time declaring his purpose to oppose Burr's enterprise with every means in his power. But, we can well conceive that the conscience of the man was not put to any sudden test, although Burr's rather extraordinarily bold programme may have startled the soldier for a moment.

The General doubtless had determined upon his course weeks prior to Swartwout's appearance—had resolved to suppress his own conspiracy and thus obtain the thanks of his countrymen! That was his usual way of advancement. Parton says:

"At the last moment, then, Wilkinson shrank from the work expected of him. The probability is strong that he always *meant* to do so. That he was a weak, vain, false, greedy man, is likely enough. That carried away by the magic of Burr's resistless *presence*, and hoping the scheme would never involve *him* in its folds, he suggested, encouraged and aided it, is very probable. That he had given Burr to understand, in some vague way, that he would strike a blow which would begin a war, whenever it should be needed, is also probable. That he chose the part he did choose from a calculation of advantages to himself, from motives mean and mercenary, rests upon evidence that convinces. Nevertheless, the fact remains, that he did *not* "strike the blow;" he did *not* involve two nations in war; he did *not* shape his course according to the wishes of Aaron Burr, instead of the orders of Thomas Jefferson. If he was a traitor, he was a traitor to his confederates, not to his country, his commission, his flag. True, the country, particularly the Western States, desired war, and would have applauded him for beginning it. But to a soldier, his country speaks only through the commands of its chief."

The author might have paused at his words "evidence that convinces." We conceive it as admitting of no denial, that the General chose his part from motives base enough to relieve his memory from the charge of once having acted the patriot's part from a patriot's sense of duty.

In spite, however, of the General's announced purpose, he did not act as promptly as his testimony would indicate. He kept Swartwout in camp for *ten* days, when the messenger was permitted to go down stream to New Orleans, fully believing in the General's good faith to Burr. After Swartwout had been gone *three* days the General resolved to dispatch information to Jefferson. Parton states:

"The messenger left camp on the 21st of October, and delivered his dispatches to the President on the 25th of November. On the 27th, Jefferson issued his proclamation, and sent it flying through the States, paralyzing the enterprise as it flew, and filling the country with consternation. It is noticeable, that neither in Wilkinson's dispatches, nor in Jefferson's proclamation, was the name of Burr mentioned.

Wilkinson, indeed, expressly and falsely wrote that he did not know who the prime mover of the conspiracy was. He admitted, afterward, that he wrote a letter to Burr after the receipt of the cypher, but, upon reflection, pursued the letter and destroyed it. The President's proclamation merely announced that unlawful enterprises were on foot in the Western States; warned all persons 'to withdraw themselves from the same without delay,' 'as they will answer the contrary at their peril, and incur prosecution with all the rigors of the law;' and commanded all officers, civil and military, to use their immediate and utmost exertions to bring the offending persons to condign punishment."

The duplicity of the man stands forth here as in almost every decisive act of his life: he wrote to Burr *after* he had resolved upon his arrest, but recalled the messenger, and thereupon debated several precious days further, took counsel of his wits and of Swartwout, then dismissed the bearer of the cypher, and, after three days' further reasoning with himself, dispatched a messenger to the President. But, even then he practiced deceit, stating that he did not know who was the prime mover of the conspiracy! He did not know himself.

After the departure of his dispatches to Washington, Wilkinson moved his army from Nachitoches to the Sabine river, where the Spaniards still remained in menacing force. He soon arranged terms of truce, much to the disgust of his men, who were eager to "wipe out" the Dons; and then departed for New Orleans, ordering Colonel Cushing to follow with the bulk of the army. On the very day that his dispatches reached the Capital the General-in-Chief dropped into New Orleans, to find the city in a state of mysterious excitement. The sturdy patriot, Andrew Jackson, had written to Claiborne, Governor of "Orleans territory," under date of Nov. 12th, in a manner to excite alarm. Jackson said, among other things:

"Put your town (New Orleans) in a state of defense, organize your militia, and defend your city as well against internal enemies as external. My knowledge does not extend so far as to authorise me to go into detail, but, I fear you will meet an attack from quarters you do not at present expect. Be upon the alert; keep a watchful eye on your General, and beware of an attack as well from your own country as from Spain. I fear there is something rotten in the State of Denmark. * * Beware of the month of December. I love my country and Government; I hate the Dons; I would delight to see Mexico reduced, but I would die in the last ditch before I would yield a foot to the Dons, or see the Union disunited."

Claiborne at once sought for explanations of Wilkinson and was admitted to the secret. It was resolved to call the citizens together to make known to them the threatened danger. This was done. Wilkinson addressed them, giving information of the cypher letter, and filling out the details with alarming amplification of impending dangers. The multitude was thoroughly aroused and readily answered the call to arms. Volunteers enrolled to man the old fortifications and to assist in erecting new stockades at various endangered points. A strong guard was dispatched to occupy the river banks above the city, there to overhaul every craft floating down stream. The Legislature of Orleans territory was called together in special session to consider a communication from Wilkinson, which contained a translation of the cypher letter. [It was this communication which Burr read at Bayou Pierre—his first intimation of Wilkinson's defection.] The fears grew; Wilkinson was in his element—was the leading spirit of the storm. He became convinced that the civil law was impotent to cope with the dangers menacing, and resolved to "take the responsibility" of declaring martial law. Swartwout, Ogden, Bollman and Adair were forcibly seized, and, in spite of the efforts of their still staunch friends, were forced on board a vessel and sent to Baltimore—prisoners with not a single proven charge against them. Writs of *habeas corpus* were scorned, and the judge who issued them, (Workman,) was placed under arrest as a *particeps criminis*, sent to the common guard house and kept imprisoned until released by the efforts of the U. S. District Judge. [Swartwout and Bollman were examined, when they reached Washington, and were at once released—no evidence of any kind being given to sustain the arrest.] A reign of terror prevailed. Citizens were arrested and placed under surveillance. Houses were visited, papers overhauled, a passport system introduced, an embargo laid upon commerce except under special restrictions: every thing was done which savored of extreme danger.

Turning from this scene of excitement to Burr's little encampment on the east side of the Mississippi just above Bayou Pierre, and beholding there less than one hundred men, a rollicing, half armed, uninformed crew, it is difficult to suppress a laugh at the discrepancy between the imaginary and the real danger.

Week after week passed at New Orleans, and yet no signs of the "invaders"—no appearance of an English fleet in the offing—no uprising of the people in favor of the Mexican scheme! The General began to grow visibly uneasy at the absence of an enemy. He began to fear for his reputation as a courageous and discreet officer. It was growing ridiculously awkward—that standing challenge for a combat which none would accept. So the Orleans papers thought, and, ere long, so they dared to speak. The grand jury presented his measures as illegal and unconstitutional; the press arraigned him as an incompetent officer and a dangerous man; the people denounced his as a second edition of Falstaff—whom he, indeed, represented in so many of his mental and physical characteristics as to excite a regret that the General had not chosen the dramatic boards for his 'field of operations.'

But, the General was not without his grain of comfort. The issue by Jefferson of the proclamation of Nov. 27th; his emission of orders of warning and of arrest to the Governors; his message of Dec. 2d, to be followed by the special message of Jan. 22d [see Appendix for message in full]; his several approbatory letters to his friend, all served to console the agent by proving that the Administration was equally excited with himself. Then the deposition of Eaton was given publicity, to add immensely to the public excitement, and Burr became, for the moment, a monster of huge proportions; his past history was revived and painted in colors dismal enough for a Mohammedan; his victims in the social circle were counted by the dozen and his natural children by the scores; his duplicity, subtelty, power of persuasion were freely canvassed even by his old political coadjutors: he became, for the day, the sum of all villainies. Such was the change which accompanied the man's fortunes. In July he was His Excellency, the ex-Vice President; in January he was Satan.

Burr, after reading in the New Orleans journal, Wilkinson's communication to the called session of the Legislature, and also the proclamations for his arrest, expressed no perturbation, although his surprise must have been complete. He conversed freely with the planter, at whose residence he obtained the news, affirming his innocence of designs against the Union, and so far won upon the planter's confidence as to secure a warm friend. After a brief conference it was decided to move the boats and men over the river, thus to place them and himself beyond the jurisdiction of the Mississippi Executive. This was done, and a little encampment made at a point about thirty miles above Natchez. From thence he addressed a letter to the public expressive of surprise at the excitement prevailing, denying that his expedition had any other than a legitimate object, and requesting that his "fellow citizens should visit his camp and boats, and by observation learn the folly of their apprehensions"; but, the Governor answered the invitation by calling out the militia of Natchez and vicinity to arrest the fugitives under the authority of the President's proclamation and special instructions. These troops gathered without delay at Cole's creek, a few miles below Bayou Pierre, opposite to which was Burr's camp. Prior to any action, however, an arrangement was made with Poindexter, Attorney-General of Mississippi Territory, for Burr to meet Governor Mead at Cole's creek. This audience took place Jan. 16th, when Burr was informed that, in spite of his location on the Louisiana side, the militia would move upon his camp at once. He therefore surrendered himself a prisoner, and was conducted for a hearing to the town of Washington, the seat of territorial government, ten miles east of Natchez. Poindexter was of opinion that the prisoner, having committed no offense in Mississippi Territory, could not be indicted; he also held "that the Supreme Territorial Court, being a court of appeals only, could not entertain original jurisdiction of the matter, and that it would be best to send Burr to the seat of the National Government, where the Supreme Court of the United States was in session, by which the proper locality for the trial of Burr might be determined. But Rodney, the judge before whom

Burr was brought, thinking differently, directed a grand jury to be summoned to attend the approaching term of the Supreme Territorial Court, and Burr to give recognizances to appear from day to day. He was not without sympathizers among the neighboring planters, and found no difficulty in obtaining sureties. When the court met, Feb. 5th, Poindexter took the same ground he did before; but, as the two judges were divided in opinion, his motion was overruled." The grand jury therefore took the case into consideration, and, after a comparitively brief sitting, returned the following extraordinary verdict:

"The grand jury of the Mississippi Territory, on a due investigation of the evidence brought before them, are of opinion that Aaron Burr has not been guilty of any crime or misdemeanor against the laws of the United States, or of this Territory; or given any just cause of alarm or inquietude to the good people of the same.

"The grand jurors present, as a grievance, the late military expedition, unnecessarily, as they conceive, fitted out against the person and property of the said Aaron Burr, when no resistance has been made to the civil authorities.

"The grand jurors also present, as a grievance, destructive of personal liberty, the late military arrests, made without warrant, and, as they conceive, without other lawful authority; and they do sincerely regret that so much cause has been given to the enemies of our glorious Constitution, to rejoice at such measures being adopted, in a neighboring Territory, as, if sanctioned by the Executive of our country, must sap the vitals of our political existence, and crumble this glorious fabric in the dust."

This was indeed a "turning of the tables." Instead of indicting the prisoner his prosecutors were arraigned! Poindexter declared the return both a disgrace and an outrage; the Judge pronounced it impertinent and useless; but their indignation did not drive the grand jury into any change of sentiment. Burr demanded his legal release, that his recognizance might be no longer binding; but, it was resolved to hold him for further proceedings, or, as Burr feared, to hand him over to Wilkinson. His release was refused by the bench and attorney. He determined to fly: fall into Wilkinson's hands he would not. Visiting his camp he informed the men of his danger, advising them to sell the boats, provisions, &c., and to go their own way—offering all who chose to go grants of soil on the Wachita purchase. He then recrossed the river; was carefully equipped by his friends (he found plenty of them among the planters), and, provided with a good guide, struck off across the wilderness for the weary journey to the Atlantic coast, or to Pensacola, as circumstances should determine. The Court on assembling next morning called the prisoner, and, upon his non-appearance, declared his recognizance forfeited. A reward of two thousand dollars was offered for his arrest. Numbers of vagabonds were soon roaming the country in the search, though none secured the coveted prize. A negro boy who had been known to act as Burr's servant appeared on the shore opposite the flotilla, wearing his master's overcoat. He was seized, when, upon search, a note was discovered stitched to the lining of the cape addressed to "C. T." and "D. F." It read:

"If you are yet together, keep so, and I will join you to-morrow night. In the mean while, put all your arms in perfect order. Ask no questions of the bearer, but tell him all you may think I wish to know. He does not know that this is from me, nor where I am."

This doubtless was designed by Burr as a blind. Colonel Comfort Tyler, and Davis Floyd, ex-member of the Indiana Legislature, still were in camp, in charge of their respective sections. Guards were set at once by the Governor to watch for the re-appearance of the chief, but he was even then well on his way to the East, accompanied by a trusty guide. C. F. and D. T. and Blennerhassett were placed under arrest; but, nothing transpiring, they soon were released. The expedition at once dissolved. The Irishman, accompanied by his now thoroughly disheartened if not disgusted wife, retained enough means to make his way back to the island. He started for the North only to be arrested in Kentucky, by orders from Washington, and was borne to Richmond to be tried for treason. Most of the adventurers found their way back, unmolested, to their homes, though a few tarried to supply that benighted region with school and music masters.

The story of Burr's arrest in the backwoods of Alabama forms, in his biographer's (Parton) version, a very romantic episode. Stripping it of embellishment it may be told as follows: One cold evening in February (the 18th) two young lawyers were playing at backgammon in a cabin, in Wakefield, the county seat of Washington county, Alabama. Their game was disturbed by the arrival, before the door, of two travellers, one of whom made inquiry for the residence of Colonel Hinson, a leading man of that vicinity. One of the lawyers, Colonel Nicholas Perkins, passed out to direct the strangers, and observed by the glare of the bright fire that the inquirer, though outwardly dressed in the rough garb of a common planter, was a person of mark. His dazzling eye, the silvery ring of his voice and correct pronunciation of his words, the delicately booted foot projecting from the homespun pantaloons, the air of superiority—all indicated the owner to be no common man. Perkins gave the required information and entered the cabin again to pronounce the words "Aaron Burr!" to his incredulous companion. A description of the man, appended to the proclamation and reward for his arrest, left no doubt of his identity. Perkins proceeded to arouse the Sheriff. These two then made their way to the house of Colonel Hinson, in pursuit of Burr and his guide. Once there Perkins was left in the woods while the Sheriff entered the house. The two travellers were warming in the kitchen by a bright fire. While Mrs. Hinson proceeded to get supper, the Sheriff entered into conversation with the suspected stranger. The officer was "fascinated," like all others who came in contact with the man; he did not return, as promised, to Perkins. Not to be thwarted, however, the young lawyer started for Fort Stoddart, on the Tombigbee, twelve miles below, where he arrived at daybreak. Lieutenant Gaines (afterward Major-General Edmund P. Gaines) then in command, with a file of dragoons, and accompanied by Perkins, started in pursuit, directing their course to the Pensacola road. Turning up this road toward Wakefield they met Burr and his companion, only two miles from Hinson's house—the Sheriff having but just left the travellers, after directing them on their way. Gaines rode forward and accosted the stranger: "I presume I have the honor of addressing Colonel Aaron Burr." "I am a traveller, sir; and do not recognise your right to question me," was the reply, as the horseman moved on. Gaines pulled from his breast pocket the proclamation, and thrusting it before the fugitive's face exclaimed: "I arrest you by authority of this proclamation, as a prisoner to the Federal Government!" Burr attempted to intimidate his captor; but the young officer was resolute, and firmly bade Burr accompany him to his quarters, where he would be treated with all the respect due the ex-Vice President of the United States. Seeing that resistance was useless the dethroned chief submitted with a good grace, and was escorted to the Fort (Feb. 19th). There he remained until March 5th, making complete captive of all, both male and female, in and around the Fort. Leading citizens visited him freely, and the ladies, generally, showered all manner of attentions upon him. His departure from the Fort, for the trip through the wilderness to the North, we are told, was a scene of affecting adieux. "The tears," says Parton, "of the ladies residing at the fort fell fast as Colonel Burr, escorted by a file of soldiers, went down to the shore and embarked on board the boat provided for the ascent of the Alabama. He had no enemies there. The men could have no ill-will to one whose offense had been a desire to terminate the hateful rule of the Spaniards; and women were always and everywhere his friends. As the boat, with its crew of soldiers, glided past the few houses on the river's bank, all the ladies, it is said, waved their handkerchiefs, except those who were obliged to put those weapons to a tenderer use. One of the ladies of the Alabama named her infant Aaron Burr; and he was not the only young gentleman in the South-west who bore through life a similar record of the events amid which he was born."

Of that novel journey through the unsettled wilds a pleasing chapter might be written. The guard of nine trusty men was officered by Colonel Perkins, in person, who would not admit any man less resolute than himself to the important mission of delivering Burr safely to the authorities at Washington. Extreme caution was used to guard against any influence over the men, as well as to avoid all settlements where a rescue might be attempted. Only one effort was made by Burr to

White del. Rogers sc.

THE ARREST OF AARON BURR.

secure his liberty, but it failed through Perkins' resolute and rapid action. After various adventures the party safely reached Fredericksburg, in Virginia. An express from Washington directed the prisoner to be taken to Richmond, where he arrived March 26th, 1807.

On Monday, March 30th, the preliminary examination took place, before Chief-Justice John Marshall, assisted by Judge Griffin, of the District Court. Burr made his own defense—at once ingenious and, apparently, ingenuous. A three days' hearing followed. Burr called to his aid Edmund Randolph, already referred to in these pages in connection with Genet's Conspiracy. The celebrated Luther Martin, of Maryland, was afterwards added to his splendid staff of counsel. The prosecution though ordered by the U. S. Attorney General, Rodney, was conducted by the District Attorney, George Hay, assisted by that man of many brilliant qualities, William Wirt, of Richmond. Lieutenant-Governor McRae afterwards was added to the prosecutor's staff. The preliminaries resulted in a decision to commit Burr for a misdemeanor, leaving to the grand jury the investigation of the charge of treason. Two leading citizens of Richmond became his bondsmen in the sum of ten thousand dollars for his appearance at the ensuing session of the U. S. Circuit Court, to sit in Richmond May 22d, 1807.

But a few days after this examination we find Jefferson adding to his singular record of mingled frenzy and folly by writing a letter to U. S. Senator Giles, of Virginia. He referred with much bitterness to the trickery shown by the Judges, in hastening the trial so as to clear Burr; he railed at the Federalists as a disappointed set who regretted Burr's failure to sever the Union, assuming, with a partisan antipathy which should shame a President, that, had Burr succeeded, even partially, the Federalists were prepared to join the Conspirator for the overthrow of a Republic which they hated and to instal "their favorite monarchy"! And much more to the same effect; showing himself, to a later generation, as to have been a very implacable man. He sunk the dignity of the President in the irritability of the politician. Throughout the entire trial his conduct was directed by the idea that the Federalists were leagued to secure Burr's acquittal—that the Chief Justice and the associate Circuit Judge were political partisans instead of grave and austere dispensers of law. The record is one which even Mr. Randall finds it difficult to reconcile with fairness and wisdom. A more impartial and upright judge than John Marshall never graced a bench; among Chief Justices he stands a Washington of legal wisdom, prudence and truth; and the writer who attempts to defend Mr. Jefferson for his aspersions of the Judge in the conduct of the Burr trial has an unenviable task before him. Burr, adverting to the *animus* of the prosecution as betrayed in the earliest stages of the trial, said:

"The most indefatigable industry is used by the agents of government, and they have money at command without stint. If I were possessed of the same means, I could not only foil the prosecutors, but render them ridiculous and infamous. The democratic papers teem with abuse against me and my counsel, and even against the Chief Justice. Nothing is left undone or unsaid which can tend to prejudice the public mind, and produce a conviction without evidence. The machinations of this description which were used against Moreau in France were treated in this country with indignation. They are practiced against me in a still more impudent degree, not only with impunity, but with applause; and the authors and abettors suppose, with reason, that they are acquiring favor with the Administration."

The trial came on as set, May 22d, Judges Marshall and Griffin on the Bench. A grand jury was impanneled after much trouble, almost all men regarding as true the declaration made by Jefferson in his Message of Jan. 22d, that Burr's "guilt is placed beyond a question." The culprit of State assumed the conduct of his own case to find use for all of his astonishing resources. He was equal to the situation: his sagacity, accumen, tenacity of memory, power of combination and command of the technicalities of law excited the astonishment even of those who knew him best; while to Jefferson (who may be called the real prosecutor) and the Attorney General's assistants, the prisoner was a very Phœnix. On the jury was placed, among others, Senator Giles. Him Burr challenged, as well as two or three equally offensive as prejujudiced censors. It was finally impanneled, and John Randolph, of Roanoke was made foreman in spite of his declaration of a belief in Burr's guilt. This consumed the first day. The second day was taken up with minor matters: nothing of importance could be done until the arrival of Wilkinson, who was looked for hourly. On the third day the prosecution made a motion to commit Burr for high treason instead of "misdemeanor." This elicited all the energies of the defense, and there followed three days of a memorable rhetorical war, in which the several combatants displayed their noblest abilities. The object, as stated, was to commit Burr to prison. Wirt assumed that, in view of Wilkinson's coming, the prosecution had no faith in Burr's intention to confront his accuser —they feared that he would forfeit his bail and escape. To this Randolph replied with much severity. He said:

> "Of James Wilkinson we are not afraid, in whatever shape he may be produced, in whatever form he may appear in this court. We are only afraid of those effects which desperation may produce in his mind. Desperation is a word of great fitness in his case. General Wilkinson we behold first acting as a conspirator to ensnare others, afterwards as a patriot to betray them from motives of patriotism. What must be the embarrassment of this man when the awful catastrophe arrives, that he must either substantiate his own innocence by the conviction of another, or be himself regarded as a traitor and conspirator in the event of the acquittal of the accused."

Mr. Randolph evidently did not know the General: he never was "embarrassed" at anything, let his failure be ever so glaring. The motion was finally disposed of by doubling the bail bond.

Still, Wilkinson did not arrive. The counsel employed their time in plot and counterplot for the advantage of position. Burr in person had visited Washington to obtain the first dispatch of Wilkinson to the President, in which the General stated that he did not know who was the prime mover of the conspiracy; but had failed to secure a copy of the document. It was moved by his counsel that the Court should issue a *subpœna duces tecum* to the President of the United States *requiring* him to furnish the said dispatch, and also copies of the orders issued to the army and navy during the late excitement. This compulsory mandate started many new and novel points of law, for which but few precedents existed, and to govern which no rule prevailed. These points were argued both with bitterness and ability. The result was a decision that the subpœna might issue. Thereat the President became exceedingly excited, and not without some reason, considering the language used by Luther Martin, which was violent and indecorous. The President conceived the idea that Martin himself must be guilty of participation in the Conspirator's schemes, hence his zeal in Burr's behalf. Indeed, Mr. Jefferson was in possession of a letter from one Graybell, a citizen of Baltimore, who testified to Martin's complicity. The Prosecuting Attorney therefore was written to (June 19th): "Shall we move to commit Luther Martin as *particeps criminis* with Burr? Graybell will fix upon him misprison of treason at least. At any rate his evidence will put down this impudent and unprincipled Federal bull dog, and add another proof that the most clamorous defenders of Burr are all his accomplices." Notwithstanding this invitation of the Executive to trap the "bull dog," Mr. Hay did not adjudge the attempt prudent. The President was getting repaid for stating, in his "Notes on Virginia," that Martin was son-in-law to Michael Cresap, the murderer of Logan's family—a statement which Martin never forgave.

The quotation above given is interesting as indicating the extremely excited state of the President's mind. After receiving Judge Marshall's decision he wrote (June 30th) to Mr. Hay, forcibly deprecating that invasion of the Executive's dignity and rights, and threatened to use force, if necessary, to protect, as Mr. Randall terms it, "the constitutional inviolability of his office." Jefferson persisted in treating the decision as a designed personal indignity, particularly in view of his precedent in a somewhat parallel case. In the prosecutions growing out of the Miranda expedition he had authorised his Secretaries of Departments not to obey any summons of a court to be present and to testify on behalf of the defense. Here the case was aggravated by the invasion of the Executive's sanctity, making him amenable to a *subpœna*. But, the President *forced* the construction of the decision. The Judge, in granting the motion, expressly stated that the summons must not be used as a means of personal annoyance; nor did he allude to any process to *compel* the President to supply the papers: all was left to his own sense of duty and dignity. The matter was, however, virtually ended before the President's indignant protest of the 20th, for he had, prior to receiving the Judge's decision, ordered all the papers demanded to be given in. Why, then, his threat to use force in event of an invasion of his prerogatives?

Wilkinson, having arrived June 15th, appeared in court June 17th, after which the witnesses were sent up to the grand jury in great numbers. The defense at once turned their whole strategy on an effort to vitiate Wilkinson's testimony, but the grand jury anticipated the attempted impeachment by returning, on the 24th, separate indictments against Aaron Burr and Herman Blennerhassett for "treason" and for "misdemeanors." This consigned the accused to prison. On the afternoon of that day Burr was given over to the city jailor for custody. Two days after, three of the prisoner's counsel made affidavit concerning the unhealthy and unfit state of his quarters, when the Court ordered a front room of the house occupied by Martin to be prepared for his safe-keeping. Before this change was effected Mr. Hay presented a resolution passed by the Virginia Council of State tendering "apartments" in the third story of the Penitentiary, and he moved Burr's commitment there. To this the prisoner's counsel strenuously objected—the quarters proposed by the Court being more convenient. The Governor, Cabell, then wrote to offer Burr a choice of the rooms in the Penitentiary, with a stipulation that he should be permitted to see only those persons whom he chose to admit. A fine suite of three rooms were fitted up on the third floor of the building, where "the confined" lived in state until Aug. 2d, when he was returned to Martin's house. This assignment to Burr of respectable quarters called forth from Jefferson an indignant and unseemly protest. He conceived that, thereafter, any prisoner would have a right to demand comfortable apartments. He viewed Burr as a malefactor and desired him to be treated as such.

After Burr's indictment true bills were found against Colonel Comfort Tyler, Jonathan Dayton, John Smith, (U. S. Senator,) Davis Floyd and Israel Smith. After which the Court adjourned (June 27th) to Aug. 3d. The interregnum was required by both parties to make up their cases and to prepare for the important crisis, which was not only to determine the fate of Burr and his accomplices but was to fix precedents and supply legal construction of the law of treason. During the interval "the confined" remained in his apartment, but was more like a convalescing prince than a prisoner. His rooms were frequented by eminent persons of both sexes—many of whom came long distances to be present at the trial. The ladies of Richmond showered luxuries upon his table. He wrote gay letters, received visitors, chatted with cheerfulness and held conference with his counsel, thus filling up every moment of the entire day. From this pleasant Penitentiary he was transferred, Aug. 2d, to quarters prepared in Martin's lodgings near the Court House. On the day of trial he entered the room accompanied by his son-in-law, Governor Alston, of South Carolina. His serenity was complete and his energies all alive to the general conduct of his own case.

To impanel a jury was a tedious process—almost every person summoned having formed an opinion. It was not until the 17th that a panel was secured and sworn in. Even then it was accepted only as the most unprejudiced that could be had! The introduction of testimony followed. Eaton, Commodore Truxton, the Morgans, Blennerhassett's gardener, groom, and Woodbridge, his chief agent, were examined—the effort being to prove the overt act. Not a shadow of proof was adduced which could secure that starting point. When the prosecution endeavored to introduce collateral and indirect evidence to sustain their case, it was resisted by the defense. A nine days' struggle followed over the right to put in secondary and inferential testimony after the primary and direct testimony had failed. The splendid debate elicited all the legal talent engaged. During the wordy contest William Wirt pronounced that speech upon the characters of Aaron Burr and Blennerhassett which has rendered his name famous in school-books, and his victim infamous. The Virginian's oratorical effort long must remain, both as a fine specimen of rhetorical beauty and as a ridiculous sacrifice of fact to fancy. Parton very correctly characterises the speech as a "brilliant fiction." The contest over the point raised was not ended until Aug. 29th. Judge Marshall's decision was rendered on the 31st. His review of the case as presented was very clear, able and impartial. He sustained the motion to exclude testimony indirect or merely corroborative, because, being incompetent to prove the overt act itself, it was *irrelevant.*

This, of course, closed the case as to the prosecution for treason, unless the prosecutors should take exception to the ruling of the Court, or should spring some other and new issue. Mr. Hay asked time for himself and associates to consider the matter, and the Court adjourned to the day following, when the Prosecuting Attorney expressed his willingness to submit the case without further contest. The jury retired and very soon returned with their verdict recorded as follows:

"We, of the jury, say that Aaron Burr is not proved to be guilty under the indictment by any evidence submitted to us. We, therefore, find him not guilty."

This singular finding for the moment excited Burr. He protested against its form and demanded that it should be rendered in the usual words, "guilty" or "not guilty." The jury positively refusing to qualify their verdict, the matter was compromised by an order of the Court to enter on the journal "not guilty."

The result, though it seemingly took none by surprise, greatly exasperated those who, like Mr. Jefferson, had resolved that he "was guilty without a shadow of doubt."[1] The President wrote to Mr. Hay, (Sept. 4th,) bidding him to pay no witness, nor to let him depart without taking a copy of his evidence,[2]

---

[1] Writing to Mr. Hay, Aug. 20th, the President said: "Before an impartial jury Burr's conduct would convict himself were not one word of testimony to be offered against him. But, to what a state will our law be reduced by party feelings in those who administer it." Considering that that jury was composed of men almost every one of whom had formed an opinion prejudicial to the prisoner, the President's advance implication of mal-administration was highly censurable, to say the least.

[2] The President's acknowledged motive for this second examination of witnesses

assuming that it was "now more important than ever"—an expression, Parton observes, betraying that "the real object of the prosecution was not so much to convict Aaron Burr of treason as to acquit Thomas Jefferson of precipitate and ridiculous credulity." The President added:

"The criminal is preserved to become the rallying-point of all the disaffected and worthless of the United States, and to be the pivot on which all the intrigues and conspiracies which foreign governments may wish to disturb us with, are to turn. If he is convicted of the misdemeanor, the judge must in decency give us respite by some short confinement of him; but we must expect it to be very short. Be assured yourself, and communicate the same assurance to your colleagues, that your and their zeal and abilities have been displayed in this affair to my satisfaction and your own honor."

The trial on the second indictment, for "misdemeanor," followed. Burr's counsel sought to prevent the arraignment on the plea that a person could not be twice tried for the same offense—that the verdict entered on the journal of "not guilty" covered the entire case. Judge Marshall, after a patient hearing of the points raised, decided for the second trial, and it proceeded. The *subpœna duces tecum* issued. Wilkinson came forward as the main witness, producing the cypher letter, and divulging all that he knew of Burr and his scheme. It will not surprise our readers to be told that the Conspirator confessed to the Court, under Burr's searching examination, to many things incompatible with his own position, and irreconcileable with an honest intent. Among other matters it was found that he had *altered* the cypher letter. He had previously sworn that his version was a true translation of the original. It is doubtless true that the detected alterations were of a minor nature; but, that he dared at all to tamper with and to

---

was: "These whole proceedings will be laid before Congress that they may decide whether the defect has been in the evidence of guilt, or in the law, or in the application of the law, and that they may provide the proper remedy for the past and the future." What "remedy" for *the past* could Congress apply, after the ruling of the Supreme Judge in Burr's case? Did the President design by some extra-Constitutional act again to arraign Burr? There was, in truth, no necessity for this re-examination of witnesses simply for their *testimony*, for the good reason that the entire trial and evidence already had been fully reported for publication, giving to Congress all the information possible. The President must have had some other motive for his suggestion than to preserve testimony.

change it proves his 'easy virtue' and adds the crime of forgery to his other sins of commission. The original was strong enough and brazen enough for its author's condemnation: that Wilkinson could make it a little stronger showed more zeal than honesty. When Burr explained, upon his first discovery of his confederate's defection: "As to any projects which may have been formed between General Wilkinson and myself heretofore, they are now completely frustrated by the perfidious conduct of Wilkinson, and the world must pronounce him a perfidious villain. If I am sacrificed my portfolio will prove him to be such," he not only expressed his own convictions but interpreted the verdict which time is affixing to the General's character.[1]

The trial for misdemeanor ended only with the last week of October, and resulted in his acquittal on the technical ground that the offense, was not, as charged in the indictment, committed in Virginia, but in Ohio. The decision of the Court was, that Burr and Blennerhassett should give bail in the sum of three thousand dollars each, for appearance in Ohio for further trial—a decision at once assailed by Jefferson's enemies and Burr's friends as a concession to the powers at Washington, whose interest in a conviction of *some* kind it must be confessed was not without a delicate relation to their own position.

The acquittal of Burr on the indictment for treason was followed by the abandonment of similar indictments against the other parties. The trial in Ohio never transpired—both

[1] Hildreth, in his "History," [2d series vol. ii. page 671] defends Wilkinson. He says: "The Federal newspapers eagerly caught up and repeated the calumnies; and, being subsequently urged by John Randolph, and other bitter and persevering enemies of Wilkinson, they became matters of investigation by committees of Congress and military courts. The honorable acquittals of Wilkinson pronounced by these tribunals, after a thorough sifting of the facts, seem well sustained by the evidence. Yet such charges, once made, are with great difficulty wholly silenced; and these insinuations against Wilkinson still continue to float in the public mind, and to be rashly repeated to his injury by writers who know very little of the facts." We fear this generally accurate writer is the one amenable to the charge of knowing "very little of the facts." The "calumnies" are now not only not known to have been calumnies but that half was not *suspected* which was true of him. See "Wilkinson's Conspiracy," page 181.

Burr and Blennerhassett forfeiting their recognizances—the matter thereupon being dropped. Floyd was tried in Indiana for misdemeanor and found guilty of having set on foot a military expedition against the provinces of Spain; but, no punishment resulted. Judge Workman, of New Orleans, was tried on a similar charge, but was acquitted. His chief offense was in sustaining the right of his court to issue writs of *habeas corpus* in spite of Wilkinson's military orders [1] for the arrest of persons *suspected* of knowing something of Burr's designs.

With this ends the story of Burr's Conspiracy. We have recorded its leading incidents; and, out of the multiplicity of documents submitted, have endeavored to give a correct interpretation to events and to testimony.

The fact that evidence sufficient for conviction was not found does not absolve the Conspirator from guilt; but, we are inclined to judge less harshly of his schemes when we consider the leading part played by Wilkinson and the immunity shown to that individual's crimes. He not only retained the confidence of Jefferson but of his successor, and only retired from the service of the United States after the disasters of 1813–14 proved his wretched incompetency. He had conceived, and labored for, the separation of the West from the East years before Burr had dreamed of such a thing; he took Spanish money, and, while holding an important office under the Federal Government, was plotting, with other leading citizens, to betray Kentucky into the hands of a foreign power. And yet, his accomplices in that infamous sale and cession were retained in important Federal offices after their guilt became known, and one of them (George Nicholas) acted as Mr. Jefferson's chief instrument in forcing through the Kentucky Legislature the resolutions of '98. When we witness the immunity shown to these conspirators, and to the honors heaped upon them by 'democratic' administrations, we can consistently call for Burr's sacrifice only after demanding that they too shall suffer, in

---

[1] It would be well for those enemies of the Administration in 1863 who declaimed against "arbitrary arrests" and denied the military right of a suspension of the writ of *habeas corpus* to study the history of Wilkinson's high handed operations in New Orleans—operations which Thomas Jefferson sanctioned.

public estimation, for their sins against the State. Burr's crime did not, in the estimation of his prosecutors, consist in levying war against Spain. Mr. Jefferson was only awaiting the proper moment to carry out the design of invading Mexico. Indeed, he had elaborated upon Burr's programme by including Cuba in the spoils. He wrote, Aug. 16th (1807):

"I had rather have war against Spain than not, if we go to war against England. Our Southern defensive force can take the Floridas, volunteers for a Mexican army will flock to our standard, and rich pabulum will be offered to our privateers in the plunder of their commerce and coasts. Probable Cuba would add itself to our Confederation."

Had Aaron Burr written such a letter it would have been pronounced 'just like the audacious adventurer.' His indictment was for treason—levying war against his own country. As that was not *proven*, as no evidence was produced to substantiate the overt act, there now really is much less testimony of Burr's actual guilt than of the guilt of the Kentucky Conspirators of 1785. It is true that, in the report afterwards made by John Quincy Adams (November 30th, 1807) as chairman of the Senate Committee to consider the case of John Smith—Senator from Ohio, charged with knowledge of, and co-operation in, Burr's schemes—the guilt of Burr was presumed to be conclusive, and vast credit was accorded to the President for his vigilance and energy in frustrating the plot; but, that report, written under the spur of the intense feeling prevailing against Burr, does not make the case of the prosecution any stronger. We who have witnessed the gigantic conspiracy of 1860–61, which fortified itself by the resolutions of '98, will be less liable to hang and quarter the adventurer of 1806–7 than the author of those revolutionary resolves: while we express our just detestation of Burr let us not forget to give him the benefit of a comparison with his successors in the crime of secession and revolution.

Burr's succeeding fortunes were those of an outlawed citizen and distrusted man. He was secreted by his friends in New York and New Jersey until the succeeding summer, when, under the disguised name of Edwards, he was placed on board of a packet ship, by a small boat, which put out from Staten Island. In this packet he reached England in safety. No sooner was he on English soil than his fertile mind began to work, and the ex-Vice President soon was an admitted guest of Prime Ministers and men of influence. But this confidence was short lived. When he supposed himself secure in favor an order came for his exile, and, against his wishes he became a wanderer over Europe, having experiences novel even to his novel life. He was reduced quite to beggary—was everywhere distrusted, and yet, was Aaron Burr through all—the accomplished gentleman and insincere friend. He returned to the United States in disguise, early in 1812, and again took up his residence in New York, where he remained—unmolested, except by his old "Mexican" creditors—up to the close of his life, Sept. 14th, 1836. He obtained a lucrative practice at the bar, and, had he been otherwise than a person reckless of his charities and waste of money, might have amassed a fortune.[1]

[1] Randall's picture of him (as given in his "Life of Jefferson," vol. iii. pages 221–22) is the merest caricature. He was not shunned of men nor an outlaw afraid of his own presence. He practiced law with extraordinary success from 1814 to 1828, when old age began to tell upon him. He had many and influential friends—not one of whom would have permitted him to want. He was cared for by a devoted female friend, whose last kind offices afford a touching relief to the wretched history of his reckless, heartless, profligate life.

THE NEW ENGLAND DISCONTENTS, 1807-14.

DISAFFECTION between the Northern and Southern States of the Union became a recognized fact at an early day. The Convention which formed the Constitution was not harmonious; nor did that instrument, after its adoption, win a unanimous acquiescence. It was a mass of *compromises;* the Federal authority conceding to that of the States—the Northern or commercial conceding to the Southern or agricultural section —the majority of the North conceding to the minority of the South, by granting a representation on Slaves. These concessions reconciled but did not satisfy men, States and sections. As the instrument had been adopted in Convention only after prolonged opposition, so it excited among the people a spirit of contention which threatened its rejection by the State Legislatures. It was regarded in the various lights of "an experiment," a "consolidated tyranny," a "centralization fatal to State independence," a "stepping stone to monarchy," &c. Washington said of it: "there are some things in it which never did and never will obtain my cordial approbation." Patrick Henry denounced it as inimical to the liberties of the people. Franklin said, in the Convention: "I consent to this Constitution because I expect no better."

The attempt to construct a *consolidated* government out of states, diverse in interests, each jealous of its sovereignty, *was* "an experiment;" and Washington's expression of surprise, that any arrangement had been made, was justified by the result eventually achieved in the adoption of the Federal organic law. He said: "It appears to me little short of a miracle that the delegates from so many States, different from each other in their manners, circumstances and prejudices, should unite in forming a system of National Government so little liable to well founded objections;" uttering, however, in the same paragraph, his own qualified acceptance of the instrument: "Nor am I yet such an enthusiastic, partial or indiscriminating admirer of it as not to perceive it is tinctured with some real though not radical defects." Many, who either assisted in the construction of the new Government, or took part in the discussions which followed, dissented while they approved—accepted because it was the best to be obtained. So strong was the desire for a "more perfect Union," so alarming the disorders threatening, that men of divers opinions struck palms in token of brotherhood and prepared conscientiously to enforce what they had created. But this enforcement excited different views regarding the powers bestowed upon the Executive, upon Congress, and reserved to the States. These differences soon assumed a "representative" form. Ere Washington's first term had expired opposition to his construction of the Constitution took up even an armed form, and force became necessary to suppress the insurrection. This conflict of opinion created an antagonistic element which expressed itself in the various forms of open and secret organizations—some of them treasonable and others quite legitimate under the assured liberty of thought and speech. They all finally centralized around Thomas Jefferson. With Aaron Burr, Madison, Geo. Clinton, Governor Miflin and others, he laid the foundation of what soon was known as the anti-Federal or Republican party, whose distinctive tenets were, in 1798, embodied in the resolutions prepared by Jefferson for the Kentucky Republicans, and in the resolutions, with their accompanying address, prepared by Madison for the Virginia Legislature. Under the force of this opposition Jefferson became President in 1801 and Aaron Burr Vice President. Under their shrewd management and patronage the party fathered by Washington, Hamilton, John Adams, Jay, Judge Marshall, &c., passed from power; and thenceforward, for a term nearly unbroken of forty years, the Republicans (or Democrats, as they preferred to be known) controlled the destinies of the Republic. That they did not control them to the satisfaction of the New England States during the period in which Virginia Presidents ruled successively, for twenty-four years, is now a matter of History.

In this paper we propose to treat of the discontent which prevailed in the North-Eastern States after the accession to power of the Republicans or Democrats—to advert to that train of causes which resulted in the Hartford Convention.

The contest of Crowns in Europe, during Napoleon's reign, affected the entire civilized world. French and English commerce having been, by the fortunes of war, mutually driven from the seas, left the carrying trade in neutral hands. The New England States of America, then an essentially commercial community, profited by this trade to an extent which quickened all the avenues of public prosperity. Their seaports became marts of busy men; their waters floated merchant fleets; their mechanics and manufacturers prospered. But, this condition of affairs was short-lived. Presuming to dictate for a world the two great powers, decreed maritime laws and principles of blockade which soon reduced neutral commerce to a shadow. In May, 1806, the Ministry of Great Britain proclaimed an Order in Council blockading the entire coast from Brest, France, to the Elbe, in Germany, and all vessels of *neutral* powers were forbidden to enter any of the ports on the line named. This was but a "paper blockade," for England had not vessels enough to spare from active service for closing one half of that coast of six hundred miles.[1] Yet, to violate that mandate in Council was to incur the penalty of reprisals and war. Napoleon retaliated, November 21st of the same year, by a decree declaring the entire British coast in a state of blockade. England thereupon repeated the terms of her paper restriction, and, by a second Order in Council—issued 7th January, 1807—forbidding neutral vessels from trading between the ports of France and her allies, or with ports in

---

[1] In view of this and similar paper blockades how sublime becomes the assurance of that portion of the British public, who, in 1862–3 demanded that our blockade of the Southern coast should be raised because it was not efficient! The student of history discovers remarkable discrepancies between the international principles of Great Britain in 1806 and 1862.

possession of French armies, or, indeed, with any port or country from which British vessels were excluded!

These purely paper blockades and maritime usurpations, characterised by injustice and tyranny, struck a death blow to the neutral commerce of Europe—as they, and succeeding decrees, were designed to do; while they severely crippled the commerce of the United States. The orders were followed by seizures which, ere long, became not only promiscuous, and irregular even under the regulations established by the decrees, but were accompanied by infractions of jurisdiction of an insolent and defiant character. Our own ports were invaded by cruisers and officers of both belligerents, pursuing one another, or seeking for plunder in our ships. English vessels-of-war, then wanting men to man them, not only arrogated the right of search, but superadded the right of impressment of all who had, *at any time*, been British subjects. Merchant ships, fishing smacks, coasters, everywhere were overhauled, and every Briton—including Irish and Scotch—was mercilessly dragged away to serve his Majesty at his Majesty's pleasure. Many so seized were American citizens, who had not even been born abroad, while the vast majority had, by their oath of allegiance and naturalization, obtained the rights of citizenship and protection guaranteed by our Constitution. But, the wrong was not confined to our merchant marine and to unarmed craft. British arrogance proceeded to the extremity of an outrage upon an American vessel of war, in American waters—an outrage until then unparalleled for its audacity and brutality. The U. S. frigate *Chesapeake*, of 38 guns, Commodore Barron commanding, having refitted at Portsmouth (Va.) Navy Yard, started for the Mediterranean station June 22d, 1807. Three British vessels of war then lay in Lynnhaven Bay, making one of our ports their rendezvous. One of them, the *Leopard*, of 50 guns, weighed anchor and stood out of the Capes ahead of the Federal frigate. When three leagues at sea the *Leopard* hailed, and sent a boat to the *Chesapeake* with "dispatches" to Barron from Vice Admiral Berkley. These dispatches simply consisted of an order to search the Federal vessel for "deserters." Barron knew of no "deserters," and replied that he should not permit his men to be mustered. The *Leopard* then gained the weather quarter and again hailed, to which Barron replied that he did not understand that second summons. A single ball was the Briton's answer, to be followed, in a moment, by his full broadside. For fifteen minutes the *Leopard's* guns were rapidly discharged, cutting the American frigate severely. Three of her crew were killed and eighteen wounded. Barron at length struck his flag, having fired but one gun. His entire decks were so cluttered with material and baggage not yet stowed away that not a single gun was in working order. Had she been in trim it is probable he would have sunk the *Leopard;* in which case he would have had to engage the two remaining ships. The surrender of the *Chesapeake* was twice refused, but four of her men were borne away. This high handed act against a nation at peace with Great Britain created an excitement without bounds. On all hands the people plead for the wrong to be avenged. Jefferson at once started a vessel with dispatches for Mr. Munroe, our Minister to England, to demand satisfaction for the outrage. This step was followed, July 2d, by a proclamation forbidding the waters of the United States to all British vessels of war unless in distress, or acting as bearer of dispatches. The Virginia militia were called out, and proceeded to Norfolk and vicinity, to assist in driving the British fleet out of Hampton Roads. Orders were issued to the commandants of New York, Charleston and New Orleans to put their defenses in the best possible order. Congress was called to meet October 26th, by which date it was thought an answer must arrive to the demand for satisfaction. Congress assembled to learn that the British Ministry would treat, but did not wish to consider together Mr. Munroe's two demands, viz.: for satisfaction and for security from further impressments. This was but a contemptible expedient to gain time. Jefferson and Congress so thought, and appropriations for harbor defence by gunboats and fortifications were passed by heavy majorities. The "Committee on Aggressions" brought forward three bills, voting, in the aggregate, one million four hundred and fifty-two thousand dollars.

In the midst of discussions on these measures Jefferson transmitted to Congress (Dec. 16th) a message containing important dispatches regarding new decrees made by the British Ministry, and new interpretations given by the French, to the Berlin decree of November 21st, 1806. The danger was so imminent that the President recommended an embargo on our commerce —thus, as he assumed, to preserve our seamen from impressment, our property from seizure and confiscation, and deny to our two enemies the food which both looked for from our plethoric graneries. This very significant and important recommendation was acted upon with almost unseemly haste. It was a deadly blow to our already crippled commerce: to New England it was the knell of her prosperity, threatening all branches of her trade and industry with overwhelming ruin. Even the coasting and fishing trade was estopped by restrictions, so radical was the measure. After only four hours' discussion the bill passed in the Senate, Dec. 18th. The House amended and passed the act Dec. 22d, by a vote of 82 to 44. The Senate concurred in the slight House amendments, the President, without an hour's delay, signed the bill, and the Embargo became the law of the land.

All this action, it will be seen, was *predicated* on the dispatches from Armstrong, our Minister to France. If its propriety was doubted all doubts for the moment were forgotten when news camo of England's new Order in Council, dated Nov. 11th, 1807, but not promulgated until Nov. 17th. These orders "prohibited any neutral trade with France or her allies, in other words, with the whole of Europe, Sweden excepted, unless through Great Britain. All neutral vessels, whatever tneir cargoes, bound to any port of France or her allies, were required, under pain of capture and condemnation, first to touch at some British or Irish port, and there to pay such re-exportation duties as might be imposed, and to obtain, by the payment of certain fees, a British license to trade to the Continent. Nor was any export to be allowed of the produce of France or her allies except in vessels which had complied with the foregoing regulation, all such vessels being further required to return to some British or Irish port, and there to unlade their cargoes, as a preliminary to shipment to the neutral country."

This edict elicited from Napoleon his celebrated Milan decree of Dec. 17th, 1807, confirming and extending the provisions of his Berlin decree. This new mandate of the ruler of Europe, and would-be ruler of the world, "denationalized and forfeited every vessel which should submit to be searched by a British cruiser, or should pay any tax, duty, or license money to the British government, or should be found on the high seas or elsewhere, bound to or from any British port. Spain and Holland, with their usual subserviency, forthwith issued similar decrees."

Under the press of these accumulated impositions the Embargo was enforced; but, not all the justification urged by its friends could reconcile the New England people to its destructive operation. It was a source of indignant comment in all circles. How to evade it soon became the study of the restless, sagacious vessel owners and officers. The more Government tried to punish violators the greater became the odium attached to the law, which was pronounced unnecessary, unconstitutional, arbitrary, and levied by the agricultural South regardless of the rights, interests and wishes of the commercial North. Town meetings denounced it; magistrates refused to lend their assistance in its enforcement; smuggling and evasion were not regarded as dishonorable. St. Mary's, in Georgia, and Eastport, in Maine, became great *entrepots* for the contraband trade. Situated on the frontiers, with navigable rivers reaching into the interior, they were very available for receiving goods and passing provisions over the line to British and Spanish hands, from whence they found their way to Halifax, on the North, and to the West Indies on the South. Large quantities also passed, by way of Lake Champlain and over the Vermont line into Canada. Three supplementary acts were passed to circumvent these violators, but, in proportion as smuggling suffered, detestation of the law increased. So furious grew the sentiment against it that not a few of its friends in Congress anxiously hoped for an early expiration of the act.

The Massachusetts Legislature upon its convention in June, 1808 immediately grappled with the anomalous position of trade and navigation, "a question," says Hildreth, "in which that State was deeply interested, as owner of more than one third of the shipping of the Union. The views of the majority were expressed in a series of able resolutions, which began by calling in question the constitutional power of Congress to impose an unlimited embargo—an experiment, so far as it had in view the coercion of foreign nations, novel and dangerous, doubtful in its effects abroad, and full of disaster at home. Supposing the embargo to be constitutional, yet the vast authority delegated to the President to regulate the coasting trade, and to grant exemptions and dispensations from the rigor of the law, was denounced as a dangerous opening for partiality, tending to prepare the country for the habitual surrender of the legislative power into a single hand. Though our true policy was a peaceful one, the people of Massachusetts would ever be ready to endure all privations, and to make every exertion to support the dignity and to enforce the reasonable pretensions of the nation. The resources of the country being fully adequate to the protection of its maritime and territorial rights, they ought to be directed and employed in such preparations as the experience of ages had demonstrated to be alone effectual for that purpose. A naval force was especially necessary, and the senators and representatives of Massachusetts were pressed to urge upon Congress effectual steps in that direction. The General Government having been expressly instituted to provide for the common defense and general welfare, and to preserve the blessings of liberty, while it secures those inestimable objects by an equal and paternal solicitude for the various sections of the Union, must be supported at every expense and every hazard; but the General Government was one thing, and the administration of it another; that administration being only entitled to the confidence of the people, when, by a full, fair, and frequent display of its purposes and policy, it preserved itself from the imputation of partiality and prejudice, and of undue fear and affection in the conduct of foreign as well as of domestic affairs."

These resolutions fairly interpreted the feeling of the people. They were bitterness itself to the President, casting in his face, as they did, a want of confidence in his use of power and in his impartiality. John Quincy Adams, then acting with the Administration party, refused to endorse the course prescribed for him and was superceded by the election of James Lloyd, a merchant and ship owner of Boston. In this procedure Adams assumed to discover the operations of the old "Essex Junto," in which the elder Adams had found an unrelenting enemy to his French treaty and concession to Democratic clamor. This Junto, John Quincy Adams regarded as treasonable—aiming to throw the country under British domination; and the Republicans (Democrats) were not slow to discover in every Federalist an enemy to the Union and Constitution. The Administration partisans resolved not to repeal but to renew these restrictions on commerce, and, in spite of the most strenuous opposition of the Federalists of New England, succeeded in forcing through Congress (Jan. 9th, 1809) what was termed the Enforcing Act. The action which followed this legislation is thus chronicled by Hildreth:

"Already, before the passage of the Enforcing Act, public meetings began to be held in the mercantile towns of New England, to protest against it. Similar meetings were also held in Albany and the city of New York. The leading Federal newspapers in Boston announced its passage with mourning columns, and with the motto, 'Liberty is dead!' General Lincoln, the collector, now very old and infirm, resigned his office, as did also the deputy collector, rather than undertake to enforce an act so unpopular. Other custom-house officers at other ports followed their example. The merchants, indeed, totally denying the constitutionality of the act, gave fair warning that, for every seizure of their property under it, they should commence suits in the State courts; a procedure, as it might be no easy matter for the officers to procure bail, likely to end in their committal to prison.

"A Boston town-meeting, regularly called, after a warm struggle between the opposers of the embargo and the friends of the Administration, in which the latter were completely beaten, agreed upon a strong memorial to the Legislature about to meet, denouncing the Enforcing Act as arbitrary and unconstitutional. This meeting resolved 'not voluntarily to assist in carrying it into execution; and that all who should do so ought to be considered as enemies of the Constitution of the

United States, enemies of the State of Massachusetts, and hostile to the liberties of the people.' "

The answer of the Legislature was equally significant. The Lieutenant-Governor, Lincoln, a Democrat—Governor Sullivan being dead—had demanded in his first message that something be done to restore the confidence of the National Administration in Massachusetts loyalty. The response was very like a threat. Says the historian:

"Care was taken explicitly to disavow any disposition to separate from the Union, or intention to encourage resistance to the laws. At the same time, it was pretty plainly intimated that the embargo and its supplements were not laws. 'The people of New England,' said the Senate, 'perfectly understand the distinction between the Constitution and the Administration. They are as sincerely attached to the Constitution as any portion of the United States. They may be put under the ban of the empire, but they have no intention of abandoning the Union.' Adherence to the Union did not, however, require even passive obedience to unconstitutional and ruinous stretches of power. 'On such occasions, passive obedience would, on the part of the people, be a breach of their allegiance, and, on our part, treachery and perjury. The people have not sent us here to surrender their rights, but to maintain and defend them; and we have no authority to dispense with the duties thus solemnly imposed.'

"At the very opening of the session, a great mass of petitions had been presented to the House from various town-meetings. Upon these petitions a report was made, concluding with a series of resolutions (in which the Senate concurred) pronouncing the late Enforcing Act to be, in many respects, 'unjust, oppressive, and unconstitutional, and not legally binding;' recommending, however, to parties aggrieved by it, 'to abstain from forcible resistance, and to apply for remedy in a peaceful manner to the laws of the commonwealth.' A strong memorial to Congress against the embargo was presently adopted, and a bill was passed, prohibiting, under high penalties, any searches of dwelling-houses, unless by virtue of warrants issued on complaints supported by oath—a particular in which the Enforcing Act was thought to trench upon the Constitutions both of the State and the Union. This bill, however, failed to become a law, by reason of the executive veto.

"An order from Washington, in consequence of the resignation of the collector of Boston, to the commandant of the fort in the harbor, to allow no vessel to pass, though countermanded a few days after, served to add to the excitement. All the ships hoisted their flags at half mast. It was not without reason that Randolph warned the Administration that they were treading fast in the fatal footsteps of Lord North."

Nor was Massachusetts alone in assuming an attitude of menace. Connecticut was equally decided in her views of the embargo and its collateral acts. Governor Trumbull declined (Feb. 4th, 1809) to comply with the President's circular for the designation of special officers of militia on whom the collectors of the customs might call for aid. He did not know, so he stated, of any authority under which such appointments could be made. Instead of detaching militia to aid the collectors, he summoned the Legislature to meet; in his opening address (Feb. 23) to which he took the ground that, on great emergencies, when the National Legislature had been led to overstep its constitutional power, it became the right and duty of the State Legislatures 'to interpose their protecting shield between the rights and liberties of the people and the assumed power of the General Government.' The session resulted in the adoption of measures very similar to those of Massachusetts." In all the New England States, indeed, as well as in New York, the reaction was very perceptibly gaining ground, and in Congress the tide began to turn; the Administration during January rapidly lost ground. Democratic members from the North deserted a restrictive policy, opposing both embargo and war. A sensible excitement pervaded Administration circles. Every effort, private and parliamentary, was used to steady the refluent tide but to no purpose. The month of February was passed in highly exciting debate, which finally ended in the ostensible repeal of the embargo by the adoption of a new act, of anomalous character, full of apparent restrictions upon commerce; but, so illy constructed was the law as to open ways and means of evasion, enough almost to satisfy the people that evasion was designed!

Pending this Congressional excitement sentiments inimical to the integrity of the Republic itself were expressed by a powerful and significant address published by the Massachusetts Legislature at the close of its session (March 2d, 1809). This document severely censured the pro-French policy and anti-Britain discrimination of the President, but found the evil to lie in the power conferred upon the Executive, and upon the Southern States which then held the scale of Congress in their keeping by virtue of the three-fifths' slave representation clause. The address declared it as an indispensable means toward a better and more equitable administration of the Government that the Constitution should be so amended as to deprive the Slave States of their exceptional representation. Other amendments were suggested which should positively "secure commerce and navigation from a repetition of invidious and destructive *theories*." The address added:

"Nothing less than a perfect union and intelligence among the Eastern States can preserve to them any share of influence in the National Government. Without influence, they can expect no regard to their interests, but are exposed to the effect of a policy whose object will be to secure power and office with a view to local and personal aggrandizement; and to make them colonial governments, subject to the worst form of domination, that of one member of a confederacy over another. Indeed, the present state of our connection is not far from that condition. The late election of Representatives to Congress, and the vote for President, plainly demonstrate the disapprobation of the present system by a great majority of the Eastern people. Mr. Madison, who was known to favor it, had not a vote in those States except in Vermont, and recent elections there afford evidence that at this moment he would have none. On the other hand, in the Southern States, from the artificial popularity of this fatal system, his majority has been triumphant. The same division is apparent in Congress. The known wishes of the Eastern States have been not merely neglected, but rejected with threatenings and contempt. Politicians of yesterday, from the backwoods and mountains, vie with each other in the language of insult and defiance; and the men whom you delight to honor, and the great majority of those who have the deepest interests at stake in the welfare of the country, are stigmatized as a corrupt and seditious part of the community. Even when those of your own representatives, who have encouraged by their countenance this presumptuous conduct, discovering their errors, are desirous to recede, repentance comes too late. Thus, under new names, but with the same views, the embargo system is still visited upon our unhappy country, in spite of the opposition of some of those who appear too late desirous of retrieving their country from ruin. Choose, then, fellow-citizens, between the condition of citizens of a Free State, possessing its equal weight and influence in the National Government, or that of a colony, free in name, but in fact enslaved by sister States."

This document awakened intense feeling. It was the germ of the Hartford Convention. Its declarations and their natural sequence, occasioned anxiety, particularly as it was seconded by a sudden increase of Federalist strength. Not only in New England but in New York, and even in Maryland, they won the popular branches of the Legislature—a result astounding to the Democrats, whose triumphs had been so complete, and whose tactics had been so potent as to lead them to ideas of a life lease on power.

These events were followed by the announcement, April 17th, that a treaty had been concluded with Mr. Erskine, the British Minister, by which all matters in dispute with his Government were provisionally settled. A proclamation issued announcing a cessation of the embargo and non-intercourse so far as related to Great Britain and her dependencies, after June 10th. This news spread like wild-fire throughout the country, giving to the seaport towns in particular the most unalloyed satisfaction.

Thus, for the moment, all things seemed propitious. Madison, the newly elected President, in negotiating with Erskine, appeared to Federalists to have abandoned the "persecuting policy" of his predecessor. Hence New England visibly subsided in excitement. The French Minister at Washington grew indignant over the Erskine treaty and growled, and Congress legislated a little for his satisfaction by an act dropping the embargo, and, with it, the provision excluding foreign armed vessels—which gave to French vessels of war the right of entry, rendezvous and supply in our ports. Congress adjourned June 28th, after its five weeks' session, in great good feeling.

All was changed again, in a few weeks of comparative quiet. July 20th the news arrived that the British Ministry had rejected Erskine's treaty! This announcement threw all circles once more into ferment. The excitement which followed was indeed great. The British Premier, Canning, refusing to accept Erskine's arrangement, insisted that his representative had exceeded his powers, and had, also, misjudged the true position of affairs. The offending minister therefore was recalled and "Copenhagen" Jackson sent in his stead. With Jackson some sharp correspondence soon succeeded. Madison insisted, much to Jackson's surprise, that all communication between them should be reduced to writing. A lengthy negotiation for explanations and new terms of accommodation of differences followed. Jackson's intercourse with the Administration was characterised by no little rhetorical severity, and, so offensive at length did he become, that our Secretary of State refused further correspondence with him (Nov. 8th) as preliminary to an application for his recall. Whereupon the British embassador withdrew to New York to await the order of his government. He addressed (Nov. 13th) a circular to the British consuls in the United States to notify them of his withdrawal, and accompanied this notification with an abstract of his last communication, made through his secretary, in reply to the notice of his rejection by our Government. This unusual procedure was construed as an insult—for, what had consuls to do with ministerial differences? It savored strongly of the offensive course pursued by the little Frenchman, Genet, in threatening an appeal from the Government to the people, during Washington's administration.

The efforts of Congress—which assembled Nov. 29th, 1809—were directed to a revision of the laws regulating, or, rather, restricting commerce. Debate of a very acrimonious character was the consequence. No distinctive party lines were drawn. The New England State representatives, assisted by members from other sections, pressed the repeal of all laws burdening trade, assuming that, in spite of the French and English retaliatory decrees, American ingenuity could and would provide for the protection of American property and honor; but, as the Democrats had embraced the embargo and the non-intercourse policy as their own, a Democratic administration could not abandon it without loss of prestige. John Randolph, of Virginia, made this presentment of the case:

"The history of that act (the Embargo) was very extraordinary. When originally introduced, not a single person had pretended that, absolutely and by itself, it was a good measure. During the debate upon it it had gained no friends, and yet it had passed by a two-thirds' vote. During the present session it had been reprobated by every body of all parties, in the House and out of it; and yet, after a five months' session, it still remained on the statute-book! And why? Because as the majority pretended, it could not be repealed without the abandonment of national honor! An unwise, passionate and ill-informed majority had brought the nation into a false and ruinous position, and the national honor required us to stay there! To give up this wretched Non-importation Act without some equally wretched substitute for it, would be, it was pretended, unconditional submission and irretrievable disgrace."

Despite Congressional restrictions, English Orders and French Decrees, an extensive American commerce was afloat during the latter part of the year 1809—much of it suddenly launched for a market under the brief relief afforded by the temporary operation of the Erskine treaty. This commerce English officers were instructed to respect under certain provisions; but Buonaparte seized every vessel, indiscriminately, which fell in French hands, no matter what her register or flag. All American craft so seized were ordered to confiscation and sale. This outrageous conduct was defended with infinite audacity by the French Prime Minister, Duke of Cadore, as necessary, because the American Government had not yet taken measures against the unprovoked aggressions of England on the rights of neutrals! and because France, who had given no cause of offense, was included in the penalties of the non-intercourse act of 1809! Our Minister to France, Armstrong, came forward with an able and high toned remonstrance against tyrannical confiscation of a neutral's property, wherever found. He pointed out, with great directness, the inconsistency of Cadore's assumptions in the matter. The only answer vouchsafed was the Rambouillet decree of March 23d, 1810, ordering the condemnation and sale of one hundred and thirty-two American vessels, with their cargoes—in all valued at about eight millions of dollars! Like confiscation was to be visited upon any American vessel caught in any French port or ports held by French arms. Wrong, insult and disregard of maritime usage could not go farther. An immediate declaration of war against France would have been justified.

But, not to dwell too closely upon the extraordinary circumstances of our European relations in 1810 and 1811, we may come to results. The pressure for war against England became, under the quickening of popular feeling, so strong as scarcely to afford a hope of peaceful reconciliation of differences with that power. That such a war was calculated immeasurably to assist Buonaparte was not denied. Said John Randolph, in his great speech delivered Dec. 11th, 1810, against the drift of the current towards a war with Great Britain:

"And shall Republicans become the instruments of him who has superseded the title of Attila to be called the scourge of God? If, instead of being as I am, my memory clouded, my intellect stupefied, my strength and spirits exhausted, I had the completest command of my faculties, I should still fail to give utterance to that strong detestation which I feel toward such characters as Genghis, Tamerlane, Kouli Khan and Buonaparte, malefactors of the human race, who grind down men into mere material of their impious and bloody ambition! Yet, under all the accumulated wrongs, and insults, and robberies of the last of these chieftains, we are about to become a party to his views, a partner in his wars!"

But, it was of no avail. The point steadily kept in view by the popular leaders was to secure a solidification of sentiment on the course adopted. Under the impetus of Southern and Western men, the Congressional attitude of war was assumed. During January, February, March, April, May and June, 1812, nothing was heard but preparations for a second measuring of strength with our old enemy. The war spirit grew rapidly. As Brackenridge truthfully said: "the habits of a people, who had been thirty years at peace, and constantly occupied in industrious callings could not be changed suddenly: but men are by nature warlike, and they cannot exist long in the midst of martial scenes without catching their spirit." This fact the leaders of the war party counted upon: by "precipitating" action they sought to render the popular voice unanimous. Legislation, however, was too reckless to escape animadversion. It soon became hasty, ill-considered and well calculated to arouse the still unawed opposition by its evidently partisan nature. New England sought for a navy, but it was denied. Extensive enlistments were ordered and heavy appropriations voted. Yet no declaration of war was made. The hope of Madison was to force England to an accommodation—to compel her, by a show of retaliation, to do us justice. To this end the President, in a confidential message to Congress, recommended an embargo, to continue in force for a term of sixty days, when, if no change was made in Britain's attitude, the declaration of war must follow. The new Embargo as it finally passed (April 4th) fixed the time for ninety instead of sixty days. It prohibited the sailing of any vessel for any foreign port except foreign vessels with such cargoes as they had on board at the passage of the acts. The measure was sweepingly complete, chaining our commerce to the docks with an irreversible knot.

Madison was measurably sustained in his course by capital made from the revelations of one John Henry, an Irishman, whose secret "mission" to Massachusetts in 1809 to stir up sedition, he had, for a doceur of *fifty thousand dollars*, divulged to the President. This mercenary professed to have been dispatched by the Governor-General of Canada, Sir James Craig, to Boston, early in 1809, to watch the course of events, to aid in developing the spirit of discontent, to labor for the disruption of the American Union and for the reannexation of New England to the Canadas! The fellow, it afterwards appeared, was in Boston at the time indicated, a frequenter of brothels and a companion of disreputable characters generally; but, with all his confessions, he implicated no one—designated no special person, act or movement calculated to add to the weight of testimony against the New England Federalists. For what the enormous sum of fifty thousand dollars was paid it is now difficult to see. In his special message transmitting the dearly paid for revelation, the President assumed that Henry's evidence proved England to have been intriguing for the base purpose of exciting sedition, first essaying to bring about an open resistance to the laws; then, "by introducing a British force, to assist in destroying the Union and forming, with the Eastern section thereof, a connection with Great Britain." This, for the moment, created renewed feeling of hostility against the English and their sympathisers in New England; but, when the whole affair was probed by the New Englanders themselves, nothing was discovered which could implicate any American born citizen in Henry's professed designs; and nothing was adduced to prove that stipendiary had told the truth. The general impression was, that the heavy sum paid for information was worse than wasted. It is well to state that Henry, having received his money, left the country for France *before* his affidavits and papers were made public.[1]

It was necessary, as Madison then stood, to sustain the war policy vigorously or fail of a nomination for the Presidency. There was no alternative. That he was at heart against the war, admits of no question. He bent before the imperious demands of the Democratic caucus, led by Henry Clay, and accepted the nomination with its implied responsibilities to press the war programme to an immediate and unconditional issue. He then indicated his adhesion by proposing the embargo. This was followed by his confidential message of June 1st, 1812, wherein were recited the causes of complaint against Great Britain; "her impressments of our seamen; her infringements upon our maritime jurisdiction, and disturbance of the peace of our coasts; her paper blockades, unsupported by any adequate force; her violations of our neutral rights by her orders in council, and her inflexible determination to maintain those orders against all appeals to her justice. Add to this her suspected instigation of Indian hostilities; and her conduct, taken together, would be found to amount to war as against us, while we remained at peace with her. Under these circumstances, it became the duty of the House to consider, as it was their constitutional right to decide, whether we should longer remain passive under those progressive and accumulated wrongs. But, while thus leading the way to war, as if to guard against the charge of French influence, so much dwelt upon by the Federalists, a caution was added against entanglement 'in the contests and views of other powers.' France not

[1] Too much has been made of this "spy" by historians. One writes: "The fact remains that the British Government had been treacherously endeavoring to destroy the Union while professing friendship," &c. The "fact" remains that the British Government knew nothing whatever of the "spy's" operations, and refused to pay him one cent for services rendered; and that refusal induced Henry to turn informer. Nor is it true that the British Government then "professed friendship:" its Orders in Council show that it both professed and practiced anything but friendship for us. Whatever Sir James Craig may have done is not material. If *he* hired a vagabond to do dirty work, and kept his "mission" a profound secret not only from the British Minister to this country, but even from the British Ministry, we can see little propriety for affixing to the British Government any responsibility in the matter.

only refused all indemnity for former wrongs, but, notwithstanding 'the repeal of her decrees as they violated the neutral rights of the United States,' she still continued to authorize illegal captures of our ships, attended by the perpetration of other outrages. The recommendation, however, of any definitive measures with regard to her was deferred, in the expectation that the result of the unclosed negotiation at Paris would speedily enable Congress to decide with greater advantage on the course due to the rights, interest and honor of the country."

John Randolph—who had struggled violently against the precipitation of hostilities and had, while disclaiming association with the New Englanders, co-operated with them in opposing the schemes of the hot-heads—moved to refer this message to the Committee of the Whole, but; as that would open it to a fierce struggle on the floor, the message was committed to the Committee on Foreign Relations. This Committee, by its Chairman, John C. Calhoun, reported (June 3d) for war, at the same time introducing a bill declaring war. The struggle in the House over this well engineered bill was brief; the friends of the measure were too strong for much opposition. A motion to include France in the declaration received *ten* votes! The vote for the bill stood 79 to 49. Its semi-sectional character was apparent upon analyzation. Pennsylvania and the States to the South and West voted 62 aye, 17 nay. The States North of Pennsylvania voted 17 aye, 32 nay. Thirteen Northern and two Southern Democrats voted nay. Many others who were opposed to war voted for the act purely for the reason that it was a "party measure." In the Senate, after various efforts to insert a clause authorising letters of marque and reprisal—to include French vessels in the clause—to substitute for the original bill such letters both against England and France, the bill was brought to a vote and passed 19 to 13—a number of Democrats voting nay. The House concurred in the letter of marque clause and the President signed the bill June 18th.

All this was done in secret session. The people, though informed by report of the probable result, awaited with intense anxiety for the denouement. It was received by Democratic partisans with favor, but otherwise by their opponents and the mercantile interest generally. Then, as at a later day, the great mass of foreign population walked their straight course to the ballot box with straight Democratic votes in their hands. The foreign element then being composed largely of Irish who had fled from the tyranny of British rule, most eagerly encouraged the idea of war with their oppressors. The old French faction, with its element of infidelity and love of revolution, suddenly revived at the clarion call, for, with them, Buonaparte, though an Emperor, still was the representative of innovation and war against the old order of things, and a war with England was to befriend him. There also was a new element abroad. The generation of Henry Clay, John C. Calhoun, Richard M. Johnson, had arisen, with their ardor for public distinction, to stir up the land by their glowing rhetoric, and to call around them the young and fiery sons of revolutionary sires for a second stroke at the hereditary foe of their independency and prosperity. Against these stirring spirits, of foreign and domestic constitution, it was futile to struggle, particularly when the old leaders—De Witt Clinton, Jefferson, Gallatin, Giles, Gerry, Macon, Findley, Sevier, Dr. Mitchell—manipulated the reins. Opposition came not so much from Federalists *as* such, as from Northern industry and commerce whose interests were to suffer, and from New England people whose territory, lying adjacent to the British frontier, would be assailed by land as well as by sea. The South, being purely agricultural in character, and having little to fear from English navies or armies of invasion, could not be a sufferer except to the extent of the slight additional taxation necessary to sustain the finances.[1] Hence war to the two sections was so differently

[1] Jefferson wrote at a later day (Nov. 28th, 1814) of the effect which a state of war had produced on Virginia prosperity: "To me this state of things brings a sacrifice of all tranquillity and comfort through the residue of life. For, although the debility of age disables me from the services and sufferings of the field, yet, by the total annihilation in value of the produce which was to give me subsistence and independence, I shall be like Tantalus, up to the shoulders in water yet dying of thirst. We can make, indeed, enough to eat, drink and clothe ourselves; but nothing for our salt, iron, groceries, and taxes, which must be paid in money. For, what can we raise for the market? Wheat? We can only give it to our horses,

viewed as to awaken the keenest and most bitter antagonisms.

Said the Federalist members of Congress, in an address to their constituents, issued at the close of the session (July 6): "If honor demands a war with England, what opiate lulls that honor to sleep over the wrongs done us by France—on land, robberies, seizures, imprisonments; at sea, pillage, sinkings, burnings? With full knowledge of the wrongs inflicted by the French, ought the Government of this country to aid the French cause by engaging in war against the enemies of France? It cannot be concealed that to engage in the present war against England is to place ourselves on the side of France, and exposes us to the vassalage of the States serving under the French Emperor."

And this, indeed, was one of the sharpest thorns in the side of men of the old Federal school—men who transferred their detestation of Robespierre, Danton and Voltaire to the Emperor who had emerged from that sea of blood around the guillotine to become the conqueror of a world: they could not become reconciled to the idea that free America was to contribute to his ascendancy. The clergy of New England, in particular, gave utterance to sentiments not well calculated to reconcile those of Puritan blood to the war.

But, these symptoms of opposition did not stay the prosecution of the contest. With a few successes chiefly at sea, disaster visited our arms too humiliating to dwell upon, during the years 1812–13. Only the gleam of Perry's noble achievement and of Harrison's brilliant campaign in recovery of Detroit, came to permanently inspirit the people. In New England the war grew daily more unpopular. From its incipient stages such opposition had been manifested as gave the General Government much anxiety. The quota (of the 100,000 men called for) to be furnished by the States of Massachusetts and Connecticut, was not forthcoming—the refusal being justified by the asserted right of State Governments to determine *when* the

as we have been ever since harvest. Tobacco? It is not worth the pipe it is smoked in. Some say whiskey, but all mankind must become drunkards to consume it. But, although we feel we shall not flinch."

exigencies of the General Government gave the President authority to call out the militia. The Governors also took umbrage at the attempt to exclude their militia field officers from all command by orders for all militia to be mustered into the United States' service, when they would be commanded by the Major-Generals and Brigadiers of Madison's own creation. It was pronounced, by the Governors, unconstitutional for the President to delegate such authority over their militia. Both of these assumptions were defended by decisions of the Supreme Court of Massachusetts. As a consequence the New England States were left in a perfectly defenseless condition, save only as far as the local forces and the organized State militia gave protection.

At the opening of the war our Government had signified its wish to negotiate for peace, and had instructed Russell, chargé d'affaires at Paris, to agree to an armistice as preliminary to an arrangement, on condition of a repeal of the Orders in Council, the discontinuance of impressments and the return of those impressed. Through one of the by-roads of diplomacy—illustrating the devious ways of diplomats—the offensive Orders in Council were discovered to have been repealed since June 23d! There stood nothing, therefore, between our country and peace but the vexed question of impressments. The British Ministry actually had sent directions, early in August, 1812, to Admiral Warren, to propose a discontinuance of hostilities on the strength of the repeal of the offensive Orders. All of these things operated on the Massachusetts mind to heighten its feeling against an Administration which refused to discontinue a war after such overtures had been given for peace. July 15th the Legislature of that State agreed upon a "Remonstrance, in which they denounced the perseverance in war, after the repeal of the British orders, as improper and impolitic, from the distrust which it exhibited of the good faith of the English nation, giving color to the charge of co-operation with France, and thereby tending to arouse the whole British nation against us; and unjust, because we had not taken, on our part, all the steps necessary to remove grounds of British complaint as to the employment of her seamen in our ships, because the question of impressment had never been presented to Great Britain as one of peace and war, between which she might choose, and because, for aught that appeared, it was still possible to settle that question by negotiation.

"It was the hope of protection to commerce which had induced the Northern people, who did not need the aid of the South for their defense, to surrender to the General Government so large a share of their sovereignty, and in agreeing to the slave representation, to yield to the South a political weight so undue. But, so far from protection, a bitter spirit of hostility to commerce had early evinced itself on the part of the central authority, ending, after a long course of harrassments, in its total destruction by war; a war which appeared to be prompted rather by a subserviency to France most dangerous to our liberties, and by a lust of conquest, than by any disposition to defend endangered rights: ill conducted, excessively expensive, and which, in risking our future enjoyment of the fisheries, the great nursery of our seamen, and means of support to thousands of our inhabitants, of vastly more value than any Canadian territory we might be able to conquer, put us in jeopardy of losing what New England never could consent to abandon.

"Under such circumstances silence toward the Government would be treachery to the people. In making this solemn representation of our sufferings and our dangers, we have been influenced only by the duty which we owe to our constituents and our country, to our consciences and the memory of our fathers. And to the Searcher of all hearts we appeal for the purity of our motives and the sincerity of our declarations!"

This was accompanied by a report from a committee, which complained of the admission of Louisiana without the *unanimous* consent of the States, as unconstitutional and unauthorized; and the admission was stigmatised, Hildreth says, as the "commencement of a process of Western annexation which threatened to swamp the political influence of Massachusetts and the Eastern States, and which could not be suffered to pass in silence, lest silence might seem to give consent."

Herein the reader has the real secret of the opposition which culminated in the Hartford Convention. The Embargo and Non-intercourse acts, and war with England to aid France, were excessively unpopular from pecuniary results; but, in the demanded and cönceded ascendancy of the South, in the reign of Virginia at the Capital; in the offensive inequality of a Congressional representation on slaves; in the apparent willingness of the pastoral South to sacrifice and override the manufacturing and trading North, we have the true source of that uprising of the old Puritan element which convened in secret conclave at Hartford. The spirit of Cotton Mather became even more apparent in the Senate resolutions, introduced by a committee of which Josiah Quincy was chairman, refusing to Captain Lawrence, afterwards of the ill-fated *Chesapeake*, a vote of thanks for his capture of the *Peacoek*, believing—in the language of the resolution—"that in a war like the present, waged without justifiable cause, and prosecuted in a manner indicating that conquest and ambition were its real motives, it was not becoming a moral and religious people to express any approbation of military or naval exploits not directly connected with the defense of our seacoast and soil." This outraged even New England bosoms, which ever had honored heroism and devotion to country. A worthy scion of the wealthy Crowningshield family, procuring a flag of truce, proceeded to Halifax and returned with the body of Lawrence, which was buried in Salem with imposing pomp—Judge Story (afterwards Chief Justice) acting as orator.

The Legislatures of other States out of New England sustained the war by their votes and resolves if not by their men and funds. But, not an army put in the field was equal to the work assigned it; not a campaign was prosecuted with means adapted to ends. Throughout the entire field of operations on the Northern frontier the country beheld, amid occasional brilliant achievements, inefficiency of general commanders, impotency of the War Department and demoralization of the troops. It was distressingly evident that, however just the war might be, it was *not* popular, else volunteers would have flocked to their country's standard and the General Government would have been sustained with ample means. If it is asserted that

New England's disaffection and refusal to fill her quotas for offensive operations brought this weakness to the army—that her discredit of Government stocks and bonds was fatal to the financial success of the National exchequer—it is to confess the preponderating importance of that section: if its sympathy and co-operation were so necessary to the success of the war why, it pertinently may be asked, were not her wishes and her influence consulted in levying the Embargo and in declaring war? [1]

During 1813 the Vermont Federalists so far gained in strength as to throw the election for Governor into the Legislature, which, being Federal, elected (Nov. 6th) Martin Chittenden to the Chief Magistracy of the State. He was no sooner in office than he issued a proclamation recalling from the United States' service a brigade of Vermont militia then thrown into Bur-

[1] The first speech made by Daniel Webster, delivered in the House of Representatives, January 14th, 1814, contained this passage:

"It was not, Sir, the minority that brought on this war. Look to your records, from the date of the Embargo in 1807 to June, 1812. Every thing that men could do they did, to stay your course. When at last they could effect no more they urged you to delay your measures. They entreated you to give yet a little time for deliberation, and to wait for favorable events. As if inspired for the purpose of arresting your progress, they laid before you the consequences of your measures just as we have seen them since take place. They predicted to you their effects on public opinion. They told you, that, instead of healing, they would inflame political dissentions. They pointed out to you what would and what must happen on the frontier. That which since has happened there, is but their prediction turned into history. Vain is the hope, then, of escaping just retribution by imputing to the minority of the Government, or to the opposition among the people, the disasters of these times. * * If the purpose be by casting these implications upon those who are opposed to the policy of the Government, to check their freedom of inquiry, discussion and debate, such purpose is also incapable of being executed. That opposition is constitutional and legal. It is also conscientious. It rests in settled and sober conviction that such policy is destructive to the interests of the people and dangerous to the being of the Government. The experience of every day confirms these sentiments. Men who act from such motives are not to be discouraged by trifling obstacles nor awed by any dangers. *They know the limit of constitutional opposition—up to that limit at their own discretion they will walk, and walk fearlessly.*"

This speech fell from the speaker's lips in an unimpassioned utterance, but its words were trip-hammer blows to the war policy. It was patriotic throughout, characterized, as all of Webster's speeches afterwards were, by thorough devotion to the *nation*; but it was a most powerful defense of New England policy. Webster then was a member from New Hampshire.

lington to sustain Hampton's and Wilkinson's movement upon Montreal. This recall was based upon the "illegality" of the requisition for militia service—the Governor denying the existence of any of the three contingencies provided for in the Constitution. But the troops proved more patriotic than their Governor; the officer bearing Chittenden's mandate was arrested by the brigade officers on charge of sedition. The expedition against Canada, however, having proved abortive through the incompetency of its directors, was abandoned, and the militia were discharged—their term of service having nearly expired. This act of the Vermont Governor aroused the authorities at Washington. It was moved in the House of Representatives (Jan. 6th, 1814) to instruct the Attorney-General to prosecute Chittenden. In answer to this Harrison Gray Otis, in the Massachusetts Senate, Jan. 14th, introduced a resolve, expressing the duty and readiness of the State "to aid with her whole power, the Governor of Vermont, and the people of that or any other State in support of constitutional rights, by whomsoever infringed"—a resolution, which, though afterwards pointed at as revolutionary, but re-echoed the sentiments which Daniel Webster uttered on that same day in the U. S. House of Representatives. Those who most loudly denounced the resolutions as treasonable were the vehement supporters of the resolutions of '98! As the sole purpose and effect of those resolves were to exalt the State above the National Government it certainly was not becoming men of Jefferson's and Calhoun's principles to complain at the Massachusetts enforcement of their doctrines. They preached—Massachusetts practiced.

The proceedings of Congress—which assembled Dec. 6th, 1813—were calculated to inflame anew the fires glowing on the Northern hills, or slumbering in their vallies. Madison, in a confidential message (Dec. 9th) adverted with some feeling and severity to the evasions of the Non-intercourse prohibitions, asserting that not only were the enemy's fleets supplied with provisions, but the importation of British goods continued through the process of smuggling and by the practice of ransoming, by which collusive captures were made, and whole cargoes of foreign goods thrown upon our markets. To remedy these evasions he proposed that an "effectual embargo" on exports be immediately enacted; that all ransoms be prohibited; and that, to claim the rights of a neutral, the master, supercargo, and at least three-fourths of the crew be actual subjects of the alleged neutral power. To meet these suggestions a bill was matured and forced through in secret session (Dec. 19th) which, if it did not answer all the expectations of the President, produced still further exasperation of mind in New England. Even the fishing-smacks were put under heavy bonds, while a most arbitrary authority or discretion was given to Custom House officials, as well as to cruisers and privateers, to overhaul any vessel, and to seize, upon mere suspicion, any goods "apparently on their way (by land or water) toward the territory of a foreign nation, or to the vicinity thereof." The next edict, it was said, might be one to search private houses in order to discover if goods of British fabric were there in use.

A gleam of peace came to relieve the public anxiety somewhat. Russia had, upon three occasions, during the summer of 1813, offered her services as mediator; but Great Britain had rejected the Czar's offices, thus adding to the war spirit against her. But, early in January, a vessel reached our shores bearing the important news of Napoleon's defeat at Leipsic and of the advance of Wellington into France. Accompanying this news came offers from the British government to treat directly with our Government, either in London or in Gottenburg. This offer gave to the opponents of the war fresh courage. Madison gladly accepted the overture, and named (Jan. 14th) as Commissioner John Quincy Adams, then Minister to Russia, and James A. Bayard, of Delaware, whose casting vote, in the celebrated seven days' ballot, gave Jefferson the Presidency. To these were added, "as special representatives of the War party," Henry Clay and Jonathan Russell. Their instructions soon were perfected, and the two last named sailed from New York, Feb. 23d. Albert Gallatin, who was then abroad, also was added to the Commission.

But, this gleam of peace did not stay the increase of the war faction. It grew steadily. As it grew, hatred of the New Englanders increased. In view of Otis' resolves several State Legislatures gave utterance to their indignation at the attitude assumed by Massachusetts. Pennsylvania (Jan. 18th) expressed astonishment at Crittenden's proclamation and Otis' resolutions, tendering, at the same time, aid to the General Government "to bring to justice all violators of the Constitution and the law, and all aiders and comforters of the enemy, whether directly or indirectly." New Jerseymen talked even more menacingly. The Legislature (Feb. 12th) expressed "their contempt and abhorrence of the roarings of an infuriated faction, whether issuing from a legislative body, a maniac governor, or discontented and ambitious demagogues," declaring their readiness "to resist internal insurrection with the same readiness as the invasion of a cruel, vindictive and savage foe." Despite these sounding anathemas the New England men pursued their opposition unflinchingly. A large number of British officers and privates having been committed to prison, by order of the President, in retaliation for the imprisonment of Americans, by the British Governor-General of Canada, several officers were consigned to the Worcester jail under an old act (1790) which placed the jails at the service of the United States. The Legislature promptly repealed the act (Feb. 7th, 1814) so far as related to prisoners of the United States' authorities other than of the judiciary, ordering all prisoners committed under the Executive authority of the United States to be dismissed within thirty days. This gave time for the General Government to remove its charges, though a general release on parole of prisoners soon followed.

The press and the pulpit did not follow the public sentiment but *led* it, in many respects. In the Boston *Gazette*, and the *Advertiser*, as well as in a number of the interior newspapers, the extremists found "organs" noisy enough—all clamorous for a direct issue to be made with the General Government as well as for a separate peace with Great Britain. In the pulpit were found many men so strongly imbued with old Puritanic notions of the rights of conscience and liberty of action as to talk most rank treason—so rank that Jefferson, in his "Ana," rather roughly writes of the "pulpit-lyings and slanderings and maniacal ravings of their Gardiners, their Osgoods and their Parishes." This latter D. D., a minister of Byfield, made himself especially conspicuous for his exhortations to arm against the Egyptian (the Administration).

Nor, should the financiers be left unnoticed in this arraignment of sinners against the integrity of the Republic—for, of sinners, they were the most *materially* dangerous, having greatly assisted in bringing the finances of the country to the verge of bankruptcy. They made a combined assault upon the public credit. Boston, as the grand *entrepot* of smugglers, was further rendered the centre of trade by British policy, which, until the Summer of 1814, left the New England coast free from blockade! This exception doubtless was to encourage indirectly the spirit of friendship which the opposition party were supposed to entertain for Great Britain, as well as to obtain supplies by the coasting trade, which freely bore flour and meat to Eastport and Halifax, until cut off by the severe act of Dec. 19th, 1813. The city was further enriched by the disposition there of "ransomed" cargoes and prizes, by which great quantities of foreign goods found their way to an American market. All these circumstances combined to render Boston a port of supply for other cities. Soon New York, Philadelphia, Baltimore and even Richmond and Charleston became heavy debtors, on the trade lists. Thus the tide of exchange sat Northward. Ere long the New England brokers, in spite of the general prostration of New England commerce, held the finances of the country in their control. The passage of the act of Dec. 19th, while it quite cut off the lucrative contraband trade of Boston, found the Middle and Southern States greatly New England's debtor; and the Yankee capitalists resolved to retaliate for the act by striking a blow at the finances. To this end they first sought to prevent the taking of the loan authorised March 14th, 1814; but, the banks of the 'Democratic' States, and the capitalists of their cities, in order to sustain the National credit subscribed to the twenty-five million loan to a considerable amount. Many men in New England and a few of the banks also contributed to it, and the loan bid fair to be a success. The Bostonians then decided to call in their loans and credits and to send home for redemption all bills, acceptances, &c., which they held of cities and individuals to the South. They acted in concert, first drawing on New York. That city, to meet the sudden demand, drew heavily on Philadelphia; Philadelphia, in turn, upon Baltimore. Thus the chain ran through the country; to the smallest merchant it was a demand at sight to pay up all dues. A panic followed which quickly deranged the credit and the confidence of the entire country. A steady current of specie slowly flowed North, to find its way into New England vaults, already full. That such was their condition the statement of the previous January proved. The annual returns of the leading banks then stood: specie $4,945,444; notes in circulation $2,000,601—"a state of things," said Matthew Carey, "probably unparalleled in the history of banking, from the days of the Lombards." This monetary crisis wrought the end designed. Banks and individuals subscribing to the loan could not comply with their engagements. Many, still able to carry out their voluntary obligations, refused to do so, not knowing what calamities the future held in store. A financial collapse was predicted and every body kept 'close in shore,' for fear of disaster. Banks throughout the Middle and Southern States were compelled to suspend specie payments, during the latter part of August, but not until Boston coffers were full to repletion. Then followed a rapid depreciation of bank paper. The best New York notes were quoted at 20 per cent., Philadelphia, 24 per cent., and Baltimore at 30 per cent. discount, by February, 1815; while U. S. Treasury six per cents stood at 40 per cent. discount, and Treasury Notes at 24 per cent. Minor banks quite generally sank into bankruptcy.

The result of all this was to bring the National finances into the perils of bankruptcy. In September the new Secretary of the Treasury, Campbell—appointed in place of Gallatin, placed on the Peace Commission—made an exhibit which proved the impending disaster to be near if something was not done to recuperate the funds. The attempt to secure six millions of the authorised loan resulted in offers for only about one-half that sum at about 80 per cent. At this ruinous rate the Secretary was compelled to sell. To obtain $2,500,000, stocks were issued to the amount of $4,266,000. Eight millions of treasury notes were offered, one half of which would fall due during the next quarter. Other obligations rendered it necessary to secure twenty-five millions, yet, combining every resource of the Treasurer, but nine millions were to be estimated as secure. The revenues already provided were greatly too small for the demands. New schemes of taxation were devised by Alexander Dallas, of Pennsylvania, who quickly took Campbell's place, to attempt what all despaired of accomplishing—the sustentation of the National credit. Notwithstanding his old anti-bank affinities, and the intense opposition of his "Democratic Societies" to Hamilton and his schemes of National finance, Dallas came forward with a plan for a National Bank, with a capital of fifty millions—*five* in specie and the rest in Government Stocks—thus to provide a circulating medium and to obtain an immediate use of loans. This proposition—so utterly at variance with all 'Democratic' precedents—possessed few virtues with many vices. It authorised Government to become a two-fifths' stockholder, in virtue of which it was to have the appointment of the President and one-third of the Directors—the Directory to be invested with power to suspend specie payment, and the bank to loan Government thirty millions of dollars. This "wild cat" enterprise greatly displeased old Republicans and Federalists alike, but, the pressure of the war party and of the Administration prevailed, and, after considerable opposition, bills were introduced (Oct. 21st) to cover Dallas' suggestions.

It is not to be inferred that the New England bankers brought all this train of monetary disaster. The great expansion of credit, consequent on a state of war and of commercial inactivity, must have produced a financial crisis sooner or later: the bankers of the North only hastened an inevitable result of carrying on a war on loans—Gallatin's idea. Gallatin, as the successor of Alexander Hamilton, was the embodiment of a 'Democratic' financier; and his failure, as well as the adoption, by Dallas, of the banking resource, did not fail to render the contrast with Hamilton's management painful. The New England men, strong in resources, had they been so inclined, would have carried the loans along triumphantly; but, they were not so inclined, and threw upon the Administration all responsibility of meeting the exigency which it had created.

An immense number of petitions for redress, protection, action against and defiance of the embargo had been sent into the Massachusetts Legislature from officers of sailing craft, from ship owners, from manufacturers, traders and citizens generally. All these were referred to a joint committee of the two houses, which reported, Feb. 16th, (1814). This document at some length reiterated, from former reports, the oppressive and destructive policy of the Government, but superadded views clearly looking either to a defiance of the Government or to a dissolution of the Union. Among other paragraphs it rang in the President's ears this chime to his Virginia resolves:

"A power to regulate commerce is abused when employed to destroy it, and a voluntary abuse of power sanctions the right of resistance as much as a direct and palpable usurpation. The sovereignty reserved to the States was reserved to protect the citizens from acts of violence by the United States, as well as for purposes of domestic regulation. We spurn the idea that the free, sovereign and independent State of Massachusetts is reduced to a mere municipal corporation, without power to protect its people, or to defend them from oppression, from whatever quarter it comes. Whenever the National compact is violated, and the citizens of this State oppressed by cruel and unauthorized enactments, this Legislature is bound to interpose its power and to wrest from the oppressor his victim. This is the spirit of our Union, and thus has it been explained by the very man who now sets at defiance all the principles of his early political life. The question, then, is not a question of power or right, but of time and expediency."

The report did not suggest, however, the remedy of immediate application. It betrayed fears of that "leap in the dark" which it decreed was inevitable, was but a question of "time and expediency." Of the three measures of redress recommended by the memorialists, viz: a remonstrance to Congress; laws to punish unconstitutional searches and seizures, under color of the embargo; and the appointment of delegates to meet such as might be appointed by the Legislatures of other States, "for the purpose of devising proper measures to procure the united efforts of the commercial States to obtain such amendments or explanations of the Constitution as will secure them from future evils"—the Committee did not accept either. Remonstrance had been tried with no result but to incur reproach; the State courts, as then administered, would afford sufficient protection against unconstitutional seizures of persons and property; a convention would be a good thing, but, as the State had elected a new Legislature, the Committee preferred to leave the matter in its hands. And so the matter was left, much to the disgust of the extremists, for the new Legislature to grapple with. This body, "fresh from the people," met May 30th, to hear from Governor Strong a message similar to his former communications—advice to acquiesce in the state of things only so far as necessary to a bare fulfillment of Constitutional obligations. This speech the two houses endorsed, in their replies, reminding the authorities at Washington that they must not suppose, because the people of Massachusetts maintained their reputation for good order by submitting to the Constitutional right of Congress to declare war and to levy taxes to carry it on, that this submission resulted either from ignorance incapable of discerning, or from pusillanimity not ready to assert their essential rights, should any such be at any time invaded.

No action was taken on the joint report of the previous session in regard to a Convention of delegates to meet such as might be appointed by other Legislatures for holding an antemortem inquest over the Constitution. The reasons given for this delay to meet the "demands of the hour" were that Madison had proposed the repeal of the embargo—that Buonaparte had been forced to abdicate, and that a general peace must soon follow. Madison had given way before the frowns of the Federalists: although but four months had passed since his confidential message had recommended and secured a searching amendment to the offending restrictive laws, he proposed (March 31st) not only the repeal of the Embargo but of the Non-importation act and the admission of imports of all kinds except enemy's property! Webster did not fail to handle these propositions with good natured severity, as a very late confession of the injustice of the acts, but more particularly as evidence that they were designed as measures to aid France —that, as the French Empire had had to succumb to English arms the Embargo *therefore* was no longer of use! Congress was not, however ready to take the responsibility of this repeal so long as the fate of negotiations then progressing in Holland were undecided, and the matter was passed over to the next session, when, Webster insinuated, the New England manufacturers (which had suddenly sprung into existence during the operation of the restrictive non-importation system) would be sacrificed and the merchant and shipping interest already had been—so distrustful was he of the *animus* of 'Democratic' legislation.

But, the disaster and gloom of the Summer and Fall of 1814, drove States into the field for self-protection. Government was powerless to give the frontier and seaboard the least security. Governors and Legislatures had to take upon themselves the duties of defense. Not only had the first ideas of the war partisans been abandoned—the conquest of Canada—but, even the programme of a defensive war was committed, in a great measure, to the States! Governor Strong, of Massachusetts, called ten thousand militia to the field, and the Legislature appropriated to the military chest one million of dollars. New York, Virginia and other States also called out their State forces, and contributed their funds. But, in New England the militia were denied to the General Government—the Governors refused to permit any other command and jurisdiction than their own. This attitude was definitively taken in consequence of the refusal (Sept. 17th) by the Secretary of War (Munroe), to allow claims for the heavy expenses of defending New England already incurred by the Governors. This repudiation was based upon the refusal of the Governors to respond to the War Department's orders for placing the militia under command of General Dearborne, in Massachusetts, and of Brigadier-General Cushing, in Connecticut. Those of the latter State, put in the field in the Summer of 1814, did not reach the number of four thousand—the quota called for; and, because the Governor (Trumbull) placed a militia Major-General over the head of the

Government Brigadier, Munroe refused all pay, supplies, &c., to those actually in service.

This conflict of authority only strengthened the opposition element in the Legislatures. Once more the idea of a Convention of New England States was revived. Washington City had been invaded, Aug. 24th, 25th, and its chief public buildings burned, with all their precious contents. British fleets were sweeping the coasts with almost unopposed fury. The Peace Commission, then assembled at Ghent, made no progress toward a settlement. England, having broken and banished Buonaparte, was free to throw all her tremendous armament upon the country. Commercial and financial disaster stared the Union in the face like a grim spectre. The ruin predicted by the New England opponents of the war policy had more than been realized—the results of what was considered a Southern rule were painfully visible in the still smoking embers of the National Capital. Yet, the party in power proposed no modification of their system of "whipping" Great Britain into a peace. The inefficiency of the General Government compared with its demand for new sacrifices aroused the "blue light Federalists" [1] to new zeal in compelling a total change of the Governmental policy, or in effecting a separate peace with England.

We now reach the proceedings directly preliminary to the Hartford Convention. Harrison Gray Otis, as chairman of a joint committee of the Legislature, reported, Oct. 8th, that, in the position in which Massachusetts then stood, "no choice was left her between submission to the enemy, which was not to be thought of, and the appropriation to her own defense of those revenues derived from her people, but which the Gene-

[1] The only National vessels of war fit for service were blockaded in various ports, by the vigilant enemy, and could not put to sea. Decatur's two frigates were fast in New London. Several times the gallant commander designed to put out during the night, or during a storm; but, *blue lights* were burned on the hills on every attempt, and thus the enemy was placed on the alert. Decatur, in a letter to the Secretary of the Navy expressed great indignation at this treasonable interference with his plans. It is not, however, *proven* that the enemy actually were signalled by shore lights burned by the Connecticut men. The inference is a fair one that English spies and signal squads did the work.

ral Government had hitherto thought proper to expend elsewhere." The report then recurred to the Convention of Delegates suggested by the Spring session. The reasons for this Convention were thus given in abstract:

"The idea of a convention of the discontented States was also revived. The Constitution of the United States, under the administration of those now in power, had failed, so this report stated, to secure to Massachusetts, and to New England generally, those equal rights and benefits, the great objects of its formation, and which could not be relinquished without ruin. The method of procuring amendments, the probable necessity for which had been foreseen, provided for in the Constitution itself, was too slow of operation for the present crisis. The safety of the people—the supreme law—would well justify, in the present emergency, the holding of a new convention to modify or amend it. Nor was the expectation presumptuous that a spirit of equity and justice, enlightened by experience, would enable such a convention to reconcile conflicting interests, and, by obviating the principal cause of those dissensions, which unfitted the Government alike for a state of peace and of war, to give to the Union vigor and duration.

"But as such a proposition, coming from a single State, might be disregarded, and as present dangers admitted of no delay, the committee recommended, in the first instance, the inviting of 'a conference between those States, the affinity of whose interests is closest, and whose habits of intercourse, from local and other causes, are most frequent, to the end that, by a comparison of their sentiments and views, some mode of defense suited to the circumstances and exigencies of those States, and measures for accelerating the return of public prosperity, may be devised; and also to enable the delegates from those States, should they deem it expedient, to lay the foundation of a radical reform in the National compact, by inviting to a future convention a deputation from all the States in the Union.'

"The amendment of the Constitution principally insisted upon was a new basis of representation. The present basis, counting three-fifths of the slaves, had been adopted, it was said, under the idea that the slave States were more wealthy than the free States, and ought, on that account, to have a greater representation in proportion to the number of citizens. This supposition of superior wealth was, however, a mistake in fact. Had representation been based either upon property, or number of free inhabitants, or upon any uniform combination of both, this war, forced by the poor slaveholding agricultural States upon the rich, free, commercial States, would never have been declared."

This report, in spite of a most strenuous opposition from the Democrats and a few Federalists, passed by a vote of three to one, and twelve delegates were named to the proposed Convention, embracing some of the most able men of the commonwealth—Otis, Nathan Dane, George Cabot, Joseph Lyman, being of the number. A circular letter followed, addressed to the Governors of all the other New England States, inviting the appointment of delegates to meet in Convention "to deliberate upon the dangers to which the Eastern section of the Union is exposed by the course of the war, and which there is too much reason to believe will thicken around them in its progress, and to devise, if practicable, means of security and defense which may be consistent with the preservation of their resources from total ruin, and adapted to their local situation, and mutual relations and habits, and not repugnant to their obligations as members of the Union." The secondary object of the Convention was to "inquire whether the interests of the New England States did not demand persevering efforts to procure such amendments of the Federal Constitution as might secure them 'equal advantages;' and if it should seem impracticable to obtain such under the existing provisions for amendment, whether 'it might not be beneficial to endeavor to obtain a Convention from all the States of the Union, or of such as might approve the measure, with a view to obtain such amendments.' 'It cannot be necessary,' the circular added, 'to anticipate objections to this measure which may arise from jealousy or fear. The Legislature is content, for its justification, to repose on the purity of its own motives, and upon the known attachment of its constituents to the National Union, and to the rights and independence of their country.'"

"Upon the known attachment of its constituents to the National Union" really was Massachusetts' sentiment; but, in view of the feelings entertained by Otis and the Legislative majority, in view of their persistent refusal to acknowledge the supremacy of the National Executive, and in view of the practical endorsement given to State Rights doctrines, the clause quoted sounded more as if put in to appease the little censor in their own hearts than because the Legislators entertained any real attachment for the Union *as then constituted and gov-*

erned. They were attached to the Union, but with a qualification which looked amazingly like disunion.

This circular was referred to a special committee, which accompanied its endorsement by a report drawn with great force and ability, in which were set forth the excuses for the Convention, and intimated the sphere of its functions. This document, thus doubly ladened with authority, was dispatched to the several North-eastern States. The Legislatures of Connecticut and Rhode Island acted at once—the first appointing seven delegates and naming the 15th day of December as the time and Hartford as the place of the session. These seven were among the best and most influential men of the State. Rhode Island, by a vote of two to one, appointed four delegates. Vermont and New Hampshire did not appoint—the Administration party being too strong in both States. Two delegates from the latter, and one from the former, were, however, informally appointed by the people.

There followed, from Boston to New Orleans, such an outburst of patriotic indignation, particularly from Administration presses, as would lead to the conclusion that Washington's Farewell Address always had been a Gospel of Faith to them—as if the resolutions of '98 were not of 'Democratic' birth and the prime principles of the 'Democratic' creed! Many good and ardent Federalists were loud in their expressions of dissatisfaction at the course being pursued, although they—in common with many others among leading Administration men—saw no serious public danger in the movement. Ex-President John Adams, and his Secretary of War (afterwards his Secretary of Treasury), Samuel Dexter, were particularly distinguished for their hostility to the Convention. Said Jefferson:

"Some apprehended danger from the defection of Massachusetts. It is a disagreeable circumstance, but not a dangerous one. If they become neutral we are sufficient for our enemy, without them, and in fact we get no aid from them now. If their Administration determines to join the enemy their force will be annihilated by equality of division among themselves. Their Federalists will then call in the English army, the Republicans ours, and it will only be a transfer of the scene of war from Canada to Massachusetts; and we can get ten men to go to Massachusetts for one who will go to Canada.[1] Every one must know, too, that we can, at any moment, make peace with England at the expense of the navigation and fisheries of Massachusetts.[2] But, it will not come to this. Their own people will put down these factionists as soon as they see the real object of their opposition; and of this Vermont, New Hampshire, and even Connecticut itself furnish proofs."

Views which events soon confirmed: "their own people" did put down the entire movement more completely than an army could have done. Madison did not entertain this happy opinion. Timid by nature, distrustful of the patriotism of the people, he apprehended the worst results from New England's procedure. Wirt has left us a distressing picture of Madison's mental condition at that time. He was tasting the fruits of the tree which he himself had planted: he was experiencing the practical application of his State supremacy faith.

The Convention of twenty-six delegates—including two from New Hampshire and one from Vermont—assembled at Hartford at the appointed time (Dec. 15th). It organized by the election of George Cabot, of Massachusetts, as President, and Theodore Dwight, of Connecticut, as Secretary. No excitement whatever, attended its proceedings. Madison had on the ground Major Jessup, nominally for recruiting, but really to watch the course of affairs, and, in event of an uprising to be ready, with the help of Governor Tompkins, the patriotic Executive of New York, to strike down insurrection at a blow. The young officer, both zealous and discreet, was not long in reaching the conclusion that the Convention was a harmless affair which would end in resolutions and remonstrances—not in revolution. So he advised the Government. The idea probably

[1] The reader will please note the force of this positive statement as indicative of the feeling which prevailed in Virginia and the South, at that time, against New England. Purely *sectional* animosity was one of the most painful facts of those times.

[2] This is a fair statement of the power wielded by "we," the 'Demecratic' States. If it was used to levy the embargo, to crush out New England prosperity, had emergencies required, it certainly would have been used to *permanently* cripple her navigation and fisheries. It was the very *power* to do her injury of which New England chiefly complained. Jefferson, it will be seen, not only admitted that strength of "we," the ascendant Virginia party, but did not hesitate to show how, by a disgraceful peace—by surrendering New England to British commercial supremacy—"we" could have proceeded against the Northern States.

struck him as ridiculous that twenty-six excellent men (twenty of whom were lawyers!) could or would effect the destruction of the Union.[1]

The Convention sat with closed doors, for twenty days, adjourning Jan. 5th, when the results became partially known in the publication of a report, directed to the Legislatures of the States represented. The entire proceedings were not, however, divulged until five years had passed, when the President of the Convention, to satisfy the public of its actual character, placed the Journal of Proceedings in the office of the Secretary of State of Massachusetts, for public inspection. From it we learn that a committee, appointed to consider "what subjects will be proper to be considered by the Convention," reported the topics proper for consideration as follows:

"The powers claimed by the Executive of the United States to determine, conclusively, in respect to calling out the militia of the States into the service of the United States; and the dividing the United States into military districts, with an officer of the army in each thereof, with discretionary authority from the Executive of the United States to call for the militia to be under the command of such officer: the refusal of the Executive of the United States to supply or pay the militia of certain States called out for their defense, on the grounds of their not having been called out under the authority of the United States, or not having been, by the Executive of the State, put under the command of the commander over the military district: the failure of the Government of the United States to supply and pay the militia of the States, by them admitted to have been in the United States service: the Report of the Secretary of War to Congress on filling the ranks of the army, together with a bill or act on that subject: a bill before Congress, providing for classifying and drafting the militia: the expenditure of the revenue of

---

[1] And yet, a less number of men actually controlled the fortunes of the Secession Revolution of 1860–61 in its incipient stages. The difference between their work and that of the Hartford Conventionists consisted less in the principles evolved than in the character of the men:—the delegates of 1814 truly wished well for their country—the conspirators of 1860 were notoriously unscrupulous demagogues who, on the *ruins* of the Union, would erect a powerful Slave-republic which Slave owners alone should rule. There is, therefore, very little parallelism between the two parties, save in their common reliance upon the Jefferson and Madison resolutions of '98 and in their mutual dislike of the Union as it existed. The Hartford men would have tinkered the Constitution and rejuvenated the Republic—the revolutionists of '60 spurned the Constitution and rejected the Union in any shape.

the nation in offensive operations on the neighboring provinces of the enemy: the failure of the Government of the United States to provide for the common defense; and the consequent obligations, necessity and burdens devolved on the separate States to defend themselves—together with the mode and the ways and means in their power for accomplishing the object."

This was considered in Committee of the Whole for several days, when (Dec. 20th) a second Committee was named to report "a general project of such measures" as it would be proper for the Convention to adopt. The report, as adopted (Dec. 24th), first declared it expedient to "prepare a general statement of the unconstitutional attempts of the Executive Government of the United States to infringe on the rights of the individual States manifested in the letter of the Secretary of War," etc., and to recommend to the Legislatures of the States the adoption of the most effectual and decisive measures to protect the militia and the States from the usurpations contained in these proceedings. Also to prepare a statement concerning the general subject of State defenses, and to recommend an earnest application to the National Government for an arrangement with the States by which they would be allowed to retain a portion of the taxes levied by Congress, to be devoted to the expenses of self-defense, and for the reimbursement of money already expended by them for such purpose. Also to amend the Constitution, so as to accomplish the following results: 1. The restriction of the power of Congress to declare and make war. 2. A restraint of the exercise of unlimited power by Congress to make new States and admit them into the Union. 3. A restraint of the powers of Congress in laying embargoes and restrictions on commerce. 4. A stipulation that a President of the United States shall not be elected from the same State two consecutive terms; and, 5. That the same person shall not be elected President a second time. 6. That alterations be made concerning slave representation and taxation. This programme was considered with great deliberation —every member present participating in the discussion. It resulted in the adoption of the Report, with Resolutions above referred to, directed to their several Legislatures. Its most salient points were as follows:

"To prescribe patience and firmness to those who are already exhausted by distress is sometimes to drive them to despair, and the progress toward reform by the regular road is irksome to those whose imaginations discern and whose feelings prompt to a shorter course. But when abuses, reduced to a system, and accumulated through a course of years have pervaded every department of government, and spread corruption through every region of the State; when these are clothed with the forms of law, and enforced by an Executive whose will is their source, no summary means of relief can be applied without recourse to direct and open resistance. It is a truth not to be concealed that a time for a change is at hand. * * * A reformation of public opinion, resulting from dear bought experience in the Southern Atlantic States at least, is not to be despaired of. They will have seen that the great and essential interests of the people are common to the South and to the East. They will realize the fatal errors of a system which seeks revenge for commercial injuries in the sacrifice of commerce, and aggravates by needless wars the injuries it professes to redress. Indications of this desirable revolution of opinion among our brethren in those States are already manifested, Finally, if the Union be destined to dissolution by reason of the multiplied abuses of bad administrations, it should be, if possible, the work of peaceable times and deliberate consent. Some new form of confederacy should be substituted among those States which shall intend to maintain a Federal relation to each other. Events may prove that the causes of our calamities are deep and permanent. They may be found to proceed not merely from the blindness or prejudice, pride of opinion, violence of party spirit, or the confusion of the times; but they may be traced to implacable combinations of individuals or of States to monopolise power and office, and to trample without remorse upon the rights and interests of commercial sections of the Union. Whenever it shall appear that the causes are radical and permanent, a separation by equitable arrangement will be preferable to an alliance by constraint among nominal friends, but real enemies, inflamed by mutual hatred and jealousy, and inviting, by intestine divisions, contempt and aggressions from abroad—but a severance of the Union by one or more States against the will of the rest, and especially in time of war, can be justified only by absolute necessity."

The Report then proceeded to consider the several subjects of complaint, chief of which was the authority over the militia claimed by the National Executive. It said:

"In this whole series of devices and measures for raising men, this Convention discerns a total disregard for the Constitution, and a disposition to violate its provisions, demanding from the individual States a firm and decided opposition. An iron despotism can impose no harder service upon the citizen than to force him from his home and his occupation to wage offensive war undertaken to gratify the pride or passions of his master. * * * In cases of deliberate, dangerous and palpable infractions of the Constitution, affecting the sovereignty of a State and the liberties of the people, it is not only the right, but the duty of such State to interpose its authority for the protection in the manner best calculated to secure that end. When emergencies occur which are either beyond the reach of the judicial tribunals, or too pressing to admit of the delay incident to their forms, States which have no common umpire must be their own judges and execute their own decisions."

[We here have not only the legitimate logical consequent of the Kentucky resolutions, but a repetition of Jefferson's very idea. He said: "As in other cases of compact between parties having no common judge, each party has an equal right to judge for itself, as well of infractions as of the mode and measure of redress." Perhaps the special pleader may be able to discover that this assumption is not that of the Hartford Convention; but, to the mass of readers, who take words in their accredited signification, the Hartford resolves will seem but Mr. Jefferson's reproduced. If any lingering doubt exists as to the extent of Mr. Jefferson's nullification sentiments, they will be dissipated by his eighth resolution, which expressly and directly declares that (the States themselves being sole judges) where Congress assumes powers not delegated by the people, "*a nullification of the act is the right remedy; and that every State has a natural right, in cases not within the compact, to nullify, of their own authority, all assumptions of power by others within their limits.*" We are at a loss, in view of this express declaration, and that which immediately follows it in the same resolution, to discover upon what authority Mr. Everett (see Address, of July 4th, 1861) denies the nullification sentiment as Mr. Jefferson's own. This we add, *par parenthesis*, in order that, in forming his judgment of the true character of the Hartford proceedings, the 'democratic' reader at least may place to the New Englanders' *credit* whatever they may have appropriated from the ideas of the "father of Democracy."]

The resolves accompanying this Report or Address we may give in abstract:

The first recommended the Legislatures of the States represented to protect the citizens of the several States from the operation of acts passed by Congress, subjecting them to forcible drafts, conscriptions or impressments, not authorized by the Constitution.

The second recommended that the States be empowered to defend themselves, and that they have for their own use their proportion of the taxes collected.

The third recommended each State to defend itself.

The fourth recommended amendments to the Constitution, as follows: 1. Apportionment of representation and taxation the basis of white population. 2. New States to be admitted by a vote of two-thirds of both houses of Congress. 3. Congress shall have no power to lay an embargo of more than sixty days' duration. 4. Congress shall not have power to interdict foreign trade without a vote of two-thirds of both houses. 5. Congress shall not make war by a less vote than two-thirds of both branches, unless in defense of territory actually invaded. 6. No naturalized citized to be eligible to any civil office under the United States. 7. No President to be elected twice or for two terms, nor to be chosen from the same State twice in succession.

The report concluded with the recommendation that if the foregoing resolutions should be unsuccessful when submitted to the General Government through the respective States, if peace should not be concluded, and the defense of the New England States be neglected, as it had been, it would be expedient for the Legislatures of the several States to appoint delegates to another Convention to meet at Boston, in June following, "with such powers and instructions as the exigency of a crisis so momentous may require."

These resolves were designed for, and were sent forth to, the Legislatures of the several States; but, like the Virginia and Kentucky resolves of '98, elicited no favorable response. Democratic Pennsylvania heaped upon them strong expressions of contempt. The Convention's report the Legislatures of Massachusetts and Connecticut accepted, and appointed (June 19th) five Commissioners to Washington to lay their wishes before the National authorities—their instructions requiring them to *request* of the General Government compliance with their wishes in regard to taxes, &c. These agents, however, never made their demands—never presented their credentials at Washington. News of the peace of Ghent, and of Jackson's victory at New Orleans sent such a thrill of joy through the public heart as rendered further proceedings on the part of the New Englanders in very bad taste and dangerously inopportune and the Commissioners wisely preferred not even to announce their mission. Those of them who had found their way to Washington quietly returned.

The great Hartford Convention Conspiracy thus dissolved. The country, which had frowned upon and feared it, now laughed at its failure; its members were derided, or pointed at in scorn, as something loathsome if not dangerous; and three generations scarcely have sufficed to quiet the public mind in regard to its assumed treasonable character. So powerfully, indeed, did public sentiment set in against the convocation and its abettors that few were hardy enough to defend the course pursued. Even Webster, it is asserted, prosecuted Theodore Lyman (son of a member of the Convention) for asserting that he (W.) had some connection with the Convention! But, despite this popular disfavor there still exists in New England a strong feeling of sympathy for the Convention, as a representative of the opposition to Jefferson's "Chinese policy."[1] Says a New England writer in a very lucid and able paper on American Navigation:[2]

"If, during the seven years of trial and suffering, from 1808 to 1815, in which nearly one-half of the wealth of New England was extinguished, her citizens became indignant at the wanton sacrifice of their means and of the best opportunity Fortune ever gave them to gain riches by commerce—if the public sentiment found expression alike through the press, in town-meetings, in legislative halls, and even in the pulpit—if the capitalist lost confidence in a government which trifled with its own resources—if the merchant refused all countenance to those who had wrought his ruin—let the blame fall on the originators of the evil. Lord North did but impose a few light taxes, place a few restrictions upon commerce, and make a few other inroads on freedom; but he set a nation in flames. The Cabinets of 1807 and 1812 warred against commerce itself, and placed an interdict on every harbor; and which of the measures of the British statesman was more arbitrary in its character, more repugnant to the spirit of freemen, or more questionable as to its

[1] Jefferson, in his "Notes on Virginia," in 1785 had expressed his views on our maritime policy in the following terms:

"You ask me what I think of the expediency of encouraging our States to become commercial. Were I to indulge my own theory, I wish them to practise neither commerce or navigation, but to stand with respect to Europe *precisely on the footing of China.*"

[2] See "Atlantic Monthly" for June, 1861.

legality, than the Enforcing Act of 1808? And if the men of New England, who had in their colonial weakness met both France and England by sea and land without a fear, saw the fruits of their industry sacrificed and the bread taken from their children's mouths by the Chinese policy of a Southern cabinet, might they not well chafe under measures so oppressive and so unnecessary that they were ingloriously abandoned?"

John Quincy Adams recurring to the proposed second convocation, to assemble at Boston in June, says: "it was turned over to the receptacle of things lost upon earth"—so utterly *dead* did the very *idea* of a second Convention become. Not that the treaty obtained of Great Britain, by our Commissioners, really accomplished anything important; but, it was *peace*, and her wand swept away the past as if it had been but a shadow. News of the arrangement reached New York, by a British sloop-of-war bearing two messengers with the treaty, as already ratified, by the British government. Without for a moment pausing to ask the terms and conditions of that treaty, the people gave way to expressions of unlimited joy. In every city bonfires, illuminations, bell-ringings, &c., followed upon the reception of the good tidings, flying by special expresses over the land. In Congress satisfaction was not less apparent. A zealous war partisan congratulated the House on the glorious termination of the most glorious war waged by any people, &c. But, the painful fact, when the treaty was published (after its ratification by Congress, Feb. 17th) became confessed that the war had ended just where it had begun—that we had "whipped" England into nothing, extorted no concessions, established no permanent principles of comity! Says Hildreth: "The Federalists, and all the more sensible Republicans, considered the country lucky in the peace, such as it was. The violent war men, greatly cooled by this time, concealed their mortification, like Troup, behind the smoke of Jackson's victory, and vague declarations about the national rights vindicated, the national character exalted, and the military and naval glory of the war. Considering the new demands of Great Britain put forward at Ghent, they seemed to esteem it a triumph to be allowed to stop where they began, leaving the whole question of impressments and neutral rights, the sole ostensible occasion of the war, without a word said upon the subject, to be settled at some more convenient opportunity; a common termination of wars, even for the most powerful and belligerent nations, and of which Great Britain herself has given more than one instance."

It is not to be inferred that the New England States furnished no troops for the war. The volunteer system found great numbers of recruits—how many will never be known, as they were sent by squads and companies to New York for muster in various regiments. During the eventful excitement of 1814, about 14,000 volunteers were secured at recruiting rendezvous, under the bounty enlistment act; and, of this number New England furnished more than all the Southern States put together! Massachusetts enlisted more than any single State in the Union, to the Grand Army, for that year.[1]

From what has been written the reader will have a clear comprehension of the *causes* of the Hartford Convention, if not of its actual aims. That these causes were potent enough to produce irritation of the body politic is not a matter of question; and the assumption, by a certain class of writers, that it was a love of England, a desire for a state of colonial dependence which induced the hostility of the New Englanders to Madison and the war, is too transparently but an assumption to merit attention. By heaping derision, insult, libel and scorn upon the Federalists, as authors of the Convention and as enemies of the Government, their opponents gained in popular force so immensely as to render them doubly secure in power: not until the 'log cabin and hard cider' campaign of 1840 was the bond broken which gave the Democrats the Executive branches of

---

[1] It has so long been the habit of Southern partisans to libel Massachusetts that one can hardly express surprise at the statements put forth by Pollard, in his "First Year of the War"—(Secession Revolution). He says:

"In the war of 1812 the North furnished 58,552 soldiers; the South 96,812—making a majority of 37,030 in favor of the South. Of the men furnished by the North, Massachusetts furnished 3,110; New Hampshire 897; Connecticut 387; Rhode Island 637; Vermont 181."

It is possible that the South, *including* Pennsylvania and New York, furnished more troops than the North for the entire period of the war, for *general operations;* but, the figures above given of the numbers contributed by the New England States are absurdly at variance with the truth. When the facts are so easily accessible we can hardly excuse such outrageous misstatements.

the Government. Even then it was severed but briefly; by the death of Harrison. a Virginian became President and the South again resumed its scarcely broken sway. There was policy, therefore, in making the most of what, at the worst, was but an embodiment of the paramount policy of the South the *right* to discredit Congressional acts and to defy the National Executive; the crime was, as we now see, not so much in the attitude of hostility assumed, as that *Massachusetts* should have assumed it. When the rebellious States of the South in 1860–61 in their Conventions resolved, and in their wrath committed, the treason of open rebellion, what a howl of defamation went up from their people and presses that their right to break up the Union should be questioned!

Time never fails to do justice. Had the nullification attitude of South Carolina in 1831–32 never been assumed—had the revolution of 1860–61 never been inaugurated—the Massachusetts Federalists of 1814 would stand forth as bad subjects of a good government; but, with the great spots on the sun of our glory caused by the disintegrating resolutions of '98, and by their practical application in the pro-slave section, we are no longer at liberty to bestow the fullest measure of our wrath and scorn upon the little Hartford Convention.

THE SLAVE INSURRECTION OF 1822.

NEGRO conspiracies and actual insurrections in the United States have been more numerous than the Southern people care to acknowledge, but only those of Denmark Vesey and Nat Turner have won historical importance. It has been the policy of the slave-holding States not only to suppress, with a relentless hand, every appearance of disaffection among their slaves, but also to keep from the light all testimony regarding the occasional slave uprisings which have not failed to occur. It is certain that eight, if not ten, very extended conspiracies have been formed among the negro bondsmen of the South; it is known that four or five have resulted in open insurrection which was suppressed only by the sacrifice of every negro implicated as a leader or abettor; but, of these exciting episodes of Southern history, only the faintest records are in existence, as if the slave masters themselves feared to read the story. Of the two terrible tragedies now associated with the names of Vesey and Turner sufficient authentic data exists to lay before the reader intelligible narratives of them, although, in their cases, the efforts afterwards made to suppress testimony, have cast doubts upon much that otherwise must have been admitted as evidence. The comparatively recent period of these events, however, has been used by a painstaking inquirer to regather, from public and private sources, incidents and circumstances enough to render the record historically accurate. This inquirer gave the results of his investigations in two articles prepared for the *Atlantic Monthly*—June and August numbers, 1861—from which we draw much of the matter for this paper, as well as of that devoted to Nat Turner's Southampton insurrection.

Early in June, 1822, Charleston, South Carolina, was deeply stirred with excitement. A painful fear of a negro uprising filled the hearts of all who were permitted to know of the matter. Leading planters and citizens armed; the authorities were on the alert; the patrol was secretly strengthened and the negroes were watched with sleepless vigilance. All this apprehension, up to the middle of June, sprang from the most vague premises. William, a negro belonging to Mr. John Paul, had uttered mysterious hints to Devany, the slave of Colonel Prioleau, of an intended insurrection. This disclosure was confided to a free black, by whose advice Devany revealed to his owner what he had been told. That sufficed to alarm the authorities. Forthwith the Mayor of Charleston summoned the Corporation (City Council), when both negroes, William and Devany, were submitted to a close examination. Nothing in addition transpired. William was successful in baffling all inquiries into his private affairs, and was remanded to prison. He was not proof against confinement and, ere long, revealed the names of Mingo Harth and Peter Boyas, as his chief informants. These two slaves were, therefore, quietly arrested, but so innocent did they appear—so well did they disguise everything, that they were discharged. They must have practiced extraordinary dissimulation, since they really were chiefs in the Conspiracy. William was pressed to make further developments, and inculpated several other negroes; but, these blacks, like Mingo and Peter, put on such an air of innocence as to confound their examiners. Enough, however, had transpired to place the authorities on the *qui vive*, and everything was prepared for an outbreak.

Had William been the only recusant the awful tragedy of a slave insurrection and massacre, fully matured and admirably ordered, would have followed; but, another informer came forward, revealing the fact that on Sunday night, June 16th, the uprising was to take place. There were but two days grace, as the revelation was made on Friday, June 14th; but it was time enough to make ready all things. The city authorities, acting in concert with the Governor, Thomas Bennet, had their arrangements so well perfected that, had the negroes appeared to any number they must have been overcome. This revelation, secretly made, was kept from all public announcement with the design of having the Conspirators divulge their entire scheme, and thus mark the leaders for punishment. But, the sagacious blacks soon discovered that their movement was betrayed. They met Sunday night, at their several rendezvous, compared notes, and resolved to abandon the project for a more propitious moment. The secret of the insurrection was kept only until the first danger was past, when all Charleston was in a furore of excitement over its happy escape from the terrors of a San Domingo butchery. The negroes became frightened, and, from some of the most timid of the guilty, enough evidence was obtained to identify ten of those implicated, who were at once arrested. An investigation followed, when the whole plot soon stood revealed. A free black[1] named Denmark Vesey, working in the city as a carpenter, was indicated as the chief Conspirator, with Mingo and Peter, already referred to, as his principal coadjutors. Their rearrest of course immediately took place.

Vesey was, in many respects, a remarkable character. When a lad of fourteen he had been stolen from Africa and borne, along with three hundred and ninety others, to Hayti for a market. His intelligence soon rendered him a pet, and he was taken by Captain Vesey—master of the slaver, and an old citizen of Charleston—into the cabin, where he was christened "Telemak," was clothed and so civilized that he was sold for a good price to a wealthy French resident of the island. Captain Vesey ere long visited Hayti with another cargo of human flesh and blood, when he learned that "Telemak" was unsound, having had epileptic fits, and would therefore be returned upon his hands. The slave boy was, thereupon, transferred to the ship again, to become the Captain's inseparable companion-servant. For nearly twenty years he faithfully

---

[1] Simms, in his History of South Carolina, describes Vesey as "a mulatto from the island of St. Domingo"—an error. The Conspirator was a native born African taken by a slave trader from his native wilds to *Hayti*, as stated in our narrative. He did not participate in the St. Domingo insurrection—having left the island *before* the revolution, or "insurrection," as it is popularly termed.

served the sailor, visiting many lands, learning several languages and never showing signs of epilepsy! In the year 1800, having drawn a prize of fifteen hundred dollars in a lottery, he paid the Captain six hundred dollars of that prize to secure his own freedom—a transfer of property which the master considered a generous act on his own part, since Telemak—or Denmark as he grew to be called—was worth more money. Thus free from a slave's bonds, the negro took up his permanent abode in Charleston, where he became a house carpenter, practicing his trade with such success as to employ several "hands" to execute his contracts. Of his life at Charleston we have only what is to be gleaned from the "official report" made, by the Mayor, of the insurrection and trial after the condemnation of the accused to the gallows. The document said: "Among those of his color he was looked up to with awe and respect. His temper was impetuous and domineering in the extreme, qualifying him for the despotic rule of which he was ambitious. All his passions were ungovernable and savage; and to his numerous wives and children he displayed the haughty and capricious cruelty of an Eastern bashaw." All of which doubtless was true. As his "numerous wives" were such by consent of their owners, and as his "numerous children" only added to the wealth of the State—all being slaves—the report does not urge his bigamy as an additional crime. We may further quote: "For several years before he disclosed his intentions to any one, he appears to have been constantly and assiduously engaged in endeavoring to embitter the minds of the colored population against the white. He rendered himself perfectly familiar with all those parts of the Scriptures which he thought he could pervert to his purpose; and would readily quote them, to prove that slavery was contrary to the laws of God—that slaves were bound to attempt their emancipation, however shocking and bloody might be the consequences—and that such efforts would not only be pleasing to the Almighty, but were absolutely enjoined and their success predicted in the Scriptures. His favorite texts, when he addressed those of his own color, were Zechariah, xiv. 1–3, and Joshua, vi. 21; and in all his conversations he identified their situation with that of the Israelites. The number of inflammatory pamphlets on slavery brought into Charleston from some of our sister States within the last four years, (and once from Sierra Leone,) and distributed amongst the colored population of the city, for which there was a great facility, in consequence of the unrestricted intercourse allowed to persons of color between the different States in the Union, and the speeches in Congress of those opposed to the admission of Missouri into the Union, perhaps garbled and misrepresented, furnished him with ample means for inflaming the minds of the colored population of this State; and by distorting certain parts of those speeches, or selecting from them particular passages, he persuaded but too many that Congress had actually declared them free, and that they were held in bondage contrary to the laws of the land. Even whilst walking through the streets in company with another, he was not idle; for if his companion bowed to a white person, he would rebuke him, and observe that all men were born equal, and that he was surprised that any one would degrade himself by such conduct—that he would never cringe to the whites, nor ought any one who had the feelings of a man. When answered, 'We are slaves,' he would sarcastically and indignantly reply, 'You deserve to remain slaves'; and if he were further asked, 'What can we do?' he would remark, 'Go and buy a spelling-book and read the fable of Hercules and the Wagoner,' which he would then repeat, and apply it to their situation. He also sought every opportunity of entering into conversation with white persons, when they could be overheard by negroes near by, especially in grog-shops—during which conversation he would artfully introduce aome bold remark on slavery; and sometimes, when, from the character he was conversing with, he found he might be still bolder, he would go so far, that, had not his declarations in such situations been clearly proved, they would scarcely have been credited. He continued this course until some time after the commencement of the last Winter; by which time he had not only obtained incredible influence amongst persons of color, but many feared him more than their owners, and, one of them declared, even more than his God."

This picture is clearly intensified in color for effect, but is true enough to prove the African to have been a man of powerful parts. His house became the resort of negroes in sympathy with him and "his work." He made converts as preliminary to conquests. His influence extended beyond Charleston; it went up the rivers, floated over the sea islands, penetrated to the interior; everywhere he was known secretly to the negroes as "one with a work to do." Yet, it does not appear that he excited any particular notice from the planters, or the Charleston authorities—a singular fact if he did talk as freely and openly as stated in the report. He succeeded in calling to his aid as co-conspirators Peter Poyas and Gullah Jack. The first named was a daring, sagacious black, to whom Vesey ultimately committed the details of the uprising—a trust executed with much military ability and decided intelligence. The other was a kind of necromancer or sorcerer, whose influence over the ignorant sons of toil grew to be quite unbounded. These three were the guiding spirits of that terrible plot, though three or four others were added whose services were specially required. Thus, Monday Gell became Secretary of the Conspiracy, performing all the necessary writing. He even wrote a letter to President Boyer, of Hayti, informing him of the intended "stroke for liberty" and seeking for his co-operation. Tom Russell, William Garner, Mingo Harth, Polydore Faber, Bacchus Hammet, Lot Forrester, Ned and Rolla Bennett, all were chosen for particular duties, to which they were assigned, and of which they were required to give a good account on pain of untold penalties.

The *initiated* embraced the most trusted of the slaves—those whose intelligence gave them unusual facilities for obtaining the confidence of masters. A monthly place of meeting was on a plantation, up one of the sea estuaries, called Bulkley's Farm, whose overseer was a black and one of those interested in the Conspiracy. "There," says the writer in the *Atlantic*, "they prepared cartridges and pikes, and had primitive banquets, which assumed a melodramatic character under the inspiriting guidance of Jack. If a fowl was privately roasted, that mystic individual (Gullah Jack) muttered incantations over it, and then they all grasped at it, exclaiming, 'Thus we pull Buckra to pieces!' He gave them parched corn and ground-nuts to be eaten as internal safeguards on the day before the outbreak, and a consecrated *cullah*, or crab's claw, to be carried in the mouth by each, as an amulet. These rather questionable means secured him a power which was very unquestionable; the witnesses examined in his presence all showed dread of his conjurations, and referred to him indirectly, with a kind of awe, as 'the little man who can't be shot.'"

The night of Sunday was chosen for the sacrifice because of the great numbers of blacks always gathered, on that day, in Charleston, whither they all came "to church," from the surrounding plantations reached by water. The Ashley and Cooper rivers were fairly alive, on the Sabbath, with negro boats. This gave the conspirators the presence of the force required for thorough work without at all alarming the whites. The magazine writer added:

"The details of the plan, however, were not rashly committed to the mass of the confederates; they were known only to a few, and were finally to have been announced after the evening prayer-meetings on the appointed Sunday. But each leader had his own company enlisted, and his own work marked out. When the clock struck twelve, all were to move. Peter Poyas was to lead a party ordered to assemble at South Bay, and to be joined by a force from James' Island; he was then to march up and seize the arsenal and guard-house opposite St. Michael's Church, and detach a sufficient number to cut off all white citizens who should appear at the alarm-posts. A second body of negroes, from the country and the Neck, headed by Ned Bennett, was to assemble on the Neck, and seize the arsenal there. A third was to meet at Governor Bennett's Mills, under command of Rolla, and, after putting the Governor and Intendant to death, to march through the city, or be posted at Cannon's Bridge, thus preventing the inhabitants of Cannonsborough from entering the city. A fourth, partly from the country and partly from the neighboring localities in the city, was to rendezvous on Gladsden's Wharf and attack the upper guard-house. A fifth, composed of country and Neck negroes, was to assemble at Bulkley's Farm, two miles and a half from the city, seize the upper powder-magazine and then march down; and a sixth was to assemble at Denmark Vesey's and obey his orders. A seventh detachment, under Gullah Jack, was to assemble in Boundary street, at the head of King street, to capture the arms of the Neck company of militia, and to take an additional supply from Mr. Duquercron's shop. The naval stores on Mey's Wharf were also to be attacked. Meanwhile a horse-company, consisting of many draymen, hostlers, and butcher-boys, was to meet at Lightwood's alley and then scour the streets to prevent the whites from assembling. Every white man coming out of his own door was to be killed, and, if necessary, the city was to be fired in several places—slow-match for this purpose having been purloined from the public arsenal and placed in accessible positions.

"Beyond this, the plan of action was either unformed or undiscovered; some slight reliance seems to have been placed on English aid—more on assistance from St. Domingo; at any rate, all the ships in the harbor were to be seized, and in these, if the worst came to the worst, those most deeply inculpated could set sail, bearing with them, perhaps, the spoils of shops and of banks. It seems to be admitted by the official narrative, that they might have been able, at that season of the year, and with the aid of the fortifications on the Neck and around the harbor, to retain possession of the city for some time."

From this it will be seen how extensive were the arrangements for the bloody retribution. The Charlestonians indeed escaped untold horrors when that Sunday night passed in peace. Not a white life was to be spared—all were to be sacrificed. Even trusted servants, faithful slaves, class leaders and church members, were to kill their households—so terribly in earnest were the helots.[1] "One prisoner is reported in the evidence to have dropped hints in regard to the destiny of the women; and there was a rumor in the newspapers of the time, that he, or some other of Governor Bennett's slaves, was to have taken the Governor's daughter, a young girl of sixteen, for his wife, in the event of success; but this is all. On the other hand, Denmark Vesey was known to be for a war of immediate and total extermination; and when some of the company opposed killing 'the ministers and the women and children,' Vesey read from the Scriptures that all should be cut off, and said that 'it was for their safety not to leave one white

---

1 The official report mentions the case of one slave who had belonged to one master for sixteen years, sustaining a high character for fidelity and affection, who had twice travelled with him through the Northern States, resisting every solicitation to escape, and who yet was very deeply concerned in the insurrection, though knowing it to involve the probable destruction of the whole family with whom he lived.

skin alive, for this was the plan they pursued at St. Domingo.' And all this was not a mere dream of one lonely enthusiast, but a measure which had been maturing for four full years among several confederates, and had been under discussion for five months among multitudes of initiated 'candidates.'"

It will be remarked as surprising that a plot, so extended in its memberships, should have existed so long without discovery. This profound reticence is, however, one of the negroes' most remarkable characteristics. However trivial he may be, with a secret involving his own destiny he is safe. "In one case it was proven that Vesey had forbidden his followers to trust a certain man, because he had once been seen intoxicated. In another case it was shown that a slave named George had made every effort to obtain their confidence, but was constantly excluded from their meetings as a talkative fellow who could not be trusted—a policy which his levity of manner, when examined in court, fully justified. They took no women into counsel—not from any distrust, apparently, but in order that their children might not be left uncared for, in case of defeat and destruction. House-servants were rarely trusted, or only when they had been carefully sounded by the chief leaders. Peter Poyas, in commissioning an agent to enlist men, gave him excellent cautions: 'Don't mention it to those waiting men who receive presents of old coats, etc., from their masters, or they'll betray us; *I will speak to them.*' When he did speak, if he did not convince them, he at least frightened them; but the chief reliance was on the slaves hired out and therefore more uncontrolled—and also upon the country negroes." How well their confidence was kept was made evident in the statement that Peter Poyas had six hundred names on his company list, yet not one of them was arrested—not one betrayed his confederates! Of all the real leaders only Monday Gell was weak enough to confess; yet, with all the art used to obtain information, with promises of forgiveness and of reward, with threats of condign punishment, it is stated that but fifteen of the Conspirators were ferreted out during twenty-one days of official examination. And, after every possible exertion but one hundred and twenty-one arrests were made. Of this number twenty-five were discharged without trial, twenty-seven acquitted and thirty-four "transported." Thirty-five only were found guilty—every one of whom were hung. The number actually enlisted is not known. One witness gave it as nine thousand; another as six thousand six hundred; but Governor Bennett placed those actually concerned at a very small estimate—a statement especially made with a view to allay public apprehension. It is certain that, from the little which was divulged, the Conspiracy was widespread and powerful in its incipient organizations, although the programme of operations as adopted stipulated a comparative restriction of "candidates," knowing, as one of the guilty confessed, that, with enough to commence their work with spirit the slaves generally would fall into the ranks—a statement startling even in its possibility of truth. If the slaves would so easily turn into insurgents what a volcano did Southern society harbor in its very bosom!

Trial followed arrest. Five *freeholders* constituted the jury-court, appointed by two Judges of the Supreme Court under provision of a Legislative act "for the better ordering and governing of negroes and *other* slaves." What "other slaves" were indicated by the act is not stated. This court, presided over by the two justices, held its sessions of life or death in Charleston—the Mayor being informant. The trials, judged by the signification of that word in common law, were the merest form. The slaves being "property" were looked after by their masters as any other property in danger of confiscation or loss, and were furnished such counsel as the case admitted; while the negroes who testified did so without oath or voucher of truth.

Some of the incidents of the trial were thus given in the official report already alluded to: "Rolla, when arraigned, affected not to understand the charge against him, and when it was at his request further explained to him, assumed, with wonderful adroitness, astonishment and surprise. He was remarkable, throughout his trial, for great presence and composure of mind. When he was informed he was convicted, and was advised to prepare for death, though he had previously (but after his trial) confessed his guilt, he appeared perfectly confounded, but exhibited no signs of fear. In Ned's behavior there was nothing remarkable; but his countenance was stern and immovable, even whilst he was receiving the sentence of death: from his looks it was impossible to discover or conjecture what were his feelings. Not so with Peter; for in his countenance were strongly marked disappointed ambition, revenge, indignation and an anxiety to know how far the discoveries had extended; and the same emotions were exhibited in his conduct. He did not appear to fear personal consequences, for his whole behavior indicated the reverse; but exhibited an evident anxiety for the success of their plan, in which his whole soul was embarked. His countenance and behavior were the same when he received his sentence, and his only words were, on retiring, 'I suppose you'll let me see my wife and family before I die?' and that not in a supplicating tone. When he was asked, a day or two after, if it was possible he could wish to see his master and family murdered, who had treated him so kindly, he only replied to the question by a smile. Monday's behavior was not peculiar. When he was before the court, his arms were folded; he heard the testimony given against him, and received his sentence with the utmost firmness and composure. But no description can accurately convey to others the impression which the trial, defense and appearance of Gullah Jack made on those who witnessed the workings of his cunning and rude address. When arrested and brought before the court, in company with another African named Jack, the property of the estate of Pritchard, he assumed so much ignorance, and looked and acted the fool so well, that some of the court could not believe that this was the necromancer who was sought after. This conduct he continued when on his trial, until he saw the witnesses and heard the testimony as it progressed against him, when, in an instant, his countenance was lighted up as if by lightning, and his wildness and vehemence of gesture, and the malignant glance with which he eyed the witnesses who appeared against him, all indicated the savage, who, indeed, had been *caught*, but not *tamed*. His courage, however, soon forsook him.

When he received sentence of death, he earnestly implored that a fortnight longer might be allowed him, and then a week longer, which he continued earnestly to solicit until he was taken from the court-room to his cell; and when he was carried to execution, he gave up his spirit without firmness or composure."

Of the demeanor of Denmark Vesey we have full particulars both in the official report and in the narrative of the presiding judge, Kennedy, afterwards given to the public. The prisoner, though greatly dejected at the total miscarriage of his plot, was not a person to betray fear. He was as calm, resolute and self possessed as a willing martyr, and managed his own case, we are told, with exceeding shrewdness. "With his arms tightly folded and his eyes fixed on the floor, he attentively followed every item of the testimony. He heard the witnesses examined by the court, and cross examined by his own counsel, and it is evident from the narrative of the presiding judge that he showed no small skill and policy in the searching cross examination which he then applied. The fears, the feelings, the consciences of those who had betrayed him, all were in turn appealed to; but the facts were too overpowering, and it was too late to aid his comrades or himself. Then turning to the court, he skilfully availed himself of the point which had so much impressed the community, the intrinsic improbability that a man in his position of freedom and prosperity should sacrifice everything to free other people. If they thought it so incredible, why not give him the benefit of the incredibility? The act being, as they stated, one of infatuation, why convict him of it on the bare word of men who, by their own showing, had not only shared the infatuation, but proved traitors to it? An ingenious defense—indeed, the only one which could by any possibility be suggested, anterior to the days of Choate and somnambulism; but in vain. He was sentenced, and it was not, apparently, till the judge reproached him for the destruction he had brought on his followers that he showed any sign of emotion. Then the tears came into his eyes. But he said not another word."

It was reported, though not so stated in any official shape, that he made threats, asserting that the insurrection would go on. It was true that, after his execution, a number of negroes were punished for wearing sack cloth. An ordinance of the city prescribed that any slave wearing a badge of mourning should be imprisoned and flogged; under which peculiarly South Carolina ordinance every negro, caught with a semblance of mourning, was given the legal thirty-nine lashes on the bare back, and ten days in darkness on bread and water.

Although the outward semblance of calm was preserved, the excitement in and around Charleston continued intense during all of July and August. Governor Bennett wrote a letter—already noticed—which was issued as a circular, with the object of allaying public fears and personal excitement. His very words were evidence of the general alarm whose existence it was vain to deny. The constant presence of strong bodies of armed men throughout all parts of the city; the re-enforcements of United States troops thrown into Fort Moultrie; the midnight removal of the arsenal arms to Castle Pinckney; the minute search for secreted weapons; the desertion, by their owners and families, of the plantations—all were painful indications of the fears which rested upon that community. It was then that some of the South Carolina people themselves dared to lift up their voices against the presence of negroes. During the Fall of 1822 an able pamphlet appeared, directed against the aggregation of slaves, and which urged the introduction of free white labor. This was written by a prominent citizen of the State, but it excited no favorable response.

Upon one thing the public was agreed, namely: the danger of permitting the negroes to learn how to read. To that privilege was traced the insurrection. Says the *Atlantic* writer:

"The editor of the first official report racked his brains to discover the special causes of the revolt, and never trusted himself to allude to the general one. The negroes rebelled because they were deluded by Congressional eloquence, or because they were excited by a church squabble, or because they had been spoilt by mistaken indulgences, such as being allowed to learn to read, 'a misguided benevolence,' as he pronounces it. So the Baptist Convention seems to have thought it was because they were not Baptists, and an Episcopal pamphleteer because they were not Episcopalians."

But, such weakness were only worthy of the bigotry or stupidity of Southern churches; that never for a moment the presence of so many negroes in South Carolina, and the bondmen's chains riveted upon them as upon beasts, were indicated as the true source of the danger, is not to the credit of South Carolina intelligence and her Christian honesty.

The trial, as stated, resulted in the condemnation of thirty-five to execution. The sentences were made by Justice Kennedy, after the freeholders had rendered their verdict. Six were hanged July 2d—the day, it was afterwards discovered, upon which a second attempt was to have been made to start the general movement of insurrection. These six were Denmark Vesey, Peter Poyas, Ned, Rollà and Batteau—the three latter slaves of the Governor.[1] Gullah Jack and John were given to the gallows July 12th. Twenty-two were hung July 26th, and four July 30th. William Garner, having escaped, was recaptured and executed August 9th. These executions transpired at different places amid much pomp of military display, and in the presence of vast numbers of slaves, who were made to witness the end of the Conspirators as a warning of the fate awaiting all who should dare to incite rebellion against their helot's estate. Thirty-four sentenced to transportation were sent, singly, to the rice swamps of lower Georgia and Alabama.

The bearing of the men on the gallows was very resolute. To the last they resisted all importunities to confess. "Do not open your lips," said Peter to his companions: "die silent as you shall see me do," and all obeyed. Two slaves among the condemned, belonging to one Ferguson, were severely flogged prior to execution, in order to compel them to divulge, but to no purpose: they were silent as men already dead. Vesey's bearing was particularly commanding. He went to the grave as one conscious of a noble sacrifice.

Thus ended the Insurrection in South Carolina. Its prompt

---

1 The Governor had, at the trial, urged the mitigation of the sentence against Batteau—a very valuable slave, saying: "I ask this, gentlemen, as an individual incurring a severe and distressing loss." The accused represented just so much money—hence the "distressing" character of the "loss."

suppression saved the State untold misery—perhaps saved the adjoining States from incendiary fires, for, once lit, they must have swept over many a league of Southern soil. Legislation against privileges to the blacks, excited by the experiences of the day, followed. Among other acts the South Carolina Legislature, in December (1822) passed one to imprison *all* colored men (free) coming from other States—by which outrageously unconstitutional statute numbers of colored men, some of them actual citizens of the Free States, were seized from vessels in South Carolina ports, imprisoned, and finally sold into slavery to pay the costs of imprisonment! [A more inhuman act, or one more at variance with the personal liberty guaranteed by the Constitution, has not disgraced any statute book.[1] That law remained upon the records unrepealed, up to the secession of the State in 1860—a standing insult to the States and a defiance of the Constitution; and yet, among other causes stated by the secession Convention in the list of grievances put upon that autocratical Commonwealth was the violation of the Constitution by the North, in not returning fugitive slaves! Presumption and stultification of moral perceptions could hardly go farther.] The slaves also were debarred the rights of education. It soon became a state's prison offense to teach a black man how to read. The usual Sunday meetings were forbidden except under the surveillance of the whites; the gathering of slaves in Charleston, from the surrounding plantations, was prohibited; police regulations on the plantations became very rigid, and cruelty soon took the place of severity in discipline. In this respect the insurrection worked much wretchedness for the slaves; it riveted their chains more firmly, it curtailed

---

[1] Massachusetts sent Mr. Hoar, an eminent lawyer, to Charleston, to procure the release of several colored men, citizens of that State, imprisoned under this odious ordinance. Mr. Hoar, accompanied by his daughter, proceeded upon his mission but was compelled to retire in haste from Charleston under threats of personal violence. No white man from a Northern State was permitted to enter South Carolina's jurisdiction, if he proposed to question the validity of her acts. That State, from the year under notice, was, practically, in rebellion, and our Government, administered by pro-slave Presidents, was pusillanimous enough to permit her outrages without the slightest effort to correct them! The day of reckoning came at last, however. *Quem Deus vult perdere, prius demontat.*

their privileges, it made them distrusted, it brought out the scourge upon the smallest provocation, it gave their masters an excuse for denying them many of the rights of civilization. The world would shudder in horror to be told of the cruelty practiced upon the slaves to inspire them with a wholesome awe of the white man's power. Not in South Carolina alone, but in every Slave State the reins tightened, and the land became a land of wo to the wretched black. It is not strange that the great majority of the dominant race should have become, in a greater or less degree, brutalized by the exercise of this power over a subject race; it were impossible for it to have been otherwise, constituted as human nature is, and ordered as Southern society was. In that respect, at least, the spirits of Denmark Vesey and Peter Poyas had their revenge.

THE CREEK DIFFICULTIES.

THE immense tracts of lands held in Georgia, Alabama, Florida and Mississippi by the Creeks, Choctaws, Chicksaw and Cherokee Indians, proved, for awhile, a source of much anxiety to Government. "Reservations" guaranteed by solemn treaty to the Indians, in the various Southern and Western States, embraced immense bodies of choice land, up to a comparatively recent period. Solemn treaties secured to the savages (and promised protection from all infringements by the whites on their domains) territories as follows:—In Georgia, nine and a half millions of acres; in Alabama, seven and a half millions; in Mississippi, fifteen and three-quarter millions; in the Territory of Florida, four millions; in the Territory of Arkansas, fifteen and a half millions; in the State of Missouri, two millions and three-quarters; in Indiana and Illinois, fifteen millions, and in Michigan, east of the lake, seven millions.

The "march of civilization" soon compassed these reservations with white settlements, and, as a matter of course, trouble followed. Encroachments would be made by the whites, covetous of the land or of its game. Indians would murder the whites and give the State authorities and the General Government plenty to do to keep them in bounds. So great became anxiety in the Southern States named, to get rid of the aborigines, that their State Legislatures demanded of Government the entire removal of the red-men from their midst to unsettled Territories around the head waters of the Arkansas river. Georgia made her demand peremptorily, since she held the Federal Government bound by a compact to relieve her. This compact stipulated that, in consideration of Georgia relinquishing her title and claims to the Mississippi Territory, the General Government would extinguish Indian titles to lands within her confines, "whenever it could be peaceably done on reasonable terms." After making that agreement Government succeeded in extinguishing the title to about fifteen million acres, and conveyed the same to the State of Georgia. There still remained 9,537,000 acres in possession of the Indians, of which 5,292,000 acres belonged to the Cherokees and the remainder to the Creek nation. Shortly before the termination of Mr. Monroe's administration, Georgia became very urgent for an entire removal of the Indians.

Delegates from the Cherokees were in Washington during March, 1824, to arrange matters in dispute. Their pretensions to the rights of civilized usage as embassadors much excited the Georgia members in Congress, and they seized the occasion not only to enter their protest against the mission of the barbarians, but to make a formal demand upon Government for it to fulfil its treaty obligations. The Georgians spoke peremptorily, and called forth from the President, James Monroe, and John C. Calhoun, Secretary of War, communications designed to set the matter before the public in its true light. Said Calhoun:

"In fulfilment of the stipulations of the 4th article (of the convention of 1802) with Georgia, there have been held seven treaties with the Creeks and Cherokees; of which five were with the former—two previous to the war with Great Britain (1812) and three since. By the two first named there were ceded to Georgia 2,713,890 acres, and by the three last named 11,735,590 acres—altogether 14,748,690 acres. With the Cherokees there have been held two treaties—both since the late war—by which Georgia has acquired 995,810 acres, which, added to that acquired by treaties with the Creeks, make 15,744,-000 acres that have been ceded to Georgia, since the date of the convention, in fulfilment of its stipulations.

"In acquiring these cessions for the State of Georgia, the United States have expended $958,954.90; to which should be added the value of 995,310 acres which were given in exchange with the Cherokees on the Arkansas river, for a quantity ceded by them to Georgia, by the treaties of 1817 and 1819—which lands estimated at the minimum price of the public lands would make $1,244,147.50. If to these we add the sum of $1,250,000 paid to Georgia under the convention, and $4,282,151.12½ paid to the Yazoo claimants, it will be found that the United States have already paid, under the convention, $7,735,243.52½—which does not include any portion of the expenses of the Creek war, by which upwards of *seven millions* of acres were acquired to the State of Georgia." [1]

But, despite this showing, Georgia was resolved to have *all* her "rights" under the convention of 1802; and, at the solicitation of her Governor, two Commissioners were appointed to make a treaty with the Creeks for the purchase of their lands. This treaty was negotiated on the 12th of Feb., 1825, the famous Chief, General William McIntosh signing it in presence of Mr. Crowell, United States Indian Agent, by which all the Creek country and several millions of acres in Alabama were ceded to the United States. Complaints followed it to Washington as having been concluded by McIntosh without any authority from the nation. The ratification of this treaty was opposed in Congress, but was finally carried by the strong vote of thirty-four to four. This sanction on reaching the ears of the discontented Creeks produced great excitement. A secret council of the nation being called, they resolved not to abide by the cession. The death of McIntosh was determined on; and, on the 30th of April, his house was surrounded by a party, who shot him together with another chief, and burned his premises. This aroused the State authorities to a determined course, and Georgia resolved to take possession of the lands by force. Troops were called out to sustain her claims. By this act the State opened a controversy with the General Government, which was bound by treaty and good faith to protect the Indians in their just rights.

When John Quincy Adams came into power he made the subject a matter of early examination, and became convinced that the Indians were right—that the treaty, as they represent-

[1] From these figures it will be perceived to what extent Georgia was indebted to the Federal Government.

ed, had been made by McIntosh without authority, and therefore that the enforcement of its provisions ought not to be urged. As Georgia had called out troops to force the savages into an acceptance and fulfillment of the cession, it only remained for the President to order a Federal force to the confines of the reservation to protect the Indians. This step aroused not only Georgia, but also the adjoining States, who were prepared, with troops and money, to assist Georgia "against the Government and the Indians."

To avoid the hazard of war, Mr. Adams succeeded in gathering at Washington, in January, 1826, the head men and responsible representatives of the Creeks, and concluded a new treaty, which was substituted for the old one, whereby all their lands in Georgia were ceded, but none in Alabama. Notwithstanding opposition from the Georgia delegation in Congress, this treaty was ratified by the Senate at the ensuing session by a vote of thirty to seven, and appropriations were made by the House of Representatives by a vote of one hundred and sixty-seven to ten. The treaty was faithfully observed by the Indians, and Georgia became possessed of their valuable land, after waiting a quarter of a century for Government to fulfill its agreement (made in 1802). At a later day the Cherokees' title was extinguished in Alabama, though their removal to the West was not accomplished until General Scott took the matter in hand (in May, 1838).

THE SOUTHAMPTON SLAVE INSURRECTION.

THE insurrection in Southampton County, Virginia, in August, 1831, headed by Nat Turner, was not, like the South Carolina uprising, the result of a carefully elaborated plot. It was the result of one night's conference in the woods, of seven black men, who proceeded to the work of slaughter almost as soon as it was determined upon and its first steps arranged. In this respect it was calculated to inspire more apprehension among slave owners, since, if one bold spirit could, at any moment, so inflame the savage instincts of the African as to impel him to murder, where was the safety in his presence? Like Vesey's plot, however, Turner's bloody revolt was conceived in religious enthusiasm, and the black murderers became, in their frenzy, ministers of divine vengeance, slaying women and children even while they regretted its necessity. In this *religious* aspect both insurrections deserve more consideration than has been given them by writers and thinkers. It is a matter of surprise that, since religious impressions and a knowledge of the Bible proved so inflamatory, the Southern Legislatures did not forbid even the shadow of a missionary to darken their lands, and did not formally banish the Holy Word as a dangerous agent in a slave's hands. But, the surprise is lessened when we reflect that, in Virginia as well as in South Carolina, it was a states' prison offense to learn slaves to read; and the further fact that such "religious instruction" was provided for the black as impressed him with proper ideas of his own unworthiness, renders it apparent that all steps practically necessary to keep the African a barbarian not only were taken but were enforced.

Nat Turner, like Denmark Vesey, was a religious devotee who had "a work to do." "He had, by his own account," says the authority before us, "felt himself singled out from childhood for some great work; and he had some peculiar marks on his person, which, joined to his great mental precocity, were enough to occasion, among his youthful companions, a superstitious faith in his gifts and destiny. He had great mechanical ingenuity also, experimentalized very early in making paper, gunpowder, pottery, and in other arts, which, in later life, he was found thoroughly to understand. His moral faculties were very strong; white witnesses admitted that he had never been known to swear an oath, to drink a drop of spirits, or to commit a theft! And, in general, so marked were his early peculiarities, that people said 'he had too much sense to be raised, and if he was, he would never be of any use as a slave.' This impression of personal destiny grew with his growth—he fasted, prayed, preached, read the Bible, heard voices when he walked behind his plough, and communicated his revelations to the awe-struck slaves. They told him in return, that, 'if they had his sense, they would not serve any master in the world.'"

It would appear, indeed, that the man was extraordinarily endowed with the religious "power" which makes men apostles and martyrs, or which, if allowed free scope, renders them great as expounders of the truth. Had Turner lived in a congenial atmosphere he must have become a veritable Martin Luther among his race. As it was he was only a slave—the property of a white man; and while he faithfully performed the offices of a slave his soul held converse with such spirits as could penetrate the darkness of his benighted life. His "confession," made after arrest and sentence of death, is a remarkable evidence of the spiritual sympathy which swayed his entire being. Just prior to the year of the insurrection he had a special season of religious experience, in which he spoke with such power as to make a convert of a white man named Brantly, whom he baptised by immersion. He said, referring to that event: "I told these things to a white man, on whom it had a wonderful effect, and he ceased from his wickedness, and was attacked immediately with a cutaneous eruption, and the blood oozed from the pores of his skin, and after praying and fasting nine days he was healed. And the Spirit appeared to me again, and said, as the Savior had been baptized, so should we be also; and when the white people would not let us be baptized by the Church, we went down into the water together, in the sight of many who reviled us, and were baptized by the Spirit. After this I rejoiced greatly and gave thanks to God."

This certainly does not savor of blood-thirstiness, yet the very enthusiasm here recorded impelled the devotee to his work of slaughter. As he neared the year of his tragedy Turner's fervor increased. He beheld in the sky black and white spirits contending, like the hosts of Gabriel and Satan, for supremacy; at the awful conflict the scene became darkened, the heavens flashed fire and thunder filled the infinite spaces with dismal echoes. "And the Holy Ghost," he said, "was with me and said: 'Behold me as I stand in the heavens!' And I looked and saw the forms of men in different attitudes. And there were lights in the sky, to which the children of darkness gave other names than what they really were; for they were the lights of the Savior's hands, stretched forth from east to west, even as they were extended on the cross on Calvary, for the redemption of sinners." On the corn he saw drops of blood—Christ's blood, a witness of the work to be done; on the leaves in the forest he discovered signs, symbols similar to those revealed to his vision in the skies. Finally the Holy Spirit appeared to him, May 12th, 1828, to announce that the mission of the Savior would fall upon him, and, when the sign appeared in the heavens, indicated by Revelation, he must begin his struggle with the Serpent. That sign was given in an eclipse of the sun, in February, 1831. This call he must obey. He set about preparing himself to slay and destroy the white host until the land was regenerated. Then, also, the seal of secrecy was broken and he was permitted to call to his aid those who seemed marked as apostles in the crusade. This was the incipience of that terrible "work" which startled the whole country with its human sacrifice.

On Sunday, August 21st, 1831, six slaves met in the woods of the plantation of Joseph Travis, ostensibly for a barbecue. The plantation was located in Southampton County, Virginia, in the neighborhood known as Cross Keys, fifteen miles from Jerusalem C. H. and as far from Petersburg. These six men awaited the coming of a seventh, who made his appearance during the afternoon, when the roast pig was ready. His demeanor, and the deference shown to him, indicated him as the man to lead. He was a dark mulatto, in the very prime of life, powerfully built in frame, with strongly marked African features, and a face indicative of intelligence and resolution. It was Nat Turner. Observing two negroes more than he had ordered to the tryst, he demanded to know why they were there? One of them, named Will, answered with a quick response, that his life was worth no more than that of others, and that his liberty was as dear to him. Hark, one of the chosen four, answered for the other negro, named Jack, and the conference proceeded with much solemnity, as the roast pig was eaten. Turner harangued the men in his earnest, moving rhetoric, depicting the wretchedness of the negroes' lot, and proving by Scripture that he was called to disenthrall. All conceded the truth of his assumption and declared themselves ready for the work. For many hours the conference continued, and the Conspirators discussed the details of their movements. "One can imagine," says the writer in the *Atlantic Monthly*, "those terrible dusky faces, beneath the funereal woods, and amid the flickering of pine knot torches, preparing that stern revenge whose shuddering echoes should ring through the land so long." Night was well advanced when at length the last words were spoken, and the seven proceeded on their mission of murder. "It was agreed," said Turner in his confession, "that we should commence at home on that night, and, until we had armed and equipped ourselves and gained sufficient force, neither age nor sex was to be spared: which was invariably adhered to." The general design was to "conquer Southampton County, as the white men did in the Revolution, and

F. O. C. Darley del. J. Rogers, sc.

NAT TURNER & HIS CONFEDERATES IN CONFERENCE.

then retreat, if necessary, to the Dismal Swamp," which was about twenty-five miles away, and in whose fastnesses the blacks supposed they could find security. They counted, however, upon success, by the flocking of slaves to their standard. Turner also had vague ideas of a Black Republic to be formed in that vicinity, where the negroes would dwell in peace, and whose country should become the refuge of all runaway slaves. It was a wild, inconsiderate, illy-defined plan, showing but little of judgment or just apprehension of results. Surrounded upon all sides by considerable towns, whose inhabitants would turn out to a man to meet the insurrectionists —with Fortress Monroe at calling distance, ready with men and artillery to sweep away whole ranks of half armed and not half led slaves—what hope of success could any sane mind have entertained? Turner was a religious fanatic—he was not sane; his plans were those of a dreamer, and, like all creations of frenzy and ignorance, ended in the overwhelming ruin of all concerned.

Says the writer already referred to, regarding that night's work: "Swift and stealthy as Indians, the black men passed from house to house—not pausing, not hesitating, as their terrible work went on. In one thing they were humaner than Indians or than white men fighting against Indians—there was no gratuitous outrage beyond the death-blow itself, no insult, no mutilation; but in every house they entered, that blow fell on man, woman and child—nothing that had a white skin was spared. From every house they took arms and ammunition, and from a few, money; on every plantation they found recruits: those dusky slaves, so obsequious to their master the day before, so prompt to sing and dance before his Northern visitors, were all swift to transform themselves into fiends of retribution now; show them sword or musket and they grasped it, though it were an heirloom from Washington himself. The troop increased from house to house—first to fifteen, then to forty, then to sixty. Some were armed with muskets, some with axes, some with scythes; some came on their masters' horses. As the number increased they could be divided, and the awful work was carried on more rapidly still. The plan then was for an advanced guard of horsemen to approach each house at a gallop, and surround it till the others came up. Meanwhile what agonies of terror must have taken place within, shared alike by innocent and by guilty! what memories of wrongs inflicted on those dusky creatures by some—what innocent participation by others, in the penance! The outbreak lasted for but forty-eight hours; but during that period fifty-five whites were slain, without the loss of a single slave."

It was truly a reign of terror, before which the whites fled in uncontrollable dismay, abandoning homes and property in the one desire to shut out from their eyes the very sight of the vengeful blacks. Seeing this comparatively slow progress of his butchery, and realizing that the alarm must, ere long, bring the whites from other districts upon him, Turner resolved to strike out for Jerusalem, the county town, where he should be able to intercept fugitives and cut off communication with Norfolk and Fortress Monroe. With a strong body of mounted men he hurried on until within three miles of the Court House, when, passing the plantation of a Mr. Parker, the men desired to stop to enlist his negroes and to murder the whites. Turner remonstrated against this delay, but, upon the promise of expedition, he halted his troop and permitted about half of them to go up the lane to the house, one-half mile away. The halt, as Turner had feared, proved disastrous. Those dispatched to the mansion were gone so long that Turner at length followed after, to hasten their movements. His own absence left the band without a leader. Eighteen mounted white men rode up, dispersed the negroes at the road gate, pressed on up to the house and confronted the entire body of blacks. The white men dismounted, and, advancing under cover, sent a volley of balls and buck-shot into the insurrectionists' ranks. This the negroes immediately returned, when their masters broke and ran, the blacks pursuing. A fresh band of whites coming up at that moment from Jerusalem stayed the pursuit, and compelled the slaves, in turn, to break and run. Those on foot soon scattered, leaving Turner, with about twenty mounted confederates. With these he determined to hold his ground, counting upon recruits enough to enable him to push on. A large number gathered, but, at some alarm, most of them again scattered. Not dismayed, the resolute leader pressed on, at daylight, to the house of Dr. Blunt, in order to enlist his men. Here the insurrectionists were most unexpectedly checked. The Doctor had armed his slaves and Turner's troop was met by a fire from the house which drove them off. Soon a company of whites appeared, and sent such a volley into the insurgent band as proved its destruction. It broke ere long into fragments, and the insurrection, for the moment, was at an end. Turner, after arranging to meet his most trusted coadjutors in the woods where the first conference had been held, ordered the entire dispersion of his dusky guard. The murderers vanished from sight, every man of them returning to his own home as if no blood had stained his hands.

The day passed and Nat proceeded to the rendezvous. All night long he waited yet not a man appeared. What a night it must have been for that turbulent spirit! But, he was not dispirited. All day long he kept his hiding place, hoping that another night would gather, at least, his trusted friends—Hark, Dred, Will, Hercules, Nelson and Sam. Another night in those dreary solitudes, waiting and hoping in vain! Not a footstep broke the stillness—not a moving form made the shadows of the forest less lifeless and oppressive. It then was apparent that his movement was a failure, and that even the refuge in the Dismal Swamp was denied him. The country, having had time to recover from its first paralysis, was now alive with men seeking for his blood. He resolved to tarry where he was, knowing where to procure food, and hoping that some friendly hand would offer to assist him in escape, either to the Swamp, or to the North. He therefore sought a good retreat, which he found in a pile of fence rails, out in a deserted field. Beneath these rails he dug a hole, and in that most forlorn spot he dwelt *six* weeks—only leaving it at night for food and drink. It was at once his dwelling, his arsenal and his meeting house.

Thus far the direct fortunes of Turner. We must now turn to trace the secondary results of his revolt. Rumors spread with mysterious rapidity all over the land, magnifying events, until the insurrection assumed most gigantic dimensions. It reached Richmond to strike such terror among all classes as to render them incapable of aid. To arm for *defense*, was their only thought. So in all other towns of Southern Virginia and Northern North Carolina—not a body of military could be put into the field until the danger had passed. United States troops from Fortress Monroe were the first in responding to the call for help. Colonel House, then in command, sent forward three companies of light artillery under Lieutenant-Colonel Worth. —dispatching them by steamer to Suffolk. Detachments of marines and sailors from the U. S. sloops-of-war *Warren* and *Natchez* were added to this force, making it about eight hundred strong. These were first on the ground, and, alone, would have mastered almost any number of insurgents. But, rumor had so magnified the revolt, in its character and the numbers engaged, that, not only were the Virginia and North Carolina militia called to arms, but distant cities volunteered —New York, Philadelphia, Baltimore, and even New London, Connecticut, all offering military aid. The militia soon were on duty, and such duty as they performed has stained the page of Virginia's history. They murdered black men, almost indiscriminately, in Southampton County. "It was," said a member of the House of Delegates, "with the utmost difficulty and at the hazard of personal popularity and esteem, that the coolest and most judicious among us could exert an influence sufficient to restrain an indiscriminate slaughter of the blacks who were suspected." A letter from a clergyman on the spot said: "There are thousands of troops searching in every direction, and many negroes are killed every day: the exact number will never be ascertained." The magazine writer heretofore quoted from, says:

"Men were tortured to death, burned, maimed, and subjected to nameless atrocities. The overseers were called on to point out any slaves whom they distrusted, and if any tried to escape, they were shot down. Nay, worse than this. A party of horsemen started from Richmond with the intention of killing every colored person they saw in Southampton County. They stopped opposite the cabin of a free colored man, who was hoeing in his little field. They called out, 'Is this Southampton County?' He replied, 'Yes, Sir, you have just crossed the line, by yonder tree.' They shot him dead and rode on. This is from the narrative of the editor of the Richmond *Whig*, who was then on duty in the militia, and protested manfully against these outrages. 'Some of these scenes,' he adds, 'are hardly inferior in barbarity to the atrocities of the insurgents.'"

Indeed, many evidences, both public and private, exist which demonstrate the sanguinary and cruel nature of that retaliation. Masters presented claims for compensation for slaves killed to the number of over one hundred; nor was it until slave owners had resolved to shoot down any unauthorised white "patrol" found on their premises, that the slaughter was stayed. Not a few of these self-constituted guardians of the peace made it a boast that they had killed their share of "niggers." Some very affecting incidents of devotion are recorded in the annals of the day, one of which we must be permitted to repeat: "In the hunt which followed the massacre, a slave holder went into the woods, accompanied by a faithful slave, who had been the means of saving his life during the insurrection. When they had reached a retired place in the forest, the man handed his gun to his master, informing him that he could not live a slave any longer, and requesting him either to free him or shoot him on the spot. The master took the gun, in some trepidation, levelled it at the faithful negro, and shot him through the heart."

The number arrested for "trial" was fifty-five, of whom seventeen were convicted and hanged, twelve "transported" to the South, twenty acquitted, and four free colored men held for further examination. One of the executed was Lucy, a slave woman, the property of Mr. John T. Barrows. Nor were the "trials" confined to Southampton County. Said the Governor, in his message of Dec. 8th, relating to the affair: "there is much reason to believe that the spirit of insurrection was not confined to Southampton. Many convictions have taken place elsewhere, and some few in distant counties." But, nothing appears in Turner's "Confession," nor was anything elicited at the trials, to show the existence of any long premeditated and widely disseminated plot. If symptoms of insurrection were exhibited at other points it was simply because the slaves were ripe for revolt. News of Turner's success would have fired a train that led over the entire South, and in every black man's breast would have been found a magazine. The wonder is that so few actual explosions occurred. Had the black enthusiast entered Jerusalem, and secured its stores of arms and money, Nat Turner's insurrection would have ended only by a general slaughter of slaves, in that region at least.

To return to the pile of rails. For six weeks it gave shelter to the outlaw. Despite the most vigilant search he eluded all observation. Large rewards were offered for his capture and hundreds of men swarmed over the country in hope of se curing the prize. Every few days an announcement of his capture would be made, but, Nat Turner was not forthcoming: those eager for his blood were not yet gratified with an extemporized gallows scene nor a burning at the stake. A dog at length proved the fugitive's ruin—or, rather, the provisions which Nat had secreted in his hole wrought the calamity. The animal, smelling the meat, made such a noise over the rail pile as to attract thither a party out on the search. Discovery at once followed (October 15th). Turner emerged from his cave like Lucifer from the bowels of the earth, and created quite as much consternation as if he had been that fallen potentate. The whole party fled in amazement, while Turner fled in the opposite direction, eluding pursuit. For ten days longer he remained hidden in a wheat stack, although hundreds of men were scouring, and closely inspecting, every rood of land in that vicinity. Here he began to despair, and hope so far deserted him that he resolved upon surrender. One night he walked within two miles of Jerusalem, to place himself in the Sheriff's hands, but retraced his steps, safely passing the patrol established along the whole route. But, these days and nights of ceaseless watchfulness wore out even his iron frame, and he became haggard almost to insanity. His usual caution seems to have deserted him, for he was discovered by the owner of the stacks (October 25th), who discharged a load of buck shot at him. Nat fell to the earth and thus escaped death, though twelve of the shot riddled his hat. He again fled, and, astonishing as it may seem, succeeded in making his escape

For five days longer the entire population, with many negroes, were on his track, but failed to discover his person. October 30th was his last day of savage freedom. A white man named Phipps, out on patrol, was passing an old pine clearing, when he beheld motion among the dry boughs. Stopping to watch he quickly discovered the fugitive's wild face and glaring eyes, emerging from a hole beneath the brush. Phipps, bringing his shot gun to bear, called out for Turner to surrender. Exhausted as he was with privation, and armed only with a sword, he could offer but little resistance. Even to have overcome the patrol would have been but to encounter others close at hand. He quietly submitted to be bound and was marched off to the nearest house.

News of the capture flew on the wings of the wind, causing great rejoicing. Governor Floyd announced the fact in the Richmond *Enquirer*, with gratulations at the auspicious event.

He was with difficulty saved from the fury of the mob who had determined to roast him alive. But, anxious to ferret out the history of the insurrection, leading citizens preferred to save him for trial; escorted by a strong guard he was lodged in the county jail at Jerusalem.

His end approached rapidly. Says the *Atlantic* writer: "When asked by Mr. T. R. Gray, the counsel assigned him, whether, although defeated, he still believed in his own Providential mission, he answered as simply as one who came thirty years after him, 'Was not Christ crucified?' In the same spirit, when arraigned before the court, he answered, 'Not guilty,' saying to his counsel that he did not feel so. But apparently no argument was made in his favor by his counsel, nor were any witnesses called—he being convicted on the testimony of Levi Waller, and upon his own confession, which was put in by Mr. Gray, and acknowledged by the prisoner before the six justices composing the court, as being 'full, free, and voluntary.' He was therefore placed in the paradoxical position of conviction by his own confession, under a plea of 'Not guilty.' The arrest took place on the thirtieth of October, 1831, the confession on the first of November, the trial and conviction on the fifth, and the execution on the following

Friday, the eleventh of November, precisely at noon. He met his death with perfect composure, declined addressing the multitude assembled, and told the Sheriff in a firm voice that he was ready. Another account says that he 'betrayed no emotion, and even hurried the executioner in the performance of his duty.' Not a limb nor a muscle was observed to move. His body, after his death, was given over to the surgeons for dissection."

The confession here mentioned was made by Turner to his counsel and was published by Mr. Gray's authority in Baltimore. Fifty thousand copies, it is stated, were disposed of—an alarming fact, in the estimation of the pro-slave press—one of which called upon grand juries generally, where a copy of the publication was found, to indict Mr. Gray. The presumption was that it "would only serve to rouse up other leaders." Here, again, the greatness of the crime of allowing negroes to read was made manifest. After that day for a negro to be caught conning over a spelling book was to devote his bare back to the lash. The pamphlet was partially reprinted in New York, but, of the original fifty thousand, only one is mentioned as in existence—so thoroughly was the war waged even against it. It was, from all the attendant circumstances, and from the character of the culprit, a remarkable document. Said Mr. Gray: "I shall not attempt to describe the effect of his narrative, as told and commented on by himself, in the condemned-hole of the prison. The calm, deliberate composure with which he spoke of his late deeds and intentions, the expression of his fiend-like face when excited by enthusiasm, still bearing the stains of the blood of helpless innocence about him, clothed with rags and covered with chains, yet daring to raise his manacled hands to heaven, with a spirit soaring above the attributes of man—I looked on him, and the blood curdled in my veins."

This is the tribute of one capable of appreciating greatness though he beheld in that greatness only the incarnation of evil. But, it fills out the picture of the Conspirator until he stands before us a personation at once sublime and appalling.

Bid their spirits "begone!"—wave away the presences which

float before the vision: it is all in vain. Nat Turner and old John Brown rise up like the fabled Nemeses, or the ghosts of Odin's bards, to fill their enemies' souls with an awe which generations will not allay.

The events of this terrible insurrection were not unmarked by political excitement in the Old Dominion State. There were those among her counsellors and legislators who read the story aright, and behind the crime saw the hateful agent which prompted it. This class of persons made a stroke at the institution of slavery. Said James McDowell, one of Virginia's brightest lights, in a powerful speech made in the House of Delegates, in January, 1832:

"Was that a 'petty affair' which drove families from their homes—which assembled women and children in crowds, without shelter, at places of common refuge, in every condition of weakness and infirmity, under every suffering which want and terror could inflict, yet willing to endure all, willing to meet death from famine, death from climate, death from hardships, preferring anything rather than the horrors of meeting it from a domestic assassin? Was that a 'petty affair' which erected a peaceful and confiding portion of the State into a military camp—which outlawed from pity the unfortunate beings whose brothers had offended—which barred every door, penetrated every bosom with fear or suspicion—which so banished every sense of security from every man's dwelling, that let but a hoof or horn break upon the silence of the night, and an aching throb would be driven to the heart, the husband would look to his weapon, and the mother would shudder and weep upon her cradle? Was it the fear of Nat Turner, and his deluded drunken handful of followers, which produced such effects? Was it this that induced distant counties, where the very name of Southampton was strange, to arm and equip for a struggle? *No, Sir, it was the suspicion eternally attached to the slave himself—the suspicion that a Nat Turner might be in every family—that the same bloody deed might be acted over at any time and in any place—that the materials for it were spread through the land, and were always ready for a like explosion.* Nothing but the force of this withering apprehension—nothing but the paralyzing and deadening weight with which it falls upon and prostrates the heart of every man who has helpless dependants to protect—nothing but this could have thrown a brave people into consternation, or could have made any portion of this powerful Commonwealth, for a single instant, to have quailed and trembled."

But it was like the feeble voice against the whirlwind. Virginia was wedded to old families, and old families were wedded to slavery with a tenacity quite unconquerable. As her soil became exhausted, and her resources contracted, the slave was made to contribute to the wealth of the State in a manner not contemplated by Virginians of the Revolutionary era. The traffic in Eastern Virginia, in human flesh, from 1820, entered into her *productive* economy; and, by 1830, the growing of slaves for market had assumed an importance not second to that of tobacco. In this trade the largest and the smallest estates participated. Another ten years witnessed the singular fact of many old and influential families living, to a great degree, off the human product of the negro huts.

The insurrection of Turner only served to fasten the chains more firmly upon the negro race; it deprived him of the confidence of the whites; it restricted his little liberties and privileges; it made the master more willing to treat his slave merely as property, and to sell him as he would have sold an animal: it was a disaster to the black, from which flowed only misery to himself and his children.

THE NULLIFICATION REBELLION.

THE conflict between the State Rights idea and the antagonistic idea of Federal supremacy it may be said was inaugurated by Mr. Calhoun, of South Carolina. Although he conceded Mr. Jefferson's resolutions of '98 to be the keystone of his political system, Mr. Calhoun was the first statesman of influence who used the principles evolved by those resolutions to build up a great schism in the Federal institution. He became the representative man of a new school in politics which assumed supremacy for a State and the right of a State to nullify acts of Congress; and he now stands forward in history as the author of a system[1] which, so long as this Republic shall last, will be the opposing element to Federal consolidation and centralization of power.

Mr. Calhoun entered Congress in 1812, and from that time onward, for a period of forty years, was one of the controlling forces in Congress and in Executive circles. Possessing a mind of extraordinary subtlety and accumen, with great powers of physical endurance, and a resolution perfectly indomitable, he was admirably formed by nature for the part he played; and the success which attended his efforts attest less the truth of his principles than the perseverance with which they were pressed upon the country. He sustained the war policy of Madison and it prevailed; he opposed Dallas' scheme for a

[1] See Calhoun's Works (6 vols. Appleton & Co., 1855), vol. i., disquisition on Government. Aside from his great speech on the Force Bill, Feb. 15th, 1832, and his reply to Webster, Feb. 26th, 1832, his Letter to Governor Hammond, of South Carolina, August 28th, 1832, as well as his "Address to the People of South Carolina," of July 26th, 1831, embody the Southern Statesman's views on the Constitution and Government. The essay above mentioned, and the four efforts here referred to, form a perfect compendium of his political philosophy.

National Bank and it was rejected; he reported a substitute and it was accepted; opposed all tariffs as unconstitutional, except Hamilton's tariff of a revenue, and, after a struggle of sixteen years [1816–1832] witnessed the practical triumph of his opposition; he opposed as unconstitutional the principle of internal improvements by the General Government, and lived to behold the success of his labors against that system; he aimed at the Presidency and served as Vice President for two terms, and must have been President but for the over-mastering influence of Andrew Jackson; he espoused the cause of State Rights in a direct issue with the General Government, and, despite the superhuman exertions made to crush the movement inaugurated by him for nullification, he had the pleasure of forcing from Congress such concessions as placed his principles on a firm footing; scorning the Missouri Compromise, and demanding the rights of the South to introduce slavery in the Territories, he lived to see the movement initiated which ended in the overthrow of that solemn contract, and the opening of the Territories to the South on the "Squatter Sovereignty" plan: work enough, truly for one man, and success enough to satisfy any other ambition than that which John C. Calhoun cherished. He only failed to disintegrate the Union, or to ingraft upon our Constitution the novel feature of a dual executive, which should secure to the Slave States one half of the Executive, with veto power, &c. But, his principles survived their master director; and, had he lived ten years more, his eager soul would have been gladdened by the secession of the Southern States according to his plans proposed and acted upon in 1831–2. Hence his life must be pronounced a gigantic success, when viewed by its results. That these results were triumphs of evil over good we are not prepared to assume; but, that the fruits of his doctrines have been pernicious to the order, stability and humanitarian spirit of the Great Republic, is not now a matter of debate among those who reverence the Union and hold obedience to the Laws a paramount duty.

The introduction to Congress of Henry Clay's tariff of 1824, was the source of much feeling throughout the South. That section being almost purely agricultural, and a heavy consumer of imported goods, felt aggrieved at duties which increased the cost of living without offering any adequate return. It was regarded as a measure to build up the commercial and manufacturing North, and, by Mr. Calhoun, was also condemned as clearly unconstitutional. The excuse urged for its adoption was the prostrate condition of the country's finances and energies, "indicated," Clay said, in his elaborate speech sustaining the new impositions (March 31st, 1824), "by the diminished exports of native produce; by the depressed and reduced state of our foreign navigation; by our diminished commerce; by successive unthrashed crops of grain perishing in our barns and barn-yards for the want of a market; by the alarming diminution of the circulating medium; by the numerous bankruptcies, not limited to the trading classes, but extending to all orders of society; by a universal complaint of the want of employment and a consequent reduction of the wages of labor; by the ravenous pursuit after public situations, not for the sake of their honors and the performance of their public duties, but as a means of private subsistence; by the reluctant resort to the perilous use of paper money; by the intervention of legislation in the delicate relation between debtor and creditor; and, above all, by the low and depressed state of the value of almost every description of the whole mass of the property of the nation, which has, on an average, sunk not less than about fifty per cent. within a few years."

After much opposition the new tariff passed by a very close vote—25 to 21 in the Senate, and 107 to 102 in the House. This measure produced such good results that, in 1828, a further revision was proposed, chiefly at the instigation of a National Convention of manufacturers and producers held at Harrisburg in July, 1827, and called to discuss the interests involved. The friends of Jackson and anti-tariff charged that the Convention was a political trick to elect John Quincy Adams, by throwing the iron, hemp and wool growing interests against the opponents of the "American System" of protection. But, it was less a political than an economical assembly, as its labors indicated. Its discussions were those of prac-

51

tical men—men whose interests were involved, and whose experience was brought forward to direct legislation. The memorial from this body praying for an augmentation of duties on various goods and manufactures specified, was sent in to Congress. This was acted upon and a bill introduced "calculated to favor the wool and hemp growers and to satisfy the iron manufacturers, but not affording the desired protection to the manufacturers of woollen and cotton goods, though it was afterwards so arranged as to be more agreeable to them." This bill elicited the best talent of both Houses in its laborious passage, and finally was adopted by an almost purely *sectional* vote. Aside from the great hemp growing State of Kentucky only three votes were given the measure by members from the Southern States, who truly represented the feeling of their section in opposing the bill at every stage of its passage. It was received at the South with such expressions of disapprobation by Legislatures, by the press and by the people as left no doubt of the intensely sectional animosity then aroused. Large meetings of planters and citizens followed throughout the cotton growing States. At one, held in the Colleton district, South Carolina, during June, 1828, to consider the best remedy for the act of Congress, Mr. Calhoun was present and contributed to give character to the proceedings. The meeting declared nullification and non-obedience to be the rightful remedy; but, policy impelled to no open action until the Presidential election was decided. Mr. Calhoun saw the danger to Jackson's and his own election if violence resulted. He counselled obedience to the law until it was certain that Jackson's administration could not or would not reduce the duties to their old standard of 1816. If, after granting this time, it was demonstrated that no reduction would be made, then he advised that the unconstitutional law be resisted and that the State, by proper action, interpose to nullify the law. At the request of William C. Preston he "prepared a paper exposing the objectionable features of the act of 1828 and the injurious effects which must result from it, and pointing out the remedy for the evil. Five thousand copies of this paper were ordered to be printed by the Legislature which met in

December, 1828, under the title of The South Carolina Exposition and Protest on the subject of the Tariff.' The Legislature then contented itself with passing a resolution declaring the tariff acts of Congress for the protection of domestic manufactures unconstitutional, and that they ought to be resisted, and inviting other States to co-operate with South Carolina in measures of resistance." Prior to this, however, he had written numerous letters to leading spirits throughout the South, for the specific purpose of bringing the public mind up to the point of resistance and co-operation when South Carolina should take her initiatory steps. One of his letters lately brought to light is in answer to Mr. Preston's request for him to prepare the document above referred to. From this letter we obtain *inside* views of the rebellion proposed, and therefore quote:

"PENDLETON, (S. C.,) Nov. 6, 1828.

"DEAR SIR: Believing as I thoroughly do, that the liberty and happiness of our country depend on the course which our State may take in this great juncture, I am prepared to contribute whatever may be in my power, to aid in giving a salutary direction to her Council.

"The particular duty, which you request me to perform, is one of the highest importance, and no small difficulty. We have the basis in the report of Mr. Madison, and the proceedings of the Virginia and Kentucky Legislatures on the 'Alien and Sedition Act.' But from the dissimilarity between the character of the encroachments of the General Government then and now, very little aid can be derived from them in drawing up a paper for the present occasion. In casting my eyes over the subject, it strikes me that with the greatest compression consistent with clearness, the document must necessarily be voluminous—so many and so important are the principles involved, and so various are its details. It will, of course, take time and labor; it will require the aid of documents not in my possession. I have but a short period to remain at home, and I am much engaged in my domestic concerns, preparatory to setting out to Washington; but I will permit nothing to prevent me from sending on such aid that my friends may think I ought. I will commence a draft immediately. * * * Your views appear to me to be perfectly correct. Excise will not do. I deem it the most dangerous recourse that could be adopted, and would certainly be followed by defeat. The remedy you refer to is the only safe and efficient one, and is abundantly adequate. I speak with confidence. It alone can save the Union. The only question is the mode and time. It seems to me clear that the State must act by convention, but also am strongly of opinion that we must take time, especially if a new administration should come in, as there can be but little doubt it will.

"All moves aiming at reform and revolution as ours is, must, to be successful, be characterized by great respect for the opinion of others. On this great question we are far in advance of the intelligence of the other States, even of those which have the same interest with ourselves. Our measures, however sound, however justified by the noble example of Virginia, in '98, will appear at first to all our friends, novel, bold and even dangerous, and to those who exact tribute from us, treasonable. Yet, thought will be put in motion. And, as our cause rests in truth and the Constitution, it will gain daily, till it will finally prevail, if we act with wisdom and moderation.

"These views are greatly strengthened on the supposition of a change of administration. It would seem but a reasonable confidence in the new administration to afford time to see what its wisdom and virtue may effect—not to afford which will be considered hostile to it, and expose the State to the imputation of dangerous designs, which ought to be especially guarded against.

"There has been heretofore a want of caution on this important point, which has exposed us to great danger, and which renders greater caution more necessary. It seems to me that all that can be done at present is an able report, fully exposing our wrongs, and unfolding our remedies, but to abstain for the present from applying it on grounds of respect for others and a sense of moderation, with the adoption of such measures as may produce harmony of opinion among the oppressed States. It seems to me it would also be judicious to approve of the course adopted by our people to raise their own supplies, and to abstain as far as may be practicable from the consumption of the articles fostered by the tariff —but accompanied with a caution not to consider it more than a temporary palliative.

"I make these suggestions with deference, knowing how much must depend on circumstances, which can only be judged of by those on the spot. If we succeed, it will constitute one of the most glorious reforms ever effected. But, if we fail, we will have the poor consolation of thinking of the greater disaster, which would have taken place, without an effort on our part—the loss of our liberty."

This was written by the Vice President of the United States, while yet exercising the functions of his high office; and its author, as the Democratic candidate for the same trust, was even then reelected. Considering the tone of Mr. Calhoun's addresses, that he was not at once arraigned for treason was due to the danger of such a course, as well as to the apparently good cause of complaint which the malcontents urged as their justification. Benton, in his "Thirty Years' View," gives us the following statement of the actual condition of the question. We cite it as presenting what time has demonstrated to have been a very fair presentment of the case:

"The South believed itself impoverished to enrich the North by this system; and certainly a singular and unexpected result has been seen in these two sections. In the colonial state the Southern were the rich part of the colonies, and expected to do well in a state of independence. They had the exports, and felt sure of their prosperity. Not so of the North, whose agricultural resources were few, and who expected privations from the loss of British favor. But in the first half century after independence this expectation was reversed. The wealth of the North was enormously aggrandized; that of the South had declined. Northern towns had become great cities; Southern cities had decayed, or become stationery; and Charleston, the principal port of the South, was less considered than before the Revolution. The North became a money-lender to the South, and Southern citizens made pilgrimages to Northern cities to raise money upon the hypothecation of their patrimonial estates. And this in the face of Southern exports since the Revolution to the value of eight hundred millions of dollars—a sum equal to the product of the Mexican mines since the days of Cortez. The Southern States attributed this result to the action of the Federal Government—its alleged double action of levying revenue upon the industry of one section of the Union and expending it on another—and especially to its protective tariffs. But the protective system, in any degree, except in favor of cotton-planting, had been in existence only twelve years, and this reversed condition of the two sections had commenced long before that time. Philosophy and observation have long since discovered the cause to be found, not in the operations of the National Government, which has always been beneficent, but in the social character and the industrial systems of the two sections. But such was the pretense—a mere pretense, as President Jackson alleged—used by Mr. Calhoun and his associates for justifying disloyal speech in Congress, and action in South Carolina."

The years intervening between 1828 and the session of 1831–2 were years of great commercial and landed prosperity; the new "System" developed manufactures and mines with astonishing rapidity and with beneficent results; on every hand out of the South the country was satisfied with "protective" results, whatever may have been the theoretic opposition of Free Trade partisans. But, in Congress, great excitement prevailed, accompanied by a corresponding feeling among the people. A New England Senator had, early in the session for 1829–30, offered a resolution of inquiry into the expediency of limiting sales of public lands to those then in market, to suspend the surveys, and to abolish the office of Surveyor General. This proposition doubtless had its political face, although it was urged that, the public revenues then being in *excess* of the General Government's needs, it would be economy to fill up the territory already opened before proceeding with farther surveys of territory. Western members "took fire" at what was deemed to be a stroke at their section's progress, which, if not stayed, would transfer the seat of political power to the west of the Alleghanies, in another decade. Crimination and recrimination resulted; the West was pitted against the East, but particularly against New England, which was severely overhauled for its Federalism, its Hartford Convention, its friendship for a foreign enemy (England) and for its unappeasable spirit of domination. This contention, promising the worst results, Webster sough to allay the tumult by moving an indefinite postponement of the entire question. Sustaining his motion with "remarks," he only added fuel to the flame, by enlarging the scope of debate. The Ordinance of 1798 and the Missouri Compromise were introduced. At once the ghost of Slavery, supposed to have been forever appeased by the "restriction" of 1822, came up and laid its manacles upon the altar. Webster, as the exponent of New England sentiment, conceived slavery to be the Republic's bane. In one of his speeches he introduced the illustration frequently quoted, of the relative progress of the Slave State of Kentucky and the Free State of Ohio—a comparison highly damaging to the cause of slave labor. This inflamed the

Southern spirit. To *propagate* their system of involuntary servitude was boldly avowed as a political and constitutional *right.* In the utterance of these sentiments the brilliant Robert Y. Hayne, of South Carolina, became conspicuous. He denounced the interference of the North with slavery—assuming that it was a State institution, and therefore was no body's business but their own. The question of State Rights came into the turbulent arena, and laid its broken bundle of *fasces* upon the altar beside the chains and manacles. The celebrated contest between Hayne and Webster was the result. The South Carolinian planted himself upon Calhoun's platform of the right of a State to pronounce upon the validity and constitutionality of National laws and to nullify them if the State should so elect. His several speeches startled the country by their boldly avowed doctrines, proving the extreme Southern States to favor, at heart, disunion.

To these alarming sentiments Webster, thoroughly aroused, replied at great length, and his two answers to Hayne (January, 1830) stand as great living texts on the powers of the Government.

In this debate Hayne doubtless spoke with the sanction and co-operation of the Vice President. His efforts were *designed* to create a broad distinctive issue, upon which to create a party whose ultimate object was to denationalize the Government, or, failing in this, to prepare the way for a peaceable division of the Union. The more to give this movement momentum it was planned to make Thomas Jefferson assume the paternity of the party, by acknowledging his resolutions of '98—as originally prepared by him—to be its fundamental principles. A dinner party was, therefore, given at the Capital (April 13th, 1830) upon the occasion of Jefferson's birth day. Many eminent men of 'Democratic' faith were present, including the President of the United States, the Vice President, three members of the Cabinet, members of Congress, &c. All, outwardly, seemed only the offering of patriotism, but, beneath it all was the spirit of disunion. The regular toasts, apparently proper for the occasion, were, upon their dissemination, discovered to be so subtly yet so strongly tinctured with the South Carolina view of State Rights that numbers of the invited guests withdrew from the feast. The President's attention being directed to the discovery he was advised to withdraw. He refused, however, to desert the table, and, as the sequel proved, for a patriotic reason. He had resolved to rebuke the disloyal spirit of the gathering. Dinner being over the regular toasts were introduced—over one half of them prepared by Mr. Calhoun. These were received with expressions of satisfaction, and nullification seemingly became a fixed fact with the Jeffersonian Democracy, so far as "regular" toasts at a Jeffersonian festival could be trusted as exponents of principles. Volunteer sentiments were then in order, when Jackson, rising, threw this bombshell into the proceedings:

"OUR FEDERAL UNION: *it must be preserved!*"

—a sentiment designed and regarded as a proclamation from the President to announce a plot against the Union. The next toast, by Mr. Calhoun, did not by any means allay the President's apprehensions. It was:

"The Union, next to our liberty, the most dear: may we all remember that it can only be preserved by respecting the rights of the States, and distributing equally the benefit and burthen of the Union."

In the language of Thomas H. Benton, who was present, "this toast touched all the tender parts of the new question—liberty before Union—only to be preserved. State Rights, inequality of burthens and benefits. These phrases connecting themselves with Mr. Hayne's speech, and with proceedings and publications in South Carolina, unveiled nullification as a new and distinct doctrine in the United States, and the existence of a new party in the field."

The Democracy, becoming alarmed at this new movement, and beholding in it the seeds of National dissolution, hastened to repudiate the Calhoun programme. Madison, still living, spoke and wrote with great earnestness against the construction put upon his Virginia resolutions and address, and strove to defend Jefferson's fair fame from the responsibility of having to father South Carolina's heresy.[1] The Virginia Legislature also passed resolves to protect Jefferson's memory, imperilled

[1] See Appendix for Madison's defense of himself and Jefferson.

by association with nullification and disunion. But, these disclaimers did not prevent the Southern party from spreading and strengthening, and, despite Madison's special plea, despite the Virginia Legislature's resolves, the new constructionists adhered to their claim upon the father of Democracy, and thirty years of contention did not deprive them of that claim.

Strengthened by their now open movement upon the State Rights' plea, and united by the still persistent denial of Congress to reduce the offensive tariff, affairs assumed a menacing aspect as the Presidential election of 1832 approached. It became evident to the most unobserving that an explosion was at hand. Calhoun's relations with Jackson were not even friendly, for the President, from the hour of that dinner party, had watched the Vice President with distrust. This feeling culminated in the conviction that Calhoun really meditated a disruption of the Union—using the tariff as a popular pretext—upon the appearance of his (Calhoun's) "Letter to Governor Hamilton," dated Fort Hill, August 28th, 1832. Its assumptions were so clearly inimical to the authority and supremacy of the General Government, that Jackson was no longer in doubt as to the stroke for "independence" meditated by the intriguants. It contained such sentiments as the following (the italics being Mr. Calhoun's own):

"On a question whether a particular power exercised by the General Government be granted by the Constitution, it belongs to the State as a member of the Union, in her sovereign capacity in convention, to determine definitively, as far as her citizens are concerned, the extent of the obligation which she contracted: and if, in her opinion, the act exercising the power be unconstitutional, to declare it null and void, *which declaration would be obligatory on her citizens.*"

"In whatever light it may be viewed, I hold it as necessarily resulting, that, in the case of a power disputed between them, the Government, as the agent, has no right to enforce its construction against the construction of the State as one of the sovereign parties to the Constitution, any more than the State government would have against the people of the State in their sovereign capacity, the relation being the same between them."

"The General Government is a case of joint agency—the joint agent of the twenty-four sovereign States. It would be its duty, according to the principles established in such cases, instead of attempting to enforce its construction of its powers against that of the States, to bring the subject before the States themselves, in the only form which, according to the provision of the Constitution, it can be—by a proposition to amend, in the manner prescribed in the instrument, to be acted on by them in the only mode they can, by expressly granting or withholding the contested power."

"Not a provision can be found in the Constitution *authorizing the General Government to exercise any control whatever over a State* by force, by veto, by judicial process, or in any other form—*a most important omission, designed and not accidental.*"

"The construction which would confer on the Supreme Court the power in question, rests on the ground that the Constitution has conferred on that tribunal the high and important right of deciding on the *constitutionality of laws.* That it possesses this power I do not deny, but I do utterly deny that it is conferred by the Constitution, either by the provisions cited, or any other. It is a power derived from the necessity of the case; and, so far from being possessed by the Supreme Court exclusively or peculiarly, it not only belongs to every court of the country, high or low, civil or criminal, but to all foreign courts, before which a case may be brought involving the construction of a law which may conflict with the provisions of the Constitution."

"The opinion that the General Government has the right to enforce its construction of its powers against a State, in any mode whatever, is, in truth, founded on a fundamental misconception of our system. At the bottom of this, and, in fact, in almost every other misconception as to the relation between the States and the General Government, lurks the radical error, that the latter is a National, and not, as in reality it is, a Confederate Government; and that it derives its powers from a higher source than the States. There are thousands influenced by these impressions without being conscious of it, and who, while they believe themselves to be opposed to consolidation, have into their conception of our Constitution almost all the ingredients which enter into that form of government."

"However dissimilar their governments, the present *Constitution is as far removed from consolidation, and is as strictly and purely a confederation, as the one which it superseded.*"

"I have now, I trust, conclusively shown that a State has a right, in her sovereign capacity, in convention, to declare an unconstitutional act of Congress to be null and void, and that such declarations would be obligatory on her citizens, as highly so as the Constitution itself, and conclusive against the General Government, which would have no right to enforce its construction of its powers against that of the State."

"I next propose to consider the practical effect of the exercise of this high and important right—which, as the great conservative principle of our system, is known under the various names of nullification, interposition and State veto—in reference to its operation viewed under different aspects: nullification, as declaring null an unconstitutional act of the General Government, as far as the State is concerned; interposition, as throwing the shield of protection between the citizen of a State and the encroachments of the Government; and veto, as arresting or inhibiting its unauthorized acts within the limits of the State."

The nullificator then proceeded to prove to the Governor, and, through him, to the people of the South, that the General Government, possessing no *power* to *enforce* its laws against a State, could not *coerce* a State by any process of the courts.[1] This, by inference, left the State free to act, without fear of punishment or "coercion." He did, indeed, make a labored and an able argument to prove that nullification did not necessitate secession—that, to nullify laws was not to reject Federal relations and responsibilities. He said, as deducible from his argument:

"Nullification leaves the members of the association or union in the condition it found them—subject to all its burdens, and entitled to all its advantages, comprehending the member nullifying as well as the others—its object being, not to destroy, but to preserve, as has been stated. It simply arrests the act of the agent, as far as the principal is concerned, leaving in every other respect the operation of the joint concern as before; secession, on the contrary, destroys, as far as the withdrawing member is concerned, the association or union, and restores him to the relation he occupied towards the other members before the existence of the association or union. He loses the benefit, but is released from the burden and control, and can no longer be dealt with, by his former associates, as one of its members."

And he added this somewhat remarkable expression:

"With institutions every way so fortunate, possessed of means so well calculated to prevent disorders, and so admirable to correct them when they cannot be prevented, *he* who would prescribe for our political disease *disunion* on the one side, *or coercion* of *a State* in the assertion of its rights on the other, *would deserve* and *will receive*, *the execrations of this and all future generations.*"

---

[1] Judge Black's opinion [quoted at length in Victor's History of the Southern Rebellion, vol. i. pages 66–69] as given to Mr. Buchanan Nov. 20th, 1860, for his guidance in the treatment of rebellion, clearly re-enunciated Mr. Calhoun's propositions—that he had no power, under the Constitution, to coerce a State to obedience. Behind that opinion the President entrenched himself to excuse his non-action for nipping the rebellion in the bud.

We characterise it as a remarkable expression in view of the practical results of nullification, which must have been as clear to Mr. Calhoun's mind as a noon-day sun to his eye. He was safe in the declaration of devotion to the Union, because the Government must strike the first blow if it would drive a State out of the right of nullification; in which event, according to Mr. Calhoun's argument and political theory, the bond of Union would be dissolved *ex necessitate rei.*[1] He was, as at the dinner party, for the Union with a qualification, which afterwards was aptly expressed in the phrase—"obedience to the Constitution but allegiance to the State."

One of Mr. Calhoun's biographers says of this letter: "This elaborate production exhausted the whole argument in defense of the position assumed by Mr. Calhoun, and, with his address, was regarded as a political text book by the nullifiers of South Carolina. They looked upon it as their *Magna Charta*, which promised them deliverance from wrong and oppression, and behind which were safety and protection." And we quite agree with the author in his opinion concerning the harmony between the South Carolinian's creed and that enunciated by Jefferson and Madison. Mr. Jenkins says: "The Virginia resolutions declared, in express terms, the right of the States to interpose, whenever their reserved powers were infringed, and to maintain 'within their respective limits, the authorities, rights and liberties, appertaining to them;' and in the Kentucky resolutions, Mr. Jefferson held, 'that in all cases of an abuse of *delegated* powers, the members of the General Government being chosen by the people, a change by the people would be the constitutional remedy; but, where powers are *assumed*, which have *not been delegated*, a *nullification* of the act is the rightful remedy that *every State* has a natural right to, in cases not in the compact (*casus non fœderis*), to nullify, of their

[1] Calhoun's life was one of warring against the doctrine of Federal supremacy, yet he found it no contravention of principle to utter Union sentiments. Thus, in his letter announcing to the South Carolina Legislature (Nov. 26th, 1842) his purpose to resign his seat in the U. S. Senate, he closed with this expression:

"That the State may long retain her high standing in the Union, and that the Union itself, with our free and happy and glorious institutions, may be transmitted to the latest generation, shall, to my last breath, ever be my ardent prayer."

own authority, all *assumptions of powers* within their limits.' " All the special pleading and protestation yet exhausted upon the question have not succeeded in disproving Mr. Calhoun's obligation to Jefferson. He differed with the Virginian in matters of detail rather than in first principles.

The revenue produced by the tariff of 1828 proved too much of a good thing. It threatened the public treasury with plethora—a condition more to be dreaded by all good citizens than financial depletion. Something must be done to stop the receipts, as well as to stay the storm brewing in South Carolina. Jackson, in his annual message, December, 1831, recommended a reduction of the duties. An attempt was made to revise the schedule so as not to affect injuriously the multitude of interests involved. After much labor an amended act passed *enhancing* the duty on woollens five per cent., but reducing that on iron and sugar, and abolishing the duty on coffee and a great number of other articles of general consumption. The vote on this was, in the House: Northern States—yeas 73, nays 35; Southern States—yeas 49, nays 20. This gave thirty-two per cent. of the Northern and thirty-eight per cent. of the Southern vote *against* reduction. In the Senate the vote was: Northern States—yeas 23, nays 1; Southern States—yeas 9, nays 15, or four per cent. of the Northern and *sixty-two* per cent. of the Southern vote *against* reduction! The result apparently demonstrated that the country, taken in the aggregate, was satisfied with the protective system.

South Carolina rebelled. Mr. Calhoun sounded the note of alarm. The moment for action had come. A test had been submitted, and Congress absolutely refused to recede from its position. There only remained for South Carolina to enforce her old threat of non-obedience to the mandates of Congress. Mr. Calhoun issued an address to the people, announcing that a protective policy might thenceforth be regarded as settled upon the country—that all hope of relief from Congress must be abandoned—that the people of the State must now act in their own behalf. This address engendered a very revolutionary feeling, though a powerful, but at first fruitless, opposition to Calhoun's views and plans was offered by a class of wealthy and influential citizens led by such spirits as Poinsett, Pettigru, Colonel Drayton, ex-Governor Manning, &c. These men sought to prevent the nullifiers from obtaining the two-thirds majority in the Legislature necessary to call a State Convention. If that call could be prevented there would be no State action, and, consequently, no resistance to the General Government, except such as the Legislature (in its legislative not sovereign capacity) might authorise the Governor to take. But, their strenuous labors were of no avail; before the great strength of Calhoun's influence nothing could stand. Meetings took place throughout the State close upon the Presidential election. The Legislature came together amid much excitement. One of its first acts was to appoint a Committee to report on the relations of the State with the General Government. It reported that the Federal Constitution was a compact originally formed, not between the people of the different States as distinct and independent sovereignties; that when any violation of the spirit of that compact took place, it was not only the right of the people, but of the State Legislature, to remonstrate against it; that the Federal Government was responsible to the State Legislatures whenever *it* assumed powers not conferred; that notwithstanding a tribunal was appointed under the Constitution to decide controversies where the United States was a party, there were some questions that must occur between the Government and the State which it would be unsafe to submit to any judicial tribunal; and finally, that there was a peculiar propriety in a State Legislature's undertaking to decide for itself, inasmuch as the Constitution had not provided any remedy.

A convention of delegates was thereupon ordered (October 22d) to assemble on the 19th of November, to act for the State, in the crisis. Meanwhile the Virginia Legislature, also, by a vote of 154 to 68, gave her assent to the principle of nullification. North Carolina declared against it and held out firmly for the Constitution and the laws. Alabama and Georgia endorsed South Carolina heartily; and their course led the country to feel that, in event of South Carolina's secession, they would follow her lead. Government had just succeeded at enormous cost, in extinguishing the Indian titles to lands in these States, and they in return, were ready to cast off the Government.

An election, by the people, of delegates resulted in an almost unanimous choice of Calhoun men. The delegates gathered at Columbia, at the appointed time, and the Convention duly organized by the election of ex-Governor Hamilton as its President. On the 21st of November, the Ordinance of Nullification was adopted. The tariff acts of 1828 and 1832 were declared null and void and not binding upon the citizens of the States. It was further declared that if the United States should attempt to enforce them by naval or military force, the Union was to be dissolved, and a convention called to form a government for South Carolina. It further provided that no appeal should be permitted to the Supreme Court of the United States in any question concerning the validity of the ordinance, or of the laws passed to give effect thereto.

Having thus discharged its duties the Convention adjourned to meet again in March after the adjournment of Congress. The Ordinance was law by the nature of the Convention, without any submission of it to the people, for acceptance or rejection. South Carolina was a democracy only in form. Even her Governor was not chosen by the people but by the Legislature, which body was, simply, the representative of property holders and "first families." Out of the forty thousand voters then in the State it is fair to say one thousand directed the entire mass, while, of this one thousand, not one hundred were uninfluenced by three or four men who directed the State's destiny. With the forms of a democracy, South Carolina, practically, and in all essential features, was an aristocracy. The Convention legislated the Ordinance into existence and the Legislature proceeded to provide for its enforcement, the legislators being convened for the especial purpose, by call of the Governor The acts adopted embraced one authorizing the Governor to call on the militia to resist any attempt on the part of the Government of the United States to enforce the revenue laws. Ten thousand stand of arms and the requisite quantity of military munitions were ordered to be purchased, and any acts done in pursuance of that law were to be held lawful in the State courts.

Says a Democratic writer:[1] "the State placed itself in an attitude of military preparation for the defense of its position; organized and armed its own physical force; and succeeded in arousing so determined and excited a state of feeling in its citizens, that we think there can be no doubt that it would have maintained its position to the last extremity—a position, manifestly, exceedingly difficult to be overcome, if thus maintained, by any physical power which could have been brought against it."

All of these things transpired with the advice and approbation of Mr. Calhoun. They embodied his programme for "strengthening the Union by purifying it," and the country beheld the sad spectacle of a State in arms defying the power of Congress.

The election for President transpired just a fortnight before the passage of the Ordinance. Jackson was reelected. Mr. Calhoun, dropped from the list of candidates, saw his rival, Martin Van Buren, elevated to the Vice Presidency. The popular vote stood: Jackson 650,028; Henry Clay 550,189—proving the protectionists in the minority, since Clay ran as their candidate on the distinct issue of the "American System." If the popular voice was any evidence of the nation's feeling and policy, Calhoun's anti-protection views were in the majority. But, the nullifiers did not propose to await the issue of an election. Having the tariff as a pretext they were not disposed to accept the tardy terms of a Congressional majority Calhoun distrusted Jackson too much to expect anything from him except opposition. His avowed reasons for this distrust were thus given in a letter lately brought to light, written to Edmund Ruffin, of Virginia:

"He (Jackson) came in, as far as my aid and that of my friends was given him, mainly to put down the (protective) system by bringing to bear against it the immense patronage in money and power which it put into the hands of the Executive; but, instead of that, he, in fact, rested his whole scheme of power on it, while he held out fair words to

[1] Democratic Review, April, 1838.

the South. In his two first messages he proposed and urged the fatal scheme, had it been adopted, of distributing the surplus revenue expressly with the view of perpetuating it, which gave him a strong hold onthe tariff interest of the North: thus taking a position which made him more acceptable to the North than any Southern individual, and more to the South than any Northern, the result was, that, do what he would, the latter would not join to turn him out of office for Webster, for Clay, or any other tariff man, nor the former for any anti-tariff, while he wielded the immense power and revenue derived from the system to build up a party personal to himself; and hence the spoils party, made up by recruits from all sides, and which had no principle but to support the authority of its chieftain."

This attitude of South Carolina created a feeling of uneasiness among the people at large, influencing the Congressional as well as the Presidential election. The majority of Representatives, returned to Congress, so far feared or endorsed Calhoun's constitutional constructions as to be prepared for concessions proper to restore peace. They assembled to find a State in open rebellion, and proceeded to the work of redressing alleged grievances. During the first day's session a bill was introduced for the reduction of the tariff, and one for a similar object soon was reported from the Committee of Ways and Means, by its Chairman, Mr. Verplanck, of New York. This was especially designed to conciliate South Carolina.

Occupying the Presidential chair was a man of nerve—one too fearless to shrink from duty, and too loyal to pettifog as to the nature of that duty. Andrew Jackson beheld the head of treason in Calhoun's movements, and, as treason, he struck at it upon the first open act. Soon after the Ordinance was promulgated the President issued (December 10th) his Proclamation of warning to those in an attitude of defiance toward the General Government, declaring the Ordinance of the State Convention subversive of the Federal Constitution, and his intention to enforce the laws at whatever hazard, and warning the people of the State against obedience to the Ordinance as involving the crime of treason against the United States. He denounced the State Rights idea, as interpreted by those whom he characterized as demagogues, to be pernicious, and assumed for an evil purpose. He said: "Eloquent appeals to your passions, to your State pride, to your native courage, to your sense of real injury, were used to prepare you for the period when the mask, which concealed the hideous features of disunion, should be taken off. It fell, and you were made to look with complacency on objects which, not long since, you would have regarded with horror." And then added a peroration characterised both by force and a rhetorical beauty. "Snatch from the archives of your State the disorganizing edict of its convention; bid its members to reassemble, and promulgate the decided expression of your will to remain in the path which alone can conduct you to safety, prosperity and honor. Tell them that, compared to disunion, all other evils are light, because that brings with it an accumulation of all. Declare that you will never take the field unless the star spangled banner of your country shall float over you; that you will not be stigmatized when dead, and dishonored and scorned while you live, as the authors of the first attack on the Constitution of your country. Its destroyers you can not be. You may disturb its peace; you may interrupt the course of its prosperity; you may cloud its reputation for stability; but its tranquility will be restored, its prosperity will return, and the stains upon its national character will be transferred and remain an eternal blot on the memory of those who caused the disorder."

To this proclamation South Carolina responded, through her newly elected Governor, ex-Senator Robert Y. Hayne, who issued his counter manifesto sustaining the position assumed by the State, and calling out twelve thousand militia as volunteers, to maintain the supremacy of the State laws.

To the seat vacated by Mr. Hayne, in the U. S. Senate, Mr. Calhoun was chosen by the Legislature, early in December, 1832. He at once proceeded to the Capital to take his seat, having first resigned his office of Vice President. His course now commanded unusual attention. Some even doubted if he would take the oath of office, while the known indignation felt against him by Jackson, added plausibility to the rumor of Calhoun's prospective arrest for high treason. But, no arrest was made, and the Senator elect took the qualifying oath with all due formality. Morally and physically he was brave. He came to Washington to do his work; no threats, public or private—no fear of results to himself or the country, deterred him from his defense of South Carolina.

He acted promptly, by soon calling upon the President, through a resolution, to lay before the Senate the Ordinance of Nullification and accompanying documents, as remitted by the Governor of South Carolina. Before action was had, Jackson sent in his message of January 16th, 1833, wherein he descanted upon the rebellious condition of affairs in the disaffected State and recommended the revival of the act of '93 to enforce the revenue laws and to crush resistance to the United States' authorities. On this message, before action thereon, Mr. Calhoun spoke at considerable length and with much feeling, defending the course of his constituency and declaring their resolve to sustain their position. When the National Government returned to the principles of '98, he assumed, then would he be the last man to abandon that Government.

In response to the message the Senate Committee on the Judiciary, of which Mr. Webster was a member, reported a bill known as the Force Bill. It answered the President's demand for authority to execute the laws, by extending the jurisdiction of the Federal Courts in cases arising under the revenue laws, and empowering the use of any additional military force necessary to maintain the peace and the supremacy of the laws. This most significant and important act was an overwhelming stroke at nullification, which Calhoun manœuvered to parry by the subtleties of his logic. As preliminary to a general discussion on the constitutionality of such an act, and with the special object of eliciting debate, he introduced a series of resolutions on the Powers of the General Government, as follows:

"Resolved, That the people of the several States composing these United States are united as parties to a constitutional compact, to which the people of each State acceded as a separate and sovereign community, each binding itself, by its own particular ratification; and that the Union, of which the said compact is the bond, is a union *between the States* ratifying the same.

"Resolved, That the people of the several States, thus united by a constitutional compact, in forming that instrument, in creating a General

Government to carry into effect the objects for which it was formed, delegated to that Government, for that purpose, certain definite powers, to be exercised jointly, reserving, at the same time, each State to itself, the residuary mass of powers, to be exercised by its own separate government; and that, whenever the General Government assumes the exercise of powers not delegated by the compact, its acts are unauthorized, void and of no effect; and that the said Government is not made the final judge of the powers delegated to it, since that would make its discretion, and not the Constitution, the measure of its powers; but that, as in all other cases of compact among sovereign parties, without any common judge, each has an equal right to judge for itself, as well of the infraction as of the mode and measure of redress.

"Resolved, That the assertions, that the people of these United States, taken collectively as individuals, are now, or ever have been united on the principle of the social compact, and, as such, are now formed into one nation or people; or that they have ever been so united in any one stage of their political existence; or that the people of the several States comprising the Union have not, as members thereof, retained their sovereignty; or that the allegiance of their citizens has been transferred to the General Government; or that they have parted with the right of punishing treason through their respective State Governments; or that they have not the right of judging, in the last resort, as to the extent of the powers reserved, and, of consequence, of those delegated, are not only without foundation in truth, but are contrary to the most certain and plain historical facts, and the clearest deductions of reason; and that all exercise of power on the part of the General Government, or any of its departments, deriving authority from such erroneous assumptions, must of necessity be unconstitutional; must tend directly and inevitably to subvert the sovereignty of the States, to destroy the Federal character of the Union, and to rear on its ruins a consolidated government, without constitutional check or limitation, and which must necessarily terminate in the loss of liberty itself."

These resolves, it will be perceived, enunciated principles which, if endorsed, rendered the Force Bill nugatory. But, as significant of the feeling entertained in the Senate, they were laid on the table by a seven-eighths vote. Debate then opened on the Force Bill, in the course of which Mr. Calhoun delivered an effective speech, (Feb. 15th, 1833) of three hours' duration; but he avoided a discussion of the principles involved in his resolutions, reserving that discussion until Webster should first canvass the subject, thus affording his antagonist the vantage ground of a reply. Webster, answering Calhoun (Feb.

16th), proceeded to discuss the whole question on the powers of the Government. His speech was a wonderful performance, characterized as truly Titanic in its majestic force of argument, truly Demosthenian in the mastery of its eloquence. He assumed the Hamiltonian ground of *consolidated* principles involved in the organism of the Union, and maintained that the Constitution was the "*supreme* law of the land," any thing in the action of the States to the contrary. The Constitution was a "compact," like that of the old Confederation, as argued by the State Rights advocates; but it was more; after its ratification *by* the States it became *fundamental law*, supreme to the extent of its delegated powers, thus binding all the ratifying States into one indivisible whole, and rendering the people in the aggregate one nation. It is well to refresh our minds, in these days of disquietude, with the great Expounder's opinions upon the point around which centres all the interest of a life and death struggle. Let us, therefore, quote: "Whether the Constitution be a compact between States in their sovereign capacity is a question which must be mainly argued from what is contained in the instrument itself. We all agree that it is an instrument which has been in some way clothed with power. We all admit that it speaks with authority. The first question then is—What does it say of itself? What does it purport to be? Does it style itself a league, confederacy, or compact between sovereign States? It is to be remembered, that the Constitution began to speak only *after* its adoption. Until it was ratified by nine States, it was but a proposal, the mere draft of an instrument. It was like a deed drawn but not executed. The Convention had framed it; sent it to Congress then sitting under the Confederation; Congress had transmitted it to the State Legislatures; and by the last, it was laid before the Conventions of the people in the several States. All this while it was inoperative paper. It had received no stamp of authority: it spoke no language. But, when ratified by the people in their respective Conventions, then it had a voice and spoke authentically. Every word in it had then received the sanction of the popular will, and was to be received as the expression of that will. What the Constitution says of itself, therefore, is as conclusive as what it says on any other point. Does it call itself a 'compact?' Certainly not. It uses the word *compact* but once, and that is, when it declares that the *States* shall enter into no 'compact.' Does it call itself a 'league,' a 'confederacy,' a 'subsisting treaty between the States?' Certainly not. There is not a particle of such language in all its pages! But, it declares itself a CONSTITUTION. What is a *Constitution?* Certainly not a league, or confederacy, but a *fundamental law.* That fundamental regulation which determines the manner in which the public authority is to be executed, is what forms the Constitution of a State. Those primary rules which concern the body itself, and the very being of the political society, the form of government and the manner in which power is to be exercised—all, in a word, which form together the Constitution of a State—these are 'fundamental laws.' This is the language of the public writers. But, do we need to be informed in this country what a *constitution* is? Is it not an idea perfectly familiar, definite and well settled? We are at no loss to understand what is meant by the Constitution of one of the States—and the Constitution of the United States speaks of itself as being an instrument of the same nature. It says, this *Constitution* shall be the law of the land, anything in the *State Constitutions* to the contrary, notwithstanding. And speaks of itself, too, in plain contradistinction *from* a 'confederation:' for, it says, all debts contracted, and all engagements entered into by the United States, shall be as valid under this *Constitution* as under the *Confederation.*' It does not say, as valid under this *compact*, or this league, or this confederation, as under the former confederation, but as valid '*under this Constitution.*'"

To this great exposition Mr. Calhoun addressed all the resources of his mind, in his speech, pronounced on a specially alloted day (Feb. 26th) *after* the passage of the Force Bill. It was, therefore, not an argument against that act, but simply and solely a reply to Webster on the principles embodied in his (Calhoun's) resolutions. Having had time for preparation, the South Carolinian delivered what is regarded as his ablest effort. It was worthy, in every sense, of the occasion. He met, squarely, every issue presented. Assuming that the Con stitution was *but* a compact, he made such a defense of the right of a State, as a State, to sit in judgment on acts of Congress and to nullify them, that, to this day, his logic has weight with a large class of thinkers even in the Northern States. Some writers have characterised his logic as "specious;" but, that is not a term to apply to the great nullificator's effort—it was exceedingly open in its enunciation of principles and perfectly direct in its defense of them. There was nothing "specious" in it *as* an argument; if his theory was amenable to that term it was not more so than any theory awaiting acceptance as a fact. We concede to Calhoun the strength of his arguments—the more willingly, now, as we have the painful experience of the Secession Revolution to prove that his principles, when practically applied, must end in national ruin. The true test is practice, or, as essayists have it, "experience is the great teacher;" and, great as were Mr. Webster's efforts to confront the evil of Calhoun's philosophy, they will be forgotten in the more overwhelming demonstration which three years of civil war adduced. That Mr. Calhoun's philosophy was responsible for the Secession revolution we conceive to be self-evident. It is fair to presume that he would have been its chief director had he been alive and in health during the winter of 1860–61.

The Force Bill passed in the Senate to its third reading, Feb. 18th, by a vote of 32 to 8—the negatives being Calhoun and Miller, of South Carolina; King and Moore, of Alabama; Troup, of Georgia; Mangum, of North Carolina; Tyler, of Virginia, and Bibb, of Kentucky. Several Senators were absentees, to avoid a vote, it was said; among them were Clay and Benton. The bill passed the Senate Feb. 20th, by 32 to 1—that one being John Tyler. It passed the House Feb. 28th, by an overwhelming affirmative vote. It at once received the signature of Jackson, and thus became not only the law of the land but a precedent in legislation to which, in all human probability, it will be the unwelcome necessity of future legislators to evoke. So long as the principles of Nullification and State Rights excite antagonisms to Federal authority so long will there be a necessity for the precedent offered by the Force Bill of 1833.[1]

We have adverted to bills offered early in the session, for a reduction of the tariff. The increasing excitement and disagreement on the subject, the apparently irreconcileable hostility of South Carolina to the principle of protection, and the danger menacing Calhoun himself of arrest for treason, all conspired to impel Clay into concessions which virtually abrogated his "American System," by substituting for the tariff of 1832 a graduated scale, detracting from the duties one-tenth each year upon all articles tariffed *over* twenty per cent., thus gradually reducing the duties until they should strike the free list, in December, 1841. That this was a triumph for the nullificators is not to be denied. The bill was designed as a compromise, but conceded most of the premises claimed by Mr. Calhoun in regard to the tariff principle. It was a great sacrifice to make, immensely involved as the Northern and Central States had become in manufactures, and dependent as thousands were upon manufacturing enterprise for maintenance. But, taking counsel of his fears, and impressed by a sense of devotion to the Union, the "great Pacificator" astounded his friends and the country by voluntarily abandoning his own distinctive system in the moment of its greatest success. This momentous abjuration was to stay a collision then impending, which must precipitate civil war—at least so Mr. Clay assumed.

---

[1] Mr. Calhoun himself was constrained to endorse, in effect, the *necessity* of coercion, in certain cases. In 1843, during the famous Dorr rebellion in Rhode Island, Mr. Calhoun, then a member of President Tyler's Cabinet, took decided ground against any attempt, on the part of any portion of our people, to redress real or fancied wrongs, or to change the institutions of the country by force, saying:

"The very complication of our system of Government—so many distinct, sovereign and independent States, each with its separate Government, and all united under one—is calculated to give force to discussion and agitation never before known, and to cause a diffusion of political intelligence heretofore unknown in the history of the world, if the Federal Government shall do its duty under the guarantees of the Constitution *by promptly suppressing physical force as an element of change*, and keeping wide open the door for the full and free action of all the moral elements in its favor. No people ever had so fair a start. All that is lacking is, that we shall understand, in all its great and beautiful proportions, the noble political structure reared by the wisdom and patriotism of our ancestors, and to have the virtue and the sense to preserve and protect it."

The vote on this important concession was as follows, by States. In the House:

North	Yeas.	Nays.	South	Yeas	Nays.
Maine	6	1	Delaware	0	1
New Hampshire	4	1	Maryland	9	0
Vermont	0	5	Virginia	20	1
Massachusetts	0	13	North Carolina	13	0
Connecticut	0	6	South Carolina	9	0
Rhode Island	0	2	Georgia	6	0
New York	11	19	Kentucky	12	0
New Jersey	0	6	Tennessee	8	1
Pennsylvania	4	21	Louisiana	3	0
Ohio	7	6	Alabama	3	0
Indiana	2	1	Missouri	0	1
Illinois	1	0	Mississippi	1	0
Total	35	81	Total	84	4

In the Senate:

North	Yeas.	Nays.	South	Yeas.	Nays.
Maine	2	0	Delaware	2	0
New Hampshire	2	0	Maryland	1	1
Massachusetts	0	2	Virginia	2	0
Connecticut	2	0	North Carolina	1	0
Rhode Island	0	2	South Carolina	2	0
Vermont	0	2	Georgia	1	0
New York	1	1	Kentucky	2	0
New Jersey	1	1	Tennessee	2	0
Pennsylvania	0	2	Louisiana	3	0
Ohio	1	1	Mississippi	2	0
Indiana	0	2	Alabama	2	0
Illinois	1	0	Missouri	0	2
Total	10	13	Total	19	3

Benton, in his "Thirty Years in the U. S. Senate," reveals what he terms the *secret history* of that compromise. The substance of this revelation was thus given: [1]

'The relative position of the National Government and South Carolina, and of the President of the United States and Mr. Calhoun, in the winter of 1833, placed the latter in great personal peril, which his friends perceived and tried to avert. Among others consulted on the subject by them was Letcher, of Kentucky, Clay's warm personal friend. He knew that South Carolina must yield, on some terms, to the authority and power of the National Government, and he conceived the idea of a compromise by which, in so yielding, she might preserve her dignity. He proposed it to Mr. Clay, who, sincerely desiring reconciliation, entertained the idea, and submitted it to Webster. The amazing intellectual plummet of the latter had fathomed the turbid waters of Nullification far deeper than had the brilliant Kentuckian, and he instantly said: "No—it will

[1] Not having Benton's volume before us at the moment of preparing this page of our article, we are constrained to use Mr. Lossing's version of the story, as given in Harper's Magazine for August, 1862.

be yielding great principles to faction. The time has come to test the strength of the Constitution and the Government." He had heartily supported the Force Bill. Although opposed, politically, to the Administration, he had said: "I believe the country in considerable danger; I believe an unlawful combination threatens the integrity of the Union. I believe the crisis calls for a mild, temperate, forbearing, but inflexibly firm execution of the laws. And, under this conviction, I give a hearty support to this Administration, in all measures which I deem to be fair, just and necessary. And in supporting these measures I mean to take my fair share of responsibility, to support them frankly and fairly, without reflections on the past and mixing other topics in their discussion." He was utterly opposed to compromising and temporizing measures with a rebellious faction, and told Mr. Clay so; and from that time he was not approached by those who were willing to shield conspirators from the sword of justice.

'Mr. Clay drew up a compromise bill and sent it to Mr. Calhoun by Mr. Letcher. Calhoun objected to parts of the bill most decidedly, and remarked that if Clay knew the nature of his objections he would at least modify those portions of the bill. Letcher made arrangements for a personal interview between these eminent Senators, who had not been on speaking terms for some time. The imperious Clay demanded that it should be at his own room. The imperiled Calhoun consented to go there. The meeting was civil but icy. The business was immediately entered upon. The principals were unyielding, and the conference ended without results.

Letcher now hastened to the President and sounded him on the subject of compromise. "Compromise!" said the stern old man, stern only toward wickedness, "I will make no compromise with traitors. I will have no negotiations. I will execute the laws. Calhoun shall be tried for treason, and hanged if found guilty, if he does not instantly cease his rebellious course." Letcher now flew to M'Duffie, Calhoun's ardent friend, and alarmed him with a startling picture of the President's wrath. That night, after he had retired to bed, Letcher was aroused by a Senator from Louisiana, who informed him that Jackson would not allow any more delay, and that Calhoun's arrest might take place any hour. He begged Letcher to warn Calhoun of his danger. He did so. He found the South Carolinian in bed. He told him of the temper and the intentions of the President, and the Conspirator was much alarmed.

'Meanwhile Mr. Clay and J. M. Clayton, of Delaware, had been in frequent consultations on the subject. Clayton had said to Clay, while his bill was lingering in the House, "These South Carolinians act very badly, but they are good fellows, and it is a pity to let Jackson hang them;" and advised him to get his bill referred to a new committee, and so modify it as to make it acceptable to a majority. Clay did so, and Clayton exerted all his influence to avert the calamity which hung over Calhoun and his friends. He assembled the manufacturers who had hurried to the Capital when they heard of the Compromise Bill, to see whether they would not yield something for the sake of conciliation and the Union. At a sacrifice of their interests, these loyal men did yield, and agreed to withdraw all opposition to the bill, and let it pass the Senate, providing the nullifiers should vote for certain amendments made by the Lower House, as well as for the bill itself. The nullifiers in committee would not yield. The crisis had arrived. The gallows was placed before Calhoun's eyes. Clayton earnestly remonstrated with him. He pointed out the danger, the folly, the wickedness of his course; and notified him that unless the amendments were adopted, and that by the votes of himself and political friends, the bill should not pass; that he (Clayton) would move to lay it on the table when it should be reported to the Senate, and that he had strength enough in that House pledged to do it. "The President will then," he said, "be left free to execute the laws in full rigor." His object, he told them plainly, was to put them squarely on the record; to make *all* the nullifiers vote for the amendments and the bill, and thus cut them off from the plea of "unconstitutionality," which they would raise if the bill and amendments did not receive their votes. Unless they were so bound he knew that the present pacification would be only a hollow truce, and that they would make this very measure, probably, a pretense for renewing their resistance to what they were pleased to call "unconstitutional measures" of the National Government, and for resuming their march toward secession and independence. He was peremptory with both Clay and Calhoun, and warned them that this was a last chance for a compromise.

'Mr. Clayton was inexorable. Clay and Calhoun agreed to the amendments. These with the bill were reported to the Senate. All the nullifiers voted for the amendments in order, until they came to the last, that of home valuation, which was so revolting to the great leader of the Conspirators. When that came up Calhoun and his friends met it with the most violent opposition. It was the last day but one of the session, and at a late hour in the day. Finding the nullifiers persistent in their opposition, Clayton, to their great consternation, suddenly executed his threat. He moved to lay the bill on the table, and declared it should continue to lie there. Mr. Clay begged him to withdraw his motion. Others entreated him to give a little more time. He was inflexible. There was fluttering in the bevy of nullifiers. Calhoun and his friends retired behind the collonade back of the Speaker's chair, over which was the portrait of Washington, the great Unionist, and there held a brief consultation. It was very brief, for time and opportunity were precious. Senator Bibb came from the trembling conclave and asked Clayton to give a little more time. This was a token of yielding, and he complied. He withdrew his motion, but with the declaration that unless the measure, in full, was voted for by all the nullifiers he should renew it. Instantly one of their friends moved an adjournment. It was carried, and the conspirators went home

—"to sleep, perchance to dream,"

on their predicament. They knew of only one way, and that a most thorny one for their pride, still open for their escape. They all knew the character of the President, and the reliability of his promises. So they concluded to vote as Mr. Clayton demanded, but begged that gentleman to spare Mr. Calhoun the mortification of appearing on the record in favor of a measure against which at that very time, and at his instance, troops were being raised in South Carolina, and because of which the politicians of that State were preparing to declare her secession from the Union! Mr. Clayton would not yield a jot. Calhoun was the chief of sinners in this matter, and he, of all others, must give the world public and recorded evidence of penitence, whatever his "mental reservations" might be. "Nothing would be conceded," Mr. Clayton said, "unless his vote appears in favor of the measure."

'The Senate met; the bill was taken up; and the nullifiers and their friends, one after another, yielded their objections on various pretenses. At length, when all had voted but Mr. Calhoun, he arose, pale and haggard, for he had had a most terrific struggle. He declared that he had then to determine which way he should vote, and at the termination of his brief remarks he gave his vote in the affirmative with the rest. It was a bitter pill for that proud man to swallow. The alternative presented to him was absolute humiliation or the gallows. He chose the former. With that act fell the great Conspiracy to break up the Government of the United States in 1832. The violent clamors raised in South Carolina and the Gulf States on the appearance of Jackson's Proclamation soon ceased. The Ordinance of Nullification was repealed, and *Nullifier* became, as it deserved to be, a term of reproach throughout most of the Union.'

All this sounds very much like a story for effect; but, written by Benton, and published during Jackson's life-time, it doubtless is, in the main, a correct version of the matter. It shows that the nullifier had to concede a little to gain much.

But, to revert to the "seat of war." Governor Hayne's troops were put in process of organization. Military pomp and circumstance reigned in Charleston. The "fiery heart" of South Carolina was ablaze, ready for the crisis. Throughout every section of the State little else was the theme of thought than "resistance to tyranny." To all this Jackson offered only the silent admonition of Moultrie's guns and Scott's presence. As early as October, 1832, the watchful eye of the President had detected the gathering cloud in the South, and then took steps to place the Charleston forts in a condition of security from seizure. The order issued to Major Heileman (October 29th) read:[1]

"It is deemed necessary that the officers in the harbor of Charleston should be advised of the possibility of attempts being made to surprise, seize and occupy the forts committed to them. You are therefore especially charged to use your utmost vigilance in counteracting such attempts. You will call personally on the commanders of Castle Pinckney and Fort Moultrie, and instruct them to be vigilant to prevent surprise in the night, or by day, on the part of any set of people whatever, who may approach the forts with a view to seize and occupy them. You will warn the said officers that such an event is apprehended, and that they will be held responsible for the defense, to the last extremity, of the forts and garrisons under their respective commands, against any assault, and also against intrigue and surprise. The attempt to surprise the forts and garrisons, it is expected, will be made by the militia, and it must be guarded against by constant vigilance, and repulsed at every hazard. These instructions you will be careful not to show to any persons, other than the commanding officers of Castle Pinckney and Fort Moultrie."

On the 7th of November two companies of artillery were ordered to proceed forthwith to Fort Moultrie. On the 12th a further order to Major Heileman directed the "citadel" in Charleston, belonging to the State, to be delivered up, with the State arms, if required, though any attack was to be resisted. On the 18th a confidential order, issued to General Scott, indicated the President's alarm at the approaching act of resistance. We quote from it:

"The possibility of such a measure furnishes sufficient reason for guarding against it, and the President is therefore anxious that the situation and means of defense of these fortifications, should be inspected by an officer of experience, who could also estimate and provide for any dangers to which they may be exposed. He has full confidence in your judgment and discretion, and it is his wish that you repair immediately to Charleston, and examine every thing connected with the fortifications. You are at liberty to take such measures, either by strengthening these defenses, or by reenforcing these garrisons with troops drawn from any other posts, as you may think prudence and a just precaution require.

"Your duty will be one of great importance, and of great delicacy. You will consult fully and freely with the collector of the port of Charleston, and with the district attorney of South Carolina, and you will take no step, except what relates to the immediate defense and security of

[1] Niles' Register, vol. 43, page 436.

the posts, without their order and concurrence. The execution of the laws will be enforced through the civil authority, and by the mode pointed out by the acts of Congress. Should, unfortunately, a crisis arise, when the ordinary power in the hands of the civil officers shall not be sufficient for this purpose, the President shall determine the course to be taken and the measures adopted. Till, therefore, you are otherwise instructed, you will act in obedience to the legal requisitions of the proper civil officers of the United States.

"I will thank you to communicate to me, freely and confidentially, upon every topic which you may deem it important for the Government to receive information."

This emanated from General Lewis Cass, then Secretary of War. Acting under it, and also of verbal instructions given by the President, Scott proceeded to Charleston, arriving there two days after the passage of the Ordinance. All was excitement, but the representation that Scott was making his annual tour of inspection of fortresses and arsenals, served to shield his presence from suspicion. He was enabled to execute his mission, without at all exciting the attention of the State authorities, or provoking the temper of an exasperated populace. He passed on to Augusta and secretly placed the arsenal there in order of defense. The fortifications of Savannah were also quietly reenforced to a state of complete security. This accomplished he returned to Charleston, where a number of armed vessels seemed to drop in *by accident*. These were so disposed as to act promptly in event of emergency. It was determined by the Collector and District Attorney to collect the revenue under the guns of Fort Moultrie, should Governor Hayne, after February 1st, attempt to nullify the laws.

Every thing being thus admirably prepared to enforce the collection of the duties, Scott sailed for New York where such other steps were taken as were necessary to insure extensive reenforcements of both army and navy if they should be required. Of course the public, generally, knew nothing of these movements: the newspapers of that day were not so "enterprising" as to pry into the most important secrets of Government, and to publish all they knew and a little more, by adding surmises to facts, to the great detriment of their country. Consequently, Scott again sailed (late in January, 1833) to

Charleston harbor unheralded, and was in Fort Moultrie for a number of days ere the Charlestonians themselves knew of his presence. Then they first awakened to a realizing sense of their condition: there *were* means, at the disposal of the Federal officers, for *enforcing* the laws, and Scott was to be the instrument of such enforcement.

The nullifiers were extremely angered at this state of affairs, while the Unionists—a strong and powerful party—were delighted. The latter had been somewhat overawed by the violence of the nullifiers, whose party comprised all the worst elements and some of the best elements of the State; but, now that the Government, to which they owed their first allegiance, had shown its ability and *willingness* to protect them, the law and order men came out boldly for the Union and the laws. This threw new force into the excitement, and, before February 1st, the people were waging among themselves a storm of factions which, for a while, threatened bloodshed and all the horrors of civil strife.

During this internecine war the United States officers and troops were extremely cautious not to give cause for any outbursts of violence toward them, on the part of the excited nullifiers. They treated all courteously, and, even rendered such implicit obedience to orders as not to resent indignities frequently offered them in the streets, and on the waters of the harbor.

The 1st of February came, when the belligerents thought it *prudent* to "wait a little longer" before inaugurating the war with Government, and a few of the leading nullifiers of Charleston, therefore, assembled, just before the 1st of February, to agree *not* to enforce the said "ordinance," passed by convention of the whole State, until after the adjournment of Congress (March 3d). So effectually was the whole movement of resistance to authority in the hands of a few men.

Scott played a most delicate and important part in this matter, for with him really rested the issue of peace or blood. One injudicious act—one hasty word—one failure to take advantage of every opportunity offered for pacification—might have proven fatal to all compromise or adjustment except at the bayonet's point. The Government chose most wisely in sending him thither, and the country has ever felt that his wisdom and prudence averted a conflict between the State and the General Government which must have cost all parties dearly.

Alas, that the same wisdom and prudence had not been permitted the control of affairs in 1860!

The fact that a few men in Charleston should temporarily suspend the Ordinance was significant of the popular feeling against it, in defiance of the overwhelming voice for the Convention. And other acts proved that the Calhoun party, though it had obtained the ascendancy, did not control the current, for a great length of time. Thus the Ordinance required citizens of South Carolina to take a test oath of allegiance to the State. This the State Court of Appeals soon set aside[1] as unconstitutional and void because inconsistent with the allegiance of the citizen to the Federal Government. In Greenville district the Union party was in the ascendant and had resolved that the Ordinance must be enforced at the bayonet's point before they would submit to it. Pettigru, Colonel Drayton, and Poinsett led the Union clubs, which, during January, became so powerful as to intimidate the nullifiers more than Scott's troopers could have done. It was apparent to South Carolinians by Feb. 1st, that the Ordinance was exploded without any action on the part of Congress, and the resolve of a few citizens of Charleston not to enforce the mandate of insurrection and rebellion simply was an unauthorized but necessary effort to save nullification from utter default by reason of its non-appearance at the summons!

Circumstances conspired auspiciously, however, to help the "fire eaters" out of their ridiculous dilemma. Virginia, although in the heat of her patriotic zeal for "Southern institutions" she had resolved (in December) to sustain South Carolina, in January resolved differently, by adopting a series of resolutions,[2] for pacification, one of which requested South Carolina to rescind her Ordinance of Nullification; another requested Congress to modify the tariff, and a third appointed a com-

[1] See 2 Hill's South Carolina Reports, i. *State* vs. *Hunt*.

[2] See Niles' Register, vol. 43, page 396.

missioner to proceed to South Carolina to use his influence for conciliation and adjustment. This commissioner, Benjamin W. Leigh, reached Charleston early in February, when the nullifiers were looking most anxiously for some honorable escape from their dilemma. The commissioner was welcomed as a friend. Ex-Governor Hamilton reassembled the Convention, and it was resolved to accept of Virginia's overtures if Congress should abate the revenue—a result so likely to occur that public excitement, even among the most ardent nullifiers, waned rapidly, and the Convention held its informal sessions in Columbia to await the final action of Congress before adjournment, March 3d.

Mr. Calhoun at the very moment of adjournment started in haste for Columbia. Travelling night and day by the most rapid modes of conveyance, he reached the State Capital to find the Convention calmly awaiting their leader's coming. He bore with him the Compromise Act, which the Convention adopted, with a sense of relief, as an honorable adjustment of differences; the Ordinance was rescinded; the militia were disbanded; the blue cockade and palmetto button disappeared; and peace once again settled within Carolina's fair domain.

THE "PATRIOT" WAR.

THE "Patriot" war is still fresh in the memory of thousands living along the northern frontier. Originating, like most revolutions, in the fertile brains of uneasy spirits, it at one time threatened to embroil this Government in serious trouble with Great Britain. The yoke of the English crown never has rested easily upon the French inhabitants of the Canadas. They are, almost without exception, rigid Roman Catholics—the English are Protestant: they are purely Gallic in blood—the English are Anglo-Saxon with a strong admixture of the stern Scotch element: they are clannish, uncompromising, unloyal—the English, equally sectional and obstinate, are loyal to their Queen to the last. It is not strange that such negatives should not assimilate, and it is not a matter of surprise that the French, in Lower Canada, should hatch revolt.

The movement took shape late in 1837, and then broke out into open insurrection. The Canadians in Upper Canada soon caught the infection. The cry of "Freedom and a Confederacy of our own" flew from Quebec to the Georgian wilds. It crossed the frontier to arouse enthusiasm and sympathy. Let the rallying cry only be "Liberty!" and our American population would co-operate in a scheme for invading Siberia, if a leader could be found for such a frigid service. The cry of "Freedom for the Canadas from British domination," awakened the echoes "Aye!" from thousands on this side of the line, and it was not long before arms, provisions, troops and means were passing over the border in aid of the insurgents, who were gathered in much strength, at several points, along the southern shore of the Lakes. Co-operation became open and undisguised, so much so that the President issued a proclamation for order and neutrality. It fell upon ears deadened to authority—"patriotism" was superior to the claims of law and order.

Late in December (1837) one Van Rensselaer organized a troop of "patriots," and passing from Schlosser over to Navy Island (British territory) in the Niagara river, occupied it. The steamer *Caroline* was engaged to transport troops, provisions, etc., to the island, from Schlosser. This movement induced the British to make a descent on the steamer—thus to cut off Van Rensselaer's supplies. Unfortunately they acted unadvisedly, for they entered upon American territory to effect their purpose. The *Caroline* was found at the dock in Schlosser, loaded with a mass of curiosity seekers and a few patriots. The crowd was unarmed, and little resistance was offered save by fists and billets of wood. One citizen was killed and eight wounded in the *melee*. Clearing the steamer of her company, she was cut loose and sent over the Falls (Dec. 27th).

This act excited the entire country, for, beyond doubt, it was a *causus belli*. News of the event reached Washington in a few days, when Major-General Scott was ordered to the frontier to repress trespass from our side, and prevent further aggressions of the British authorities, while our Government took immediate steps to demand atonement of Great Britain for the outrage on the *Caroline*. He hastened to the Niagara frontier accompanied by Governor Marcy, of New York, by whom volunteers were furnished for any emergency which might arise. Scott determined to act to the fullest extent of his authority in suppressing American co-operation with the revolutionists. His sudden appearance on the scene caused considerable stir among the "patriots," who soon became painfully aware of their liability to arrest and imprisonment. In consequence, their movements were considerably restricted, and the spring of the year 1838 found them disorganized and powerless.

Immediately after the affair of the *Caroline*, British troops gathered in considerable force, opposite the western end of Navy Island, where three armed schooners were also anchored, to intercept the passage up the river of the steamer *Barcelona.* This steamer had been taken from Buffalo down to Schlosser for the use of the forces still on Navy Island. Scott had, however, forestalled the "patriots," by chartering her before they could arrange to indemnify her owners from loss. He immediately ordered her to return to Buffalo, at the same time advising the British commander that he should instantly repel any attack made in American waters upon our vessels or citizens. The little steamer came up (January 16th), in the American channel of the river. Scott had anchored a battery opposite the Canadian encampment, prepared to open fire the moment the British should throw a ball at the *Barcelona.* This determined action caused them to let the steamer pass, although fires were lit and matches were ready for the bombardment, on both sides.

The day previous (January 15th) Van Rensselaer and his troop of a few gentlemen and many vagabonds, had recrossed from the island to the American shore, where they were arrested by the U. S. Marshal.

During the winter Scott was tireless in his efforts to appease popular excitement along the frontier, and to prevent infractions of the neutrality laws. He had to co-operate with him Generals Brady, Wool, Worth and Eustis, who were placed in charge of special sections of the border, while he passed to and fro along the entire line, from Detroit to Vermont, exercising his authority, unaided by troops, against a populace determined upon giving aid and comfort to the Canadians. His exertions were crowned with success, so far as to save the Americans from actual trespass. By April the British authorities succeeded in suppressing the revolt for the moment.

Scott acted throughout with great prudence and wisdom, and was freely complimented for his services. Probably no other man in America could have stayed, so effectually, the rush to arms on this side of the border—an act which, if it had not been repressed, would have involved the United States in a war with the British crown. His great personal popularity, his tireless vigilance, his numberless speeches, his firmness and unconquerable will bore all before him; and the revolution in

Canada was paralyzed as much from want of co-operation on this side of the Niagara and the Lakes as from the determined action of the British Government in suppressing the rebellion by force of arms and by banishing the leaders of the movement to Van Dieman's Land.

DORR'S REBELLION.

THIS merely local "Rebellion" deserves mention rather from its peculiar nature than from its importance. Its circumstances were as follows:

Down to 1833 the government of Rhode Island was based upon the original charter of settlement, granted by Charles II. in 1663, by which the elective franchise was restricted to persons possessed of real estate to a specified amount, and to their eldest sons. This disfranchised fully two thirds of the actual citizens. Yet, so prevalent were old prejudices, so powerful old associations, that the Legislature steadily refused to substitute a more modern and republican constitution for the old, but simple and strong government of the Charter. Thomas W. Dorr, an attorney at law, of Providence, and a member of the Assembly, sought to introduce a reform; but, for a long time labored in vain. When brought to a vote his proposition for a change obtained only seven out of seventy votes. Not to be thwarted, Dorr then appealed to the people, agitating the question of change and reform in several mass conventions, held in 1840–41. When the movement had gained sufficient strength, a Convention of Delegates was called, which prepared a State Constitution to be submitted to a regular vote of the people. It obtained 14,000 votes—said to have been a clear majority of the regular citizens of the State. The Chartists pronounced the entire proceedings seditious and declared the vote, illegal as it was, to have been largely fraudulent. Dorr decided otherwise; and, with true Puritan pertinacity, proclaimed the Constitution to be the law of the State. He ordered, accordingly, an election to be held for State officers.

Dorr was chosen Governor, and a Legislature composed exclusively of his supporters, was elected, to meet at Providence on the first Monday of May, 1842. The Charter party also held an election for State officers, polling 5,700 votes, while the suffrage party claimed to have polled 7,300.

On the 3d of May, Dorr's Government attempted to organize at Providence and seize the reins of power. They were resisted by the legal State Government, which assembled at Newport on the same day, and at the head of which was Governor Samuel W. King. Both sides appealed to arms. The excitement was intense, and the people flocked to the respective standards in large numbers from various New England States. Governor King proclaimed the State under martial law, called out the militia and asked and obtained the aid of the United States to suppress the treason. On the 13th of May a portion of the Suffrage party assembled at Providence under arms and attempted to seize the arsenal, but were dispersed by Governor King and a military force. They assembled again, to the number of several hundred, May 25th, 1842, at Chepachet Hill, ten miles from Providence, but again dispersed on the approach of the State forces. Three days afterwards the affair was over. Dorr fled from the State, and took refuge first in Connecticut, and then in New Hampshire. A reward of $4000 being offered for his apprehension by Rhode Island, he voluntarily returned home, was tried, convicted of high treason, and sentenced to imprisonment for life. In 1847 he was pardoned, and, in 1852, the Legislature restored him to his civil rights, and ordered the record of his sentence to be expunged. He lived to see a liberal constitution and his party in possession of the reins of government.

THE KANSAS-NEBRASKA STRUGGLE.

THE early history of the Western States is full of tragedies, but that of Kansas is, literally written in blood. The war of sections which raged within her lines during her territorial term, and the commingled outrage, crime and political wrong through which she passed to attain her present position in the Union have conspired to render her very name synony mous with violence.

To understand fully the nature of the matter it will be necessary to revert to the first legislation affecting her destiny—the Compromise act of 1820.

In 1818 the territory of Missouri, comprising the Northern portion of what was the old French-Spanish domain of Louisiana, came forward with a constitution for admission to the Union as a State. Louisiana, running from the Gulf to as far north as the undefined lines of the great "North West Territory," was purchased from France in 1803, not more to command the entire course of the Mississippi river than to add to the Slave States new territory, by which to preserve their "balance of power" in the Union—by which simply was meant the ascendancy of Slave States in the Congress and the perpetuation of their control exercised over the Executive chair.[1]

[1] It is, as Mr. Everett has stated: "Out of seventy-two years (up to the date of Mr. Lincoln's election) since the organization of this Government the Executive chair has, for sixty-four years, been filled nearly all the time by Southern Presidents, or when not by Southern men, by those possessing the confidence of the South. For a still longer period the controlling influences of the Legislative and Judicial Departments of the Government have centered in the same quarter. Of all the offices in the gift of the central power, in every department, far more than her proportionate share has always been enjoyed by the South."

As slavery existed in the French domain it was with some astonishment that Southern men beheld any opposition to the admission of Missouri because of a slave clause in her constitution. Her admission was opposed for the reason that the act would amount to a recognition of the *right* of slave extension over the Territories of the United States. The anti-Slave States and element had resolved to grant no further "rights" in the matter—holding that slavery was a wrong not to be extended. The South, equally determined, resolved the State should have Slavery if it wanted it, thereby assuming that position which it ever after persistently maintained—of a Slave *right* in the Territories. The issue, thus squarely presented, was met in the House of Representatives by a bill (introduced, Feb. 1819, by Mr. Tallmadge, of New York,) prohibiting Slavery, "except for the punishment of crimes; and that all children born in the said State after the admission thereof into the Union, shall be free at the age of twenty-five years." This passed the House, but was lost in the Senate. For eighteen months the discussion was continued in both branches of Congress with great ability, and not without great excitement, which extended to every section of the Union.

On the one hand, it was contended that the ordinance of 1787, which excluded Slavery from all territory north-west of the river Ohio, was a public recognition of the principles of the people of the United States in regard to the establishment of Slavery in new States and Territories in that region, and that the proposal to establish it in Missouri was a direct violation of those fundamental principles. On the other hand, it was urged that Slavery was incorporated in the system of society when Louisiana was purchased from the French; and that, as the faith of the United States was pledged by treaty to all the inhabitants of that wide domain to maintain their rights and privileges on the same footing with the people of the rest of the country, it would be a violation of that faith and those rights to abolish the institution of Slavery without their consent.

The storm of words and passion which followed baffles description. It was the South struggling for supremacy against a North already much the stronger. Threats were freely uttered of a dissevered Union. Tallmadge, as the leader of his section, dauntlessly replied:

"Sir, has it already come to this: that in the Congress of the United States—that, in the Legislative councils of Republican America, the subject of slavery has become a subject of so much feeling—of such delicacy—of such danger that it cannot safely be discussed? Are members who venture to express their sentiments on this subject, to be accused of talking to the galleries, with intention to excite a servile war; and of meriting the fate of Arbuthnot and Ambrister? Are we to be told of the dissolution of the Union,, of civil war and of seas of blood?

"Sir, extend your view across the Mississippi, over your newly acquired Territory—a Territory so far surpassing in extent, the limits of your present country, that country which gave birth to your nation—which achieved your Revolution—consolidated your Union—formed your Constitution, and has subsequently acquired so much glory, hangs but as an appendage to the extended empire over which your Republican Government is now called to bear sway. Look down the long vista of futurity; see your empire, in extent unequaled, in advantageous situation without a parallel, and occupying all the valuable part of one continent. Behold this extended empire, inhabited by the hardy sons of American freemen, knowing their rights, and inheriting the will to protect them—owners of the soil on which they live, and interested in the institutions which they labor to defend; with two oceans laving your shores, and tributary to your purposes, bearing on their bosoms the commerce of our people; compared to yours, the governments of Europe dwindle into insignificance, and the whole world is without a parallel. But, sir, reverse this scene; people this fair domain with the slaves of your planters; extend *Slavery*, this bane of man, this abomination of heaven, over your extended empire, and you prepare its dissolution; you turn its accumulated strength into positive weakness; you cherish a canker in your breast; you put poison in your own bosom; you place a vulture preying on your own heart—nay, you whet the dagger, and place it in the hands of a portion of your population, stimulated to use it by every tie, human and divine. The envious contrast between your happiness and their misery, between your liberty and their slavery, must constantly prompt them to accomplish your destruction. Your enemies will learn the source and the cause of your weakness. As often as external dangers shall threaten, or internal commotions await you, you will then realize that, by your own procurement, you have planted amidst your families, and in the bosom of your country, a population producing at once the greatest cause of individual danger, and of national weakness. With this defect, your Government must crumble to pieces, and your people become the scoff of the world."

This illustrates the spirit which, at that day, swayed the hearts of the people of both sections. On the part of the South were extreme violence of threat and vituperation; on the part of the North a resolve neither to be cajoled nor bullied into a recognition of the right of Slavery extension.

This struggle was revived at the next session of Congress—debates during December 1819 and January 1820 being very acrimonious, with no prospect of agreement. Mr. Thomas, of Illinois, then came forward with a 'compromise' measure, proposing to admit Missouri as a Slave State, but, as compensation to the North therefor, to exclude the institution forever, north of the parallel of 36° 30'. The act contained this section:

"That in all that Territory ceded by France to the United States under the name of Louisiana, which lies north of thirty-six degrees thirty minutes north latitude, excepting only such part thereof as is included within the limits of the State contemplated by this act, Slavery and involuntary servitude, otherwise than in the punishment of crime where of the party shall have been duly convicted, shall be and is hereby forever prohibited."

This was acquiesced in by the Free State members, after a further resistance, as a settlement of the vexed question; and it was supposed, on all sides, that there would be no more agitation in regard to Slavery. The act gave up to Slavery the region, now embraced in Arkansas, which, in 1836, was admitted as a Slave State without a word of demur because the act of 1820 had settled the matter forever. A second excitement occurred when, in November, 1820, the State Constitution of Missouri was presented for approval. It contained, among other clauses, one preventing the emigration to the State, for residence or settlement, of free men of color. This exclusion was offensive to those States wherein colored men, under various qualifications, had obtained rights of citizenship. The statute provision, therefore, amounted to a prohibition for citizens of certain States to enter the limits of Missouri. This fire-brand was extinguished by Henry Clay, who interposed a kind of straw compromise—exacting of the Missouri Legislature a pledge that "no advantage should be taken of its Constitution"! and that it should pass no act 'to exclude any of the *citizens* of either of the States' from the enjoyment of the privileges they enjoy under the Constitution of the United States.' [1] This most remarkable, and, in many respects, preposterous collocation of words, was accepted by members enough to constitute a majority, and thus Missouri came into the Union. The vote was: in the House, 86 to 82; in the Senate, 28 to 14.

State by State had been added to the South to retain its balance of power and to maintain its supremacy, at least in the Senate. Kentucky was ceded by Virginia to "independence" in order to make an additional Slave State. Alabama and Mississippi were purchased from the Indians and Georgia [see page 391] for the same express purpose; Tennessee was set off from North Carolina that the same result might follow; then Louisiana was secured, and admitted; after the severe struggle of 1820–21, she succeeded in contributing two more States to the Slave section; then the Florida swamps and lagunes were absorbed and purchased from Spain to add its quota of two slave members to the United States Senate.

But, in spite of these enormous accessions, the South was doomed to a minority in Congress unless *more* Slave States could be secured. The steady prosperity and rapid developement of the Free States threatened to overcome this territorial aggrandisement of the Slave section by the mere force of preponderating masses, and the census of 1840 came, with its startling array of figures, like a hand writing on the wall to "Southern institutions." What remained for the South but final abjuration of its minority rule? More territory must be secured or all was lost. To the North the Slave owners could not go, since Jefferson's beneficent act of 1798 prohibited them from the entire North-west Territory, and the sentiment of the

---

[1] What "rights" did the black man then "enjoy under the Constitution"? If he enjoyed any "right" how could Missouri deprive him of it? Therefore the preposterous character of the "compromise." The other features of the compromise—a *pledge* that the Legislature should not take advantage of *its own Constitution* was, in law, an absurdity. What had the *Legislature* to do with its State Constitution? A provision to exclude negroes could be enforced by any petty officer or citizen, and the Legislature could not help itself! That this "compromise" satisfied a majority proves how easily some men's scruples are put at rest. The compromise introduced by Mr. Thomas was understood to have emanated from Mr. Clay. It was worthy the name of 'compromise'; but, the last arrangement to overcome an objection may truly be characterised as absurd.

people there was extremely hostile to a slave system. To the West they could not proceed, for Government had pledged that section to the Indians. Conquest alone must come to the rescue. Texas, an immense domain, fitted to make five States, must be won. The scheme of its "annexation" was soon conceived and perfected. War was declared upon a flimsy pretext against a weak and distracted neighbor. One hundred millions of dollars were spent, and Texas was given over to the Slave power to be made into States, as emergencies should require; while New Mexico, with her boundless plains, lay to the west, to await the necessity for her introduction to a slave proprietary.

But, even this absorption of an empire did not suffice. The census of 1850 again sent consternation into the "balance of power" ranks, and excited their leaders to renewed zeal. More territory *must* be had, at any sacrifice. Kansas and Nebraska alone offered the soil, but there stood that Gibraltar, the "Compromise Act" of 1821, guaranteeing all that region to *Freedom* FOREVER. Still, the emergency was imperative. Kansas at least must be represented on the floors of Congress by a slave delegation. The tremendous expansion of the North, in Iowa, Wisconsin, Michigan and Minnesota, threatened, by its astonishing vigor, to leap at once into an uncontrolled majority. Kansas lost, all was lost, since Texas could not, for years, gain population enough to allow of her subdivision into several States. The scheme was, hence, matured for the repeal of the Compromise Act. The ground to be taken was first, its unconstitutionality, despite its acceptance by a Southern 'Democratic' President and the endorsement by his Cabinet; second, its non-recognition of the *right* of the South in the Territories; third, the right of the people of a Territory to make their own laws and to choose their own institutions. The sole intent of the South, in abrogating the Compromise, was territorial aggrandisement, thus to preserve its superiority in the Senate;[1]

[1] The fortunes of war placed the country in possession of many letters and documents which the Southern leaders doubtless never designed should have publicity. We have had occasion already to quote from several of such "closet confessions." In a letter written by Mr. Toombs, of Georgia, dated Washington, May 21st, 1858,

but, to render a repeal of a time-honored contract palatable, some *popular* issue was necessary—some plea to commend it to the masses and thus to control them at the ballot box. This was found in the idea of "Squatter Sovereignty"—the right of the people of a *Territory* to choose their own institutions—slaves, polygamy or whatever might be to their taste. With this the question of repeal was sprung upon Congress—U. S. Senator Stephen A. Douglas, as Chairman of the Committee on Territories, becoming sponsor for the new child of politics.

One of Mr. Douglas' biographers disclaims for the Illinois Senator the credit or discredit of originality for the measure. He says: "Though Mr. Douglas has gained all the credit and all the opprobrium of the 'Nebraska Bill,' and to a great extent his name is more prominently associated with that, than with any previous act of public interest, the truth is, that the Kansas-Nebraska Act and its repeal of the Missouri restriction was not an original measure. It was but a second volume in the history of the struggle for popular right, commenced in the contest over the Compromise of 1850; it was but another act in the grand drama which in 1850 had ended with a full recognition of the freedom of the American people, whether in State or Territory, to regulate their own domestic relations without interference by Congress. The Kansas-Nebraska Act was nothing more nor less than an act to extend to the people of Kansas and Nebraska the same rights and privileges which, in 1850,

---

occurs this passage: "When the results of the Mexican war brought us new territory, and undoubtedly what is called 'free territory,' the North asserted and endeavored to maintain the right to exclude slavery therefrom by act of Congress, called sometimes 'the Ordinance of 1787,' at others, 'Missouri Restrictions or Compromise,' and again, 'the Wilmot Proviso.' Under all these names the substance was the same—*i. e.*, the prohibition of slavery in the Territories. The whole whig party of the North and all of the democrats, except about half a dozen, held this doctrine ten years ago; and as late as the opening of the sessions of 1849–50, a large majority of the House of Representatives held it. In 1850 we only defeated the application of the principle of prohibition to the new Territories while they continued in their territorial condition, and maintained the doctrine that when they came into the Union they might come in with or without slavery, as their constitutions might prescribe. In 1854 we advanced a step further, and repealed the prohibition in all the Louisiana purchase lying north of 30 degrees 30 minutes north latitude, while in a territorial state; reaffirmed the principle of 1850 as to State constitutions."

by the advice, by the aid and support of the patriot, Henry Clay, had been extended to the people of Utah and New Mexico." Yet the biographer confesses the Senator's responsibility of authorship, saying: "Whatever question or doubt may have existed or may now exist as to the authorship of the Compromise Acts of 1850 respecting the Territories, there is not the slightest question as to where the responsibility—the honor or blame, the credit or odium—for the Kansas-Nebraska Act, belongs. No one has denied that to Stephen A. Douglas belongs whatever fame that justly attaches to an act of legislation, which has been more celebrated (for the censure by its enemies, and praise by its friends) than any act of Congress since the foundation of the Government. During its pendency it was used as a pretext by the fanatics of the North for the wildest exhibition of ungovernable fury. It drew upon its author the most unbounded abuse and denunciation; while it was pending in Congress a storm, such as has never been known in the political annals of the country was gathering, and it broke with all its force upon his head. Undismayed by threats, he followed the chart that he had laid down, and has lived to see himself the political hero and leader of his own party in all those States where the storm beat fastest and raged the fiercest."

The picture here presented, of the excitement which grew out of the measure, is not overdrawn. Its remembrance is still vividly fresh in our minds. We can hardly class it among the things of the past, since it seems, by some scarcely definable process, to have become part and substance of the tremendous outburst of elements which, in 1860–61, shook the foundations of the Republic to their very base. The bill reported by Mr. Douglas (Jan. 4th, 1854) was a modification of one introduced to the Senate, by Mr. Dodge, of Iowa, Dec. 14th, 1853, proposing to organize all territory north of 36° 30′, south of 43° 30′ and west of Iowa to the summit of the Rocky Mountains into the Territory of Nebraska. Mr. Douglas' bill met with stern opposition and underwent much change, until finally he introduced the bill organizing, out of the country specified, the Territories of Kansas and Nebraska, and abrogating, in express words, the Missouri restriction. As finally adopted (May 25th, 1854) the act contained this clause:

"That the Constitution and all the laws of the United States which are not locally inapplicable, shall have the same force and effect within the said Territory of Nebraska, as elsewhere within the United States, except the eighth section of the act preparatory to the admission of Missouri into the Union, approved March sixth, eighteen hundred and twenty, which being inconsistent with the principles of non-intervention by Congress with Slavery in the States and Territories, as recognized by the legislation of eighteen hundred and fifty, commonly called the Compromise Measures, is hereby declared inoperative and void; it being the true intent and meaning of this act not to legislate Slavery into any Territory or State, nor to exclude it therefrom, but to leave the people thereof perfectly free to form and regulate their domestic institutions in their own way, subject only to the Constitution of the United States; Provided, That nothing herein contained shall be construed to revive or put in force any law or regulation which may have existed prior to the act of sixth of March, eighteen hundred and twenty, either protecting, establishing, prohibiting or abolishing Slavery." [1]

This act was signed by President Pierce May 30th, and thus became law. The country in both sections (slave and free) was thoroughly alive to the crisis. The South, with the aid of the Northern Democracy, had opened to slavery soil guaranteed, by solemn contract, to freedom forever. Nothing therefore remained for the North, if it would save the soil to freedom and a Free State representation in Congress, but to avail of the "Squatter Sovereignty" clause, and, by peopling the Territory with Northern men, to thwart the Southern intriguants. From every section of New England, from New York, from Ohio and her sister States, the cry went up: "Ho! for

[1] Singular as it may appear the Missouri "restriction" had been overridden, years before—proving that, practically, the act was inoperative. June 7th, 1836, a bill was crowded through both Houses of Congress, almost unnoticed, ceding to Missouri a triangular district of land lying west of the Missouri river, out of which six counties were constituted. The district was, of course, free soil by virtue of the Compromise Act; yet, it was deliberately absorbed by Missouri, the Indian titles extinguished at heavy cost by the General Government, and soon became one of the most populous *slave* sections of the whole State. It played a leading part in the Kansas war by supplying that horde whose brutal interference at the ballot-box, whose blockade of the Missouri river, and whose relentless persecution of Free State emigrants, won for them the appellation of "Border Ruffians." A more ignorant and thoroughly cruel class of "citizens" never cursed any community with their malign presence.

Kansas!" and soon a strong tide of emigration set in for the new Territories, chiefly by way of the Missouri river. This emigration was encouraged by the formation, in New England and Ohio particularly, of "Emigrant Aid Societies," which supplied means for all who chose to people the new country, secured the land, and assisted in developing the soil until its settlers should be self-sustaining. The town of Lawrence was founded, August 1st, by thirty persons, members of one of these societies, and thereafter became a kind of nucleus of settlement around which, in constantly extending circles, the Free State men gathered.

But, the South was not idle. The very act of dividing the Territory into Nebraska and Kansas was designed to make the latter a Slave State, as, by the nature of its climate and soil, Nebraska must become a Free State. Says Gihon, in his "History of Kansas:" "Many members of the pro-slavery party, believing it to have been a matter understood and fixed by certain contracting powers and the heads of the General Government, that Kansas was to become a Slave State, in order to keep up an equilibrium of Northern and Southern sectional and political interests, conscientiously supposed that, instead of its being a criminal offense, it was not only justifiable, but a virtue, to persecute, even to death, all Northern people who should enter the Territory with a disposition to defeat or thwart that object. All such were regarded as intruders, whom it was proper to remove at all hazards and by whatever means, however cruel or oppressive, that could be employed. This sentiment was not confined to Kansas and the adjoining State of Missouri, but was entertained by persons high in authority elsewhere, and especially at the seat of the Federal Government. By many it was freely acknowledged and boldly advocated."

The inhabitants of the border counties of Missouri had not been slow to avail themselves of Kansas' fertile fields. Immediately after the passage of the Act they crossed over the border and "squatted" great farms, upon the soil of which the Indian titles had not yet been extinguished. Soon discovering that Free State men were passing into the Territory, these Missouri guardians of the public weal convened at Westport, Missouri, early in July, organised into an association and passed the following:

"Resolved, That this association will, whenever called upon by any of the citizens of Kansas Territory, hold itself in readiness together to assist to remove any and all emigrants who go there under the auspices of the Northern emigrant aid societies.

"Resolved, That we recommend to the citizens of other counties, particularly those bordering on Kansas Territory, to adopt regulations similar to those of this association, and to indicate their readiness to operate in the objects of this first resolution."

Succeeding this meeting were others, at which originated secret societies of a seditious character, designed to interfere with the Northern settlers, by violence and persecution. Says the Report of the Congressional Committee on the Kansas Outrages:

"About the same time, and before any election was or could be held in the Territory, a secret political society was formed in the State of Missouri. It was known by different names, such as 'Social Band,' 'Friends' Society,' 'Blue Lodge,' 'The Sons of the South.' Its members were bound together by secret oaths, and they had passwords, signs and grips, by which they were known to each other. Penalties were imposed for violating the rules and secrets of the Order. Written minutes were kept of the proceedings of the Lodges, and the different Lodges were connected together by an effective organization. It embraced great numbers of the citizens of Missouri, and was extended into other Slave States and into the Territory. Its avowed purpose was not only to extend Slavery into Kansas, but also into other territory of the United States; and to form a union of all the friends of that institution. Its plan of operating was to organize and send men to vote at the elections in the Territory, to collect money to pay their expensès, and, if necessary. to protect them in voting. It also proposed to induce pro-slavery men to emigrate into the Territory, to aid and sustain them while there, and to elect none to office but those friendly to their views. This dangerous society was controlled by men who avowed their purpose to extend Slavery into the Territory at all hazards, and was altogether the most effective instrument in organizing the subsequent armed invasions and forays. In the Lodges in Missouri, the affairs of Kansas were discussed, the force necessary to control the election was divided into bands, and leaders selected; means were collected, and signs and badges were agreed upon. While the great body of the actual settlers of the Territory were relying upon the rights secured to them by the organic law, and had formed no organization or combination whatever, this conspiracy against their rights was gathering strength in Missouri, and would have been sufficient at their first election to have overpowered them, if they had been united to a man."

These meetings and secret organizations were abetted by the press of Western Missouri, whose editorials, in their own peculiar style of 'bowie knife rhetoric,' called upon Missourians to exterminate the "invaders." Under their influence many bad deeds were perpetrated which, otherwise, never would have been conceived. What could be expected of a people, notoriously addicted to whiskey, fast horses and negro trading, when the press applauded their ruffianism as "devotion to the South"?

In spite of these proceedings Northern men daily made their way into the Territory, chiefly by the river. During October, however, the Missourians offered such outrages to the emigrants—taking from them, first their arms, then their goods—that river travel was quite suspended, and even supplies were denied a transit except through well known 'Southern' hands for 'Southern' towns. The emigrants then were compelled to take the overland journey through Iowa and Nebraska—a tedious and expensive route, but one used freely during the spring and summer of 1855.

In pursuance of the policy indicated, President Pierce appointed to territorial offices men of undoubted "Democratic" sympathies. Andrew H. Reeder, the first Governor, arrived at Fort Leavenworth October 6th, to find a state of affairs quite distracted enough to distract him. Two parties were in the field contesting for the supremacy—one composed of Free State men, another of pro-slavery propagandists. The first was quiet but determined; the other violent and ready for any deed of blood against what they termed "Northern aggression." It was in vain that Governor Reeder plead the right of Northern men, under the organic act, to settle the Territory. According to the Southern sentiment Kansas was not designed for a Free State, therefore free-soilers had no rights there which Southern men were bound to respect. Reeder, though a Democrat of sterling faith, and devoted to administration interests, could not yield to the proscriptive and outrageous faction then led by one John W. Whitfield, an Indian Agent and employee of the General Government, whose sentiments were expressed in one of his popular harangues, as follows:

> "We can recognise but two parties in the Territory—the pro-slavery and the anti-slavery parties. If the citizens of Kansas want to live in this community at peace and feel at home, they *must* become pro-slavery men; but if they want to live with gangs of thieves and robbers, they must go with the abolition party. There can be no third party—no more than two issues—slavery and no slavery, in Kansas Territory."

The first election for delegate to Congress, was appointed for Nov. 29th, 1854. The Territory was divided into seventeen election districts. At the appointed time voting took place with a result disagreeably illustrative of the operation of 'squatter sovereignty.' Of two thousand eight hundred and seventy-one votes cast, one thousand seven hundred and twenty-nine were afterwards ascertained to have been illegal! Thus, district No. II., with a census of thirty-five legal voters, cast two hundred and thirty-five votes for Whitfield, the pro-slavery candidate; district No. IV., having thirty legal voters, cast one hundred and forty votes for Whitfield; district No. VII., having twenty legal voters, cast five hundred and ninety-seven votes for Whitfield! Of course Whitfield was "elected," and he went to Washington as the accredited delegate to represent the interests of his constituents. These illegal votes were polled by Missourians, or the boxes were simply "stuffed," and false lists returned. This course was determined upon before hand. For two weeks prior to the election Western Missouri (the old triangle and river counties) was canvassed by David R. Atchison (ex-Democratic Vice President of the United States) and by "General" B. F. Stringfellow, who openly called upon the people of Missouri to "enter every election district in Kansas, in defiance of Reeder and his vile myrmidoms, and vote at the point of the bowie knife and revolver"; "it was enough that the slave-holding interest wills it, from which there is no appeal"; for, if the Free State men should triumph "then Missouri and the other Southern States will have shown themselves recreant to their interests and will deserve their fate." These words reveal as once the baseness of the fraud perpetrated and the design of that fraud—to make Kansas a Slave State at all hazards.

It was not until *after* this invasion by "Border Ruffians" that blood began to be shed. Up to that period much violence had been shown and many outrages committed. The town of Lawrence had been approached by a considerable body of Missourians, bent upon its destruction, but they had been intimidated by the preparations to receive them. Free State men generally stood upon the defensive, and, in but few instances, up to Dec. 1st, resented the indignities put upon them. After that date, however, the 'hatchet was dug up,' and a war was waged whose details it is sickening to record. Robbery, pillage, arson, murder, became matters of frequent occurrence, increasing in number and atrocity as the months passed; and the struggle only ended when the Free State element became so overwhelmingly in the ascendant, during 1857, as to render Rorder Ruffian presence and Executive baseness no longer dangerous. Dr. John H. Stringfellow, having a paper at his command, published at Atcheson, Kansas, thus expressed the determination of the Southern men:

"We can tell the impertinent scoundrels of the *N. Y. Tribune* that they may exhaust an ocean of ink, their Emigrant Aid Societies spend their millions and billions, their representatives in Congress spout their heretical theories till doomsday, and His Excellency Franklin Pierce appoint abolitionist after free soiler as our Governor, *yet we will continue to lynch and hang*, to tar and feather, and drown every white-livered abolitionist who dares to pollute our soil."

Here we have the true animus of that class against whom the Northern settlers had to contend: *to lynch and hang, tar and feather*," became their conception of law. These inhuman announcements, and the numerous evidences of a settled design, on the part of the Missourians, to keep out and suppress Free State men, elicited, from the authorities at Washington, not a word of reproof, not a sign of warning, not an order to establish and preserve peace. The land was given up passively as slave soil, and Northern immigrants were compelled, if they would save themselves from massacre, to take up arms in their own defense.

[We have explored all avenues of information in public

documents, letters, speeches and written records—we have consulted with men who acted a leading part in the drama, both as Northern and Southern partisans—we have listened to the stories which almost every household along the Missouri and Kansas rivers has to tell—all, to discover a satisfactory *reason* for Presidential complicity with Stringfellow, Titus, Cato and Lecompt. Not a vestige of organic law, not a shadow of constitutional procedure, not a trace of humane regard for human rights, can we elicit from that shocking reign of terror which now stands like a burning spot upon our National honor. Governors rapidly appointed, and as rapidly removed—the refusal to guarantee the sanctity of the ballot box—the uses of the military (regulars) to suppress Free State meetings and to arrest Northern men—the removal of the commander of the department for suspected sympathy with the Northern men—the employment of a band of Georgia desperados as a *posse comitatus* to enforce "obedience"—the instructions issued to the several Governors and the forced misconstruction of them by the National Executive—all are incidental witnesses which no political sorcery can allay: they rise up, along with the ghosts of murdered settlers and their heart broken wives, to impeach the memories of two Presidents with proofs of high crimes against the State and against humanity.]

A second step in the organization of the Territory was the election of a General Assembly. This, Governor Reeder ordered for March 20th, 1856. It was accompanied by incidents well calculated to bring the elective franchise into disgrace. As preliminary to a protection of the people against illegal interference at the ballot box, the Governor ordered a census to be taken (during January and February) of the inhabitants and qualified voters of the Territory. The result was as follows:

Total population	8501
Total voters	2905
Natives of the United States	7161
Of foreign birth	409
Slaves	242
Free negroes	151

Of the election which followed the Congressional Committee spoke as follows:

"On the same day the census was completed, the Governor issued his proclamation for an election to be held on the 30th of March, A. D. 1855, for members of the Legislative Assembly of the Territory. It prescribed the boundaries of the districts, the places for polls, the names of judges, the appointment of members and recited the qualifications of voters. If it had been observed, a just and fair election would have reflected the will of the people of the Territory. Before the election, false and inflammatory rumors were busily circulated among the people of Western Missouri. The number and character of the emigration then passing into the Territory were grossly exaggerated and misrepresented. Through the active exertions of many of its leading citizens, aided by the secret societies before referred to, the passions and prejudices of the people of that State were greatly excited. Several residents there have testified to the character of the reports circulated among and credited by the people. These efforts were successful. By an organized movement, which extended from Andrew county in the north to Jasper county in the south, and as far eastward as Boone and Cole counties, companies of men were arranged in regular parties and sent into every council district in the Territory, and into every representative district but one The numbers were so distributed as to control the election in each district. They went to vote, and with the avowed design to make Kansas a Slave State. They were generally armed and equipped, carried with them their own provisions and tents, and so marched into the Territory. The details of this invasion from the mass of the testimony taken by your committee are so voluminous that we can here state but the leading facts elicited."

These "leading facts" were considered enough to prove to the most incredulous that, in most of the districts, the election was worse than a mockery—it was a crime. So apparent was this from the returns and the known presence of bodies of Missourians, that Governor Reeder felt called upon to order special elections in several of the districts where invasion, box stuffing and forged lists were too undisguised to pass them with Executive sanction. This second election was set for May 22d. Of course it aroused the pro-slavery men to violent opposition. A meeting was held at Leavenworth, April 30th, of those representing "Southern rights." It was, as stated by local papers, "ably and eloquently addressed by Chief Justice Lecompt, Colonel J. N. Burns, of Weston, Missouri, and others"—Judge

F. O. C. Darley del. John Rogers. sc

MISSOURIANS GOING TO KANSAS TO "VOTE".

J. B. Torrey, Publisher 13 Spruce St. New York

Lecompt being Mr. Pierce's appointee to the high office of Chief Justice of the Territory. The meeting resolved:

"That the institution of slavery is known and recognised in this Territory; that we repel the doctrine that it is a moral and political evil, and we turn back with scorn upon its slanderous authors the charge of inhumanity; and we warn all persons not to come to our peaceful firesides to slander us, and sow the seeds of discord between the master and the servant; for, as much as we deprecate the necessity to which we may be driven, we cannot be responsible for the consequences."

And to carry out the resolve a committee of thirty was appointed whose special duty it was to spy out and report all such as should, "by the expression of abolition sentiments produce a disturbance to the quiet of the citizens, or danger to their domestic relations; and all such persons, so offending, shall be notified, and made to leave the Territory." Under the operations of this committee a tyranny was instated as relentless as ever prevailed on a rice plantation. Orders were issued to large numbers of Free State men, who were instructed to leave the Territory in a specified number of days or suffer the penalty of death. Large numbers of settlers were driven from their homes, barely escaping with their wives and children, leaving behind them, to be appropriated by the Southern vagabonds, their homes and property. One case may be cited as an instance. Among those who signed a protest against the election held in Leavenworth (March 20th) was a lawyer named William Phillips. He was, of course, among the first of those "warned" by the self-constituted committee. Whereupon "he was, on the 17th of May, seized by a band of men chiefly from Missouri, who carried him eight miles up the river to Weston, where they shaved one half of his head, tarred and feathered him, rode him on a rail, and sold him at a mock auction by a negro, all of which he bore with manly fortitude and bravery, and then returned to Leavenworth and persisted in remaining, notwithstanding his life was constantly threatened and in danger. He was subsequently murdered in his own house, by a company of 'law and order' men, or 'territorial militia,' under command of Captain Frederick S. Emory, simply for refusing to leave the town." Eight days after this outrage on his person, a second meeting was held in Leavenworth, over which the member elect to the Assembly Council presided. Judge Lecompte again "eloquently addressed" the assembly, and the following resolutions, presented by another member elect to the Assembly, were passed unanimously:

"*Resolved*, That we heartily endorse the action of the committee of citizens that shaved, tarred and feathered, rode on a rail, and had sold by a negro, William Phillips, the moral perjurer.

"*Resolved*, That we return our thanks to the committee for faithfully performing the trust enjoined upon them by the pro-slavery party.

"*Resolved*, That the committee be now discharged.

"*Resolved*, That we severely condemn those pro-slavery men who, from mercenary motives, are calling upon the pro-slavery party to submit without further action.

"*Resolved*, That in order to secure peace and harmony to the community, we now solemnly declare that the pro-slavery party will stand firmly by and carry out the resolutions reported by the committee appointed for that purpose on the memorable 30th."

This local action was responded to very generally by Missourians, and the right of invasion sustained. Numerous meetings were held by them at which addresses were made by prominent citizens. Dr. Gihon, in his "History of Kansas," quotes the following resolves, passed by a large public meeting held in Clay county, Mo., as giving a just impression of the ideas and feeling which prevailed:

"Those who, in our State, would give aid to the abolitionists by inducing or assisting them to settle in Kansas, or would throw obstacles in the way of our friends, by false and slanderous misrepresentations of the acts of those who took part in and contributed to the glorious result of the late election in that Territory, should be driven from amongst us as traitors to their country.

"That we regard the efforts of the Northern division of the Methodist Episcopal Church to establish itself in our State as a violation of her plighted faith, and, plédged as its ministers must be to the anti-slavery principles of that church, we are forced to regard them as enemies to our institutions. We therefore fully concur with our friends in Platte county in resolving to permit no person belonging to the Northern Methodist Church to preach in our county.

"That all persons who are subscribers to papers in the least tinctured with free-soilism or abolitionism, are requested to discontinue them immediately."

Shocking instances of violence occurred against their own citizens. All who ventured to signify a disapproval of these outrages upon Kansas settlers and the ballot box were condemned as enemies to the South and were visited with persecution in various ways. Thus public sentiment was stifled, for few even of the wealthy and influential class cared to court the vengeance of the mob which presumed to hold the destiny of Kansas in its keeping. A newspaper office was mobbed in Parkeville, Platte county, because its venerable editor, Mr. Parke, had, in perfectly respectful terms, condemned the March invasion. The press, types, &c., were thrown into the river and the mob would have killed the assistant editor but for the interference of citizens. Mr. Parke being absent escaped lynching. His assistant was permitted to leave the town under penalty of death should he dare to return. Why did not the Governor of Missouri punish such crimes? Because they were committed in behalf of the Southern cause! Why did not the law abiding citizens arm themselves against such villainy? Because they would have been assassinated, their houses burned, their stock killed, by the incomparable scoundrels who shamed the Camanches in their revelry of wrong doing. Claiborne F. Jackson, afterwards Governor of Missouri, headed one of the companies which invaded District No. I., March 30th. Said the Congressional Committee of this event: "The evening before and the morning of the day of election, about one thousand men from the above counties arrived at Lawrence, and encamped in a ravine a short distance from town, near the place of voting. They came in wagons—of which there were over one hundred—and on horseback, under command of Colonel Samuel Young, of Boone county, Missouri, and Claiborne F. Jackson, of Missouri. They were armed with guns, rifles, pistols and bowie knives, and had tents, music and flags with them. They brought with them two pieces of artillery, loaded with musket balls." It is not a matter of surprise that this Jackson should, as Governor of his State, afterwards have conspired to carry Missouri into the Southern Confederacy. He truly was a fit instrument for any political baseness. The surprise is that a man of his character should have been chosen Governor. Let us hope the day of public prostitution to such representatives of hateful elements is past, for Missouri.

Against this second election numerous protests were entered; and so palpably illegal were the returns that, in such instances as properly signed protests were filed, the Governor refused to issue certificates to members whose election was thus contested. This action resulted, as might have been expected, in excessive swearing on the part of the pro-slavery faction, who denounced Reeder as "an Abolitionist," and who had the base ingratitude to charge upon the President a design to make Kansas a Free State—the cruelest of returns for what the President had done for Southern interests. Notwithstanding these threats, Reeder ordered a third election to be held in six of the contested districts. One of the Missouri papers thereupon exclaimed:

"We learn, just as we go to press, that Reeder has refused to give certificates to four of the Councilmen and thirteen members of the House. He has ordered an election to fill their places on the 22d of May. This infernal scoundrel will have to be hemped yet."

It was determined by the Southern party to let the special election, ordered for May 22d, go by default, as the committee on elections in their Assembly would deny seats to all Free State men elected under it. Only in Leavenworth did the pro-slavery men go to the polls, but there they went only for mischief and the destruction of the ballot box. True to their decision *every man then elected was denied a seat in the Assembly*, which assembled at Pawnee, July 2d, 1855. The committee on elections, under various pretexts, deprived of seats every free-soiler except one, and this one, owing to the personal peril by which he was constantly surrounded, was compelled quickly to resign! This gave the legislation of the territorial organic laws into the hands of the pro-slave propagandists, and the Assembly at once proceeded to the work of "making their own laws and forming their own institutions." It was in session for a term of fifty days, and legislated in that short space of time enough to fill three portly volumes. The laws adopted occupied in bulk over one thousand octavo pages. This would seem to indicate extreme industry as well as executive ability on the part of the Assemblymen; but, when the fact transpired that those "laws" were, simply, an adaptation of the Missouri code, with slight alterations and a few most scandalous additions, we are undeceived as to the character and ability of that legislative body. Referring to these extraordinary proceedings in organizing the Territory, the Congressional Committee state:

"The material differences in the Missouri and Kansas statutes are upon the following subjects: The qualifications of voters and of members of the Legislative Assembly; the official oath of all officers, attorneys and voters; the mode of selecting officers and their qualifications; the slave code, and the qualifications of jurors.

"Upon these subjects, the provisions of the Missouri code are such as are usual in many of the States. But by the 'Kansas Statutes' *every office in the Territory, executive and judicial, was to be appointed by the Legislature, or by some officer appointed by it.* These appointments were not merely to meet a temporary exigency, but were to hold over two regular elections, and until after the general election in October, 1857, at which the members of the new council were to be elected. The new Legislature is required to meet on the first Monday in January, 1858. Thus, by the terms of these "laws," the people have no control whatever over either the Legislature, the executive or the judicial departments of the Territorial Government until a time before which, by the natural progress of population, the Territorial Government will be superseded by a State Government.

"No session of the Legislature is to be held during 1856, but the members of the House are to be elected in October of that year. A candidate, to be eligible at this election, must swear to support the fugitive slave law; and each voter, if challenged, must take the same oath. The same oath is required of every officer elected or appointed in the Territory, and of every attorney admitted to practice in the courts.

"A portion of the militia is required to muster on the day of election. 'Every free white male citizen of the United States, and every free male Indian who is made a citizen by treaty or otherwise, and over the age of twenty-one years, and who shall be an inhabitant of the Territory and of the county and district in which he offers to vote, and shall have paid a Territorial tax, shall be a qualified elector for all elective offices.' Two classes of persons were thus excluded, who by the organic act were allowed to vote, viz.: those who would not swear to the oath required, and those of foreign birth who had declared on oath their intention to become citizens. Any man of proper age who was in the Territory on the day of election, and who had paid one dollar as a tax to the Sheriff, who was required to be at the polls to receive it, could vote as an 'inhabitant,' although he had breakfasted in Missouri, and intended to return there for supper. There can be no doubt that this unusual and unconstitutional provision was inserted to prevent a full and fair expression of the popular will in the election of members of the House, or to control it by non-residents.

"All jurors are required to be selected by the Sheriff, and 'no person who is conscientiously opposed to the holding of slaves, or who does not admit the right of holding slaves in the Territory, shall be a juror in any cause' affecting the right to hold slaves, or relating to slave property."

It is not in the order of human events that men, in whose breasts remain one spark of self respect, should submit, as subjects, to such shocking perversions of law.[1] We should have been surprised had the Free State settlers tamely abandoned, in that crisis, all their hopes and their rights under the Kansas-Nebraska Act. They moved quietly and resolutely forward, in the *only* path open for escape from lawlessness and usurpation. After the invasion of March 30th, they circulated for signatures a memorial to Congress, citing, with graphic force

---

[1] John M. Clayton, U. S. Senator from the State of Delaware, afterwards referring to these laws thus characterised them: "Now, Sir, let me allude to that subcect which is the great cause of all this discord between the two Houses. The unjust, iniquitous, oppressive and infamous laws enacted by the Kansas Legislature, as it is called, ought to be repealed before we adjourn. * * * What are these laws? One of them sends a man to hard labor for not less than two years for daring to discuss the question whether Slavery exists or does not exist in Kansas: not less than two years—it may be fifty; and if a man could live to be as old as Mathuselah, it might be over nine hundred years. That act prohibits all freedom of discussion in Kansas, on the great subject directly referred to the exclusive decision of the people in that Territory; strikes down the liberty of the press, too; and is an act egregiously tyrannical as ever was attempted by any of the Stuarts, Tudors or Plantagenets of England, and this Senate persists in declaring that we are not to repeal that!

"Sir, let us tender to the House of Representatives the repeal of that and of all other objectionable and infamous laws that were passed by that Legislature. I include in this denunciation, without any hesitation, those acts which prescribe that a man shall not even practice law in the Territory unless he swears to support the Fugitive Slave Law; that he shall not vote at any election, or be a member of the Legislature, unless he swears to support the Fugitive Slave Law; that he shall not hold any office of honor or trust there, unless he swears to support the Fugitive Slave Law; and you may as well impose just such a test oath for any other and every other law. * * * I will not go through the whole catalogue of the oppressive laws of this Territory. I have done that before to-day. There are others as bad as those to which I have now referred. * * * I will not, on the other hand, ever degrade myself by standing for an instant by those abominable and infamous laws which I denounced here this morning. What I desire now is, that the Senate of the United States shall wash its hands of all participation in these iniquities by repealing those laws."

and much minuteness of specification, the wrongs and disabilities put upon them, praying for relief. And when the character of the Assembly legislation became apparent the Northern settlers resolved to initiate a movement for the formation of a *State* Government, and to apply for admission at the coming session of Congress. Meetings were held in various localities, when the subject was canvassed in a thorough manner. No violence was betrayed in their proceeding—only a spirit of determination to preserve their rights under the Constitution against the tyranny of Missourian and outside interference. A mass convention of Free State citizens and actual settlers was held at Lawrence, August 15th, 1855. A large representation of the best inhabitants of the Territory was present. The following were adopted:

"Whereas, The people of Kansas have been, since its settlement, and now are, without any law-making power, therefore be it

"Resolved, That we, the people of Kansas Territory, in masi meeting assembled, irrespective of party distinctions, influenced by common necessity, and greatly desirous of promoting the common good, do hereby call upon and request all *bona fide* citizens of Kansas Territory, of whatever political views and predilections, to consult together in their respective Election Districts and in mass conventions or otherwise, elect three delegates for each representative to which said Election District is entitled in the House of Representatives of the Legislative Assembly, by proclamation of Governor Reeder, of date 19th of March, 1855; said delegates to assemble in convention, at the town of Topeka, on the 19th day of September, 1855, then and there to consider and determine upon all subjects of public interest, and particularly upon that having reference to the speedy formation of a State Constitution, with an intention of an immediate application to be admitted as a State into the Union of the United States of America."

This action was endorsed by other assemblies of settlers and *bona fide* inhabitants, and delegates formally elected as designated. The convention met at Topeka, Sept. 19th, 1855, and proceeded in regular form, to the work of preliminary organization for a State Government. An Executive Committee, composed of seven leading and able citizens, was named and duly authorized, under prescribed regulations, to take steps for an election to be held on the second Tuesday of October following "for members of a Convention to form a Constitution, adopt a Bill of Rights for the people of Kansas, and take all needful measures for organizing a State Government preparatory to the admission of Kansas into the Union as a State." This Committee acted promptly, by issuing a proclamation addressed to the legal voters of Kansas, requesting them to meet at their several precincts, at the time and places named in the proclamation, then and there to cast their ballots for members of a Constitutional Convention, to meet at Topeka on the 4th Tuesday of October following. The proclamation also designated the places of elections, appointed judges, recited the qualifications of voters and the apportionment of members of the Convention. This call and action were responded to, by the *actual settlers*, with great unanimity. Proof upon this point appears to be incontestible. The inhabitants felt that it was the lawful way to proceed, and all entered into the election with great good spirit. These elections passed off with harmony, very full votes being polled in every district except two, where pro-slavery feeling reigned triumphant under the rule of a floating mob having no visible means of support nor any claims to citizenship except their temporary presence on Kansas soil. According to regulations prescribed, the Executive Committee proclaimed the results of that election, and issued an order requiring the members elect to convene at Topeka, October 23d, 1855, as a "Constitutional Convention," duly elected and legally constituted. The Convention accordingly met, and addressed itself to the work of forming a State Constitution. This being accomplished a respectful memorial was addressed to Congress praying for the admission of Kansas to the Union, under the Constitution adopted. As preliminary to this application to Congress, the Constitution was submitted to a vote of the people Dec. 15th, 1855, with a result as follows: For Constitution 1731—against 46; for General Banking Law 1120—against 564; for Exclusion of Negroes and Mulattoes from rights of citizenship 1287—against exclusion 453; total number of votes cast 1778. In Leavenworth the poll book was destroyed. After this acceptance an election was ordered by the Executive Committee for State Officers (to be held Jan. 15th, 1856) and for members of a General Assembly.

This was duly held and the result announced, *pro forma*, by the Committee. The members elect met at Topeka, March 1st, 1856, and organized the first General Assembly. Dr. Charles Robinson, Governor elect, took the oath of office. An election of United Senators was held, by which ex-Governor Reeder and James H. Lane were chosen to take their seats when the State should be admitted to the Union. After transacting much important business the Assembly adjourned, to meet again on the 4th of July following.

The reader is now in possession of the leading facts concerning the organization of the two Governments, Territorial and State. One, done under the apparent sanction of the Organic Act was, in reality, in contravention of the entire spirit of our democratic institutions. The other, without appealing to the Organic Act for authority, proceeded, in the usual form, to organize a government and to apply for admission to the Union directly as a State. That the latter represented a majority of the *actual settlers* of Kansas—the men who have since constituted the State's best population, has not been successfully denied. That the former was the offspring of fraud and outrage upon the elective franchise is equally unquestionable.

The Pawnee Assembly so legislated as to strip the Governor of power to do "the cause" harm. They made, as we have seen, territorial offices legislative appointments so far as it was possible to do so under the Organic Act. This was aimed at Reeder, who was regarded by the Missourians as inimical to their proceedings. It was a useless step, however. Reeder was, upon a baseless pretext of land speculation, removed, July 31st, 1855. From that moment, until after October, '57, a period of over two years, as Dr. Gihon truthfully states, "*there was but one man, and he the post-master at Lawrence, who held an office either under the Federal Government or by appointment of the Legislature, or through their agents, who was not in favor of introducing Slavery into the Territory and through any means by which it could be effected!*" This simple fact should be borne in mind, as it is the key that unlocks the Pandora box of mischief which followed.

The Free State movement was taken, as stated, to avert the

calamities threatening. Its proceedings, looking, as they did, to a total evasion of the territorial laws, were met by the pro-slavery partisans with threats of wholesale arrests for treason. Violence was to be expected; yet the movement inaugurated at Lawrence gradually assumed definite shape. On the 9th of October, 1855, an election for delegates to Congress—ordered by the Executive Committee already referred to—resulted in the election of ex-Governor Reeder, by the vote of 2827. In this election the Southern partisans did not participate. Their election for the same office transpired, by order of the Shawnee Mission Assembly,[1] October 1st, when Whitfield was returned by over three thousand votes—nearly or quite one thousand of them absolutely illegal. These two delegates went on to Washington, in December, but both, though paid mileage fees, were rejected by Congress. The Free State Constitution—accepted Dec. 15th, 1855, by vote of the people thereon—resulted in the gathering at Topeka March 1st of the officers elect of the new government and of the newly elect State Legislature, at which the proceedings already recorded were had.

Governor Reeder was removed July 30th, and Wilson Shannon appointed in his stead. Shannon was then a resident of the Territory, and a partisan of the pro-slave faction. He was a man of bad precedents, dissolute and reckless. Why such a person should have been named to the responsible trust only those in power at Washington manipulating Kansas affairs, can tell. His reign, though brief, was characterised by a perfect confraternity with all the worst elements in the Territory. He addressed himself to the task of suppressing the Free State movement, and soon found an opportunity of calling out "the militia," by which was meant taking into his employ about eight hundred as wretched creatures as ever shouldered a musket. The direct pretext for this act was the rescue, by his friends, from the hands of "Sheriff" Samuel J. Jones, of an old man named Branson, a Free State settler. This man, Jones, upon a "peace" warrant, had arrested and was bearing off to

[1] Pawnee was deserted by vote of the Assembly July 4th, 1855, and Shawnee Mission chosen as the temporary seat of the territorial Government. Reeder vetoed this act of removal, but it was repassed over his veto.

prison, when he was quietly taken from Jones' custody. The facts of the case rendered the arrest one of outrageous impudence. Coleman, a pro-slave ruffian, deliberately and in cold blood shot down a young man named Dow. Branson took the body into his house, from whence it was buried. Coleman, after the horrid deed, fled and placed himself under the *protection* of Sheriff Jones. The murderer had two accomplices, who soon joined him. One of them swore out a peace warrant against Branson, as having threatened his life, and upon this warrant Jones, in company with a band of seven, including the two accomplices to the murder, proceeded to arrest Branson! The Free State men at once rallied and, without violence, rescued their friend. Whereupon Jones called upon Governor Shannon (Nov. 27th) for *three thousand* men to "carry out the laws"! Shannon at once ordered out "Major-General" Wm. P. Richardson, a citizen of Missouri, but also a member of the Kansas Council, and, by virtue of legislative appointment, Major-General of the territorial militia. As there were no "militia" in the Territory the programme was to introduce armed partisans from Missouri. The most outrageous falsehoods were disseminated in regard to the rescue affair and the belligerent attitude of the Free State men. Shannon published numerous orders calculated to fan the excitement, and, on the 29th of Nov. issued his Proclamation calling upon all "good citizens" to come forward to assist him in reclaiming the prisoner. The friends of "law and order"—as the Southern partisans called themselves—spread the alarm. Missouri was expected to furnish men for the crisis. Numerous meetings were held along the border and down the Missouri river to raise "troops for the war." The following circular was scattered, by special expresses, widely over the surrounding counties:

"INDEPENDENCE, Mo., Dec. 2d.

"An express, in at ten o'clock last night, says all the volunteers, ammunition, &c., that can be raised will be needed. The express was forwarded by Governor Shannon to Colonel Woodson, and by Woodson to this place, to be transmitted to various parts of the country. Call a meeting, and do everything you can.

"DRS. MCMURRY AND HENRY."

The Woodson here referred to then was a member of Congress from Missouri but an active promoter of the several "invasions." A second circular was issued as follows, from the same headquarters of patriotism, viz.:

"INDEPENDENCE, Dec. 3, 8 P. M.

"Jones will not make a move until there is sufficient force in the field to ensure success. We have not more than three hundred men in the Territory. You will, therefore, urge all who are interested in the matter to start immediately for the seat of war. There is no doubt in regard to having a fight, and we all know that a great many have complained because they were disappointed heretofore in regard to a fight. Say to them, now is the time to show game, and, if we are defeated this time, the Territory is lost to the South."

These appeals threw into Kansas about fifteen hundred cut-throats ready for the work of "wiping out the Abolitionists." The grand provocation had been offered; and, as the circular last quoted said: "if defeated this time the Territory is lost to the South," it was a question of "Southern rights" to be decided—a State to be lost or won. Shannon, afterwards seeking to exculpate himself from responsibility in this disgusting episode of his reign, said: "These men came to the Wakarusa camp to fight; they did not ask peace; it was war—*war to the knife*. They *would* come; it was impossible to prevent them. What, then, was my policy? Certainly this; to mitigate an evil which it was impossible to suppress, by bringing under military control these irregular and excited forces. This was only to be accomplished by permitting the continuance of the course which had already been adopted, without my knowledge, by Generals Richardson and Strickler; that is, to have the volunteers incorporated, as they came in, into the already organized command. A portion of these men were mostly from Jackson county, Mo., reported themselves to Sheriff Jones, by giving in a list of their names, as willing to serve in his *posse*; and he, after taking legal advice upon the question, determined to receive them. They were accordingly enrolled." And thus these assassins were adopted for the Governor's service. Kansas, for the moment, was at mercy of a mob over whose actions the Governor himself presumed to exercise no direct authority. "Sheriff" Jones alone was their accepted leader, under whose auspices the "Wakarusa War" was to be waged.

Against this fierce horde the Free State men resolved to stand. "Governor" Robinson and "Senator" Lane rapidly gathered at Lawrence a body composed of nearly one thousand men, armed with Sharpe's rifles. Rude fortifications were thrown up on Oread Hill and everything arranged for a defense of the town against the destruction impending. Shannon saw this with dismay. What would the country—the world—say to his complicity in thus exciting a resort to arms? He resolved to call in United States troops (regulars) to preserve the peace, and dispatched urgent appeals to Colonel (afterwards Major-General) Sumner, commanding at Fort Leavenworth, for aid. This step the Southern men of course disapproved, and efforts were made to intercept Shannon's dispatches to Sumner. The U. S. officer resolved, however, not to interfere without orders from the War Department at Washington. Still desirous of preventing a collision, and acting under advice of Sumner, Shannon issued orders to General Richardson and "Sheriff" Jones to proceed no further until he should receive instructions from Washington. The "Sheriff" protested, in a note dated Camp Wakarusa, Dec. 4th, against any delay; he insisted upon orders to go forward and make his "arrests," for which he had prepared a pocket full of warrants. But he was denied such orders; and matters remained in *statu quo*, while various negotiations were pending between Shannon and the Free State leaders, for a peaceful adjustment of differences. This was finally effected, and a document, "done in Lawrence, K. T., Dec. 8th, 1855," signed by Wilson Shannon, Charles Robinson and J. H. Lane, was published, setting forth the terms of treaty adopted. It was a most extraordinary instrument of agreement, if, as Shannon and the pro-slave partisans averred, the Free State men were in rebellion. The Governor, on the 9th, issued orders to Jones and Richardson to disband their forces.[1] To the former he said: "Having made satisfactory arrangements by which all legal processes in your hands, either now

[1] See Executive Documents No. I. 3d session of 34th Congress (1856–7) pages 45 to 173, for the entire correspondence, orders, &c., concerning the "Wakarusa war" and subsequent events up to Nov. 7th, 1856. The documents accompanied by message of Dec. 2d, 1856, comprise the entire correspondence and dispatches of Shannon and a portion of those of his successor, Governor Geary.

or hereafter, may be served without the aid of your present *posse*, you are hereby required to disband the same." On the same day the Governor announced the following:

"*To C. Robinson and J. H. Lane, Commanders of the Enrolled Citizens of Lawrence:*

"You are hereby authorized and directed to take such measures and use the enrolled forces under your command in such manner, for the preservation of the peace and the protection of the persons and property of the people in Lawrence and its vicinity, as in your judgment shall best secure that end. WILSON SHANNON.

"Lawrence, Dec. 9th, 1855."

Considering the late call to arms, and the Governor's proclamation of Nov. 29th, denouncing the "numerous associations of lawless men, armed with deadly weapons and supplied with all the implements of war, combined and confederated together for the avowed purpose of opposing by force and violence, the execution of the laws of this Territory," this latter authorization and the disbanding of the Southern *posse* was a most remarkable evidence of the Governor's weakness or of the Free State strength. The *posse* disbanded in rage and disgust, making open threats that they soon would see town in ashes, in spite of Shannon.

To the personal rencontres, the combats of parties representing the two elements of discord, the house burnings and outrages perpetrated upon persons and property we cannot advert. Their briefest mention would necessitate a long chapter, whose perusal might gratify a taste craving for excitement, but could not add to the strength or clearness of the record which we desire to present.

The application to Washington for permission to use the U. S. troops was answered satisfactorily. Shannon received, in February, 1856, authority to employ the Federal military to enforce the laws of the Shawnee Legislature—thus confirming that Assembly in its assumptions. The President had, in his annual message Dec. 31st, 1855, and in his special message of Jan. 24th, argued the case of the territorial organization, giving to the Southern men the most unqualified sympathy in their struggle with "fanaticism." His last message, indeed, read as if it had emanated from Messrs. Atcheson and Stringfellow—so strongly did it condemn the movement and programme of the Free State settlers. He followed this up with a proclamation denouncing the acts of the Topeka Convention and setting forth the territorial or Shawnee Mission Assembly as the only legal legislative power of the Territory. Orders were sent forward to the Western Military department for its commander to sustain Shannon in his efforts to enforce the laws of the Shawnee Assembly and to suppress the Topeka convocation. This action was sustained, in the Senate, by the majority report made by Mr. Douglas, March 12th, 1856, from the Committee on Territories, to which had been referred the special message on Kansas affairs. In this report the President's view of matters was, substantially, endorsed. It went into a somewhat minute history of Congressional legislation and the subsequent proceedings in Kansas up to the date of the message. It defended the course pursued by the Southern men as being efforts to *counteract* incendiary proceedings of Northern States and "Emigrant Aid Societies." The minority report of this same committee (composed of Judge Collamer of Vermont) gave a most thorough *expose* of the whole system by which the Kansas struggle was thrust upon the country. It forms one of the leaves of current history, embodying, as it does, a presentment of the case which ultimately triumphed in defiance of the tremendous power and patronage of two Presidents secretly committed to delivering Kansas over to the South.

In the House a fierce struggle was waged over Kansas affairs. While the Senate was applauding the Shawnee Mission Assembly, and seeking to enforce its monstrous legislation at the point of Federal bayonets, the House was struggling to secure justice for the oppressed Free State settlers. Not, however, until March 19th, 1856, was a final vote had on the proposition of the Committee on Elections to send for persons and papers. It was then so modified as to appoint a special committee of three to proceed to Kansas, with full powers to take testimony and to compel attendance of witnesses. On this commission were placed Wm. A. Howard, of Michigan, John Sherman, of Ohio, and Oliver, of Missouri—the latter a known sympathiser with the Southern faction. This commission reached Lawrence April 17th, and at once entered upon its most onerous as well as dangerous duties. The Southern partisans viewed it with extreme distrust. Well they might, since the revelations made by the committee came before the country to prove, beyond cavil, the worst charges preferred against the National and Territorial Executives and the ruffians whose reign of terror had made Kansas soil red with blood.

Just prior to the arrival of the commission in Kansas there passed into the Territory a regiment of desperados recruited chiefly in South Carolina, Georgia and Alabama by one "Colonel" Buford. By whose order they were thus recruited none cared to confess. The fact that they were, on their arrival, adopted by the U. S. Marshal Donalson, as a *posse*, and were armed by Governor Shannon with United States muskets, proved their advent to have been part of the programme for making Kansas a Slave State. A few of them, it is stated, came as honest settlers, to better their fortunes; but, the great majority were arrant villains who long proved a pest to the Territory as assassins, highway robbers, horse thieves and rogues ready for any bad service. During the session of the commission the outrages against Northern settlers culminated in "official" acts of great severity. Armed with authority from Washington to enforce the acts of the Shawnee Assembly, Shannon felt secure, and "Sheriff' Jones proceeded to put in force his long threatened arrest for treason of leading Free State men. As preliminary to this arrest Donalson placed Buford's vagabonds in quarters around Lawrence, where they soon became a terror to all inhabitants. Judge Lecompte, on the 5th of May, delivered his charge to a grand jury convened in Douglas county. His words were:

"This Territory was organized by an act of Congress, and so far its authority is from the United States. It has a Legislature elected in pursuance of that Organic act. This Legislature, being an instrument of Congress, by which it governs the Territory, has passed laws; these laws therefore, are of United States authority and making, and all that resist these laws, resist the power and authority of the United States, and are, therefore, guilty of high treason. Now, gentlemen, if you find that any persons *have* resisted these laws, then must you, under your oaths, find bills against such persons for high treason. If you find that no such resistance has been made, but that combinations have been formed for the purpose of resisting them, and individuals of influence and notoriety have been aiding and abetting in such combinations, then must you still find bills for constructive treason, as the courts have decided that to constitute treason the blow need not be struck, but only the *intention* be made evident."

This sentiment was reciprocated fully by the Missouri jurymen, who were not long in concocting a presentment "that, from the evidence before them" they had to report the two Free State journals—*The Herald of Freedom* and *The Kansas Free State*—were demoralizing and seditious sheets, which they (the jurymen) recommended should be abated as nuisances. Also that the building in Lawrence known as the "Free State Hotel" was constructed with a view to regular military occupation and defense, and it was therefore a nuisance also to be abated! Writs were soon secured "from the proper authorities" against many prominent Free State citizens in Lawrence and vicinity and their service committed to the proper representative of Marshal Donalson. The citizens of Lawrence were reputed to be prepared for this advent of their old enemy, hence the Deputy Marshal did not attempt to enter the town. Donalson then issued a call to the people of Kansas, May 11th, 1846, commanding all "law abiding citizens of the Territory" to appear at Lecompton, as soon as practicable and in numbers sufficient for the execution of the law.

At the very moment of this call Buford's men and several other organized military bodies were close to Lawrence ready for duty. Their near vicinity called from the people of the town and the farmers around an address to the Governor, stating that these men were but robbers and asking from him protection by the United States' troops at his disposal. The Governor flatly refused all protection so long as the citizens were in arms to resist the laws. That the entire proceeding of Lecompte, Donalson and Shannon was a gross libel on the acts and circumstances of the Lawrence men the reader need hard ly be told. A meeting of the citizens held May 13th, adopted the following explicit resolution:

"Resolved, By this public meeting of the citizens of Lawrence, held this thirteenth day of May, 1856, that the allegations and charges against us, contained in the aforesaid proclamation, are wholly untrue in fact, and the conclusion which is drawn from them. The aforesaid deputy marshal was resisted in no manner whatever, nor by any person whatever, in the execution of said writs, except by him whose arrest the said deputy marshal was seeking to make. And that we now, as we have done heretofore, declare our willingness and determination, without resistance, to acquiesce in the service upon us of any judicial writs against us by the United States Deputy Marshal for Kansas Territory, and will furnish him with a *posse* for that purpose, if so requested; but that we are ready to resist, if need be, unto death, the ravages and desolation of an invading mob. J. A. WAKEFIELD, President."

This was sent to Shannon and Donalson. A letter, signed by a large committee of the best citizens, was addressed to the Marshal, also, explicitly denying that any opposition had been offered to any legal process, or that any such would be offered, and asking protection from the mob. Donalson's reply was, like Shannon's, a pledge to give no quarter to men armed with Sharpe's rifles and bound together by oaths and pledge to resist the laws. As if the Free State settlers would have been unarmed in view of the dangers by which they had for months been surrounded! As for being banded together to "resist the laws," the solemn declarations above cited disprove the charge.

The *pre-determined* purpose of all that demonstration was *not* to "enforce the laws" but to *sack and burn Lawrence*, and thus, by one decisive stroke, to get rid of the Free State faction. That was the sole *intent* of Lecompte's charge, of the writs of arrest issued, and of the presence before Lawrence of that large armed mob composed almost exclusively of non-residents of the Territory, and who gathered for the openly acknowledged object of clearing the Territory of all "abolitionists." Writs were obtained upon the affidavit of any pro-slavery rascal who coveted his neighbor's goods. These the "Sheriff" served, with a large *posse* always at his side, and soon the jail at Lecompton was filled with Northern men—many of them perfectly guiltless of any act which even the "friends of the South" could construe into an offense. Soon, gathering assurance, this officer visited Lawrence and made numbers of arrests for alleged petty offenses. On the 23d of April he came in with a strong guard of United States dragoons from the fort and arrested several leading citizens, for "resistance to the laws," for "inciting sedition," for "being dangerous to the public peace," &c., &c. This last arrest greatly excited the populace, who read in it the fate in store for every man who had taken a part in the State movement. The prisoners were borne to the "Sheriff's" camp and quartered among his *posse*, subjected to insults and occasional acts of violence. Some one, during the night, shot into Jones' tent, wounding him slightly. This act awakened a second frenzy among the pro-slave press, which teemed with articles eulogistic of the brave Jones and defaming Northern men. The moment for sacking and burning Lawrence had come. Several murders followed of a most atrocious character—the victims being Northern settlers.

On the morning of May 21st Marshal Donalson ordered the advance upon Lawrence. Mount Oread had been seized during the night and two cannon planted there. "Governor" Robinson's house, located on the hill, was seized and converted at once to the uses of the armed mob. By eight o'clock the town was surrounded. No resistance was, or had been, offered. The parade was useless since the inhabitants of the place had resolved to submit to the course of "justice" and trust to the future to restore them their liberty and their rights. A Deputy Marshal, with a strong *posse*, proceeded to make arrests of two active Free State partisans. This done the Marshal ordered his "forces" to retire; the U. S. dragoons withdrew, but Jones soon appeared on the scene, accompanied by ex-Vice President David R. Atchison. This latter addressed the mob, using the coarsest language, informing them that the time had arrived to "wipe out the accursed Abolitionists." Led by Jones and Atchison the ruffians then proceeded to the work of destruction. The "Free State Hotel," and the two newspaper offices already named as having been indicted by Judge Lecompte's jury, were soon a mass of ruins. The affair was thus chronicled by the *Lecompton Union*, Judge Lecompte's "organ."

"During this time appeals were made to Sheriff Jones to save the Aid Society's Hotel. This news reached the company's ears, and was received with one universal cry of 'No, no! blow it up! blow it up!'

"About this time a banner was seen fluttering in the breeze over the office of *The Herald of Freedom.* Its color was a blood-red, with a lone star in the centre, and South Carolina above. This banner was placed there by the Carolinians—Messrs. Wrights and a Mr. Cross. The effect was prodigious. One tremendous and long continued shout burst from the ranks. Thus floated in triumph the banner of South Carolina—that single white star, so emblematic of her course in the early history of our sectional disturbances. When every Southern State stood almost upon the verge of ceding their dearest rights to the North, Carolina stood boldly out, the firm and unwavering advocate of Southern institutions.

"Thus floated victoriously the first banner of Southern rights over the abolition town of Lawrence, unfurled by the noble sons of Carolina, and every whip of its folds seemed a death stroke to Beecher propagandism and the fanatics of the East. O! that its red folds could have been seen by every Southern eye!

"Mr. Jones listened to many entreaties and finally replied that it was beyond his power to do any thing, and gave the occupants so long to remove all private property from it. He ordered two companies into each printing office to destroy the press. Both presses were broken up and thrown into the street, the type thrown in the river, and all the material belonging to each office destroyed. After this was accomplished, and the private property removed from the hotel by the different companies, the cannon was brought in front of the house and directed their destructive blows upon the walls. The building caught on fire, and soon its walls came with a crash to the ground. Thus fell the abolition fortress; and we hope this will teach the Aid Society a good lesson for the future."

Then followed a promiscuous plunder and sacking of the town, from which the inhabitants had fled in terror. Stores were gutted, private houses pillaged, and what could not be borne away was destroyed by mutilation or smashing. This work of ruin was only stayed by the absolute weariness or drunkenness of the rioters, who were acting under the forms of territorial law. At night the heavens were lit up by the burning of Robinson's fine house on Mount Oread. The drunken horde then disappeared bearing with them stolen wagons loaded with stolen plunder, drawn by stolen horses.

What a picture for American citizens to contemplate! The creatures who perpetrated this outrage upon law and upon society acted *by virtue of* the orders of United States authority, enforcing the mandates of a Chief Justice named by the President and long after continued in office by him and his successor. The miscreants whose hands wrought the deed were in the pay of the recognized government, and were mostly armed with United States muskets. Governor Shannon made no interference—the United States troops were not permitted to interpose, and the deed passed as a just retribution for the abolitionists. Said Jones, as he witnessed the work of destruction: "This is the happiest day of my life. I determined to make the fanatics bow before me in the dust and to kiss the territorial laws, and I have done it."

After these proceedings there was an end of peace. The young and most ardent of the Free State settlers, stung to desperation by their wrongs, apparently gave up all hopes of *any* confraternity with the Southern rights' representatives, and, with the resolve of men ready to test their principles with their strength, took up arms to wage a war of extermination. Some of the leading citizens and most reputable settlers condemned, in strong terms, this reign of violence, and sought, by every means in their power, to stay it; but without avail. A carnival of robbery, pillage, arson and murder, succeeded.

Old John Brown then first appeared, clearly outlined against the dark background, as the spirit of vengeance. Around him rallied a small troop of determined characters, who, led by the old man's invincible will, soon became a territorial terror. Brown's four sons had moved into Kansas early in the Spring of 1855 to become permanent residents, having with them valuable stock, implements, &c., but no arms. Settling in Lykins county, on the Pottawattomie creek, about eight miles from Ossawattomie, they were exposed to the visits of marauders, and suffered so many outrages that the boys united in a letter to their father—a man then fifty-five years of age—urging him to come to them with arms for all. The old man heard "the call," and, by the help of Gerritt Smith, of New York State, proceeded to Kansas, accompanied by three more of his sons. He was in Lawrence during the "siege" ready for fight, but, the Free State men having resolved, after conference, not to be the first to precipitate the conflict, submitted peaceably, as we have seen, to the writs and violence of the territorial authorities. After the sacking of Lawrence Old John Brown entered upon "his work" in earnest,[1] by leading a small company of resolute spirits with which to sweep over the Territory. The first act of his agents was to seize and slay a party of Southern desperados who, as a self constituted vigilance committee, had arranged to murder a number of Free State immigrants. These desperados richly deserved death but the summary proceeding of Brown's men failed to command the assent of many of the settlers. The old man was not present at the slaughter, but endorsed it as necessary and just. This act aroused the Missourians to new deeds of retailation. New invasions followed, more tragedies ensued, and the United States dragoons were called upon to disperse contending hosts of the two factions. The first "army" of Missourians, under command of one H. Clay Pate, after committing many outrages and crimes, was bagged by Old Brown in a skirmish. Another and a more formidable force, gathered by Whitfield, then took the field. The town of Franklin became their rendezvous and depot. On it Old Brown fell during the night of June 2d, and captured the place with its stores. A gathering of forces followed, with the intent of fighting a pitched battle, which Brown was anxious to bring on; but the Federal dragoons interfered and easily induced the Missourians to retire. In leaving they took Ossawattomie in their course and sacked the town (June 9th) with every mark of brutality. Says Dr. Gihon: "There were but few men in the town, and the women and children were treated with the utmost brutality. Stores and dwellings were alike entered and pillaged. Trunks, boxes and desks were broken open, and their contents appropriated or destroyed. Even rings were rudely pulled from the ears and fingers of the women, and some of the apparel from their persons. The liquor found was freely drank, and served to incite the plun-

[1] Says his biographer, James Redpath: "He had only two objects in going to Kansas: first, to begin the work for which, as he believed, he had been set apart, by so acting as to acquire the confidence of the friends of freedom, who might thereby subsequently aid him; and, secondly, because to use his own language, 'with the exposures, privations, hardships and wants of pioneer life, he was familiar, and thought he would benefit his children, and the new beginners from the older parts of the country, and help them to shift and contrive in their new home.'"

derers to increased violence in the prosecution of their mischievous work. Having completely stripped the town, they set fire to several houses, and then beat a rapid retreat, carrying off a number of horses, and loudly calling each other to greater haste, as 'the d—d abolitionists were coming!' There are hundreds of well authenticated accounts of the cruelties practised by this horde of ruffians, some of them too shocking and disgusting to relate, or to be accredited, if told. The tears and shrieks of terrified women, folded in their foul embrace, failed to touch a chord of mercy in their brutal hearts, and the mutilated bodies of murdered men, hanging upon the trees, or left to rot upon the prairies or in the deep ravines, or furnish food for vultures and wild beasts, told frightful stories of brutal ferocity from which the wildest savages might have shrunk with horror."

The state of affairs during June and July was truly distressing. In all localities under jurisdiction of Southern or territorial emissaries, the families of Northern men suffered every degree of indignity. Numbers of citizens of Leavenworth were sent on board of steamers, without warning, and shipped down the river. Others were imprisoned and their possessions seized. All passengers arriving from below were searched, and, if Free State men, were robbed of their money and goods. It was truly a reign of the *canaille.* 'Life, liberty and the pursuit of happiness' were permitted to no Free State man except as a special favor. The Federal authorities removed Colonel Sumner for his openly avowed disgust at the proceedings of the Missourians and the territorial officials. General Persifer F. Smith, a pro-slave partisan, was given the command and arrived in July just after the Topeka Legislature had been dispersed by the United States' dragoons. This Legislature, it will be remembered, was adjourned to meet July 4th. It did so meet, but Colonel Sumner, acting under orders from Washington, entered Topeka on that day and forbade the assembly. The legislators therefore dispersed. "Governor" Robinson and several others of the actors in the State movement having been arrested were imprisoned at that time, but ex-Governor Reeder and James W. Lane, were fortunate enough to have escaped the writs of Donalson and made their way to Washington, to urge the adoption of the State Constitution by Congress. That Mr. Pierce did not order their arrest in the National Capital probably was owing to a fear of consequences. Yet, under the forms of the National Constitution in what respect had they sinned?

The contest in Congress was keenly renewed late in June. In the House, the Committee on Territories, through Mr. Grow, its Chairman, reported a bill for the admission of Kansas as a State under the Constitution submitted. The debate which succeeded was acrimonious and persistent, and, after various manœuvres by its opponents, the bill was lost: yeas 106 nays 107. This vote was, by strenuous efforts of Northern men, reconsidered, and, on July 3d, the second vote on the act for admission resulted in its adoption: yeas 99, nays 97.

The State movement fared adversely in the Senate. Mr Douglas, as Chairman of the Committee on Territories, reported a bill appointing five commissioners to take a census of the legal voters of the Territory; the Territory to be apportioned into fifty-two districts, which should elect delegates to decide upon a State Constitution; the delegates to meet in December, 1856, and to have power to decide if it was expedient to form a Constitution; and, if so, to proceed with the formation of that instrument. This bill was adopted July 3d, after an ineffectual but tenacious opposition from the Northern free soil members. Being sent to the House, it remained on the Speaker's table untouched at the day of adjournment, Aug. 18th. On the 8th of July Mr. Douglas reported the House bill to admit Kansas, and offered an amendment striking out all after its enacting clause, substituting the Senate bill above referred to as adopted July 3d. Against this the free soil Senators struggled fruitlessly; the substitute passed by the vote of yeas 32, nays 13. This vote of course amounted to a rejection of the Kansas State Constitution, and in leaving the Shawnee Mission legislators in uncontrolled supremacy. How they exercised that supremacy is written in the story of blood which we have had to record.

But, the friends of Free Kansas did not give over the struggle in Congress. Having a bare majority in the House they sought, by various means, to restrain the Administration from pushing its cruel mandates to the extremes of enforcing the odious territorial laws. Yet, all efforts failed. There stood the heavy pro-slave majority of the Senate in the way, and no act for the relief of the oppressed people could pass a chamber so long accustomed to Southern rule that a free soil member was regarded as an interloper. In the House, however, was vested a power which even the Senate could not override nor the Executive defy. Toward the close of its turbulent and long-protracted session the annual appropriation bills came up. To these the House attached provisions calculated to effect what the due course of direct legislation could not accomplish. Provisos were inserted abolishing, repealing or suspending the most obnoxious features of the territorial Legislature. These provisions the Senate resisted and successfully so, as far as general appropriations were concerned; but, one item, of $20,000, to pay the *next* session of that infamous territorial legislative body was abandoned by the Senate in order to save the civil appropriation bill from total defeat. But the two Houses came to a dead lock on a proviso "forbidding the employment of the army to enforce the acts of the Shawnee Mission assemblage, claiming to be a territorial Legislature of Kansas, when at noon on the 18th of August the Speaker's hammer fell, announcing the termination of the session, leaving the army bill unpassed. But President Pierce immediately issued a proclamation convening an extra session on the 21st (Thursday), when the two Houses reconvened accordingly, and a full quorum of each was found to be present. The House promptly repassed the army bill, again affixing a proviso forbidding the use of the army to enforce the disputed territorial laws, which proviso the Senate as promptly struck out, and the House as promptly reinserted. The Senate insisted on its disagreement, but asked no conference, and the House (Aug. 22d) by a close vote decided to adhere to its proviso, yeas 97, nays 93; but one of the yeas (Bocock, of Va.) was so given in order to be able to move a reconsideration; so that the true division was 96 to 94, which was the actual division on a motion by Mr. Cobb, of Ga., that the House recede from its position. Finally, a motion to reconsider was made and laid on the table; yeas 97, nays 96, and the House thereupon adjourned."

"The struggle for the passage of the bill with or without the proviso continued until Saturday, Aug. 30th, when, several members, hostile to the proviso, and hitherto absent, unpaired, having returned, the House again passed the Army bill with the proviso modified as follows:

"'Provided, however, that no part of the military force of the United States, for the support of which appropriations are made by this act, shall be employed in aid of the enforcement of any enactments heretofore made by the body claiming to be the Territorial Legislature of Kansas.'

"The bill passed as reported (under the previous question): yeas 99, nays 79, and was sent to the Senate, where the above proviso was stricken out, yeas 26, nays 7, and the bill thus returned to the House, when the Senate's amendment was concurred in, yeas 101, nays 97.

"So the proviso was beaten at last, and the bill passed, with no restriction on the President's discretion in the use of the army in Kansas; just as all attempts of the House to direct the President to have a *nolle prosequi* entered in the case of the Free State prisoners in Kansas charged with aiding the formation and adoption of the Free State Constitution as aforesaid had been previously beaten, after prevailing in the House—the Senate striking them out, and the House (by union of nearly all the supporters of Fillmore with nearly or quite all those supporting Buchanan) finally acquiescing."[1]

This result left the Free State party in Kansas under the ban of the law, and those in authority, for a few months, held wild riot in their success. Shannon was removed during August for incapacity and drunkenness. Woodson, his secretary, was acting Governor until the new appointee, John W. Geary, of Pennsylvania, should arrive. He was a wretched substitute, a leader of the Missouri raids, a servile tool of faction, and a bitter enemy of the Free State men. August 16th, just five

[1] Political Text Book for 1860.

days prior to his receiving the seal of office, Atchison, Colonel Boone, Colonel Russell and "General" B. F. Stringfellow, had issued a circular from Westport, Missouri, announcing that James H. Lane had entered Kansas with a large army—had captured Lecompton, and had liberated the State prisoners there confined—had committed other acts demanding vengeance. The circular therefore called upon all "true men" to rally to their several rendezvous, there to organize to meet the daring liberator.[1] This call Woodson repeated in a proclamation dated August 25th, declaring the Territory in a state of rebellion and insurrection and calling for help to put down the insurrectionists and to bring to condign punishment all who were engaged with them. It was all a well concerted programme, to sanction a second overwhelming invasion. This Governor's call found about eleven hundred ruffians already gathered at Little Santa Fe, on the Missouri border, who soon were on their mission of "extermination." A section of Atchison's army, composed of about three humdred, with one field piece, advanced under command of General Reed on Ossawattomie, hoping to capture Old John Brown, who was reported to be at that place with his body guard of about thirty men. The wary old campaigner was not caught, however. He retired into the wood bordering the Marais des Cygnes creek,

---

[1] A circular was issued, also, in Lexington, Missouri, Aug. 17th, whose closing paragraph read:

"Meet at Lexington on Wednesday, August 20, at 12 o'clock. Bring your horses, your guns and your clothing—all ready to go on to Kansas. Let every man who can possibly leave home, go now to save the lives of our friends. Let those who cannct go hitch up their wagons and throw in a few provisions, and get more as they come along by their neighbors, and bring them to Lexington on Wednesday. Let others bring horses and mules, and saddles and guns—all to come in on Wednesday. We must go immediately. There is no time to spare, and no one must hold back. Let us all do a little, and the job will be light. We want two hundred to three hundred men from this county. Jackson, Johnson, Platte, Clay, Ray, Saline, Carroll and other counties are now acting in this matter. All of them will send up a company of men, and there will be a concert of action. New Santa Fe, Jackson county, will be the place of rendezvous for the whole crowd, and our motto this time will be, "No quarter." Come up, then, on Wednesday, and let us have concert of action. Let no one stay away. We need the old men to advise, the young men to execute. We confidently look for eight hundred to one thousand citizens to be present."

and, for three hours held the Missourians at bay. Not overcome, but in danger of being outflanked, he was compelled, under a sharp fire, to pass the creek, losing two of his party, killed. The Missourians' scouts, led by a preacher named White, a member of the Kansas Legislature, had, prior to the appearance of Reid's force, come upon Brown's youngest son, Frederick, a boy of eighteen, and four others. These young men were not attached to any military command. Young Brown was killed, together with one of his companions, who was shockingly mutilated. Another was left for dead in the road. Old Brown at that time was about two miles away, with only fifteen men. He fell back upon the town, hoping to defend it; but, finding the enemy too powerful, he took to the woods, where, joined by twelve mounted men, he maintained the fight as above noted.

After the "victory" Reid's men entered the village, burned between twenty and thirty houses, robbed the post office, plundered the stores, seized all the horses, cattle and wagons, and, loaded with spoils made off in haste to Missouri to boast of having "wiped out another d—d abolition hole." It cost the ruffians between twenty and thirty lives to secure that "glorious result."

The main division of Atchison's forces marched toward Bull creek, to which spot Lane also directed his course with three hundred men. Before this array of Northern muskets the Missourians retreated in haste, with a cowardice discreditable even to them. Thus this invasion temporarily ended. Lane then pushed on to Lecompton, whither a number of Free State men again had been carried as prisoners. On the morning of Sept. 4th he appeared, with his cannon, on Court House hill, commanding the town. "General" Richardson refused to fight and threw up his commission in disgust at the running away of his constituents. Another "General" was found, who treated with Lane, agreeing to deliver up all the prisoners in his keeping. This he did, by sending them into Lawrence the next day, under an escort of United States dragoons! Lane returned to Lawrence, but kept the field with his vigilant force until Governor Geary issued his Inaugural Address, and Proclamation of Sept. 11th, 1856. These documents seemed so reassuring of peace that Lane disbanded his men and countermanded orders then dispatched to Lawrence for men and cannon to proceed against a party of Missourians strongly housed at Hickory Point. The countermand came too late. Captain Harvey, with one hundred and ten men, left Lawrence Saturday, and, by a forced march, reached the point indicated, Sunday morning. A short, sharp conflict resulted in the capture of the Missourians, but Harvey's men were, in turn secured by a force of dragoons dispatched from Lecompton by orders of Governor Geary. The Governor regarded these men as the aggressors, and held them prisoners for trial.

At the moment these exciting incidents were transpiring great excitement prevailed in the vicinity of Lawrence. The approach of a large body of Missourians was announced during Sunday. As Lane and Harvey were absent with the best fighting material of the town much alarm was felt for its safety. Old John Brown, however, was in the place and, under his active direction the citizens of the town were put into the extemporised defenses, while, with a force of about fifty riflemen, Brown proceeded to an advanced position on the prairie to engage the invaders. By five o'clock a considerable body of the Missouri "militia" had crossed the Wakarusa. These the Lawrence men soon engaged to advantage, and darkness came to find the fight pressed sharply by the riflemen. Though full three hundred strong, and mounted, the Missourians were outmanœuvred by Brown's excellent arrangements and were forced to retire upon their main body, then at Franklin..

A messenger, dispatched in haste to the Governor, at Lecompton, informed him of this threatened attack. He at once ordered forward the dragoons under Colonel Cook, with instructions to prevent a collision. Colonel Cook reached Lawrence Sunday evening to find the Lawrence men under Brown already engaging their enemy. Ordering, in the name of the Governor, the Missourians to retire to their main camp beyond Franklin, the Colonel dispatched a messenger for the Governor, informing him that about twenty-seven hundred men were assembled only four miles from Lawrence, under command of

"Generals" Heiskell, Reid, Atchison, Richardson and Stringfellow, "determined to exterminate that place (Lawrence) and all its inhabitants." Said Geary, in his dispatch to Mr. Marcy, of Sept. 16th, 1856: "Fully appreciating the awful calamities that were impending, I hastened with all possible dispatch to the encampment, assembled the officers of the militia, and in the name of the President of the United States, demanded suspension of hostilities. I had sent in advance, the secretary and adjutant-general of the Territory, with orders to carry out the spirit and letter of my proclamations; but, up to the time of my arrival, these orders had been unheeded, and I could discover but little disposition to obey them. I addressed the officers in council at considerable length, setting forth the disastrous consequences of such a demonstration as was contemplated, and the absolute necessity of more lawful and conciliatory measures to restore peace, tranquillity and prosperity to the country. I read my instructions from the President, and convinced them that my whole course of procedure was in accordance therewith. and called upon them to aid me in my efforts, not only to carry out those instructions, but to support and enforce the laws, and the Constitution of the United States. I am happy to say, that a more ready concurrence in my views was met, than I had at first any good reason to expect. It was agreed, that the terms of my proclamations should be carried out by the disbandment of the militia; whereupon the camp was broken up, and the different commands separated, to repair to their respective homes."

Geary's arrival in the distracted Territory was, indeed, opportune. He was, seemingly, well qualified for his mission of peace. Had the President named him to the trust committed to the wretched Shannon, much of the tragedy of Kansas never would have been written. His first dispatch to the War Department, dated Sept. 9th, confessed affairs to be in a shocking condition. To show the reader that the record which we have presented has not exceeded or misconstrued the reality, we may quote from that communication:

"I find that I have not simply to contend against bands of armed ruffians and brigands, whose sole aim and end is assassination and robbery

—infatuated adherents and advocates of conflicting political sentiments and local institutions—and evil-disposed persons, actuated by a desire to obtain elevated positions; but, worst of all, against the influence of men who have been placed in authority, and have employed all the destructive agents around them to promote their own personal interests, at the sacrifice of every just, honorable and lawful consideration.

"I have barely time to give you a brief statement of facts as I find them. The town of Leavenworth is now in the hands of armed bodies of men, who, having been enrolled as militia, perpetrate outrages of the most atrocious character under shadow of authority from the territorial Government. Within a few days these men have robbed and driven from their homes unoffending citizens; have fired upon and killed others in their own dwellings; and stolen horses and property under the pretence of employing them in the public service. They have seized persons who have committed no offense; and, after stripping them of all their valuables, placed them on steamers, and sent them out of the Territory. Some of these bands, who have thus violated their rights and privileges, and shamefully and shockingly misused and abused the oldest inhabitants of the Territory, who had settled here with their wives and children, are strangers from distant States, who have no interest in, nor care for the welfare of Kansas, and contemplate remaining here only so long as opportunities for mischief and plunder exist.

"The actual pro-slavery settlers of the Territory are generally as well disposed persons as are to be found in most communities. But there are among them a few troublesome agitators, chiefly from distant districts, who labor assiduously to keep alive the prevailing sentiment.

"It is also true that among the free soil residents are many peaceable and useful citizens; and if uninfluenced by aspiring demagogues, would commit no unlawful act. But many of these, too, have been rendered turbulent by officious meddlers from abroad. The chief of these is Lane, now encamped and fortified at Lawrence, with a force, it is said, of fifteen hundred men. They are suffering for provisions, to cut off the supplies of which, the opposing faction is extremely watchful and active.

"In isolated or country places, no man's life is safe. The roads are filled with armed robbers, and murders for mere plunder are of daily occurrence. Almost every farm-house is deserted, and no traveller has the temerity to venture upon the highway without an escort."

The reader will infer that the Governor's views, as to Lane's brigandism, underwent a change ere a month had passed, by which time he discovered that it was that leader's prowess alone which had saved the town of Lawrence from destruction and the Territory from utter subjugation by a foreign host. If the

Governor afterwards prosecuted Harvey's men, whom he held as prisoners to be tried as violators of the peace, it was because they were so; and that he permitted the army assembled before Lawrence for its destruction to depart, was for the reason that those ruffians were there by virtue of the proclamation of the acting Governor Woodson—therefore they could not be arrested. That the Lawrence people welcomed the Governor—that Lane hastened to obey the injunctions of Geary's inaugural message and proclamation, are incidents which show the character of the Free State men; while the curses heaped upon the Governor by the invaders and the pro-slave faction generally, are evidences of their innate dislike of law and peace. Says Dr. Gihon (who was the Governor's private secretary and accompanied Geary to the scene of hostilities before Lawrence):

"There, in battle array, were ranged at least three thousand armed and desperate men. They were not dressed in the usual habiliments of soldiers, but in every imaginable costume that could be obtained in that western region. Scarcely two presented the same appearance, while all exhibited a ruffianly aspect. Most of them were mounted, and manifested an unmistakable disposition to be at their bloody work. In the background stood at least three hundred army tents and as many wagons, while here and there a cannon was planted, ready to aid in the anticipated destruction. Among the banners floated black flags to indicate the design that neither age, sex nor condition would be spared in the slaughter that was to ensue. The arms and cannon also bore the black indices of extermination.

"In passing along the lines, murmurs of discontent and savage threats of assassination fell upon the Governor's ears; but, heedless of these, and regardless, in fact, of everything but a desire to avert the terrible calamity that was impending, he fearlessly proceeded to the quarters of their leader. * * * To Atchison, he especially addressed himself, telling him that when he last saw him he was acting as Vice President of the Nation, and President of the most dignified body in the world, the Senate of the United States; but now with sorrow and pain he saw him leading on to a civil and disastrous war an army of men, with uncontrollable passions, and determined upon wholesale slaughter and destruction. He concluded his remarks by directing attention to his proclamation, and ordered the army to be disbanded and dispersed. Some of the more judicious of the officers were not only willing but anxious to obey this order; whilst others, resolved upon mischief, yielded a very reluctant assent. General Clarke said he was for pitching into the United States troops, if necessary, rather than abandon the objects of the expedition. General Maclean didn't see any use of going back until they had whipped the d—d abolitionists. Sheriff Jones was in favor, now they had a sufficient force, of "wiping out" Lawrence and all the Free State towns. And these and others, cursed Governor Geary in not very gentle expressions, for his untimely interference with their well laid plans. They, however, obeyed the order, and retired, not as good and law-loving citizens, but as bands of plunderers and destroyers, leaving in their wake ruined fortunes, weeping eyes and sorrowing hearts."

The history of Geary's brief administration is one of exceeding novelty, as illustrative of the peculiar faculty for crime and disorder of the pro-slave partisans and the extraordinary facility with which the Judges, United States Attorney and Marshal baffled the Governor's endeavors to bring criminals to justice. Only in a few instances did the Executive succeed in securing the trial of men whose hands were red with Free State blood; but, even in the case of these awful criminals, Judge Lecompte's acceptance of worthless bail, or a pro-slave and packed jury, soon relieved the prison of its just prey. Yet, there was great progress toward order, and, by a rigid surveillance of the municipal and preliminary jurisdictions, a flattering state of affairs rapidly succeeded the Governor's efforts. An election, ordered by proclamation, came off October 6th. It was to elect members of the territorial House of Representatives, a delegate to Congress and also to decide upon the question of a State Convention. About twenty-five hundred votes were polled—almost exclusively by pro-slave men. The members elect were, therefore, of the old order of things. Whitfield was re-elected as delegate, and the Shawnee Mission laws were triumphant.

In this election the Free State men did not participate, as their policy, at that time, was to ignore the entire territorial government as a usurpation and a foreign body. They still adhered to their Topeka State organization, although it was outlawed and powerless. The Governor made an extended tour through the Territory, consuming the time from Oct. 17th to Nov. 8th. He reported to the War Department a favorable feeling, and spoke hopefully of the future. On the 20th of Nov. a large meeting of citizens was held in Leavenworth City, at which, among other resolutions passed, were the following:

"Resolved, That we cordially approve any and all measures that may have a tendency to restore peace and harmony among the citizens of Kansas; that in view of the past and impressed with the importance of the present, we earnestly implore our fellow-citizens, without distinction of party, to aid in the preservation of peace and order by adopting a policy of conciliation.

"Resolved, That whatever difference of opinion may prevail touching the circumstances that resulted in the adoption of existing laws, we deem it the duty of every man to support and sustain these laws, in preference to having no laws at all, and continuing the anarchy that has too long prevailed.

"Resolved, that we believe the existing territorial laws contain provisions that should be repealed, and we have confidence that the Legislature, at the next session, will, with a spirit of justice and moderation, correct oppressive legislation."

The meeting of the "adjourned session" of the Topeka Legislature came off Jan. 6th, 1857. It was arranged by the Governor to dissolve the assembly simply by proclamation, with troops in reserve at Lecompton to enforce his order if it were resisted. But, "Sheriff" Jones pressed his unwelcome presence upon the public once more. Having obtained from Judge Cato writs for the arrest of the legislators for treason, he proceeded to Topeka on the opening day and served his processes. No opposition was offered, greatly to Jones' discomfiture. He had calculated upon a resistance to his officious intermeddling, and a second outbreak in consequence—thus deranging the Governor's peaceful programme. Quiet submission to arrest averted the solicited outbreak and preserved the peace. Previous to this descent of the vulture the legislators had assembled in informal meeting and prepared a second memorial to

Congress. As prisoners of State the assemblymen were conveyed by Jones to Tecumseh and were kept under arrest until the next day, when all were admitted to bail on their own recognizances. A *nolle prosequi* afterwards was entered by the district attorney, and thus the designed outrage ended as a farce. The whole proceeding met with Geary's disapproval.

The Shawnee Mission Territorial Assembly convened at Lecompton Jan. 12th, 1857—the Mission having ceased to be the capital. Governor Geary sent in his message. It was a document of so much force and pertinency as greatly to excite the Assembly. The Governor denounced their "territorial militia," and refused to regard their "law and order" partisans otherwise than as bandits. He also failed to denounce the Free State settlers for having arms and using them in their own defense. Six thousand copies of the unpalatable message were ordered to be printed, but the printers of State (the *Lecompton Union* office) conveniently neither had paper nor types for the performance of the order—hence, the message was not circulated. A secret caucus of the members resolved to disregard the Governor's apprehended vetoes of their pre-determined legislation, and afterwards acted upon the understanding by repassing at once every vetoed act. As already stated, the legislators, exercising the rights of "sovereigns," had passed acts stripping the Governor of all power except what was vested in him by the Organic act; but this act was so printed and construed as to deny him the usual power of pardon or remission of sentence. Then the rogues resolved to use their usurped authority by depriving him of the veto power itself! Said Dr. Gihon: "The Governor was apprised of this fact, but scarcely believing so infamous a measure possible, attempted to arrest several bills, by offering the most tangible objections, which only served to excite the merriment of members and call down upon his own head the most violent anathemas. Indeed, the greater portion of the time of the session was taken up with long speeches denunciatory of his Excellency for his supposed impartiality, or, rather, his unwillingness to 'go in' heart and soul, with all his ability, influence and power, to advance the interests of the pro-slavery cause. So entirely were they devoted to this peculiar object, that it was a common expression of the idlers of the town, when no better employment was on hand, to say to each other, 'Come, let us go over to the House to hear Jenkins,' or Brown, or Anderson, or O'Driscoll, or Johnson, or some other prominent orator, 'abuse the Governor.'"

Thus passed the term of this session of drunkards—a body of bad men chiefly directed by such designing knaves as Atchison, Woodson, Whitfield, Stringfellow, Calhoun, etc., who, in turn, were but ministers of that powerful pro-slave coterie at Washington which controlled President, Cabinet and Senate. The entire legislation proved so corrupt, so wicked, so repugnant to every sense of justice as to shock even the legislators themselves when they had time to dissipate the fumes of Jack Thompson's whiskey. Their acts stand on the historic record only as additional evidence of the disgusting debasement of all law and justice at the hands of those "friends of Southern institutions." And that class only was recognised by the President as law-givers for the Territory! The story of that Winter is so filled with violence and blood, personal outrages upon the Governor and his friends, infamous official proceedings and defilement of all the avenues of law, as to render its repetition humiliating. We pass it over with the sense of relief which one experiences when conscious that a leper has ceased to taint the air with his presence.

To one act we must refer, owing to its connection with succeeding political events of vital significance. The Legislature was supplied (from Washington it is said) with a census bill, providing for an enumeration of the inhabitants as preliminary to an election of delegates to a Convention for forming a State Constitution. The bill possessed highly objectionable features, and the Governor asked a conference with the chairmen of the House and Council Committees. The act, as then matured, forbid the people of the State to vote upon the Constitution, after its adoption by the Convention. This popular exclusion was engrafted upon the act to prevent the Free State expression, and was so confessed to the Governor by the chairmen, in their conference. They stated, in their interview with Geary, that the question of submission to a vote of the people had been fully considered, and that it would not be admitted since it "would defeat the only object of the act, which was to secure, beyond any possibility of failure, the Territory of Kansas to the South as a Slave State. Any alteration in the bill would be fatal to their projects. Even should they allow the Spring immigration to take part in the election, their plans would be frustrated. This, they said, was their last hope, and they could not let the opportunity pass unimproved. They had already, in anticipation of the passage of the bill, so apportioned the Territory, and made such other preliminary arrangements, that the success of this grand project was placed beyond the reach of any contingency that might now occur." The census act, therefore, passed as first ordered. Geary vetoed it in a message setting forth, with much force and with perfect conclusions, its injustice and violation of all precedent; but, the Assembly repassed it without hesitation, over the veto, and it became the law. Under that act the mockery of a true census was taken—the Legislature naming all the processes of the enumeration, the officers, &c. Governor Geary, sickened and dismayed at this reign of faction, and obtaining from Washington only implied censure for his "obstinacy," resigned, under date of March 4th—the resignation to take effect March 20th. He was forced to this step apparently by circumstances which could have been averted only by his utter abjuration of self-respect and honesty. That his reign was one of *designed* good is not now gainsayed: if he accomplished but little it was because he labored without co-operation, and, ultimately, was left helpless before the power of the most wicked and most reckless body of legislators ever recognized by a civilized government.

How the census act was enforced we are told by numerous writers. All agree that it had not even the farce of form to commend it; it was a mockery unworthy even of "border ruffian" dishonesty. Out of thirty-eight organised counties but twenty-six were entered for representation in the Constitutional Convention. Of these twenty-six the actual census was taken in ten only. In some of these ten only a partial enumeration was made. In six other counties the poll list was made up from the *old poll books!* No registry was made in the fine and well settled counties south of the Kansas river, for they were peopled with Free State families. By this manipulation of the "territorial authorities," quite three-fifths of the people were given no voice in the election of delegates. A strong pro-slave delegation of course was returned. So outrageous was the entire proceeding that, in counties where the Free State men were permitted to vote, they refused to participate and the election was all on one side. Yet, James Buchanan, President of the United States, in referring to this abstinence charged it to a revolutionary spirit, at the same time characterising the census act as, in the main, fair and just! Let us quote his words:

"On the 19th of February previous, the territorial Legislature had passed a law providing for the election of delegates on the first Monday of June, to a convention to meet on the first Monday in September, for the purpose of framing a Constitution preparatory to admission into the Union. This law was in the main fair and just; and it is to be regretted that all the qualified electors had not registered themselves and voted under its provisions.

"At the time of the election for delegates, an extensive organization existed in the Territory, whose avowed object it was, if need be, to put down the lawful government by force, and to establish a government of their own, under the so-called Topeka Constitution. The persons attached to this revolutionary organization abstained from taking any part in the election."

They did abstain; for what citizen, respecting the boon of an elective franchise, could participate in that prostitution of it to the most undemocratic ends? The opinion, however, prevailed—and that opinion was sustained by the new Governor, Robert J. Walker, late of Mississippi—that the Constitution, by the Organic act, *must* be submitted to a vote of the people. The Free State men, therefore, were satisfied to await the vote upon ratification when they might, as legal voters, put their veto upon the whole "territorial" proceeding. It was enough for them to reply to Governor Walker's earnest request for them to go the polls June 15th, 1857, to vote for delegates, that in nineteen out of thirty-eight counties no registry even had been made, and that, in fifteen of the nineteen counties, no census had been taken—hence those counties could not be represented in the Convention. As those counties, lying south of the Kansas river, were filled with Free State towns and were teeming with Free State industry, it is not a matter of surprise that the friends of the Topeka Free State movement abstained from the mockery of voting for delegates to that proscriptive Convention.

The entire vote cast at the election for delegates was but 2200. The delegates elect assembled in Convention at Lecompton, Sept. 5th, but soon adjourned over to October, to await the result of the territorial election on the first Monday of that month. At this territorial election both parties nominated candidates. At the request of Governor Walker, two thousand U. S. troops were in the Territory, and they were stationed so as to protect the polls as much as possible. Over eleven thousand votes were polled, after rejecting twenty-eight hundred as fraudulent and irregular, sixteen hundred of which were returned from the Oxford precinct, where, according to the census, there were but forty-three voters, and twelve hundred from McGee county, where no poll was opened. The result of this election was the Free State party carried the Legislature and the delegate to Congress.

"The Convention reassembled in October, according to adjournment, and formed the Constitution now so famous as the Lecompton Constitution. When it became known that the Convention had refused to submit the entire Constitution to a vote of the people for ratification or rejection, and had submitted only a proposition in regard to slavery, and that in a form and under a test oath which would prevent the Free State people from voting, there was great excitement in the Territory, threatening bloodshed. Under these circumstances acting Governor Stanton called (Governor Walker had resigned) an extra session of the territorial Legislature. The Legislature assembled Dec. 17th, and passed an act to submit the Lecompton Constitution fairly to a vote of the people on the 4th of January next, following, the time fixed by the Lecompton Convention for the election of State officers under that Constitution.

"On the 21st of Dec. the vote was taken in the manner prescribed by the Convention, and resulted as follows:

"'For the Constitution with Slavery' - - - -	6266
"'For the Constitution without Slavery' - - -	567
"Total vote, - - - - - - - -	6793

"Jan. 4th, 1858, in accordance with the act of the territorial Legislature, the people voted as follows:

"For the Lecompton Constitution with Slavery - -	138
" " " without Slavery -	24
"Against the Lecompton Constitution - - -	10,226

"Being over ten thousand majority against the Lecompton Constitution." [1]

Here we have, in brief, the whole story of the celebrated "Lecompton Constitution." It was born of a Convention illegally constituted, contained features repugnant to the sense of the people, was sought to be forced upon the people despite their wishes, but, when they came to vote squarely on it, the thing was rejected by the overwhelming majority of over ten thousand! Yet, despite this emphatic expression, James Buchanan used his tremendous influence as President to constrain Congress to accept the repudiated instrument. One month after that contemptuous rejection of it by the people, to wit: on Feb. 2d, 1858, he transmitted the Lecompton instrument to Congress, accompanied by a carefully prepared and labored argument urging its acceptance. In that Executive endorsement the President assumed the office of patron to the pro-slave faction. His words were:

"When we speak of the affairs of Kansas, we are apt to refer merely to the existence of two violent political parties in that Territory, divided on the question of slavery, just as we speak of such parties in the States. This presents no adequate idea of the true state of the case. The dividing line there, is not between two political parties, both acknowledging the lawful existence of the Government, but between those who are loyal to this Government and those who have endeavored to destroy its existence by force and by usurpation—between those who sustain, and those who have done all in their power to overthrow, the Territorial Government established by Congress. This Government they would long since have subverted had it not been protected from their

[1] Political Text Book for 1860.

assaults by the troops of the United States. Such has been the condition of affairs since my inauguration. Ever since that period a large portion of the people of Kansas have been in a state of rebellion against the Government, with a military leader at their head, of most turbulent and dangerous character. They have never acknowledged, but have constantly renounced and defied, the Government to which they owe allegiance, and have been all the time in a state of resistance against its authority. They have all the time been endeavoring to subvert it and to establish a revolutionary Government, under the so-called Topeka Constitution, in its stead. Even at this very moment, the Topeka Legislature are in session. Whoever has read the correspondence of Governor Walker with the State Department, recently communicated to the Senate, will be convinced that this picture is not overdrawn."

All of which either was wilful prevarication of the truth, or a shocking misapprehension of the character of the Free State settlers' resistance. They proposed to subvert no just authority, for, to call that territorial Assembly a "Government" was degrading to the idea. Nor was the "revolutionary" Topeka movement illegal. It was a clearly constitutional association, and had a perfect right to memorialize Congress as an informal body–other than that it never had nor ever preferred any claims. The force in the field under Lane was composed of men resolved, not upon revolution but upon obtaining order and rights guaranteed by the Organic act itself—the rights of actual settlers to make their own laws and to dictate the institutions of the new State. That this class of men thus libeled by the President constituted the immense majority of the people not only was proven by the vote of Jan. 4th, 1858, but by the succeeding vote of Aug. 3d, 1858, referred to hereafter—evidence not to be gainsayed. But, overwhelming as was this voice of the "squatter sovereigns," it failed to convince President, Cabinet, and the Southern party in Congress, and Kansas was doomed to a further two years' struggle to obtain what was clearly her rights and for her best interests.

One act of the Lecompton instrument as sent into the Senate for ratification was of four sections, as follows:

"§ 1. The right of property is before and higher than any constitutional sanction, and the right of the owner of a slave to such a slave and its increase is the same, and is inviolable, as the right of the owner of any property whatever.

"§ 2. The Legislature shall have no power to pass laws for the emancipation of slaves without the consent of their owners, or without paying their owners, previous to emancipation, a full equivalent in money for the slaves so emancipated. They shall have no power to prevent emigrants to the State from bringing with them such persons as are deemed slaves by the laws of any one of the United States or Territories so long as any persons of the same age or description shall be continued slaves by the laws of this State; provided, that such person or slave be the *bona fide* property of such emigrant; and provided, also, that laws may be passed to prohibit the introduction of slaves into this State who have committed high crimes in other States or Territories. They shall have power to permit the owners of slaves to emancipate them, saving the rights of creditors, and preventing them from becoming a public charge. They shall have power to oblige the owners of slaves to treat them with humanity—to provide for their necessary food and clothing—to abstain from all injuries to them, extending to life or limb—and, in case of neglect or refusal to comply with the direction of such laws, to have such slave or slaves sold for the benefit of the owner or owners.

"§ 3. In the prosecution of slaves for crimes of higher grade than petit larceny, the Legislature shall have no power to deprive them of an impartial trial by a petit jury.

"§ 4. Any person who shall dismember or deprive a slave of life shall suffer such punishment as would be inflicted in case the like offense had been committed on a free white person, and on the like proof, except in case of insurrection of such slave."

It was this provision alone which the Convention resolved to submit to the *registered* voters, Dec. 21st, 1857, with the result already chronicled. The reader will not fail to observe this feature of that election: the ballots were "Constitution with Slavery" and "Constitution with no Slavery"—a vote for either being, a vote to *adopt the Constitution*, only rejecting, in the latter ballot, the sections in regard to slavery. By what process of reasoning could the Northern settlers be required to vote on that specially privileged occasion? Yet, for not so voting, they were censured by the President as malcontents! The feature above adverted to was but one of several odious proscriptions of the Lecompton instrument. Provisions were inserted to render any possible Free State majority or vote powerless to change the "peculiar institution."

This Constitution, as submitted by the President, was reported on favorably in the Senate, by the Committee on Territories, who introduced, Feb. 17th, an act known as the Lecompton bill, accepting the Constitution as submitted, defining the boundaries of the new State and giving it its apportionment in the House. This bill passed the Senate March 23d, 1858, by the vote thirty-three to twenty-five—Mr. Douglas voting in the negative. John J. Crittenden, of Kentucky, offered and pressed a substitute for the bill, providing in substance that the Constitution be submitted to the people at once, and, if approved, the President to admit Kansas by proclamation. If rejected, the people to call a Convention and frame a Constitution. The substitute made special provision against frauds at the election.

This was lost by a vote of yeas 24, nays 34. The bill as passed by the Senate was taken up in the House April 1st, when, after various efforts to strangle it, a substitute was offered similar in character and language with that submitted by Mr. Crittenden in the Senate. This was, finally, adopted, by a vote of 120 to 112. With this bill the Senate resolved at once (April 2d) to disagree, by a vote of 34 to 22. The House thereupon voted (April 7th) to adhere to its amendment, by the vote of 119 to 111. On the 13th of April the Senate voted to insist on its resolve to disagree, and asked for a committee of conference, by the vote 30 to 24. To this the House tried to reply by a second vote on adherence, with a call for the previous question. This call was lost by the casting vote of the Speaker, when Mr. English, of Indiana, moved the appointment of a committee of conference, calling the previous question on the motion. This prevailed by the casting vote of the Speaker. The conference was then accepted. It resulted in the adoption of a new scheme, submitting the Constitution to a direct vote of the people of Kansas, Aug. 3d, 1858, and providing, if the Lecompton instrument was *accepted*, very liberal donations of land; if it was not accepted the act provided that Kansas then should not be permitted to come in as a State until she should actually have 93,340 inhabitants. Mark the result. Notwithstanding the bribe offered in lands—notwithstanding the threat to keep the Territory in its embryo condition for years, the vote was *over ten thousand majority against the Lecompton Constitution.* That election determined, beyond any question, the character and purposes of the vast majority of Kansas' inhabitants, and demonstrated to a certainty how meagre was the number of settlers and authorised voters who had, by the aid of Government bayonets, reigned in terror over the land. But even that expression failed to stay the hand of oppression in its design to make Kansas a Slave State, and in defiance of the promised rights guaranteed by the Organic Act, that immense majority was doomed to a further prolongation of the reign of ignorance and vice called the Lecompton Legislature.

Governors were rapidly changed. Walker resigned in disgust and indignation in the Summer of 1858. His secretary, Stanton, reigned a brief period only, to enter his most solemn protest against the Southern order of affairs. Denver assumed the office to find it too much even for his faith in the Administration. He was followed, in the Fall of 1858, by Samuel Medary, the "wheel horse" of Ohio Democracy, whose rule was a commingled record of folly and inefficiency. He was chosen to "sustain the Administration"—as if, in the face of an overwhelming Free State population, any Governor, or even Federal bayonets could compel that population to accept the Lecompton reign! During Denver's, and the first months of Medary's term of office, intense excitement prevailed in the Southern counties. In the Summer of 1856 all Free State settlers were driven from that section, abandoning claims, cultivated fields and houses. These were seized and appropriated by the Missouri borderers. Becoming reassured by their greatly increased numbers, the Northern immigrants, during the Summer following, began to return to their old possessions, to find them tenanted by Missourians. They resolved to settle upon their original claims and then to submit their squatter rights to the Land Office for decision. Seeing this, and determined to prevent Northern men from getting a hold upon the counties—for, once there, what should prevent the "Yankees" from swarming over into the fine domain of the Indian Territory?—the Southern men conspired for a second stand against their free soil emigration. Fort Scott was used as headquarters, from which, and the country adjacent, sallied parties who committed atrocities of the most cold blooded nature. Cattle and other property were first stolen to provoke an outbreak, when, under the old dodge of writs from "the authorities," Federal bayonets could be called into requisition to enforce the Southern programme. All this worked auspiciously for awhile. But, a "Free State Squatter Court" organized early in November, whose summary justice sent terror into the pro-slave ranks. A deputy U. S. Marshal, with a strong *posse*, essayed to break up the court, but was repulsed; when the United States forces were ordered out by Governor Denver to assist in suppressing the 'illegal and riotous combination.' At this call Lane again took the field, and, for a moment there threatened a decisive civil war. This attitude of the Free State men alarmed both the Governor and the Missourians, and no attempt was made to enforce any Fort Scott processes of arrest or ejectment. A bitter partisan war followed, and Captain James Montgomery entered the service to catch and punish any Missouri assassin prowling around the settlement. Several shocking murders occurred during the Winter of 1857–8, perpetrated by bands led, in some instances, by members of the Lecompton Legislature. Montgomery succeeded in securing several of these bandits, and, it is said, made short work of them. He was, at length, pursued (in April, 1858) by a body of dragoons from the Fort. These, with eight sharp shooters, he repulsed, killing one and wounding five. Governor Denver then again determined to "suppress" the guerilla, and dispatched a messenger to the Fort to arrange plans for Montgomery's capture. This was answered satisfactorily, by the officer in command, and the messenger started on his return, bearing a letter detailing arrangements for the capture. This unluckily fell into Montgomery's hands. He opened the epistle and reenclosed it, accompanied by a note to the Governor, stating that he had only to protect Free State settlers in their rights and their peace to secure his withdrawal from the field—that, until such time, he would not permit his band to be dissolved.

The dreadful massacre of the Marais des Cygnes creek succeeded. Hamilton, a member of the Lecompton Legislature, entered the Territory at the head of twenty-five men, passed to the settlements on the creek, seized eleven settlers, took them into a retired spot, formed them into a line and shot them. Five were killed, five wounded and one escaped by feigning death. The ruffians retired, unmolested, from their deed of blood; nor was any action ever taken in the matter by Governor or President. This aroused a feeling of intense animosity in the breasts of Northern men. Captain Montgomery found his strength fully equal to any emergency, but no action for retaliation followed. Governor Denver, alarmed for the peace of the Territory, hastened to Montgomery's quarters, and, through the co-operation of Free State men, induced the Captain to sign a treaty of amnesty, in which it was agreed that the past should be forgotten—that all obnoxious officers should be removed, all processes destroyed, and no more disturbance permitted. All of which, for a while, seemed to answer a good purpose. Montgomery's men returned to their homes; the Captain himself worked his farm in peace. But, in October the slave power broke out anew. A court assembled at Fort Scott found a jury to indict the Captain and a number of his men. A reign of violence ensued. With a resolution characteristic of the times, Montgomery gathered a party of resolute followers, proceeded to the fort, seized court and jury, burned the indictments and thus ended that tribunal of territorial dignitaries. The settlements were once again under arms. Marauders from Missouri came in, eager for plunder and still anxious to "wipe out the abolitionists." Old John Brown took the field and fortified several good positions on the Little Osage river and the Little Sugar creek, not far from the Missouri border, where he might watch the "enemy." Montgomery also prepared for a renewal of his guerilla operations. Against both of these restless and uncompromising haters of the Missourians, the Free State men north of the Kansas began to experience a feeling of distrust, and many of that class, it is asserted, volunteered in a Sheriff's *posse*, dispatched by the new Governor, Medary, to arrest the two Captains as disturbers of the peace. The adventure failed, for both Brown and Montgomery were absent from their quarters when the descent was made.

One of the latter's men was seized and imprisoned in Fort Scott. Dec. 15th, Montgomery, with one hundred and fifty followers, made his sudden appearance at the fort and released the Free State partisan. This act greatly incensed the Governor. He ordered down from Fort Leavenworth four companies of dragoons, and called into the field four companies of independent militia. These assembled at Fort Scott. A large body of Missourians gathered on the border ready to co-operate in the threatened arrest of every Free State man found in arms or who had participated in the rescue of Montgomery's man. Thus matters indeed looked serious, for, both guerilla Captains were resolved to fight to the last. Suddenly, dispatches arrived from Washington, ordering a recal of the troops. The dragoons returned to Leavenworth, while the militia disbanded. But, a body of Missourians having taken possession of the house of a blacksmith named Snyder, near the scene of the Marais des Cygnes butchery, the owner of the cabin fell upon it; the Missourians refused to surrender and opened fire on the Free State party. Snyder set fire to the premises and four of the inmates were consumed.

John Brown, watching the still powerful body of Missourians assembled at Falls' store, only eight miles from his quarters in Bourbon county, now performed an act which, at the time, created more of a sensation than any event of the year—'firing the Southern heart' to a degree of eruptive fury. He invaded Missouri and ran off the slaves of two plantations. His story of the liberation we may repeat:

"On Sunday, December 19, a negro man called Jim came over to the Osage settlement, from Missouri, and stated that he, together with his wife, two children and another negro man, was to be sold within a day or two, and begged for help to get away. On Monday, (the following) night, two small companies were made up to go to Missouri and forcibly liberate the five slaves, togethes with other slaves. One of these companies I assumed to direct. We proceeded to the place, surrounded the buildings, liberated the slaves, and also took certain property supposed to belong to the estate.

"We, however, learned, before leaving, that a portion of the articles we had taken belonged to a man living on the plantation, as a tenant, and who was supposed to have no interest in the estate. We promptly returned to him all we had taken. We then went to another plantation, where we found five more slaves, took some property and two white men. We moved all slowly away into the Territory for some distance, and then sent the white men back, telling them to follow us as soon as they chose to do so. The other company freed one female slave, took some property, and, as I am informed, killed one white man (the master), who fought against the liberation."

The old campaigner thereupon instituted "a parallel," recalling the Marais des Cygnes massacre, in these significant terms:

"Eleven persons are forcibly restored to their natural and inalienable rights, with but one man killed, and all 'hell is stirred from beneath.' It is currently reported that the Governor of Missouri has made a requisition upon the Governor of Kansas for the delivery of all such as were concerned in the last-named 'dreadful outrage.' The Marshal of Kansas is said to be collecting a posse of Missouri (not Kansas) men at West Point, in Missouri, a little town about ten miles distant, to 'enforce the laws.' All pro-slavery, conservative Free State and doughface men, and Administration tools, are filled with holy horror."

The panic which followed this invasion was ridiculous, considering its provocation. A general stampede of slaves was apprehended; consequently the two counties of Bates and Vernon were soon quite cleared of their "chattels," which were sent into the interior or shipped to the South for sale. Brown, however, made no further "reprisals," but proceeded at once to remove his colored colony to Canada. The Governor of Missouri offered a reward of three thousand dollars for his arrest—a sum afterwards increased by the President by an additional reward of two hundred and fifty dollars. Proceeding north by way of Lawrence, Brown left that place Jan. 20th, *en route* for Canada through Nebraska, Iowa, Illinois and Michigan—all of which States he traversed with his body guard. Though closely followed by men thirsting for his blood, as well as eager for the rewards, his slow march over the States was unimpeded—it was like a little triumphal procession. The negroes were safely delivered into Victoria's dominions and became thriving settlers.

This act was the finishing blow to Missouri violence. John

Brown evidently had calculated results when he made the reprisal. Frightened for the future security of their "property," the pro-slave borderers became suddenly peaceful, anxious to recover the good will of their too-evidently invincible opponents, and bearing, with as good a grace as possible, the unpalatable fortune of a Free State on their western border. An "Amnesty Act" was adopted, pardoning all "political offenses;" the Governor proclaimed it, and peace dwelt permanently in those fair domains.

We approach the end of this most painful chapter in our National history. The election of August, 3d, 1858, was so emphatic a protest against minority reign that only the form of electing members to that territorial body was necessary to secure in it a majority of Free State representatives. This being gained, steps at once could be taken for a new State Constitutional Convention, to repudiate the past, and to offer to Congress such an instrument as it could not, in good faith, reject. At the succeeding election, therefore, for assemblymen, the Free State men participated and elected members enough to override the Missouri intruders. An act was passed (Feb. 11th, 1859) "to refer the question to the people of a new Constitutional Convention, the election to be held on the first Tuesday in March, 1859. The election was held, and resulted in a majority of 3881 in favor of a Convention." This result being ascertained, the Governor issued his proclamation for an election of delegates. The old party organizations were now abandoned, and those of Republicans and Democrats substituted, and it was on this basis that the canvass for the election of delegates proceeded. The Convention was to consist of fifty-two delegates. The Democrats proclaimed themselves disciples of Mr. Douglas and his Territorial Sovereignty doctrine, and decidedly opposed to making Kansas a Slave State. The Leavenworth district—where, through its contractors for army supplies, the Government exercised a great influence, and which from its population was entitled to ten delegates—elected the Democratic ticket, not, however, without the aid of fraudulent votes. But the Republicans, by their predominance in other parts of the Territory, succeeded in securing a majority in the Convention of thirty-five to seventeen."

This Convention met at Wyandot July 5th, and continued in session twenty-two days. The debates were somewhat acrimonious, owing to efforts of the "opposition" to absorb as much of Nebraska as lay south of the Platte river, and for including within the lines, on the west, all the Pike's Peak region. Being composed exclusively of Democrats, the opposition also sought to engraft a provision in the Constitution excluding free negroes from the State, and also to prohibit all bank issues. But, the Free State (Republican) majority was too great. The Constitution, adopted by a vote of 34 to 13, was a straight-forward, democratic affair, embodying the best features of the organic laws of the older States. To it was prefixed a bill of rights which included a prohibition of Slavery and made competent for testimony before the courts of persons of any religious belief.

This instrument was submitted to a vote of the people on the first Tuesday in October following. The result was its ratification by over four thousand majority. An election for members of the Territorial Legislature transpired in November, when the Free State men elected the delegate to Congress and a majority of the Legislators. This latter election was regarded as but a mere form, for it was expected that Congress would accept the Wyandot Constitution at an early moment. An election for State officers was held Dec. 6th, 1859, which resulted in the choice of an entire Free State (Republican) ticket, on which stood Dr. Charles Robinson for Governor, and M. F. Conway for Congress. The Legislature chosen was largely Republican.

The Constitution was accepted, by the House of Congress, April 11th, 1860, by a vote of 174 to 73—the Southern members and a few Northern "Democrats" voting against it. But, in the pro-slave Senate the acceptance was resisted successfully. Mr. Seward (Feb. 21st, 1860), from the Committee on Territories, introduced the House bill for the admission of Kansas under the Wyandot Constitution. The matter lay over to June 5th, when it came up in its order. It was opposed by the notorious blackguard, Wigfall, of Texas, on the ground that he did not want his State to associate with Kansas under any circumstances! Hunter, of Virginia, moved to postpone the question, and it was so postponed, yeas 32, nays 27—a strict party vote, only two Northern Democrats being among the nays. June 7th, Mr. Wade, of Ohio, again moved to take up the bill, but, the motion was lost by the same vote as above; and Congress adjourned leaving Kansas still a Territory.

Thus, the Senate, which had repealed the time honored Compromise Act of 1822 in order to open the Western Territories for competition in their settlement, refused to receive Kansas with a Constitution prohibiting Slavery. Putting the first and last acts together, and throwing in as incidental testimony the extraordinary efforts made by two Administrations to fasten the Lecompton laws upon Kansas, we have irrefragible proof of the collusion of Northern men with the South for the *purpose* of Slavery extension. This is now the historic verdict, unpalatable as it may be to those who co-operated with Mr. Toombs in his crusade against *any* restrictions to Slavery [See letter of Toombs, quoted on page 457, foot note]. It was not until the session of 1860–61 when the Senate, by the secession of Southern members, permitted Kansas to enter the Union. During January, in the midst of extraordinary events transpiring in Congress and in the Southern States, the friends of Kansas pressed the bill for its admission to its successful passage. The Territory became a State, by approval of the President, January 29th, 1861, and Kansas soon was a commonwealth, as remarked for its loyalty to the General Government as for its fortitude under the awful visitations of those who had failed to make her a slave pen, and who gravitated toward the "Confederate" cause as naturally as sharks toward an infected ship.

The failure to secure Slave States west of Missouri hastened the pro-slave rebellion. The only hope for the South as a section, in the Union, was in the United States Senate: controlling that branch of Congress it might continue to exercise its supremacy in National affairs in spite of the immense numerical majority of the North. The secession programme doubtless would have been sprung in 1852 had there not been held out to Toombs and his confederates the prospect of Southern accessions to the west by a co-operation of Northern votes. Throughout the entire struggle in Kansas Southern men strained every nerve to secure the Territory, and they were sustained, by all the power of two administrations, as if both Presidents had solemnly agreed to make Kansas a Slave State. That they *were* pledged to the South we entertain not a shadow of doubt—the pledge was the price of their acceptance by the South, and they were voted for by that section with a full understanding that pro-slave interests were to be sustained.[1] How impotent all conspiracy and usurpation were we have seen. Truly

"there 's a Divinity that shapes our ends
Rough hew them as we will,"

---

[1] The following letter from James M. Mason, of Va., to the then Secretary of War, Jefferson Davis, explains itself:

"SELMA, NEAR WINCHESTER, VA., Sept. 30, 1856.

"MY DEAR SIR: I have a letter from Wise, of the 27th, full of spirit. He says the Governments of North Carolina, South Carolina and Louisiana, have already agreed to rendezvous at Raleigh, and others will—this in your most private ear. He says, further, that he had officially requested you to exchange with Virginia, on fair terms of difference, percussion for flint muskets. I don't know the usage or power of the Department in such cases, but if it can be done, even by liberal construction, I hope you will accede. Was there not an appropriation at the last session for converting flint into percussion arms? If so, would it not furnish good reason for extending such facilities to the States? Virginia probably has more arms than the other Southern States, and would divide, in case of need. In a letter yesterday to a Committee in South Carolina, I gave it as my judgment, in the event of Fremont's election, the South should not pause, but proceed at once to 'immediate, absolute and eternal separation.' So I am a candidate for the first halter

"Wise says his accounts from Philadelphia are cheering for Old Buck in Pennsylvania. I hope they be not delusive. *Vale et Salute,*

(Signed) "J. M. MASON.

"Colonel DAVIS."

THE CONSPIRACY OF JOHN BROWN.

THE attempt of John Brown to excite a servile insurrection in Virginia was a revival of Nat Turner's scheme of a Negro independency in the South. It was not, as generally reported at the time of his arrest, trial and execution, a mere plan to run off slaves to Canada. The old man was, as we shall show, no "chattel thief" of this sort. His plans rather embraced a heavy accession *from* Canada of able bodied and resolute negroes to form the mountain army of his contemplated permanent occupation. There was a wildness in the conception which savored of insanity; but, the plan was not conceived in a moment of frenzy—it was the matured enterprise of several years of thought and of much conference with certain eminent abolitionists. If it failed, and ended in the execution of all who survived the first conflict, it was, 1st, because, as in Nat Turner's case, the slaves did not rally to his call, and 2d, because he had underestimated the odds against him. Had the first stroke been successful he might have maintained hold upon Virginia soil. News of this success would have impelled great numbers of slaves and free negroes to his standard; accessions would have passed in from the North both of whites and free negroes, and thus his dream would have been realized of a liberating army too strong to be driven out yet too dangerous to be permitted to remain. Then would have followed the conflict which the old man counted on as necessary to spread the spirit of revolt among the plantations, and his beacon fires would have been lit along the Alleghanies from the Potomac to the Georgian Hills as rallying points for the swarms of black humanity which must answer to his call. The first stroke was a disaster with which fell a scheme that Federal arms alone could have suppressed.

As early as the year 1839 John Brown had determined upon this slave insurrection, as we are expressly informed by his accredited biographer, Redpath, who states:

"It was in 1839 that he conceived the idea of becoming a Liberator of the Southern slaves. He had seen, during the twenty-five years that had elapsed since he became an abolitionist, every right of human nature, and of the Northern States, ruthlessly trodden under the feet of the tyrannical slave power. He saw it blighting and blasting the manhood of the nation; and he listened to 'the voice of the poor that cried.' He heard Lafayette loudly praised, but he saw no helper of the bondman. He saw the people building the sepulchres of the fathers of '76, but lynching and murdering the prophets that were sent unto them. He believed that:

'Who would be free, themselves must strike the blow.'

But the slaves, scattered, closely watched, prevented from assembling to conspire, without arms, apparently overpowered, at the mercy of every traitor, knowing the white man only as their foe, seeing every where and always, that (as the Haytian proverb pithily expresses it,) '*Zie blanc, bouille negues*'—the eyes of the whites burn up the negroes—in order to arise and strike a blow for liberty, needed a positive sign that they had friends among the dominant race, who sympathized with them, believed in their right to freedom, and were ready to aid them in their attempt to obtain it. John Brown determined to let them know that they had friends, and prepared himself to lead them to liberty. From the moment that he formed this resolution, he engaged in no commercial speculations, which he could not, without loss to his friends and family, wind up in fourteen days. He waited patiently. 'LEARN TO WAIT: I have waited twenty years,' he often said to the young men of principle and talent, who loved and flocked around him when in Kansas."

He only went to Kansas in 1855, at the call of his sons, for their defense, and to "win the confidence" of those on whose personal co-operation he must depend for primary success in his great undertaking. [See page 490, foot note.] He was then residing in North Elba, in New York, on a sheep farm—having failed in business as a wool speculator, a few years previously. Though poor in worldly goods, yet he possessed the will of a Hercules, the faith of an Aaron. All accounts agree in ascribing to him a character remarkable for moral purity and for the invincible tenacity of his will. He had courage, patience, self-denial and power of command to an almost unlimited degree. He had age to render him venerable yet his frame was capable of great endurance. All were mastered by the deep devotion to an idea, or rather to a principle—that of war against human slavery. This principle was the compass of his life; it rankled in his soul like a subterranean fire; it impregnated his religion, his politics, his relations to man; it was his Golden Rule and his sword of flame. Men called him a monomaniac; but his mania was identical with that which sways the actions of all intense natures. Luther, Melancthon, Peter the Hermit, Savonarolla, Joan d'Arc, Cromwell, were monomaniacs; but, unlike these, Brown was not a man of powerful intellectual perceptions; he was an irreconcilable zealot, possessed neither of a statesman's powers nor of a politician's discretion. He occupies a place in history beside the religious enthusiast, Nat Turner, rather than an association with those named above. His admirers have exalted him to the Valhalla of the Great; a few New England idealists have classed him with that rare race of individuals of whom one occasionally appears to impersonate the revolutionary idea which marks the progress of human events toward perfect order; lasting honor has crowned his career by embalming his memory in the rude lyric which moves men and masses like an inspiration: [1]

John Brown's body lies mouldering in the grave,
John Brown's body lies mouldering in the grave,
John Brown's body lies mouldering in the grave,
But his soul is marching on.
Glory, glory hallelujah,
Glory, glory hallelujah,
Glory, glory hallelujah,
His soul is marching on.

[1] The origin of this song is a mystery. Like those lyrics which have become immortal from their interpretation of national emotion, it seems to have taken form insensibly, as the utterance of feeling otherwise unutterable. The sublime cadences of that wild song, chaunted by whole divisions, were the inspiration of the "Army of the Union" when it went into battle. No battle anthem ever so stirred men up to deeds of greatness. The leaders of the Union army acknowledge its superhuman power for inspiriting the ranks. One of the most eminent of Department commanders has said that that song "made heroes of all his men."

John Brown's knapsack is strapped upon his back,
John Brown's knapsack is strapped upon his back,
John Brown's knapsack is strapped upon his back,
And his soul is marching on

Glory, glory hallelujah,
Glory, glory hallelujah,
Glory, glory hallelujah,
His soul is marching on.

He 's gone to be a soldier in the army of the Lord,
He 's gone to be a soldier in the army of the Lord,
He 's gone to be a soldier in the army of the Lord,
And his soul is marching on.

Glory, glory hallelujah,
Glory, glory hallelujah,
Glory, glory hallelujah,
His soul is marching on.

But, considering his entire character and career, we attribute his posthumous fame less to any true greatness of his nature than to the fact that his "martyrdom" was rapidly followed by, if it did not, indeed, hasten, the shot on Sumter's walls. In some indefinable manner the Southern Rebellion came to be regarded as a fulfilment of his prophecies. He, hence, became a Jeremiah, who, though dead in the body, still lived in the hearts of the people: "his soul is marching on," was but the refrain of the grand emotion swelling and surging in the popular breast.

Brown's Kansas experiences doubtless served to confirm his purposes in regard to a slave insurrection. He there received new impressions regarding the baleful effects of the institution upon whites as well as blacks. The men who represented 'Southern interests' and clamored lustily for slavery were vicious and dissolute to a degree almost incomprehensible to a Northern mind. His impressions were much intensified by seeing and *knowing* these men, and he returned from Kansas to the East late in the Fall of 1856 to impart to the 'friends of freedom' what he had learned, as well as to perfect arrangements for the deliverance of the Territory from the grasp of the 'enemies of man.' During the Winter following he visited many places and addressed large audiences convened to hear the story of his experiences. Everywhere he made a profound impression, although a large class conceived him a dangerous, because an "incendiary", character. Said a leading free soil paper in Cleveland, Ohio, on the occasion of his visit to that place:

"He was so demented as to suppose he could raise a regiment of men in Ohio to march into Missouri to make. reprisals against the slave forces, and even asked a friend if the power of the State could not be enlisted in that matter. He was then told by many that he was a madman, and the poor man left, sorrowing that there was no sympathy here for the oppressed."

And his own half-brother, a well-to-do farmer and a person of intelligence, regarded him as demented. He said—writing after the fatal termination of the Harper's Ferry *emeute:*

"After his return to Kansas he called on me, and I urged him to go home to his family and attend to his private affairs; that I feared his course would prove his destruction and that of his boys. This was about two years ago. He replied that he was sorry that I did not sympathize with him; that he knew he was in the line of his duty, and he must pursue it, though it should destroy him and his family. He stated to me that he was satisfied that he was a chosen instrument in the hands of God to war against slavery. From his manner and from his conversation at this time, I had no doubt he had become insane upon the subject of slavery, and gave him to understand this was my opinion of him."

But, he was not demented. He was, on the contrary, very clear headed. He saw things with a vision different from those around him; and he was too self-denying, too persistent, to let any consideration move him from his conceived path of duty. Such men are rare in these days of mammon worship; yet, are numerous enough to vitalize the great crust of society and keep it from settling down into the dull, heavy, mass which presages social dyspepsia. He was neither insane nor impractical; rather he was eminently rational and methodical. His conduct proves nothing against his sanity save that he loathed slavery with a sublime sense of dislike; and the future, whatever may be the legal verdict upon his career, will not cease to admire the soul which could press on to its conceived mission with such patient reliance upon the idea that moved him.[1]

[1] The testimony of his most hateful enemy, C. L. Vallandigham, of Ohio, is worthy of citation. After the capture of Brown at Harper's Ferry, Mr. V. proceeded in haste to the spot to gain from him a knowledge of his accomplices, with the ul-

When in Boston, during January, 1857, he said: "I believe in the Golden Rule and the Declaration of Independence. I think they both mean the same thing; and it is better that a whole generation should pass off the face of the earth—men, women and children—by a violent death, than that one jot of either should fail in this country."

This was his idea, and he pursued it to the gallows. Was he insane for entertaining it?

In this visit to the East it is known that Brown conferred with leading abolitionists regarding his proposed descent on Virginia and received so much encouragement as to arrange, somewhat definitively, for his long-contemplated crusade. He failed, however, to obtain funds, and returned to Kansas in the Summer of 1857 to form the nucleus of his liberating host. He there met by agreement Colonel Hugh Forbes, an English adventurer who had participated in the Hungarian and Italian revolutions, and had a good knowledge of Garabaldi's system of guerilla warfare. Brown sought to call around him those young men whom he already had tried and found 'true as steel,' though it would seem that some of the men were not informed as to the ultimate object of their organization. Want of means restricted movements so much that Brown retired to the "abolition" village of Tabor, in Iowa, where he remained from August to November, when Colonel Forbes abandoned the conspiracy for reasons variously stated. He afterwards became an informer against Brown, and compelled the temporary suspension of the plot in 1858.

In the Spring of 1858 the company, composed of nine, started from Tabor, for the East, taking with them considerable

timate design of their arrest and extradition to Virginia for trial. He closely and cruelly pressed the old man, as he lay wounded on the floor of the guard house, but learned not a word to use as evidence against his political antagonists whom he hoped to see in Virginia dungeons. After his inquisition he wrote:

"It is in vain to underrate either the man or the conspiracy. Captain John Brown is as brave and resolute a man as ever headed an insurrection, and in a good cause, and with a sufficient force, would have been a consummate partisan commander. He has coolness, daring persistency, the stoic faith and patience, and a firmness of will and purpose unconquerable. He is the farthest possible remove from the ordinary ruffian, fanatic or madman. Certainly it was one of the best planned and best executed conspiracies that ever failed."

stores, arms and ammunition, which Brown and his friends had gathered. The arms consisted of about two hundred Sharpe's rifles and the same number of navy revolvers. These were transported to Ashtabula county, Ohio, thence to be borne, at the proper moment, to the rendezvous near Harper's Ferry.

From Ohio Brown passed over into Canada West, where a preconcerted convention was held May 8th, 1858. This convocation was an important feature in the conspiracy. Its general nature and action were thus referred to by Cook, one of the Conspirators afterwards caught and hanged by the Virginians. In his confession he stated:

"The place of meeting was in one of the negro churches in Chatham. The convention, I think, was called to order by J. H. Kagi. Its object was then stated, which was to complete a thorough organization and the formation of a Constitution. The first business was to elect a President and Secretary. Elder Monroe, a colored minister, was elected President, and J. H. Kagi, Secretary. The next business was to form a Constitution. Captain Brown had already drawn up one, which, on motion, was read by the Secretary. On motion it was ordered that each article of the Constitution be taken up, and separately amended and passed, which was done. On motion, the Constitution was then adopted as a whole. The next business was to nominate a Commander-in-Chief, Secretary of War, and Secretary of State. Captain John Brown was unanimously elected Commander-in-Chief, J. H. Kagi, Secretary of War, and Richard Realf, Secretary of State. Elder Monroe was to act as President until another was chosen. A. M. Chapman, I think, was to act as Vice President. Dr. M. K. Delaney was one of the Corresponding Secretaries of the Organization. There were some others from the United States, whose names I do not now remember. Most of the delegates to the Convention were from Canada. After the Constitution was adopted, the members took their oath to support it. It was then signed by all present. During the interval between the call for the Convention and its assembling, regular meetings were held at Barbour's Hotel, where we were stopping, by those who were known to be true to the cause, at which meetings plans were laid and discussed. There were no white men at the Convention, save the members of our company. Men and money had both been promised from Chatham and other parts of Canada. When the Convention broke up, news was received that Col. H. Forbes, who had joined in the movement, had given information to the Government. This, of course delayed the time of attack. A day or two afterwards most of our party took the boat to Cleveland—J. H.

Kagi, Richard Realf, William H. Leeman, Richard Robertson and Captain Brown remaining. Captain Brown, however, started in a day or two for the East. Kagi, I think, went to some other town in Canada to set up the type and to get the Constitution printed, which he completed before he returned to Cleveland. We remained in Cleveland for some weeks, at which place, for the time being, the company disbanded."

Among the papers of Brown found at Harper's Ferry were minutes of the proceedings of this Convention, a list of its members, and copies of the "Constitution" as adopted. [See Appendix for so much of this instrument as the Virginia authorities permitted to be published.] But, there is yet much mystery concerning the affair. The Constitution itself was a queer document, judged by the light thus far shed upon it. It is probable, however, the conspiracy was but half unfolded—that the movement which miscarried at its first stroke, was one planned for ultimate results of an extended political as well as social nature. If further developements shall be made—as is not likely—what now in the Constitution and in Brown's proceedings appear singular will assume at least an air of consistency.

After the Chatham gathering it was not Brown's design to repair to Kansas, but, at once, to direct his steps to Harper's Ferry. The discovery of Forbes' defection and revelations to the President of the United States regarding the perfected plans of the "Liberators," compelled a change in their programma. Aside from this defection, when the moment for action came Brown found that numerous friends, in the East and in Ohio, failed to come forward with their promised means. He went East, from Cleveland, during May, to confer with some of these friends, and then hastened to Kansas, having first dispatched Cook to Harper's Ferry to reconnoitre, to indicate depots for arms, and to report—all of which he did. The horrible massacre of ten Free State men on the Marais-des-Cygnes creek, in May, 1858, aroused all the lion in Brown's soul, and he again repaired to Kansas to enlist in its defense. His proceedings there are detailed in the preceding article. He literally "carried the war into Africa," and struck the blow which ended all further Missouri raids over the border. The forcible abstraction by him, of eleven slaves, from Missouri soil—the march to Detroit, Michigan, with his prize, defying not only all pursuers but even the Fugitive Slave law and the United States authority, illustrates the resolution and the sympathies of the man. He safely delivered the slaves at Windsor.

The moment then seemed to have arrived for the initiation of his schemes. He therefore earnestly set about gathering material resources for his anti-slave crusade. From March to midsummer he pressed his arrangements so secretly and so successfully as to excite not a ripple of alarm among the opponents of his enterprise, who, at that time, comprised nineteen-twentieths of the people. Yet, he did not proceed in disguise. Late in March he appeared, in company with his intelligent and devoted confederate, Kagi, at Cleveland, Ohio, and made a speech to the multitude convened to express sympathy with several leading citizens of Oberlin, then in prison by United States processes for assisting in the escape of runaway slaves. His words were those of scorn of the institution which made chattels of human beings. He related the particulars of his late expedition of liberation, and remarked that, though very poor, he still was worth three thousand two hundred and fifty dollars—that being the price fixed upon his head by the Governor of Missouri and the President of the United States. He was received with a "storm of applause." From Cleveland he proceeded first to Astabula county, Ohio, where he found friends and advisers in several well known men, and where his temporary depot of arms then was. Passing on to the East, he delivered a speech at Rochester, N. Y., and spent a brief period with his friend Gerritt Smith, at Peterboro, from whom he doubtless, received such final aid as enabled him to hasten the consummation of his plans. He visited Boston and New York city. At Collinsville, Conn., he ordered to be completed the one thousand pikes, which, though contracted for in March, 1857, he had not been able to pay for—hence they were not finished. After a somewhat extended tour to the East, and a brief visit to his family at North Elba, New York, he returned to Northern Ohio—thence he made his way to Chambersburg, Penn., where he was joined by two of his sons and

Captain Anderson. With these he proceeded to Hagerstown, Md.—there assuming the name of *Smith.* He was carried to Harper's Ferry in a public hack, and represented to inquirers that, tired of farming in Western New York, he was seeking for a sheep farm in that vicinity. Said the man who drove the adventurers over to the Ferry:

"After looking around Harper's Ferry a few days, and prowling through the mountains in search of minerals, as they said, they came across a large farm with three unoccupied houses—the owner, Dr. Booth Kennedy, having died in the Spring. These houses they rented from the family till next March, and paid the rent in advance, and also purchased a lot of hogs from the family for cash, and agreed to take care of the stock until a sale could be had; *and they did attend most faithfully to them, and have it all in first rate order; were gentlemen, and kind to every body.* After living there a few weeks, others joined them, until as many as twelve were in these three houses, and every few days a stranger would appear and disappear again without creating the least surprise."

This Kennedy farm was located about five miles from the Ferry, on the Maryland side, in a well settled but somewhat wild region. It was an admirably chosen rendezvous, accessible yet not too exposed. The men there quietly gathered, but kept from sight, spending much time in wandering singly, over wide distances of the mountainous regions around the Ferry, to become well acquainted with its wild and intricate features. Their goods, arms, ammunition and stores, were carted, without notice, from Chambersburg to the farm, which soon became quite an arsenal.

Here the conspirators remained undisturbed until the hour of action. Says Brown's biographer: "It was the original intention of Captain Brown to sieze the arsenal at Harper's Ferry on the night of the 24th of October, and to take the arms there deposited to the neighboring mountains, with a number of the wealthier citizens of the vicinity, as hostages, until they should redeem themselves by liberating an equal number of their slaves. When at Baltimore, for satisfactory reasons, he determined to strike the blow that was to shake the slave system to its foundations, on the night of the 17th. One of the men who fought at Harper's Ferry gave me as the chief reason for the precipitate movement, that they suspected there was a Judas in their company. That the reasons were just and important, the prudence that John Brown had always hitherto manifested satisfactorily proves. But this decision, however necessary, was unfortunate; for the men from Canada, Kansas, New England and the neighboring Free States, who had been told to be prepared for the event on the 24th of October, and were ready to do their duty at Harper's Ferry at that time, were unable to join their Captain at this earlier period.

"Many, who started to join the Liberators, halted half way; for the blow had already been struck, and their Captain made a captive. Had there been no precipitation, the mountains of Virginia, to-day, would have been peopled with free blacks, properly officered and ready for field action.

"The negroes, also, in the neighboring counties, who had promised to be ready on the 24th of October, were confused by the precipitate attack; and, before they could act in concert—which they can only do by secret nocturnal meetings—were watched, overpowered, and deprived of every chance to join their heroic Liberators.

"Having sent off the women who lived at their cabins—Cook's wife and others—the neighbors began to talk about the singularity of the proceeding; and it became necessary, on that account, also, to precipitate an attack on Harper's Ferry."

On the evening of the 17th, Brown convened his friends and gave them his general as well as specific instructions—among which was to take no life not actually necessary to their own self-preservation—an injunction followed to the letter.

At night fall, October 17th, 1859, the Conspirators passed from the farm to the Ferry. The number detailed to the town was twenty-two, viz.: seventeen whites, and five blacks. Several squads were dispatched to positions above and below the town for the purpose of cutting away the telegraph wires and for tearing up the railway track—thus to sever all communication with the Ferry and to give the Conspirators time to consummate their work. The first steps were to sieze the town and some of its citizens as hostages for the safety of any "Liberator" who might be captured; to capture the Government arsenal with its rich stores of cannon, muskets and munitions, thus to obtain the necessary equipments for the powerful force which it was conceived would soon be at the leader's disposal, composed of whites and negroes on their way from the North, and of slaves for whose liberation the movement was made; then, all having been accomplished, the armed host was to retire to the fastnesses of the mountains before the militia which would, it was supposed, gather for an attack. The general plan, as divulged by Cook, Brown and Kagi,[1] comprised a *permanent occupation of the Virginia mountains;* no slaves were to be run off to Canada, except such as preferred to go; communications with the North, through Pennsylvania, were to be preserved; the standard of revolt was to be borne along the mountains to the South, but no war was to be made other than one of strict defense, and such as might be necessary to aid the negroes in making their way from the plantations to the mountains. This was the general scheme conceived by the daring leader. That it could have succeeded is, indeed, most questionable; for, had Brown been able to retire, as arranged, to the mountains, and had he proven too strong for the militia, the Federal Government itself must have assumed the offensive. It doubtless was expected by the friends of the movement that, in event of the General Government calling out its forces, a large accession of Northern men, to Brown's numbers would at once take place and thus render him too formidable for suppression. However, nothing is now in existence to prove that it was his design actually to resist the Federal Government in the field, though we can well conceive that the permanent occupation arranged for, and the "provisional government" ordained by the Chatham Convention, meant nothing if not war against all comers. Kagi, in his revelation, it is true, put a less revolutionary face on the movement. Thus, the authority who reports his evidence, says:

"As fast as possible other bands besides the original ones were to be formed, and a continuous chain of posts established in the mountains.

[1] Kagi was killed early in the first affray. Before leaving Kansas, in 1858, he divulged the programme of deliverance and of operations in Virginia. This programme was followed out so closely as to make it appear that Kagi's revelation embodied the main features of Brown's stupendous plans.

They were to be supported by provisions taken from the farms of the oppressors. They expected to be speedily and constantly reenforced; first, by the arrival of those men, who, in Canada, were anxiously looking and praying for the time of deliverance, and then by the slaves themselves. The intention was to hold the egress to the Free States as long as possible, in order to retreat when that was advisable. Kagi, however, expected to retreat southward, not in the contrary direction. The slaves were to be armed with pikes, scythes, muskets, shot guns and other simple instruments of defense; the officers, white or black, and such of the men as were skilled and trustworthy, to have the use of the Sharpe's rifles and revolvers. They anticipated procuring provisions enough for subsistence by forage, as also arms, horses and ammunition. Kagi said one of the reasons that induced him to go into the enterprise was a full conviction that, at no very distant day, forcible efforts for freedom would break out among the slaves, and that slavery might be more speedily abolished by such efforts than by any other means. He knew by observation in the South, that in no point was the system more vulnerable than in its fear of a slave rising. Believing that such a blow would soon be struck, he wanted to organize it so as to make it more effectual, and also, by directing and controlling the negroes, to prevent some of the atrocities that would necessarily arise from the sudden upheaval of such a mass as the Southern slaves. The Constitution adopted at Chatham was intended as the framework of organization among the emancipationists, to enable the leaders to effect a more complete control of their forces. Ignorant men, in fact all men, were more easily managed by the forms of law and organization than without them. This was one of the purposes to be served by the Provisional Government. Another was to alarm the Oligarchy by the discipline and the show of organization. In their terror they would imagine the whole North was upon them pell-mell, as well as all their slaves. Kagi said John Brown anticipated that by a system of forbearance to non-slaveholders many of them might be induced to join them."

The company detailed to the town performed its work quietly. All street lights were first extinguished and the armory secured—its watchmen being taken prisoners and locked up in the guard house. A watchman on the railway bridge over the Potomac also was seized. A second watchman coming on at midnight was ordered to surrender, but ran and gave the first alarm at the hotel, though nothing followed. A passenger train from the West, bound to Baltimore and Washington, reached the bridge after midnight to find it in possession of an armed guard. The train was delayed several hours, greatly to the alarm of its passengers, but Brown's habitual kindness prevailed over his sense of prudence, it would appear, for he finally permitted it to pass. It then flew on its way to the east to spread the alarm, and, early on the 18th, the country was electrified with most startling announcements of the "insurrection." Newspaper "extras" issued in the cities. East, west, north and south the excitement which succeeded was boundless. The most eager curiosity prevailed for more news, and more news soon was forthcoming; each hour added to the store of reports "from the scene of conflict." Great numbers of adventurers and newspaper reporters took early trains to reach the centre of interest.

The first steps taken by Brown were followed by the arrest of every citizen who appeared on the street. By day-break about fifty had thus been borne to the guard house. As the morning progressed, so quietly had affairs been managed, that numbers of workmen turned out for their day's labor, unconscious, until taken prisoners, that the town was under martial occupancy. The detail of squads for guarding important points was necessarily small. Thus, Brown, his two sons, Aaron D. Stevens and two blacks held the armory; John Kagi, with Wm. H. Leeman, Stewart Taylor, Lewis Leary, Anderson and Copeland (the two latter colored men) held the rifle works and patrolled the lower town; John E. Cook, with Owen Brown, C. P. Tidd, F. J. Merriam and Barclay Coppoc remained at the Kennedy farm cabins and school house to care for the property there and to act as a reserve; a few men stood on guard at the bridge and street corners. What an army of invasion!

During the forenoon shots were fired by citizens who began to pluck up resolution. A man named Barclay who fired upon the guard was killed instantly. About half a dozen Virginians, gathered in a building commanding the armory grounds, succeeded in killing one of Brown's men and in mortally wounding his son Watson. This random firing continued until after mid-day. Shortly after noon a detachment of militia from Charlestown, Va., arrived, one hundred strong. This was the beginning of the end. These troops, in conjunction with citizens, soon obtained possession of the Shenandoah bridge, the rifle works and other available points. Brown, seeing his position untenable, retired to the armory engine house. Kagi and his men, pressed into the river, swam to rocks in its centre, which four of them reached. They were there met by the fire of one hundred muskets. Kagi literally was riddled with balls. His body floated down stream, soon to be accompanied by that of Anderson. Leary was mortally wounded and Copeland taken prisoner. Leeman's brains were blown out by a German militiaman. Having been sent to confer with Brown, he was wounded and was pursued into the water there to be shot down. The engine house soon was under siege. One by one the "Liberators" began to fall. Newby, a negro, and Jim, Colonel Washington's coachman, fell early in the afternoon. Also a free negro. All of these negroes fought intrepidly. Two Virginians were killed in the first assault on the engine house, viz.: Captain Turner and Mr. Beckman, Mayor of the town. In revenge, William Thompson, one of Brown's men, held as a prisoner, was taken out on the bridge and shot, with many accompaniments of atrocity. A townsman held as a hostage prevailed on Brown to let Stevens and himself pass out, under a flag of truce, to try and arrange matters. Brown consented, when Stevens and the citizen passed out. The flag was violated; Stevens was shot, and the citizen failed to return to Brown's quarters. Night at length came to find the lion-hearted old warrior closely besieged by a force of over one thousand well armed and infuriated men. His case was hopeless. Why he did not escape to the mountains before he became so helplessly hemmed in is not known. Should he hold out until morning then the force against him would be two thousand men, for the President of the United States, the Governor of Virginia and the City of Baltimore all had dispatched troops to the spot. Said Redpath: "The result of the day's fight to the Liberators looked extremely gloomy. In the rivers floated the corpses of Kagi, Leeman, Stewart Taylor and Wm. Thompson. Imprisoned, and near to death, lay Lewis Leary and Stevens. Copeland was a captive. On the street lay the dead bodies of Hazlitt and Newby. In the engine house were the remains of Oliver Brown and Dauphin Thompson; while

Watson, the Captain's son, lay without hope of recovery. The only unwounded survivors of the Liberators in the engine house were Captain Brown, Jerry Anderson, Edwin Coppoc, and Shields Green, the negro. Eight Virginia hostages, and a small number of armed negroes were with them."

The morning of Tuesday, October 19th, brought, as was expected, such an array as would have appalled any other heart than that of John Brown. There was no tremor in his nerves. He calmly awaited the last shock, determined, with his three unwounded men, to receive the charge of the host without but not to surrender. A company of United States troops, having arrived during the night, with two pieces of artillery, took position before the engine house, but forbore to open on it as within were Colonel Washington and seven other Virginians, held as hostages. A parley was called, therefore, under a flag of truce. Brown was pressed earnestly to surrender. He firmly refused except upon terms equivalent to his escape, viz.: to be permitted to march out with his men and arms, taking his prisoners with him; to proceed to the second toll gate be yond the bridge, where he would free the prisoners; there the troops might enter upon the pursuit and catch the "Liberators" if they could.

The direct assault followed. A heavy ladder used as a battering ram laid open the doors and the United States troops entered. One only of the assailants was seriously wounded, although four rifles were fired into the crowd. One of Brown's men was killed, and he himself shockingly cut by sabre strokes on his head after he had ceased resistance, and, after he was down, was twice bayonetted. Only Coppoc and Green escaped unhurt to be reserved for the gallows. Brown was borne to the guard house, where he found the wounded Stevens. Watson Brown was, a few hours later, removed, in a dying condition, to the same place. In front of the engine house lay the other son's dead body. No beds were provided for the wounded men; they were treated with great severity. Had it not been for the presence of Colonel Robert E. Lee, of the U. S. army, it is probable the militia would have hung on the spot every survivor. Cook and his party, informed of Brown's fate, fled to the mountains, to become a seven days' terror, and to enlist, in his pursuit, half the able bodied inhabitants of the surrounding country, as well as several bodies of militia and the United States' marines.

It is needless here to detail the incidents which followed this capture. That they were numerous and exciting is true, but they belong rather to local than to general history. Governor Wise and U. S. Senator Mason, both of Virginia, hastened to the Ferry, where they held an interview with Brown and Stevens in the guard house.[1] They learned nothing aside from what Brown confessed to be his general design to liberate slaves. The premises at Kennedy's farm were searched, and, in a carpet bag filled with papers, were found copies of the Chatham Constitution, which Brown acknowledged to be his own conception. He produced on his visitors, by his fearless but kind demeanor, an impression singularly at variance with the hate of the infuriated crowd who gathered to "get a sight of the monster." Said the Governor, after his return to Richmond:

"They are themselves mistaken who take him to be a madman. He is a bundle of the best nerves I ever saw, cut and thrust, and bleeding and in bonds. He is a man of clear head, of courage, fortitude and simple ingenuousness. He is cool collected and indomitable, and it is but just to him to say, that he was humane to his prisoners, as stated to me by Colonel Washington and Mr. Mills, and he inspired me with great trust in his integrity as a man of truth. He is a fanatic, vain and garrulous, but firm, and truthful and intelligent. His men, too, who survive, except the free negroes with him, are like him. He professes to be a Christian, in communion with the Congregational Church of the North, and openly preaches his purpose of universal emancipation: and the negroes themselves were to be the agents, by means of arms, led on by white commanders."

There were found stored in the buildings at the farm, and in the log school house near by, a considerable quantity of arms, munitions, &c. Also two fine horses, wagon and other personal property. All was "confiscated."

After lying in the guard house until Wednesday afternoon, Oct. 20th, the surviving Conspirators were borne to Charles-

[1] Vallandigham, the Ohio Congressman, already referred to, was present at this interview. He was anxious to implicate others, but Brown and Stevens were too discreet to give the politician any comfort.

town jail, accompanied by Governor Wise and a strong escort of U. S. marines. Watson Brown had died in the guard house Wednesday morning. His body was given over to the doctors for dissection.[1] The remaining bodies were gathered and buried together in a pit. A preliminary 'court' composed of eight justices of the peace, convened on the 25th of October. This court was but a form to bind the prisoners over to the Circuit Court. Brown protested against it. His fearless speech in the court room has often been cited. He said:

"If a fair trial is to be allowed us, there are mitigating circumstances, that I would urge in our favor. But if we are to be forced with a mere form—a trial for execution—you might spare yourselves that trouble. I am ready for my fate. I do not ask a trial. I beg for no mockery of a trial—no insult—nothing but that which conscience gives or cowardice would drive you to practise.

"I ask again to be excused from the mockery of a trial. I do not know what the special design of this examination is. I do not know what is to be the benefit of it to the Commonwealth. I have now little further to ask, other than that I may not be foolishly insulted, only as cowardly barbarians insult those who fall into their power."

The examination, however, proceeded. The evidence of course was such as to commit all for final trial, before the higher tribunal, which assembled at once—so hurried were the proceedings. Great alarm existed in the community. Rumors of the wildest character prevailed regarding a rescue by Northern men, and also in regard to the strength of Cook, still in the mountains. Said a dispatch from the Charlestown telegraph office:

"There is an evident intention to hurry the trial through, and bxecute the prisoners as soon as possible—fearing attempts to rescue them. It is rumored that Brown is desirous of making a full statement of his motives and intentions through the press, but the court has refused all access to reporters—fearing that he may put forth something calculated to influence the public mind, and to have a bad effect on the slaves."

"The reason given for hurrying the trial is, that the people of the whole country are kept in a state of excitement, and a large armed force is required to prevent attempts at rescue."

1 The students of Winchester Medical College skinned the body, separated the muscular and venous systems and injected the veins, dried and varnished the bones, and kept the whole on exhibition in their anatomical museum. The skin was to have been stuffed, but was, it is understood, prepared into leather and used for making various articles of *virtu*.

The grand jury was called at two o'clock P. M., Tuesday, (Oct. 25th,) and charged by Judge Parker. The charge was a queer commingling of judicial honesty and pro-slave prejudgment. While it demanded for Brown an impartial hearing, it assumed his guilt as certain, and used such terms as must inflame the minds of Virginians against the prisoners. The jurymen did not perfect their indictment until noon of Wednesday, the 26th, when a "true bill" was reported against each of the prisoners arraigned: first, for conspiring with negroes to incite an insurrection; second, for treason to the Commonwealth of Virginia; third, for murder. Upon *all* these counts of the indictment the trial at once proceeded—not upon one, as is usual. Brown, still ill and feeble from wounds, asked for a short delay to recover his strength and to prepare his case; but, it was refused. The prisoners all plead "not guilty." Their appearance was thus noticed by a correspondent of a Richmond paper:

"The prisoners were brought into court, accompanied by a body of armed men. Cannon were stationed in front of the court house, and an armed guard were patrolling round the jail. Brown looked something better, and his eye was not so much swollen. Stevens had to be supported, and reclined on a mattress on the floor of the court room—evidently unable to sit. He has the appearance of a dying man, breathing with great difficulty. The prisoners were compelled to stand during the indictment, but it was with difficulty. Stevens being held upright by two bailiffs."

The State elected to try Brown first, when Lawson Botts, the counsel assigned for his defense, by the court, asked for delay, citing Brown's unfitness for trial. No respite, however, was permitted. The court evidently deemed it impolitic to give the culprit chance for sturdy defense. A jury was impanneled during the afternoon, after much labor to obtain those who "had not been at Harper's Ferry." Mr. Botts, while he tried to do his duty, evidently did not care to face public sentiment; the jury was impanneled and sworn in without a challenge.

On Thursday morning, October 27th, John Brown's trial opened. It is unnecessary to detail the proceedings. Counsel for the prisoners, which had been sent for, almost hourly was expected; but, no suspension of the trial was permitted. Thursday and Friday were spent in the examination of witnesses. Brown's counsel elicited many facts going to prove his client's humanity; but, before the court stood those who had witnessed, or participated in, the conflict of Monday and Tuesday: no Virginia jury could be expected to regard Brown, in the face of their testimony, other than as a criminal of the worst class. One of those who had assisted in the murder of Thompson, confessed the deed and its brutal circumstances; but, not a thought prevailed of crime in his case. Counsel for Brown arrived Friday. A brief respite was asked by them to look into the case; still, all delays, for any cause, were denied. During Saturday witnesses for the defense were introduced. The most sought to be proven by them was Brown's freedom from malice in his acts and his merely defensive attitude in all cases where life was taken. These points appear to have been well sustained. His counsel (composed of Messrs. George H. Hoyt, of Boston, Hiram Griswold, of Cleveland, O., and Sam'l Chilton, of Washington City) sought, by various technicalities, to gain time—to try on one count only, &c., but, all efforts failed. Monday the prosecution and defense made their arguments. At two o'clock the jury retired, and, in less than an hour, returned with a verdict of guilty on all the counts of the indictment. One present wrote of the proceedings, at this point:

"Not the slightest sound was heard in the vast crowd as this verdict was returned and read. Not the slightest expression of elation or triumph was uttered from the hundreds present, who, a moment before, outside the court, joined in heaping threats and imprecations on his head; nor was this strange silence interrupted during the whole of the time occupied by the forms of the court. Old Brown himself said not even a word, but, as on any previous day, turned to adjust his pallet, and then composedly stretched himself upon it.

"Mr. Chilton moved an arrest of judgment, both on account of errors in the indictment and errors in the verdict. The objection in regard to the indictment has already been stated. The prisoner had been tried for an offense not appearing on the record of the grand jury. The verdict was not on each count separately, but was a general verdict on the whole indictment."

This motion was argued on the succeeding day but denied,

and Brown was remanded to jail for sentence. Coppoc's case was then taken up (Nov. 1st) and ended (Nov. 2d) in his conviction. Brown, to save time, was brought into court for sentence, during the absence of the jury in the second case. He was able to stand, and addressed the court. We may quote:

"In the first place, I deny every thing but what I have all along admitted—the design on my part to free the slaves. I intended certainly to have made a clear thing of that matter, as I did last Winter, when I went into Missouri, and there took slaves without the snapping of a gun on either side, moved them through the country, and finally left them in Canada. I designed to have done the same thing again, on a larger scale. That was all I intended. I never did intend murder or treason, or the destruction of property, or to excite or incite slaves to rebellion, or to make insurrection.

"I have another objection: and that is, it is unjust that I should suffer such a penalty. Had I interfered in the manner which I admit, and which I admit has been fairly proved—(for I admire the truthfulness and candor of the greater portion of the witnesses who have testified in this case)—had I so interfered in behalf of the rich, the powerful, the intelligent, the so-called great, or in behalf of any of their friends, either father, mother, brother, sister, wife or children, or any of that class, and suffered and sacrificed what I have in this interference, it would have been all right, and every man in this court would have deemed it an act worthy of reward rather than punishment.

"This court acknowledges, as I suppose, the validity of the Law of God. I see a book kissed here which I suppose to be the Bible, or, at least, the New Testament. That teaches me that all things 'whatsoever I would that men should do unto me, I should do even so to them.' It teaches me further, to 'remember them that are in bonds as bound with them.' I endeavored to act up to that instruction. I say, I am yet too young to understand that God is any respecter of persons. I believe that to have interfered as I have done, as I have always freely admitted I have done, in behalf of His despised poor, was not wrong, but right. Now, if it is deemed necessary that I should forfeit my life for the furtherance of the ends of justice, and mingle my blood further with the blood of my children, and with the blood of millions in this slave country whose rights are disregarded by wicked, cruel and unjust enactments—I submit: so let it be done.

"Let me say one word further.

"I felt entirely satisfied with the treatment I have received on my trial. Considering all the circumstances, it has been more generous than I expected. But I feel no consciousness of guilt. I have stated from the first what was my intention and what was not. I never had any design against the life of any person, nor any disposition to commit treason, or excite slaves to rebel, or make any general insurrection. I never encouraged any man to do so, but always discouraged any idea of that kind.

"Let me say, also, a word in regard to the statements made by some of those connected with me. I hear it has been stated by some of them that I have induced them to join me. But the contrary is true. I do not say this to injure them, but regretting their weakness. There is not one of them but joined me of his own accord, and the greater part at their own expense. A number of them I never saw, and never had a word of conversation with, till the day they came to me, and that was for the purpose I have stated.

"Now I have done."

He was sentenced to be hanged on Friday, Dec. 2d. He was kept a close prisoner, and a powerful military guard was detailed for duty. The excitement which waited upon these proceedings was prodigious. In every section of the South all classes were anxious for news. The Virginians, fearing a rescue, acted with extreme caution. Brown was kindly treated; wrote and received many letters; had free frequent interviews with visitors and friends; and, would appear to have enjoyed perfect serenity of mind. His letters, indeed, are remarkable evidences of his clear understanding, his devotion to what he deemed duty, and his resignation. They are, at once, very inspiriting and very pathetic, and have not failed to extort from his worst enemies words of admiration. One other significant feature of his case must be mentioned: the letters of condolence and of money contributions which flowed in upon him from most unexpected sources. These letters proved that sympathy for him and *his work* was wide spread: if Brown was insane so were his thousand sympathisers.[1] Many ministers of

[1] In the report of his interview with a son of Governor Wise, we have this testimony: "Brown said he did not recognize any slaveholder, lay or clerical, or any man sympathizing with slavery, as a Christian. He gave the same reason yesterday for his refusal to accept the services of some clergymen who called upon him. He also said he would as soon be attended to the scaffold by blacklegs or robbers of the worst kind as by slaveholding ministers, or ministers sympathizing with slavery, and that if he had his choice he would prefer being followed to the scaffold by barefooted, barelegged, ragged negro children, and their old gray-headed slave-mother, than by clergymen of this character. He would feel, he said, much prouder of such an escort, and wished he could have it." There is an Apostolic sublimity in this.

the Gospel, among others, gained access to his room—some of them to argue the divine right of man in man. All of these Brown dismissed peremptorily. He refused, in all instances, the prayers of every man who was of pro-slavery views. His stern, outspoken hate of the "accursed institution" excited the astonishment, we are told, of Virginians.

By November 24th excitement became so great that the military force in and around Charlestown was largely augmented and martial law was proclaimed. After that it was difficult to obtain access to the town, and we only have detached pictures of his life up to the day of execution. He spent the latter portion of his days in preparing a document for his family —understood to be not so much a defense as an exposition of his acts and his views. This interesting document never reached its direction. It doubtless was destroyed by the Virginia authorities, who, in court and out of it, betrayed much anxiety to suppress the utterance of anti-slavery views. Upon that point comment might prove interesting.

Wednesday before the execution, Mrs. Brown, under escort of the military, reached Charlestown and had an interview with her husband. It was a very sad meeting, but Brown was thoroughly resigned and resolute. His wife bore the affliction with a fortitude worthy of all praise.

The execution took place on the day allotted by law, in the midst of an imposing military display. The spot chosen was on a hill-side near to the town, from which the vast concourse of spectators could behold the sight. Brown was invincible to the last—betraying not a shadow of fear. He went into eternity like one gliding off into repose. After death the body was given over to Mrs. Brown, and, by her, borne to their farm at North Elba, N. Y., where it was buried with circumstances of profound interest. Wendall Phillips, of Boston, pronounced the funeral oration—one of the most impressive and eloquent orations ever uttered on this continent. By him, and by abolitionists of the radical school, Brown was crowned with the laurels of martyrdom.

Cook was captured on Friday, Oct. 28th. He was seized in Pennsylvania by men on his track for the reward offered. His trial quickly followed, and he was hung, along with Hazlitt, Dec. 16th. Their bodies were sent to New Jersey for burial. The execution of Stevens, Copeland, and Green passed off without much notice—the excitement having culminated in Brown's exit from life.

Thus closed the tragedy of John Brown's scheme for slave liberation. Its sad results elicited, from a large majority of the North, not a word of regret. The act of Brown was at war with the peace of society and the comity of States; it had for its aim the overthrow of recognized institutions and the instatement of a reign of terror; its ends could only be attained through desolation and blood. But a select few were "radcal" enough to sustain his course, much as the majority of men might have admired his heroism and his truth of soul. For a season abolitionists of the Garrisonian school reposed under a load of obloquy, and it appeared as if slavery were strengthened by the war of words which succeeded. When Congress assembled the subject was introduced, and Mr. Douglas, by a bill to punish sedition, sought to render further invasions high State crimes. In the debates which ensued partisan capital was sought to be made against the party then for the first time in the ascendancy—the anti-slavery, or "Republican" party. But, the Republican leaders disclaimed any sympathy with Brown, whose cause they censured as revolutionary and reprehensible. A feeling of uneasiness prevailed in Southern circles; some danger seemed impending; vague apprehensions of further invasion were entertained; and such intimations were made by Mr. Mason and other Southern Senators as induced the appointment (Dec. 15th) by the Senate, (agreeable to resolutions introduced by Mason, Dec. 5th, 1859,) of a committee of inquiry, to investigate the Harper's Ferry affair and its ramifications, and to report if any cause for further alarm existed. This committee, in the prosecution of its investigations, summoned as witnesses, among others, Thaddeus Hyatt, of New York, John Brown, Jr., of Ohio, F. B. Sanborn and James Redpath, of Massachusetts. These men all failed to answer the summons, and writs for their arrest for contempt of authority, were issued by vote of the Senate, Feb.

15th, 1860. Great excitement followed attempts to seize these persons. Brown and his neighbors armed, and defied the officer detailed for his arrest. Sanborn was seized at Concord, N. H., at night, but was rescued by his neighbors, and, under a writ of *habeas corpus*, had a hearing before Chief Justice Shaw, who declared the arrest illegal. Redpath eluded the writ of arrest. Hyatt was borne to Washington. March 9th he appeared, with eminent counsel, before the Senate, to answer, 1st, why he had refused to obey the first summons to testify, and 2d, if he was then willing to appear before the committee and to answer such questions as might be required of him. Very exciting proceedings ensued. Hyatt's reply was, in substance, that the committee was commissioned with "powers such as were never before known or contemplated in this Republican Government; powers that were inimical to freedom, subversive of liberty and in violation of the fundamental law of the land; and to be resisted, 1st, because contrary to reason, and 2d, because contrary to the Constitution." In support of this he submitted his written argument—a very able paper, surveying the whole question involved, of congressional powers and personal rights. In view of this protest Mason introduced a resolution to commit Hyatt to the common jail of the District, there to be kept in close custody until he should signify his willingness to answer such questions as might be propounded by the select committee. Pending discussion on this order of incarceration, Hyatt was remanded to the custody of the Sergeant at Arms. March 12th, the resolution for close confinement was passed, by a vote of 44 to 10. Hyatt, accordingly, was committed to the common jail, and was, in most respects, treated as a common felon. An effort was made, May 28th, to grant him the privilege of the city limits as his bounds, but the motion failed of consideration. He was kept in prison until June 15th, when the select committee of five, through its chairman, Mason, reported—Mr. Doolittle, for himself and Collamer, the two Republican members, at the same time putting in their minority report. Mason moved Hyatt's discharge, because the select committee of five being dissolved there was no other committee before which Hyatt could be cited. He was thereupon, released, having been incarcerated three months. Mason's report was a lengthy document, the concluding portions of which we give in the Appendix. It is interesting as presenting the Southern view of the affair.

APPENDIX.

JEFFERSON'S KENTUCKY RESOLUTIONS OF '98.

In the paper on the "Alien and Sedition Troubles" we refer to the celebrated Kentucky Resolutions of Nullification and State Supremacy, which have ever since formed one of the fundamental principles of the "democratic" party. Their importance requires their repetition here at length. As passed, in their modified form, by the Kentucky Legislature (Nov. 10th, 15th, 1798), they read:

1. *Resolved,* That the several States composing the United States of America, are not united on the principle of unlimited submission to their general government; but by compact, under the style and title of a Constitution for the United States, and of amendments thereto, they constituted a general government for special purposes, delegated to that government certain definite powers, reserving, each State to itself, the residuary mass of right to their own self-government; and, that whensoever the General Government assumes undelegated powers, its acts are unauthoritative, void and of no force; that to this compact each State acceded as a State, and is an integral party; that this government, created by this compact, was not made the exclusive or final judge of the extent of the powers delegated to itself; since that would have made its discretion, and not the Constitution, the measure of its powers; but, that, as in all other cases of compact among parties having no common judge, each party has an equal right to judge for itself, as well of infractions as of the mode and measure of redress.

2. *Resolved,* That the Constitution of the United States having delegated to Congress a power to punish treason, counterfeiting the securities and current coin of the United States, piracies and felonies committed on the high seas, and offenses against the laws of nations, and no other crimes whatever; and it being true, as a general principle, and one of the amendments to the Constitution having also declared, "that the powers not delegated to the United States by the Constitution, nor prohibited by it to the States, are reserved to the States respectively, or to the people," therefore also the same act of Congress, passed on the 14th day of July, 1798, and entitled "An act in addition to act entitled An act for the punishment of certain crimes against the United States;" as also the act passed by them on the 27th day of June, 1798, entitled "An act to punish frauds committed on the Bank of the United States," (and all other their acts which assume to create, define or punish crimes other than those enumerated in the Constitution,) are altogether void and of no force, and that the power to create, define and punish such other

crimes is reserved, and of right appertains solely and exclusively, to the respective States, each within its own territory.

3. *Resolved,* That it is true, as a general principle, and is also expressly declared by one of the amendments to the Constitution, that "the powers not delegated to the United States by the Constitution, nor prohibited by it to the States, are reserved to the States respectively, or to the people;" and that no power over the freedom of religion, freedom of speech, or freedom of the press being delegated to the United States by the Constitution, nor prohibited by it to the States, all lawful powers respecting the same did of right remain, and were reserved to the States or to the people; that thus was manifested their determination to retain to themselves the right of judging how far the licentiousness of speech and of the press may be abridged without lessening their useful freedom, and how far those abuses which cannot be separated from their use should be tolerated rather than the use be destroyed; and thus also they guarded against all abridgement by the United States of the freedom of religious principles and exercises, and retained to themselves the right of protecting the same, as this State, by a law passed on the general demand of its citizens, had already protected them from all human restraint or interference; and that, in addition to this general principle and express declaration, another and more special provision has been made by one of the amendments to the Constitution which expressly declares, that "Congress shall make no laws respecting an establishment of religion, or prohibiting the free exercise thereof. or abridging the freedom of speech or of the press," thereby guarding in the same sentence, and under the same words, the freedom of religion, of speech and the press, insomuch that whatever violates either, throws down the sanctuary which covers the others; and that libels, falsehood and defamation, equally with heresy and false religion, are withheld from the cognizance of Federal tribunals. That therefore the act of the Congress of the United States, passed on the 14th of July, 1798, entitled "An act in addition to the act entitled An act for the punishment of certain crimes against the United States," which does abridge the freedom of the press, is not law, but is altogether void and of no force.

4. *Resolved,* That alien friends are under the jurisdiction and protection of the laws of the State wherein they are; that no power over them has been delegated to the United States, nor prohibited to the individual States distinct from their power over citizens; and it being true, as a general principle, and one of the amendments to the Constitution having also declared, that "the powers not delegated to the United States by the Constitution, nor prohibited to the States, are reserved to the States respectively, or to the people," the act of the Congress of the United States, passed the 22d day of June, 1798, entitled "An act concerning aliens," which assumes power over alien friends not delegated by the Constitution, is not law, but is altogether void and of no force.

5. *Resolved,* That in addition to the general principle as well as the express declaration, that powers not delegated are reserved, another and more special provision inferred in the Constitution, from abundant caution has declared, "that the migration and importation of such persons as any of the States now existing shall think proper to admit, shall not be prohibited by the Congress prior to the year 1808." That this commonwealth does admit the migration of alien friends described as the subject of the said act concerning aliens; that a provision against prohibiting their migration, is a provision against all acts equivalent thereto, or it

would be nugatory; that to remove them when migrated is equivalent to a prohibition of their migration, and is, therefore, contrary to the said provision of the Constitution, and void.

6. *Resolved,* That the imprisonment of a person under the protection of the laws of this commonwealth on his failure to obey the simple order of the President to depart out of the United States, as is undertaken by said act, entitled, "An act concerning aliens," is contrary to the Constitution, one amendment in which has provided, that "no person shall be deprived of liberty without due process of law," and that another having provided, "that in all criminal prosecutions, the accused shall enjoy the right to a public trial by an impartial jury, to be informed as to the nature and cause of the accusation, to be confronted with the witnesses against him, to have compulsory process for obtaining witnesses in his favor, and to have assistance of counsel for his defense," the same act undertaking to authorize the President to remove a person out of the United States who is under the protection of the law, on his own suspicion, without jury, without public trial, without confrontation of the witnesses against him, without having witnesses in his favor, without defense, without counsel, is contrary to these provisions also of the Constitution, is therefore not law, but utterly void and of no force.

That transferring the power of judging any person who is under the protection of the laws, from the courts to the President of the United States, as is undertaken by the same act concerning aliens, is against the article of the Constitution which provides, "that the judicial power of the United States shall be vested in the courts, the judges of which shall hold their office during good behavior," and that the said act is void for that reason also; and it is further to be noted that this transfer of judiciary power is to that magistrate of the General Government who already possesses all the executive, and a qualified negative on all the legislative powers.

7. *Resolved,* That the construction applied by the General Government (as is evident by sundry of their proceedings) to those parts of the Constitution of the United States which delegate to Congress power to lay and collect taxes, duties, imposts, excises; to pay the debts, and provide for the common defense and general welfare of the United States, and to make all laws which shall be necessary and proper for carrying into execution the powers vested by the Constitution in the Government of the United States, or any department thereof, goes to the destruction of all the limits prescribed to their power by the Constitution: That words meant by that instrument to be subsidiary only to the execution of the limited powers, ought not to be so construed as themselves to give unlimited powers, nor a part so to be taken as to destroy the whole residue of the instrument: That the proceedings of the General Government under color of those articles, will be a fit and necessary subject of revisal and correction at a time of greater tranquility, while those specified in the preceding resolutions call for immediate redress.

8. *Resolved,* That the preceding resolutions be transmitted to the senators and representatives in Congress from this commonwealth, who are enjoined to present the same to their respective Houses, and to use their best endeavors to procure at the next session of Congress a repeal of the aforesaid unconstitutional and obnoxious acts.

9. *Resolved lastly,* That the Governor of this commonwealth be, and is hereby authorized and requested to communicate the preceding resolutions to the Legis-

latures of the several States, to assure them that this commonwealth considers union for special National purposes, and particularly for those specified in their late Federal compact, to be friendly to the peace, happiness and prosperity of all the States—that, faithful to that compact, according to the plan, intent and meaning in which it was so understood and acceded to by the several parties, it is sincerely anxious for its preservation; that it does also believe, that to take from the States all the powers of self-government, and transfer them to a general and consolidated Government, without regard to the special delegations and reservations solemnly agreed to in that compact, is not for the peace, happiness or prosperity of these States; and that, therefore, this commonwealth is determined, as it doubts not its co-States are, to submit to undelegated and consequently unlimited powers in no man or body of men on earth; that if the acts before specified should stand, these conclusions would flow from them; that the General Government may place any act they think proper on the list of crimes and punish it themselves, whether enumerated or not enumerated by the Constitution as cognizable by them; that they may transfer its cognizance to the President or any other person, who may himself be the accuser, counsel, judge and jury, whose suspicions may be the evidence, his order the sentence, his officer the executioner, and his breast the sole record of the transaction; that a very numerous and valuable description of the inhabitants of these States, being by this precedent reduced as outlaws to the absolute dominion of one man, and the barriers of the Constitution thus swept from us all, and no rampart now remains against the passions and the power of a majority of Congress, to protect from a like exportation or other grievous punishment the minority of the same body, the Legislatures, judges, governors and counsellors of the States, nor their other peaceable inhabitants who may venture to reclaim the constitutional rights and liberties of the States and people, or who, for other causes, good or bad, may be obnoxious to the views or marked by the suspicions of the President, or be thought dangerous to his or their elections or other interests, public or personal; that the friendless alien has been selected as the safest subject for a first experiment; but the citizen will soon follow, or rather has already followed; for, already has a Sedition act marked him as a prey: that these and successive acts of the same character, unless arrested on the threshold, may tend to drive these States into revolution and blood, and will furnish new calumnies against republican governments, and new pretexts for those who wish it to be believed that man cannot be governed but by a rod of iron; that it would be a dangerous delusion were a confidence in the men of our choice to silence our fears for the safety of our rights; that confidence is everywhere the parent of despotism; free government is founded in jealousy and not in confidence; it is jealousy and not confidence which prescribes limited constitutions to bind down those whom we are obliged to trust with power; that our Constitution has accordingly fixed the limits to which, and no farther, our confidence may go; and let the honest advocates of confidence read the Alien and Sedition acts, and say if the Constitution has not been wise in fixing limits to the government it created, and whether we should be wise in destroying those limits? Let him say what the government is, if it be not a tyranny, which the men of our choice have conferred on the President, and the President of our choice has assented to and accepted over the friendly strangers, to whom the mild spirit of our country and its laws has pledged hospitality and protection; that the men of our choice have more respected the bare suspicions of the President than the solid rights of innocence, the claims of justification, the sacred force of truth, and the forms and substance of law and justice. In questions of power, then, let no more be said of confidence in man, but bind him down from mischief by the chains of the Constitution. That this commonwealth does therefore call on the co-States for an expression of their sentiments on the acts concerning aliens, and for the punishment of certain crimes hereinbefore specified, plainly declaring whether these acts are or are not authorized by the Federal compact. And it doubts not that their sense will be so announced as to prove their attachment to limited government, whether general or particular, and that the rights and liberties of their co-States will be exposed to no dangers by remaining embarked on a common bottom with their own; but they will concur with this commonwealth in considering the said acts as so palpably against the Constitution as to amount to an undisguised declaration, that the compact is not meant to be the measure of the powers of the General Government, but that it will proceed in the exercise over these States of all powers whatsoever. That they will view this as seizing the rights of the States and consolidating them in the hands of the General Government, with a power assumed to bind the States (not merely in cases made Federal) but in all cases whatsoever, by laws made, not with their consent, but by others against their consent; that this would be to surrender the form of government we have chosen, and live under one deriving its powers from its own will, and not from our authority; and that the co-States, recurring to their natural rights in cases not made Federal, will concur in declaring these void and of no force, and will each unite with this commonwealth in requesting their repeal at the next session of Congress.

MADISON'S VIRGINIA RESOLUTIONS OF '98.

Following up the Kentucky Resolutions above given, Madison, in concert with Jefferson, proposed this series of resolves which were passed by the Virginia Legislature Dec. 21st, 24th, 1798:

Resolved, That the General Assembly of Virginia doth unequivocally express a firm resolution to maintain and defend the Constitution of the United States, and the Constitution of this State, against every aggression, either foreign or domestic; and that they will support the Government of the United States in all measures warranted by the former.

That this Assembly most solemnly declares a warm attachment to the Union of the States, to maintain which it pledges its powers; and, that for this end, it is their duty to watch over and oppose every infraction of those principles which constitute the only basis of that Union, because a faithful observance of them can alone secure its existence and the public happiness.

That this Assembly doth explicitly and peremptorily declare, that it views the powers of the Federal Government, as resulting from the compact to which the States are parties, as limited by the plain sense and intention of the instrument constituting that compact, as no further valid than they are authorized by the grants enumerated in that compact; and that, in case of a deliberate, palpable and dangerous exercise of other powers not granted by the said compact, the

States, who are parties thereto, have the right, and are in duty bound, to interpose, for arresting the progress of the evil, and for maintaining within their respective limits the authorities, rights and liberties appertaining to them.

That the General Assembly doth also express its deep regret, that a spirit has, in sundry instances, been manifested by the Federal Government, to enlarge its powers by forced constructions of the constitutional charter which defines them; and that indications have appeared of a design to expound certain general phrases (which having been copied from the very limited grant of powers in the former Articles of Confederation, were the less liable to be misconstrued) so as to destroy the meaning and effect of the particular enumeration which necessarily explains and limits the general phrases, and so as to consolidate the States by degrees into one sovereignty, the obvious tendency and inevitable result of which would be, to transform the present republican system of the United States into an absolute, or at best, a mixed monarchy.

That the General Assembly doth particularly protest against the palpable and alarming infractions of the Constitution, in the two late cases of the "Alien and Sedition Acts," passed at the last session of Congress; the first of which exercises a power nowhere delegated to the Federal Government, and which, by uniting legislative and judicial powers to those of the executive, subverts the general principles of free government, as well as the particular organization and positive provisions of the Federal Constitution; and the other of which acts exercises, in like manner, a power not delegated by the Constitution, but, on the contrary, expressly and positively forbidden by one of the amendments thereto; a power which, more than any other, ought to produce universal alarm, because it is leveled against the right of freely examining public characters and measures, and of free communication among the people thereon, which has ever been justly deemed the only effectual guardian of every other right.

That this State having by its Convention, which ratified the Federal Constitution, expressly declared, that among other essential rights, "the liberty of conscience and the press cannot be canceled, abridged, restrained, or modified by any authority of the United States," and from its extreme anxiety to guard these rights from every possible attack of sophistry or ambition, having with other States recommended an amendment for that purpose, which amendment was, in due time, annexed to the Constitution, it would mark a reproachful inconsistency and criminal degeneracy, if an indifference were now shown to the most palpable violation of one of the rights, thus declared and secured; and to the establishment of a precedent which may be fatal to the other.

That the good people of this Commonwealth having ever felt, and continuing to feel, the most sincere affection for their brethren of the other States, the truest anxiety for establishing and perpetuating the Union of all, and the most scrupulous fidelity to that Constitution which is the pledge of mutual friendship and the instrument of mutual happiness, the General Assembly doth solemnly appeal to the like dispositions in the other States, in confidence that they will concur with this Commonwealth in declaring, as it does hereby declare, that the acts aforesaid are unconstitutional; and that the necessary and proper measures will be taken by each for co-operating with this State, in maintaining, unimpaired, the authorities rights and liberties, reserved to the States respectively, or to the people.

That the Governor be desired to transmit a copy of the foregoing resolutions to the executive authority of each of the other States, with a request that the same may be communicated to the Legislatures thereof; and that a copy be furnished to each of the Senators and Representatives representing this State in the Congress of the United States.

These resolves were sent out to the States accompanied by an Address, prepared also by Madison, setting forth the reasons for their adoption and urging responses from the several States. *None* of the States responded favorably to the resolutions, but, on the contrary, Maryland, Delaware, Pennsylvania, New Jersey, New York, Connecticut, Rhode Island, Massachusetts, New Hampshire and Vermont disavowed the doctrine set up of a right in the State Legislatures to decide upon the validity of acts of Congress. The reply of Massachusetts, likewise, maintained the constitutionality of the Alien and Sedition Laws as being justified by the exigency of the moment, and by the power of Congress to provide for the common defense.

JAMES MADISON'S DEFENSE.

Throughout all of Madison's career, from the date of his service as President up to his decease, he wrote powerfully to combat the heresies of secession and nullification. His published works (Congressional edition) contain numerous papers valuable as expositions of the Constitution, of the power of Congress, of the Judiciary, &c. Did we not know that he was the author of the Virginia Resolutions of '98, and of the Address accompanying them, we should give them double weight as authority.

In a letter to Nicholas P. Trist, not given in the "Madison Papers," we have the ex-President's views directly on the issues excited by South Carolina's attitude of nullification, in 1832, and also his own interpretation of the Virginia resolves. We quote this letter in order to place before our readers Madison's defense of himself and Jefferson against the construction placed upon their '98 labors by the opponents of the State Rights dogmas.

MONTPELIER, Dec. 23d, 1832.

DEAR SIR: I have received yours of the 19th, inclosing some South Carolina papers. There is in one of them some interesting views of the doctrine of secession, among which, one that had occurred to me, and which for the first time I have seen in print; namely, that if one State can at will withdraw from the others, the others can withdraw from her, and turn her, *nolentem volentem*, out of the Union. Until of late there is not a State that would have abhorred such a doctrine more than South Carolina, or more dreaded an application of it to herself. The same may be said of the doctrine of nullification, which she now preaches as the only doctrine by which the Union can be saved.

I partake of the wonder that the men you name should view secession in the light mentioned. The essential difference between a free government and governments not free, is, that the former is founded in compact, the parties to which are mutually and equally bound by it. Neither of them, therefore, can have a greater right to break off from the bargain than the other or others have to hold him to it. And certainly there is nothing in the Virginia resolutions of '98 adverse to this principle, which is that of common sense and common justice. The fallacy which draws a different conclusion from them, lies in confounding a single party with the parties to the constitutional compact of the United States. The latter having made the compact, may do what they will with it. The former, as one of the parties, owes fidelity to it till released by consent, or absolved by an intolerable abuse of the power created. In the Virginia resolutions and report, the plural number (States) is in every instance used, whenever reference is made to the authority which presided over the Government. As I am now known to have drawn those documents, I may say, as I do with a distinct recollection, that it was intentional. It was in fact required by the course of reasoning employed on the occasion. The Kentucky resolutions, being less guarded, have been more easily perverted. The pretext for the liberty taken with those of Virginia is the word "respective" prefixed to the "rights," &c., to be secured within the States. Could the abuse of the expression have been foreseen or suspected, the form of it would doubtless have been varied. But what can be more consistent with common sense, than that all having the rights, &c., should unite in contending for the security of them to each?

It is remarkable how closely the nullifiers, who make the name of Mr. Jefferson the pedestal for their colossal heresy, close their eyes and lips whenever his authority is ever so clearly and emphatically against them. You have noticed [1] what he says in his letters to Monroe and Carrington (p. 43 and 202, vol. 2d) with respect to the power of the old Congress to coerce delinquent States; and his reasons for preferring for the purpose a naval to a military force; and moreover, his remark that it was not necessary to find a right to coerce in the Federal articles, that being inherent in the nature of a compact. It is high time that the claim to secede at will should be put down by the public opinion, and I am glad to see the task commenced by one who understands the subject.[2]

I know nothing of what is passing at Richmond, more than what is seen in the newspapers. You were right in your foresight of the effect of passages in the late proclamation. They have proved a leaven for much fermentation there, and created an alarm against the danger of consolidation balancing that of disunion. I wish with you the legislature may not seriously injure itself by assuming the high character of mediator. They will certainly do so, if they forget that their real influence will be in the inverse ratio of a boastful interposition of it.

---

1 In a note to this reference Mr. Trist says: "These passages had been made use of in combating nullification, and in rescuing the fame of Jefferson and my native State from the 'deep disgrace' of the paternity of that monstrous doctrine, which, as preached at this period, was a product—one of many similar products—of the fungus-breeding brain of the most pestilent of all the pestilent sophists by whom God's highest gift to man, the faculty of speech, has ever been perverted. The most pestilent, not from superior ability—for as a thinker, he was among the shallowest of the shallow—but from the magnitude of the theater upon which the accident of birth-place threw him, and the immensity, the incalculable immensity, of the human interests, in sporting with which his unholy ambition found its delight.

"I have said 'in rescuing' that immortal name, instead of saying 'in endeavoring to rescue

JEFFERSON'S MESSAGE ON BURR'S CONSPIRACY.

On Tuesday, January 22d, 1807, the President sent in to Congress a special message relating to the Conspiracy of Aaron Burr and the action taken to bring the Conspirator to justice. It was as follows:

To the Senate and House of

Representatives of the United States:

Agreeably to the request of the House of Representatives, communicated in their resolution of the 16th instant, I proceed to state under the reserve therein expressed, information received touching an illegal combination of private individuals against the peace and safety of the Union, and a military expedition planned by them against the territories of a power in amity with the United States, with the measures I have pursued for suppressing the same.

I had for some time been in the constant expectation of receiving such further information as would have enabled me to lay before the Legislature the termination as well as the beginning and progress of this scene of depravity, so far as it has been acted on the Ohio and its waters. From this, the state of safety of the lower country might have been estimated on probable grounds; and the delay was indulged the rather, because no circumstance had yet made it necessary to call in the aid of the legislative functions. Information, now recently communicated, has brought us nearly to the period contemplated. The mass of what I have received in the course of these transactions, is voluminous; but little has been given under the sanction of an oath, so as to constitute formal and legal evidence. It is chiefly in the form of letters, often containing such a mixture of rumors, conjectures and suspicions, as renders it difficult to sift out the real facts, and unadvisable to hazard more than general outlines, strengthened by current information, on the particular credibility of the relator. In this state of the evidence, delivered sometimes, too, under the restriction of private confidence, neither safety nor justice will permit the exposing names, except that of the principal actor, whose guilt is placed beyond question.

Some time in the latter part of September, I received intimations that designs were in agitation in the Western country unlawful and unfriendly to the peace of the Union; and that the prime mover in these was Aaron Burr, heretofore distinguished by the favor of his country. The grounds of these intentions being inconclusive, the objects uncertain, and the fidelity of that country known to be firm,

---

it.' For the seeming arrogance of this locution, some apology, if not a perfect warrant, will be found in the following extract from another letter of Mr. Madison, dated Sept. 23, 1831:

"'Interruptions from my rheumatism, and a succession of less unwelcome guests, have delayed the thanks now rendered for your several printed communications; particularly the pamphlet of Mr. Everett, and the paper headed "Nullification Theory." The former is an able and well written performance, and will be denied this character by few of the adverse party. If the latter does not silence the adversary, the explanation will lie between an impenetrable stupidity and an incurable prejudice. I hope the antidote will find its way into the channels which have most successfully circulated the poison.'"

2 This refers to an article on "secession," under the signature "One of the '98 School," which had appeared in the Richmond *Enquirer* a few days before. Mr. Trist was the writer of the article.

the only measure taken was to urge the informants to use their best endeavors to get further insight into the designs and proceedings of the suspected persons, and to communicate them to me.

It was not till the latter part of October, that the objects of the conspiracy began to be perceived; but still so blended and involved in mystery, that nothing distinct could be singled out for pursuit. In this state of uncertainty as to the crime contemplated, the acts done, and the legal course to be pursued, I thought it best to send to the scene, where these things were principally in transaction, a person in whose integrity, understanding and discretion, entire confidence could be reposed, with instructions to investigate the plots going on, to enter into conference (for which he had sufficient credentials) with the Governors and all other officers, civil and military, and, with their aid, to do on the spot whatever should be necessary to discover the designs of the conspirators, arrest their means, bring their persons to punishment, and to call out the force of the country to suppress any unlawful enterprise in which it should be found they were engaged. By this time it was known that many boats were under preparation, stores of provisions collecting, and an unusual number of suspicious characters in motion on the Ohio and its waters. Besides dispatching the confidential agent to that quarter, orders were at the same time sent to the Governors of the Orleans and Mississippi Territories, and to the commanders of the land and naval forces there, to be on their guard against surprise, and in constant readiness to resist any enterprise which might be attempted on the vessels, posts, or other objects under their care; and on the 8th of November instructions were forwarded to General Wilkinson, to hasten an accommodation with the Spanish commandant on the Sabine, and as soon as that was effected, to fall back with his principal force to the hither bank of the Mississippi, for the defense of the interesting points on that river. By a letter received from that officer on the 25th of November, but dated October 21st, we learnt that a confidential agent of Aaron Burr had been deputed to him with communications, partly written in cypher and partly oral, explaining his designs, exaggerating his resources, and making such offers of emolument and command, to engage him and the army in his unlawful enterprise, as he had flattered himself would be successful. The General, with the honor of a soldier and fidelity of a good citizen, immediately dispatched a trusty officer to me, with information of what had passed, proceeding to establish such an understanding with the Spanish commandant on the Sabine, as permitted him to withdraw his force across the Mississippi, and to enter on measures for opposing the projected enterprise.

The General's letter, which came to hand on the 25th of November, as has been mentioned, and some other information received a few days earlier, when brought together, developed Burr's general designs, different parts of which only had been revealed to different informants. It appeared that he contemplated two distinct objects, which might be carried on either jointly or separately, and either the one or the other first, as circumstances should direct. One of these was the severance of the Union of these States by the Alleghany mountains; the other an attack on Mexico A third object was provided, merely ostensible, to wit, the settlement of a pretended purchase of a tract of country on the Wachita, claimed by a Baron Bastrop. This was to serve as the pretext for all his preparations, an allurement for such followers as really wished to acquire settlements in that country, and a cover under which to retreat in the event of a final discomfiture of both branches of his real design.

He found at once that the attachment of the Western country to the present Union was not to be shaken; that its dissolution could not be effected with the consent of its inhabitants, and that his resources were inadequate, as yet, to effect it by force. He took his course then at once, determined to seize on New Orleans, plunder the bank there, possess himself of the military and naval stores, and proceed on his expedition to Mexico, and to this object all his means and preparations were now directed. He collected from all the quarters where himself or his agents possessed influence, all the ardent, restless, desperate and disaffected persons, who were ready for any enterprise analagous to their characters. He seduced good and well meaning citizens, some by assurances that he possessed the confidence of the Government, and was acting under its secret patronage, a pretence which procured some credit from the state of our differences with Spain; and others by offers of land in Bastrop's claim on the Wachita.

This was the state of my information of his proceedings about the last of November, at which time, therefore, it was first possible to take specific measures to meet them. The proclamation of November 27th, two days after the receipt of General Wilkinson's information, was now issued. Orders were dispatched to every interesting point on the Ohio and Mississippi, from Pittsburg to New Orleans, for the employment of such force, either of the regulars or of the militia, and of such proceedings also of the civil authorities, as might enable them to seize on all the boats and stores provided for the enterprise, to arrest the persons concerned, and to suppress, effectually, the further progress of the enterprise. A little before the receipt of these orders in the State of Ohio, our confidential agent, who had been diligently employed in investigating the conspiracy, had acquired information sufficient to open himself to the Governor of that State, and apply for the immediate exertion of the authority and power of the State to crush the combination. Governor Tiffin and the Legislature, with a promptitude, an energy, and patriotic zeal, which entitle them to a distinguished place in the affection of their sister States, effected the seizure of all the boats, provisions, and other preparations within their reach, and thus gave a first blow, materially disabling the enterprise in its outset.

In Kentucky a premature attempt to bring Burr to justice, without a sufficient evidence for his conviction, had produced a popular impression in his favor, and a general disbelief in his guilt. This gave him an unfortunate opportunity of hastening his equipments. The arrival of the proclamation and orders, and the application and information of our confidential agent, at length awakened the authorities of that State to the truth, and then produced the same promptitude and energy of which the neighboring State had set the example. Under an act of their Legislature, of December 23d, militia was instantly ordered to different important points, and measures taken for doing whatever could yet be done. Some boats (accounts vary from five to double or treble that number) and persons (differently estimated from one to three hundred) had in the mean time passed the Falls of Ohio, to rendezvous at the mouth of the Cumberland, with others expected down that river.

Not apprised, till very late, that boats were building on the Cumberland, the effect of the proclamation had been trusted to for some time in the State of Tennessee. But, on the 19th of December, similar communications and instructions, with those to the neighboring States, were dispatched by express to the Governor, and a General officer of the Western division of the State; and, on the 23d of December, our confidential agent left Frankfort for Nashville, to put into activity the means of that State also. But, by information received yesterday, I learn that on the 23d of December, Mr. Burr descended the Cumberland with two boats merely of accommodation, carrying with him from that State no quota toward his unlawful enterprise. Whether, after the arrival of the proclamation, of the orders, or of our agent, any exertion which could be made by that State, or the orders of the Governor of Kentucky for calling out the militia at the mouth of the Cumberland, would be in time to arrest these boats, and those from the Falls of the Ohio, is still doubtful.

On the whole, the fugitives from the Ohio, with their associates from Cumberland, or any other place in that quarter, cannot threaten serious danger to the city of New Orleans.

By the same express of December 19th, orders were sent to the Governors of Orleans and Mississippi, supplementary to those which had been given on the 25th of November, to hold the militia of their Territories in readiness to co-operate, for their defense, with the regular troops and armed vessels then under command of General Wilkinson. Great alarm, indeed, was excited at New Orleans by the exaggerated accounts of Mr. Burr, disseminated through his emissaries, of the armies and navies he was to assemble there. General Wilkinson had arrived there himself on the 24th of November, and had immediately put into activity the resources of the place, for the purpose of its defense; and, on the 10th of December, he was joined by his troops from the Sabine. Great zeal was shown by the inhabitants generally; the merchants of the place readily agreeing to the most laudable exertions and sacrifices for manning the armed vessels with their seamen; and the other citizens manifesting unequivocal fidelity to the Union, and a determined spirit of resistance to their expected assailants.

Surmises have been hazarded that this enterprise is to receive aid from certain foreign powers. But these surmises are without proof or probability. The wisdom of the measures sanctioned by Congress at its last session, has placed us in the paths of peace and justice with the only powers with whom we had any differences; and nothing has happened since which makes it either their interest or ours to pursue another course. No change of measures has taken place on our part; none ought to take place at this time. With the one, friendly arrangement was then proposed, and the law, deemed necessary on the failure of that, was suspended to give time for a fair trial of the issue. With the same power friendly arrangement is now proceeding, under good expectations, and the same law deemed necessary on failure of that, is still suspended, to give time for a fair trial of the issue. With the other, negotiation was in like manner then preferred, and provisional measures only taken to meet the event of rupture. With the same power negotiation is still preferred, and provisional measures only are necessary to meet the event of rupture. While, therefore, we do not deflect in the slightest degree from the course we then assumed, and are still pursuing, with mutual consent, to restore a good understanding, we are not to impute to them practices as irreconcilable to interest as to good faith, and changing necessarily the relations of peace and justice between us to those of war. These surmises, are, therefore, to be imputed to the vauntings of the author of this enterprise, to multiply his partisans by magnifying the belief of his prospects and support.

By letters from General Wilkinson, of the 14th and 18th of December, which came to hand two days after the date of the resolution of the House of Representatives, that is to say, on the morning of the 18th instant, I received the important affidavit, a copy of which I now communicate, with extracts of so much of the letters as comes within the scope of the resolution. By these it will be seen that of three of the principal emissaries of Mr. Burr, whom the General had caused to be apprehended, one had been liberated by *habeas corpus*, and two others, being those particularly employed in the endeavor to corrupt the General and Army of the United States, have been embarked by him for ports in the Atlantic States, probably on the consideration that an impartial trial could not be expected during the present agitation of New Orleans, and that that city was not as yet a safe place of confinement. As soon as these persons shall arrive, they will be delivered to the custody of the law, and left to such course of trial, both as to the place and progress, as its functionaries may direct. The presence of the highest judicial authorities, to be assembled at this place within a few days, the means of pursuing a sounder course of proceedings here than elsewhere, and the aid of the Executive means, should the judges have occasion to use them, render it equally desirable for the criminals as for the public, that, being already removed from the place where they were first apprehended, the first regular arrest should take place here, and the course of proceedings receive here the proper direction.

TH. JEFFERSON.

JACKSON'S MESSAGE ON NULLIFICATION.

The Message submitted to Congress January 16th, 1833, by President Jackson, in transmitting his Proclamation, is a document of so much importance that we here lay before our readers those portions of it which have special reference to our text.

Since the date of my last annual Message, I have had officially transmitted to me by the Governor of South Carolina, which I now communicate to Congress, a copy of the ordinance passed by the convention which assembled at Columbia, in the State of South Carolina, in November last, declaring certain acts of Congress therein mentioned, within the limits of that State, to be absolutely null and void, and making it the duty of the Legislature to pass such laws as would be necessary to carry the same into effect from and after the 1st of February next.

The consequences to which this extraordinary defiance of the just authority of the Government might too surely lead, were clearly foreseen, and it was impossible for me to hesitate as to my own duty in such an emergency.

The ordinance had been passed, however, without any certain knowledge of the recommendation which, from a view of the interests of the nation at large, the Executive had determined to submit to Congress; and a hope was indulged that, by frankly explaining his sentiments, and the nature of those duties which the crisis would devolve upon him, the authorities of South Carolina might be induced to retrace their steps. In this hope, I determined to issue my proclamation of the 10th of December last, a copy of which I now lay before Congress.

I regret to inform you that these reasonable expectations have not been realized, and that the several acts of the Legislature of South Carolina, which I now lay before you, and which have, all and each of them, finally passed, after a knowledge of the desire of the Administration to modify the laws complained of, are too well calculated, both in their positive enactments, and in the spirit of opposition which they obviously encourage, wholly to obstruct the collection of the revenue within the limits of that State.

Up to this period, neither the recommendation of the Executive in regard to our financial policy and impost system, nor to the disposition manifested by Congress promptly to act on that subject, nor the unequivocal expression of the public will, in all parts of the Union, appears to have produced any relaxation in the measures of opposition adopted by the State of South Carolina; nor is there any reason to hope that the ordinance and laws will be abandoned.

I have no knowledge that an attempt has been made, or that it is in contemplation, to reassemble either the convent on or the Legislature; and it will be perceived that the interval before the 1st of February is too short to admit of the preliminary steps necessary for that purpose. It appears, moreover, that the State authorities are actively organizing their military resources, and providing the means, and giving the most solemn assurances of protection and support to all who shall enlist in opposition to the revenue laws.

A recent proclamation of the present Governor of South Carolina has openly defied the authority of the Executive of the Union, and general orders from the head quarters of the State announced his determination to accept the services of volunteers, and his belief that, should their country need their services, they will be found at the post of honor and duty, ready to lay down their lives in her defense. Under these orders, the forces referred to are directed to "hold themselves in readiness to take the field at a moment's warning;" and in the city of Charleston, within a collection district and a port of entry, a rendezvous has been opened for the purpose of enlisting men for the magazine and municipal guard. Thus South Carolina presents herself in the attitude of hostile preparation, and ready even for military violence, if need be, to enforce her laws for preventing the collection of the duties within her limits.

Proceedings thus announced and matured must be distinguished from menaces of unlawful resistance by irregular bodies of people, who, acting under temporary delusion, may be restrained by reflection, and the influence of public opinion. In the present instance, aggression may be regarded as committed when it is officially authorized, and the means of enforcing it fully provided.

Under these circumstances, there can be no doubt that it is the determination of the authorities of South Carolina fully to carry into effect their ordinance and laws after the 1st of February. It therefore becomes my duty to bring the subject to the serious consideration of Congress, in order that such measures as they, in their wisdom, may deem fit, shall be seasonably provided; and that it may be thereby understood that, while the Government is disposed to remove all just cause of complaint, as far as may be practicable consistently with a proper regard to the interests of the community at large, it is, nevertheless, determined that the supremacy of the laws shall be maintained.

In making this communication, it appears to me to be proper not only that I should lay before you the acts and proceedings of South Carolina, but that I should also fully acquaint you with those steps which I have already caused to be taken for the due collection of the revenue, and with my views of the subject generally, that the suggestions which the Constitution requires me to make, in regard to your future legislation, may be better understood.

This subject having early attracted the anxious attention of the Executive, as soon as it was probable that the authorities of South Carolina seriously meditated resistance to the faithful execution of the revenue laws, it was deemed advisable that the Secretary of the Treasury should particularly instruct the officers of the United States in that part of the Union as to the nature of the duties prescribed by the existing laws.

Instructions were accordingly issued on the 6th of November to the Collectors in that State, pointing out their respective duties, and enjoining upon each a firm and vigilant, but discreet performance of them in the emergency then apprehended.

I herewith transmit copies of these instructions, and of the letter addressed to the District Attorney requesting his co-operation. These instructions were dictated in the hope that, as the opposition to the laws by the anomalous proceeding of nullification was represented to be of a pacific nature, to be pursued, substantially, according to the forms of the Constitution, and without resorting, in any event, to force or violence, the measures of its advocates would be taken in conformity with that profession; and, on such a supposition, the means afforded by the existing laws would have been adequate to meet any emergency likely to arise.

It was, however, not possible altogether to suppress apprehehsion of the excesses to which the excitement prevailing in that quarter might lead; but it certainly was not foreseen that the meditated obstruction to the laws would so soon openly assume its present character.

Subsequently to the date of those instructions, however, the ordinance of the convention was passed, which, if complied with by the people of that State, must effectually render inoperative the present revenue laws within her limits.

* * * * * * * * * *

This solemn denunciation of the laws and authority of the United States has been followed up by a series of acts on the part of the authorities of that State, which manifest a determination to render inevitable a resort to those measures of self-defense which the paramount duty of the Federal Government requires; but, upon the adoption of which, that State will proceed to execute the purpose it has avowed in this ordinance, of withdrawing from the Union. * * *

I transmit a copy of Governor Hamilton's message to the Legislature of South Carolina, of Governor Hayne's inaugural address to the same body, as also of his proclamation, and a general order of the Governor and commander-in-chief, dated the 20th of December, giving public notice that the services of volunteers will be accepted under the act already referred to.

If these measures cannot be defeated and overcome by the power conferred by the Constitution on the Federal Government, the Constitution must be considered as incompetent to its own defense, the supremacy of the laws is at an end, and the rights and liberties of the citizens can no longer receive protection from the Government of the Union. They not only abrogate the acts of Congress, commonly called the tariff acts of 1828 and 1832, but they prostrate and sweep away at once and without exception, every act, and every part of every act, imposing any amount whatever of duty on any foreign merchandise; and, virtually, every existing act which has ever been passed authorizing the collection of the revenue, including the act of 1816, and also, the collection law of 1799, the constitutionality of which has never been questioned. It is not only those duties which are charged to have been imposed for the protection of manufactures that are thereby repealed, but all others, though laid for the purpose of revenue merely, and on articles in no degree suspected of being objects of protection. The whole revenue system of the United States in South Carolina is obstructed and overthrown; and the Government is absolutely prohibited from collecting any part of the public revenue within the limits of that State. Henceforth, not only the citizens of South Carolina and of the United States, but the subjects of foreign States, may import any description or quantity of merchandise into the ports of South Carolina, without the payment of any duty whatsoever. That State is thus relieved from the payment of any part of the public burdens, and duties and imposts are not only rendered not uniform throughout the United States, but a direct and ruinous preference is given to the ports of that State over those of all the other States of the Union, in manifest violation of the positive provisions of the Constitution.

In point of duration, also, those aggressions upon the authority of Congress, which, by the ordinance, are made part of the fundamental law of South Carolina, are absolute, indefinite, and without limitation. They neither prescribe the period when they shall cease, nor indicate any conditions upon which those who have thus undertaken to arrest the operation of the laws are to retrace their steps, and rescind their measures. They offer to the United States no alternative but unconditional submission. If the scope of the ordinance is to be received as the scale of concession, their demands can be satisfied only by a repeal of the whole system of revenue laws, and by abstaining from the collection of any duties and imposts whatsoever.

It is true, that in the address to the people of the United States by the Convention of South Carolina, after announcing the "fixed and final determination of the State in relation to the protecting system," they say "that it remains for us to submit a plan of taxation, in which we would be willing to acquiesce, in a liberal spirit of concession, provided we are met in due time, and in a becoming spirit, by the States interested in manufactures." In the opinion of the convention, an equitable plan would be, that "the whole list of protected articles should be imported free of all duty, and that the revenue derived from import duties should be raised exclusively from the unprotected articles, or that whenever a duty is imposed upon protected articles imported, an excise duty of the same rate shall be imposed upon all similar articles manufactured in the United States." The address proceeds to state, however, that "they are willing to make a large offering to preserve the Union, and with a distinct declaration that it is a concession on our part, we will consent that the same rate of duty may be imposed upon the protected articles that shall be imposed upon the unprotected, provided that no more revenue be raised than is necessary to meet the demands of the Government for constitutional purposes, and provided also that a duty substantially uniform be imposed upon all foreign imports."

It is also true, that, in his message to the Legislature, when urging the necessity of providing "means of securing their safety by ample resources for repelling force by force," the Governor of South Carolina observes that he "cannot but think that, on a calm and dispassionate review by Congress, and the functionaries of the General Government, of the true merits of this controversy, the arbitration, by a call of a convention of all the States, which we sincerely and anxiously seek and desire, will be accorded to us."

From the diversity of terms indicated in these two important documents, taken in connection with the progress of recent events in that quarter, there is too much reason to apprehend, without in any manner doubting the intentions of those public functionaries, that neither the terms proposed in the address of the convention, nor those alluded to in the message of the Governor, would appease the excitement which has led to the present excesses. It is obvious, however, that, should the latter be insisted on, they present an alternative which the General Government of itself can by no possibility grant, since, by an express provision of the Constitution, Congress can call a convention for the purpose of proposing amendments only "on the application of the Legislatures of two-thirds of the States." And it is not perceived that the terms presented in the address are more practicable than those referred to in the message.

It will not escape attention that the conditions on which it is said, in the address of the convention, they "would be willing to acquiesce," form no part of the ordinance. While this ordinance bears all the solemnity of a fundamental law, is to be authoritative upon all within the limits of South Carolina, and is absolute and unconditional in its terms, the address conveys only the sentiments of the convention in no binding or practical form; one is the act of the State, the other only the expression of the opinion of the members of the convention. To limit the effect of that solemn act by any terms or conditions whatever, they should have been embodied in it, and made of import no less authoritative than the act itself. By the positive enactments of the ordinance, the execution of the laws of the Union is absolutely prohibited; and the address offers no other prospect of their being again restored, even in the modified form proposed, than what depends upon the improbable contingency, that, amid changing events and increasing excitement, the sentiments of the present members of the convention, and of their successors, will remain the same.

It is to be regretted, however, that these conditions, even if they had been offered in the same binding form, are so undefined, depend upon so many contingencies, and are so directly opposed to the known opinions and interests of the great body of the American people, as to be almost hopeless of attainment. The majority of the States and of the people will certainly not consent that the protecting duties shall be wholly abrogated, never to be re-enacted at any future time, or in any possible contingency. As little practicable is it to provide that "the same rate of duty shall be imposed upon the protected articles that shall be imposed upon the unprotected;" which, moreover, would be severely oppressive to the poor, and, in time of war, would add greatly to its rigors. And though there can be no objection to the principle, properly understood, that no more revenue shall be raised than is necessary for the constitutional purposes of the Government, which principal has been already recommended by the Executive as the true basis of taxation, yet it is very certain that South Carolina alone cannot be permitted to decide what these constitutional purposes are. * * * * *

By these various proceedings, therefore, the State of South Carolina has forced the General Government unavoidably, to decide the new and dangerous alternative of permitting a State to obstruct the execution of the laws within its limits, or seeing it attempt to execute a threat of withdrawing from the Union. That portion of the people at present exercising the authority of the State, solemnly assert their right to do either, and as solemnly announce their determination to do one or the other.

In my opinion, both purposes are to be regarded as revolutionary in their character and tendency, and subversive of the supremacy of the laws and of the integrity of the Union. The result of each is the same; since a State in which, by a usurpation of power, the constitutional authority of the Federal Government is openly defied and set aside, wants only the form to be independent of the Union.

The right of a people of a single State to absolve themselves at will, and without the consent of the other States, from their most solemn obligations, and hazard the liberties and happiness of the millions composing this Union, cannot be acknowledged. Such authority is believed to be utterly repugnant both to the principles upon which the General Government is constituted, and to the objects which it is expressly formed to attain.

Against all acts which may be alleged to transcend the constitutional power of the Government, or which may be inconvenient or oppressive in their operation, the Constitution itself has prescribed the modes of redress. It is the acknowledged attribute of free institutions, that, under them, the empire of reason and law is substituted for the power of the sword. To no other source can appeals for supposed wrongs be made, consistently with the obligations of South Carolina; to no other can such appeals be made with safety at any time; and to their decisions, when constitutionally pronounced, it becomes the duty, no less of the public authorities than of the people, in every case to yield a patriotic submission.

That a State, or any other great portion of the people, suffering under long and intolerable oppression, and having tried all constitutional remedies without the hope of redress, may have a natural right, when their happiness can be no otherwise secured, and when they can do so without greater injury to others, to absolve themselves from their obligations to the Government, and appeal to the last resort, needs not, on the present occasion, be denied.

The existence of this right, however, must depend upon the causes which may justify its exercise. It is the *ultima ratio*, which presupposes that the proper appeals to all other means of redress have been made in good faith, and which can never be rightfully resorted to unless it be unavoidable. It is not the right of the State, but of the individual, and of all the individuals in the State. It is the right of mankind generally to secure, by all the means in their power, the blessings of liberty and happiness; but when, for these purposes, any body of men have voluntarily associated themselves under a particular form of Government, no portion of them can dissolve the association without acknowledging the correlative right in the remainder to decide whether that dissolution can be permitted consistently with the general happiness. In this view, it is a right dependent upon the power to enforce it. Such a right, though it may be admitted to pre-exist, and cannot be wholly surrendered, is necessarily subjected to limitations in all free governments, and in compacts of all kinds, freely and voluntarily entered into, and in which the interest and welfare of the individual become identified with those of the community of which he is a member. In compacts between individuals, however deeply they may affect their relations, these principles are acknowledged to create a sacred obligation; and in compacts of civil government, involving the liberties and happiness of millions of mankind, the obligation cannot be less.

Without adverting to the particular theories to which the Federal compact has given rise, both as to its formation and the parties to it, and without inquiring whether it be merely federal, or social, or national, it is sufficient that it must be admitted to be a compact, and to possess the obligations incident to a compact; to be "a compact by which power is created on the one hand, and obedience exacted on the other; a compact freely, voluntarily and solemnly entered into by the several States, and ratified by the people thereof, respectively; a compact by which the several States, and the people thereof, respectively, have bound themselves to each other, and to the Federal Government, and by which the Federal Government is bound to the several States, and to every citizen of the United States." To this compact, in whatever mode it may have been done, the people of South Carolina have freely and voluntarily given their assent: and to the whole and every part of it, they are, upon every principle of good faith, inviolably bound. Under this obligation they are bound, and should be required to contribute their portion of the public expense, and to submit to all laws made by the common consent, in pursuance of the Constitution, for the common defense and general welfare, until they can be changed in the mode which the compact has provided for the attainment of those great ends of the Government and the Union. Nothing less than causes which would justify revolutionary remedy, can absolve the people from this obligation; and for nothing less can the Government permit it to be done without violating its own obligations, by which, under the compact, it is bound to the other States, and to every citizen of the United States.

These deductions plainly flow from the nature of the Federal compact, which is one of limitations, not only upon the powers originally possessed by the parties thereto, but also upon those conferred on the Government, and every department thereof. It will be freely conceded that, by the principles of our system, all power is vested in the people; but to be exercised in the mode, and subject to the checks which the people themselves have prescribed. These checks are, undoubtedly, only different modifications of the same great popular principle which lies at the foundation of the whole, but are not, on that account, to be less regarded or less obligatory.

Upon the power of Congress, the veto of the Executive, and the authority of the Judiciary, which is to extend to all cases in law and equity arising under the Constitution, and laws of the United States made in pursuance thereof, are the obvious checks; and the sound action of public opinion, with the ultimate power of amendment, is the salutary and only limitation upon the powers of the whole.

However it may be alleged that a violation of the compact, by the measures of the Government, can affect the obligations of the parties, it cannot even be pretended that such violation can be predicated of those measures until all the constitutional remedies shall have been fully tried. If the Federal Government exercise powers not warranted by the Constitution, and immediately affecting individuals, it will scarcely be denied that the proper remedy is a recourse to the judiciary. Such, undoubtedly, is the remedy for those who deem the acts of Congress laying duties and imposts, and providing for their collection, to be unconstitutional. The whole operation of such laws is upon the individuals importing the merchandise. A State is absolutely prohibited from laying imposts or duties on imports or exports, without the consent of Congress, and cannot become a party, under these laws, without importing in her own name, or wrongfully interposing her authority against them By thus interposing, however, she cannot rightfully obstruct the operation of the laws upon individuals. For their disobedience to, or violation of, the laws, the ordinary remedies through the judicial tribunals would remain. And in a case where an individual should be prosecuted for any offense against the laws, he could not set up, in justification of his act, a law of the State, which, being unconstitutional, would therefore be regarded as null and void. The law of a State cannot authorize the commission of a crime against the United States, or any other act which, according to the supreme law of the Union, would be otherwise unlawful. And it is equally clear, that, if there be any case in which a State, as such, is affected by the law beyond the scope of judicial power, the remedy consists in appeals to the people, either to effect a change in the representation, or to procure relief by an amendment of the Constitution. But the measures of the Government are to be recognized as valid, and, consequently, supreme, until these remedies shall have been effectually tried; and any attempt to subvert those measures, or to render the laws subordinate to State authority, and, afterwards, to resort to constitutional redress, is worse than evasive. It would not be a proper resistance to "a Government of unlimited powers," as has been sometimes pretended, but unlawful opposition to the very limitations on which the harmonious action of the Government, and all its parts, absolutely depends. South Carolina has appealed to none of these remedies, but, in effect, has defied them all. While threatening to separate from the Union, if any attempt be made to enforce the revenue laws otherwise than through the tribunals of the country, she has not only appealed in her own name to those tribunals which the Constitution has provided for all cases in law or equity arising under the Constitution and laws of the United States, but has endeavored to frustrate the proper action on her citizens, by drawing the cognizance of cases under the revenue laws to her own tribunals, specially prepared and fitted for the purpose of enforcing the acts passed by the State to obstruct those laws, and both the judges and jurors of which will be bound, by the import of oaths previously taken, to treat the Constitution and laws of the United States in this respect as a nullity. Nor has the State made the proper appeal to public opinion, and to the remedy of amendment. For, without waiting to learn whether the other States will consent to a convention, or, if they do, will construe or amend the Constitution to suit her views, she has, of her own authority, altered the import of that instrument, and given immediate effect to the change. In fine, she has set her own will and authority above the laws, has made herself arbiter in her own cause, and has passed at once over all intermediate steps to measures of avowed resistance, which, unless they be submitted to, can be enforced only by the sword.

In deciding upon the course which a high sense of duty to all the people of the United States imposes upon the authorities of the Union, in this emergency, it cannot be overlooked that there is no sufficient cause for the acts of South Carolina, or for her thus placing in jeopardy the happiness of so many millions of people.

Misrule and oppression, to warrant the disruption of the free institutions of the Union of these States, should be great and lasting, defying all other remedy. For causes of minor character, the Government coutd not submit to such a catastrophe without a violation of its most sacred obligations to the other States of the Union who have submitted their destiny to its hands.

There is, in the present instance, no such cause, either in the degree of misrule or oppression complained of, or in the hopelessness of redress by constitutional means. The long sanction they have received from the proper authorities, and from the people, not less than the unexampled growth and increasing prosperity of so many millions of freemen, attest that no such oppression as would justify or even palliate such a resort, can be justly imputed either to the present policy or past measures of the Federal Government. The same mode of collecting duties, and for the same general objects, which began with the foundation of the Government, and which has conducted the country, through its subsequent steps, to its present enviable condition of happiness and renown, has not been changed. Taxation and representation, the great principle of the American Revolution, have continually gone hand in hand; and at all times, and in every instance, no tax of any kind, has been imposed without their participation; and in some instances which have been complained of, with the express assent of a part of the Representatives of South Carolina in the councils of the Government. Up to the present period, no revenue has been raised beyond the necessary wants of the country and the authorized expenditures of the Government. And as soon as the burden of the public debt is removed, those charged with the administration have promptly recommended a corresponding reduction of revenue.

That this system, thus pursued, has resulted in no such oppression upon South Carolina, needs no other proof than the solemn and official declaration of the late Chief Magistrate of that State, in his address to the Legislature. In that he says, that "the occurrences of the past year, in connection with our domestic concerns, are to be reviewed with a sentiment of fervent gratitude to the Great Disposer of human events; that tributes of grateful acknowledgment are due for the various and multiplied blessings he has been pleased to bestow on our people; that abundant harvests, in every quarter of the State, have crowned the exertions of agricultural labor; that health, almost beyond former precedent, has blessed our homes; and that there is not less reason for thankfulness in surveying our social condition." It would, indeed, be difficult to imagine oppression where, in the social condition of a people, there was equal cause of thankfulness as for abundant harvests, and varied and multiplied blessings with which a kind Providence had favored them.

Independently of these considerations, it will not escape observation that South Carolina still claims to be a component part of the Union; to participate in the national councils, and to share in the public benefits, without contributing to the public burdens; thus asserting the dangerous anomaly of continuing in an association without acknowledging any other obligation to its laws than what depends upon her own will.

In this posture of affairs, the duty of the Government seems to be plain. It inculcates a recognition of that State as a member of the Union, and subjects her to its authority; a vindication of the just power of the Constitution; the preservation of the integrity of the Union; and the execution of the laws by all constitutional means.

The Constitution, which his oath of office obliges him to support, declares that the Executive "shall take care that the laws be faithfully executed," and in providing that he shall, from time to time, give to Congress information of the state of the Union, and recommend to their consideration such measures as he shall judge necessary and expedient, imposes the additional obligation of recommending to Congress such more efficient provision for executing the laws as may, from time to time, be found requisite.

The same instrument confers on Congress the power not merely to lay and collect taxes, duties, imposts and excises, to pay the debts, and provide for the common defense and general welfare, but "to make all laws which shall be necessary and proper for carrying into effect the foregoing powers, and all other powers vested by the Constitution in the Government of the United States, or in any department or officer thereof;" and also to provide for calling forth the militia for executing the laws of the Union. In all cases similar to the present, the duties of the Government become the measure of its powers; and whenever it fails to exercise a power necessary and proper to the discharge of the duty prescribed by the Constitution, it violates the public trusts not less than it would in transcending its proper limits. To refrain, therefore, from the high and solemn duties thus enjoined, however painful the performance may be, and thereby tacitly permit the rightful authority of the Government to be contemned, and its laws obstructed by a single State, would neither comport with its own safety, nor the rights of the great body of the American people.

It being thus shown to be the duty of the Executive to execute the laws by all constitutional means, it remains to consider the extent of those already at his disposal, and what it may be proper further to provide.

In the instructions of the Secretary of the Treasury to the collectors in South Carolina, the provisions and regulations made by the act of 1799, and also the fines, penalties and forfeitures, for their enforcement, are particularly detailed and explained. It may be well apprehended, however, that these provisions may prove inadequate to meet such an open, powerful, organized opposition, as is to be commenced after the 1st of February next.

Subsequently to the date of these instructions, and to the passage of the ordinance, information has been received, from sources entitled to be relied on, that, owing to the popular excitement in the State, and the effect of the ordinance declaring the execution of the revenue laws unlawful, a sufficient number of persons, in whom confidence might be placed, could not be induced to accept the office of inspector, to oppose with any probability of success, the force which will, no doubt, be used when an attempt is made to remove vessels and their cargoes from the custody of the officers of the customs; and, indeed, that it would be impracticable for the collector, with the aid of any number of inspectors whom he may be authorized to employ, to preserve the custody against such an attempt.

The removal of the custom house from Charleston to Castle Pinckney was deemed a measure of necessary precaution; and though the authority to give that direction is not questioned, it is nevertheless apparent that a similar precaution cannot be observed in regard to the ports of Georgetown and Beaufort, each of which, under the present laws, remains a port of entry, and exposed to the obstructions meditated in that quarter.

In considering the best means of avoiding or of preventing the apprehended obstruction to the collection of the revenue, and the consequences which may ensue, it would appear to be proper and necessary, to enable the officers of the customs to preserve the custody of vessels and their cargoes, which, by the existing laws, they are required to take, until the duties to which they are liable shall be paid or secured. The mode by which it is contemplated to deprive them of that custody, is the process of replevin, and that of *capias in withernam*, in the nature of a distress from the State tribunals organized by the ordinance.

Against the proceeding in the nature of a distress, it is not perceived that the collector can interpose any resistance whatever; and against the process of replevin authorized by the law of the State, he, having no common law power, can only oppose such inspectors as he is by statute authorized, and may find it practicable to employ; and these, from the information already adverted to, are shown to be wholly inadequate.

The respect which that process deserves must, therefore, be considered.

If the authorities of South Carolina had not obstructed the legitimate action of the courts of the United States, or if they had permitted the State tribunals to administer the law according to their oath under the Constitution, and the regulations of the laws of the Union, the General Government might have been content to look to them for maintaining the custody, and to encounter the other inconveniences arising out of the recent proceedings. Even in that case, however, the process of replevin from the courts of the State would be regular and unauthorized. It has been decided by the Supreme Court of the United States that the courts of the United States have exclusive jurisdiction of all seizures made on land or water for a breach of the laws of the United States, and any intervention of a State authority, which, by taking the thing seized out of the hands of the United States officer, might obstruct the exercise of this jurisdiction, is unlawful; that, in such case, the court of the United States having cognizance of the seizure, may enforce a re-delivery of the thing by attachment or other summary process; that the question under such a seizure, whether a forfeiture has been actually incurred, belongs exclusively to the courts of the United States, and it depends on the final decree whether the seizure is to be deemed rightful or tortuous; and that not until the seizure be finally judged wrongful, and without probable cause, by the courts of the United States, can the party proceed at common law for damages in the State courts.

But by making it " unlawful for any of the constituted authorities, whether of the United States or of the State, to enforce the laws for the payment of duties, and declaring that all judicial proceedings which shall be hereafter had in affirmance of the contract made with purpose to secure the duties imposed by the said acts, are, and shall be, held utterly null and void," she has, in effect, abrogated the judicial tribunals within her limits in this respect—has virtually denied the United States access to the courts established by their own laws, and declared it unlawful for the judges to discharge those duties which they are sworn to perform. In lieu of these, she has substituted those State tribunals already adverted to, the judges whereof are not merely forbidden to allow an appeal, or permit a copy of their record, but are previously sworn to disregard the laws of the Union, and enforce those only of South Carolina; and thus deprived of the function essential to the judicial character, of inquiring into the validity of the law, and the right of the matter, become merely ministerial instruments in aid of the concerted obstruction of the laws of the Union.

Neither the process nor authority of these tribunals, thus constituted, can be respected, consistently with the supremacy of the laws, or the rights and security of the citizen. If they be submitted to, the protection due from the Government to its officers and citizens is withheld, and there is, at once, an end, not only to the laws, but to the Union itself.

Against such a force as the sheriff may, and which, by the replevin law of South Caralina, it is his duty to exercise, it cannot be expected that a collector can retain his custody with the aid of the inspectors. In such case, it is true, it would be competent to institute suits in the United States courts against those engaged in the unlawful proceeding; or the property might be seized for a violation of the revenue laws, and, being libelled in the proper courts, an order might be made for its redelivery, which would be committed to the marshal for execution. But, in that case, the fourth section of the act, in broad and unqualified terms, makes it the duty of the sheriff "to prevent such recapture or seizure, or to redeliver the goods, as the case may be," "even under any process, order or decrees, or other pretext, contrary to the true intent and meaning of the ordinance aforesaid." It is thus made the duty of the sheriff to oppose the process of the courts of the United States; and, for that purpose, if need be, to employ the whole power of the county; and the act expressly reserves to him all power which, independently of its provisions, he could have used. In this reservation, it obviously contemplates a resort to other means than those particularly mentioned.

It is not to be disguised that the power which it is thus enjoined upon the sheriff to employ, is nothing less than the *posse comitatus*, in all the rigor of the ancient common law. This power, though it may be used against unlawful resistance to judicial process, is, in its character, forcible, and analogous to that conferred upon the marshals by the act of 1795. It is, in fact, the embodying of the whole mass of the population, under the command of a single individual, to accomplish, by their forcible aid, what could not be effected peaceably, and by the ordinary means. It may properly be said to be the relict of those ages in which the laws could be defended rather by physical than moral force, and, in its origin, was conferred upon the sheriffs of England to enable them to defend their country against any of the King's enemies when they came into the land, as well as for the purpose of executing process. In early and less civilized times, it was intended to include "the aid and attendance of all knights and others who were bound to have harness." It includes the right of going with arms and military equipment, and embraces larger classes and greater masses of population than can be compelled by the laws of most of the States to perform militia duty. If the principles of the common law are recognized in South Carolina, (and from this act it would seem they are,) the power of summoning the *posse comitatus* will compel, under the penalty of fine and imprisonment, every man over the age of fifteen, and able to travel, to turn out at the call of the sheriff, and with such weapons as may be necessary; and it may justify beating, and even killing, such as may resist. The use of the *posse comitatus* is, therefore, a direct application of force, and cannot be otherwise regarded than as the employment of the whole militia force of the country, and in an equally efficient form under a different name. No proceeding which resorts to this power, to the extent contemplated by the act, can be properly denominated peaceable.

The act of South Carolina, however, does not rely altogether upon this formidable remedy. For even attempting to resist or obey—though by the aid only of the ordinary officers of the customs—the process of replevin, the collector and all concerned are subjected to a further proceeding, in the nature of a distress of their personal effects; and are, moreover, made guilty of a misdemeanor, and liable to be punished by a fine of not less than one thousand, nor more than five thousand dollars, and to imprisonment not exceeding two years, and not less than six months; and even for attempting to execute the order of the court for retaking the property, the marshal, and all assisting, would be guilty of a misdemeanor, and liable to a fine of not less than three thousand dollars, nor more than ten thousand, and to imprisonment not exceeding two years, nor less than one; and, in case the goods should be retaken under such process, it is made the absolute duty of the sheriff to retake them.

It is not to be supposed that, in the face of these penalties, aided by the powerful force of the county, which would doubtless be brought to sustain the State officers, either that the collector would retain the custody in the first instance, or that the marshal could summon sufficient aid to retake the property, pursuant to the order or other process of the court.

It is, moreover, obvious that in this conflict between the powers of the officers of the United States and of the State, (unless the latter be passively submitted to,) the destruction to which the property of the officers of the customs would be exposed, the commission of actual violence, and the loss of lives, would be scarcely avoidable.

Under these circumstances, and the provisions of the act of South Carolina, the execution of the laws is rendered impracticable even through the ordinary judicial tribunals of the United States. There would certainly be fewer difficulties, and less opportunity of actual collision between the officers of the United States and of the State, and the collection of the revenue would be more effectually secured —if indeed it can be done in any other way—by placing the custom-house beyond the immediate power of the county.

For this purpose, it might be proper to provide that whenever, by any unlawful combination or obstruction in any State, or in any port, it should become impracticable faithfully to collect the duties, the President of the United States should be authorized to alter and abolish such of the districts and ports of entry as should be necessary, and to establish the custom-house at some secure place within some port or harbor of such State; and, in such cases, it should be the duty of the collector to reside in such place, and to detain all vessels and cargoes until the duties imposed by law should be secured or paid in cash, deducting interest; that in such cases it should be unlawful to take the vessel and cargo from the custody of the proper officer of the customs, unless by process from the ordinary judicial tribunals of the United States; and that, in case of an attempt otherwise to take the property by a force too great to be overcome by the officers of the customs, it should be lawful to protect the possession of the officers by the employment of the land and naval forces, and militia, under provisions similar to those authorized by the 11th section of the act of the 9th of January, 1809.

This provision, however, would not shield the officers and citizens of the United

States, acting under the laws, from suits and prosecutions, in the tribunals of the State, which might thereafter be brought against them; nor would it protect their property from the proceeding by distress; and it might well be apprehended that it would be insufficient to insure a proper respect to the process of the constitutional tribunals in prosecutions for offenses against the United States, and to protect the authorities of the United States, whether judicial or ministerial, in the performance of their duties. It would, moreover, be inadequate to extend the protection due from the Government to that portion of the people of South Carolina, against outrage and oppression of any kind, who may manifest their attachment, and yield obedience to the laws of the Union.

It may, therefore, be desirable to review, with some modifications betted adapted to the occasion, the 6th section of the act of the 3d of March, 1815, which expired on the 4th of March, 1817, by the limitation of that of the 27th of April, 1816; and to provide that, in any case, where suit shall be brought against any individual in the courts of the State, for any act done under the laws of the United States, he should be authorized to remove the said cause, by petition, into the circuit court of the United States, without any copy of the record, and that the courts should proceed to hear and determine the same as if it had been originally instituted therein. And that in all cases of injuries to the persons or property of individuals for disobedience to the ordinance, and laws of South Carolina in pursuance thereof, redress may be sought in the courts of the United States. It may be expedient, also, by modifying the resolution of the 3d of March, 1791, to authorize the marshals to make the necessary provision for the safe keeping of prisoners committed under the authority of the United States.

Provisions less than these, consisting, as they do, for the most part, rather of a revival of the policy of former acts called for by the existing emergency, than of the introduction of any unusual or rigorous enactments, would not cause the laws of the Union to be properly respected or enforced. It is believed these would prove inadequate, unless the military forces of the State of South Carolina authorized by the late act of the Legislature, should be actually embodied and called out in aid of their proceedings, and of the provisions of the ordinance generally. Even in that case, however, it is believed that no more will be necessary than a few modifications of its terms, to adapt the act of 1795 to the present emergency, as, by that act, the provisions of the law of 1792 were accommodated to the crisis then existing; and by conferring authority upon the President to give it operation during the session of Congress, and without the ceremony of a proclamation, whenever it shall be officially made known to him by the authority of any State, or by the courts of the United States, that, within the limits of such State, the laws of the United States will be openly opposed, and their execution obstructed, by the actual employment of military force, or by any unlawful means whatsoever, too great to be otherwise overcome.

In closing this communication, I should do injustice to my own feelings not to express my confident reliance upon the disposition of each department of the Government to perform its duty, and to co-operate in all measures necessary in the present emergency.

The crisis undoubtedly invokes the fidelity of the patriot and the sagacity of the statesman, not more in removing such portions of the public burden as may be necessary, than in preserving the good order of society, and in the maintenance of well-regulated liberty.

While a forbearing spirit may, and I trust will, be exercised towards the errors of our brethren in a particular quarter, duty to the rest of the Union demands that open and organized resistance to the laws should not be executed with impunity.

The rich inheritance bequeathed by our fathers has devolved upon us the sacred obligation of preserving it by the same virtues which conducted thsm through the eventful scenes of the Revolution, and ultimately crowned their struggles with the noblest model of civil institutions. They bequeathed to us a Government of laws, and a Federal Union founded upon the great principle of popular representation. After a successful experiment of forty-four years, at a moment when the Government and the Union are the objects of the hopes of the friends of civil liberty throughout the world, and in the midst of public and individual prosperity unexampled in history, we are called to decide whether these laws possess any force, and that Union the means of self-preservation. The decision of this question by an enlightened and patriotic people cannot be doubtful. For myself, fellow-citizens, devoutly relying upon that kind Providence which has hitherto watched over our destinies, and actuated by a profound reverence for those institutions I have so much cause to love, and for the American people, whose partiality honored me with their highest trust, I have determined to spare no effort to discharge the duty which, in this conjuncture, is devolved upon me. That a similar spirit will actuate the representatives of the American people, is not to be questioned; and I fervently pray that the Great Ruler of nations may so guide your deliberations, and our joint measures, as that they may prove salutary examples, not only to the present, but to future times; and solemnly proclaim that the Constitution and the laws are supreme, and the Union indissoluble.

ANDREW JACKSON.

WASHINGTON, January, 1833.

JOHN BROWN'S PROVISIONAL GOVERNMENT CONSTITUTION.

Reference is made, in the body of this work, [see pages 527, 528, &c.] to the Constitution adopted at the Chatham, C. W. Convention. Copies of this document were found among John Brown's effects at the Kennedy farm, but, notwithstanding many calls for its publication, only a *partial* copy has been permitted the light. We quote it as printed by the Virginia authorities:

PROVISIONAL CONSTITUTION AND ORDINANCES FOR THE PEOPLE OF THE UNITED STATES.

PREAMBLE.—Whereas, Slavery, throughout its entire existence in the United States, is none other than the most barbarous, unprovoked and unjustifiable war of one portion of its citizens against another portion, the only conditions of which are perpetual imprisonment and hopeless servitude, or absolute extermination, in utter disregard and violation of those eternal and self-evident truths set forth in our Declaration of Independence:

Therefore, We, the citizens of the United States, and the oppressed people, who, by a recent decision of the Supreme Court, are declared to have no rights which the white man is bound to respect, together with all the other people degraded by the laws thereof, do, for the time being, ordain and establish for ourselves the following Provisional Constitution and ordinances, the better to protect our people, property, lives and liberties, and to govern our actions.

Article I. Qualifications of Membership.—All persons of mature age, whether proscribed, oppressed and enslaved citizens, or of proscribed and oppressed races of the United States, who shall agree to sustain and enforce the Provisional Constitution and ordinances of organization, together with all minor children of such persons, shall be held to be fully entitled to protection under the same.

Art. II. Branches of Government.—The Provisional Government of this organization shall consist of three branches, viz.: the Legislative, the Executive and the Judicial.

Art. III. The Legislature.—The Legislative branch shall be a Congress or House of Representatives, composed of not less than five, nor more than ten members, who shall be elected by all the citizens of mature age and sound mind connected with this organization, and who shall remain in office for three years, unless sooner removed for misconduct, inability or death. A majority of such members shall constitute a quorum.

Art. IV. Executive.—The Executive branch of the organization shall consist of a President and Vice President, who shall be chosen by the citizens or members of this organization, and each of whom shall hold his office for three years, unless sooner removed by death, or for inability, or for misconduct,

Art. V. Judicial.--The Judicial branch consists of one Chief Justice of the Supreme Court, and four Associate Judges of the said Court, each of them constituting a Circuit Court, They shall each be chosen in the same manner as the President, and shall continue in office until their places have been filled in the same manner by an election of citizens.

Art. XIII. to XXV. provide for the trial of the President and other officers, and Members of Congress, the impeachment of Judges; the duties of the President and Vice President, the punishment of crimes, Army appointments, salaries, &c., &c. These articles are not of special interest, and are therefore omitted.

Art. XXVI. Treaties of Peace.—Before any treaty of peace shall take full effect, it shall be signed by the President, Vice President, Commander-in-Chief, a majority of the House of Representatives, a majority of the Supreme Court, and a majority of the general officers of the army,

Art. XXVII. Duty of the Military.—It shall be the duty of the Commander-in-Chief, and all the officers and soldiers of the army, to afford special protection, when needed, to Congress, or any member thereof, to the Supreme Court, or any member thereof, to the President, Vice President, Treasurer and Secretary of War, and to afford general protection to all civil officers, or other persons having a right to the same.

Art. XXVIII. Property.—All captured or confiscated property, and all the property the product of the labor of those belonging to this organization, and of their families, shall be held as the property of the whole equally, without distinction, and may be used for the common benefit, or disposed of for the same object. And any person, officer or otherwise, who shall improperly retain, secrete, use, or needlessly destroy such property, or property found, captured or confiscated, belonging to the enemy, or shall wilfully neglect to render a full and fair statement of such property by him so taken or held, shall be guilty of a misdemeanor, and, on conviction, shall be punished accordingly.

Art. XXIX. Safety or Intelligence Fund.—All money, plate, watches or jewelry captured by honorable warfare, found, taken or confiscated, belonging to the enemy, shall be held sacred, to constitute a liberal safety or intelligence fund; and any person who shall improperly retain, dispose of, hide, use or destroy such money or other article above named, contrary to the provisions and spirit of this article, shall be deemed guilty of theft, and, on conviction thereof, shall be punished accordingly. The Treasurer shall furnish the Commander-in-Chief at all times with a full statement of the condition of such fund, and its nature.

Art. XXX. The Commander-in-Chief and the Treasury.—The Commander-in-Chief shall have power to draw from the Treasury the money and other property of the fund provided for in Article XXIX., but his orders shall be signed also by the Secretary of War, who shall keep a strict account of the same, subject to examination by any member of Congress or General Officer.

Art. XXXI. Surplus of the Safety or Intelligence Fund.—It shall be the duty of the Commander-in-Chief to advise the President of any surplus of the Safety or Intelligence Fund, and he shall have power to draw the same, his order being also signed by the Secretary of State, to enable him to carry on the provisions of Article XXII.

Art. XXXII. Prisoners,—No person, after having surrendered himself a prisoner, and who shall properly demean himself or herself as such, to any officer or private connected with this organization, shall afterwards be put to death, or be subjected to any corporeal punishment, without first having had the benefit of a fair and impartial trial; nor shall any prisoner be treated with any kind of cruelty, disrespect, insult or needless severity; but it shall be the duty of all persons, male and female, connected herewith, at all times, and under all circumstances, to treat all such prisoners with every degree of respect and kindness that the nature of the circumstances will admit of, and insist on a like course of conduct from all others, as in fear of the Almighty God, to whose care and keeping we commit our cause.

Art. XXXIII. Volunteers.—All persons who may come forward, and shall voluntarily deliver up slaves, and have their names registered on the books of this organization, shall, so long as they continue at peace, be entitled to the fullest protection in person and property, though not connected with this organization, and shall be treated as friends, and not merely as persons neutral.

Art. XXXIV. Neutrals,—The persons and property of all non-slaveholders who shall remain absolutely neutral shall be respected as far as circumstances can allow of it, but they shall not be entitled to any active protection.

Art. XXXV. No needless Waste.—The needless waste or destruction of any useful property or article by fire, throwing open of fences, fields, buildings or needless killing of animals, or injury of either, shall not be tolerated at any time or place, and shall be promptly and peremptorily punished.

Art. XXXVI. Property Confiscated.—The entire personal and real property of all persons known to be acting, either directly or indirectly, with or for the enemy, or found in arms with them, or found wilfully holding slaves, shall be confiscated and taken, whenever and wherever it may be found, in either Free or Slave States.

Art. XXXVII. Desertion.—Persons convicted, on impartial trial, of desertion to the enemy after becoming members, acting as spies, of treacherous surrender of property, arms, ammunition, provisions or supplies of any kind, roads, bridges, persons or fortifications, shall be put to death, and their entire property confiscated.

Art. XXXVIII. Violation of Parole of Honor.—Persons proved to be guilty of taking up arms, after having been set at liberty on parole of honor, or after the same to have taken any active part with or for the enemy, direct or indirect, shall be put to death, and their entire property confiscated.

Arts. XXXIX., XL. and XLI. require all labor for the general good, and prohibit immoral actions.

Art. XLII. The Marriage Relation—Schools—The Sabbath.—Marriage relations shall be at all times respected, and families shall be kept together as far as possible, and broken families encouraged to reunite, and intelligence offices shall be established for that purpose. Schools and churches shall be established as may be, for the purpose of religious and other instruction, and the first day of the week shall be regarded as a day of rest, and appropriated to moral and religious instruction and improvement, to the relief of the suffering, the instruction of the young and ignorant, and the encouragement of personal cleanliness; nor shall any person be required on that day to perform ordinary manual labor, unless in extremely urgent cases.

Art. XLIII. To carry Arms openly.—All persons known to be of good character, and of sound mind and suitable age, who are connected with this organization, whether male or female, shall be encouraged to carry arms openly.

Art. XLIV. No Persons to carry Concealed Weapons.—No person within the limits of conquered territory, except regularly appointed policemen, express officers of army, mail carriers, or other fully accredited messengers of Congress, the President, Vice-President, members of the Supreme Court, or commissioned officers of the Army, and those under peculiar circumstances, shall be allowed at any time to carry concealed weapons; and any person not specially authorised so to do, who shall be found so doing, shall be deemed a suspicious person, and may at once be arrested by any officer, soldier or citizen, without the formality of a complaint or warrant; and may at once be subjected to thorough search, and shall have his or her case thoroughly investigated, and be dealt with as circumstances on proof shall require.

Art. XLV. Persons to be seized.—Persons living within the limits of territory holden by this organization, and not connected with this organization, having arms at all, concealed or otherwise, shall be seized at once, or be taken in charge of by some vigilant officer, and their case thoroughly investigated; and it shall be the duty of all citizens and soldiers, as well as officers, to arrest such parties as are named in this and the preceding sections or article, without formality of complaint or warrant; and they shall be placed in charge of some proper officer for examination, or for safe keeping.

Art. XLVI. These Articles not for the Overthrow of Government.—The foregoing articles shall not be construed so as in any way to encourage the overthrow of any State Government, or of the General Government of the United States, and look to no dissolution of the Union, but simply to amendment and repeal, and our flag shall be the same that our fathers fought under in the Revolution.

Art. XLVII. No Plurality of Offices.—No two offices specially provided for by this instrument shall be filled by the same person at the same time.

Art. XLVIII. Oath.—Every officer, civil or military, connected with this organization, shall, before entering upon the duties of office, make solemn oath or affirmation to abide by and support the Provisional Constitution and these ordinances. Also, every citizen and soldier, before being recognized as such, shall do the same.

Schedule.—The President of this Convention shall convene, immediately on the adoption of this instrument, a Convention of all such persons as shall have given their adherence by signature to the Constitution, who shall proceed to fill by election all offices specially named in said Constitution—the President of this Convention presiding and issuing commissions to such officers elect; all such officers being hereafter elected in the manner provided in the body of this instrument.

REPORT OF THE SELECT COMMITTEE (U. S. SENATE) ON THE HARPER'S FERRY AFFAIR.

As stated (page 545) the reports of the Committee appointed to investigate the Harper's Ferry scheme of John Brown, were presented to the Senate June 15th. The majority report, signed by Messrs. Mason, Davis and Fitch, was a very lengthy document. Only its conclusion need here be cited. We quote:

Upon the whole testimony, there can be no doubt that Brown's plan was to commence a servile war on the borders of Virginia, which he expected to extend, and which he believed his means and resources were sufficient to extend through that State and throughout the entire South. Upon being questioned, soon after his capture, by the Governor of Virginia, as to his plans, he rather indignantly repelled the idea that it was to be limited to collecting and protecting the slaves until they could be sent out of the State as fugitives. On the contrary, he vehemently insisted that his purpose was to retain them on the soil, to put arms in their hands, with which he came provided for the purpose, and to use them as his soldiery. (Pp. 61, 62.)

This man (Brown) was uniformly spoken of, by those who seemed best to have known him, as of remarkable reticence in his habits, or, as they expressed it, "secretive." It does not appear that he intrusted even his immediate followers with his plans, fully, even after they were ripe for execution. Nor have the committee been enabled clearly to trace knowledge of them to any. The only exception would seem to be in the instance of the anonymous letter received by the Secretary of War in the Summer preceding the attack, referred to in his testimony. The Secretary shows that he could get no clue to the writer; nor were the committee enabled in any way to trace him. Considering that the letter was anonymous, as well as vague and apparently incoherent in its statements, it was not at all remarkable, in the opinion of the committee, that it did not arrest the attention of the officer to whom it was addressed.

The point chosen for the attack seems to have been selected from the twofold inducement of the security afforded the invaders by a mountain country, and the large deposit of arms in the arsenal of the United States there situated. It resulted in the murder of three most respectable citizens of the State of Virginia without cause, and in the like murder of an unoffending free negro. Of the military force brought against them, one marine was killed, and one wounded; whilst eight of the militia and other forces of the neighborhood were wounded, with more or less severity, in the several assaults made by them.

Of the list of "insurgents" given in Colonel Lee's report, (fourteen whites and five negroes,) Brown, Stevens and Coppic, of the whites, with Shields, Green and Copeland, of the negroes, captured at the storming of the engine house, were subsequently executed in Virginia, after judicial trial; as were also John E. Cook and Albert Hazlett, who at first escaped, but were captured in Pennsylvania and delivered up for trial to the authorities of Virginia—making in all seven thus executed. It does not seem to have been very clearly ascertained how many of the party escaped. Brown stated that his party consisted of twenty-two in number. Seven were executed, ten were killed at the Ferry: thus leaving five to be accounted for. Four of these five, it is believed, were left on the Maryland side in charge of the arms when Brown crossed the river, and who could not afterwards join him; leaving but one, who, as it would appear is the only survivor of the party who accompanied Brown across the bridge, and whose escape is not accounted for.

The committee, after much consideration, are not prepared to suggest any legislation, which, in their opinion, would be adequate to prevent like occurrences in the future. The only provision in the Constitution of the United States which would seem to import any authority in the Government of the United States to interfere on occasions affecting the peace or safety of the States, are found in the eighth section of the first article, among the powers of Congress "to provide for calling for the militia to execute the laws of the Union, suppress insurrections, and repel invasions;" and in the fourth section of the fourth article, in the following words: "The United States shall guaranty to every State in this Union a republican form of Government, and shall protect each of them against invasion, and, on the application of the Legislature or of the Executive, (when the Legislature cannot be convened,] against domestic violence." The "invasion" here spoken of would seem to import an invasion by the public force of a foreign power, or (if not so limited and equally referable to an invasion by one State of another) still it would seem that public force, or force exercised under the sanction of acknowledged political power, is there meant. The invasion (to call it so) by Brown and his followers at Harper's Ferry, was in no sense of that character. It was simply the act of lawless ruffians, under the sanction of no public or political authority—distinguishable only from ordinary felonies by the ulterior ends in contemplation by them, and by the fact that the money to maintain the expedition, and the large armament they brought with them, had been contributed and furnished by the citizens of other States of the Union, under circumstances that must continue to jeopard the safety and peace of the Southern States, and against which Congress has no power to legislate.

If the several States, whether from motives of policy or a desire to preserve the peace of the Union, if not from fraternal feeling, do not hold it incumbent on them after the experience of the country, to guard in future by appropriate legislation against occurrences similar to the one here inquired into, the committee can find no guaranty elsewhere for the security of peace between the States of the Union.

So far, however, as the safety of the public property is involved, the committee would earnestly recommend that provision should be made by the Executive, or, if necessary, by law, to keep under adequate military guard the public armories and arsenals of the United States, in some way after the manner now practiced at the navy yards and forts.

Before closing their report, the committee deem it proper to state that four persons summoned as witnesses, to wit: John Brown, jr., of Ohio, James Redpath, of Massachusetts, Frank B. Sanborn, of Massachusetts, and Thaddeus Hyatt, of New York, failing or refusing to appear before the committee, warrants were issued by order of the Senate for their arrest. Of these, Thaddeus Hyatt only was arrested; and on his appearance before the Senate, still refusing obedience to the summons of the committee, he was, by order of the Senate, committed to the jail of the District of Columbia. In regard to the others, it appeared by the return of the marshal of the northern district of Ohio, as deputy of the Sergeant-at-Arms, that John Brown, jr., at first evaded the process of the Senate, and afterwards, with a number of other persons, armed themselves to prevent his arrest. The marshal further reported in his return that Brown could not be arrested unless he was authorized in like manner to employ force. Sanborn was arrested by a deputy of the Sergeant-at-Arms, and afterwards released from custody by the Judges of the Supreme Court of Massachusetts on *habeas corpus*. Redpath, by leaving his State, and otherwise concealing himself, successfully evaded the process of the Senate.

www.ingramcontent.com/pod-product-compliance
Lightning Source LLC
LaVergne TN
LVHW021232110826
845150LV00002B/316

* 9 7 8 1 4 2 5 5 6 2 5 9 5 *